The US Foreign Investment in Real Property Tax Act
A Practical Guide

The US Foreign Investment in Real Property Tax Act
A Practical Guide

Angela W. Yu

Wolters Kluwer

Published by:
Kluwer Law International B.V.
PO Box 316
2400 AH Alphen aan den Rijn
The Netherlands
Website: www.wolterskluwerlr.com

Sold and distributed in North, Central and South America by:
Wolters Kluwer Legal & Regulatory U.S.
7201 McKinney Circle
Frederick, MD 21704
United States of America
Email: customer.service@wolterskluwer.com

Sold and distributed in all other countries by:
Quadrant
Rockwood House
Haywards Heath
West Sussex
RH16 3DH
United Kingdom
Email: international-customerservice@wolterskluwer.com

The information contained herein is of a general nature and is based on authorities that are subject to change. Applicability of the information to specific situations should be determined through consultation with your professional adviser. This work represents the views of the author only, and does not necessarily represent the views or advice of KPMG LLP.

Printed on acid-free paper.

ISBN 978-90-411-8464-1

e-Book: ISBN 978-90-411-8465-8
web-PDF: ISBN 978-90-411-8466-5

© 2017 Kluwer Law International BV, The Netherlands

All rights reserved. No part of this publication may be reproduced, stored in a retrieval system, or transmitted in any form or by any means, electronic, mechanical, photocopying, recording, or otherwise, without written permission from the publisher.

Permission to use this content must be obtained from the copyright owner. Please apply to: Permissions Department, Wolters Kluwer Legal, 76 Ninth Avenue, 7th Floor, New York, NY 10011-5201, USA. Website: www.wolterskluwerlr.com

Printed in the United Kingdom.

To Geoff and Alex

Foreword

As commonly recognized, the interest of foreign investors in U.S. real estate has increased exponentially over the years. It is essential that these investors and their advisors fully understand the U.S. tax implications of their investments in order to implement the correct structure to maximize their returns, avoid unnecessary withholding and comply with applicable requirements.

Therefore, I was delighted when Angela agreed to develop a comprehensive guide to FIRPTA. A clear-cut pathway to a thorough understanding of this complex set of rules is long overdue, and I cannot think of anyone more qualified for that task than Angela, with whom I have had the pleasure to work closely over the years on numerous cross-border real estate transactions, many of which have raised unusual issues under the FIRPTA rules. The result is an invaluable resource that should benefit all interested parties for years to come.

Angela has succeeded in clearly articulating the operation and transactional implications of FIRPTA and its interaction with various other regimes (for example, the REIT and publicly traded partnership regimes). In this volume, she sets forth for the reader real life situations, and points out potential traps, always in a readily graspable format. I am confident that you will find this compendium valuable in identifying and formulating the correct strategies for yourselves or your clients with respect to investments in the U.S. real estate market.

Peter H. Blessing

About the Author

Angela Yu is a tax partner of KPMG's New York office. Prior to her current role, she was an international tax partner with KPMG's Washington National Tax practice and Vancouver U.S. tax practice. Angela also served as a member of the U.S. Congressional staff of the Joint Committee on Taxation.

Angela has extensive experience providing integrated tax advice to clients on cross-border transactions. Her expertise includes FIRPTA planning; income tax treaty interpretations; structuring mergers and acquisitions, reorganizations and joint ventures; evaluating financing options and repatriation strategies; and subpart F, PFIC and foreign tax credit planning.

Angela has published various articles on FIRPTA, income tax treaties and the branch profits tax. She is a frequent speaker on U.S. tax issues and has addressed many professional organizations including the American Bar Association, International Fiscal Association, Tax Executives Institute, and the Internal Revenue Service.

Angela is a member of New York State Society of CPAs. She received her MBA and BS, magna cum laude, from New York University.

Table of Contents

Foreword		vii
About the Author		ix
Author's Note		xix

Chapter 1
The Genesis of FIRPTA and Related Background — 1

§1.01	Overview	1
	A. What Are We Talking About	1
	B. The Organization of This Book	3
§1.02	Foreign Investment Tax Act	5
§1.03	FIRPTA: The Early Years	5
§1.04	The 1986 Tax Reform Act	6
	A. Repeal of the *General Utilities* Doctrine	7
	B. The Enactment of the Branch Profits Tax	8
§1.05	The FIRPTA Regulations	9
§1.06	Recent Legislative Amendments	11
§1.07	Will FIRPTA Be Repealed?	12

Chapter 2
Structuring Foreign Investments in the United States — 13

§2.01	Overview	13
§2.02	Taxation of Operating Income	14
	A. General Rule	15
	B. Branch Profits Tax	18
	1. General Rule	18
	2. Branch Termination Exception	22
§2.03	Real Estate Investments Funds	23
	A. Attribution of US Trade or Business to Investors	23
	B. Sale of Fund Interests	25
§2.04	Investment Vehicles	26
	A. Foreign Corporations Investing Directly in USRPIs	27
	B. Investing through a US Partnership	28

	C. Investing through a US Corporation	30
	D. Investing through a US REIT	31
§2.05	Summary	33
	A. Fund Investment Platform	34
	B. Corporate Investment Platform	35
Appendix 2-A		36

Chapter 3
Definition of a US Real Property Interest — 43

§3.01	Overview	43
§3.02	The Operative Rule	44
§3.03	Definition of a USRPI	45
	A. The Statute	45
	B. The Regulatory Framework	46
	1. Land and Improvements	47
	2. Personal Properties Associated with the Use of Real Property	50
	C. Interest Other Than Solely as a Creditor in USRPI	51
§3.04	Treatment of Intangibles	53
	A. Rights in Governmental Permits	55
	B. Treatment of Infrastructure Projects	57
	C. Case Study	58
	1. Facts	58
	2. The Comprehensive Agreement	58
	3. The Project Funding	59
	4. Take Away	60
§3.05	Summary	61

Chapter 4
Definition of a US Real Property Holding Company — 63

§4.01	Overview	63
§4.02	The Operative Rule	64
§4.03	Definition of a USRPHC	66
	A. General Rule – 50% Fair Market Value Test	66
	B. Elective Rule – 25% Book Value Test	68
	C. Trade or Business Assets	69
§4.04	Look-Back Period and Determination Dates	71
§4.05	The Look-Through Rules	73
	A. Look-Through Rules for Controlled Corporations	73
	B. No Look-Through for Non-Controlled Corporations	74
	C. Look-Through Rules for Partnerships, Trusts and Estates	75
§4.06	Summary	76

Chapter 5
Using REITs to Invest in the US — 79

§5.01	Overview	79
§5.02	Foreign Investors' Use of REITs	83
	A. Initial Assessment on Using a REIT	83
	B. REIT Conversion and the Sting Tax	85
	C. Restrictions on REIT Spin-Offs	87

§5.03	REIT Qualifications	89
	A. Organizational/Ownership Requirements	89
	B. Quarterly Asset Tests	90
	C. Income Tests	93
	D. Annual Distribution Requirements	95
	E. Special Rules Applicable to TRS	97
	1. Tenant Services	98
	2. Eligible Independent Contractors	99
§5.04	Taxation of Foreign Investors' Income and Gain from REITs	100
	A. Ordinary Dividends	100
	B. Capital Gain Dividends	101
	1. General Rule	101
	2. FIRPTA Tax on Gain Distributed	102
	C. Gain from the Sale of REIT Stock	108
§5.05	Summary	108

Chapter 6
Exceptions to FIRPTA   109

§6.01	Overview	109
§6.02	Original FIRPTA Exceptions	110
	A. The Cleansing Exception	110
	B. The Publicly Traded Exception	112
	1. The Trading Requirements	113
	2. The Ownership Requirements	114
	3. Application to Partnership Interests	116
	C. The Domestically Controlled QIE/REIT Exception	116
	1. General Rule	116
	2. 2015 PATH Act Changes	120
§6.03	New Exceptions under the 2015 PATH Act	123
	A. QFPF Exemption	123
	1. General Rule	123
	2. Unanswered Questions	126
	B. Qualified Shareholder Exemption	127
	1. General Rule	127
	2. Who Will Benefit?	129
§6.04	Other Special Rules	130
	A. Foreign Sovereign Exemption	131
	1. Definition of Foreign Government	132
	2. Controlled Entities v. Controlled Commercial Entities	133
	3. The *Per Se* Rule for Controlled Commercial Entities	135
	4. Commercial Activities	136
	5. Treatment of a Sovereign as a Foreign Corporation	137
§6.05	Summary	138

Chapter 7
FIRPTA Nonrecognition Rules   139

§7.01	Overview	140
§7.02	General Code Nonrecognition Provisions	141
	A. Contributions to Corporations	141

	B. Corporate Reorganizations	142
	C. Corporate Liquidations	144
§7.03	The FIRPTA Nonrecognition Rules	145
	A. Exchanges of USRPIs in Code Section 351 Transfers and Acquisitive Reorganizations	147
	1. Transfers of USRPIs to a US Corporation in a Code Section 351 Exchange or B Reorganization	147
	2. Foreign-to-Foreign Nonrecognition Exchanges	148
	a. Transfer of USRPHC Stock in a Code Section 351 Exchange or B Reorganization	148
	b. Acquisitive Asset Reorganizations	149
	3. D and F Reorganizations	150
	4. A and C Reorganizations	152
	B. Foreign-to-Foreign Liquidations	153
	C. Inbound Liquidations and Reorganizations	154
	1. The General Rules	154
	2. The Way Forward?	156
	D. Code Section 355 Distributions	157
	E. Other Transfers to and from US Corporations	159
	1. E and F Reorganizations of USRPHCs	159
	2. Outbound Liquidations of US Corporations	160
§7.04	Other Special Rules	160
	A. The Filing Requirement	160
	B. The Section 897(i) Election	162
§7.05	Summary	163
Appendices		165

Chapter 8
FIRPTA Withholding   189

§8.01	Overview	190
§8.02	Purchaser's Responsibility to Withhold	192
	A. Dispositions of Interests in USRPIs	192
	B. Dispositions of Interests in Partnerships	193
§8.03	Special Rules Relating to Certain Dispositions and Distributions	194
	A. Dispositions by Partnerships	194
	B. Dispositions by Trusts	195
	C. Distributions of USRPIs by Foreign Corporations	196
	D. Distributions by USRPHCs	197
§8.04	Exemptions from FIRPTA Withholding	198
	A. Sale of USRPIs	199
	1. Certification of Non-Foreign Status	199
	2. Certification of Non-USRPHC Interests	201
	B. Distributions with respect to USRPIs	202
	1. Certification of Non-Foreign Status	202
	2. Certification of Non-USRPHC Status	202
	C. Notice of Nonrecognition Transfer	203
	D. Foreclosures	205
	E. Government Transferors	207
§8.05	The Withholding Certificate	207

	A. Request Submitted Prior to the Transfer	209
	B. Request Submitted After the Transfer	209
§8.06	Coordination with FATCA	210
	A. FIRPTA Generally Overrides FATCA	210
	B. Certain Real Estate Related Payments Are Subject to FATCA	212
§8.07	Summary	213
Appendices		214

Chapter 9
Impact of US Income Tax Treaties — 253

§9.01	Overview	254
§9.02	US Treaty Interpretation	255
§9.03	Limitation on Benefits	256
	A. Qualified Persons	256
	B. Limited Benefits for Non-Qualified Persons	258
	1. Active Trade or Business Test	259
	2. Derivative Benefits Provision	263
	3. Competent Authority Relief	264
§9.04	Provisions that Affect Real Estate Gains	264
	A. Relief for Capital Gains	264
	B. Non-Discrimination Provisions	266
	C. Branch Profits Tax	266
	D. Business Profits and Permanent Establishment	268
§9.05	Treaty Benefits for FDAP Income	269
	A. Real Estate Rental Income	269
	B. Interest Income	270
	1. Amounts Paid by US Corporations	271
	2. Amounts Paid by Foreign Corporations	272
	C. Dividend Income	273
	D. Special Rules for Tax-Exempt Organizations and Pensions	274
§9.06	2016 US Model	275
	A. Special Tax Regimes	275
	B. Revisions to LOB Provisions	276
	1. New Derivative Benefits Test	276
	2. New Headquarters Company Test	277
	3. Active Trade or Business and Publicly Traded Company Subsidiary Tests	278
	C. Triangular Permanent Establishments	278
	D. Denial of Treaty Benefits Following Law Change	279
	E. Dividend Article	279
§9.07	Summary	280
Appendix 9-A		281

Chapter 10
Entity Classifications and Interest Deductions — 283

§10.01	Overview	283
§10.02	Entity Classification Rules	284
§10.03	Debt Equity Considerations	286
	A. Common Law and the Codification of Section 385	287

	B. The 385 Regulations	288
	1. Documentation Requirements	289
	2. Recast Rules	290
§10.04	Other Applicable Doctrines	292
	A. Transfer Pricing – Section 482	293
	B. Acquisitions Made to Evade or Avoid Tax – Section 269	294
	C. Economic Substance Doctrine – Section 7701(o)	295
§10.05	Limitations on Interest Deductions	295
	A. Interest Owed to Related Person	296
	B. Earnings Stripping Limitation	297
§10.06	Withholding Tax on Interest	299
	A. Portfolio Interest Exemption	299
	B. Anti-Conduit Financing Rules	301
§10.06	Summary	303
Appendix 10-A		305

Chapter 11
Tax Administration, Penalties, and Interest   307

§11.01	Overview	307
§11.02	Types of Tax Authorities	308
	A. Legislative Authorities	309
	B. Administrative Authorities	309
	1. Regulations	310
	2. Generic Guidance	311
	3. Taxpayer Specific Guidance	312
	C. Judicial Authorities	313
§11.03	Common Types of Penalties	313
	A. Penalties Related to the Filing of Tax Returns	313
	1. Delinquency Penalties	314
	2. Reasonable Cause Exception	315
	B. Accuracy-Related Penalties	316
	1. Penalty for Negligence and Disregard of Tax Rules or Regulations	317
	2. Penalty for Substantial Understatement of Income Tax	319
	3. Penalty for Transactions Lacking Economic Substance	320
	4. Penalty for Undisclosed Foreign Financial Assets	321
	5. Special Rules for Tax Shelters	321
§11.04	Summary	322

Chapter 12
State and Local Tax Considerations   323

§12.01	Application of FIRPTA to State and Local Taxes, Generally	323
	A. Overview	323
	B. Effect of Tax Treaties on State and Local Taxation	324
§12.02	State and Local Tax Considerations on Sales of Real Property	324
§12.03	State and Local Withholding on Sales of Real Property	325
	A. California	325
	B. Delaware	327
	C. Hawaii	328
	D. New York State	330

Table of Contents

§12.04	State and Local Transaction Taxes on Sales of Real Estate	331
	A. Direct Transfer of Realty	332
	B. Indirect Transfer of Realty	332
	C. Long-term Lease	332
	D. Exemptions	333
§12.05	Selected State-Specific Real Estate Transfer Tax Provisions	333
	A. California	333
	1. Los Angeles	334
	2. San Francisco	335
	B. New York	336

Chapter 13
Income and Transfer Tax Issues Applicable to Foreign Individual Investors   339

§13.01	Overview	339
§13.02	Income Taxation	340
	A. Definition of a Resident Alien	341
§13.03	Estate and Gift Taxation	348
	A. Gift Tax	348
	1. Application to a US Citizen or Domiciliary	348
	2. Application to a Non-Domiciled Foreign Citizen	349
	B. Estate Tax	350
	1. Application to a US Citizen or Domiciliary	350
	2. Application to a Non-Domiciled Foreign Citizen	350
	C. Generation-Skipping Transfer Tax	351
§13.04	Estate and Gift Tax Treaties	352
§13.05	Summary	354

Index   355

Author's Note

Over my 30 years as a tax advisor, I have spoken with hundreds of foreign investors about their investments in U.S. real properties. Many of my clients, especially those who were unfamiliar with U.S. tax rules, were dismayed by the breadth and complexity of the regime. Truth be told, I agree with them.

Surprisingly, I have not encountered any materials that address FIRPTA and the related tax issues in a comprehensive way that is accessible to non-tax professionals. Although FIRPTA is a fairly self-contained set of rules, it does not exist in isolation within the U.S. tax system. Foreign investors in U.S. real property must also deal with myriad other tax rules, including those that govern the taxation and reporting of U.S. source income that arises during the lifespan of the investment, as well as the U.S. withholding tax imposed on income, gains and disposition proceeds. At times, the U.S. tax system can feel like a game of Whac-A-Mole – whenever you address one aspect of the rules, a different challenge arises.

When Wolters Kluwer approached me to see if I was interested in creating the first practical guide to FIRPTA, I decided to give it a try. With FIRPTA as the main focus, this book attempts to present, in a single volume, an introduction to the common U.S. tax issues that affect foreign investors in U.S. real property. I tried to convey the information in a straightforward and concise manner. I stayed away from discussing narrow technical issues that may only apply in limited circumstances. I hope that foreign investors and their advisors will use this book as a road map to identify their issues and conduct further research if necessary.

This book could not have been written without the encouragement and mentorship of Peter H. Blessing and Raymond D. Jasen. Other KPMG colleagues who reviewed earlier drafts of the chapters include Stephen M. Massed, John DerOhanesian, Jesse F. Eggert, David W. Lee, Douglas G. Holland, Tracy T. Stone, Benedict Francis, Danielle Nishida, Shirley K. Sicilian, Harve M. Lewis and Marianne Evans (Marianne actually wrote the chapter on state and local taxation). I also wish to thank Matthew I. Weiss, Anna Nellums, Evangeline Hu and Sashka Koleva for their valuable assistance in researching various issues. Any omissions and mistakes, however, are entirely mine.

This book represents the views of the author only, and does not necessarily represent the views or professional advice of KPMG LLP. The information contained herein is of a general nature and based on technical authorities that are subject to change. Applicability of the information to specific situations should be determined through consultation with your tax advisor.

Angela W. Yu
August 2017

Chapter 1
The Genesis of FIRPTA and Related Background

§1.01	Overview	1
	A. What Are We Talking About	1
	B. The Organization of This Book	3
§1.02	Foreign Investment Tax Act	5
§1.03	FIRPTA: The Early Years	5
§1.04	The 1986 Tax Reform Act	6
	A. Repeal of the *General Utilities* Doctrine	7
	B. The Enactment of the Branch Profits Tax	8
§1.05	The FIRPTA Regulations	9
§1.06	Recent Legislative Amendments	11
§1.07	Will FIRPTA Be Repealed?	12

§1.01 OVERVIEW

A. What Are We Talking About

Investing in US real estate can generate stable and attractive returns. Foreign investors continue to make significant investments in US real estate.[1] Countries with an income tax system generally preserve the right to tax the gain from a disposition of real estate located within their borders. The US is no exception. The Internal Revenue Code, however, is unique relative to other countries' tax laws in the sense that the US tax

---

1. High-profile real estate deals include the purchase of the Rockefeller Center and Pebble Beach Country Club by Japanese purchasers in the late 1980s and, more recently, the 2015 purchase of the Waldorf Astoria hotel by an insurance company based in the People's Republic of China. *See* Chelsey Dulaney, *Waldorf Astoria Hotel Sale Completed*, The Wall Street Journal (February 11, 2015) (available at http://www.wsj.com/articles/waldorf-astoria-hotel-sale-completed-1423705536).

rules are very broad and very complex. The Foreign Investment in Real Property Tax Act, or FIRPTA,[2] rules exemplify that really well.

FIRPTA is a complex and multi-faceted regime. Some people think of FIRPTA as a mere withholding tax imposed on the sale of US real estate by foreign persons and that is all there is to it. This book hopes to dispel that notion completely. FIRPTA is a substantive tax that is imposed on the *sale or deemed sale* of a 'US real property interest' or USRPI.[3] In many cases, the party that acquires the USRPI is required to withhold a percentage of the *gross proceeds* from the transaction as a mechanism to collect the FIRPTA substantive tax.[4] The amount so withheld often does not equal the foreign person's final tax liability, and the foreign owner is required to file a US tax return to report the sale and settle the tax.[5]

If a foreign investor is not careful (or not aware of the rules), it can end up incurring a significantly higher tax burden on the US real estate investment than expected.[6] The fact that FIRPTA is imposed on a transaction whereby the foreign owner is *deemed* to have sold the USRPI suggests that a foreign owner that transfers a USRPI in certain transactions that may otherwise be non-taxable can be viewed as having sold the USRPI for US tax purposes. Such a transaction could trigger FIRPTA tax on the full appreciation of the USRPI.[7] Even in the case of an actual sale, the combined effective US tax rate that is imposed on the transaction can be in excess of 70% without any advance planning.[8] There are planning ideas that may minimize a foreign investor's US tax burden on the income and gain generated by the USRPI.[9] However, all US tax planning ideas require continuous proper implementation throughout the course of the investment or the anticipated benefit could easily be reduced or denied.

There is no one-size fits all approach to structure US real estate investment.[10] Hence, tax structuring advice regarding the acquisition, holding and exit of a US

---

2. Foreign Investment in Real Property Tax Act of 1980. H.R. Rep. No. 96-1167 2d Sess., at 530 (1980). This book refers to the amounts that may be subject to the FIRPTA regime as 'FIRPTA gains,' the tax imposed by I.R.C. §897(a) as the 'FIRPTA tax' or 'FIRPTA substantive tax' and the withholding tax imposed by I.R.C. §1445 as the 'FIRPTA withholding tax.'
3. See Chs. 3 and 4, *infra*, for definitions of USRPIs and US real property holding company, respectively.
4. See Ch. 8, *infra*, for a discussion of the withholding tax rules.
5. See Ch. 11, *infra*, for a discussion of the statute of limitations and key penalties relating to underpayment of taxes.
6. See Ch. 7, *infra*, for a discussion of the special rules applicable to nonrecognition transactions involving a transfer of USRPIs.
7. The investor also should take into account its resident country taxation (including whether the country gives a credit for any FIRPTA tax incurred) in assessing the overall tax burden with respect to the investment.
8. See Example 5.5, *infra*, for an illustration of the calculation.
9. See Ch. 6, *infra*, for a discussion of the exceptions to FIRPTA. In addition, Ch. 10, *infra*, also includes a discussion regarding US rules applicable to US debt versus equity rules and the rules that limit US interest deductions. If done properly, using some level of internal leverage may reduce the overall US tax burden with respect to certain investments in USRPI.
10. In some countries, such as the United Kingdom, a nonresident investor may avoid local country tax on the gain from a disposition of real estate investments if the property is held

real estate investment must be custom tailored to suit a foreign investor's specific profile, investment objectives and risk tolerance. A foreign-based multinational may be tempted to work through the US tax rules and drive the structuring of the US real estate investment on their own. Such an approach is analogous to driving on a super highway with a blindfold. No matter how talented and dedicated the members of the team are, they are not familiar with the US tax landscape with the many twists and turns that constantly show up when they are least expected. Without an experienced US tax professional navigating the course, there is no guarantee that the approach will stay on track.

Many informative (and some scholarly) articles have been written over the years about different technical aspects of FIRPTA,[11] but there does not seem to be an up-to-date, comprehensive and practical treatise that contains the various aspects of investing in US real estate in a single volume. The goal of this book is to provide a straightforward and accessible guide for readers to navigate the US tax issues that confront foreign investors in US real estate. Although FIRPTA is the key focus here, certain other related issues apply to foreign investors that invest in USRPIs. For example, the branch profits tax can significantly increase the tax burden of a foreign corporate investor on the gain from the sale of a USRPI,[12] but an investor that is eligible for treaty benefits may reduce or even eliminate that layer of incremental tax.[13] In addition, an overview of the real estate investment trust (or REIT)[14] rules is appropriate as those rules may reduce the overall US effective tax rate of the earnings distributed to a foreign investor during the course of the investment.[15]

B. The Organization of This Book

The discussion herein primarily focuses on foreign corporate investors which is the largest investor class in US real estate assets.[16] The book uses simplified examples from both real life situations and existing authorities to highlight the US tax consequences directly or indirectly affecting foreign investors in USRPIs. While the book covers the FIRPTA-specific issues more extensively, by necessity it merely highlights some of the related technical areas to raise the readers' awareness on those issues. Subsequent editions will include more real life examples and, depending on

---

by a company organized under the laws of a non-UK company, e.g., Jersey, and certain other conditions are met. When the Jersey company sells the real estate located in the UK, both the UK and Jersey would not impose tax on the gain realized from the sale. A foreign investor might avoid FIRPTA tax if it disposes of the shares of a foreign corporation that owns USRPI. However, the buyer is likely going to demand a price concession because the US tax basis of the USRPI would not be stepped up to the fair market value.

11. This book will refer to the work of many others who have provided insights on various technical issues.
12. *See* discussion in §2.02.B., *infra*.
13. *See* discussion in Ch. 9, *infra*.
14. As defined in I.R.C. §856(a).
15. *See* discussion in Ch. 5, *infra*.
16. However, Ch. 13, *infra,* discusses some of the key US tax issues that a foreign individual investor may come across.

readers' feedback, may also adjust the topics included. This remainder of this book is organized as follows:

- Chapter 2 describes the different structures and vehicles that foreign investors use to invest in US real estate and summarizes the overall US federal income tax consequences regarding the structures.
- Chapter 3 discusses the definition of a US Real Property Interest, or USRPI,[17] (other than a US Real Property Holding Company or USRPHC[18]) which is the basis of the FIRPTA regime.
- Chapter 4 discusses the definition of a US Real Property Holding Company.
- Chapter 5 provides a summary of the REIT rules and highlights certain interactions between the FIRPTA and REIT regimes.
- Chapter 6 discusses the exemptions to FIRPTA as well as special rules applicable to foreign governmental investors.
- Chapter 7 discusses the FIRPTA nonrecognition provisions that apply in addition to other Code provisions that would grant nonrecognition tax treatment regarding USRPIs.
- Chapter 8 discusses the FIRPTA withholding taxes that are jointly and severally liable for the buyers and sellers of USRPIs.
- Chapter 9 discusses certain treaty provisions that may impact foreign investors that are residents of a country that has entered into an income tax treaty with the US.
- Chapter 10 discusses certain entity classification issues and various restrictions on interest deductions by a US corporation.
- Chapter 11 summarizes certain US tax reporting standards and potential penalties for non-compliance.
- Chapter 12 provides a high-level discussion of state and local tax issues relating to US real estate investments.
- Chapter 13 provides a high-level discussion of certain income and transfer tax issues that affect foreign individuals who invest in US real estate.

US policies regarding the taxation of foreign investments have been somewhat inconsistent over the last half century. Congress amended the inbound tax rules in the 1960s to encourage the inflow of foreign capital. Less than two decades later, sentiment turned against foreign investment in US real estate with the enactment of FIRPTA. Then came the 1986 Tax Reform Act and the introduction of the branch profits tax which had the effect of significantly increasing the US tax burden of certain foreign investors. Fast forward to 2015, Congress amended the FIRPTA rules to relax the taxation of investments in REIT and other US real estate assets for certain foreign investors. This discussion below provides a background with respect to this progression and highlights how some of these changes affect the way the FIRPTA rules currently operate.

---

17. As defined in I.R.C. §897(c)(1).
18. As defined in I.R.C. §897(c)(2).

1. The Genesis of FIRPTA and Related Background

§1.02 FOREIGN INVESTMENT TAX ACT

Prior to 1966, the tax treatment of a foreign person's income depended on whether they were engaged in a US trade or business.[19] If a foreign person was not engaged in a US trade or business, then the foreign person would be subject to tax on the gross amount of only certain types of US source passive income, which included rental income but not gains from the sale of capital assets.[20] Conversely, if a foreign person engaged in a US trade or business, all US source passive income (including capital gains) and US source business income was subject to tax in a manner similar to that of a US resident (i.e., on a net basis after deductions at progressive income tax rates). This 'force of attraction' principle created a potentially onerous tax burden: US passive investments could be subject to the high marginal tax rates in effect at the time even though such passive investments were completely unrelated to the taxpayer's US trade or business.

In an effort to increase the flow of foreign capital into the US, Congress changed how foreign taxpayers engaged in a US trade or business were taxed in the Foreign Investor Tax Act of 1966 (FITA).[21] Under FITA, a foreign taxpayer engaged in a US trade or business was only subject to graduated income tax rates on a net basis if it received income effectively connected with the conduct of that US trade or business referred to as ECI.[22] FITA also added an election to treat real estate rental income as ECI.[23] This election was not necessarily favorable to the taxpayer at the time because it would subject gain from the sale of US real estate to US income tax, which, prior to FIRPTA, was rather easily avoided under the pre-FIRPTA Internal Revenue Code.[24]

§1.03 FIRPTA: THE EARLY YEARS

In the late 1970s, public opinion toward foreign investment started to move in the opposite direction compared to the prevailing attitudes when FITA was enacted. Specifically, there was public concern that US farmers were being priced out of the market due to increased foreign purchases of US farmland.[25] This apprehension in the general public led to a study by the Treasury Department in 1978 that concluded foreign investors had a tax advantage over US investors under the laws in effect at that time.[26]

Congress enacted FIRPTA in 1980 to level the playing field between US and foreign investors in US real estate.[27] FIRPTA treats gain or loss from the disposition of

---

19. *See* Dale, *Effectively Connected Income*, 42 Tax L. Rev. 689 (1987).
20. *Id.* at 690.
21. P.L. 89-809, 80 Stat. 1539 (enacted Nov. 13, 1966).
22. *See* Ch. 2, *infra*, for a further discussion of ECI and related issues.
23. *See* Dale, fn 19, at 708.
24. *Id.*
25. *See*, e.g., U.S. Department of the Treasury, Taxation of Foreign Investment in U.S. Real Estate (May 4, 1979) p. 47.
26. *Id.*
27. The 1980 Senate Finance Committee Report accompanying the enactment of FIRPTA explicitly stated that: '[t]he Committee believes that it is essential to establish *equity* of tax treatment in U.S. real property between foreign and domestic investors. The Committee

a USRPI by a foreign individual or foreign corporation as ECI, regardless of whether the foreign individual or foreign corporation was engaged in a US trade or business.[28] Immediately after the enactment of FIRPTA, taxpayers began engaging in transactions to avoid the application of the FIRPTA rules (e.g., contributing USRPIs to the capital of a foreign corporation). As a result, the Economic Recovery Tax Act of 1981[29] made a number of technical corrections to the FIRPTA regime, including:

- redefining USRPI to include real property located in the US or the Virgin Islands;
- making clear the Treasury's authority to provide for recognition of gain when a carryover basis transaction is for the purpose of avoiding federal income tax;
- adding that, under certain circumstances, a foreign investor may recognize gain when contributing USRPIs to the capital of a foreign corporation; and
- permitting some foreign corporations to elect to be treated as a US corporation for limited purposes.

Prior to 1984, the FIRPTA rules were enforced through a complex regime of reporting requirements. The Tax Reform Act of 1984 repealed these reporting requirements and added Code section 1445. Code section 1445(a) generally requires a purchaser of a USRPI from a foreign individual or foreign corporation to withhold a percentage of the gross proceeds paid to the seller and remit such amount to the IRS.[30] Additionally, Code section 1445(e) generally requires corporations, partnerships and trusts to withhold on distributions to foreign shareholders at the corporate tax rate (currently 35%). The withholding rules add their own set of complexity in addition to the underlying FIRPTA rules and are discussed in more detail in Chapter 8.

§1.04 THE 1986 TAX REFORM ACT

Within six years of the enactment of FIRPTA, much of the Internal Revenue Code was rewritten and reorganized by the Tax Reform Act of 1986 (TRA of 1986)[31] which generally lowered federal income tax rates[32] and broadened the tax base by removing certain perceived loopholes that effectively reduced taxable income. In fact, the changes were so vast that the Code itself was renamed the Internal Revenue Code

---

    does not intend by the provisions of Title IX to impose a penalty on foreign investors or to discourage foreign investors from investing in the United States' (emphasis added). S. Rep. No. 504, 96th Cong., 1st Sess. 6 (1979), at 511 H.R. Rep. No. 96-1167 2d Sess., at 530 (1980).
28. I.R.C. §897(a). *See* Ch. 3, *infra*, for a more detailed discussion of the definition of USRPI.
29. P.L. 97-34, 95 Stat. 172 (enacted Aug. 13, 1981).
30. H.R. Rep. No. 98-861, at 940-947 (1984).
31. P.L. 99-514, 100 Stat. 2085, enacted October 22, 1986.
32. The highest marginal tax rate for individuals was lowered to 28% for in 1986 (only to increase to 39.5% in 1987). *See* P.L. 99-514, 100 Stat. 2096, §101. Similarly, the highest marginal tax rate for corporations was lowered to 34% for tax years beginning after July 1, 1987. *See* P.L. 99-514, 100 Stat. 2249, §601.

of 1986.[33] Although the FIRPTA statute itself was not amended, the TRA of 1986 did introduce certain changes that indirectly increased the US tax burden that foreign investors in US real estate may face. Some of the changes relevant to the investment in US real estate are the repeal of the so-called *General Utilities* doctrine[34] and the introduction of the branch profits tax, discussed below.

A. Repeal of the *General Utilities* Doctrine

When FIRPTA was originally enacted, a corporate taxpayer generally could avoid paying corporate-level tax upon a sale of its assets if it liquidated within one year of the sale under the *General Utilities* doctrine. Under that doctrine, a foreign corporation that owned a USRPI could sell the property and liquidate without being subject to US corporate-level tax on the gain recognized.[35] To address this issue, Congress enacted Code section 897(d)[36] which prevents taxpayers from getting a tax-free step up in the basis of USRPI using the *General Utilities* doctrine for distributions made after June 18, 1980.[37] Code section 897(d) generally requires a foreign corporation that distributes a USRPI to recognize gain, *notwithstanding any other income tax provisions of the Code*, unless specific conditions are met. In a nutshell, FIRPTA repealed the *General Utilities* doctrine for foreign corporations that owned USRPIs.

The TRA of 1986 took a step further and repealed the *General Utilities* doctrine for *all* corporations. After the repeal, gain generally is recognized on liquidating distributions of appreciated property under Code section 336(a), except in the case of a corporation that makes a liquidating distribution to its 80% parent-corporation in a transaction to which Code section 332 applies.[38] Nonetheless, the Code section 897(d) rules have never been revised to take into account the *General Utilities* repeal. Subsequent guidance continues to ignore the fact that the *General Utilities* doctrine was repealed three decades ago. As discussed in Chapter 7, these FIRPTA Nonrecognition Rules contain some of the most complicated provisions of the FIRPTA regime. Absent satisfying the additional hurdles provided under these rules, any appreciation on the US real properties transferred in an otherwise tax-free transaction would be subject to FIRPTA tax. As a result, these rules increase the chances that the same gain is subject to double taxation (by both the US and the resident country

---

33. There were three previous overhauls of the Internal Revenue Code before 1986: one in 1954, one in 1939, and one in 1926.
34. In *General Utilities & Operating Co. v. Helvering*, 56 S. Ct. 185 (1935), the US Supreme Court held that a corporation did not have to recognize any gain when it distributed appreciated property to its shareholders.
35. On the other hand, the buyer was able to step up the tax basis of the property to the fair market value paid for such property.
36. The rest of this book refers to the provisions of I.R.C. §897(d) and (e), a companion provision which limits the application of certain nonrecognition involving one or more USRPIs, as the FIRPTA Nonrecognition Rules.
37. *See* Feingold and Glicklich, *An Analysis of the Temporary Regulations under FIRPTA: Part I*, 69 J.Tax'n 262 (October 6, 1988) for a discussion of the issues.
38. *See* I.R.C. §337. The TRA of 1986 also amended I.R.C. §367(e)(2) to provide that unless provided in regulations, the nonrecognition rules of I.R.C. §337 will not apply in the context of a liquidation involving a subsidiary of a foreign corporation.

of the foreign taxpayer). One commentator observed that '[W]hatever the merits of Regs §1.897-5T(c) might have been in the 1980s, it is today an anachronism that should be eliminated.'[39]

B. The Enactment of the Branch Profits Tax

The Tax Reform Act of 1986 introduced the 30% branch profits tax under Code section 884. The branch profits tax is imposed on the Dividend Equivalent Amount of a US branch (or deemed US branch)[40] of a foreign corporation.[41] The branch profits tax is intended to mirror the withholding tax imposed on a US subsidiary corporation paying dividends to its foreign parent corporation. Although that objective may have been attained at certain levels, the branch profits tax rules do not give rise to identical tax consequences between a US branch versus a US subsidiary of a foreign corporation in many situations.

The branch profits tax rules are very complex[42] and use a formula to determine whether a US branch is deemed to have repatriated any of its earnings to the foreign head office[43] for purposes of triggering the tax. As a result, it is possible for a foreign corporation to incur a branch profits tax liability in a year that it has not made any actual repatriation.[44] Furthermore, the branch termination rules contain various requirements that are not applicable to the liquidation of a US corporation.[45] The computation of a foreign corporation's Dividend Equivalent Amount generally includes all ECI, but excludes the gain from the sale of the shares of a USRPHC. As a result, FIRPTA gain, other than the gain from the sale of USRPHC shares, is potentially subject to the branch profits tax.

Without careful planning, a foreign investor may end up in a situation where the combined federal income tax imposed is 54.5% of the amount of appreciation

---

39. See Blanchard, FIRPTA in the 21st Century – Installment One: A Closer Look at Regs. §1.897-5T(c), Tax Management International Journal, 10/12/2007.
40. The language of I.R.C. §884 does not refer to a branch but, instead, refers to a foreign corporation that is subject to US tax under I.R.C. §882, i.e., one that is engaged in a US trade or business.
41. See Ch. 2 and Ch. 9, respectively, for a general discussion of the branch profits tax rules and for treaty provisions that may affect the branch profits tax rate.
42. See New York State Bar Association (NYSBA), Report on Temporary Branch Profits Tax Regulations, no. 596 dated December 8, 1988, which states, inter alia, that 'We question the need for the length and the complexity of the temporary regulations.'
43. This is treated as a 'disinvestment' from the US operations under the branch profits tax rules.
44. See Example 2.3, infra, for a numerical illustration of this phenomenon. This is in contrast with the situation involving a US subsidiary that generally may control when to make a dividend distribution to its foreign parent corporation, assuming that the US subsidiary is a regular US Subchapter C corporation (sometimes referred to as a 'C corporation' in this book) as opposed to a corporation that is subject to special rules such as a REIT.
45. See discussion in Ch. 2, infra, for a discussion of the branch termination rules. A foreign corporation that qualifies for the branch termination rules would not be subject to the branch profits tax for the year of termination and all subsequent years.

1. The Genesis of FIRPTA and Related Background

of the US real property.[46] In light of the fact that a stated goal of the TRA of 1986 is to generally lower the effective federal income tax rates, a foreign corporate investor subject to the branch profits tax may be surprised to learn the onerous US income tax burden.[47] The comparison is particularly striking when viewed in contrast with tax-efficient structures available to invest in other developed countries such as the UK.

§1.05 THE FIRPTA REGULATIONS

The Treasury Department and the IRS exercised their authority to promulgate regulations under Code section 897 over several decades, starting with proposed regulations in 1982 (which were partially amended in 1983 and finalized in 1984), followed by temporary regulations issued in 1988 and, most recently, new final regulations in 2003.[48] As discussed throughout this book, the regulations vastly expanded the reach of FIRPTA, sometimes in ways that were unforeseen.[49] Portions of the regulations have been updated by rulings, notices and announcements, and some other portions of the regulations are outdated because of recent legislative changes. A complete overhaul of the regulations would be very helpful but would represent a major undertaking. It is not clear if that would be a priority for the Treasury Department and the IRS in the near future.

Proposed Treasury regulation section 1.897-1 was issued in 1982 to provide more detailed definitions for the terms used in the statute. New proposed Treasury regulations issued in 1983 amended the 1982 proposed Treasury regulation to address comments requesting more detailed guidance on the definition of real property (i.e., land, unsevered natural products of land, land improvements, and personal property associated with the use of real property constitute 'real property'). The 1983 proposed Treasury regulations also removed an anti-abuse provision from the definition of an 'interest other than solely as a creditor.'[50]

Final Treasury Regulations under section 1.897-1 were issued in 1984, and largely maintained the same definitions as provided in the amended proposed regulations, including: 'real property,' 'real property interest,' and 'interest other than

---

46. *See* discussions in Chs. 2 and 9, *infra*, on the impact of the branch profits tax with and without the benefits of an income tax treaty, respectively.
47. T.D. 9082. Applicable state and local tax may increase the combined rate to closer to 60%. *See* Ch. 11 for a summary of these taxes. In addition, a foreign investor with ECI, including FIRPTA gain, is also required to file US income tax returns to report such income and gains. *See* discussion in Ch. 12, *infra*, for some of penalties for failure to satisfy US compliance requirements.
48. Other regulatory changes occurred in 1986, 1996 and 2016, which generally consisted of technical corrections and conforming amendments to recent statutory changes.
49. For example, the regulations expanded the definition of what constitutes a USRPI. *See* Ch. 3, *infra*, for a more detailed discussion of this issue. As another example, the regulations narrowed the application of the FIRPTA Nonrecognition Rules. *See* Ch. 7, *infra*, for a discussion of those issues.
50. Under the former anti-abuse rule, if a taxpayer had any interest in a USRPI other than solely as a creditor, then all of its interests in that USRPI would be treated as interests other than solely as a creditor.

an interest solely as a creditor.'[51] Some of these definitions, while more expansive than the definitions provided in the statutory language, create more ambiguity for the application of FIRPTA in certain instances.[52] Proposed Treasury Regulation section 1.897-2, also issued in 1982, provided procedures for determining whether a corporation was not a USRPHC. These proposed regulations were likewise amended in 1983, and finalized in 1984. Some of the points expanded on in Proposed Treasury Regulation section 1.897-2 include an alternative test to determine USRPHC status, when USRPHC status is determined, the treatment of assets held indirectly through attribution, and rules concerning the termination of USRPHC status.[53]

In 1988, the Treasury Department issued Temporary Treasury regulations which provide more detailed guidance with respect to the application of the FIRPTA rules in the context of corporate distributions and nonrecognition transactions, respectively.[54] Temporary Treasury Regulation section 1.897-5 expands on the rules in section 897(d), specifically the treatment of distributions of USRPIs by US corporations (including USRPHCs), foreign corporations, and foreign corporations electing to be treated as US corporations for FIRPTA purposes. Temporary Treasury Regulation section 1.897-6 was added to expand on Code section 897(e) and provide guidance on other nonrecognition transactions involving USRPIs. Despite the statutory language, the regulations only allow nonrecognition treatment when a USRPI is exchanged for another USRPI. In addition, the regulations add an exception to this general rule for exchanges between two foreign entities, in which case nonrecognition treatment is allowed only if the USRPI being exchanged is still subject to tax in the hands of the new owner. Despite the guidance provided in the temporary regulations, a lot of subsequent guidance has been issued by the IRS on a piecemeal basis, making this area of the FIRPTA regime particularly challenging to navigate.[55]

The Treasury Department and the IRS issued proposed and temporary regulations to implement the FIRPTA withholding tax under Code section 1445 in 1984. These regulations were finalized in 1986.[56] Additional withholding tax regulations were issued in 1990 to provide guidance on distributions by REITs and publicly traded partnerships.[57] A point of contention in the 1990 final regulations is the requirement to withhold an amount that could be designated as a capital gain dividend[58] by a REIT as a surrogate for the FIRPTA tax imposed by Code section 897(h)(1). Criticisms of this requirement include questions regarding the statutory authority to support the rule and the fact that the amount withheld does not represent a good measurement of the FIRPTA substantive tax imposed.[59]

---

51. These terms are discussed in greater detail in Ch. 3, *infra*.
52. For example, the regulations include language that makes it difficult to determine whether certain intangibles are USRPIs. See §§3.03.C and 3.04, *infra*, for a more detailed discussion of this issue.
53. *See* Ch. 4, *infra*, for a detailed discussion of these rules.
54. *See* T.D. 8198.
55. *See* Ch. 7, *infra*, for a discussion of the nonrecognition provisions under FIRPTA.
56. See T.D. 8113.
57. See T.D. 8321.
58. As defined in I.R.C. §857(b)(3)(C).
59. See Blanchard, *Is There A FIRPTA Tax on REIT Distributions?*, 112 Tax Notes 1071 (Sept. 18, 2006).

§1.06 RECENT LEGISLATIVE AMENDMENTS

The American Jobs Creation Act of 2004 (2004 Jobs Act) contained the next set of changes to FIRPTA tax with respect to REIT distributions.[60] Code section 897(h)(1) generally imposes a FIRPTA tax on distributions made by a REIT to foreign persons to the extent the amount is attributable to the sale or exchange of a USRPI by the REIT (the REIT Distribution Look-through Rule). Prior to the 2004 Jobs Act, all capital gains dividends attributable to the sales of a USRPI by a REIT were subject to tax under FIRPTA. The 2004 Jobs Act created an exception to this rule for distributions with respect to REIT stock regularly traded on an established securities market for shareholders owning no greater than 5% of such class of stock during the tax year.[61] The 2004 Jobs Act also expanded the REIT Distribution Look-through Rule to apply to 'qualified investment entities' which includes regulated investment companies, or RIC, as well as REITs.[62] In 2006, Congress enacted Code section 1445(e)(6) to apply withholding tax to, among other things, REIT distributions that are subject to substantive FIRPTA tax imposed by Code section 897(h)(1). This raises the question of whether the final regulations issued under 1.1445-8(c)(2)(ii)(A) in 1990 before the statute of Code section 1446(e)(6) was actually enacted have sufficient legislative support.[63]

Most recently, the Protecting Americans from Tax Hikes Act of 2015 (the 2015 PATH Act)[64] arguably made the most significant changes to the FIRPTA regime since its enactment. The changes included a number of provisions that favor foreign investments in REITs which, despite their humble beginning as vehicles to facilitate investments by small investors, have become an attractive vehicle for foreign investors.[65] Other significant changes include an exemption for qualified foreign pension funds (or QFPFs)[66] as well as an increase in FIRPTA withholding tax to 15% of the gross proceeds from 10%.[67] Additional clarifications and guidance are needed to implement a number of these new provisions. Some, such as a number of unanswered questions with respect to the qualification of QFPFs, should be issued in the foreseeable future.

---

60. P.L. 108-357, 118 Stat. §418, enacted October 22, 2004.
61. *Id.* at §418(a).
62. *Id.* at §411(c). The Distribution Look-through Rules under FIRPTA apply to RICs in order to prevent circumvention of FIRPTA by investing in RICs. Unless otherwise indicated, the rest of this book will refer only to REITs for ease of discussion where the rules apply to qualified investment entities.
63. *See* Blanchard, footnote 59 *supra*, for a further discussion of this issue.
64. Protecting American from Tax Hikes Act of 2015, P.L. 114-113, 129 Stat. 2242.
65. Ch. 5, *infra,* includes a summary of the REIT rules and a discussion of the overlap between the FIRPTA and REIT regimes.
66. These changes are discussed in more detail in Ch. 6, *infra*.
67. The increase in the withholding tax makes it even more attractive for taxpayers to consider obtaining a withholding certificate prior to the transaction to avoid any excess withholding tax. *See* Ch. 8, *infra,* for a discussion regarding FIRPTA Withholding Certificates.

§1.07 WILL FIRPTA BE REPEALED?

The call to repeal FIRPTA was first made within a few years of its enactment.[68] Similar comments have been made in recent years.[69] None of these suggestions have made any serious impact so far. Until they do, foreign investors who are well versed or well advised with respect to the regime have a better chance of avoiding incurring an unnecessary US tax burden on their return from the US real estate investments.

---

68. In 1984, Senator Wallup, one of the original sponsors of FIRPTA stated that the legislation '…has grown into a gorilla which terrorizes foreign investors, treaties, and the free market, to the detriment of all but the tax technicians.' Repeal of Foreign Investment in Real Property Tax Act, 1984: Hearing Before the Subcomm. on Energy and Agricultural Taxation of the Senate Comm. on Finance, 98th Cong., 2d Sess., 947 (1984).
69. Taylor, *Suppose FIRPTA Was Repealed*, 14 Fla. Tax Rev. 1, 6 (2013).

Chapter 2
Structuring Foreign Investments in the United States

§2.01	Overview	13
§2.02	Taxation of Operating Income	14
	A. General Rule	15
	B. Branch Profits Tax	18
	1. General Rule	18
	2. Branch Termination Exception	22
§2.03	Real Estate Investments Funds	23
	A. Attribution of US Trade or Business to Investors	23
	B. Sale of Fund Interests	25
§2.04	Investment Vehicles	26
	A. Foreign Corporations Investing Directly in USRPIs	27
	B. Investing through a US Partnership	28
	C. Investing through a US Corporation	30
	D. Investing through a US REIT	31
§2.05	Summary	33
	A. Fund Investment Platform	34
	B. Corporate Investment Platform	35
Appendix 2-A		36

§2.01 OVERVIEW

Foreign investors generally associate investment in US real estate with FIRPTA, which taxes a foreign investor's gain on the disposition of its USRPI. However, if the USRPI generates income prior to the disposition, which is often the case with developed real estate, such income is also subject to US federal income tax at 35%. A foreign corporation's gain and operating income of its USRPI may be subject to an additional 30% branch profits tax unless an exception applies. The taxation of the income from the pre-disposition period and the branch profits tax apply outside of the FIRPTA regime but, where applicable, they also affect a foreign investor's return on its US real estate investment. The structure of the investment can have a significant impact on the overall US tax burden.

When FIRPTA was enacted in 1980, the level of foreign ownership in US real estate was significantly lower and the investment structures were also simpler.[1] Today, foreign investors[2] with different profiles acquire diverse US real estate assets via different structures. For example, foreign-based real estate companies that own and operate US office buildings may hold such assets through wholly owned US subsidiaries. Passive investors, such as pension funds, may own interests in an investment fund that itself invests in real estate assets or other entities that own such assets.

This chapter discusses some of the real estate ownership structures used by investors today. As there are many building blocks to a structure (the type of income, entity used to hold the real estate and intermediary entities, etc.), it is helpful to understand the US tax issues with respect to the operating income and/or disposal gains from these structures. Because this chapter precedes the discussion of the substantive FIRPTA rules, readers may want to refer to later chapters that describe the various rules for context. Some of the nomenclature introduced in this chapter, e.g., US Blocker Corporation,[3] will be used throughout the book.

§2.02 TAXATION OF OPERATING INCOME

There are several issues applicable to the operating income generated by a USRPI. Depending on the ownership structure and the type of asset, the income may be categorized as active business income, i.e., ECI, or passive income. As discussed below, these two categories of income are taxed very differently.

Foreign taxpayers that have ECI or deemed ECI are also required to report the amount on a US income tax return. US tax compliance requirements can be rather complicated. The filing of the tax return generally starts the three years statute of limitation for the IRS to examine the tax return and assess any additional tax due.[4] If a taxpayer does not file a required tax return, then the statute of limitations will not begin, giving the IRS an unlimited window to assess the tax due. Even if a return is timely filed, there is a perception that the IRS can be aggressive in asserting penalties if a taxpayer fails to properly comply with the US tax rules.[5]

Many foreign taxpayers, particularly those who only have passive US investments, prefer not to have such US filing obligations or interactions with the tax authorities to the extent possible. For example, a foreign corporate investor that

---

1. Recall that the initial concern of FIRPTA was to address foreign ownership of US farm land.
2. The term 'investor' is used loosely in this context and does not refer to a person who is treated as an investor (versus a developer or dealer) under US tax principles.
3. Unless otherwise specified, the term Blocker Corporation or Blocker refers to Subchapter C corporations in this book. In this context, a corporation is a 'blocker' because it is the person that reports any income from the specific underlying USRPI on its own US income tax return and pays the associated US tax liabilities; hence, it 'blocks' the ultimate foreign investor from these obligations.
4. I.R.C. §6501(a).
5. *See*, e.g., discussion in §11.03.A., *infra*, for penalties relating to a failure to file tax returns.

expects to have ECI from its USRPI during the pre-disposition period may choose to use a US Blocker Corporation to own the asset directly. That way, the Blocker is responsible for reporting the income on its own US tax return and the ultimate foreign parent of the Blocker need not bear such responsibilities.

A.   General Rule

In broad terms, a foreign taxpayer is generally subject to US tax on two types of income earned either directly or indirectly (e.g., through an investment fund):

- US source income that is fixed or determinable annual or periodical (FDAP) income subject to a 30% *gross*-basis tax;[6] and
- income effectively connected with a US trade or business (ECI) subject to a 35%[7] *net*-basis tax.[8]

FDAP income describes a broad spectrum of income items.[9] The statute enumerates specific items of FDAP income including interest, dividends, rents, premiums, annuities and compensations.[10] The most common types of FDAP income that a foreign investor in real estate may receive are rental income, interest and dividends. A foreign investor that owns a USRPI directly may receive rental income while a foreign investor that owns its USRPI through a US Blocker Corporation is likely to receive dividend income from the Blocker.[11]

The rules can be tricky when it comes to the characterization of rental income. The statute specifically lists rent as a type of FDAP income.[12] Hence, rental income may be subject to the 30% gross-basis tax. However, this characterization is not automatic but, instead, should be determined based on the facts and circumstances of each case. For instance, the Treasury Department and the IRS have held that a foreign person who owned a net lease for a US real property on a long-term basis was not engaged in a US trade or business because the activities conducted in the US were not 'considerable, continuous and regular.'[13] As a result, rental income from a triple net lease may be treated as FDAP income.

---

6. I.R.C. §§871(a)(1) and 881(a). An applicable income tax treaty may reduce or even eliminate the US tax imposed on such income. *See* Ch. 9, *infra*, for further discussion on application of treaties.
7. Technically speaking, 35% is the top marginal tax rate for corporations. *See* I.R.C. §11(b). The rest of this book refers to the corporate federal income tax rate as 35% for ease of discussion. *See* discussion in Ch. 13, *infra*, regarding US individual income tax rates.
8. A taxpayer may deduct appropriate expenses in determining its taxable income which is effectively connected with a US trade or business. I.R.C. §882(c)(1).
9. For US withholding tax purposes, FDAP income generally includes all items of US source gross income except gains from the sale of property. *See* Treas. Reg. §1.1441-2(b).
10. I.R.C. 881(a).
11. The foreign investor also may receive US source interest income from the Blocker Corporation if there is internal leverage. See discussion in Ch. 10, *infra*.
12. I.R.C. §§871(a) and 881(a).
13. *See* Rev. Rul. 73-522, 1973-2, C.B. 225. As a result, the ruling concluded that expenses paid by the lessee and netted against the rent are expenses of the lessee and not treated as income or expenses of the lessor. Outside of a true net lease context, the courts

A foreign corporation that operates a building through the activities of its employees or agents in the US is considered to be engaging in a US trade or business. In that case, the rental income will constitute ECI.[14] The Code does not provide an affirmative definition of a US trade or business, but does provide guidance on what does *not* constitute a US trade or business.[15] US tax principles also impute activities of an agent to its principal.[16] If a foreign corporation is engaged in a US trade or business, certain US source FDAP income and US source capital gains may be treated as ECI if the income is derived from assets held in the conduct of the US trade or business, or the activities of such trade or business were a material factor in the realization of the income.[17] In addition, all US source income, gain or loss, other than FDAP income and capital gain or loss also shall be treated as ECI under a limited 'force of attraction' rule.[18]

A special rule allows a taxpayer to affirmatively treat passive rental income as ECI.[19] The benefit of this election is the taxpayer's ability to offset the rental income with deductions. The type of deductions that are generally allowable include mortgage interest, depreciation, real property taxes, utilities, and other ordinary and necessary business deductions associated with operating the property. Although the deductions can reduce the US income tax base, a foreign corporation that makes this election also may subject what is otherwise passive income to the branch profits tax.[20] It is advisable to model-out the expected US income tax liabilities under both scenarios prior to deciding whether to make the election.[21]

Assume that George Inc., **Example 2.1**, is a foreign corporation that acquired an office building in Atlanta, Georgia for USD 100 million at the end of 2015. The

---

determination of whether a taxpayer is engaged in a US trade or business is based on the facts and circumstances of each case. See *Lewenhaupt v. Commissioner*, 20 T.C. 151 (1953), aff'd, 221 F.2d 227 (9th Cir. 1955); *Herbert v. Commissioner*, 30 T.C. 26 (1958); and *De Amodio v. Commissioner*, 34 T.C. 894 (1960), aff'd, 299 F.2d 623 (3rd Cir. 1962).

14. See I.R.C. §864(c).
15. See I.R.C. §864(b). The concept of a 'trade or business' has been developed through US case law and is generally accepted to mean the active pursuit of profit through regular and continuous activities. *See*, e.g., *Higgins v. Commissioner, 312 U.S. 714* (S. Ct. 1941). *See* §9.04.D., *infra*, for a discussion of the US taxation of business profits of a treaty resident.
16. For example, in *InverWorld, Inc. v. C.I.R. T.C. Memo*, 1996-301 (US Tax Ct., 1996), the Tax Court concluded that an indirect US subsidiary of a Cayman Islands corporation was acting as the latter's dependent agent. Consequently, the foreign principal was considered to be engaging in a US trade or business. The IRS has applied a similar principle to impute activities of independent agents to foreign principals in other situations. *See* EMISC 2009-010. In addition, I.R.C. §875(1) also treats a foreign person that is a member of a partnership as engaged in a US trade or business if the partnership is so engaged. *See* discussion in §2.03.A., *infra*.
17. I.R.C. §864(c)(2).
18. I.R.C. §864(c)(3).
19. I.R.C. §882(d). This is the net-basis election (also referred to as the ECI election sometimes) that was enacted by FITA. *See* discussion in §1.02, *supra*.
20. See §2.02.B., *infra*, for a discussion of the branch profits tax which applies to a foreign corporation's business profits. An income tax treaty may reduce or eliminate the branch profits tax burden. *See* discussion in Ch. 9, *infra*.
21. Compare Example 2.1 to Example 2.2.

purchase price was allocated 80% and 20% to the building and land, respectively. In addition, 60% of the purchase price was financed by a mortgage debt with a 5% fixed interest rate. The building is externally managed and generates USD 8 million of gross rental revenue annually. The analysis of whether to make the net-basis election to treat the rental income as ECI may look like this.

Example 2.1

	No Election	Net-Basis Election
	(in USD millions)	
Gross Rent Income	8	8
Less:		
– Depreciation	–	(2)[22]
– Mortgage Interest	–	(3)
ECI	n/a	3
30% Gross-Basis Tax	(2.4)	n/a
35% Net-Basis Tax	n/a	(1.05)
Residual Cash	2.6[23]	3.95

This example does not take into account any US branch profits tax that may apply to a foreign corporation that generates ECI during the holding period of a USRPI. See **Example 2.2** for a calculation that does.

A special rule applies to determine a foreign corporation's interest expense that may be allocated to and deducted against its ECI.[24] In general, a foreign corporation determines its US interest deduction based on the formula prescribed under Treasury regulations regardless of the actual amount accrued or paid by its US business.[25] The formula uses a detailed three-step process that treats a portion of the corporation's worldwide interest expense as incurred by its US business.[26]

---

22. USD 80 million purchase price allocated to the building is depreciated over a recovery period of 39 years. See I.R.C. §168(c).
23. George Inc. may not deduct the USD 3 million mortgage interest that it paid but the amount still reduces its cash flow.
24. *See* I.R.C. §882(c).
25. *See* Treas. Reg. §1.882-5.
26. At a high level, the interest deduction is computed by: Step (1) determining assets that generate ECI; Step (2) determining liabilities that are effectively connected with the conduct of a US trade or business; and Step (3) determining an average US interest rate, which is applied to US-connected liabilities determined in Step (2). This formula also affects the foreign corporation's branch profits tax calculation. *See* discussion in §2.02.B.1., *infra*.

A foreign corporation is required to report its ECI on a timely filed US tax return.[27] A failure to file the returns could result in interests and penalties.[28] A special rule requires a foreign corporation to file its federal income tax return within eighteen months of the original due date or lose its ability to use any deductions to offset its ECI.[29] A foreign corporation that does not derive any ECI in a tax year may file a tax return within the prescribed period to protect its rights to claim deductions and credits if it later determines that the original determination was incorrect (i.e., it discovered later that it did have ECI in that year).[30] By contrast, a foreign corporation that has only FDAP income in a year generally does not have any US tax compliance obligations.[31]

If the USRPI is owned directly by a US Blocker, then the US Blocker is the entity that reports the income and pays the US income tax associated with the annual profit or loss generated.[32] Using a US Blocker to report the equivalent of the ECI generally should not result in a higher US federal income tax liability. Using a US Blocker may be simpler because it avoids the application of the US branch profits tax.[33] Such a structure also may provide an easier path in the event of an IRS income tax examination.[34]

B. Branch Profits Tax

1. *General Rule*

The purpose of the branch profits tax is to subject foreign corporations operating in the US in branch form to similar taxation as foreign corporations operating there in subsidiary form. The rules intend to impose an additional layer of tax when the US branch of a foreign corporation repatriates its business profits overseas to its head office. However, as discussed below, the complex formula used to determine a

---

27. *See* I.R.C. §§6012(a)(2) and 6072(c).
28. *See* Ch. 11, *infra*, for a discussion of some of the penalty provisions.
29. Treas. Reg. §1.882-4(a)(3)(i). The IRS Commissioner or his or her delegate may waive the filing deadline if the foreign corporation can establish that, based on the facts and circumstances, it acted reasonably and in good faith in failing to file a US income tax return (including a protective tax return) within the eighteen-month window. Treas. Reg. §1.882-4(a)(3)(ii). *See Swallows Holdings, Ltd. v. Comm'r* 515 F.3d 162 (3d Cir. 2008).
30. Treas. Reg. §1.882-4(a)(3)(vi).
31. Treas. Reg. §1.6012-2(g)(2)(i).
32. A foreign corporation that has FIRPTA gain is required to file a US income tax return to report the gain which is treated as ECI under I.R.C. §897(a).
33. A foreign person is generally subject to a 30% US withholding tax on US source dividends. *See* I.R.C. §881(a). The withholding tax is imposed on the amount actually paid by a US corporation as compared to the branch profits tax which is imposed on the amount deemed paid by a US branch. As shown in Example 2.3, it is possible to incur a branch profits tax even though a foreign corporation has reinvested all of its earnings in its US operations.
34. If the taxpayer is a US Blocker Corporation, then presumably the IRS should be examining the books and records of the Blocker instead of the books and records of the ultimate foreign investor which may have other non-US businesses and assets.

foreign corporation's branch profits tax can give rise to a tax liability in a year when no repatriation has actually occurred.

Under this regime, a foreign corporation is subject to 35% federal tax on its net ECI and an additional 30% branch profits tax when the income is repatriated or deemed repatriated. Thus, if branch profits tax applies in a taxable year, a foreign corporation's US federal tax rate on the ECI can be as high as 54.5%.[35] This additional branch tax could apply even if the US ECI earnings are not actually distributed; by contrast, the after-tax earnings of a US subsidiary of a foreign corporation are only subject to an additional 30% tax when they are distributed to a foreign parent.[36] **Example 2.2** illustrates the consequences if George Inc. in **Example 2.1** had repatriated all of its effectively connected earnings and profits generated in 2015 to its head office which is located in a non-treaty country.

Example 2.2

	Regular Corporate Tax	*Regular and Branch Profits Tax*
	(in USD millions)	
Gross Rent Income	8	8
Less:		
– Depreciation	(2)	(2)
– Mortgage Interest	(3)	(3)
ECI	3	3
30% Gross-Basis Tax	n/a	n/a
35% Net-Basis Tax	(1.05)	(1.05)
Dividend Equivalent Amount	3.95	3.95
30% Branch Profits Tax	n/a	(1.19)
Residual Cash	3.95	2.76

The branch profits tax is levied on a foreign corporation's Dividend Equivalent Amount which generally equals its earnings and profits that are effectively connected with the conduct of a US trade or business.[37] The foreign corporation's Dividend Equivalent Amount is adjusted as follows:

---

35. (100% − 35%) x 30% + 35%.
36. A US corporation that has not made an election to be taxed as a REIT is generally not required to distribute its earnings each year. See Ch. 5, *infra*, for a discussion of the REIT rules. See §8.03.D., *infra*, for a discussion of the ordering rules on distributions of a corporation's earnings.
37. I.R.C. §884(a) and (b).

- decreased by amounts reinvested in the foreign corporation's US Net Equity;[38] and
- increased by any disinvestment in the foreign corporation's US Net Equity;[39]

US Net Equity is the amount of a foreign corporation's US Assets[40] reduced by its US Liabilities.[41] In general, USRPIs[42] are treated as US Assets only if the property produces effectively connected *operating* income.[43] Shares of a USRPHC are not US Assets.[44] Depreciable and/or amortizable intangible properties are treated as US Assets in the same proportion that the amount of depreciation or amortization allowable as a deduction that is effectively connected with the conduct of a US trade or business bears to the total depreciation or amortization of the property.[45] If a foreign corporation makes an installment sale of a US Asset, all of the gain (including the deferred portion) is included in the corporation's effectively connected earnings and profits.[46] A foreign corporation that is a partner in a partnership must allocate the adjusted basis of its partnership interest between US and non-US Assets.[47]

A foreign corporation's US Liabilities is determined as the product of its US Assets multiplied by a fraction. The fraction may be either: (1) a fixed ratio of 50% for a foreign corporation that is neither a bank nor an insurance company,[48] or (2) the actual ratio of the corporation's worldwide liabilities to its worldwide assets.[49] As a result, the amount of a corporation's US Liabilities for branch profits tax purposes is

---

38. A foreign corporation is considered to have reinvested in the US if its US Net Equity as of the close of the tax year exceeds the amount of its US Net Equity as of the beginning of its tax year. I.R.C. §884(b)(1).
39. I.R.C. §884(b)(2)(B) limits the increase in the Dividend Equivalent Amount to the difference between post-1986 effectively connected earnings and profits and the aggregate Dividend Equivalent Amount for previous years.
40. The term US Assets is defined as money and the aggregate adjusted basis of property used by the foreign corporation that is treated as effectively connected with the conduct of a US trade or business. I.R.C. §884(c)(2). In general, an asset is a US Asset if all income from the use, and all gain from the disposition of the property on the determination date is (or would be) effectively connected with the conduct of a US trade or business. Treas. Reg. §1.884-1(d)(1)(i). The determination date is usually the close of the foreign corporation's taxable year. Treas. Reg. §1.884-1(c)(3) and (d)(1).
41. I.R.C. §884(c)(1).
42. The ones described in I.R.C. §897(c)(1)(A)(i).
43. For example, a condominium owned by a foreign corporation is not a US Asset if it is not part of a US trade or business activity, e.g., because it is used by the foreign corporation's shareholders as a residence. Treas. Reg. §1.884-1(d)(2)(xi), Example (3).
44. Because gain on the disposition of such shares is specifically excluded from the definition of effectively connected earnings and profits. *See* I.R.C. §884(d)(2)(C).
45. *See* Treas. Reg. §1.884-1(d)(2)(i).
46. I.R.C. §312(n)(5).
47. The allocation may be done using either the asset or the income method. *See* Treas. Reg. §1.884-1(d)(3). The basis of a foreign corporation's partnership interest is determined under I.R.C. §705 with adjustments set forth in Treas. Reg. §1.884-1(d)(3)(vi).
48. The fixed liability ratio for a bank or an insurance company is 95%. *See* Treas. Reg. §§1.884-1(e)(1) and 1.882-5(c)(4).
49. All amounts are stated at the end of the foreign corporation's taxable year. Treas. Reg. §1.884-1(c)(3).

2. Structuring Foreign Investments in the United States

driven by a formula and has no relationship to the liabilities recorded on the books of the US branch.

Not all of the increase in a foreign corporation's US Assets is treated as reinvestment into its US Net Equity based on the above formula. It is easier to use an example to illustrate this point. In **Example 2.3**, Harper Ltd. is a non-treaty country corporation that engages in various businesses both abroad and in the US. In 2016, Harper Ltd.'s US trade or business has generated effectively connected earnings and profits of USD 500,000 all of which is reinvested in the US. There are no other increases in Harper Ltd.'s US Assets. Harper Ltd. elects to use the 50% fixed liability ratio to compute its US interest deduction (and, hence, its US Liabilities).[50]

Example 2.3

Under the branch profits tax rules, Harper Ltd.'s US Assets have increased by USD 500,000 as of 12/31/16, but its US Liabilities are deemed to have increased by only USD 250,000.[51] As a result, Harper Ltd.'s US Net Equity also increased by only USD 250,000.

Harper Ltd.'s 2016 Dividend Equivalent Amount is USD 250,000 (USD 500,000 of effectively connected earnings and profits less USD of 250,000 increase in its US Net Equity). The amount of Dividend Equivalent Amount is subject to the 30% branch profits tax or USD 75,000.

Amounts Per Books
(in USD 000s)

	12/31/15	12/31/16	Increase
US Assets	40,000	40,500	500
US Liabilities	(24,000)	(24,000)	—
US Net Equity	16,000	16,500	500

Calculations Per Regulations

	12/31/15	12/31/16	Increase
US Assets	40,000	40,500	500
US Liabilities	(20,000)	(20,250)	(250)
US Net Equity	20,000	20,250	250

Harper Ltd. may have avoided any branch profits tax liability in 2016 if it operated its US business through a US subsidiary instead of a branch; that is because no US withholding would apply since the US subsidiary has not made any distributions. Alternatively, if Harper Ltd. is a single purpose foreign company that operates

---

50. This election makes it easier to determine the amount of interest expense allocable to Harper Ltd.'s ECI.
51. Computed as 50% of USD 500,000 because Harper Ltd. elects to use the 50% fixed liability ratio of Treas. Reg. §1.882-5(c)(4) to determine its interest expense calculation.

exclusively in the US, and it uses the actual liability ratio to determine its interest deduction (and, hence, its US Liabilities),[52] then the result should be the same as operating through a US subsidiary. In other words, the increase in the foreign corporation's US Net Equity would also be USD 500,000 which would equal the increase in its US Assets.

2. *Branch Termination Exception*

The Branch Termination Exception is a special rule that exempts a foreign corporation from the branch profits tax in the year that it completely terminates its US trade or business. If this exception applies, any non-previously taxed accumulated effectively connected earnings and profits as of the close of the termination year are extinguished and exempt from the branch profits tax.[53]

The foreign corporation must satisfy a number of conditions to qualify for the Branch Termination Exception. Among other things, the foreign corporation and its 10%-or-greater related corporations may not use, directly or indirectly, any of the US Assets of the terminated US trade or business, or property attributable thereto or to effectively connected earnings and profits earned by the foreign corporation in the year of complete termination, in the conduct of a US trade or business at any time during a three-year period from the close of the year of complete termination[54] (also referred to as the Reinvestment Rule).[55]

The Branch Termination Exception is an attempt to provide comparable US tax treatment to complete liquidation of a US subsidiary of a foreign corporation.[56] However, some have observed that the rules 'can discriminate against foreign corporations conducting a branch business in the United States in favor of those doing business here through U.S. subsidiaries.'[57] Amongst the most criticized of the Branch Termination Exception is the Reinvestment Rule.

The exception is drafted broadly and prohibits reinvestment in any US business regardless of whether the new business is similar to the old business that was terminated. There is no similar reinvestment prohibition when a US subsidiary sells its business and liquidates into a foreign corporate parent.[58] Therefore, a foreign corporation should be very mindful of the requirements of the Reinvestment Rule in planning its exit from the US in order to qualify for the Branch Termination Exception.

---

52. Under Treas. Reg. §1.882-5(c)(2).
53. Temp. Treas. Reg. §1.884-2T(a)(1).
54. Temp. Treas. Reg. §1.884-2T(a)(2)(i)(A) provides that a foreign corporation's year of complete termination may include the tax year as of the close of which the foreign corporation has no US Assets or its shareholders have adopted an irrevocable resolution to completely liquidate and dissolve the corporation and the immediately succeeding tax year in which all of its US Assets are either distributed, used to pay off liabilities or cease to be US Assets.
55. *See* Temp. Treas. Reg. §1.884-2T(a)(2)(i)(B), and (iv).
56. In general, the accumulated earnings and profits of a US subsidiary are treated as a dividend when the subsidiary distributes the amount to its foreign parent corporation in a complete liquidation. *See* I.R.C. §331(b).
57. *See* NYSBA report, Ch. 1 footnote 42, *supra*.
58. *See* I.R.C. §332.

In some instances, it may be possible to use a foreign corporation to own a single USRPI and liquidate the foreign corporation after the sale of the USRPI to demonstrate that the liquidation satisfies the Reinvestment Rule.

§2.03 REAL ESTATE INVESTMENTS FUNDS

Investing in US real estate through a fund is a common investment route for foreign investors. Conceptually, a fund is any vehicle that enables a sponsor to pool capital from different parties to invest in a portfolio of assets. A US fund is generally established as a limited partnership or a limited liability corporation. In some cases, foreign partnerships also may be formed, e.g., in the Cayman Islands, to facilitate investments by foreign investors.[59] A recent example is the use of vehicles such as Singapore listed REITs to raise capital from Asian investors.[60] Regardless of the place of organization, a fund entity almost always elects to be classified as a partnership for US federal income tax purposes in order to avoid corporate-level tax on the income and gains from the investment.[61]

Because a partnership is a pass-through entity for tax purposes, a foreign partner of a partnership is the party that is subject to tax on its allocable share of US source income, gain or loss of the partnership. US partnership taxation rules are very complex and a discussion is beyond the scope of this book. However, in the context of foreign investment in US real estate, two aspects of the US partnership tax rules that directly impact foreign investors should be mentioned: (1) attribution of the US trade or business of the fund to its foreign investors; and (2) taxation of the sale of the partnership interests in the fund.

A. Attribution of US Trade or Business to Investors

US tax principles attribute the business of a partnership to its foreign partners. Hence, a foreign corporation is deemed to be engaged in a US trade or business if it is a partner in a partnership that is so engaged.[62] When the partnership entity (e.g., either a joint venture entity or a real estate fund) disposes of any of the underlying USRPI, the *foreign partner* will be subject to FIRPTA tax with respect to its allocable share of the gain. The *foreign partner* also will have US tax reporting obligations in the year of disposition. In addition, if the partnership entity generates ECI during

---

59. Some feeder funds may be formed in jurisdictions such as Luxembourg or Ireland to satisfy European Union regulatory requirements and to attract European investors. An example is the Alternative Investment Fund Managers Directive or AIFMD requirements. 2011/61/EU is an EU directive on the financial regulation of hedge, private equity, real estate and similar funds undertaken by G20 nations following the global financial market meltdown in 2008.
60. *See* Jeevan Vasagar, *US assets set to form larger part of Singapore REITs market,* Financial Times (21 June 2016).
61. The legal form of the entity does not control the US tax classification of the entity. The partnership tax characterization is always used because it avoids US entity-level tax. *See* §10.02, *infra,* for a discussion on the US Check-the-Box rules.
62. *See* I.R.C. §875(1).

the pre-disposition period prior to the sale (e.g., rental income or a sale of a portion of the underlying USRPI), the foreign partner also may be required to file US tax returns to report its allocable portion of income or loss that is considered effectively connected with the underlying US trade or business.

A foreign investor that enters into a private joint venture that engages in a US trade or business (e.g., the development of residential high rises) with a few partners generally performs the necessary due diligence with respect to the investment. Such an investor/partner may learn about the US tax exposures with respect to the investment during the course of the due diligence. Most of the time, the foreign investor forms a US Blocker Corporation to own the partnership interest. The US Blocker becomes the alter ego of the foreign investor and handles US tax reporting and pays US taxes associated with the investment.[63]

On the other hand, a foreign investor that owns a small equity interest in a large investment fund[64] is unlikely to set up its own US Blocker solely for purposes of owning the US partnership investments. An investment fund that intends to attract foreign investors sometimes sets up one or more foreign corporations (also referred to as Foreign Feeder Corporations) into which foreign investors may invest directly to achieve similar results. In such a structure, the Foreign Feeder Corporation will file the necessary US tax returns to report any ECI and FIRPTA gain from the sale of the underlying investment. Some of these entities are formed as partnerships legally but elect to be treated as corporations *solely* for US tax purposes.[65]

There is another wrinkle regarding investment in real estate funds. If the fund, classified as a partnership for tax purposes, itself is engaged in a trade or business,[66] then the partnership must withhold quarterly tax payments on the amount of *any* ECI (i.e., not just ECI attributable to USRPIs) that is allocable to foreign partners.[67] The withholding tax is paid quarterly based on the amount of the partnership's net ECI allocable to its foreign partners;[68] however, a special rule allows the partnership to take into consideration certain *partner-level* deductions and losses that may reduce the amount of withholding tax liability.[69] A coordination rule provides that

---

63. *See* Ch. 10, *infra*, for various leveraging and interest deduction issues applicable to US Blocker structures.
64. Some of these investment funds own primarily real estate assets while others invest in various asset classes including real estate.
65. *See* discussion in Ch. 10, *infra*, regarding the US Check-the-Box rules to elect corporate or pass-through status of an entity solely for US tax purposes. Such an election does not have any impact for non-US tax purposes; as a result, the entity still may be treated as a pass-through entity for foreign tax purposes (referred to as a Reverse Hybrid Entity), and may avoid entity-level tax in the foreign country under whose laws it is organized, etc.
66. As opposed to merely engaging in investment activities.
67. I.R.C. §1446. The withholding tax rate for ECI allocable to corporate foreign partners is 35%. Special rules apply to publicly traded partnerships. *See* Treas. Reg. §1.1446-4 and discussion in Ch. 8, *infra*.
68. Treas. Reg. §1.1446-3(b)(1).
69. See Treas. Reg. §1.1446-6(c)(1) which requires, *inter alia*, that the partner certifies that the partner-level deductions and losses may reduce the amount of I.R.C. §1446 withholding tax liability.

this withholding tax overrides the FIRPTA withholding tax in a situation when both rules apply.[70]

B. Sale of Fund Interests

Under the 'aggregate' theory of partnership taxation, a partnership is treated as an aggregate of its partners. In contrast, under the 'entity' theory, a partnership is treated as an entity distinct from its partners. US tax principles are a blend of aggregate and entity treatment for partners and partnerships.[71] The Code generally applies the entity theory with respect to the sale of a partnership interest by a partner. The statute generally requires a partner to treat the gain or loss from the sale of a partnership interest as the amount from the sale of a capital asset.[72] Hence, a foreign partner is generally subject to US federal income tax on the sale of the partnership interest only if the gain is ECI.[73]

There is no statutory provision that treats any portion of a foreign partner's gain with respect to the sale of partnership interest as ECI. Notwithstanding the lack of statutory authority, the Treasury Department and the IRS issued a revenue ruling that applied a hybrid aggregate and entity approach to the sale of a partnership interest by a foreign partner. In Revenue Ruling 91-32,[74] the IRS ruled that a foreign partner's gain or loss from a sale of its partnership interest[75] generally is treated as ECI in an amount equal to the foreign partner's hypothetical distributive share of ECI as if the partnership had disposed of all its assets in transactions in which gain or loss was recognized in full.[76]

The IRS reached the conclusion in Revenue Ruling 91-32, in part, by reasoning that because a partner is engaged in the trade or business of the partnership by virtue of Code section 875(1), the partner is also considered to have a US office or fixed place of business if the partnership's trade or business is conducted through such a US office or fixed place of business.[77] It then further attributed the income from the sale of the partnership interest to such US office or fixed place or business. In one of the situations in the ruling (Situation 3), the IRS extended the same holding to a foreign partner that is resident in a treaty country. The treaty permits source

---

70. Treas. Reg. §1.1446-3(c)(2).
71. *See.* e.g., Rev. Rul. 89-85, 1989-2 C.B. 218, 219 and *Casel v. Commissioner*, 79 T.C. 424 (1982).
72. *See* I.R.C. §§741 and 751.
73. The issue is similar to the one that existed with respect to the US taxation of gain from a disposition of US real property prior to the codification of I.R.C. §897 by FIRPTA.
74. 1991-1 C.B. 107. *See* Appendix 2-A.
75. As an initial matter, the Treasury Department and the IRS applied the entity theory of I.R.C. §741 to determine the overall amount of the gain or loss from the sale of the partnership interest.
76. At this point, the Treasury Department and the IRS looked through the partnership to only tax the portion of the overall gain attributable to ECI-generating assets. They cited I.R.C. §897(g) as support for applying the aggregate theory to the sale.
77. According to the IRS, this is based on case law such as *Donroy, Ltd. v. United States*, 301 F. 2d 200 (9th Cir. 1962) and *Unger v. Commissioner*, T.C. Memo, 1990-15 58 TCM 1157, 1159.

country taxation of business profits only to the extent attributable to a permanent establishment. The IRS attributed the partner's gain from the sale of the partnership interest to the partnership's permanent establishment in that situation.

The facts of Revenue Ruling 91-32 did not involve USRPI and, hence, FIRPTA was not directly implicated. However, the IRS did cite Code section 897(g), which applies the aggregate principle to determine the amount of FIRPTA gain from a sale of a partnership interest, as support for reaching its conclusion in the ruling. Accordingly, Code section 897(g) should apply a similar methodology and treat as ECI the portion of the gain from a sale of the partnership interest based on the same ratio from a hypothetical distributive share of ECI as if *the partnership* sold all of the underlying assets.

The conclusions of the revenue ruling are controversial and some have questioned the statutory basis for the positions.[78] The Obama Administration included a proposal to codify the rule set forth in the revenue ruling in the 2012 Green Book.[79] The Green Book explained that taxpayers may take a contrary position to the holding of the revenue ruling '[B]ecause no Code provision explicitly provides that gain from the sale or exchange of a partnership interest by a nonresident alien individual or a foreign corporation is treated as ECI.' This statement and the proposal highlight the fact that the authority for the revenue ruling may not be have been as strong as the IRS would have liked. As of July 2017, the proposal to codify Revenue Ruling 91-32 has not yet been enacted into legislation.

In a recent case, *Grecian Magnesite Mining, Co. v. Comm'r*,[80] the Tax Court rejected the IRS's position in Revenue Ruling 91-32 and held that a foreign corporation was not subject to US federal income tax on the gain that it realized upon the redemption of its interest in a US partnership that is engaging in a US mining business (except to the extent that gain was attributable to the USRPI held by the partnership). At the time of this writing, it is not clear whether the IRS will appeal the decision.

§2.04 INVESTMENT VEHICLES

The choice of investment vehicle affects the US tax costs associated with the investment. As discussed earlier, the type of underlying property and income, as well as the profile of the investors that participate in the fund impact the decision on the type of investment vehicle. Key considerations for structuring a real estate fund include:

- identifying the profile of investors who will participate in the fund;[81]

---

78. *See* Bell and Shoemaker, *Revenue Ruling 91-32: Right Result For the Wrong Reasons*, 9 J. Partnership Tax'n 80 (1992), Reavey and Elliott, *Sale of U.S. Partnership Interests by Foreign Partners: New Rules After Rev. Rul. 91-32?*, 91 TNI 50-27 (Dec. 1991) and Harris and Wirtz, *The Interplay Between Partnership and International Tax Rules in the Internal Revenue Code: Revenue Ruling 91-32*, 20 Tax Management Int'l J. 345 (No. 8, Aug. 9, 1991).
79. Dept. of the Treasury, *General Explanations of the Administration's Fiscal Year 2013 Revenue Proposals*, at 96 (Feb. 2012).
80. 149 T.C. 3 (July 13, 2017).
81. Investors in US real estate funds may include US taxable and tax-exempt investors, foreign taxable investors, QFPFs and foreign sovereign investors. *See* I.R.C. §892 and discussion in §6.04.A., *infra*, for a discussion on the tax issues relating to foreign sovereign investors.

- identifying the type of properties and associated revenue stream;
- identifying an appropriate investment vehicle;
- exploring possible fund structures; and
- understanding real estate specific tax considerations.

Real estate investment funds are sometimes categorized based on the type of income and expected return from the underlying investments. In that regard, a 'core' fund generally targets well leased investments in strong locations, primarily involves institutional grade properties and utilizes modest levels of debt. A core fund is typically expected to generate stable annual income plus modest appreciation. For example, an office building that has steady long-term tenants that generates a consistent rental yield may be put into a core fund. Depending on the level of services provided and other factors, it also may be suitable to use a REIT to own the building.[82] A 'value' fund typically engages in active strategies to create value in their underlying property investments. A value fund may produce a broad range of returns and typically use modest to high levels of leverage. An 'opportunistic' fund is typically structured as a closed end fund that targets higher risk strategies, such as development, highly leveraged financing or similar transactions. An opportunistic fund typically targets higher net internal rates of return.

The discussion below highlights some of the potential US federal income tax burdens and compliance requirements applicable when a foreign corporation owns its USRPI through different types of legal entities. It is assumed, for purposes of this discussion, that the underlying USRPIs generate only business rental income that is treated as ECI (e.g., leasing of office buildings, or rental of multi-family complexes or hotel operations). As a result, the immediate entity that owns the real estate asset will have US tax compliance obligations to report the income annually. A full discussion of the US tax compliance requirements is beyond the scope of this book.[83] The summary below only highlights the entities that are responsible for reporting the rental income as a reminder.

A. Foreign Corporations Investing Directly in USRPIs

A foreign corporation may own US real property directly or through a disregarded entity.[84] While the US tax consequences of both structures are practically the same, there may be non-tax reasons to hold the property in a separate legal entity, e.g., to have limited legal liability with respect to the underlying business operations. The general US tax consequences of this ownership structure are as follows:

US tax-exempt investors, other than the state-sponsored investor (the so-called 'super tax-exempt' investors) also may have their own tax sensitivities such as the preference to avoid any unrelated business income and income from debt-financed properties. The objective of this book is to address tax issues relating to foreign investments in US real estate; accordingly, it will not cover topics that do not directly affect foreign investors.

82. *See* Ch. 5, *infra*, for a discussion on REIT qualifications and benefits.
83. US tax compliance requirements are complex and different requirements apply to different types of entities. *See* Ch. 11, *infra*, for a general discussion of certain common penalties applicable to a failure to comply with the reporting requirements.
84. *See* Ch. 10, *infra*, for a discussion of the US entity classification rules.

- The foreign corporation is subject to 35% US federal income tax plus the 30% (or a lower treaty rate)[85] branch profits tax on its Dividend Equivalent Amount on the net rental income from the property.[86]
- The foreign corporation is subject to any applicable state and local income or franchise tax[87] on the net rental income from the property.
- When the foreign corporation sells the US real property, it will be subject to 35% US federal income tax (the FIRPTA tax) plus the 30% (or a lower treaty rate) branch profits tax unless the Branch Termination Exception applies.
- The foreign corporation is also subject to any applicable state and local tax on the gain from a sale of the property.
- The foreign corporation is required to file US federal, state and local income tax returns to report its net taxable income annually and the gain from the sale.[88]

Example 2.4

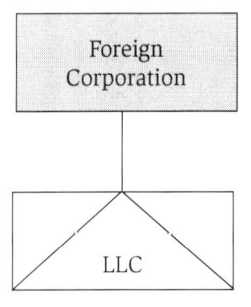

```
       ┌──────────────┐
       │   Foreign    │
       │ Corporation  │
       └──────┬───────┘
              │
       ┌──────┴───────┐
       │     LLC      │
       └──────────────┘
```

This structure is simple and is often the default structure if there is no advance planning prior to making the investment.

B.   **Investing through a US Partnership**

A foreign corporation may own US real property through a legal partnership or limited liability company that is classified as a partnership for US tax purposes.[89] The foreign

---

85. See Ch. 9, *infra*.
86. The foreign corporation may deduct interest expense, depreciation and other ordinary and necessary business expenses in determining its net taxable income. See Ch. 10, *infra*, for a discussion of some of the principles and limitations with respect to these matters.
87. See Ch. 12, *infra*, for a discussion on state and local tax issues.
88. The applicable federal corporation income tax return is Form 1120F. Annual US income tax returns and instructions are updated at least once a year and may be accessed at the IRS's website.
89. The US tax issues are generally the same regardless of whether the partnership is formed under the laws of the US or a foreign jurisdiction.

investor has similar US tax and reporting consequences as a foreign corporation that owns US real estate directly[90] *except* as follows:

- The partnership makes quarterly withholding payments on the ECI allocable to the foreign corporate partner.[91]
- The partnership files an annual information tax return to report the net rental income from the operations and the gain/loss from the sale of the property. The partnership also reports the amount of income, gains, losses and other items allocable to each partner.[92]
- In the event the partnership sells the real property, the foreign corporation will be subject to 35% US federal income tax and the 30% (or a lower treaty rate) branch profits tax on its pro-rata share of the gain on the sale of property unless the Branch Termination Exception applies.
- In the event the foreign corporation sells the partnership interest, it will be subject to 35% US federal income tax[93] and the 30% (or a lower treaty rate) branch profits tax on the gain from the sale of the entity unless the Branch Termination Exception applies.
- The foreign corporation also will be subject to any applicable state and local tax if the partnership sells the underlying property or if it sells the partnership interest.

Example 2.5

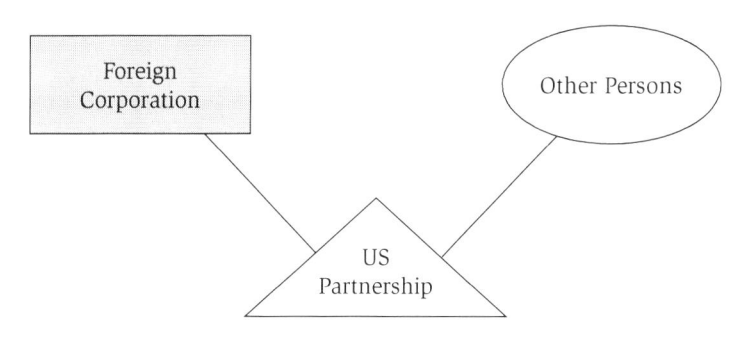

[Diagram: "Foreign Corporation" (rectangle) and "Other Persons" (oval) both connected to "US Partnership" (triangle).]

This structure is similar to investing directly by a foreign corporation as shown in **Example 2.4**, *supra*.

---

90. For example, the foreign corporation is still required to report its pro-rata share of net ECI allocated by the partnership annually on Form 1120F and pay its federal income tax liability associated with the income.
91. *See* I.R.C. §1446.
92. The applicable federal partnership information tax return is Form 1065.
93. *See* I.R.C. §897(g).

C. **Investing through a US Corporation**

A foreign corporation may own real property through a private[94] US Blocker Corporation. The general, US tax consequences of this ownership structure are as follows:

- The US Blocker Corporation is generally subject to 35% US federal income tax, plus any applicable state and local tax, on its worldwide income (including net rental income and any gains from the sale of the real property). There is no branch profits tax under this structure.
- The US Blocker Corporation will file annual US federal income tax returns[95] and any applicable state and local income or franchise tax returns.
- The US Blocker Corporation may, but is not required to, distribute its after-tax earnings as a dividend to the foreign corporation. The dividend constitutes FDAP income generally subject to a 30% (or a lower treaty rate) withholding tax.[96]
- The foreign corporation is not required to file any US tax returns to report the dividend or interest income it receives from the US Blocker Corporation provided the latter withholds the proper amount of gross-basis tax imposed on such payments.
- The foreign corporation may sell its stock in the US Blocker Corporation. Because the stock of the US Blocker Corporation is USRPI,[97] the foreign corporation will be subject to 35% FIRPTA tax on the gain unless an exception applies.[98] The foreign corporation is required to file a US federal income tax return to report the ECI.[99]
- The US Blocker Corporation may sell the underlying real property and pay 35% federal income tax and any applicable state and local taxes on the gain from the sale and liquidate.[100]

Advantages of this structure

- The US Blocker Corporation is the US tax reporting entity.
- The parties may use internal leverage to lower the US corporation-level tax. The US Blocker Corporation generally may deduct any arm's-length interest payments made to the foreign corporation.[101] Interest paid to the foreign

---

94. If the US corporation is publicly traded, then a foreign investor may avoid FIRPTA if it owns no more than 5% of the publicly listed stock of the corporation that is regularly traded on an established securities market. *See* I.R.C. §897(c)(3) and discussion in Ch. 6, *infra*.
95. The applicable tax return is Form 1120.
96. I.R.C. §§881, 1441 and 1442.
97. *See* discussion in Chs. 3 and 4, *infra*, with respect to the definition of USRPI and USRPHC, respectively.
98. There is no branch profits tax on the gain from the sale of the stock of a USRPHC. See I.R.C. §884(d)(2)(C).
99. The applicable tax return is Form 1120F in the year of the sale.
100. *See* discussion in Ch. 6, *infra*, with respect to the Cleansing Exception.
101. *See* discussion in Ch. 10, *infra*, on limitations imposed on the amount of such interest deductions such as I.R.C. §163(j).

2. Structuring Foreign Investments in the United States

corporation is generally subject to a 30% (or lower treaty rate) withholding tax.[102]
- The parties generally may control the timing of any dividend distributions and, thus, can avoid triggering any withholding tax inadvertently.[103]
- The liquidation rules for a US Blocker Corporation are more favorable than the Branch Termination Exception.[104]
- The FIRPTA exemption is available for the sale of the shares of a non-controlled USRPHC[105] by a foreign shareholder that qualifies as a foreign governmental entity.[106]
- The FIRPTA exemption is available for the sale of the shares of any USRPHC by a QFPF.[107]

Example 2.6

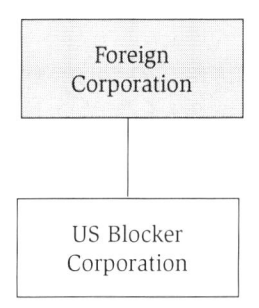

```
┌─────────────┐
│   Foreign   │
│ Corporation │
└──────┬──────┘
       │
┌──────┴──────┐
│ US Blocker  │
│ Corporation │
└─────────────┘
```

D. Investing through a US REIT

A foreign corporation may invest in US real estate through owning an equity interest in a REIT.[108] Although REITs were originally established as vehicles to pool investment from small investors, it has become a favored investment vehicle in recent years and it is becoming more common for foreign investors to compare the benefits (operational, tax and administrative) of using a REIT versus US Blocker Corporation to own its USRPI.[109] Depending on the level of investment, the REIT may be a private

---

102. *Id.*
103. In contrast, as discussed above, the formula approach used to determine whether a US branch is deemed to have repatriated to its foreign head office may inadvertently trigger the branch profits tax.
104. *See* I.R.C. §332 and discussion, *supra*, in §2.02.B.
105. Generally ownership of less than 50% of the vote and value. *See* I.R.C. §892(a)(2)(B).
106. *See* I.R.C. §892(a)(2)(B) and discussion in Ch. 6, *infra*.
107. *See* discussion in Ch. 6, *infra*, with respect to this exemption available under I.R.C. §897(l).
108. The REIT rules are discussed in Ch. 5, *infra*.
109. *Id.*

REIT[110] or a publicly traded REIT.[111] The general US tax consequences of a private REIT ownership structure are as follows:

- A REIT generally may avoid entity-level tax with respect to its operating income if it satisfies a number of requirement and distributes all of its taxable income to its shareholders.[112]
- The REIT files an annual US federal income tax return[113] and any applicable state and local income or franchise tax returns (i.e., the REIT also operates as a Blocker Corporation).
- The REIT's ordinary dividends distributed to foreign shareholders are generally subject to 30% (or a lower treaty rate) US withholding tax.[114] There is no branch profits tax on the ordinary dividends.
- A REIT is generally not subject to US tax on the gain from the sale of real property if it distributes the gain to its shareholders. However, the foreign corporation is subject to 35% FIRPTA tax on any distribution attributable to the capital from a disposition of a USRPI.[115] This distribution generally is subject to the 30% (or lower treaty rate) branch profits tax.
- A liquidating distribution of a REIT to the foreign corporation also is subject to 35% FIRPTA tax to the extent the distribution is attributable to the gain from the sale (or deemed sale) of the real property.[116]
- Gain from the sale of REIT stock is subject to FIRPTA tax unless an exception applies.[117]
- A foreign corporation generally does not have any US tax reporting obligation with respect to ordinary dividend income from a REIT. However, the foreign corporation generally is required to file US income tax returns to report a capital gain distribution (either liquidating or non-liquidating) or gains/losses from a sale of it REIT stock.[118]

Advantages of this structure

- The US REIT is the US tax reporting entity.
- The REIT may avoid US corporate-level tax; instead, the foreign shareholder is generally subject to 30% US withholding tax on annual ordinary REIT

---

110. The foreign corporation may own up to 100% of the common stock of the REIT provided that all the other REIT requirements including the one-hundred-shareholder rule and the closely held requirements are satisfied. *See* discussion in Ch. 5, *infra*.
111. Foreign ownership of publicly traded REIT is becoming more common. *See* discussion in Chs. 5 and 6, *infra*, regarding some of the relevant issues for such ownership.
112. *Id.*
113. The applicable tax return is Form 1120 REIT.
114. Some US income tax treaties reduce the withholding rate on ordinary REIT dividends if certain conditions are met. *See* discussion in Ch. 9, *infra*.
115. *See* §897(h)(1) and discussion on this issue in Ch. 5, *infra*.
116. *See* IRS Notice 2007-55, 2007-2 CB 13, 6/13/07, and discussion in Ch. 5, *infra*.
117. *See* discussion in Ch. 6, *infra*, regarding exceptions to FIRPTA tax.
118. The applicable tax return to file in the year of the sale is Form 1120F. There is no branch profits tax on the gain from the sale of the stock. *See* I.R.C. §884(d)(2)(C).

2. Structuring Foreign Investments in the United States

dividends. Everything being equal, this structure generally produces the lowest US effective tax rate for non-liquidating distributions of operating profits.
- The parties may use internal leverage to lower the US withholding tax on REIT's ordinary dividends.[119]
- The parties generally may control the timing of any dividend distributions and, thus, can avoid inadvertently triggering any withholding tax.[120]
- The liquidation rules for REITs are more favorable than the Branch Termination Exception.
- There is a FIRPTA exemption available for the sale of the shares of non-controlled REITs by a foreign shareholder that qualifies as a foreign governmental entity.[121]
- There is a FIRPTA exemption available for the sale of the shares of any REIT by a QFPF or a qualified shareholder.[122]
- There is a FIRPTA exemption available for the sale of less than 50% of the value of a domestically controlled REIT.[123]
- There is a FIRPTA exemption available for the sale of up to 10% of the shares of a publicly listed REIT that is regularly traded on an established securities market.[124]

Example 2.7

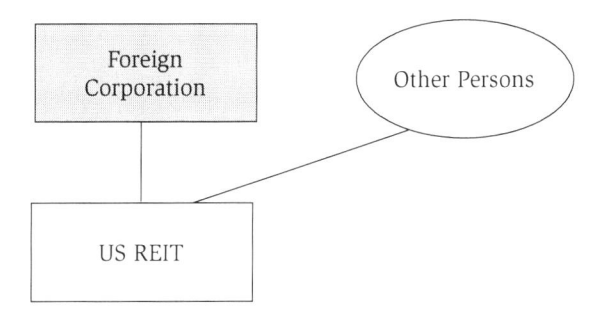

```
    ┌─────────────┐           ╱────────────╲
    │   Foreign   │          (  Other Persons )
    │ Corporation │           ╲────────────╱
    └──────┬──────┘                │
           │                       │
           │                       │
        ┌──┴────────────┐          │
        │    US REIT    │──────────┘
        └───────────────┘
```

§2.05 SUMMARY

In practice, a real estate investment fund platform or a foreign corporate owner of USRPIs combine a number of different entities to build a structure that suits their

---

119. *See* Ch. 10, *infra*.
120. In contrast, as discussed above, the formula approach used to determine whether a US branch is deemed to have repatriated to its foreign head office may inadvertently trigger the branch profits tax.
121. *See* I.R.C. §892(a), Treas. Reg. §1.892-3T and discussion in Ch. 6, *infra*, with respect to this exemption.
122. *See* I.R.C. §897(k) and (l) and discussion in Ch. 6, *infra*, with respect to these exemptions.
123. *See* I.R.C. §897(h)(2) and discussion in Ch. 6, *infra*, with respect to this exemption.
124. *See* I.R.C. §897(k)(1)(A) and discussion in Ch. 6, *infra*.

particular objectives. From a US tax perspective, the goals are: (1) minimize the foreign investors' overall tax burden during the pre-disposition period and upon a sale of the investment; and (2) alleviate the US tax return filing obligation of the investors to the extent possible. The two examples below illustrate what real life investment structures in USRPIs may look like.

A. Fund Investment Platform

Example 2.8 illustrates a real estate fund platform. The Foreign Investors invest in a US Blocker Corporation which, in turn, invests in the US Master Fund. The US Master Fund owns various USRPIs and shares of a US REIT:

- The US Blocker Corporation files annual US corporation income tax returns to report its allocable share of partnership income from the US Master Fund.
- Dividends paid by the US Blocker Corporation to Foreign Investors are FDAP income subject to US gross-basis withholding tax.
- Foreign Investors' gain on the sale or deemed sale of the stock in the US Blocker Corporation is FIRPTA gain taxed as ECI. Each Foreign Investor must report the gain on his/her/its US tax return.[125]

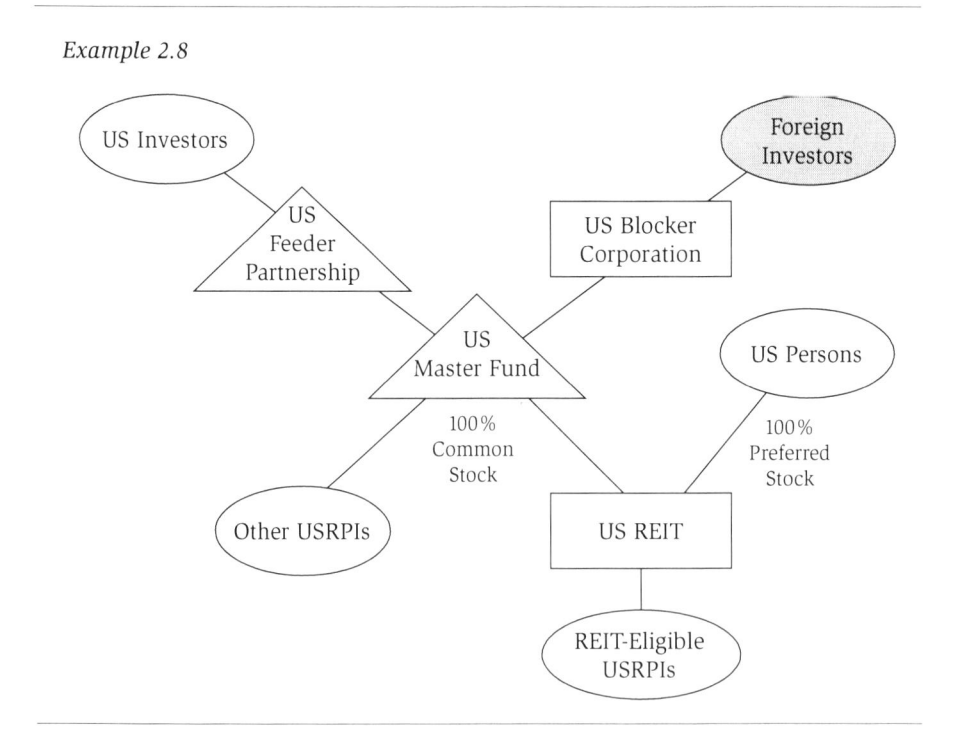

Example 2.8

```
      US Investors                              Foreign Investors

           │                                          │
           ▼                                          ▼
      US Feeder                              US Blocker
      Partnership                            Corporation
           │                                          │
           └──────────────┬───────────────────────────┘
                          ▼
                    US Master Fund                      US Persons
                    ╱         ╲                             │
              100%              100%                         │
              Common            Preferred                    │
              Stock             Stock                        │
                ╱                  ╲                         │
         Other USRPIs            US REIT ◄──────────────────┘
                                    │
                                    ▼
                              REIT-Eligible
                                 USRPIs
```

---

125. Unless the Cleansing Exception applies to the stock of US Blocker Corporation. *See* §6.02.A., *infra*, for a discussion of the exception.

2. Structuring Foreign Investments in the United States

B. Corporate Investment Platform

Foreign Corporation in **Example 2.9** owns office buildings and a residential construction business in the US. The REIT owns the office buildings which are rented to unrelated tenants. The USRPHC owns the residential construction business:

- the REIT and the USRPHC each files annual US corporation income tax returns to report their respective taxable income;
- the REIT distributes 100% of its taxable income as ordinary dividends[126] annually to Foreign Corporation and to US Persons. The dividends paid to Foreign Corporation are FDAP income subject to US gross-basis withholding tax;
- the USRPHC reinvests most of its earnings in the construction business and distributes its excess cash to Foreign Corporation once every three to four years. The distributions are dividends and are FDAP income subject to US gross-basis withholding tax; and

Foreign Corporation is subject to FIRPTA tax on any gain from an actual or deemed sale of the stock of the REIT and the USRPHC. Foreign Corporation must report the gain as ECI to gain on its US federal income tax return in the year of disposition.

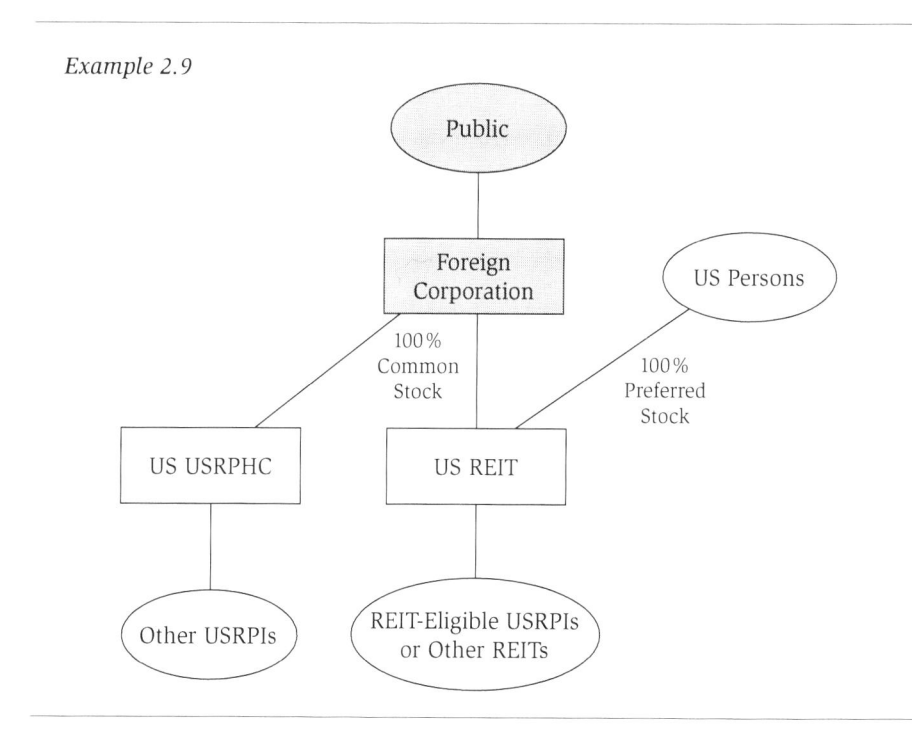

Example 2.9

```
                         ┌─────────┐
                         │ Public  │
                         └────┬────┘
                              │
                    ┌─────────────────┐
                    │    Foreign      │          ┌───────────┐
                    │  Corporation    │          │ US Persons│
                    └────┬────────┬───┘          └─────┬─────┘
                         │        │                    │
                   100%  │        │  100%              │ 100%
                  Common │        │  Common          Preferred
                   Stock │        │  Stock            Stock
                         │        │                    │
        ┌──────────┐     │        │   ┌──────────┐    │
        │ US USRPHC│─────┘        └───│ US REIT  │────┘
        └─────┬────┘                  └─────┬────┘
              │                             │
        ┌───────────┐              ┌──────────────────┐
        │   Other   │              │ REIT-Eligible    │
        │  USRPIs   │              │ USRPIs or        │
        │           │              │ Other REITs      │
        └───────────┘              └──────────────────┘
```

---

126. *See* discussion in §5.04.A., *infra*.

APPENDIX 2-A

Revenue Ruling 91-32

Rev. Rul. 91-32; 1991-1 C.B. 107; 1991 IRB LEXIS 223; 1991-20 I.R.B. 20

January 1991

[*1]

A.   Subject Matter

Definitions and Special Rules

B.   Summary

At issue was the U.S. tax consequences of the disposition of a foreign partner's interest in a domestic or foreign partnership that conducted a business through a fixed place of business or had a permanent establishment in the U.S. The IRS held that under I.R.C. §864(c)(2), gain or loss in a situation in which where a foreign partner was engaged in a business through a fixed place of business under I.R.C. §875(1) would be U.S. source gain that was effectively connected with the conduct of a U.S. business (ECI gain) or would be a loss that was allocable to the ECI gain to the extent that the partner's distributive share of unrealized gain or loss would be attributable to ECI (United States source) property of the partnership. In a situation in which the foreign partner had a distributive share of the income, gain, loss, deduction, and credit of the partnership and in which certain appreciated assets other than those used by the partnership in its U.S. trade or business were located outside the U.S., a 25 percent portion of the gain realized by the partner would be foreign source capital gain that was not effectively connected with the conduct of a trade or business in the U.S.

C.   Applicable Sections

Section 864.-Definitions and Special Rules
        26 CFR 1.864-4: U.S. source income effectively connected with U.S. business. (Also Sections 701, 702, 704, 741, 865, 875.)

D.   Text

Partnership effectively connected income lookthrough. Gain or loss of a foreign partner from a disposition of an interest in a partnership that conducts a trade or business through a fixed place of business or has a permanent establishment in the U.S. is gain effectively connected with such trade or business (or loss allocable to such gain) or is gain attributable to a permanent establishment (or loss allocable to such gain).

1.   Issue

What are the United States tax consequences of the disposition of a foreign partner's interest in a domestic or foreign partnership that conducts a trade or business through a fixed place of business or has a permanent establishment in the United States?

2. Facts

Situation 1

FP1, a nonresident alien individual, is a partner in partnership PS1. PS1, which is not a publicly traded partnership within the meaning of section 7704 of the Internal Revenue Code, is engaged in a trade or business through a fixed place of business in the United States. PS1 owns appreciated real and personal property located in [*2] Country X. PS1 also owns appreciated personal property located in the United States that is used or held for use in PS1's trade or business within the United States (collectively, the "ECI property"). PS1 does not trade in stocks, securities or commodities. None of the ECI property is a United States real property interest within the meaning of section 897 of the Code. FP1 disposes of his partnership interest in a transaction entered into after March 18, 1986.

Situation 2

The facts are the same as those in Situation 1. In addition, *FP1* has a distributive share of 25 percent of the income, gain, loss, deduction and credit of PS1. The assets of PS1 consist of the following:

	Basis	Value
Cash	$300,000	$300,000
Real property outside the United States	500,000	1,000,000
Machinery outside the United States	500,000	100,000
Personal property used in its United States trade or business	200,000	500,000
Total	$1,500,000	$1,900,000

FP1 did not contribute property to the partnership in anticipation of deriving a United States tax benefit under these rules from a subsequent sale of his partnership interest. *FP1*'s adjusted basis in his partnership interest is $375,000. *FP1* sells its partnership interest for $475,000.

Situation 3

FP2, [*3] an alien individual resident in Country Y, is a partner in partnership PS2. The United States and Country Y are parties to a treaty whose provisions are identical to those of the Draft United States Model Income Tax Treaty (June 16, 1981) (the Treaty). PS2, which is not a publicly traded partnership within the meaning of section 7704 of the Code, has a permanent establishment in the United States within the meaning of the Treaty. The assets of PS2 consist of immovable and movable property located in Country Y, and movable property located in the United States that are assets of the permanent establishment. FP2 disposes of his partnership interest in a transaction entered into after March 18, 1986.

3. Law and Analysis

Situation 1

Section 701 of the Code provides that a partnership is not subject to income tax, but instead its partners are liable for the tax in their separate or individual capacities. Each partner must take into account separately the partner's distributive share of the items of income, gain, loss, deduction or credit of the partnership, as described in section 702 and the regulations thereunder. A partner's distributive share of such items is determined pursuant to section 704 [*4] and the regulations thereunder.

The determination of the source and character of a foreign partner's income from the disposition of a partnership interest depends upon the application of sections 864, 865, 875 and 741 of the Code.

Pursuant to section 875 (1) of the Code, a nonresident alien individual or foreign corporation that is a partner in a partnership engaged in a trade or business in the United States is itself considered to be so engaged. Because PS1 is engaged in a trade or business in the United States, FP1 is also so engaged since he is a partner in PS1.

For foreign persons other than a controlled foreign corporation within the meaning of section 957 (a) of the Code, section 865 applies to transactions entered into after March 18, 1986. Pub. L. No. 99-514, section 1211 (c) (2), 100 Stat. 2085, 2536. Section 865 (e) (2) provides, inter alia, that income from the sale of personal property by a nonresident will be sourced in the United States if the nonresident has a fixed place of business in the United States and if the income is attributable to such fixed place of business. A foreign partner of a partnership that is engaged in a trade or business through a fixed place of business [*5] in the United States itself has a fixed place of business in the United States, since the foreign partner is considered to be engaged in such trade or business pursuant to section 875 (1). Income from the disposition of a partnership interest by the foreign partner will be attributable to the foreign partner's fixed place of business in the United States. See section 865 (e) (3); cf. *Unger v. Commissioner*, T. C. Memo. 1990-15, T.C. Memo 1990-15, 58 TCM 1157, 1159. Accordingly, to the extent provided below, income from *FP1*'s disposition of his partnership interest will be sourced in the United States.

Section 864 (c) (2) of the Code provides that certain gain or loss from sources within the United States from the sale or exchange of a capital asset is gain that is effectively connected with the conduct of a United States trade or business ("ECI gain"), or is loss that is allocable to ECI gain ("ECI loss"). Factors considered in determining whether the gain or loss is ECI gain or ECI loss within the meaning of section 864 (c) (2) include whether the gain or loss is derived from an asset that is used or held for use in the conduct of a trade or business in the United States, or whether [*6] the activities of that trade or business were a material factor in the realization of the gain or loss. The rules of section 1.864-4 (c) (2) of the regulations apply to determine whether an asset is used or held for use in the conduct of a trade or business within the United States, while the rules of section 1.864-4 (c) (3) apply to determine the character of gain or loss realized directly from the active conduct of the trade or business.

Since a foreign partner's gain or loss from the disposition of its interest in a partnership is not gain or loss realized directly from the active conduct of a trade or business within the United States, the character of the foreign partner's gain or loss must be determined pursuant to the rules of section 1.864-4 (c) (2) of the regulations.

By virtue of its interest in the partnership, the foreign partner is considered to be engaged in a trade or business through the partnership's fixed place of business in the United States. Moreover, the value of the trade or business activity of the partnership affects the value of the foreign partner's interest in the partnership. Consequently, an interest in a partnership that is engaged in a trade or business [*7] through a fixed place of business in the United States is an ECI asset of a foreign partner. See section 1.864-4 (c) (2) of the regulations.

A partnership, however, may also own property that, if disposed of by the partnership, would produce foreign source income that generally would not be subject to United States tax. Amounts received by a foreign partner from a disposition of its partnership interest may thus be attributable to unrealized gain or loss of the partnership representing the foreign partner's potential distributive share of foreign source items that, if realized by the partnership, generally would not be gain or loss to the foreign partner described in section 864 (c).

Subchapter K of the Code is a blend of aggregate and entity treatment for partners and partnerships. Compare section 751 of the Code with section 741. For purposes of applying provisions of the Code not included in subchapter K, a partnership may be treated as an aggregate of its partners or as an entity distinct from its partners, depending on the purpose and scope of such provisions. Rev. Rul. 89-85, 1989-2 C.B. 218, 219; see *Casel* v. *Commissioner*, 79 T.C. 424 (1982). The treatment of amounts received [*8] by a foreign partner from a disposition of a partnership interest must therefore be considered in connection with the general purpose and scope of section 864 (c) and section 865 (e). Pursuant to section 865 (e) (3) the principles of section 864 (c) (5) are applied to determine whether gain or loss from a sale is attributable to an office or fixed place of business for purposes of section 865 (e) (1) and (2), so the same analysis applies to both sections 864 (c) and 865 (e).

Characterizing the entire amount of gain or loss from a foreign partner's disposition of a partnership interest as United States source ECI gain or ECI loss would effectively subject to the tax jurisdiction of the United States items that may not be de scribed in section 864 (c) of the Code, a result which Congress did not intend. *See* S. Rep. No. 1707, 89th Cong., 2d Sess. 17 (1966). Furthermore, treating the gain or loss realized by a foreign partner from the disposition of an interest in a partnership that is engaged in a United States trade or business entirely as United States source EC1 gain or EC1 loss may be conceptually inconsistent with other sections of the Code. For example, section 897 (g) of the Code, [*9] which governs the treatment of a foreign partner's disposition of an interest in a partnership that has a United States real property interest, generally treats as ECI gain or ECI loss the amount that is attributable to a United States real property interest of the partnership. This provision evidences the view of Congress that a foreign partner's gain or loss from the disposition of an interest in a partnership that is engaged in a trade or business through a fixed place of business in the United States need not always be treated as ECI gain or ECI loss from United States sources in its entirety.

Accordingly, in applying sections 864 (c) and 865 (e) of the Code, it is appropriate to treat a foreign partner's disposition of its interest in a partnership that is engaged in a trade or business through a fixed place of business in the United States as a disposition of an aggregate interest in the partnership's underlying property for purposes of determining the source and ECI character of the gain or loss realized by the foreign partner. The determination of the source and the ECI character of gain or loss of a foreign partner from the disposition of a partnership interest will therefore [*10] be determined in the manner described below.

A foreign partner's gain or loss from the disposition of an interest in a partnership that is engaged in a trade or business through a fixed place of business in the United States will be ECI (United States source) gain or loss to the extent such gain or loss is attributable to ECI (United States source) property of the partnership. The gain or loss attributable to the ECI property of the partnership is an amount that bears the same ratio to gain or loss realized by the foreign partner from the disposition of its partnership interest as the foreign partner's distributive share of partnership net ECI gain or loss would have borne to the foreign partner's distributive share of partnership net gain or loss if the partnership had itself disposed of all of its assets at fair market value at the time the foreign partner disposes of its partnership interest. In computing the foreign partner's distributive share of net gain or loss of the partnership, net ECI gain or loss and net non-ECI gain or loss are computed separately. Thus, net non-ECI loss will not offset ECI gain, and net ECI loss will not offset net non-ECI gain.

Further, if a foreign partner [*11] realizes a loss on the disposition of its partnership interest, and if its distributive share of ECI gain or loss from the deemed disposition of ECI assets by the partnership would be a net ECI gain, then none of the loss realized by the foreign partner on the disposition of the partnership interest shall be ECI loss. If a foreign partner realizes a gain on the disposition of its partnership interest, and if its distributive share of ECI gain or loss from the deemed disposition of ECI assets by the partnership would be a net ECI loss, then none of the gain realized by the foreign partner on the disposition of the partnership interest shall be ECI gain.

In applying these rules, a foreign partner's gain on the disposition of an interest in a partnership that is engaged in a U.S. trade or business will be presumed to be U.S. source ECI gain in its entirety, and a foreign partner's loss on such a disposition will be presumed to be foreign source non-ECI loss in its entirety, unless the partner is able to produce upon request information showing the distributive share of net ECI and net non-ECI gain or loss that such partner would have been allocated if the partnership sold all of its assets. [*12] This presumption is a specific application of the general principle that the burden of proof is on the taxpayer.

Note that if a foreign partner contributes property to the partnership in anticipation of a subsequent sale of its partnership interest to derive a United States tax benefit under the approach taken under this ruling, the contribution may be disregarded under general tax principles in determining the tax consequences of the subsequent sale.

For purposes of these rules, the ECI (United States source) property of a partnership does not include United States real property interests held by the partnership. The rules of section 897 (g), rather than the rules described in this ruling, govern the treatment of amounts received from (he disposition of an interest in a partnership that are attributable to a United States real property interest of the partnership, and are applied before the rules described in this ruling are applied.

Situation 2

The character of the $100,000 gain realized by *FPI* is determined under section 741 and section 751 of the Code, and is capital gain in this case. *FPI's* gain from the disposition of his partnership interest that is attributable to the ECI property [*13] of *PSI* is an amount that bears the same ratio to the gain realized by *FPI* from the disposition of his partnership interest as *FPI's* distributive share of partnership net ECI gain would have borne to his distributive share of partnership net gain if the partnership had disposed of all of its assets at fair market value on the date *FPI* disposes of his partnership interest.

Upon a disposition of its ECI asset, the partnership would realize United States source ECI gain of $300,000 (fair market value of PSI's ECI property of $500,000 less basis of $200,000), of which 25 percent, or $75,000, would represent *FPI's* distributive share. Upon a disposition of all of its non-ECI assets, the partnership would realize a net gain of $100,000 (fair market value of machinery and real property outside the United States of $1,100,000 less basis of $1,000,000), of which *FPI's* 25 percent distributive share is $25,000.

FPI's gain from the disposition of his partnership interest that is attributable to ECI (United States source) property of the partnership is an amount that bears the same ratio to $100,000 (FPI's gain from the disposition of its partnership interest) as $75,000 *(FPI's* distributive share of [*14] the partnership's ECI (United States source) gain) bears to $100,000 (the sum of *FPI's* distributive share of the partnership's net ECI gain and net non-ECI gain). Accordingly, the portion of *FP1's* gain from the disposition of his partnership interest that is attributable to the ECI property of PS1 equals $75,000. Note that if the partnership's assets included United States real property interests, *FP1* also would be subject to tax pursuant to section 897 (g) on the amount attributable to the United States real property interests of the partnership. In this case, because the appreciated assets other than those used by PS1 in its United States trade or business are located outside the United States, the remaining $25,000 gain realized by *FP1* will be foreign source capital gain that is not effectively connected with the conduct of a trade or business in the United States.

Situation 3

The Treaty generally exempts from United States tax gain from the disposition of movable property by a resident of the United States treaty partner. See Article 13 (3) (Gains) of the Treaty. However, this rule does not apply if such gain is from the alienation of movable property that are assets of a permanent [*15] establishment in the United States.

A foreign partner of a partnership that has a permanent establishment in the United States is treated as itself having a permanent establishment. *Donroy, Ltd.* v. *United States*, 301 F.2d 200 (9th Cir. 1962); see Rev. Rul. 85-60, 1985-1 C.B. 187. More particularly, "the office or permanent establishment of a partnership is the office of each of its partners, whether general or limited", *Unger* v. *Commissioner*, T. C. Memo. 1990-15, T.C. Memo 1990-15, 58 TCM 1157, 1159, citing *Donroy, Ltd.* v. *United States,* supra. Accordingly, FP2 is considered to have a permanent establishment in the United States because he is a partner in PS2.

The determination whether gain from the alienation of movable property is attributable to a permanent establishment in the United States is generally made by applying principles analogous to those governing whether an item is effectively connected with the conduct of a trade or business in the United States, though the "attributable to" concept of the Treaty is more limited in its scope than the "effectively connected" concept of the Code. See Rev. Rul. 81-78, 1981-1 C.B. 604. The principles applied are substantially similar, however, [*16] when the amounts at issue are those that would be described in section 864 (c) (2) of the Code if the Treaty were not applied. Accordingly, for the reasons discussed in Situation 1, a disposition of an interest in a partnership that has a permanent establishment in the United States will be treated as resulting in gain that is attributable to the permanent establishment to the extent provided below.

It is appropriate under the Treaty to look to a foreign partner's interest in the assets of the partnership to determine the amount of the foreign partner's gain from the disposition of its partnership interest that is attributable to a United States permanent establishment. Cf. Commentary on Article 1 of the OECD Model Double Taxation Convention on Income and Capital, paragraphs 2-5 (1977). Gain of FP2 from the disposition of its interest in PS2 will thus be subject to United States tax only to the extent such gain is attributable to the unrealized gain of the partnership's assets attributable to the partnership's permanent establishment, and loss will be allocable to FP2's gain from sources within the United States that is attributable to a permanent establishment of FP2. Such gain or [*17] loss is to be determined in the manner described in Situation 1.

4. *Holdings*

Situation 1

Gain or loss of a foreign partner that disposes of its interest in a partnership that is engaged in a trade or business through a fixed place of business in the United States will be United States source ECI gain or will be ECI loss that is allocable to United States source ECI gain, to the extent that the partner's distributive share of unrealized gain or loss of the partnership would be attributable to ECI (United States source) property of the partnership.

Situation 2

FP1's gain from the disposition of his partnership interest that is attributable to ECI (United States source) property of the partnership is an amount that bears the same ratio to $100,000 (*FP1*'s gain from the disposition of its partnership interest) as $75,000 (*FP1*'s distributive share of the partnership's ECI (United States source) gain) bears to $100,000 (the sum of *FP1*'s distributive share of the partnership's net ECI gain and net non-ECI gain). Accordingly, the portion of *FP1*'s gain from the disposition of his partnership interest that is attributable to the ECI property of PS1 equals $75,000.

Situation 3

Under the Treaty, gain of [*18] a foreign partner that disposes of its interest in a partnership that has a United States permanent establishment is gain that is attributable to a permanent establishment and is subject to United States tax under the Treaty, to the extent that the partner's potential distributive share of unrealized gain of the partnership is attributable to the partnership's permanent establishment.

Chapter 3
Definition of a US Real Property Interest

§3.01	Overview	43
§3.02	The Operative Rule	44
§3.03	Definition of a USRPI	45
	A. The Statute	45
	B. The Regulatory Framework	46
	1. Land and Improvements	47
	2. Personal Properties Associated with the Use of Real Property	50
	C. Interest Other Than Solely as a Creditor in USRPI	51
§3.04	Treatment of Intangibles	53
	A. Rights in Governmental Permits	55
	B. Treatment of Infrastructure Projects	57
	C. Case Study	58
	1. Facts	58
	2. The Comprehensive Agreement	58
	3. The Project Funding	59
	4. Take Away	60
§3.05	Summary	61

§3.01 OVERVIEW

Whether a property is a USRPI is the first step in assessing a foreign investor's US tax exposure upon a sale of the property. In general, one typically thinks of real estate as land, buildings or other permanent structures that are tangible properties. In the FIRPTA context, however, a variety of properties other than traditional real estate assets fall within the definition of a USRPI. The breadth of this definition is what makes FIRPTA a trap for the unwary and necessitates a careful review of its provisions. According to the statute, the term USRPI generally means:

– an interest in real property located in the United States or the Virgin Islands; and

– an interest (other than solely as a creditor) in any US corporation unless the shareholder establishes that the corporation was not a USRPHC at any time during the shorter of (1) the shareholder's holding period in the stock, or (2) the five-year period ending on the date of the disposition of the stock.[1]

The stated policy of FIRPTA is to create parity between the US taxation of gain on a disposition of USRPI by foreign and US investors. FIRPTA subjects gain from any disposition of USRPI by a foreign investor[2] to US federal income tax at rates applicable to ECI unless an exception applies. The FIRPTA statute contains a complicated set of rules to implement this policy. The Treasury Department and the IRS have gone further and created regulations and other administrative guidance that broadens the reach of the original legislation in many aspects.

The Treasury Department and the IRS continue to issue guidance to expand the scope of the FIRPTA regime and, as discussed in this chapter, even the definition of USRPI is not always clear cut. It is interesting that new legislation has been enacted in 2015 to exclude certain foreign taxpayers from FIRPTA with the intention of attracting foreign investments in US infrastructure assets.[3] At the same time, however, there are a lot of uncertainties regarding whether intangible assets, including those associated with infrastructure projects, should constitute USRPI. Foreign investors, particularly those investing through private equity funds, are becoming more cautious in their investment decisions.

§3.02 THE OPERATIVE RULE

The statute generally recharacterizes any gain or loss realized by a foreign investor from the disposition of a USRPI as if the gain or loss was ECI for US federal income tax purposes, regardless of whether the seller actually engages in a US trade or business and regardless of whether the gain or loss is in fact connected with any actual US trade or business of the foreign seller.[4] The foreign seller may aggregate the gain or loss from the sale with any income or loss from its other US trade or business and report these transactions on a US tax return in the year of disposition.

A foreign investor's gains from the disposition of a USRPI is subject to the FIRPTA tax unless an exception applies. The scope of FIRPTA is very broad and treats any transfer that would constitute a disposition by the transferor for any purpose of the Code and the regulations thereunder.[5] Examples of transactions affected by this rule include a distribution made by a corporation to its shareholder in excess of the payor corporation's earnings and profits and the shareholder's tax basis in the corporation, which is treated as a gain from the shareholder's disposition of the stock.[6]

---

1. I.R.C. §897(c)(1)(A).
2. The statute refers only to dispositions by a foreign corporation and a nonresident alien. See I.R.C. §897(a)(1).
3. See §6.03, *infra*, for a discussion on the new exceptions to FIRPTA enacted in 2015.
4. I.R.C. §897(a)(1).
5. Treas. Reg. §1.897-1(g). The severance of crops or timber and the extraction of minerals do not alone constitute the disposition of a USRPI.
6. See I.R.C. §301(c)(3).

3. Definition of a US Real Property Interest

A foreign shareholder would be subject to FIRPTA tax if the distributing corporation is a USRPHC. Chapter 7 discusses the nonrecognition provisions application to FIRPTA.[7]

The amount of gain or loss subject to FIRPTA tax should be determined in accordance with general US income tax rules.[8] Amounts that are treated as principal and interest on all debt obligations, including any contingent interest, do not generally give rise to gain or loss that is subject to FIRPTA tax.[9] This is true even if the contingent interest is determined based on the appreciation of the underlying real estate. If a foreign investor holds US real estate primarily for sale to customers in the ordinary course of his trade or business[10] the investor will be considered a dealer and any gain it realizes from the disposition of such inventory real estate will be taxed at US ordinary income tax rates.[11] A particular investor may be able to establish that, although it holds one real property as a dealer, it holds other property for investment, i.e., as a capital asset.[12]

§3.03   DEFINITION OF A USRPI

A.   The Statute

Code section 897(c)(6)(A) provides that 'an interest in real property' *includes* fee ownership, co-ownership, and leaseholds of land or improvements thereon, as well as options to acquire land, leaseholds, or improvements thereon. Code section 897(c)(6)(B) then states that 'real property' *includes* movable walls, furnishings, and other personal property associated with the use of the real property. The statutory language is clear that these rules are inclusive and maybe even expansive.[13]

---

7. *See* I.R.C. §897(d) and (e).
8. *See* I.R.C. §1001(a) and (b).
9. Treas. Reg. §1.897-1(h). An exception applies to principal payments on certain installment payments.
10. I.R.C. §1221.
11. A corporation is subject to the same 35% federal income tax rate on capital gain and ordinary income currently. Note that capital loss may only offset capital gain. *See* I.R.C. §1222. On the other hand, an individual and an entity that is taxed as an individual for US tax purposes, e.g., certain foreign trusts, may be eligible for a reduced federal income tax rates on capital gains.
12. *See* Fellows, *Ordinary Income vs. Capital Gain: The Storied History Continues*, 44 Real Est. L.J. 69 (2015); *Pool v. Comm'r*, T.C. Memo. 2014-3 (2014) (denying capital gain treatment with respect to proceeds from the sale of land based on the intent of the owner in acquiring and holding the property, frequency and continuity of sales, the nature of the taxpayer's business and substance of the transaction); *Boree v. Comm'r*, T.C. Memo. 2014-85, (2014) (denying capital gain treatment with respect to proceeds from the sale of land based on the facts and circumstances test, focusing on the frequency and substantiality of sales by the taxpayers). *See* also, *Rice v. Comm'r*, T.C. Memo. 2009-142 (finding that proceeds from the sale of land are entitled to capital gains treatment based on the taxpayers' intent to building their home on the land, infrequent sales of lots of land, full-time jobs outside the real estate industry, among other factors).
13. It was pointed out that, shortly after the enactment of FIRPTA, the statutory language contains a 'difficult interpretive question' because it will be necessary to distinguish when personal property is viewed as 'associated with the use of real property.' *See* Feder and

The legislative history states that real property, for FIRPTA purposes, is supposed to have the same meaning as that in the 1977 United States Treasury Model Tax Treaty (the 1977 US Model).[14] Article 6 of the 1977 US Model uses the term 'immovable property' to refer to real property. Under the article, the term should have the same meaning under the law of the country in which the property is situated.[15] In addition, the term also should include property 'accessory to immovable property... rights to which the provisions of general law respecting landed property apply, usufruct of immovable property and rights to variable of fixed payments as consideration for the working of, or the right to work, mineral deposits, sources and other natural resources; ships, boats and aircraft shall not be regarded as immovable property.'

Both the statutory language and the related legislative history appear to suggest that conventional real estate asset is the bedrock of USRPI a disposition of which would lead to FIRPTA tax. Neither the statute nor the legislative history provided any hints that FIRPTA applies to cover rights that are not, in some way, directly tied to the ownership of the underlying real property.[16] However, as discussed later in this chapter, the question of what constitutes USRPI, particularly with respect to intangibles, has become increasing difficult to answer based on the existing rules.

B. The Regulatory Framework

The regulations contain a set of rules that considerably expand the scope of what constitutes a USRPI. Part of the issue is that the regulations introduce a potpourri of concepts that apply to *both* USRPI and USRPHC.[17] Some of these concepts overlap and intertwine together making their application confusing. The discussion below first lays out the organization of the regulations and then analyzes some of the specific items that are of particular interest.

- Treasury Regulation section 1.897-1(b) provides the general definition of 'real estate.' This is the corresponding provision to Code section 897(c)(6)(B) and adds a litany of hard assets that qualify as real estate for FIRPTA purposes.
- Treasury Regulation section 1.897-1(c) provides the definition of 'US real property interest.' This may be the corresponding rule to Code section 897(c)(6)(A). In an important deviation from the statute, this regulation states that

---

Parker, *The Foreign Investment in Real Property Tax Act of 1980*, Tax Lawyer, Vol. 35, No. 3 pg. 552.

14. H.R. Rep. No. 96-1479, 96th Cong., 2d Sess. 186 (1980).
15. Although this is circular, it appears that the intent is to refer to the type of property that constituted real property under US law in 1980. According to one commentator, the US Treasury Department had not fully exercised its authority to expressly define what constitutes real property for treaty purposes prior to the enactment of FIRPTA. *See* Taylor, Ch. 1 footnote 69, *supra*, pg. 15.
16. According to one commentator, even the fact that the statutory definition of an 'interest in real property' includes 'option to acquire land' is 'odd, since options are not ordinarily viewed as ownership; and the inclusion in an "interest" of any interest other than an interest solely as a creditor (which obviously duplicates the inclusion of options) took the potential scope of FIRPTA far beyond what had been the rule before.' *Id.* pgs. 15 -16.
17. *See,* e.g., Treas. Reg. §1.897-1(c)(1).

the term USRPI also includes any interest, other than an interest solely as a creditor, in real property located in the United States (or the Virgin Islands).[18]
- Treasury Regulation section 1.897-1(d) provides the definition of 'an interest other than solely as a creditor' as the term applies to *both* USRPI and USRPHC.
- Treasury Regulation section 1.897-1(e) provides a series of look-through rules for the purpose of determining whether a US corporation is a USRPHC.[19]
- Treasury Regulation section 1.897-1(f) provides special definitions to categorize three specific groups of assets for the purpose of determining whether a US corporation is a USRPHC. *This is the only place in the regulations that contains a special rule addressing the treatment of intangibles such as goodwill and going concern, licenses and similar assets.*

The regulations also add a rule that treats any class of interests in a partnership or trust that is regularly traded on an established securities market as interests in publicly traded corporations.[20] On the other hand, the statute applies the partnership aggregate theory and subjects the amount that a foreign investor realizes on the disposition of an interest in a partnership, trust, or estate to FIRPTA tax to the extent the amount is 'attributable to' USRPIs held by the partnership, trust, or estate.[21] No guidance has been issued to determine the amount of distribution to a foreign investor that is 'attributable to' the gain from the disposition of USRPI.

In a way, the regulations can be viewed as a continuum. The rules start out by providing guidance on the classification of various tangible real properties and certain associated personal properties as USRPIs (i.e., a fairly straightforward area). The focus then turns on the use of the phrase 'an interest other than a creditor' to modify an interest in USRPIs as well as USRPHC (i.e., a more ambiguous area), and ends with vague references regarding certain intangible rights (i.e., an unsettled area).

1. Land and Improvements

Local law definitions of the term 'real property' will not be controlling for FIRPTA purposes.[22] In general, the definition of 'real property' includes three categories of property:

(i) land and unsevered natural products of the land;
(ii) improvements to real property; and
(iii) certain personal property associated with the use of real property.[23]

---

18. *See* Treas. Reg. §1.897-1(c)(1). (Emphasis added.)
19. These rules are discussed in Ch. 4, *infra*.
20. Treas. Reg. §1.897-1(c)(2)(iv).
21. *See* I.R.C. §897(g) and Notice 88-72, 1988-2 C.B. 383. An interest in a partnership may be treated as a USRPI in its entirety, solely for purposes of withholding under I.R.C. §1445, if: (a) 50% or more of the value of the gross assets of the partnership consist of USRPIs; and (b) 90% or more of the value of the gross assets consists of USRPIs plus cash or cash equivalents. *See* Ch. 8, *infra*, for a discussion regarding the FIRPTA withholding rules.
22. The regulations provide practical guidance by including a catalog of real estate related assets modeled after the former investment tax credit (ITC) rules. See Treas. Reg. §1.897-1(b)(1).
23. Id.

The first category of real property includes land, growing crops and timber, and mines, wells and other natural deposits.[24] Crops and timber that are severed from the land and ores and minerals extracted from the ground are no longer considered to be real property. Storage of severed or extracted crops, timber or minerals on real property will not cause those items to be characterized as real property.

The second category of real property covers improvements to land which are further broken down into three subcategories: buildings, inherently permanent structures, or structural components of either buildings or inherently permanent structures.[25] Buildings, for this purpose, means 'any structure or edifice enclosing space within its walls, and usually covered by a roof, the purpose of which is, for example, to provide shelter or housing or to provide working, offices, parking, display, or sales space.'[26] An 'inherently permanent structure' generally is any property that is affixed to real property and will ordinarily remain affixed for an indefinite period of time.[27] In addition to this general rule, any property not otherwise described in the regulations that constitutes 'other tangible property' under former Code section 48(a)(1)(B) and Treasury Regulation section 1.48-1(c) and (d), is treated as an inherently permanent structure for FIRPTA purposes.[28] This greatly expands what is real property for FIRPTA purposes. Examples of inherently permanent structures in these regulations include swimming pools, paved parking and other paved areas, special foundations for heavy equipment, bridges, fences, railroad tracks and signals, and telephone poles.[29]

An inherently permanent structure does not include property in the nature of machinery or essentially an item of machinery or equipment under the ITC regulations.[30] There is no guidance on the application of these exceptions as applied in the FIRPTA context. Therefore, taxpayers must rely on guidance provided that interprets these provisions in the context of the ITC regulations. Courts have generally found property to be in the nature of machinery if the primary function of the property is mechanical or is accomplished through mechanical means.[31] Generally, property that

---

24. *Id.*
25. The regulations generally model after the ITC rules in determining whether an item of property constitutes an improvement for this purpose. *See* Treas. Reg. §1.897-1(b)(3)(i).
26. Apartment houses, factories, office buildings, warehouses and stores are all examples of 'buildings' under the regulations. Further, any structure that is classified as a building under the ITC rules is treated as a building for FIRPTA purposes. *See* Treas. Reg. §1.897-1(b)(3)(ii).
27. A structure held to real property by its own weight is considered affixed for purposes of the regulations. *See* Treas. Reg. §1.897-1(b)(3)(iii)(A).
28. *See* Treas. Reg. §1.897-1(b)(3)(iii)(B).
29. *Id.*
30. *See* Treas. Reg. §1.897-1(b)(3)(iii)(B). The ITC regulations listed as examples gasoline pumps, hydraulic car lifts, and automatic vending machines as properties 'in the nature of machinery.' *See* Treas. Reg. §1.48-1(c). *See also* Rev. Rul. 85-93, 1985-2 C.B. 9, which held that snowmaking guns and hoses, power transformers, pumps, compressors, control equipment, plumbing and wiring in around a pumphouse used to produce artificial snow all constituted property in the nature of machinery.
31. *See*, e.g., *Munford v. Comm'r*, 87 T.C. 463 (1986), *aff'd* 849 F.2d 1398 (11th Cir. 1988) (inquiring whether property performed a machine type function). Further, property that appears to be 'permanent' in nature and form may be treated as property in the nature of

is not in the nature of machinery may constitute 'essentially an item of machinery or equipment' if the property is 'so specially designed that [it is] in essence a part of the machinery or equipment with which [it is] associated.'[32] If the precedents under the ITC rules do not provide adequate guidance regarding the classification of an item of property, the determination of whether the property constitutes an inherently permanent structure is made by taking into account all the facts and circumstances. In making this determining, the following six factors must be considered:

(i) the manner in which the property is affixed to real property;
(ii) whether the property was designed to be easily removable or to remain in place indefinitely;
(iii) whether the property has been moved since its initial installation;
(iv) any circumstances that suggest the expected period of affixation (e.g., a lease that requires removal of the property upon its expiration);
(v) the amount of damage that removal of the property would cause to the property itself or to the real property to which it is affixed; and
(vi) the extent of the effort that would be required to remove the property, in terms of time and expense.[33]

Structural components of buildings and other inherently permanent structures, as defined in the ITC regulations, constitute real property for FIRPTA purposes.[34] For this purpose, structural components include walls, partitions, floors, ceilings, windows, doors, wiring, plumbing, central heating and central air conditioning systems, lighting fixtures, pipes, ducts, elevators, escalators, sprinkler systems, fire escapes and other components relating to the operation or maintenance of a building.[35] However, structural components do not include machinery installed solely for the purpose of maintaining minimum temperature or humidity requirements which are essential for the operation of other machinery or the processing of materials or foodstuffs.[36] This exception applies even if the machinery incidentally provides for the comfort of employees or serves to an insubstantial degree areas where such temperature or humidity requirements are not essential.[37]

---

machinery if the property is so closely related or integral to associated machinery that the machinery could not function without the other property. *See*, e.g., *Weirick v. Comm'r*, 62 T.C. 446 (1974) (finding that towers supporting ski lift lines were in the nature of machinery because the towers were so closely related to the mechanical components of the ski lifts that they could not be treated as separate groups of assets); *Marineland of Pacific, Inc. v. Comm'r*, T.C. Memo. 1975-288 (finding that the tower that supports an amusement park ride was property in the nature of machinery because the tower was 'an integral part of the whole apparatus' and 'no portion of the physical property was capable of operation without the rest').

32. *See* Rev. Rul. 79-183, 1979-1 C.B. 44. Rev. Rul. 69-557, 1969-2 C.B. 3.
33. *See* Treas. Reg. §1.897-1(b)(3)(iii)(C).
34. *See* Treas. Reg. §1.897-1(b)(3)(iv).
35. *Id.*
36. *Id.*
37. *Id.*

2. *Personal Properties Associated with the Use of Real Property*

Certain personal properties such as movable walls, furnishings and other personal property that are associated with the use of real property are categorized as real property for FIRPTA purposes.[38] The regulations provide that the term 'personal property associated with the use of real property' applies only if the property falls within one of the four subcategories:

(i)   property used in mining, farming, and forestry;[39]
(ii) property used in the improvement of real property;[40]
(iii) property used in the operation of a lodging facility;[41] and
(iv) property used in the rental of furnished office and other work space.[42]

All four subcategories require that the property be 'predominantly' used for the indicated activity.[43] In addition, personal property will be considered associated with the use of real property only where both the personal property and the real property with which it is associated are held by the same person or by related persons.[44]

Personal property associated with real property generally will be treated as real property for FIRPTA purposes regardless of whether or not its disposition accompanies

---

38. I.R.C. §897(c)(6)(B).
39. Treas. Reg. §1.897-1(b)(4)(i)(A). Personal property is associated with the use of real property if it is predominantly used to exploit unsevered natural products in or upon the land. This includes mining equipment, farm machinery, draft animals and equipment used in the growing and cutting of timber. Personal property used to process or transport minerals, crops or timber after severance is not associated personal property.
40. Treas. Reg. §1.897-1(b)(4)(i)(B). Personal property is used in the improvement of real property if it is predominantly used to construct or otherwise carry out improvements. Such property includes property used to clear and prepare raw land as well as construction equipment.
41. Treas. Reg. §1.897-1(b)(4)(i)(C). Property used in the operation of a lodging facility includes property used in the living quarters, such as beds, refrigerators and ranges, as well as property used in the common areas of a facility, such as laundry equipment. Such property constitutes personal property associated with the use of real property in the hands of the owner or operator of the facility, not of the tenant or guest. A lodging facility is an apartment house or apartment, hotel, motel, dormitory, residence, or any other facility (or part thereof) predominantly used to provide, at a charge, living and/or sleeping accommodations, whether on a daily, weekly, monthly, annual or other basis. The term does not include a personal residence occupied solely by its owner, or a facility used primarily as a means of transportation (such as aircraft, vessel or railroad car). The term also does not include any portion of a facility that constitutes a non-lodging commercial facility available to persons not using the lodging facility (such as a restaurant in a lodging facility).
42. Treas. Reg. §1.897-1(b)(4)(i). Office furniture and equipment included in the rental of furnished space is 'associated with' property in the hands of the lessor, not of the lessee.
43. Property is used 'predominantly' in an activity if it is devoted to that activity during at least half of the time in which it is in use during a calendar year. Treas. Reg. §1.897-1(b)(4)(i).
44. Treas. Reg. §1.897-1(b)(4)(i)(A). Persons are considered to be related in accordance with I.R.C. §267(b) and (c) or I.R.C. §707(b)(1) for partners or partnerships. Treas. Reg. §1.897-1(i).

the disposition of the real property with two exceptions:[45] (1) where the otherwise associated personal property is disposed of either more than one year before or after the disposition of the associated real property,[46] or (2) where the personal property and associated real property are separately sold within a ninety-day period to unrelated persons.[47] The determination of whether personal property has been associated with the use of real property is made on the date the personal property is disposed of and on each applicable determination date.[48]

C. Interest Other Than Solely as a Creditor in USRPI

In using the phrase 'any interest, other than an interest solely as a creditor' to modify *both* an interest in a USRPI and an interest in a USRPHC, the regulations differ from the statute which uses the same phrase to modify *only* an interest in a USRPHC.[49] This wording is a bit odd and there is no analogous description of ownership in other areas of US tax rules. The regulations introduce a number of concepts to describe the phrase. Under the regulations, 'an interest in real property, other than an interest solely as a creditor,' includes a fee ownership, co-ownership, or leasehold interest in real property, a time sharing interest in real property, a life estate, remainder, or reversionary interest in such property. Significantly, the term also includes:

> [A]ny direct or *indirect right to share* in the appreciation in the value, *or in the gross or net proceeds or profits generated by*, the real property.[50]

The rest of this chapter refers to the above language as the 'Indirect Right to Share Rule' and an interest in an asset that is covered by this rule as an 'Indirect Right to Share Interest.' It is evident, from the language, that the rule is as broad as it is vague. Under the Indirect Right to Share Rule, a loan that includes any direct or indirect right to share in the appreciation of the value of, or the gross or net proceeds, or profits generated by, an interest in real property of the debtor or of a related person is treated an interest in real property other than solely as a creditor in its *entirety*.[51] The

---

45. Treas. Reg. §1.897-1(b)(4)(ii)(A).
46. Where the associated real property is disposed of more than one year prior to the disposition of the personal property, the personal property will be considered real property if any right to use or occupy the real property is reacquired within the one-year period. Treas. Reg. §1.897-(1)(b)(4)(ii)(C). However, personal property will not be considered real property if the reacquisition is made in foreclosure or pursuant to some other contractual or judicial remedy.
47. The purchasers must be unrelated to each other and to the transferor within the meaning of Treas. Reg. §1.897-1(i). A transferor may rely upon this rule unless he has reason to know that the purchasers are related or intend to re-associate the personal property with the real property within one year of the date of disposition of the personal property.
48. Treas. Reg. §1.897-1(b)(4)(iii).
49. For further discussion on this point, see Guy A. Bracuti, *Infrastructure and Alternative Energy in the 21st Century: Does 20th Century U.S. Tax Policy Leave Us Tilting at Windmills?* 40 Tax Mgmt. Int'l J. 3 (1/14/11).
50. Treas. Reg. §1.897-1(d)(2). (Emphasis added.)
51. *See*, generally, Treas. Reg. §1.897-1(d). The regulations include an example to show the operation of this rule. In the example, a US citizen borrows a loan from a foreign person

regulations also contain special rules, summarized below, regarding whether seven enumerated rights in certain properties constitute an Indirect Right to Share Interest.

(i) Mineral production payments, described in Code section 636, generally will *not* constitute 'an interest in real property other than solely as a creditor' unless it conveys a right to share in the appreciation in the value of the mineral property.[52]

(ii) Installment obligations arising from the disposition of an interest in real property generally will constitute 'an interest in real property other than solely as a creditor.'[53] In that case, each installment payment should be treated as a disposition of an interest in real property to the extent of gain required to be recognized under Code section 453. However, if the transferor elects out of installment treatment so that gain (or loss) is recognized on the disposition of the property, the installment obligation will constitute 'an interest solely as a creditor.' If the original holder of the installment obligation disposes of the obligation to an unrelated person and recognizes gain or loss,[54] the obligation will constitute an interest solely as a creditor in the hands of the subsequent holder.[55]

(iii) An option, a contract, or a right of first refusal to acquire any interest in real property (other than an interest solely as a creditor) will itself constitute 'an interest in real property other than solely as a creditor.'[56]

(iv) A security interest to repossess or foreclose on real property under a mortgage, security agreement, financing statement, or other collateral instrument securing a debt will *not* be considered 'an interest in real property other than solely as a creditor.'[57] In addition, a mortgagee in possession will *not*, for that reason alone, be considered to hold 'an interest in real property other than solely as a creditor.'

(v) An interest [in an instrument] that bears *a rate of interest* tied to an index intended to reflect general inflation or deflation of prices and interest rates (such as the Consumer Price Index) will *not* be viewed as a right to share in the appreciation in, the value of, or gross or net proceeds or profits generated by real property.[58] However, if an interest in real property bears an interest that is tied to an index the *principal purpose* of which is to reflect changes in real property values, the real property interest will be within the scope of

---

to purchase a condominium located in the United States. The terms of the loan provide for the payment of 13% annual interest each year for ten years and 35% of the appreciation in the value of the property at the end of the ten-year period. Under these facts, the foreign person is deemed to have an interest in the property other than solely as a creditor in the condominium.

52. Treas. Reg. §1.897-1(d)(2)(i).
53. Treas. Reg. §1.897-1(d)(2)(ii)(A).
54. *See* I.R.C. §453B.
55. Treas. Reg. §1.897-1(d)(2)(ii)(A).
56. Treas. Reg. §1.897-1(d)(2)(ii)(B).
57. Treas. Reg. §1.897-1(d)(2)(ii)(C).
58. Treas. Reg. §1.897-1(d)(2)(ii)(D).

3. Definition of a US Real Property Interest

the Indirect Right to Share Rule and, hence, will constitute a USRPI.[59] The rest of this chapter refers to this as the Interest Rate Rule.
(vi) Where the assets of a trust or estate consist of real property, the right to reasonable compensation for services rendered as a trustee or in a similar capacity is *not* a real property interest.[60]
(vii) A right to receive a commission, brokerage fee or similar payment for services rendered in connection with the financing, purchase, sale, or lease of real property is *not* 'an interest in real property other than solely as a creditor' even if the amount of the fee or payment is based on a percentage of the real estate sales price or rent. However, if the fee is contingent upon the amount of appreciation, proceeds or profits arising after the date of the transaction, the fee will constitute an interest in real property other than solely as a creditor.[61] The rest of this chapter refers to this as the Commission Rule.

The Commission Rule is interesting. The language of the rule suggests that because the commission is to compensate the real estate agent for the services rendered, the amount should not be considered *generated by* real estate even though the amount of the commission is calculated based on a percentage of the sales price of the real estate. In other words, although the amount can be viewed as *an indirect right to share in the gross or net proceeds* as a result of the sale of a real estate asset, it should represent compensation income and, thus, is *not generated by* real estate. It would be more helpful if there is affirmative guidance that spells out the circumstances under which a type of income is considered *generated by* real estate.

The special rules in section 1.897-1(d) of the regulations do not make any specific reference to the treatment of a license or similar intangibles. Instead, Treasury Regulation section 1.897-1(f)(1)(ii), which addresses treatment of assets for purposes of determining the USRPHC status of a corporation, states that intangibles such as goodwill, franchises, licenses and similar assets are generally considered assets used in a trade or business of a corporation and are *not* real property interests. Although there is no explicit rule that coordinates the application of Treasury Regulation section 1.897-1(f)(1)(ii) and section 1.897-1(d)(2) (which defines the Indirect Right to Share Rule), the clear implication is that both parts of the regulation should apply to determine whether an asset constitutes an USRPI. As a result, goodwill, franchises, licenses and similar assets are excluded from the definition of a USRPI under the FIRPTA regulation.

§3.04 TREATMENT OF INTANGIBLES

Besides the regulations, the IRS has issued very little guidance regarding the treatment of intangibles as USRPIs. One such authority is a revenue ruling that

---

59. *Id.*
60. Treas. Reg. §1.897-1(d)(2)(ii)(F).
61. Treas. Reg. §1.897-1(d)(2)(ii)(E). *See also* Private Letter Ruling 199951027, Sept. 27, 1999, (management agreements were USRPI because the manager was entitled to a percentage of gross revenue of the real property and incentives determined based on revenues in excess of certain specified amounts, and where the manager had a right to acquire the underlying real property).

addresses the treatment of notional principal contracts. Although the conclusion is favorable, as discussed below, this ruling leaves taxpayers pondering over a number of issues.

The IRS held, in Revenue Ruling 2008-31,[62] that an interest in a notional principal contract whose return is calculated by reference to an index of data from a broad range of United States real estate is not a USRPI.[63] A notional principal contract is a financial instrument that provides for the payment of amounts by one party to another at stated intervals calculated by reference to a specified index upon a notional principal amount in exchange for a specified consideration or a promise to pay similar amounts. Examples of notional principal contracts include interest rate swaps, currency swaps, basis swaps, interest rate caps, interest rate floors, commodity swaps, equity swaps and similar agreements.[64]

The revenue ruling addressed an unspecified index that is published widely and is intended to measure the appreciation and depreciation of residential or commercial real estate values within certain geographic areas of the United States. The index in the revenue ruling measures the fluctuation in values within a metropolitan statistical area, a combined statistical area (both as defined by the United States Office of Management and Budget) or a similarly large geographic area within the United States. The metropolitan statistical area, combined statistical area or similarly large geographic area each has a population exceeding one million people. The index is calculated by reference to sales prices obtained from public records, appraisals and reported income, or similar objective financial information. That information is derived from a wide range of real property assets, held by unrelated owners within the relevant geographic area during the relevant testing period.

The facts of the revenue ruling involve a foreign corporation that entered into a notional principal contracts with an unrelated US counterparty. The foreign corporation would profit if the index appreciates over certain levels, and would suffer a loss if the index depreciates or fails to appreciate more than at a specified rate. The revenue ruling stated that the counterparty did not directly or indirectly own or lease a material percentage of the real property whose values were reflected in the index. The IRS concluded that, because of the broad-based nature of the index, the notional principal contract did not fit the definition of an Indirect Right to Share Interest and, hence, did not constitute 'an interest in real property other than solely as a creditor.'

Although the conclusion in the revenue ruling is taxpayer favorable, the exact implication of the ruling is unclear. First of all, the IRS did not explain what constituted a 'broad-based' index for this purposes. In addition, there is no mention of how the revenue ruling reconciles with the Interest Rate Rule which treats an index the *principal purpose* of which is to reflect changes in real estate values will be considered to be an Indirect Right to Share Interest.[65] As a result, it is not clear if the IRS and Treasury Department intended for the revenue ruling to provide *an*

---

62. 2008-1 CB 1180.
63. *See* Rubinger, *IRS Rules Total Return Swap Tied to Real Estate Index Is Not Subject to FIRPTA,* 109 J. Tax'n 149 (2008).
64. Treas. Reg. §1.446-3(c)(1)(i).
65. *See* Treas. Reg. §1.897-1(d)(2)(ii)(D).

example of a notional principal contract that does not fit the definition of an asset that satisfies the Interest Rate Rule (because the index on which the contract is based is so broad), or if the intent is for the revenue ruling to *expand* the Interest Rate Rule to apply to all types of notional principal contracts (while the Interest Rate Rule appears to apply only to instrument with indexed *interest rates*).

A.   Rights in Governmental Permits

In an announcement also issued in 2008, the Treasury and the IRS indicated that they were considering the issuance of proposed regulations to treat certain rights granted by a governmental unit and related to the lease, ownership or use of toll roads, toll bridges, and certain other physical infrastructure as USRPIs. Announcement 2008-115, Infrastructure Improvements under Section 897,[66] describes a *typical* transaction[67] in which a partnership with US corporate partners (owned by foreign shareholders) leases (or purchases) both certain US infrastructure assets and the associated land (collectively referred to as the Specified Infrastructure) from a local government. The partnership then obtains a governmental permit for the right to charge and collect tolls as one of the conditions to operate the Specified Infrastructure (e.g., a toll bridge). The announcement states that in cases where the physical attributes of the Specified Infrastructure give rise to no other commercial use, the value of the partnership's leasehold interest in the Specified Infrastructure should be derived from the value of the governmental permit.

The Treasury and the IRS claim that foreign shareholders have taken the position that gains from the sale of shares of the US corporate partners should not be subject to FIRPTA tax. These taxpayers allegedly treat a governmental permit to operate Specified Infrastructure as an intangible asset that is used in a trade or business[68] and not a USRPI, and allocated the vast majority of the value of the partnership interest

---

66. 2008-2 C.B. 1228.
67. According to Wikipedia, the term 'infrastructure' refers to:

    [S]tructures, systems, and facilities serving the economy of a business, industry, country, city, town, or area, including the services and facilities necessary for its economy to function. It is typically a term to characterize the existence or condition of *costly 'technical structures'* such as road, bridges, tunnels, or other constructed facilities such as loading docks, cold storage chambers, electrical capacity, fuel tanks, cranes, overhead clearances, or components of water supplies, sewers, electrical grids, telecommunications, and so forth. Infrastructure thus consists of improvements with significant cost to develop or install that return an important value over time. [Emphasis added.]

    An infrastructure project may encompass any of the above structures and is generally substantial in scale. Each project is unique and the details of one project may differ significantly from those of another project. Furthermore, as the private sector's involvement in the infrastructure space increases over time, the practice also evolves and the arrangements between the parties may deviate more from the 'typical' transaction described in the announcement.
68. *See* Treas. Reg. §1.897-1(f) which provides that certain licenses and similar intangibles are treated as assets used in a trade or business for purposes of determining whether a corporation is a USRPHC.

to the governmental permit.[69] This position allows the US corporate partner to avoid USRPHC status.[70] The announcement concludes that the governmental permit may properly be characterized as a USRPI in some of the transactions at issue. To counter such practice, the IRS proposed to tie the value of the governmental permit to the value of the leasehold interest of the underlying real property in cases where the leasehold interest would otherwise have no potential alternative commercial use. According to the announcement, the IRS and Treasury Department were considering issuing proposed regulations to address the USRPI characterization of certain *licenses, permits, franchises,* or other similar rights granted by a governmental unit that are related to the value of the use or ownership of an interest in real property and have requested comments on the scope of this regulatory project.

Many commentators criticized the announcement. For example, one commentator wrote that 'toll rights are not rights inherent in and specific to the underlying real property. Rather, they are typically separately bargained-for rights that need to be obtained from relevant governmental agency.'[71] The same commentator also suggested that the IRS and Treasury should clarify that toll rights, like licenses and franchises, should be classified as Code section 197 intangibles instead of USRPIs.[72] Another commentator argued that a contract to earn income, including toll revenue, should be treated as an intangible analogous to business goodwill rather than an interest in real property.[73]

The New York State Bar Association Tax Section issued a report to provide comments to the announcement (the NYSBA Toll Rights Report).[74] The NYSBA Toll Rights Report discussed many different treatments of toll rights under FIRPTA and made a number of recommendations.[75] The report's primary recommendation

---

69. This comment suggests that the IRS is concerned that taxpayers are overvaluing the amount of the intangible and misclassifying the property as non-USRPI.
70. Specifically, for purposes of determining USRPHC status of a corporation, I.R.C. §897(c)(4)(B) requires the assets held by the US partnership to be treated as held proportionately by its corporate partners, including its US corporate partners with foreign shareholders. Thus, the US partnership, by allocating more value to the government permit (i.e., non-USRPI asset or a business asset) than the Specified Infrastructure assets (i.e., USRPI), enables its US corporate partners to avoid USRPHC status because the value of such partners' proportional share of the partnership's business assets invariably will exceed their proportional share of the partnership's USRPIs.
71. Hollender, *Privatizing Our Infrastructure: Taxing the Toll or Tolling the Tax,* 122 Tax Notes 1479, (Mar. 23, 2009).
72. Id.
73. Blanchard, *Infrastructure and FIRPTA: Advanced Notice of Proposed Rulemaking,* 38 Tax Mgmt. Intl. J. 166 (2009), for an overview of the debate. *See also* Bracuti, footnote 49, *supra.*
74. *See* NYSBA, *Report on IRS Announcement 2008-115 on FIRPTA Treatment of Rights Granted by a Governmental Unit,* no. 1195, dated November 16, 2009.
75. One of NYSBA Toll Rights Report's primary recommendations is that the treatment of toll rights under FIRPTA should be consistent with other provisions, e.g., I.R.C. §§197, 1031 and the REIT provisions. The IRS and Treasury did not adopted this recommendation when they finalized the regulations on what constitute 'real estate asset' for REIT purposes. See discussion in §5.03.B., *infra.*

was to treat toll right as part of a single asset inseverable from the underlying real estate to which it relates; as a result, the combined asset would be characterized as a USRPI. According to the report, even if the IRS and Treasury Department find a toll right to be an asset severable from the underlying real property, a toll right of the type in the announcement should still be characterized as USRPI for a variety of reasons.[76]

In some ways, the debate on the treatment of permits and licenses fundamentally stems from the fact that there is no affirmative guidance on what constitutes appreciation or proceeds *generated by* real estate. Hence, a broad spectrum of rights that are remotely associated with real estate may be caught by the Indirect Right to Share Rule and treated as an Indirect Right to Share Interest. To date, the IRS and the Treasury Department have not issued any regulations under the announcement.[77] The lack of clear guidance in this area creates a host of tax issues for the affected parties. Some of the issues are discussed in the section below.

B. Treatment of Infrastructure Projects

This section contains a case study with a simplified fact pattern to illustrate that it can be very difficult to determine whether certain intangible rights in an infrastructure project constitutes a USRPI. At a higher level, the taxpayer in the example has agreed to finance the various costs of the project (which are substantial) in return for the right to collect tolls for a fixed number of years, but has not made a lump sum payment upfront to lease or acquire the underlying real estate which was the practice when these so called public private party (PPP) projects first began in the US around 2004.[78] The example differs from the specific fact pattern in Announcement 2008-115 as the taxpayer in the example *has not* leased or purchased any infrastructure assets.

---

76. According to the NYSBA Toll Rights Report, a toll right described in the announcement that is severed from the underlying real estate property may be characterized as USRPI under current or amended regulations under I.R.C. §897 because the right can be viewed as either a 'traditional real property interest', an 'interest in real property other than solely as a creditor' or personal property that is 'inextricably linked' to the underlying real estate property (the last point is based on the standard articulated in the preamble to the current regulations).
77. *See* Joint Comm. on Tax'n, *Overview of Selected Provisions Relating to the Financing of Surface Transportation Infrastructure Scheduled for a Public Hearing Before the Senate Committee on Finance on June 25, 2015*, JCX-97-15, fn 21.
78. Macquarie Infrastructure Group, an Australian enterprise, and Cintra Concesiones de Infraestructuras de Transporte S.A., a Spanish corporation, signed a USD 1.8 billion contract with the city of Chicago to maintain and operate the Chicago Skyway in exchange for the related toll revenues under a 99-year lease. See, *Chicago Privatizes Skyway Toll Road in $1.8 Billion Deal,* The Associated Press, Oct. 7, 2004.

C. Case Study

1. Facts

The Department of Transportation of State X (the DOT) has contracted with Operator, a US partnership, to build a new bridge across River Y. Two of Operator's partners are US publicly traded corporations. The other partner, USS, is a newly formed US subsidiary of a foreign corporation FC. USS has one outstanding class of common stock all of which is owned by FC. DOT and Operator sign a forty-year comprehensive agreement (CA) which divides the project into two phases: the Construction Phase and the Operation and Maintenance Phase lasting 60 months and 420 months, respectively. Operator's primary responsibility for the first phase is to finish construction of the bridge, and it is responsible for the operating and maintaining the bridge in the second phase.

2. The Comprehensive Agreement

Operator also assumes substantial financial, technical and operational risks in the project throughout the entire term of the CA. The estimated construction costs of the project is USD 1 billion of which USD 300 million is to be provided by DOT.[79] Operator is entitled to 70% of the toll revenues throughout the Operations and Maintenance Phase. Operator also has the following additional rights, among others, under the CA to:

- access to all land that the DOT owns or has acquired in connection with the constructing the toll bridge;
- develop, finance, maintain, improve, equip, modify, repair and operate the toll bridge for the term of the CA;
- hire and supervise any subcontractors to perform the construction of the bridge;
- fix and charge tolls and other fees for vehicles using the toll bridge; and
- pledge, sell or otherwise transfer solely the toll revenues available for distribution to Operator's owners.

The CA provides that Operator's property interests under the agreement are solely those of a licensee, and the DOT and Operator are expressly *not* co-venturers, partners, lessor-lessee or principal-agent. Operator does *not* have fee title, leasehold estate, easement or other real property interest of any kind in or to the toll bridge or associated real properties such as the toll bridge right of way. Operator's property interests under the agreement are limited to contract rights constituting intangible personal property to charge, collect and enforce payment of toll revenues. Operator's toll revenues are gross revenues that are based on a variable pricing model that is dependent solely on the classification of vehicles that pass on the bridge and levels

---

79. There are different ways that DOT may fund its USD 300 million commitment under the CA. For example, it may receive a grant from the federal government or it may raise a public bond or a combination of both.

of traffic at different times of the day. In essence, the parties intend that Operator provides services for the construction, operation and maintenance of the toll bridge for forty years. Operator's compensation for the services consists of the tolls that it collects as the project enters into the Operation and Maintenance Phase after the completion of the Construction Phase.

3. The Project Funding

Operator receives USD 150 million of total capital contribution from the three partners and borrows USD 550 million from a line of credit obtained from a syndicate of banks.[80] Operator completes the first phase of the project on time and places the toll bridge in service by the end of the sixtieth month. Based on the projections, Operator's cash intake from the tolls should exceed the amount of expenses involved in maintaining and operating the bridge during the second phase. FC, USS's parent, is interested in monetizing its investment in the project and is negotiating with an unrelated party to sell all the common stock in USS. FC's US tax consequences on the sale depend on whether USS's outstanding common stock is USRPI;[81] if so, then any gain FC recognizes from the sale would be subject to FIRPTA tax.

USS common stock would be considered a USRPI if 50% or more of its real estate and business assets is made up of USRPIs (i.e., if it satisfies the definition of a USRPHC or former USRPHC).[82] USS will look through its partnership interest in Operator for the purpose of determining whether it owns USRPIs.[83] As a result, it is necessary to determine whether the CA is treated as a USRPI. This exercise involves examining a number of different provisions. At the end of the day, the overriding consideration here is whether the interest in the CA constitutes an 'interest in real property other than solely as a creditor.' As discussed earlier, Treasury Regulation section 1.897-1(d)(2) generally defines an 'interest in real property other than solely as a creditor' as:

(i) one of the items among a list of seven items stipulated in the regulations;[84]
(ii) a traditional type of real estate asset such as a fee ownership, co-ownership, or leasehold interest in real property; or
(iii) an Indirect Right to Share Interest.

The bundle of rights in the CA is not one of the seven specific items listed in Treasury Regulation section 1.897-(d)(2)(i) and (ii). Therefore, the first rule in the above list is not applicable. As stated earlier, Operator's interests under the CA are solely those of a licensee and the parties have not entered into an actual lessor/

---

80. FC contributes USD 50 million of cash to USS which uses the money to fund its capital contribution to Operator. DOT has provided USD 300 million to Operator in accordance with the terms of the CA.
81. The determination is based on whether USS is a USRPHC. See I.R.C. §897(c)(2). The answer to this question, in turn, depends on whether the CA itself is a USRPI. See Ch. 4, *infra*, for a discussion of the rules applicable to USRPHC.
82. *Id.*
83. I.R.C. §897(c)(4)(B) and Treas. Reg. §1.897-2(e)(2). See discussion in §4.05.C., *infra*.
84. *See* Treas. Reg. §1.897-1(d)(2)(i) and (ii).

leasee arrangement. Therefore, in form, Operator does not have a traditional type of real estate asset such as a leasehold. Notwithstanding that, it is necessary to review the substance of the transaction to determine whether Operator could be deemed to have a leasehold interest under US tax principles.[85] Assuming the CA does not qualify as a type of leasehold interest for tax purposes, the second rule above also does not apply.

The final step is to determine whether the CA is an Indirect Right to Share Interest. This is a much more difficult question. Operator does not have any right to share in the appreciation of the underlying real property (e.g., the toll bridge); however, the question that needs to be answered is whether the right to collect tolls is treated as an interest to 'share in the gross or net proceeds or profits *generated by* the real property.'[86] An argument can be made that Operator's right to collect tolls is *generated by* the services that it provides under the terms of the CA. Under that argument, the toll income may be analogous to the commission income that a real estate agent receives from a sale of a real estate asset even though the amount of the income is measured by the proceeds related to the operations of the bridge.[87]

4. Take Away

As of July 2017, there is no definitive rule to deal with the characterization of the CA described in the case study or similar contracts. This issue may become more prevalent as foreign investors are encouraged to increase the amount of investment in US infrastructure projects.[88] As the infrastructure sector requires a significant amount of new investments, the capital raising platforms may offer new vehicles or instruments that reflect the performance of certain aspects of the projects that relates to the underlying real estate. It would be interesting to see what, if any, new guidance the Treasury and the IRS will issue to address the US tax treatment of these new investments.

Foreign investors should evaluate whether a particular investment constitutes, in whole or in part, a USRPI prior to committing their capital in order to assess the associated US tax consequences which, in turn, affect their return on the investment. If a foreign investor is investing in an investment fund that invests in infrastructure projects, the investor should ask for a copy of the tax opinion and any related analysis that concludes whether the underlying investment is classified as a USRPI.

---

85. This analysis requires application of common law principles and other statutory provisions (e.g., I.R.C. §7701(e) which codifies a list of factors developed by case law for purposes of determining when a services contract is more properly treated as a lease for tax purposes). This determination is very fact specific, and largely depends on the specific terms of the underlying contract.
86. *See* Treas. Reg. §1.897-1(d)(2).
87. *Id.*
88. *See* discussion in Ch. 6, *infra.*

§3.05 SUMMARY

The reach of FIRPTA has grown over the last three decades as the definition of USRPI keeps expanding. Despite that, it is still unclear what type of intangible assets constitute a USRPI. The definition can have a significant impact regarding the taxation of foreign investments in the infrastructure sector. Recent tax legislative amendments, enacted with earlier stated intent to encourage foreign investment in US infrastructure projects, resulted in exempting certain categories of foreign investors (instead of categories of investments) from FIRPTA.[89] As foreign investments in the infrastructure sector increases, it becomes even more important to have clear guidance in this area.

Foreign investors need to be very focused in getting answers to the question as to whether a particular investment constitutes a USRPI. The foreign investor's resident country analysis and taxation of the income from the investment is also relevant. When an investment constitutes a USRPI, there is a potential for double taxation unless the resident country allows the investor to credit the FIRPTA tax against its own income tax.[90] In a case where FIRPTA taxes the gain in one year but the resident country postpones the taxation of the transaction until another year (e.g., in the case of a transaction that is tax-deferred under the laws of the resident country), the mismatch in the timing may increase the possibility of double taxation. Foreign investors who pay attention to these issues and engage in careful planning ahead of the transaction may avoid getting caught in the situation of incurring an excess tax burden on a disposition or transfer of their USRPIs.

---

89. *See* Ch. 6, *infra*, for a discussion of the 2015 PATH Act amendments to FIRPTA.
90. I.R.C. §861(a)(5) generally treats the gain taxable under FIRPTA as US source income. As a result, any foreign tax paid by a foreign investor on its gains from the sale or other disposition of a USRPI is not allowable as a foreign tax credit under I.R.C. §904 except to the extent that such foreign tax is imposed other than solely by reason of the nationality or residence of the seller. *See* I.R.C. §906(b)(1).

Chapter 4
Definition of a US Real Property Holding Company

§4.01	Overview	63
§4.02	The Operative Rule	64
§4.03	Definition of a USRPHC	66
	A. General Rule – 50% Fair Market Value Test	66
	B. Elective Rule – 25% Book Value Test	68
	C. Trade or Business Assets	69
§4.04	Look-Back Period and Determination Dates	71
§4.05	The Look-Through Rules	73
	A. Look-Through Rules for Controlled Corporations	73
	B. No Look-Through for Non-Controlled Corporations	74
	C. Look-Through Rules for Partnerships, Trusts and Estates	75
§4.06	Summary	76

§4.01 OVERVIEW

In general, a US Real Property Holding Company, or USRPHC, is any US corporation if the fair market value of its USRPIs equals or exceeds 50% of the aggregate fair market value of its:

- USRPIs;
- foreign real property interests (FRPIs);[1] and
- other assets used or held for use in the corporation's trade or business (Trade or Business Assets).[2]

---

1. This is defined as an interest other than solely as a creditor, as defined in Treas. Reg. §1.897-1(d), in real property located outside the US or the Virgin Islands. Therefore, this FIRPTA rules apply in determining whether an interest in *foreign* real estate is viewed as real estate interest for purposes of this determination.
2. I.R.C. §897(c)(2).

$$\frac{\text{Fair Market Value of USRPIs}}{\text{Fair Market Value of USRPIs + FRPIs + Trade or Business Assets}} \geq 50.0\%$$

As discussed in Chapter 3, the definition of a USRPI includes an interest, other than solely as a creditor, in a US corporation that is treated as a USRPHC or former USRPHC.[3] In general, an interest in a US corporation is presumed to be a USRPI unless the foreign seller establishes otherwise.[4] This means that the seller has the burden of proving that the US corporation is not a current or former USRPHC.[5] While the formula used to compute USRPHC status is mechanical, the overall determination of whether a corporation is a USRPHC can be quite involved.

The USRPHC analysis incorporates all the issues regarding the definition of a USRPI, other than the stock of a US corporation,[6] plus additional considerations such as whether each of the non-real estate assets should be treated as Trade or Business Assets of the tested corporation. Uncertainties regarding the characterization of an asset, e.g., certain intangibles in an infrastructure project,[7] as a USRPI or a Trade or Business Asset impacts the determination of whether a corporation is a USRPHC. This determination, in turn, affects the US taxation of a foreign owner of the corporation because gain from a sale of the stock of a US corporation that is not a USRPI is not subject to US tax.

This chapter discusses the issues with respect to the definition and determination of a USRPHC. Chapter 5 discusses the issues surrounding REITs, many of which also qualify as USRPHCs. Chapter 6 discusses the exemptions from FIRPTA including those applicable to USRPHCs and REITs.

§4.02 THE OPERATIVE RULE

Generally speaking, a US Blocker Corporation, i.e., a US corporation formed solely for purposes of owning one or more USRPIs, qualifies as a USRPHC.[8] The determination is not as straightforward in cases where the US corporation also owns non-real estate assets. As a first step, the denominator of the fraction used to determine a corporation's USRPHC status is all of the corporation's non-real estate assets minus assets that do not satisfy the definition of Trade or Business Assets. Special rules apply to determine whether an asset constitutes a corporation's Trade or Business Asset for this purpose. If a corporation owns an interest in another entity, a detailed

---

3. A former USRPHC is a US corporation that was a USRPHC at some point during a Five-Year Look-Back Period. See I.R.C. §897(c)(1)(A)(ii) and discussion in §4.04, *infra*. In practice, a former USRPHC is often just referred to as a USRPHC.
4. Treas. Reg. §1.897-2(g)(1)(i)
5. Treas. Reg. §1.897-2(g)(1)(i).
6. See discussion in Ch. 3, *supra*.
7. See discussion in §3.04.B. and §3.04.C., *supra*. The fact pattern in IRS Announcement 2008-115 involves a US corporation that is a partner in a partnership that contracts with a governmental entity to engage in an infrastructure project.
8. See Ch. 10, *infra*, for a discussion on various tax issues regarding US Blocker Corporations (also referred to as Blockers).

set of rules applies to determine whether to look through the interest in order to determine the USRPHC status of the owner corporation.[9]

Absent an applicable exception, the sale by a foreign investor of an interest, other than an interest solely as a creditor, in a USRPHC (or a former USRPHC) will be treated as generating ECI gain or loss. In that case, *all* of a foreign investor's gain (i.e., not just the portion that is attributable to US real property) from the disposition of any non-creditor interest in that entity is subject to FIRPTA tax in its *entirety* (i.e., a minority investor is taxed the same as a majority shareholder).[10] This is the case even where a substantial portion of the entity's assets are not USRPIs at the time of the sale, and regardless of whether all or a substantial part of the gain realized on the sale of the stock or other interest in the entity is attributable to appreciation in the value of non-real estate assets of the corporation. This is in direct contrast with the treatment of a foreign investor's sale of an interest in a partnership, trust or estate in which only the gain attributed to the USRPIs that have appreciated in value may be subject to FIRPTA tax.[11]

A non-creditor interest in a domestic corporation is presumed to be a USRPI; however, a foreign person may establish that the interest it is selling is not a USRPI as of the date of the disposition by requesting and obtaining from the domestic corporation a statement that the interest was not a USRPI as of that date (i.e., a non-USRPI Statement).[12] A domestic corporation must, within a reasonable time period after receipt of a request from a foreign person, inform that person whether the interest constitutes a USRPI.[13] If a foreign interest holder requests that a domestic corporation make a USRPI determination, the domestic corporation must provide a notice of such determination to the IRS within thirty days of mailing the USRPI determination to the foreign interest holder.[14] A foreign person that requests and obtains such a statement is not required to forward the statement to the IRS and is not required to take any further action to establish that the interest disposed of was not a USRPI.[15]

If a domestic corporation does not respond to a foreign investor's request within thirty days, the foreign investor may request a determination by the Director, Foreign

---

9. While a non-controlling interest will be either a USRPI in its entirety or not at all, a controlling interest will trigger an analysis of the subsidiary's assets. *See* §4.05, *infra*, for a discussion of these rules.
10. *See* Ch. 6, *infra*, for a discussion of the applicable exceptions.
11. I.R.C. §897(g).
12. Treas. Reg. §1.897-2(g)(1)(ii).
13. Treas. Reg. §1.897-2(h)(1)(i). To qualify under Treas. Reg. §1.897-2(g)(1), the foreign person must obtain the corporation's statement no later than the date, including any extensions, on which a tax return would otherwise be due with respect to a disposition.
14. Treas. Reg. §1.897-2(h)(2). The domestic corporation's failure to timely mail the notice to the IRS will cause the statement provided to the foreign interest holder to become an invalid statement.
15. If it later turns out that the corporation's statement is incorrect, the foreign holder is not excused from filing a return or paying taxes, although no penalties will be assessed unless the holder knew or had reason to know that the corporation's statement was incorrect. Treas. Reg. §1.897-2(g)(1)(ii)(A).

Operations District of the IRS (Director).[16] In order to qualify for a determination, the original request to the domestic corporation must have been made no later than ninety days before the date on which the foreign investor's tax return would be due with respect to the disposition in question.[17] In any event, a foreign investor who has requested such a determination from the Director is not excused from filing a US tax return and paying any taxes due. If the Director determines that the interest in question was not a USRPI, the foreign investor will be entitled to a refund of taxes, penalties and interest. If the Director is unable to make a determination as to the corporation's status based on the Director's records, the foreign investor must treat the interest as a USRPI unless the foreign investor can supply information satisfactory to the Director.[18]

§4.03   DEFINITION OF A USRPHC

A.   General Rule – 50% Fair Market Value Test

Whether a US corporation is a USRPHC at any given time depends on the makeup of the corporation's assets. As shown earlier, the USRPHC calculation may be expressed as a fraction, the numerator of which is the fair market value of the corporation's USRPIs, and the denominator of which is the sum of the fair market values of the corporation's USRPIs, FRPIs, and Trade or Business Assets. Any asset that is not a USRPI,[19] a FRPI, or a Trade or Business Asset, is excluded from the USRPHC calculation.[20]

The USRPHC fraction has two components: a definitional component and a valuation component. Hence, a foreign investor that owns multiple USRPIs, FRPIs and Trade or Business Assets may attempt to arrange and maintain these assets among different US corporations so that less than 50% of the fair market value of each corporation consists of USRPIs under the above formula. A successful execution of such an arrangement may avoid USRPHC classification for one or more US corporations; and, as a result, the foreign investor may dispose of the stock of such US corporations without triggering US federal income tax.[21]

If a person holds both an equity interest and an interest solely as a creditor of a US corporation, the interests generally are respected as separate interests.[22] Under an anti-abuse rule, the IRS may effectively treat a creditor-type interest as an interest *other than* solely as a creditor, and aggregate that interest with the equity interest if it

---

16. Treas. Reg. §1.897-2(g)(1)(i)(B) and -2(g)(1)(iii).
17. Treas. Reg. §1.897-2(g)(1)(iii)(B).
18. Treas. Reg. §1.897-2(g)(1)(iii)(C). Presumably, an interest holder might supply information drawn from annual reports, financial statements or other records of the corporation.
19. For example, the stock of a domestically controlled REIT is not a USRPI and, hence, is not included in the numerator of the fraction. *See* Ch. 6, *infra,* for a discussion of Domestically Controlled REITs.
20. *See* §4.03.C, *infra,* for a discussion of the definition of Trade or Business Assets for this purpose.
21. The gain with respect to the sale of these stock is foreign source income under I.R.C. §865(a)(2).
22. Treas. Reg. §1.897-1(d)(4).

determines that the interests had been separated in order to avoid the application of FIRPTA.[23] On the other hand, if the creditor-type interest has an arm's-length interest rate and repayment schedule, it will not be aggregated with an equity-type interest.[24]

The fair market value of a property, for USRPHC determination purposes, is its gross value reduced by the outstanding balance of certain debts secured by the property.[25] Gross value means the price at which property would change hands between an unrelated willing buyer and seller. In the case of Trade or Business Assets, going concern value is generally considered to provide the best measure of value.[26] The gross value of a corporation's property is reduced by the outstanding balance of debts that are secured by a mortgage (or other security interest) on the property and that were either (i) incurred to acquire the property, or (ii) otherwise incurred in direct connection with the property (such as property tax liens) or in order to maintain or improve the property.[27]

Under an anti-abuse rule, the outstanding balance of any debt will reduce the gross value of FRPIs or Trade or Business Assets where the debt was incurred for the principal purpose of acquiring the assets in order to avoid the application of the FIRPTA rules. Whether the principal purpose of avoiding the FIRPTA rules exists is determined based on all the facts and circumstances of the case.[28] Debts that are incurred in a corporation's ordinary course of its acquisition of assets used or held for use in its trade or business will not be considered to be entered into for the principal purpose of avoiding the FIRPTA rules.[29]

Special rules apply to the determination of fair market value for leases, options to purchase property, and for intangible assets. In the case of leasehold interests, the fair market value is generally the present value, over the period remaining on the lease, of the difference between the rental income provided for in the lease and the current rental value of the real property.[30] Thus, a lease that provides for market (or above-market) rates will have a zero value for this purpose. A leasehold interest bearing restrictions on assignment or sublease also may have a fair market value of zero if the restrictions preclude the lessee's ability to transfer the lease at a gain.[31] The fair market value for an option to acquire real property is the price at which the option could be sold, or generally the difference between the option price and the fair market value of the property.[32] There are three methods to value intangible assets used or held for use in a trade or business:

---

23. Id. A person is deemed to own any interest held by a related person for purposes of this aggregation rule.
24. Id. An interest rate that does not exceed 120% of the applicable federal rate under I.R.C. §1274(d) will be presumed to be an arm's-length rate.
25. Treas. Reg. §1.897-1(o)(2)(i).
26. Treas. Reg. §1.897-1(o)(2)(ii).
27. Treas. Reg. §1.897-1(o)(2)(iii). Debts owed to related persons may be taken into account to reduce the gross value of property only if the lender has made similar loans to unrelated persons on similar terms and conditions.
28. See Treas. Reg. §1.897-1(o)(2)(iv).
29. Treas. Reg. §1.897-1(o)(2)(iv).
30. Treas. Reg. §1.897-1(o)(3).
31. Id.
32. Id.

(i) intangibles acquired by purchase from an unrelated purchaser may be valued at the purchase price;[33]
(ii) intangibles acquired from unrelated parties, other than goodwill and going concern value, may be valued at the amount at which they are carried on financial accounting records under US generally accepted accounting principles;[34] or
(iii) intangibles may be valued at any other reasonable method reflecting true fair market value.[35]

If an alternative valuation method is used for intangibles, special notification requirements may apply.[36]

B. Elective Rule – 25% Book Value Test

The statute refers only to a fair market value test for purposes of determining a corporation's USRPHC status. The regulations added an alternative book value test presumably for taxpayers' convenience. The alternative test generally allows a corporation to rely on the amounts used for its internal accounting purposes, instead of establishing the fair market value, of the relevant assets to determine its USRPHC status.

Under the book value test, a domestic corporation is not considered a USRPHC if, on an applicable 'determination date',[37] the total book value of its USRPIs is 25% or less of the aggregate book value of its USRPIs, FRPIs, and Trade or Business Assets.[38] Book value, for this purpose, is the value at which an item is carried on the financial accounting records of the corporation if such value is determined in accordance with generally accepted accounting principles as applied in the United States.[39] For assets that a corporation is deemed to own indirectly, book value means the corporation's share of the book value of the assets as reported on the books of the entity that directly holds the asset.[40]

A domestic corporation that satisfies the book value test is presumed not to be a USRPHC. However, if the IRS later determines that the presumption does not accurately reflect the corporation's USRPHC status, the IRS will notify the corporation

---

33. Treas. Reg. §1.897-1(o)(4)(i). The purchase price must be adjusted by amortization required by US generally accepted accounting principles. Intangible assets acquired by purchase include amounts allocated to goodwill or going concern value pursuant to I.R.C. §338(b)(3).
34. Treas. Reg. §1.897-1(o)(4)(ii). This method does not apply to assets acquired from a related party.
35. Treas. Reg. §1.897-1(o)(4)(iii).
36. *See* Treas. Reg. §1.897-2(h)(5)(i) and (ii).
37. *See* §4.04, *infra*, for a brief discussion of the rules with respect to a 'determination date' for this purpose.
38. Treas. Reg. §1.897-2(b)(2)(i).
39. Treas. Reg. §1.897-2(b)(2)(ii). While value must be computed with reference to US generally accepted accounting principles, the entity need not keep all of its books in accordance with such principles so long as the value of the relevant assets is determined in accordance therewith.
40. Treas. Reg. §1.897-2(b)(2)(ii).

that it may not rely upon the presumption.[41] The corporation then must determine whether it was a USRPHC pursuant to the 50% value test on the last 'determination date' and notify the IRS of its conclusion no later than 90 days after receiving such notification. If the corporation finds that it was not a USRPHC based on the 50% value test, it may continue to rely on the alternative book value test unless the IRS raises the issue again.[42] If the corporation determines that it was a USRPHC pursuant to the 50% value test, then the corporation must notify its shareholders that it was a USRPHC as of its most recent determination date no later than the 180th day following the IRS's notification.[43]

Generally, a corporation that has properly satisfied the alternative book value test will not be subject to any penalties if it is later determined to be a USRPHC under the fair market value test.[44] However, a corporation will remain subject to possible penalties if the corporation had reason to believe that under the 50% value test it would probably be a USRPHC, because it knew that the book value of relevant assets was substantially higher or lower than the fair market value of those assets.[45] Information with respect to the fair market value is considered to be known by a corporation if the information is included on any books and records of the corporation or its agents, is known by its directors or officers, or is known by employees who in the course of their employment have reason to know such information. There is no affirmative duty to determine the fair market value if such values are not otherwise known.[46]

C. Trade or Business Assets

Trade or Business Assets increase the denominator of the USRPHC fraction; thus, the higher the amount of a corporation's Trade or Business Assets, the less likely it

---

41. Treas. Reg. §1.897-2(b)(2)(iii). The IRS makes such determination based on the information as to the fair market values of a corporation's assets.
42. Id.
43. Id.
44. Treas. Reg. §1.897-2(b)(2)(iv). In fact, a later determination will be prospective only. A foreign investor that relies in good faith on a corporation's determination of its USRPHC status is still required to file a tax return and pay any taxes due in the event the corporation's determination is found to be incorrect. Treas. Reg. §1.897-2(g)(1)(ii)(A). However, such reliance will be taken into account in determining whether the foreign investor is subject to any penalty, unless the investor had reason to know that the corporation's reliance upon the book value presumption was unreasonable. Id.
45. Treas. Reg. §1.897-2(b)(2)(iv)(B). The regulations provide an example of the 'knowledge' standard. A domestic corporation engaged in manufacturing has a fifty-year-old building and some recently purchased equipment. Where the building is located in a deteriorated downtown area and the corporation has no knowledge of facts indicating a fair market value of the building substantially higher than book value, the corporation can rely on the alternative book value test. However, if the facts indicate that the downtown area has become subject to an extensive urban renewal program and the president of the corporation has been offered a price for the building far in excess of book value by a developer planning to convert the building into condominiums, then the corporation would not be entitled to the alternative book value presumption. See Treas. Reg. §1.897-2(b)(2)(iv)(B) Examples 1 and 2.
46. Id.

will be a USRPHC. The regulations define what constitutes Trade or Business Assets, for purposes of determining USRPHC status, to prevent situations where a taxpayer uses passive assets to dilute the USRPHC fraction. Under the regulations, an item of property (other than a USRPI) is a Trade or Business Asset for purposes of the USRPHC fraction if the property falls within one of three categories of property identified and the property is used or held for use in the corporation's trade or business.[47]

The first category of property means: (i) stock in trade or other property of a kind which would properly be included in inventory at year end or held primarily for sale to customers in the course of the company's trade or business, (ii) depreciable property used or held for use in the trade or business as described in Code section 1231(b)(1) (without regard to that provision's holding period requirements), and (iii) certain livestock, including poultry, used or held for use in a trade or business for draft, breeding, dairy, or sporting purposes.[48]

The second category includes goodwill, going concern value, patents, inventions, formulas, copyrights, literary, musical, or artistic compositions, trademarks, trade names, franchises, licenses, customer lists, and similar intangible property, but only to the extent such property is used or held for use in the entity's trade or business.[49] The final category includes cash, securities, receivables of all kinds, options or contracts to acquire cash, securities, or receivables, and options or contracts to acquire commodities, to the extent such assets are used or held for use in the corporation's trade or business and do not constitute USRPIs.[50]

An asset is considered to be used or held for use in a trade or business for this purpose only if the asset is:

(i) held for the principal purpose of promoting the present conduct of the trade or business;
(ii) acquired and held in the ordinary course of that business as, e.g., an account or note receivable arising from that trade or business; or
(iii) otherwise held in a direct relationship to the current, and not future, needs of the trade or business.[51]

An asset is considered to be held in direct relationship to a trade or business only if the asset is needed in that trade or business.[52] An asset is considered to be needed in a trade or business only if the asset is held to meet the present needs of that trade or

---

47. *See* Treas. Reg. §1.897-1(f).
48. *See* Treas. Reg. §1.897-1(f)(1)(i). I.R.C. §1231(b)(1) generally defines property used in a trade or business as property of a character which is subject to depreciation under I.R.C. §167, but which is not any of the following: inventory, property held for sale to customers in the ordinary course of business, artistic works or copyrights, timber, coal, iron ore, livestock, and unharvested crops.
49. *See* Treas. Reg. §1.897-1(f)(1)(ii). Any intangibles not specifically enumerated should be evaluated under the test mentioned above for depreciable property that is described in I.R.C. §1231(b)(1).
50. *See* Treas. Reg. §1.897-1(f)(1)(iii).
51. *See* Treas. Reg. §1.897-1(f)(2) which applies the principles of Treas. Reg. §1.864-4(c)(2) for this determination.
52. *Id.*

business and not its anticipated future needs.[53] For example, an asset is not considered as needed in a trade or business if the asset is held for the purpose of providing for future diversification into a new trade or business, future expansion of the trade or business activities, future plant replacement, or future business contingencies.[54]

While the general rule requires judgment to determine the amount of Trade or Business Assets, the regulations also include a safe harbor rule which objectively provides that 5% of the cash and other liquid assets (those listed above in the final category of Trade or Business Assets above) are presumed to be used or held for use in a corporation's trade or business.[55] Another special rule treats all cash and other liquid assets as used or held for use in an entity's trade or business if the principal business of the entity is trading or investing in such assets for its own account.[56] An entity's principal business is presumed to be trading or investing in such assets if the fair market value of the entity's cash and other liquid assets equals or exceeds 90% of the sum of the fair market values of the entity's USRPIs, FRPIs, and all its Trade or Business Assets.[57]

§4.04 LOOK-BACK PERIOD AND DETERMINATION DATES

The applicable 'look-back' period, for purposes of determining a corporation's USRPHC status, is the shorter of: (i) the period during which the foreign person held such interest, or (ii) the five-year period ending on the date that the foreign person disposes of the interest (the Five-Year Look-Back Period).[58] An interest in a domestic corporation is a USRPI if the corporation was a USRPHC on any 'determination date' during the applicable look-back period ending on the date specified in the interest-holder's request (or on the date such request was received if no date is specified).[59] Whether a corporation is a USRPHC is to be determined on the last day of the corporation's tax year and any date that:

(i) the corporation acquires a USRPI (with a cumulative value above a certain threshold as discussed below in this section);
(ii) the corporation disposes of a FRPI or Trade or Business Asset (with a cumulative value above a certain threshold); and
(iii) would be a determination date for any entity the assets of which are proportionately attributed to the corporation under the partnership or 'controlling interest' rules discussed below.[60]

---

53. Id.
54. Id.
55. See Treas. Reg. §1.897-1(f)(3)(i). This safe harbor does not apply, however, to any liquid assets that are held or acquired for the principal purpose of avoiding I.R.C. §§897 or 1445.
56. Treas. Reg. §1.897-1(f)(3)(ii). It is generally difficult to qualify for this presumption due to the high percentage requirement of non-real estate investment assets.
57. Id.
58. I.R.C. §897(c)(1)(A). Treas. Reg. §1.897-1(d) defines an interest, for this purpose, as other than an interest solely as a creditor.
59. Treas. Reg. §1.897-2(h)(1)(ii).
60. See Treas. Reg. §1.897-2(c)(1)(i)-(iv).

The regulations specify a variety of transactions that will not give rise to a USRPHC determination date. For example, the disposition of inventory (including livestock) or the satisfaction of accounts receivable arising from the disposition of inventory or from the performance of services do not trigger a USRPHC determination date;[61] nor does the disbursement of cash to meet the regular operating needs of the business (such as to acquire inventory or to pay wages).[62]

The regulations apply a sliding scale to determine the amount of USRPIs that a US corporation generally may acquire, or the amount of Trade or Business Assets that a US corporation may dispose of, without triggering a USRPHC determination date for such corporation:[63]

- If a corporation, on its most recent USRPHC determination date, was considered to hold USRPIs having a fair market value that was less than 25% of the fair market value of all its assets, then the corporation may acquire USRPIs in an amount up to 10% (referred to as the 'applicable limitation amount') of the value of all its USRPIs, or may dispose of Trade or Business Assets up to 10% of its total Trade or Business Assets without triggering a new USRPHC determination date.
- If the fair market value of a corporation's USRPIs was 25% or more, but less than 35% of all its assets on its last USRPHC determination date, the applicable limitation amount is 5% without triggering a new USRPHC determination date.
- If the fair market value of a corporation's USRPIs was 35% or more of all its assets, the applicable limitation amount is 2%.
- If a corporation is not a USRPHC under the alternative book value test, then the applicable limitation amount is 10% of the book value of all its Trade or Business Assets or all USRPIs (as applicable) held by the corporation.[64]

Under an alternative method, a corporation may elect to determine its USRPHC status at the end of each calendar month.[65] An electing corporation also must make a determination as of the date on which, pursuant to a single transaction (consisting of one or more transfers) where USRPIs are acquired or interests in FRPIs and/or Trade or Business Assets are disposed of, the total fair market value of the assets acquired and/or disposed of exceeds 5% of the total fair market values of all these assets.[66]

---

61. Treas. Reg. §1.897-2(c)(2)(i)(A) and (B).
62. Treas. Reg. §1.897-2(c)(2)(i)(C).
63. Treas. Reg. §1.897-2(c)(2)(iii).
64. Treas. Reg. §1.897-2(c)(2)(iii)(A) through (D). Once a USRPHC determination date is triggered, the computation of the amount of Trade or Business Assets disposed of or USRPIs acquired after that date begins at zero. Treas. Reg. §1.897-2(c)(2)(iii). For examples of the USRPHC determination date calculation, see Treas. Reg. §1.897-2(c)(2)(iii) Examples (1) and (2).
65. Treas. Reg. §1.897-2(c)(3)(ii).
66. Treas. Reg. §1.897-2(c)(3)(iii).

§4.05 THE LOOK-THROUGH RULES

As mentioned earlier, detailed look-through rules apply in determining the USRPHC status of a corporation that owns an interest in another entity. These rules are extensive and cover a corporation's direct or indirect ownership of controlling interests in subsidiary corporations, ownership of non-controlling interests in other corporations and ownership of interests in partnerships, estates and trusts.

A. Look-Through Rules for Controlled Corporations

A corporation (referred to as the first corporation) that owns 50% or more of the fair market value of all classes of stock of another corporation (referred to as the second corporation) is generally deemed to own the controlling interest of the second corporation for purposes of determining whether the first corporation is a USRPHC.[67] In such a case, the first corporation's shares of stock owned in the second corporation generally are disregarded, and the first corporation generally will be treated as owning a proportionate share of all of the second corporation's assets for purposes of determining the USRPHC status of the first corporation.

Under this look-through rule, the first corporation will be treated as using such assets, or holding them for use, in its trade or business if the second corporation uses such assets, or holds them for use, in its own trade or business.[68] The look-through rule applies successively to all lower-tier subsidiaries, domestic or foreign, connected to the first corporation being tested by a chain of 50% or more ownership to determine the USRPHC status of a corporation.[69]

Special constructive ownership rules also apply to determine whether a first corporation owns a controlling interest in another corporation. The applicable constructive ownership rules are a modified version of the Code section 318 rules substituting the ownership threshold from 5% for 50% for purposes of triggering certain attribution rules.[70] Although this look-through rule may be intended to be taxpayer favorable, it may be difficult for a taxpayer to obtain the necessary

---

67. I.R.C. §897(c)(5) and Treas. Reg. §1.897-2(e)(3). Under a special rule, the first corporation shall not be treated as holding a proportionate share of assets that, in the hands of the second corporation, are treated as Trade or Business Assets under the safe harbor rule for investment companies as provided in Treas. Reg. §1.897-1(f)(3)(ii). In addition, the regulations do not specify whether the 50% test should be applied to the sum of all different classes of stock of the second corporation or on a class-by-class basis to each class of stock. Compare, e.g., Rev. Rul. 59-259, 1959-2 C.B. 115 which provides that for purposes of the I.R.C. §368(c) control requirement, the test with respect to 'all classes' of stock is applied to 'each class' of stock of the relevant corporation.
68. I.R.C. §897(c)(5)(A)(iii).
69. Id.
70. Treas. Reg. §1.897-2(e)(3), which generally modifies the attribution of I.R.C. §318(a)(2)(C) and (3)(C), from partnerships and corporations and to partnerships and corporations, respectively. In addition, a corporation that does not directly hold any interest in the second corporation shall not be treated as holding a controlling interest in the second corporation by reason of I.R.C. §318(a)(3)(C); thus, brother-sister corporations will not be considered to own controlling interests in each other through the common parent.

information to make a proper determination in cases where the second corporation is not wholly owned by the first corporation.

B.   No Look-Through for Non-Controlled Corporations

Where the first corporation owns less than a controlling stock interest (i.e., less than 50%) in the second corporation that is a US corporation, and the second corporation is a USRPHC, such stock interest is treated as a USRPI of the first corporation. In addition, a less than controlling stock interest in a foreign corporation that would be a USRPHC if it were a US corporation is also treated as a USRPI for this purpose.[71] The entire amount of non-controlling stock interests in such USRPHCs (or in such foreign corporations that are deemed USRPHCs for testing purposes) will be counted as USRPIs regardless of the actual asset mix of the second corporation. This is very different from the look-through rule above that would apply if the first corporation holds a controlling interest in the second corporation in question.

On the other hand, if the first corporation owns a non-controlling interest in a second corporation that is not a USRPHC, the full value of the interest in the second corporation will be taken into account in determining whether the first corporation is a USRPHC only if the first corporation uses, or holds for use, the stock of the second corporation in its trade or business (i.e., as a Trade or Business Asset included in the denominator of the USRPHC fraction).[72] As discussed further below, a non-controlling interest in a corporation is presumed to be a USRPI unless the shareholder establishes that such interest is not a USRPI.[73]

As illustrated by an example in the regulations,[74] these rules appear to be drafted to avoid situations where taxpayers use tiers of foreign corporations to own primarily USRPIs. In situations where this assumption is not true, the presumption that a lower-tier foreign corporation as a USRPHC until proven otherwise may unjustly cause the top-tier US corporation to be a USRPHC because, in practice, it may be very difficult for the US corporation to obtain the necessary information to determine the USRPHC status of all of the lower-tier corporations in which it does not own a controlling interest.

In general, the first corporation may follow the same procedure as any foreign holder (discussed above) and obtain a statement from the second corporation in which it owns a non-controlling interest to determine whether the second corporation is treated as a USRPI.[75] Alternatively, the first corporation may make its own determination as to the status of the interest it owns in the second entity. The determination must be based on the best evidence available, drawn from annual reports, financial statements, etc. that demonstrate to a reasonable certainty that the interest in the second corporation is not a USRPI.[76]

---

71. I.R.C. §897(c)(4)(A) and Treas. Reg. §1.897-2(e)(1).
72. I.R.C. §897(c)(2)(B)(iii).
73. Treas. Reg. §1.897-2(e)(1).
74. *See* Treas. Reg. §1.897-2(e)(1) Example (2).
75. Treas. Reg. §1.897-2(g)(2)(i).
76. Treas. Reg. §1.897-2(g)(2)(iv). If the IRS subsequently determines that the corporation's independent determination was incorrect, it will be subject to penalties only if the

C. Look-Through Rules for Partnerships, Trusts and Estates

Where a corporation owns any interest in a partnership, trust or estate, the corporation is treated as owning a proportionate share of all of the assets held by the partnership, trust or estate for purposes of determining its USRPHC status.[77] Similar to the look-through rule for a controlling interest in a corporation, the corporate partner or beneficiary will be treated as using such assets, or holding them for use, in its a trade or business if the partnership or trust or estate uses such assets, or holds them for use, in its own Trade or Business Assets.[78] In addition, this look-through rule applies successively through tiers of partnerships, trusts or estates that are above the first partnership, trust or estate in a chain thereof.[79]

Generally, a person's proportionate share of the assets of a partnership, trust or estate equals the person's percentage ownership interest multiplied by the fair market value of assets held by the entity. A person's percentage ownership interest in a partnership is the percentage equal to the ratio of the liquidation value of all interests held by the person to the total liquidation value of the partnership.[80] A proper determination of such liquidation value generally requires an understanding of the terms of the partnership agreement and access to information with respect to the fair market value of the underlying partnership assets. **Example 4.1**, adopted from the regulations, illustrates the application of this rule.

Example 4.1

A, a US person, and B, a foreign person, form a partnership in Year 1 to purchase undeveloped land located in the United States for USD 300,000 (which is the partnership's only asset). The capital interests of A and B in the partnership are 25% and 75%, respectively; however, A and B each have a 50% profits interest in the partnership. The partnership agreement provides that, upon liquidation, any unrealized gain will be distributed in accordance with the partners' respective profits interests. In Year 5, the partnership has no items of income or deduction, and the fair market value of the undeveloped land is USD 500,000.

Accordingly, B's percentage ownership interest is 65% – the ratio of USD 325,000 (USD 100,000 profits interest plus USD 225,000 capital interest) to USD 500,000.[81]

A person's percentage ownership interest in a trust or estate generally equals the ratio of the actuarial value of the entity's assets (minus liabilities to creditors) to

---

 determination was unreasonable in view of the facts that the corporation knew or had reason to know.
77. I.R.C. §897(c)(4)(B) and Treas. Reg. §1.897-2(e)(2).
78. Id.
79. Id.
80. Treas. Reg. §1.897-1(e)(2)(ii).
81. Treas. Reg. §1.897-1(e)(2)(iii) Example (2).

the entity's overall net assets.[82] Special rules apply to a trust or estate that grants certain options or conversion rights as well as those that entitle an interest holder to a disproportionate distribution of USRPI upon liquidation.[83] The regulations include an anti-abuse rule that treats a beneficiary in a discretionary trust or estate generally as deemed to own all of the entity's discretionary assets. An example in the regulation illustrates the application of this rule. A simplified version of the example is provided below.

Example 4.2

A, a US person, established a discretionary trust in Year 1 and contributed a USRPI with a value of USD 10,000 to the trust. The terms of the trust provide that the unrelated trustee may, in its discretion, retain trust income or distribute it to X, a foreign person. Upon the death of X the remainder is to go in equal shares to foreign persons Y and Z. Assume that the actuarial values of the remainder interests are definitely ascertainable – USD 1,000 for Y and USD 500 for Z. X's income interest has no definitely ascertainable actuarial value. The difference between the USD 10,000 value of the trust and the USD 1,500 ascertainable value is treated under the FIRPTA regulations as owed by each beneficiary.

Accordingly, X's percentage ownership interest is 85% (USD 8,500 divided by USD 10,000), Y's is 95% (USD 8,500 plus USD 1,000 divided by USD 10,000), and Z's is 90% (USD 8,500 plus USD 500 divided by USD 10,000).[84]

§4.06 SUMMARY

The USRPHC definition has important implications. A foreign investor's share of the gain from the sale of the stock of a US corporation is exempt from US tax if the corporation is not a USRPHC or a former USRPHC.[85] Notwithstanding the general premise that a corporation is a USRPHC if the majority of its assets is USRPI, the actual determination of whether a corporation is a USRPHC can be challenging. In a situation where a corporation owns a significant amount of real estate, e.g., a mining company or a hotel, the determination may be straightforward. Conversely, the analysis can be quite complicated, if, e.g., the corporation owns:

- stock in one or more non-controlled subsidiaries, then it is necessary to determine whether each non-controlled subsidiary is itself a USRPHC;[86]

---

82. Treas. Reg. §1.897-1(e)(3)(ii).
83. *Id.*
84. Treas. Reg. §1.897-1(e)(3) Example.
85. Some investment funds have mandates not to acquire shares of any companies if the gain from a subsequent sale of the stock would give rise to FIRPTA.
86. *See* discussion in §4.05.B., *supra*.

4. Definition of a US Real Property Holding Company

- real estate interests that appreciate at a different rate than its other assets;[87]
- a sizable amount of personal property associated with the use of real property;[88] or
- interests in certain intangible rights;[89]

Although it is not required to do so,[90] a US corporation that is trying to raise capital, publicly or privately, should conduct a formal analysis for the 5-year 'look back' period to determine its USRPHC status. If the corporation determines that it is not a USRPHC during such period, it could make it findings available to potential investors prior to the capital raise to alleviate any potential concern that the corporation maybe a USRPHC. Ideally, the corporation should also provide periodic updates of its USRPHC status to its investors.

---

87. The requirement to use fair market value to determine the USRPHC fraction of a company necessitates having information regarding the fair market of each of the company's assets. Using the 25% alternative book value test obviates the need for such information, but a US corporation is more likely going to constitute a USRPHC under the alternative test.
88. It is necessary to determine whether the personal property falls within a certain category of assets that are used predominantly for certain activities. Treas. Reg. §1.897-1(b)(4)(i) and discussion in §3.03.B.2., *supra*.
89. It is necessary to determine whether the right constitutes an Indirect Right to Share Interest. *See* discussion in §3.03.C., *supra*.
90. The rule that requires a US corporation to respond to a foreign investor's inquiry about its USRPHC status prior to an investor's *sale* of the stock does not provide the information in a timely manner for investors that wish to avoid acquiring the stock of a USRPHC. *See* Treas. Reg. §1.897-2(g)(1)(i)(A).

Chapter 5
Using REITs to Invest in the US

§5.01	Overview	79
§5.02	Foreign Investors' Use of REITs	83
	A. Initial Assessment on Using a REIT	83
	B. REIT Conversion and the Sting Tax	85
	C. Restrictions on REIT Spin-Offs	87
§5.03	REIT Qualifications	89
	A. Organizational/Ownership Requirements	89
	B. Quarterly Asset Tests	90
	C. Income Tests	93
	D. Annual Distribution Requirements	95
	E. Special Rules Applicable to TRS	97
	1. Tenant Services	98
	2. Eligible Independent Contractors	99
§5.04	Taxation of Foreign Investors' Income and Gain from REITs	100
	A. Ordinary Dividends	100
	B. Capital Gain Dividends	101
	1. General Rule	101
	2. FIRPTA Tax on Gain Distributed	102
	C. Gain from the Sale of REIT Stock	108
§5.05	Summary	108

§5.01 OVERVIEW

Created by Congress in 1960 as a vehicle to enable small investors to pool their resources together to invest in passive real estate assets investments, a real estate investment trust (REIT)[1] is an entity that owns primarily passive real estate invest-

---

1. *See* I.R.C. §§856-860. A REIT that owns rental real estate is referred to as an equity REIT and a REIT that owns mortgages is referred to as a mortgage REIT.

ments such as rental real estate assets and real estate mortgages. Although a REIT is generally treated as a corporation for US tax purposes[2] it may reduce or eliminate its taxable income if it pays out its earnings and profits as dividends to its shareholders (this is referred to as a 'dividend paid deduction').[3] This tax-favored[4] vehicle has gained popularity in recent years.

A number of Subchapter C corporations that own non-traditional real estate assets have converted into REITs.[5] In some of these transactions, a publicly traded Subchapter C corporation contributed the real estate it owned to a new subsidiary and distributed the stock of the subsidiary to its shareholders in a tax-free transaction.[6] Some have questioned the appropriateness of using REITs in these so-called 'opco-propco' structures. The concern was whether the REIT rules that are intended to benefit passive real estate businesses can be used to benefit operating businesses that own real estate. For example, an article in the press stated that '[a] small but growing number of American corporations, operating in businesses as diverse as private prisons, billboards and casinos, are making an aggressive move to reduce – or even eliminate – their federal tax bills.'[7] In response to this concern, the 2015 PATH Act enacted a provision that generally prevents a REIT from being eligible to participate in a tax-free spin-off as discussed in more detail below.

Foreign ownership in REITs also has increased in recent years. Many foreign investors now use private REITs to own office buildings, shopping centers, residential properties, hotels and industrial properties. Effective use of a REIT structure may result in the following benefits:

- a lower effective US tax rate for distributed rental income earned during the holding period of the investment;

---

2. Generally, a US corporation is subject to entity level tax under Subchapter C of Chapter 1 of the IRC. This 'classic system' imposes two levels of tax on corporate income: once at the entity level and then again on dividends paid by the corporation to the shareholders.
3. See I.R.C. §561. As a result of the dividend paid deduction, a REIT may avoid corporate-level tax on its taxable income that is distributed. Instead, the REIT's shareholders pay one level of tax on the dividends received.
4. The REIT platform is tax-favored because it generally eliminates the corporate-level taxation and imposes only one level of tax on the shareholders. Example 5.1 illustrates this principle.
5. These non-traditional real estate assets included electricity transmission system, data center property, natural gas pipeline system, wireless and broadcast communications infrastructures system, outdoor advertising display, floating gaming facility, correctional facility, and record storage facility. For example, of the current six publicly traded data-center REITs, five completed their initial public offerings during the past ten years, while one converted from a Subchapter C corporation to a REIT effective in 2015. Omotayu Okusanya and David Shamis, *REITs: What's Next in the REIT Conversion Phenomenon?* Jefferies, at 2 (Apr. 10, 2013).
6. See I.R.C. §355. After the spin, the subsidiary elects REIT status and leases the real estate back to the Subchapter C corporation.
7. See, *Restyled as Real Estate Trusts, Varied Businesses Avoid Taxes*, published by *The New York Times* on April 21, 2013.

5. Using REITs to Invest in the US

- a foreign recipient of ordinary REIT dividends does not have to file a US tax return to report the ordinary dividend income;[8] and
- a foreign investor also may potentially reduce or even eliminate its US tax burden if it sells REIT shares when it is ready to exit the investment in USRPI.[9]

Example 5.1

	Subchapter C Corporation	REIT
	(in USD 000s)	
Gross Rent Income	120	120
Less:		
– Expenses	(20)	(20)
– Federal income tax	(35)	n/a
Earnings and profits	65	100
30% US withholding	(19.5)	(30)
Net cash distribution	45.5	70
Effective tax rate	54.5%	30%

This example does not take into account any depreciation expense and state and local tax savings which would generally increase the benefits of using a REIT. In addition, US tax treaties may reduce the withholding tax on dividends paid by a Subchapter C corporation or, to a lesser extent, by a REIT.[10]

As illustrated in Example 5.1, using an equity REIT can offer significant tax savings to a foreign investor in a USRPI.[11] Such tax savings come at a cost. The REIT regime has very detailed and prescriptive requirements that must be satisfied continuously

---

8. *See* discussion in §2.02.A., *supra*, for a discussion of the general reporting rules applicable to foreign investors.
9. For example, if the REIT qualifies as a Domestically Controlled Qualified Investment Entity then the foreign investor may be exempt from US tax on the gain upon a sale of the REIT stock. *See* I.R.C. §897(h)(2) and discussion in §6.02.C, *infra*, regarding this exception.
10. See Ch. 9, *infra*, regarding the application of US income tax treaties on dividends paid to foreign persons.
11. A mortgage REIT effectively converts the character of the underlying interest income into ordinary REIT dividends which is typically subject to a higher US tax when the income is distributed to foreign investors but does not generally cause foreign investors to be engaged in a trade or business in the United States. Hence, mortgage REITs generally do not offer US tax savings to foreign investors. *See* Chs. 9 and 10, respectively, for discussions on US withholding tax under an applicable treaty and the Portfolio Interest Exemption on interest payments. Unless indicated otherwise, the discussion in this chapter is intended to cover only equity REITs.

in order to preserve the REIT status. A REIT that fails to satisfy all the qualification requirements would lose its REIT status. Such an entity would be taxed as a Subchapter C corporation for the year unless the failure is due to reasonable cause and not due to willful neglect. Certain exceptions may allow a taxpayer to cure inadvertent failures to satisfy specific REIT qualification requirements.[12] If none of the exceptions apply, the failed entity generally may not reelect REIT status until the fifth year following the year it lost the REIT status but does not incur any other monetary penalty.[13]

If the failure is discovered in a later year after the REIT already distributed its earnings and profits to its shareholders, then the result could be rather messy.[14] Using the facts from **Example 5.1**, the REIT distributed USD 100,000 in Year 1 (USD 30,000 withheld and the remaining USD 70,000 was paid to its foreign shareholder)[15] and had no earnings and profits in Years 2 and 3. Now assume that the IRS determined, in Year 4, that the REIT failed its REIT status in Year 1 and should have been taxed as a Subchapter C corporation in that year. The situation could end up looking like this:

- At the entity level, the former REIT would owe USD 35,000 of federal corporate income tax plus interest.[16] The former REIT's earnings and profits would be reduced to USD 65,000.[17]
- At the shareholder level, there would be an overpayment of USD 10,500 FDAP withholding tax (i.e., imposed on dividends).[18] Of the USD 70,000 that the foreign shareholder received from Year 1, only USD 45,500 would constitute dividend income.[19] The difference of USD 24,500 would be treated first as a return of capital, and any excess would be capital gain subject to FIRPTA tax.

This chapter discusses some of the considerations that affect a foreign investor's decision to use a REIT as the investment vehicle to own its USRPI, provides a high-level review of the key REIT qualification requirements and operating issues and then summarizes certain recent tax issues affecting REITs.[20] Readers should be

---

12. *See*, e.g., I.R.C. §856(c)(6), (c)(7), and (g)(5).
13. I.R.C. §856(g)(3).
14. If the Subchapter C corporation in Example 5.1 does not distribute its earnings to its shareholders in a year and waits until it liquidates to distribute all of its accumulated cash to its shareholders, the amount distributed would not be characterized as dividends for US tax purposes. Instead, the liquidating distributions would be treated as proceeds received from a sale or exchange of the stock under I.R.C. §331(b) which would be exempt from US withholding tax.
15. This assumes that the REIT has one foreign shareholder that owns all of its common stock and ignores any dividends paid to the 100 preferred shareholders.
16. The IRS also may attempt to impose various penalties. *See* Ch. 11, *infra*, for a general discussion of the penalties potentially applicable.
17. Determined as pre-tax earnings of USD 100,000 less federal corporate income tax of USD 35,000.
18. USD 30,000 paid less USD 19,500 (USD 65,000 x 30%).
19. USD 65,000 of the Year 1 redetermined earnings and profits less USD 19,500 of withholding tax imposed.
20. The 2015 PATH Act included a number of changes to the REIT regime.

aware that the REIT rules are complex and a full discussion of the rules is beyond the scope of this book.

§5.02 FOREIGN INVESTORS' USE OF REITs

A. Initial Assessment on Using a REIT

A foreign person, let's call him Cole, who is a Canadian tax resident, wishes to acquire a class A office building in Manhattan with some co-investors. The group intends to lease the space in the building to unrelated tenants. Cole and his co-investors should always consider whether it is appropriate to use a REIT to own the building directly in light of the tax benefits afforded. The extent of the tax benefits of the REIT structure depends on factors including whether the group wants to have the cash from the operations repatriated at least once a year, and whether members of the group are eligible for treaty benefits.[21] On the other hand, if the group expects to reinvest the funds from the building's operations in the US, then the tax benefit of the REIT structure would be reduced.

The detailed REIT requirements can be intimidating. The actual complexities of the structure vary depending on a variety of factors including the investor's ownership structure and the type of properties that the REIT owns. For example, it is generally easier to identify any issues that arise with respect to a single-property REIT versus a REIT that owns a large portfolio of assets. It is generally helpful for a foreign investor to evaluate certain threshold issues to form a preliminary view as to whether a REIT structure may be suitable for the particular investment contemplated.

The first step is to determine whether the underlying property constitutes a real estate asset for REIT purposes, and whether the asset generates REIT eligible income. Although the definitions of 'real property assets'[22] for REIT purposes, and 'interest in real property,'[23] for FIRPTA purposes, overlap to some degree, there are important differences. In other words, not all USRPIs are REIT-able assets. Furthermore, outside of the leasing of traditional real estate assets such as an office or an apartment building, it is sometimes difficult to differentiate whether an item of income constitutes pure rental income or some other type of income, e.g., certain services,[24] which may adversely impact the entity's ability to satisfy the various REIT income tests. For example, a REIT that provides space in its facilities to customers for storage of physical items and certain related services[25] in exchange for a storage fee

---

21. For example, if the foreign investor is eligible for 5% reduced dividend withholding tax on dividends paid by a Subchapter C corporation under a US income tax treaty, then the tax benefit of using the REIT structure would be reduced.
22. I.R.C. §856(c)(5)(B) defines 'real estate assets', for REIT purposes, to include interests in real property and also direct and indirect interests in mortgages, mortgage securitizations, shares in other REITs and temporary investments of new capital.
23. See I.R.C. §897(c)(6)(A) and discussion in §3.03.A., supra.
24. Separate charges for services customarily furnished in connection with the rental of real property are also considered rents from real property. I.R.C. §856(d)(1)(B).
25. Such services may include the handling of the stored items for customers who need to regain physical custody of the contents of the stored items, courier operations with respect

may be receiving part rental income and part services income. In such a situation, the REIT may use a taxable REIT subsidiary, or TRS, to conduct certain business activities in connection with the rental of space.[26] A TRS is a corporation, the stock of which is directly or indirectly owned by a REIT.[27] The IRS held privately that a data storage facility REIT that uses its TRS to provide related services to its customers is considered to receive rents from real property.[28]

Under a special rule, 50% of the stock of a REIT (measured by value) may not be owned by five or fewer individuals.[29] Look-through rules apply to determine the ownership. If a single family's ultimate ownership, through a group of entities (including public corporations), of a US entity exceeds the 50% threshold, then such an entity would not be eligible to elect REIT status. In our example, if Cole and his four brothers ultimately own 50% or more of the investment, then this restriction would kick in and they may not use a REIT to own the building. The result would be very different if Cole is the executive of an investment company that intends to set up a Canadian income trust with numerous investors who own units of the trust. Separately, if a widely held foreign investor (including a public corporation) intends to use a REIT structure that qualifies for the Domestically Controlled Qualified Investment Entity exception,[30] it must carefully observe the requirements during the requisite holding period to be eligible for the benefit.

The next step is to determine how to structure the ownership of the real estate asset. If the investment involves one or more newly acquired assets, then a new entity may be formed to acquire the asset, and the new entity simply elects to be treated as a REIT. On the other hand, if the structure involves a conversion of an existing Subchapter C corporation, then it is necessary to address any potential issues regarding the Built-in Gains Tax (also referred to as the Sting Tax).[31] Finally, if the investment involves a portfolio of assets, then it may be worth considering whether multiple REITs or single-property REITs should be used to facilitate the exit of the investment.[32]

---

      to the stored items at a customer's request, and secured shredding of sensitive or outdated documents.

26. The TRS provisions were added in December 1999 and became effective for 2001 to relax the restrictions against a REIT rendering non-customary services to tenants and certain other limitations.
27. There is no minimal percentage ownership threshold with respect to a REIT's ownership percentage of its TRS. A TRS election is made jointly by the REIT on Form 8875. I.R.C. §856(l)(1). The TRS election automatically applies to any corporate subsidiaries in which the TRS has a greater than 35% ownership (by voting power or value). I.R.C. §856(l)(2).
28. PLR 201503010 (1/16/15).
29. *See* discussion in §5.03.A., *infra,* for a brief discussion of the prohibition against closely held REITs.
30. *See* I.R.C. §897(h)(2) and discussion in §6.02.C., *infra.*
31. See discussion in §5.02.B., *infra,* for a brief discussion of the rules applicable to Sting Tax.
32. See discussion §5.04.B., *infra,* regarding the application of I.R.C. §897(h)(1) upon a sale of the properties by the REIT followed by a distribution of the proceeds.

B.   REIT Conversion and the Sting Tax

A newly formed entity that is otherwise taxable as a domestic corporation may elect REIT status effective the first date that it generates any income or acquires any assets. Such an entity would not have to deal with any conversion issues. On the other hand, a Subchapter C corporation with existing assets may convert to become a REIT. There are two common ways to effectuate the conversion. In a straight conversion transaction, the Subchapter C corporation may make a prospective REIT election on its federal income tax return.[33] Certain requirements must be met in such a transaction, e.g., the entity must distribute all of its earnings and profits accumulated while it was a Subchapter C corporation. The distribution is generally taxable as dividends to the shareholders.

Alternatively, the conversion may take the form of an umbrella partnership REIT structure (an UPREIT).[34] In a typical UPREIT transaction, a property owner (including an existing Subchapter C corporation) contributes its real estate assets to a partnership in exchange for partnership units.[35] Meanwhile, a newly formed domestic corporation issues stock[36] to raise cash which it contributes to the same partnership in exchange for partnership units.[37] The newly formed corporation elects REIT status effective on the incorporation date. The newly formed REIT would not have any non-REIT earnings and profits to distribute. In addition, the UPREIT structure allows more flexibility in the overall ownership because there is no restriction regarding the concentration of ownerships of the partnership below the REIT.[38]

A REIT is generally subject to the Built-in-Gains Tax (or the Sting Tax), if it disposes of property owned by a Subchapter C corporation predecessor during the 'recognition period.'[39] Instead of the Sting tax, the Subchapter C corporation that is converting to become a REIT may elect[40] to recognize gain or loss as if it had sold

---

33. See I.R.C. §856(a)(1).
34. The UPREIT structure is sanctioned by the partnership anti-abuse rules. See Treas. Reg. §1.701-2(d) Example 4. Also see Rubin, Whiteway and Forrest, *Tax Planning for the Property Owner in REIT Acquisitions*, Practising Law Institute Seventh/Eighth Annual Real Estate Forum (No. 6155) for a detailed discussion of the issues relating to an UPREIT structure.
35. The partnership units are typically convertible into the REIT stock to provide liquidity to the party that contributed the assets. While the initial contribution of the assets to the partnership is tax-deferred, a contributing partner is generally subject to US tax on the deferred gain when it converts the partnership units into REIT stock.
36. This can be done in an initial public offering or in a private placement. In many cases, the partnership units that the Subchapter C corporation receives in exchange for the property contributed are convertible into the shares of the REIT.
37. The partnership generally uses the cash to pay down existing liabilities or in another manner that avoids the application of the disguised sale rules to the person(s) that contributed the properties. See I.R.C. §707(a)(2)(B).
38. As compared to the prohibition against closely held ownership of a REIT. See I.R.C. §856(a)(6).
39. Treas. Reg. §1.337(d)-7(a)(1) and (c)(1).
40. The election is available for a REIT or a Subchapter C corporation that is not otherwise required to recognize gain, i.e., as part of an I.R.C. §355 distribution subject to the new I.R.C. §337(d) regulations discussed later.

the converted properties at their fair market value on the date of the conversion.[41] Code section 337(d) and the regulations thereunder contain the rules for this special tax.[42] The Treasury and the IRS have always stated that the recognition period for the Sting Tax for REITs should parallel the treatment of the Built-in Gains Tax for Subchapter S corporations.[43] The recognition period for the S corporation Built-in Gains Tax was originally ten years but had been shortened to seven years for 2009 and 2010 tax years. The recognition period was subsequently shorted to five years thereafter.[44]

The Sting Tax is 35% of the REIT's 'net recognized built-in gain'[45] for a taxable year.[46] The amount of the Sting Tax incurred by a REIT is treated as a loss that reduces the REIT's taxable income and earnings and profits for that year.[47] If the asset sold during the recognition period is also a USRPI, then FIRPTA tax also may apply if the proceeds are distributed to a foreign shareholder.[48] **Example 5.2** compares the federal tax consequences when a REIT disposes of an asset with a USD 100,000 of gain that is: (1) not subject to the Sting Tax, (2) subject to the Sting Tax, and (3) subject to both the Sting Tax and the FIRPTA tax.

The application of the Sting Tax (and FIRPTA tax) significantly reduces the tax benefits of using a REIT. A foreign investor that is acquiring the shares of a converted REIT should inquire about any unexpired recognition period as well as any potential Sting Tax exposure during the due diligence phase. A foreign investor that purchases a USRPI that it contributes to a newly formed corporation that elects REIT status may avoid this altogether because there is no conversion. A REIT also may engage in Code Section 1031 Like-Kind Exchanges with respect to a property with built-in gain to avoid triggering any Sting Tax.

---

41. For instance, a Subchapter C corporation with expiring net operating loss carryover may elect immediate recognition and offset the built-in gain with the carryover losses.
42. As discussed in Ch. 1, *supra,* Congress repealed the *General Utilities* doctrine in 1986. After the repeal, appreciated property owned within corporate solution is generally subject to corporate-level tax when the property is distributed to the corporation's shareholders. As part of the repeal, Congress granted the Secretary of Treasury the authority to prescribe regulations under I.R.C. §337(d) to carry out the purpose of the amendments in a manner that would prevent taxpayers from using special corporate entities, such as REITs to circumvent the repeal.
43. *See* Notice 88-19, 1988-1, C.B. 486. The regulations under I.R.C. §337(d) have incorporated the reference to I.R.C. §1374 since 2000. In addition, the IRS ruled privately that the shortened period applied to a REIT's acquisition of a Subchapter C corporation's property in a carryover basis transaction where no deemed sale election was made. *See* PLR 201202014 (January 13, 2012).
44. *See* I.R.C. §1374(d)(7)(B) prior to the passage of the 2015 PATH Act. *See* I.R.C. §1374(d)(7)(A).
45. *See* I.R.C. §1374(d)(2).
46. I.R.C. §1374(b).
47. Treas. Reg. §1.337(d)-7(b)(3)(ii).
48. *See* I.R.C. §897(h) and corresponding discussion in §5.04.B, *infra.*

5. Using REITs to Invest in the US

Example 5.2

	REIT (in USD 000s)		
	A. No Sting Tax	B. Sting Tax	C. Sting Tax & FIRPTA Tax
Built-in gain	100	100	100
Less:			
– Sting Tax	n/a	(35)	(35)
Earnings and profits	100	65	65
30% US withholding	(30)	(19.5)	n/a
35% FIRPTA tax	n/a	n/a	(22.75)
Net cash distribution	70	45.5	42.25
Effective tax rate	30%	54.5%	57.75%

This example illustrates the US federal income tax consequences with respect to the amount taxable from a REIT's sale of a built-in-gain asset followed by a distribution of the remainder amount to a foreign corporate shareholder.

A. The built-in-gain asset is *not* a USRPI, and it is sold six years after the former Subchapter C corporation converted to be a REIT. Therefore, the REIT is not subject to the Sting Tax, and the distribution is treated as ordinary REIT dividend to the foreign corporate shareholder.

B. The built-in-gain asset is *not* a USRPI, but it is sold four years after the former Subchapter C corporation converted to be a REIT. Therefore, the REIT is subject to the Sting Tax. In addition, the distribution is treated as ordinary REIT dividend to the foreign corporate shareholder.

C. The built-in-gain asset, a USRPI, is sold in Year 4 after the REIT conversion. Therefore, the REIT is subject to the Sting Tax. In addition, the distribution is subject to FIRPTA tax in the hands of the foreign corporate shareholder.

C.   Restrictions on REIT Spin-Offs

A corporation generally is required to recognize gain on the distribution of appreciated property, including the stock of a subsidiary, to its shareholders subsequent to the repeal of the *General Utilities* doctrine in 1986,[49] as if the corporation had sold the property for its fair market value. Code section 355 provides a special exception to this general rule which allows for the tax-free distribution of the stock in a controlled corporation (referred to as 'Controlled') by the distributing parent corporation (referred to as 'Distributing') to its shareholders if various requirements are met.

---

49. *See* Ch. 1, *supra*, for the background on the repeal of the *General Utilities* doctrine.

The 2015 PATH Act includes certain provisions that severely limit the ability of REITs to engage in tax-free spin-offs under Code section 355.[50] Under these rules, a REIT may not participate in a tax-free spin-off transaction as either a Distributing or Controlled corporation unless: (1) both the Distributing and Controlled are REITs immediately following the spin; or (2) Controlled was a TRS of the REIT and certain conditions are satisfied.[51] In addition, neither a Distributing nor a Controlled corporation may elect REIT status during the ten-year period following a tax-free spin-off transaction (other than an election for the controlled when both the Distributing and Controlled are REITs immediately following the distribution).[52]

The Treasury Department and the IRS issued final Code section 337(d) regulations in January 2017. The final regulations deem a Subchapter C corporation that engages in a Conversion Transaction[53] involving a REIT within ten years of a Code section 355 tax-free spin-off transaction to have sold its assets on the date of the conversion. In other words, the Deemed Sale Election became the only rule applicable and the converting corporation is required to recognize the built-in gain on its appreciated assets immediately. Under a special exception to this new rule, the Subchapter C corporation is not subject to this deemed sale treatment if:

- the Distributing and Controlled corporations are both REITs immediately after the Code section 355 distribution (including by reason of making the REIT elections after the related Code section 355 distribution that are effective before the related Code section 355 distribution) and at all times during the two years thereafter;
- the transaction involves a REIT's distribution of an 'old and cold' controlled TRS; or
- the distribution occurred before December 7, 2015, or is described in a ruling request initially submitted to the IRS on or before December 7, 2015.[54]

These amendments aim to curtail the type of REIT conversion activities that allowed taxpayers to obtain tax benefits for operating businesses that own real estate.[55] However, in a situation where there is minimal appreciation in either the real estate or the operating business, a taxable spin-off of a controlled entity by a corporation

---

50. Besides curtailing REITs' eligibility to participate in spin-off transactions, the 2015 PATH Act generally includes a number of favorable amendments to the REIT rules. *See* Ch. 6, *infra*, for a discussion of these changes.
51. I.R.C. §355(h) effective for distributions on or after December 7, 2015.
52. I.R.C. §856(c)(8) effective for distributions on or after December 7, 2015.
53. Defined as the qualification of a Subchapter C corporation as a RIC or REIT or the transfer of property owned by a Subchapter C corporation to a RIC or REIT. *See* Treas. Reg. §1.337(d)-7(a)(2)(ii).
54. This request must not have been withdrawn and the ruling must have not been issued or denied in its entirety as of December 7, 2015.
55. Joint Committee on Taxation, *Technical Explanation of the Revenue Provisions of the Protecting Americans from Tax Hikes Act of 2015, House Amendment #2 to the Senate Amendment to H.R. 2029 (Rules Committee Print 114-40)*, (JCX-144-15), December 17, 2015, at pg. 264, provides that '[F]ollowing the spin-off, income from the assets held in the REIT is no longer subject to corporate level tax (unless there is a disposition of such assets that incurs tax under the built-in-gain rules.)' Also *see* discussion in §5.01, *supra*.

may achieve the desired post-spin structure (i.e., an 'opco-propco' structure) without triggering a significant amount of corporate-level tax. The shareholders that receive the stock of the controlled entity generally include the fair market value of the stock received as dividend income to the extent of the distributing corporation's earnings and profits.[56]

§5.03 REIT QUALIFICATIONS

Generally speaking, an entity otherwise taxable as a US corporation[57] that satisfies certain requirements with respect to its organization and ownership, assets, income and distributions may elect to be treated as a REIT in a tax year. The REIT rules are very technical and detailed. A foreign investor that decides to pursue a REIT structure after exploring the above issues should consider the actual REIT qualification requirements, including those summarized below, in depth with a tax advisor who is experienced in implementing REIT structures.[58]

A.   Organizational/Ownership Requirements

A REIT generally must have at least one hundred beneficial owners.[59] The one-hundred-shareholder requirement is waived for the REIT's first taxable year but must be in place before the end of the first month in the second twelve-month year.[60] This requirement may be satisfied by small investors owning a class of preferred shares of the REIT regardless of the size of the REIT.[61] Many privately owned REITs, including those owned by foreign investors, issue non-voting preferred shares to 125 unrelated individuals[62] for a stated amount of investment, e.g., USD 1,000 per share, to satisfy this requirement. The preferred stock typically pays a fixed rate of dividend.[63]

Under a special rule that guards against closely held structures, five or fewer *individual* owners cannot own more than 50% in the value of the REIT's outstanding

---

56. I.R.C. §301(b)(1).
57. I.R.C. §856(a)(3). Many REITs are currently formed as limited liability companies.
58. Reliance on experience is crucial in REIT implementations; e.g., prevailing industry practices play a key role in determining whether certain activities are customary and may be deemed to generate qualifying rents from real property. See discussion in §5.03.C., *supra*.
59. I.R.C. §856(a)(5).
60. I.R.C. §856(h)(2). This is generally January 31 of the second year because REITs are required to use a calendar year-end.
61. *See* PLR 200507004 (February 18, 2005).
62. Although technically a REIT only needs one hundred shareholders, many REITs issue preferred stock to 125 shareholders in case some of the shareholder redeem their shares prematurely.
63. The cost for establishing the structure and the on-going expenses involved in maintaining such a structure, although generally manageable, is a reduction in the REIT's return on its investments. Therefore, such a structure may not be suitable if the amount of the underlying investment, or the expected annual return on the investment, is relatively small.

shares during the last half of any taxable year of the REIT.[64] Constructive ownership rules apply for the purposes of this requirement.[65] For example, if five individual shareholders held their REIT interests through an intermediate corporation which owns more than 50% in the value of a REIT's outstanding shares, the REIT will fail the ownership test. The corporation in this case is not treated as an owner for purposes of this rule. This rule is waived for the first year of the REIT.[66]

Many REITs include a special 'excess shares' provision in their charters. The provision generally prohibits any person (other than a person who has been granted an exception) from owning more than 9.8% of the aggregate of the outstanding shares of its stock to avoid failing the closely held rule.[67]

B. Quarterly Asset Tests

The legislative history makes it clear that REITs should earn 'passive income from real estate investments, as contrasted to income from the active operation of a business involving real estate.'[68] The regime includes specific rules to prevent REITs from engaging directly in activities that would be considered an active business, and includes a number of gross income and asset tests to ensure that a REIT's investments consist primarily of real estate and real estate mortgages, and income derived therefrom.

If a REIT is a partner in a partnership, the REIT is deemed to own its proportionate share (based on capital interest) of the assets and income of the partnership for purposes of the asset and income tests.[69] Further, a corporation that is wholly owned by a REIT (other than a TRS) is a qualified REIT subsidiary (QRS) which is disregarded as an entity separate from the REIT for US federal income tax purposes.[70] Accordingly, assets, liabilities, and items of income, deduction, and credit of a QRS are treated as assets, liabilities, and such items of the REIT.[71] A REIT must meet various asset tests, including the ones below, at the end of each quarter of a tax year.[72]

- At least 75% of the value of its total assets[73] must be real estate assets (including shares of another REIT), cash and cash items (including ordinary receivables), and US government securities (the '75 Percent Asset Test').

---

64. I.R.C. §856(a)(6).
65. *See* I.R.C. §§856(h) and 544.
66. I.R.C. §856(h)(2).
67. *See*, e.g., PLRs 9621032 (May 24, 1996) and 9534022 (May 31, 1995).
68. *See* H.R. Rep. No. 86-2020, at 3 (1960).
69. Treas. Reg. §1.856-3(g).
70. I.R.C. §856(i).
71. *Id.*
72. I.R.C. §856(c)(7) generally allows a REIT that inadvertently failed to meet one of the asset tests for a particular quarter to cure such failure if, *inter alia*, the failure is due to reasonable cause and a penalty tax of at least USD 50,000 per failure is paid.
73. Total assets, for this purpose, means the gross assets of the REIT determined in accordance with generally accepted accounting principles. *See* Treas. Reg. §1.856-2(d)(3).

5. Using REITs to Invest in the US

- Securities of TRSs must not represent more than 25% of the value of the REIT's total assets. The 2015 PATH Act reduced this amount to 20% for taxable years beginning after December 31, 2017.
- Not more than 25% of the value[74] of the REIT's total assets can be represented by securities (other than those qualifying for the 75 Percent Asset Test).
- Not more than 25% of the value of the REIT's total assets can be represented by nonqualified publicly offered REIT debt instruments.
- Securities of another issuer held by the REIT (other than securities of TRSs or those qualifying for the 75 Percent Asset Test) must not represent (1) more than 5% of the value of the REIT's total assets, or (2) more than 10% of the total voting power or the total value of the outstanding securities of such issuer.[75]

Because of the increasing interest in REIT conversions involving non-traditional assets and the related publicity,[76] the IRS, in June 2013, suspended its letter ruling request process and formed a working group to study the standards it was using in defining 'real property' for REIT qualification purposes. In November 2013, the IRS resumed the letter ruling process followed by the release of the proposed regulations in May 2014, clarifying the definition of 'real property'. On August 30, 2016, the Treasury Department and the IRS published final regulations retaining much of proposed regulations.[77]

Real estate assets, for REIT purposes, include an interest in real property which is defined to include fee ownership and co-ownership of land or improvements, leaseholds of land or improvements, and options to acquire leaseholds of land or improvements, but does not include mineral, oil, or gas royalty interests.[78] An interest in real estate assets also includes debt instruments issued by publicly offered REITs, interests in mortgages on real property interests and property attributable to the temporary investment of new capital.[79]

As mentioned above, a threshold question of whether a foreign investor could use a REIT to own its USRPI depends on whether the USRPI qualifies as a real estate asset for REIT purposes. The FIRPTA and REIT regimes contain separate and distinct definitions of what constitutes real property for their respective purposes and the rules do not always coincide. For instance, in the case of intangible assets,[80] the final

---

74. I.R.C. §856(c)(5)(A).
75. Value, for this purpose, means with respect to assets (other than securities with readily available market quotations) fair value as determined in good faith by the trustees. *See* I.R.C. §856(c)(4).
76. *See* footnote 7, *supra*.
77. T.D. 9784. For a non-traditional asset REIT owning data centers, cold storage warehouses, or pipeline systems, the examples provided in the final Treasury regulations under I.R.C. §856 may eliminate the need for a separate letter ruling. The framework adopted by the regulations for classifying real property for REIT purposes should be helpful for other non-traditional assets and for considering the potential use of the REIT structure for owning and operating these assets.
78. I.R.C. §856(c)(5)(B) and (C).
79. I.R.C. §856(c)(5)(B).
80. *See* discussion in §3.04., *supra*, regarding the issues concerning the FIRPTA characterization of intangible assets.

Treasury Regulations under Code section 856 provide that an intangible asset is real property or an interest in real property if it:

(1) derives its value from real property or an interest in real property;
(2) is inseparable from that real property or interest in real property; and
(3) does not produce or contribute to the production of income other than consideration for the use or occupancy of space.[81]

The final regulations also contain a specific rule for licenses and permits which provides that '[a] license, permit or other similar right that is solely for the use, enjoyment, or occupation of land or an inherently permanent structure and that is in the nature of a leasehold or easement generally is an interest in real property. A license or permit to engage in or operate a business is not real property or an interest in real property if the license or permit produces or contributes to the production of income other than consideration for the use of space'.[82] A simplified version of an example that demonstrates the application of this rule is provided in **Example 5.3**.

Example 5.3

REIT X receives a government permit to place a cell tower on Federal Government land that abuts a federal highway. The permit is not a lease of the land but is a permit to use the land for a cell tower. The government reserves the right to cancel the permit and compensate the REIT if the site is needed for a higher public purpose. The REIT leases space on the tower to various cell service provides. The permit does not produce, or contribute to the production of any income other than the REIT's receipt of payments from the cell service providers in consideration for their being allowed to use space on the tower.

The permit is *in the nature* of a leasehold that allows the REIT to place a cell tower in a specific location on government land. Therefore, the permit is an interest in real property.[83]

Prior to the issuance of the final regulations, the IRS has observed that goodwill associated with real properties may be inextricably linked to the tangible real property and should constitute a real estate asset for REIT purposes. In one private letter ruling, the taxpayer, a data-center REIT, had intangible assets including tenant relationships, trademarks, favorable land leases, and goodwill related to its trade or business as a lessor of real property. The IRS reasoned that these intangibles could be characterized for purposes of the REIT income and asset tests based upon the characterization of the underlying activities. The IRS reasoned that, because these intangibles related solely to the business of leasing and providing customary services to tenants in their data centers, they qualified as real estate assets and interests in real property.[84]

---

81. Treas. Reg. §1.856-10(f)(1).
82. Treas. Reg. §1.856-10(f)(2).
83. Treas. Reg. §1.856-10(g), Example 12. (Emphasis added.)
84. *See*, e.g., PLR 201314002 (April 5, 2013).

5. Using REITs to Invest in the US

The treatment of intangibles as real estate assets for REIT purposes is important for a variety of reasons. For example, if a REIT sells its entire operations and there is residual gain attributable to the goodwill of the operations, the gain that is attributable to goodwill would constitute good REIT income only if the goodwill is treated as a real estate asset. Hence, the treatment of intangibles as real estate assets protects inadvertent disqualification of REIT status. On the other hand, the treatment of any intangible as interest in real property for FIRPTA would subject the gain from a sale of the intangible to US tax as ECI. As discussed earlier, there is no clear guidance regarding the FIRPTA treatment of various intangibles including licenses and permits used in certain infrastructure projects.[85] It would be helpful, if the Treasury Department and the IRS would issue definitive guidance on the classification of these intangibles for both FIRPTA[86] and REIT purposes simultaneously.

Another area where the FIRPTA and REIT definitions of real property differ pertains to the treatment of personal properties, including certain structural components to a building. Under the REIT rules, if rents from personal property are treated as rents from real property under Code section 856(d)(1)(C), then such personal property will be treated as real property for purposes of the 75 Percent Asset Test.[87] Additionally, an obligation secured by a mortgage on both real and personal property will be treated as a real estate asset for purposes of the 75% Asset Test (and the interest income from such obligation will be treated as income that satisfies the 75% income test discussed below) if the fair market value of such personal property does not exceed 15% of the total fair market value of all such property.[88] Under the FIRPTA rules, the determination of whether a personal property will be treated as real property under Code section 897(c)(6)(C) is based on whether the property is associated with the use, improvement, operations or rental of specific types of real property.[89]

C.   Income Tests

In general, a REIT's gross income should be derived predominantly from rents from real property, interest on mortgages and, to some degree, capital gains from the sale of real estate assets. Specifically, a REIT is required to meet all of the following income tests, among others, annually:[90]

---

85. *See* discussion in §3.04.B., *supra*.
86. The IRS has announced that it is considering issuing proposed regulations to address, among other things, the definition of a USRPI to include certain licenses, permits, franchise, or other similar rights granted by a governmental unit that are related to the value of the use or ownership of an interest in real property. However, the IRS has not yet issued any regulations or other guidance to date regarding the treatment of such governmental licenses or permits for FIRPTA purposes. *See* IRS Announcement 2008-115. 2008-2 C.B. 1228 and discussion in §3.04.A., *supra*.
87. I.R.C. §856(c)(9)(A).
88. I.R.C. §856(c)(9)(B). The fair market value is determined in the same manner as fair market value is determined for purposes of apportioning interest income between real and personal property under I.R.C. §856(c)(3)(B).
89. *See* Treas. Reg. §1.897-1(b)(4)(i) and discussion in §3.03.B.2. *supra*.
90. I.R.C. §856(c)(6) generally allows a REIT that inadvertently failed to meet one of the asset tests for a particular quarter to cure such failure if, *inter alia*, the failure is due to

- At least 75% of its gross income must be derived from rents from real property, mortgage interest, gain on the sale of real property (but not including gain on sales of dealer property), dividends from shares in other REITs, amounts received in consideration for entering into agreements to make loans on real property, or to lease real property, and certain qualified temporary investment income.
- At least 95% of its gross income must be from items satisfying the 75% test, plus other interest and dividends (i.e., passive income from securities).[91]

In essence, no more than 5% of a REIT's income can be from *nonqualifying* sources such as service fees or a non-real estate business, including revenues from asset management, leasing, janitorial services, etc. This type of non-real estate income is typically earned by a TRS.[92] A REIT, through its employees or agents, may conduct only usual and customary services[93] related to the use of space for occupancy, provided such services are not rendered primarily for the convenience of the tenant.[94] For REIT qualification purposes, rents from real property are generally amounts received for the use of, or the right to use, real property and include charges (whether separately stated or not) for services customarily furnished in connection with the rental of real property.[95] Services performed would be considered customary if, in the geographical market where the building is located, tenants in the buildings which are of a similar class are customarily provided with the service. Thus, the determination is based, in part, on the facts and circumstances of each case.[96]

Rents from real property generally exclude amounts received or accrued, directly or indirectly, with respect to any real property (or personal property leased in connection with real property) if the determination of the amount depends, in whole or in part, on the income or profits derived by any person from the property.[97] However, any amount determined based on a fixed percentage or percentages or receipts or sales may qualify as rents from real property.[98]

Rents from real property also exclude amounts received or accrued directly or indirectly by the REIT from any person in which it owns, directly or indirectly, an interest of 10% or more (i.e., a related tenant).[99] However, as discussed in more detail below, rents paid by a REIT's TRS with respect to a REIT's leasing of its qualified lodging facility or qualified healthcare facility to its TRS are not excluded if that

---

reasonable cause and a penalty tax is paid.
91. I.R.C. §856(c)(2) and (3).
92. *See* discussion in §5.03.E., *infra*.
93. This 'customary' determination technically is not based on the geographic market, which is for the added sentence.
94. I.R.C. §856(d)(7)(C)(ii).
95. I.R.C. §856(d)(1)(B) and Treas. Reg. §1.856-4(b)(1).
96. Examples of customary services include the furnishing of utilities, cleaning and maintenance of common areas, trash collection, parking and swimming pools. *See* Treas. Reg. §1.856-4(b)(1).
97. Treas. Reg. §1.856-4(b)(3).
98. *Id.*
99. I.R.C. §856(d)(2)(B).

facility is operated by an eligible independent contractor (EIK).[100] Furthermore, rents from real property include rent attributable to personal property, but only if the rent attributable to the personal property does not exceed 15% of the total rents under the lease. For this purpose, the amount considered attributable to the personal property is calculated based on the relative fair market values of the personal and real property.[101]

As REITs were created to pool resources together to invest in passive real estate activities, there is a special rule that discourages a REIT from holding property for sale to customers.[102] Under this special rule, a REIT may be subject to a 100% tax on the net income derived from the sale or other disposition of property that is held primarily for sale to customers in the ordinary course of business.[103] The tax is intended to preclude a REIT from retaining any profit from ordinary retailing activities such as sales to customers of condominium units or subdivided lots in a development tract.[104] A REIT also may not deduct the net loss from such transactions in determining its net income derived from prohibited transactions subject to the 100% tax.[105] Safe harbor provisions are available to exclude certain property sales from this prohibited transactions tax.[106]

D. Annual Distribution Requirements

A REIT must distribute at least 90% of its REIT taxable income (REITTI) determined before the dividends paid deduction and excluding net capital gain annually.[107] The distribution requirement is the cornerstone provision that enables a REIT to operate as a pseudo pass-through entity for tax purposes. A REIT first determines its taxable income under general Subchapter C principles,[108] and then makes adjustments to arrive at its REITTI.[109] A REIT that distributes all of its REITTI, determined before the

---

100. I.R.C. §856(d)(8)(B). See I.R.C. §856(d)(9) for a definition of the term EIK which is similar to the definition of an independent contractor, or IK, as defined in I.R.C. §856(d)(3).
101. I.R.C. §856(d)(1)(C).
102. An exception applies to foreclosure properties. I.R.C. §857(b)(6)(B)(iii).
103. I.R.C. §857(b)(6)(A). Whether an asset is held primarily for sale to customers in the ordinary course of a taxpayer's trade or business may be determined by a number of factors including the nature and purpose of the acquisition of the property and the duration of the ownership, the extent and nature of the taxpayer's efforts to sell the property, the number, extent, continuity, and substantiality of the sales, and the time and effort the taxpayer habitually devoted to the sales. See, e.g., Cottle v. Commissioner, 89 T.C. 467, 489 (1987).
104. A REIT's ownership of dealer property does not always have an adverse impact on the entity's qualification as a REIT.
105. I.R.C. §857(b)(6)(B)(ii).
106. A sale may qualify for one of the safe harbor provisions if it satisfies certain statutory requirement which includes owning the property for at least two years. See I.R.C. §857(b)(6)(C). The IRS has issued a number of private letter rulings in which it concluded that a REIT's proposed sale of its assets pursuant to a plan of liquidation would not constitute prohibited transactions under I.R.C. §857(b)(6)(B). See PLRs 201609004 (February 26, 2016), 201346005 (November 22, 2013) and 201340004 (October 4, 2013).
107. I.R.C. §857(a)(1).
108. Treas. Reg. §1.856-1(e)(1).
109. I.R.C. §857(b)(2).

dividends paid deduction, in a taxable year is not subject to corporate-level tax. In general, only dividends that are paid out of a REIT's earnings and profits are eligible for the dividend paid deduction.[110]

A REIT that incurs a net operating loss for a year may carryforward such losses up to twenty years to offset any REITTI arising during the carryover period.[111] A REIT deducts the amount of its dividends paid before it uses the net operating loss carryforward to determine its REITTI.[112] A REIT that has net operating loss carryforward in excess of its current year earnings may use the loss carryforward to offset its REITTI and not make any distributions.[113] In addition, a REIT that has net operating loss carryforward and no current year ordinary earnings may use the loss carryforward to offset the gain from the sale of one or more appreciated USRPIs; when that occurs, the REIT does not have to make distributions that otherwise would have been subject to FIRPTA tax under Code section 897(h)(1).[114]

A REIT receives a deduction for dividends paid to its shareholders.[115] To the extent that a REIT distributes at least 90%, but less than 100%, any undistributed earnings will be subject to tax at ordinary corporate income tax rates imposed on a Subchapter C corporation under Code section 11.[116] Effective for taxable years beginning after December 31, 2015, the overall amount of dividends designated by a REIT (including Capital Gains Dividends) is limited to the total amount of dividends paid for the year (including dividends deemed paid under Code section 858).[117]

Dividends paid during a year are generally taken into account to determine a REIT's distribution requirement. In addition, certain payments made by a REIT after the tax year also may be taken into account for this purpose. For example, certain dividends declared in October, November or December of a year and paid during January of the following year may be taken into account in the first year.[118] The statute also allows a REIT to take into account dividends declared and paid in the

---

110. *See* I.R.C. §§561 and 562. Distributions with respect to preferential dividends are generally not deductible. A preference is generally deemed to exist if any rights to preference inherent in any class of stock are violated. The disallowance, where any preference exists, extends to the entire amount of the distribution and not just a portion of the distribution. *See* Treas. Reg. §1.562-2(a).
111. I.R.C. §172(b)(1)(A)(ii). A net operating loss cannot be carried back to any tax year for which the taxpayer has elected REIT status. I.R.C. §172(b)(1)(B)(ii).
112. *See* I.R.C. §172(d)(6)(A).
113. The REIT in this case may be subject to the alternative minimum tax (AMT) of I.R.C. §55. In general, the AMT is a 20% corporate-level tax which is imposed on the taxpayer's taxable income taking into account certain adjustments including net operating loss carryforward; however, a taxpayer may only offset up to 90% of its AMT taxable income with any net operating loss carryforward.
114. *See* §5.04.B., *infra*, regarding the rules on taxation of Capital Gain Dividends and the application of I.R.C. §897(h)(1). The net operating loss also may offset any built-in gains of a pre-conversion asset sold during the recognition period.
115. I.R.C. §857(a)(1). Note that a REIT's liquidating distributions also may be deducted against its REITTI under I.R.C. §562(b).
116. I.R.C. §857(b)(1). A REIT, or its shareholders, also may be subject to the AMT of I.R.C. §55(b)(2).
117. I.R.C. §857(g).
118. I.R.C. §857(b)(9).

following year if certain conditions are satisfied.[119] If a REIT's taxable income in a year is adjusted from a 'determination', then the REIT may elect to make a deficiency dividend to prevent inadvertent disqualification of its REIT status.[120] A determination, for this purpose, may include a final court determination, a final agreement with respect to an IRS examination, or a statement by the REIT itself, filed with the IRS.[121]

Special provisions also allow a REIT to satisfy the distribution requirement without paying a cash dividend. Such provisions include the consent dividend provision which generally allows a common stockholder of a REIT to agree to include in its US taxable income an amount equal to a hypothetical distribution made by the REIT.[122] The consenting shareholder will pay US tax with respect to the amount of the consent dividend which it is deemed to have contributed to the paid in capital of the REIT.[123] The deemed contribution, in turn, will increase the shareholder's US tax basis in the REIT's stock.

If a REIT fails to make certain required distributions in a year, it will be subject to a non-deductible 4% excise tax.[124] The required distribution is the sum of 85% of the REIT's ordinary income for the calendar year, 95% of its capital gain for the calendar year plus any undistributed taxable income in prior years. The 4% excise tax is imposed on the difference between the amount of required distributions and the REIT's distributed amount[125] for the calendar year.

E. Special Rules Applicable to TRS

As discussed earlier, a REIT may operate a business through a TRS and still avoid corporate-level tax with respect to its rental income.[126] Under an anti-abuse rule, a 100% excise tax maybe imposed on certain amounts that would be subject to reallocation under US transfer-pricing principles to prevent taxpayers from shifting income or deductions between the TRS and the REIT to reduce the overall US tax burden. For example, if a REIT underpays its TRS for services provided to tenants or provided to (or on behalf) of the REIT, allocates an excess amount of deductions to the TRS, or charges excessive interest to the TRS on intercompany debt, such amounts may be subject to the excise tax.[127] It is critical that taxpayers have contemporaneous transfer pricing studies to substantiate the position that the REIT and its TRS conduct their transactions in accordance with the US arm's-length standard to avoid the penalty. Certain common uses of TRSs are discussed below.

---

119. I.R.C. §858.
120. I.R.C. §860.
121. I.R.C. §860(e).
122. See I.R.C. §565 and the regulations thereunder.
123. Treas. Reg. §1.565-3(a).
124. See I.R.C. §4981.
125. A REIT's distributed amount generally equals the amount it actually distributed and the amount of income that the REIT retained on which corporate income tax is imposed. I.R.C. §4981(c)(1).
126. See I.R.C. §856(c)(4)(B)(ii) which limits the value of a REIT's ownership in TRS securities to 20% of all of its assets.
127. I.R.C. §857(b)(7)(A).

1. Tenant Services

Services or property management activities that are not considered customary, or that may be considered rendered for the primary convenience of a tenant, are referred to as 'impermissible tenant services income' or ITSI.[128] The amount of ITSI must not exceed a *de minimis* threshold (i.e., 1% of all amounts from such property) or the REIT must contract with a TRS or an IK to perform the services.[129] Services or property management activities that do not meet these requirements may cause all the rents from a particular property to be treated as nonqualifying income for the REIT.[130]

In order to avoid violating the ITSI rule, a REIT may enter into an agreement with its TRS to provide all non-customary services (or services considered rendered for the primary convenience of a tenant) to tenants of the REIT's buildings. For example, employees of the TRS may perform all of the housekeeping services for the tenants of a residential building, and the TRS pays all costs of providing the services. Charges to the tenants for the housekeeping services are not separately stated from the rents that the tenants pay to the REIT for the use of their apartments.

In the event the REIT and the TRS provide customary and non-customary services to the tenants, respectively, it would be important to keep detailed records with respect to the services performed. In addition, the REIT and the TRS should properly document that the transactions satisfy the arm's-length standard to avoid the 100% penalty tax mentioned earlier. Although using a TRS may increase the overall tax burden of the structure, it is generally best practice to use such an entity to avoid inadvertently running afoul of the REIT income tests.

Special rules apply to a REIT that owns a qualified lodging facility or a qualified healthcare property. Both of these are special types of properties that offer extensive personal services to the users of the properties, e.g., hotel guests, nursing home occupants and/or patients. Absent this special rule, revenues ordinarily generated by these types of properties would not qualify as rental income of the REIT. Under the special rules, a REIT may lease a qualified lodging facility or a qualified health care property to its TRS. The rent from such leases may qualify as rents from real property for REIT income test purposes provided that the TRS contracts with one or more EIKs to operate the property.

Generally speaking, a qualified lodging facility means a lodging facility – such as a hotel, motel, or other establishment that has more than one-half of its dwelling units being used on a transient basis, provided no authorized gambling activities are being conducted.[131] The term 'transient' generally means a rental period of less than thirty days.[132] Hence, a qualified lodging facility includes an establishment if

---

128. I.R.C. §856(d)(7)(A).
129. The test may apply to the value of such services if there is no separately determined income.
130. I.R.C. §856(d)(7)(B).
131. I.R.C. §856(d)(9)(D).
132. This originates from the former investment tax credits rules. *See* Joint Comm. Staff, Description of the Tax Technical Correction Act of 2007, as passed by the House of Representatives (JCX-119-07), 12/18/2007, p.12.

more than one-half of its dwelling units are used by guests staying less than thirty days. There are a number of undefined concepts in this area. For example, there is no clear guidance on what constitutes as 'an establishment' for this purpose.

A qualified healthcare facility generally means any hospital, nursing facility, assisted living facility, congregate care facility, qualified continuing care facility, or other licensed facilities eligible to participate in Medicare.[133] Some of these terms are not defined in the statute or in the regulations. The IRS has issued a limited number of private letter rulings concerning whether the described age-restricted residential communities would constitute congregate care facilities.[134] The facts in those rulings encompassed age-restricted facilities providing varying degrees of dining, wellness and medical care services for the residents that clearly distinguishes these facilities from the typical multi-family rental property.

As the foreign ownership and operations of hotels, long-term residences and assisted living facilities continue to expand in the US, a greater number of these facilities are formed as REITs. Taxpayers considering using a REIT structure to operate a qualified lodging facility or a qualified healthcare facility should ensure that the transactions between the REIT and its TRS satisfy the arm's-length standards. These taxpayers may wish to avoid running into the uncertain areas or seek private letter rulings to avoid running afoul of the requirements.

2.   *Eligible Independent Contractors*

As discussed above, the qualified lodging or healthcare facility exception requires the facility to be operated by an EIK if the facility is leased from the REIT. A REIT generally may not derive income from an EIK and the relationship between the REIT and the contractor must be arm's length.[135] Thus, the REIT may not receive any dividends or any key money from the EIK. However, a REIT may derive income from certain entities affiliated with an EIK (e.g., parent or brother/sister entity) provided that the EIK is a separate tax entity, maintains its own bank accounts, books and records, and has its own employees under its separate control.[136] An EIK must be adequately compensated for its services, and must not be an employee of the REIT (i.e., the manner in which he carries out his duties must not be subject to the control of the REIT).[137] In addition, an EIK means any independent contractor (or a related person of an independent contractor):

- that is actively engaged in the trade or business of operating qualified lodging or healthcare facilities, as applicable, for persons not related to the REIT or TRS at the time of entering into an agreement with the TRS to operate the facility.[138]

---

133. I.R.C. §856(e)(6)(D).
134. *See* PLRs 201147015 (November 25, 2011), 201429017 (July 18, 2014), and 201509019 (February 27, 2015).
135. Treas. Reg. §1.856-4(b)(5).
136. *See*, e.g., Rev. Rul. 75-136, 1975-1 C.B. 195 and Rev. Rul. 73-194, 1973-1 C.B. 355.
137. PLR 201129031 (July 22, 2011).
138. I.R.C. §856(d)(9)(A).

For this purpose, an independent contractor means any person:

- that does not own, directly or indirectly, more than 35% of the REIT's shares; and
- not more than 35% of the person's equity interest is owned, directly or indirectly, by the same party (or parties) that owns 35 % or more of the shares of the REIT.[139]

The IRS has reasoned that the tax-free spin-off standard for the active trade or business requirement of Code section 355 is instructive in determining whether an independent contractor is actively engaged in the trade or business of operating qualified lodging facilities in a private letter ruling.[140] To satisfy such standard, the company's own employees, i.e., not independent contractors, generally should perform substantial management and operational activities directly.[141]

§5.04 TAXATION OF FOREIGN INVESTORS' INCOME AND GAIN FROM REITs

Turning back to our hypothetical Canadian friend Cole, he is now an executive of a publicly traded Canadian multinational corporation and has engaged a team of professionals to perform comprehensive tax due diligence with respect to several class A office buildings in Manhattan. The due diligence confirms that 100% of the buildings' gross revenue qualifies as real property rental income from unrelated tenants. All the services provided to the tenants, e.g., cleaning service, are considered customary and performed by independent contractors from whom the property owner does not derive any income. Cole's company decided to use a newly created private REIT to own the buildings.[142] Cole also engaged US tax advisors to ensure that all the other REIT requirements are satisfied. The REIT is now operational. The discussion below focuses on the US taxation of the REIT's majority shareholder, i.e., Cole's company.

A. Ordinary Dividends

As discussed above, a REIT may avoid corporate-level tax on its ordinary income due to the dividend paid deduction and, instead, the distributions are taxed in the hands of the REIT's shareholders. A REIT's distributions to its shareholders are characterized as follows:[143]

---

139. I.R.C. §856(d)(3). Modified ownership attribution rules are apply for purposes of determining the qualification of an operator as an independent contractor. See I.R.C. §856(d)(5).
140. PLR 200825034 (June 20, 2008). The statute and the regulations do not define what constitutes 'actively engaged' for purposes of establishing EIK status. See also PLR 201125013 (June 24, 2011).
141. Treas. Reg. §1.355-3(b)(2)(iii).
142. Cole's company owns all of the voting common stock of the REIT and 100 unrelated investors own all of the non-voting preferred stock of the REIT.
143. The same ordering rules governing distributions made by Subchapter C corporations apply to REITs. See Treas. Reg. §1.856-1(e)(2).

(1) first out of the REIT's earnings and profits[144] which are treated as taxable dividends to the shareholders;
(2) any distribution in excess of earnings and profits are treated as non-taxable return of capital up to each shareholder's adjusted basis is the stock; and
(3) any remaining amount is treated as capital gain to the shareholders.[145]

The amount of ordinary REIT dividend paid to a foreign investor is treated as FDAP income which generally is subject to a 30% US statutory withholding tax under Code sections 871 or 881.[146] A number of existing US tax treaties reduce the rate to 15%, 10% or 5% if certain special conditions are satisfied.[147] As a result, the highest US federal income tax rate applicable to net income distributed to a foreign shareholder of a REIT is 30%.[148] As show in **Example 5.1**, this is significantly lower than the 54.5% US federal income tax rate applicable to income earned and distributed on a current (non-liquidating) basis if a foreign investors uses a US corporate subsidiary to own or operate USRPI.[149]

If a REIT makes a consent dividend to a foreign shareholder, the REIT is required to remit an amount of tax equal to the withholding tax that would have been imposed (i.e., generally 30%) as if an actual cash distribution had been paid to the shareholder on the last day of the corporation's tax year.[150]

B.   Capital Gain Dividends

1.   General Rule

A REIT may elect to pay corporate-level tax on any net capital gain it has in a taxable year.[151] To the extent a REIT retains its net capital gain and pays corporate-level tax on the capital gain, it may elect to treat such gain as being distributed. In such case, each shareholder includes its share of the undistributed capital gain in income, receives a credit for the corporate level tax paid, and steps up the basis of the shareholder's REIT stock for the amount included in income.[152]

---

144. A REIT generally determines its earnings and profits in the same manner as a Subchapter C corporation with special adjustments. *See* Treas. Reg. §1.856-1(e)(6) and I.R.C. §857(d).
145. *See* I.R.C. §301(c)(1), (2) and (3).
146. *See* discussion in §2.02.A., *supra*.
147. The US-Canada income tax treaty currently in force does not reduce the US withholding rate on ordinary REIT dividends paid to a corporate shareholder that owns more than 10% of the stock of the REIT. *See* Art. X, para. 7, of the Convention between the United States of America and Canada with respect to taxes on income and capital, signed on September 16, 1980, as amended by protocols signed on June 14, 1983, March 23, 1984, March 17, 1995, July 19, 1997, and September 21, 2007 (referred to as the US-Canada Treaty).
148. Some states also exempt REITs from entity-level tax.
149. However, a Subchapter C corporation is generally not required to distribute its earnings and profits annually. *See* footnote 14, *supra*.
150. Treas. Reg. §1.565-5. The amount of consent dividend also may be eligible for reduced US withholding tax under an applicable income tax treaty. *See* Ch. 9, *infra*.
151. I.R.C. §857(b)(3).
152. I.R.C. §857(b)(3)(D)(iii).

Alternatively and more commonly, instead of paying the tax itself, a REIT may choose to distribute all, or a portion, of its net capital gain to its shareholders and designate the amount as a Capital Gain Dividend, deductible by it, if certain conditions are met.[153] A Capital Gain Dividend is treated as gain from the sale or exchange of a capital asset held for more than one year in the hands of the REIT's shareholders.[154] This rule is intended to preserve the character of the income or gain earned at the REIT level when such income is distributed to the shareholders.[155]

The amount designated as a Capital Gain Dividend may not exceed a REIT's 'net capital gain' generated in the taxable year.[156] The REIT provisions do not contain a specific definition of 'net capital gain' for this purpose. General US tax principles define net capital gain as the excess of a taxpayer's 'net long-term capital gain' over its 'net short-term capital loss' for the same year.[157] The amount of 'net short-term capital loss' includes capital losses carried forward from a prior year.

Code section 857(b)(3)(E) contains a special rule which permits a REIT to pay Capital Gain Dividends without taking into account its net operating loss.[158] Code section 857(g)(1), enacted by the 2015 PATH Act, limits the aggregate amount of dividends designated by a REIT (e.g., a Capital Gain Dividend) for a taxable year to the amount of *dividends paid* with respect to the taxable year. As discussed above, a REIT's dividend is determined by its earnings and profits[159] which take into account any current-year net operation loss deductions. The 2015 PATH Act's legislative history does not mention how the new rule would interact with the special provision of Code section 857(b)(3)(E). Thus, it is not clear the effects this newly enacted provision may have on a REIT's ability to designate Capital Gain Dividends and preserve net operating loss when it lacks sufficient earnings and profits to treat all of its distributions as dividends.

2. FIRPTA Tax on Gain Distributed

To the extent a REIT is not subject to corporate-level tax on its net capital gain with respect to the sale of its USRPIs, Congress deemed it appropriate to impose FIRPTA tax on the gain when the amount is distributed to the REIT's foreign shareholders. Code section 897(h)(1), enacted to implement this policy, is triggered if a REIT, or a lower-tier REIT that is owned by the REIT, sells one or more USRPI for gain and

---

153. I.R.C. §857(b)(3). However, a Capital Gain Dividend is not taken into account in determining the 90% annual distribution requirement of I.R.C. §857(a)(1)(A)(i).
154. I.R.C. §857(b)(3)(B).
155. Accordingly, shareholders who are individuals may be taxed at a lower capital gains rate with respect to such income.
156. I.R.C. §857(b)(3). See I.R.C. §1212(a)(1) and (a)(4) for capital loss carryforward and carryback rules applicable to REITs.
157. I.R.C. §1222(11).
158. The intent of this rule is to permit a REIT to pass through the maximum amount of capital gain to its shareholders. For example, in PLR 200534013 (August 26, 2005) the IRS permitted a REIT to designate a Capital Gain Dividend notwithstanding the fact that it lacked sufficient earnings and profits to treat the amount of the distribution as a dividend.
159. See I.R.C. §316(a).

the REIT makes a distribution to a foreign shareholder.[160] However, the tax only applies to the amount of the distribution that is *attributable to* the gain from the REIT's sale of its USRPI.[161] Although this provision was part of the original FIRPTA statute enacted in 1980, the precise mechanism to determine the FIRPTA tax under this rule has been elusive.

A REIT determines its annual earnings and profits (on which its dividend paid deduction is determined) based on its operating results of the year taking into account any gains and losses from sales of its assets. Hence, each dividend paid by a REIT theoretically reflects a portion of the overall results. There is no mechanism to isolate the amount of gain or loss from the sale of any one particular asset from the overall earnings and profits calculation. As a result, there is no easy way to determine the portion of the distribution that is attributable to the gain from a sale of a USRPI.

In a case where a REIT has only a single asset which is a USRPI, the rule may work like this. When the REIT sells its USRPI for a gain and distributes all of the proceeds from the sale to its foreign shareholder and liquidates, the foreign shareholder includes the gross amount it receives as a distribution. Although the rules are not entirely clear, it would seem appropriate for the foreign shareholder to determine the amount of its FIRPTA gain by subtracting the tax basis of the REIT stock from the gross amount of the distribution.[162] As a result, the foreign shareholder's FIRPTA tax liability would be based on the net gain from the sale of the USRPI.

The same determination becomes more difficult if the facts are even slightly different. For instance, if Cole's company's REIT sells two of several buildings it owns in the same year, one for a gain and the other for a loss, and distributes the total proceeds to its foreign shareholder. The statute does not explicitly state whether the FIRPTA tax applies on an asset-by-asset basis or if it applies only if there is a net gain from both sales. Some believe the wording of Code section 897(h)(1) suggests that the rule applies on an asset-by-asset basis.[163] On the other hand, the legislative history of FIRPTA specifically uses the term 'net capital gains' as the amount to which Code section 897(h)(1) is applicable which suggests a netting of the gains and losses.[164] The issues become even more complicated if the REIT also

---

160. *See* I.R.C. §897(h)(1), second sentence, (k)(1)(B), (k)(2)(A)(ii), and (l). Prior to 2004, this rule only applied to REITs. The American Jobs Creation Act of 2004 expanded the statute to include regulated investment companies, or RICs, and the term qualified investment entity, or QIE, was incorporated into the statute. As this chapter discusses various provisions affecting only REITs, the term REIT, instead of QIE, is used. *See* the discussion in Ch. 6 on exceptions to I.R.C. §897(h)(1).
161. If the stock of the REIT is publicly traded and the so-called Publicly Traded Exception applies to the disposition of the REIT shares, then the distribution is taxed as a dividend (i.e., FDAP income instead of FIRPTA gain) to a foreign shareholder that owns 10% or less of the class of publicly traded REIT shares. *See* I.R.C. §857(b)(3)(F) and discussion in §6.02.B. *infra*
162. The REIT continues to be a USRPI after it disposes of its asset. *See* I.R.C. §897(c)(1)(B)(iii); hence, a liquidation of the REIT is treated as a taxable sale or exchange to the foreign shareholder. *See* I.R.C. §897(e)(1). The sale should result in an effectively connected loss to the shareholder. See I.R.C. §897(a)(1).
163. *See* Blanchard, Ch. 1 footnote 59, *supra*.
164. The Conference Committee Reports specifically uses the term 'net capital gains' as the amount to which I.R.C. §897(h)(1) is applicable. The 1980 Conference Report, page 187.

has ordinary operating profits or losses from its normal operations. Although these are common fact patterns, no guidance has been issued to determine how much of the REIT's distributions should be considered *attributable to* gain from the sale of USRPI(s) where the REIT has other results that may interact with this determination.

The FIRPTA *withholding tax* regulations, on the other hand, require a REIT to withhold 35% on the largest amount of a REIT's distribution that *could be designated* as a Capital Gain Dividend regardless of the amount of such dividends actually designated.[165] Such an amount is the REIT's net capital gain for the year, which does not take into consideration any ordinary operating losses. Some practitioners believe that most foreign shareholders simply report the amount of Capital Gain Dividend designated by their REITs as the amount that is also subject to FIRPTA *substantive* tax.[166] This approach could result in an overpayment of the FIRPTA tax liability which should be based on the amount distributed by the REIT (i.e., net of any operating losses incurred).

The Treasury Department and the IRS issued Notice 2007-55 (referred to as the '2007 Notice')[167] which provides that Code section 897(h)(1) applies to all distributions including liquidating distributions under Code sections 331 and 332 (i.e., not just dividend distributions). In essence, the 2007 Notice applies a look-through approach that treats liquidating distributions by a REIT as proceeds from an asset sale instead of from a stock sale. The 2007 Notice generated a significant amount of comments from tax practitioners. The Tax Section of the American Bar Association provided an in-depth analysis of the issues raised by the notice (referred to as the 'ABA 2008 Report').[168] The following points raised by the report are of particular interest:

(1) a key reason that the Treasury Department and the IRS issued the 2007 Notice was to address a loophole that was available under the Cleansing Exception[169] applicable to REITs prior to the 2015 PATH Act;[170]

---

165. Treas. Reg. §1.1445-8(c)(2)(ii).
166. *See* Peter J. Genz, *Request for Guidance on Certain Tax Issues Arising in REIT Liquidations, Including Issues Relating to Notice 2007-55*, ABA Sec. Tax. Rep. (June 10, 2008) (also referred to as the ABA 2008 Report in the text) pg. 20. Another commenter questions whether the FIRPTA withholding rule of Treas. Reg. §1.1445-8(c)(2)(ii) is even authorized by the statue in the first place. *See* Blanchard, Ch. 1 footnote 59, *supra*.
167. *See* ABA 2008 Report, footnote 166, *supra*.
168. *Id*.
169. I.R.C. §897(c)(1)(B). Also *see* discussion in Ch. 6, *infra*.
170. The ABA 2008 Report stated, among other things, that '[W]e see a reasonable policy justification for applying section 897(h)(1) to Non-Dividend Distributions in the case of a foreign controlled REIT that is a USRPHC or a former USRPHC,...otherwise the foreign shareholders could avoid US tax entirely (both at the corporate and shareholder levels) by causing the REIT to sell or distribute its property after adopting a plan of complete liquidation, zeroing out REIT-level taxable income with the dividends paid deductions, and relying on the *Cleansing Exception* to avoid FIRPTA tax at the shareholder level. It is doubtful that Congress intended such a result.' *See* pg. 26 of the report. (Emphasis added.)

(2) the 2007 Notice's interpretation of Code section 897(h)(1) exposes a foreign corporate shareholder to branch profits tax on a liquidation or redemption of REIT shares;[171] and

(3) there is no compelling policy reason to extend the Code section 897(h)(1) FIRPTA tax to non-dividend distributions if the Cleansing Exception is repealed with respect to REITs.[172]

REITs are no longer eligible for the Cleansing Exception effective for dispositions on and after December 18, 2016.[173] As a result of this 2015 PATH Act amendment, the shares of a REIT remain a USRPHC even after the REIT has sold all of its underlying USRPIs. This change closes the loophole previously available to REITs. The change also may support subjecting any gain from the liquidation/deemed sale of the REIT shares to FIRPTA tax under *Code section 897(a)*. However, such treatment would be in conflict with the 2007 Notice[174] which subjects the taxation of a REIT's liquidating proceeds to tax under *Code section 897(h)(1)*. Although the amount of the FIRPTA tax should be the same under either Code section 897(a) or 897(h)(1), the difference is the potential imposition of the branch profits tax.[175]

As discussed earlier, the branch profits tax is a 30% surrogate withholding tax for amounts deemed repatriated by a fictional US subsidiary to its fictional foreign parent.[176] The gain on a sale of the shares of a USRPHC, including a REIT, is specifically exempt from branch profits tax. On the other hand, FIRPTA gain from liquidating REIT distributions is generally subject to branch profits tax unless an exemption applies. In a case that the foreign corporation does not satisfy the Branch Termination Exception (e.g., a related person reinvests in the US within three years of the sale), the branch profits tax could significantly increase the US tax burden of a foreign investor with respect to the gain from a disposition of USRPI, particularly if a treaty reduction in the rate is not available.[177] See **Example 5.4**.

---

171. This result is particularly onerous when compared to the fact that gain on a sale of REIT shares is exempt from branch profits tax. *Id*, pg. 28.
172. *Id.*, pg. 29.
173. *See* discussion in §6.02.A., *infra*.
174. Unless an applicable income tax treaty eliminates the branch profits tax or the Branch Termination Exception applies. *See* Ch. 9, *infra,* for a discussion of income tax treaty provisions.
175. I.R.C. §884(d)(2)(C).
176. I.R.C. §897(c)(1)(B). Also *see* discussion in Ch. 2, *supra*.
177. *Id.*

Example 5.4

	REIT (in USD 000s)	
	A. FIRPTA Tax	B. FIRPTA Tax & Branch Profits Tax
Gain	100	100
Earnings and profits	100	100
35% FIRPTA tax	(35)	(35)
30% branch profits tax	n/a	(19.5)
Net cash received	65	45.5
Effective tax rate	35%	54.5%

This example illustrates the US federal income tax consequences with respect to the amount taxable from a REIT's sale of a USRPI followed by a distribution of the remainder amount to a foreign corporate shareholder.

A. The foreign corporate shareholder is subject to FIRPTA tax.[178] The foreign corporate shareholder is eligible for the Branch Termination Exception;[179] hence, it is not subject to the branch profits tax.[180]

B. The foreign corporate shareholder fails to meet the requirements for the Branch Termination Exception; hence, it is subject to the branch profits tax. US tax treaties may provide a reduced or nil rate tax from the 30% statutory rate shown.

In the event the REIT that sold the USRPI was a former Subchapter C corporation and the sale occurred with the Recognition Period, then the Sting Tax also could apply to the transaction. As **Example 5.5** illustrates, the aggregate federal income tax burden on such a sale can be in excess of 70%. Although this could occur only in limited situations, the result is abominable. Taxpayers should be very careful to avoid running into such a situation and explore other options, e.g., the use of a tax-free Code section 1031 Like-Kind Exchange provisions to defer triggering recognition of gain, to the extent possible.

---

178. I.R.C. §897(h)(1).
179. Temp. Treas. Reg. §1.884-2T(a).
180. I.R.C. §884(a).

5. Using REITs to Invest in the US

Example 5.5

| | REIT (in USD 000s) ||
	A. Sting Tax & FIRPTA Tax	B. Sting Tax, FIRPTA Tax & Branch Profits Tax
Built-in gain	100	100
Less:		
– Sting Tax	(35)	(35)
Earnings and profits	65	65
35% FIRPTA tax	(22.75)	(22.75)
30% branch profits tax	n/a	(12.67)
Net cash contribution	42.25	29.58
Effective tax rate	57.75%	70.42%

This example illustrates the US federal income tax consequences with respect to the amount taxable from a REIT's sale of a USRPI which is also a built-in-gain asset followed by a distribution of the remainder amount to a foreign corporate shareholder. The REIT is subject to the Sting Tax.

A. The foreign corporate shareholder is subject to FIRPTA tax but is eligible for the Branch Termination Exception.

B. The foreign corporate shareholder is subject to FIRPTA tax, but fails to meet the requirements for the Branch Termination Exception and, thus, the branch profits tax applies. US tax treaties may provide a reduced or nil rate tax from the 30% statutory rate shown.

The ABA 2008 Report provided a number of suggestions on how to determine the amount of a REIT's distributions that should be treated as attributable to gain from its sales or exchanges of USRPIs.[181] The NYSBA Tax Section also issued a report offering suggestions about future guidance in implementing the 2007 Notice and Code section 897(h)(1).[182] Until the Treasury Department and the IRS issue further guidance on how to determine the amount of a REIT's distribution that is attributable to the entity's gain from a sale or disposition of USRPI, it remains unclear on how taxpayers may calculate the substantive FIRPTA tax liability imposed by Code section 897(h)(1). Foreign investors that use a single-property REIT may avoid the issue as the gain will come from the only property the REIT owns.

---

181. A positive outcome with respect to the issuance of the 2007 Notice is that it generated many thoughtful comments on the manner of how to determine the amount of REIT distributions that should be considered attributable to the gain from a disposition of USRPI.
182. NYSBA, *Report on Notice 2007-55 and Possible Administrative Guidance Addressing Sections 897(h)(1) and 1445(e)(6),* no. 1296, dated January 7, 2014.

C. Gain from the Sale of REIT Stock

The above discussion illustrates that a foreign shareholder that sells the shares of a REIT avoids the complexities and the additional tax burden that apply when a shareholder receives distributions from a REIT from a sale of its underlying USRPIs. In practice, some foreign sellers have stipulated in the purchase and sale contract that a buyer of REIT shares must not liquidate the REIT for a period of time (e.g., twelve to eighteen months) to avoid any potential recast of the share sale as an asset sale. Finally, as discussed in Chapter 6, a number of FIRPTA exceptions apply to the sale of REIT stock. The application of one of these exceptions further increases the US tax benefits of using a REIT.

§5.05 SUMMARY

REITs are generally tax efficient vehicles for investors, domestic and foreign, particularly if the goal is to repatriate the funds from the operations annually to the investors. The trade-off for the tax efficiency is that the myriad REIT rules must be strictly complied with throughout the period for which REIT benefits are claimed. Failure to do so could result in losing the expected REIT tax benefits (i.e., avoiding corporate-level tax) and potentially subject to interest and penalties.

A foreign investor may wish to consider certain threshold issues to assess whether a REIT structure is suitable for the particular investment contemplated. Once the investor believes it is beneficial to use a REIT to own one or more USRPIs, the investor should perform a comprehensive due diligence to ascertain that: (1) A REIT structure is optimal for the particular investment, and (2) how to structure the REIT including whether it is necessary to use a TRS to operate certain business activities.[183]

The interaction between FIRPTA and REIT regimes raises complex technical issues some of which do not have clear answers. A lot of the complexities surround the taxation of REIT distributions attributable to gains from a sale of USRPIs. These issues can be avoided if the exit strategy is to sell the REIT shares instead of having the REIT sell the USRPI and liquidate. Furthermore, foreign shareholders of REITs also may enjoy special FIRPTA exceptions when they sell REIT shares.[184] Investors that use single-property REITs have more flexibility selling each REIT to a different buyer. Such a structure is more costly to maintain and may warrant a cost/benefit analysis to support the determination.

---

183. If there is uncertainty as to whether a type of service provided to the tenants is considered customary, a prudent investor may choose to have the TRS provide the service in order to protect the REIT status. The costs involved to maintain the TRS, including any tax leakage, must be balanced against the tax savings provided by the REIT.
184. *See* discussion in Ch. 6, *infra*.

Chapter 6
Exceptions to FIRPTA

§6.01	Overview	109
§6.02	Original FIRPTA Exceptions	110
	A. The Cleansing Exception	110
	B. The Publicly Traded Exception	112
	1. The Trading Requirements	113
	2. The Ownership Requirements	114
	3. Application to Partnership Interests	116
	C. The Domestically Controlled QIE/REIT Exception	116
	1. General Rule	116
	2. 2015 PATH Act Changes	120
§6.03	New Exceptions under the 2015 PATH Act	123
	A. QFPF Exemption	123
	1. General Rule	123
	2. Unanswered Questions	126
	B. Qualified Shareholder Exemption	127
	1. General Rule	127
	2. Who Will Benefit?	129
§6.04	Other Special Rules	130
	A. Foreign Sovereign Exemption	131
	1. Definition of Foreign Government	132
	2. Controlled Entities v. Controlled Commercial Entities	133
	3. The *Per Se* Rule for Controlled Commercial Entities	135
	4. Commercial Activities	136
	5. Treatment of a Sovereign as a Foreign Corporation	137
§6.05	Summary	138

§6.01 OVERVIEW

As stated in the beginning of this book, the intent of FIRPTA is to level the playing field regarding the taxation of US and foreign investors on the gain from a sale of US real estate. A US seller, unless it is an entity that is exempt from federal income tax, is generally subject to US tax on gain from the sale of appreciated real estate. The same principle applies to a foreign seller. Under the FIRPTA regime, foreign sellers, except a particular type of pension plan investors, are generally subject to US tax on the sale of appreciated USRPIs.

Generally speaking, a foreign corporation pays between 35%[1] and 70%[2] of FIRPTA tax on the gain from a disposition of its USRPI. There are a number of exceptions that may reduce the FIRPTA tax. Three of the exceptions were enacted with FIRPTA in 1980 (i.e., the original exceptions). The 2015 PATH Act modified all the original exceptions and added two new ones.[3] Foreign sovereign investors may be exempt from FIRPTA tax on the sale of the shares of less-than-50% owned USRPHCs. A foreign investor that wishes to obtain the benefits under any of the exceptions must keep meticulous records to prove that it qualifies for the exception.

§6.02 ORIGINAL FIRPTA EXCEPTIONS

The three original exceptions to FIRPTA tax all pertain to the disposition of an interest, other than an interest solely as a creditor, of a USRPHC.[4] The discussion below describes each of these exceptions and the associated amendments made by the 2015 PATH Act.

A. The Cleansing Exception

A foreign seller is not subject to FIRPTA tax when it disposes of an interest in a US corporation that was a former USRPHC[5] if the Cleansing Exception applies. The policy of this exception is that if a US corporation disposed of its USRPIs in one or more taxable transactions, the gain with respect to the USRPIs had already been subject to US tax. Hence, the corporation's foreign shareholder should not be subject to FIRPTA tax again upon a subsequent sale of the interest in the corporation.

The Cleansing Exception is intended to impose a single level of tax on the sale of a USRPI. There are two methods for a US corporation to cleanse its USRPHC taint. Under the first cleansing method, an interest in a former USRPHC will cease to be treated as a USRPI *immediately* if, as of the date that a foreign shareholder disposes of the interest in the stock, the US corporation:

---

1. See Example 5.4, *supra*.
2. See Example 5.5, *supra*.
3. The Tax Technical Corrections Act of 2016 was introduced on December 6, 2016 in the House of Representatives as H.R. 6439 and in the Senate as S. 3506 (referred to as the 2016 TCA). The 2016 TCA contains a number of technical corrections to the 2015 PATH Act. As of July, 2017, the 2016 TCA has not been enacted into law. The discussion in this chapter includes the provisions of the 2016 TCA as well as the current law prior to the amendment.
4. The remainder of this chapter refers to all interests in USRPHCs, including those that are other than an interest solely as a creditor, that is generally subject to FIRPTA tax as the 'interests' in the USRPHC to simplify the discussion.
5. The stock of a domestic corporation is generally treated as a USRPI if the corporation was a USRPHC on any 'determination date' during the applicable Five-Year Look-Back Period ending on the date of the sale of such interest. See I.R.C. §897(c)(1)(A)(ii). See also discussion in §4.04., *supra*, regarding the look-back period and determination dates.

(1) no longer owns any USRPIs;
(2) previously disposed of all of the USRPIs it owned in fully taxable transactions;[6] and
(3) neither such corporation nor any predecessor was a REIT in the five years preceding the disposition.[7]

Prior to the 2015 PATH Act, some taxpayers took the position that a REIT may dispose of all its assets and the gain could completely escape US tax under the Cleansing Exception. Here is how it worked. A REIT disposed of all its USRPIs in a taxable transaction.[8] The REIT then made a liquidating distribution of the proceeds from the sale to its shareholders. The liquidating distribution completely eliminated the REIT's taxable income.[9] The foreign shareholders of the REIT treated the liquidating distribution as proceeds realized from the sale of an interest in a corporation which had cleansed its USRPHC taint under the Cleansing Exception.[10] Accordingly, the gain from the sale of the USRPIs escaped US tax at both the REIT and the foreign shareholder levels. This is inconsistent with the policy of the Cleansing Exception. As a result, the 2015 PATH Act added condition (3) above to prevent this abuse.

Under the second cleansing method, a US corporation loses its USRPHC taint five years[11] after the fair market value of its USRPIs no longer equals or exceeds 50% of all of its includible assets.[12] Under this rule, taxable transactions that *reduce* the level of a US corporation's USRPIs to less than 50% of its includible assets does *not* get rid of the corporation's USRPHC status immediately. A corporation that is a former USRPHC at any time in the Five-Year Look-Back Period also needs to avoid accidentally owning any interests in USRPIs, such as certain leasehold interest[13] or receivables[14] from a sale of its USRPIs in order to qualify for this second cleansing rule.

---

6. The fact that the former USRPHC disposed of all of its USRPIs in fully taxable transactions satisfies the policy of the Cleansing Exception to impose one level of tax on the sale of USRPIs even though the tax is imposed on a US seller. This result is consistent with the stated policy of FIRPTA to level the playing field between US and foreign investors in US real estate. *See* Ch. 1, *supra,* for a general discussion of the background of FIRPTA.
7. The rule also applies to regulated investment companies, or RICs, that are USRPHCs. As a practical matter, it is not common for a RIC to qualify as a USRPHC. Therefore, the remainder of this chapter refers only to REITs, to which the FIRPTA rules most often apply.
8. I.R.C. §897(c)(1)(B).
9. I.R.C. §562(b)(1)(B). *See* also discussion in §5.03.D., *supra*, regarding REIT distribution requirements.
10. In other words, these taxpayers took the position that I.R.C. §897(c)(1)(B) overrides I.R.C. §897(h)(1).
11. The statute states that the taxpayer must establish that the corporation was not a USRPHC during the shorter of: (1) the period after June 18, 1980, during which the taxpayer held such interest, or (2) the five-year period ending on the date of the disposition of such interest (i.e., the Five-Year Look-Back Period). *See* I.R.C. §897(c)(1)(A).
12. *Id.*
13. A corporation that disposes of all its USRPIs other than a lease that has a fair market value of zero will be considered to have disposed of all of its USRPIs, provided the leased property is used in the conduct of a US trade or business. *See* Treas. Reg. §1.897-2(f)(2).
14. If a corporation sold its own USRPIs under the installment method during the Five-Year Look-Back Period but has not collected all the installment payments, its shares also will

B. The Publicly Traded Exception

The Publicly Traded Exception exempts the gain from a sale of certain publicly traded USRPHCs from FIRPTA tax. This exception traditionally benefited a relatively small segment of investors that owned no more than 5% of the stock of certain publicly traded USRPHCs that are either Subchapter C corporations or REITs.[15] A corresponding rule exempted a foreign shareholder that owned 5% or less of a publicly traded REIT at any time during the one-year period ending on the date of the distribution from FIRPTA tax imposed by Code section 897(h)(1) (referred to as the Publicly Traded Distribution Exception).[16]

The 2015 PATH Act increased the ownership threshold for REIT stock. A foreign investor of a publicly traded REIT is now exempt from FIRPTA tax if the investor owns no more than 10% of the REIT stock.[17] In addition, the ownership threshold for the corresponding Publicly Traded Distribution Exception is also increased to no more than 10% of the stock of a publicly traded REIT. The amount of the distribution that is exempt from FIRPTA tax under the Publicly Traded Distribution Exception is treated as an ordinary REIT dividend, i.e., FDAP income, subject to gross-basis withholding tax.[18]

A foreign shareholder must meet several requirements in order to be eligible for the benefit available under this seemingly simple exception. To qualify for the Publicly Traded Exception, the taxpayer needs to demonstrate the following:

(1) the shares of a class of stock in a domestic corporation that otherwise would be a USRPHC is *Regularly Traded* on an *Established Securities Market*,[19] and
(2) the taxpayer does *not* own more than either 5% or 10% of that class of stock of a regular Subchapter C corporation or a REIT,[20] respectively, *at any time* during the Five-Year Look-Back Period.

The discussion below focuses on the key aspects of these requirements.

---

continue to constitute USRPHC because it has not recognized all the gain from the sale. See Treas. Reg. §1.897-1(d)(2)(ii)(A) and (3)(ii)(A). As another example, a corporation would not qualify for the Cleansing Exception if it made a taxable, non-installment sale of its USRPI and took back a mortgage as part of the transaction if the mortgage constitutes a USRPI because it has a right to share in the appreciation of the USRPI. See Treas. Reg. §1.897-1(d)(2) and discussion in §3.03.C., *supra*.

15. I.R.C. §897(c)(3).
16. I.R.C. §857(b)(3)(F).
17. I.R.C. §897(k)(1).
18. I.R.C. §857(b)(3)(F).
19. I.R.C. §897(c)(3).
20. The 2015 PATH Act expansion of the Publicly Traded Exception to cover the ownership of 10% of the REIT stock is effective on December 18, 2015. See I.R.C. §897(k)(1)(A). This expansion aligns well with a typical provision in many REIT charters that limits ownership of the REIT by any single shareholder to 9.8% to avoid violating the closely held test which prohibits ownership of more than 50% of the value of the REIT by five or fewer individuals. See I.R.C. §542(a)(2) and discussion in §5.03.A., *supra*.

1. The Trading Requirements

The stock in question must be traded on a US or foreign stock exchange that qualifies as an Established Securities Market. This includes shares traded on a stock exchange, the over-the-counter market, and a foreign national securities exchange which is officially recognized, sanctioned, or supervised by a governmental authority.[21] A class of stock that is traded on a US Established Securities Market is considered to be Regularly Traded during any calendar quarter if it is regularly quoted by brokers or dealers making a market in such interests.[22] On the other hand, a class of interests that is traded on a foreign Established Securities Market is considered to be Regularly Traded during any calendar quarter if *all* of the following conditions are met:

(1) trades in such class are effected, other than in *de minimis* quantities, on at least fifteen days during the calendar quarter;
(2) the aggregate number of interests in such class traded is at least 7.5%[23] of the average number of interests in such class outstanding during the calendar quarter;[24] and
(3) the interests traded are in registered form and the corporation meets specified reporting requirements.[25]

The reporting requirements are satisfied if the corporation has registered under section 12 of the Securities Exchange Act of 1934 or meets a series of specific alternative requirements.[26] To meet the alternative requirements, a corporation must attach to its tax return a statement including information as to the identity of each person

---

21. Under Treas. Reg. §1.897-1(m), the term includes a national securities exchange which is registered under Sec. 6 of the Securities Exchange Act of 1934 (15 U.S.C. §78f) and any over-the-counter market. An over-the-counter market is any market reflected by the existence of an interdealer quotation system; that is, a system of general circulation to brokers and dealers which regularly disseminates quotations of stocks and securities by identified brokers or dealers, other than by quotation sheets prepared by a broker or dealer which contain only quotations of such preparer.
22. Temp. Treas. Reg. §1.897-9T(d)(2). A broker or dealer makes a market in such interests only if the broker or dealer holds himself out to buy or sell interests in such class at the quoted price. Shares of certain RICs are considered regularly traded. Id.
23. If a class of interests is held by 2,500 or more record shareholders, the test is 2.5% or more instead of 7.5% or more (this is sometimes referred to as the closely held prong of the publicly traded exception). Temp. Treas. Reg. §1.897-9T(d)(1)(ii)(A).
24. If, at any time during the calendar quarter, 100 or fewer persons own 50% or more of the outstanding shares of a class of interests, such class is not considered to be regularly traded. Temp. Treas. Reg. §1.897-9T(d)(1)(ii)(B). TAM 9639010 (September 27, 1996), in ruling on a separate issue, asserted that the closely held prong is an exception only to the general rule of Temp. Treas. Reg. §1.897-9T(d)(1), and does not constitute an exception to the domestic exchange provision of Temp. Treas. Reg. §1.897-9T(d)(2). Under an anti-abuse rule, trades between related persons and arrangements designed to comply with the literal requirements of Temp. Treas. Reg. §1.897-9T(d)(1) are disregarded for purposes of determining whether the shares are considered regularly traded for this purpose. *See* Temp. Treas. Reg. §1.897-9T(d)(1)(iii).
25. Temp. Treas. Reg. §1.897-9T(d)(1).
26. Temp. Treas. Reg. §1.897-9T(d)(3).

who, at any time during the corporation's taxable year, was the beneficial owner of more than 5% of any class of interests of the corporation; the title, and the total number of shares issued, of any class of interest so owned; and with respect to each beneficial owner of more than 5% of any class of interests of the corporation, the number of shares owned, the percentage of the class represented thereby, and the nature of the beneficial ownership of each class of shares so owned.[27]

2. The Ownership Requirements

The exception applies to *a person* that owns no more than 5% or 10%, respectively, of the publicly traded stock of a Subchapter C corporation or a REIT. This wording raises a number of questions some of which are discussed below. In addition, a number of special rules apply to determine whether this condition is met.

The definition of a person includes an individual, a trust, estate, partnership and a corporation.[28] As such, the exception applies to a partnership that owns no more than the permitted percentage of stock of a publicly traded entity. There does not seem to be any look-through rule that would test the ownership of the publicly traded stock at the partner level. Thus, the percentage limitation applies regardless of the ultimate foreign ownership of the partnership. In other words, to qualify for the exception, a partnership may own no more than 5% of the stock of a publicly traded Subchapter C corporation regardless of whether 1% or 99% of its partners are foreign persons. Commentators have suggested that the Treasury Department and the IRS issue regulations that provide a look-through approach similar to that available for the Portfolio Interest Exemption.[29]

Attribution rules apply to treat stock owned by related individuals and entities as owned by a foreign investor for purposes of testing whether the foreign investor owned more than the permitted percentage of the regularly traded stock during the Five-Year Look-Back Period.[30] Specifically, the statute applies the constructive ownership rules of Code section 318, except that the threshold of applying the attributable rules has been lowered so that stock may be attributed from a corporation to a 5%, instead of 50%, or greater shareholder and from such shareholder to the corporation. As a result, it is easier for a foreign investor to exceed the 5% or 10% threshold, as the case may be, under this modified attribution rule.[31]

It may be useful to illustrate some of the operative aspects of the attribution rules using an example. Bobby, a private equity fund manager, wishes to acquire the stock of USRPHC1 which is publicly traded on a US stock exchange. Bobby understands that the stock is a USRPI and he wants to make sure that the foreign investors in his family of funds are exempt from FIRPTA tax on the disposition of

---

27. Id.
28. I.R.C. §7701(a)(1).
29. Treas. Reg. §1.871-14(g)(3). See Blanchard, *FIRPTA in the 21st Century – Installment Two: The 5% Public Shareholder Exception*, 37 Tax Mgmt. Intl. J. 44 (2008). Ms. Blanchard's article also discusses various other issues regarding the Publicly Traded Exception.
30. *See* I.R.C. §897(c)(6)(C) and Treas. Reg. §1.897-1(c)(2)(iii). *See* Ch. 10, *infra*, for a discussion of the Portfolio Interest Exemption.
31. The I.R.C. §318 rules are complex and may reattribute the ownership to another party in a number of situations. *See, e.g.,* I.R.C. §318(a)(5).

6. Exceptions to FIRPTA

the stock under the Publicly Traded Exception. **Example 6.1** illustrates the structure of the funds that Bobby manages.

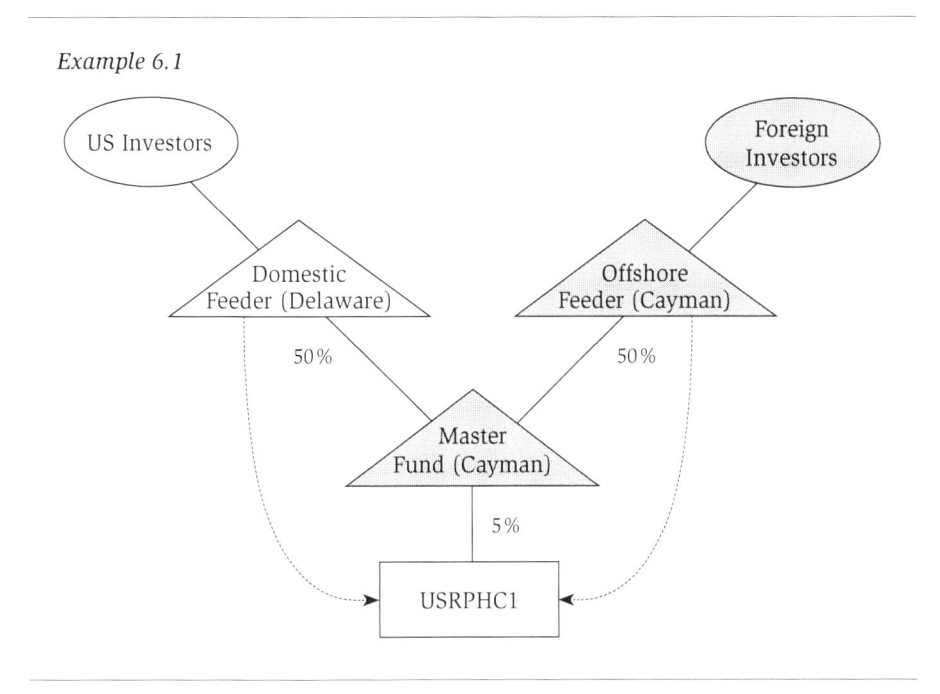

Example 6.1

```
   US Investors                                Foreign Investors

   Domestic                                    Offshore
   Feeder (Delaware)                           Feeder (Cayman)

              50%                    50%

                    Master
                    Fund (Cayman)

                         5%

                    USRPHC1
```

Any USRPHC1 stock owned by Domestic Feeder or Offshore Feeder in **Example 6.1** may be attributed to Master Fund.[32] However, any stock that is owned by Domestic Feeder that is attributed to Master Fund *may not be* reattributed to the Offshore Feeder.[33] Therefore, the Offshore Feeder may qualify for the Publicly Traded Exception if it owns up to 5% of the USRPHC1 stock. At the same time, the Domestic Feeder also may own additional USRPHC1 stock without causing the Offshore Feeder to violate the 5% ownership threshold.

Bobby compared this with the situation in which the Master Fund acquires USRPHC1 stock directly. In that case, Master Fund may qualify for the Publicly Traded Exception if it owns up to 5% of the USRPHC1 stock. However, any USRPHC1 stock that Domestic Feeder or Offshore Feeder acquires would be attributed to Master Fund for purposes of the Publicly Traded Exception.[34] After thinking it through, Bobby decided to have the Offshore Feeder and the Domestic Feeder each acquire

---

32. I.R.C. §318(a)(3)(A) attributes the stock owned, by or for a partner, to the partnership. Under this rule, a partnership is considered to own all the stock owned by the partner regardless of the interest the partner owns in the partnership.
33. I.R.C. §318(a)(5)(C) provides that the stock attributed to a partnership under I.R.C. §318(a)(3)(A) may not be reattributed to another partnership of the same partnership under I.R.C. §318(a)(2)(A).
34. *See* I.R.C. §318(a)(3)(A).

5% of the stock of USRPHC1. As a result, the Offshore Feeder is still eligible for the Publicly Traded Exception on the gain from the sale of the USRPHC1 stock even though Bobby's family of funds own 10% of the class stock in total.

Where a person acquires separate blocks of different equity interests[35] in a corporation for a principal purpose of avoiding the ownership threshold, the equity interests generally will be aggregated in determining whether the 5% or 10% ownership threshold, respectively, for Subchapter C corporations and REITs has been exceeded. However, equity interests acquired in transactions more than three years apart will not be aggregated.[36]

3. Application to Partnership Interests

The statute applies the Publicly Traded Exception only to stock of corporations.[37] The Treasury regulations created a parallel exception for interests in publicly traded partnerships and trusts.[38] This parallel exception overrides the look-through rule that otherwise applies to partnerships and trusts, and treats a sale of an interest in publicly traded partnerships and trusts as either taxable or exempt under FIRPTA in its entirety.[39]

As a result of the parallel rule, a foreign investor in a publicly traded partnership or trust must first determine whether the publicly traded entity would qualify as a USRPHC based on the value of the entity's ownership in USRPIs relative to its ownership in FRPIs and Trade or Business Assets under the same rules used to determine the USRPHC status of a US corporation.[40] Hence, a publicly traded partnership or trust that wishes to attract foreign investments should maintain such information at the entity level which it may provide to the investors.

C. The Domestically Controlled QIE/REIT Exception

1. General Rule

This can be viewed as the most generous of the original FIRPTA exceptions. Under the Domestically Controlled QIE[41] Exception, a foreign investor could own up to

---

35. For example, this includes different classes of non-regularly traded class of interests of a corporation. See Temp. Treas. Reg. §1.897-9T(b).
36. Id.
37. See I.R.C. §897(c)(3).
38. Treas. Reg. §1.897-1(c)(2)(iv).
39. I.R.C. §897(g) only taxes a foreign investor's gain on the disposition of an interest in a partnership to the extent the gain is attributable to the foreign partner's share of the partnership's USRPIs. See discussion in §2.03.B., supra.
40. See discussion in §4.03, supra.
41. I.R.C. §897(h)(4)(A). The 2015 PATH Act permanently extended the application of the Domestically Controlled QIE exception to RICs effective for sales occurring on or after January 1, 2015.

6. Exceptions to FIRPTA

almost half of the value of a QIE/REIT[42] and still avoid FIRPTA tax on the gain from a disposition of its entire interest in the entity provided that the balance of the interest was not owned directly or indirectly by foreign persons. Assume that the REIT 2 stock in **Example 6.2** has appreciated in value by USD 100. If the Domestically Controlled REIT Exception applies, then USD 49 of the *overall* gain would be exempt from US tax.

Example 6.2

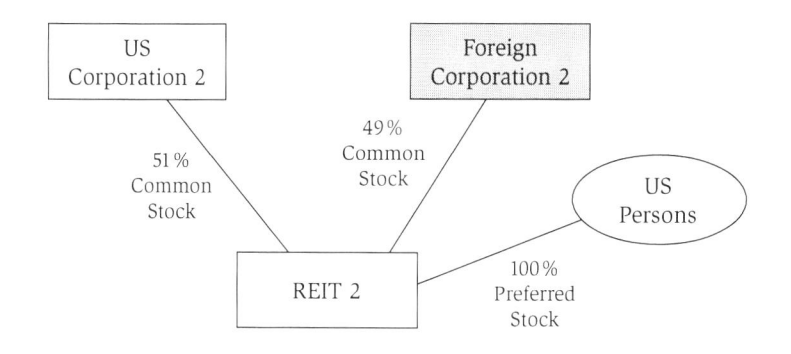

```
        US                      Foreign
    Corporation 2            Corporation 2
                    49%
         51%      Common
       Common      Stock                    US
        Stock                             Persons

                                  100%
                REIT 2          Preferred
                                  Stock
```

A Domestically Controlled REIT is a REIT where *at all times* during the testing period less than 50% in value of its shares was held directly or indirectly by foreign persons.[43] The testing period, for this purpose, is the shorter of: (i) the five-year period ending on the date of disposition or distribution, or (ii) the period during which the REIT was in existence.[44] There is no guidance on how a taxpayer should demonstrate the level of the REIT's domestic ownership *at all times* during the testing period. Interestingly, the regulations provide that Domestically Controlled REITs are not required to respond to requests from a foreign investor for a determination as to whether the shares are USRPIs.[45]

Many foreign investors in USRPIs that are REIT-eligible are interested in using the Domestically Controlled REIT structure. Because the statute defines domestically controlled by looking to the value of the stock that is owned *directly or indirectly* by foreign persons, the logical question is what constitutes indirect ownership for this purpose. The tax community, in pondering the meaning of indirect ownership in

---

42. Even though the statute refers to Domestically Controlled QIE, there are not a lot of RICs that also qualify as USRPHCs. Hence, the discussion herein refers only to the impact of this exception on REITs.
43. I.R.C. §897(h)(4)(B). Unlike the test for USRPHCs, there are no specific determination dates in determining whether a REIT is a Domestically Controlled REIT; instead, the test applies continuously during the requisite testing period which is more challenging. See discussion in §4.04., *supra*, for a discussion of the determination dates applicable to USRPHCs.
44. I.R.C. §897(h)(4)(D).
45. Treas. Reg. §1.897-2(h)(3).

The US Foreign Investment in Real Property Tax Act: A Practical Guide

this context, is really asking whether Foreign Corporation 3 in **Example 6.3** would be viewed as owning 49% or 100% of the common stock of REIT 3 for purposes of applying the Domestically Controlled REIT Exception.

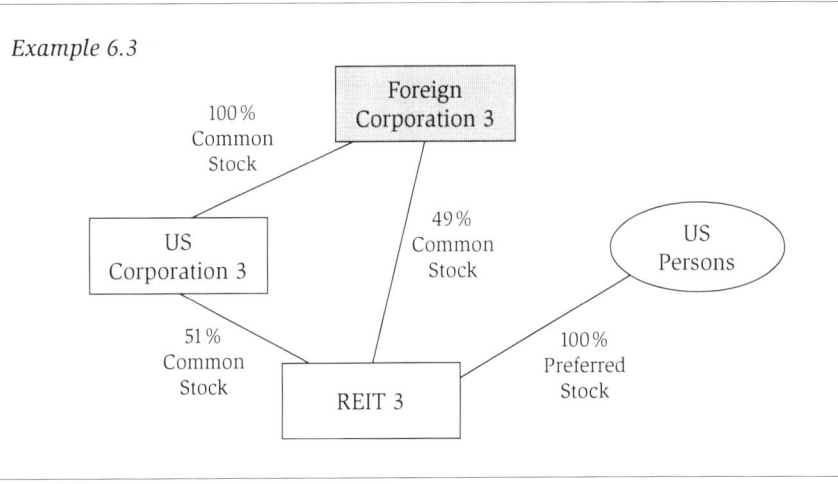

Example 6.3

```
                            Foreign
          100%              Corporation 3
          Common
          Stock
                              |
                              | 49%
     US                       | Common         US
Corporation 3                 | Stock       Persons

     51%                               100%
     Common                            Preferred
     Stock          REIT 3             Stock
```

The statute that governs the Domestically Controlled REIT Exception, in contrast to the one that governs the Publicly Traded Exception, does *not* refer to any type of attribution or constructive ownership rules in determining the ownership of a Domestically Controlled REIT.[46] Both of these exceptions were enacted at the same time, and both exempt the gain from the disposition of the interests in certain USRPHCs, including REITs, from FIRPTA taxation. If Congress intended to incorporate any attribution or constructive ownership rules to determine the amount of foreign ownership in a Domestically Controlled REIT, it would make sense that the applicable statute[47] would contain a reference to those rules.

The FIRPTA regulations provide that, for purposes of determining indirect ownership in this context, 'the *actual* owners of stock, as determined under section 1.857-8, must be taken into account.'[48] Regulation section 1.857-8(b), in turn, provides that:

> [t]he actual owner of stock of a real estate investment trust is the person who is required to include in gross income in his return the dividends received on the stock. Generally, such person is the shareholder of record of the real estate investment trust...

---

46. As discussed above, incorporating the modified constructive ownership rules in the Publicly Traded Exception caused the exception to be less accessible to taxpayers. Incorporating some form of constructive ownership rules in the Domestically Controlled REIT Exception would have a similar result.
47. *See* I.R.C. §897(h)(4)(B). The legislative history of FIRPTA also did not suggest that a constructive ownership rule should be used to determine a foreign person's ownership for purposes of the Domestically Controlled REIT Exception.
48. *See* Treas. Reg. §1.897-1(c)(2)(i). (Emphasis added).

6. Exceptions to FIRPTA

There is no further explanation regarding the reference to the REIT regulation for purposes of determining the ownership of a Domestically Controlled REIT. The language of Treasury Regulation section 1.857-8(b), however, is clear that an actual owner need not be the record owner of the stock of a REIT. Thus, read narrowly, the term 'indirect' may refer to ownership of stock through a nominee for purposes of determining the domestic ownership of a REIT. Although this interpretation stems from a literal application of the specific authority referenced in the FIRPTA regulations,[49] it is not clear if that is the proper interpretation.

This issue was resolved favorably for one taxpayer which sought a private letter ruling. In PLR 200923001,[50] the IRS concluded that a REIT whose common stock was directly owned by two Subchapter C corporations was a Domestically Controlled REIT notwithstanding that the two Subchapter C corporations were ultimately owned 100% by foreign persons. The ownership structure of the REIT as described in the private letter ruling is shown in **Example 6.4**.

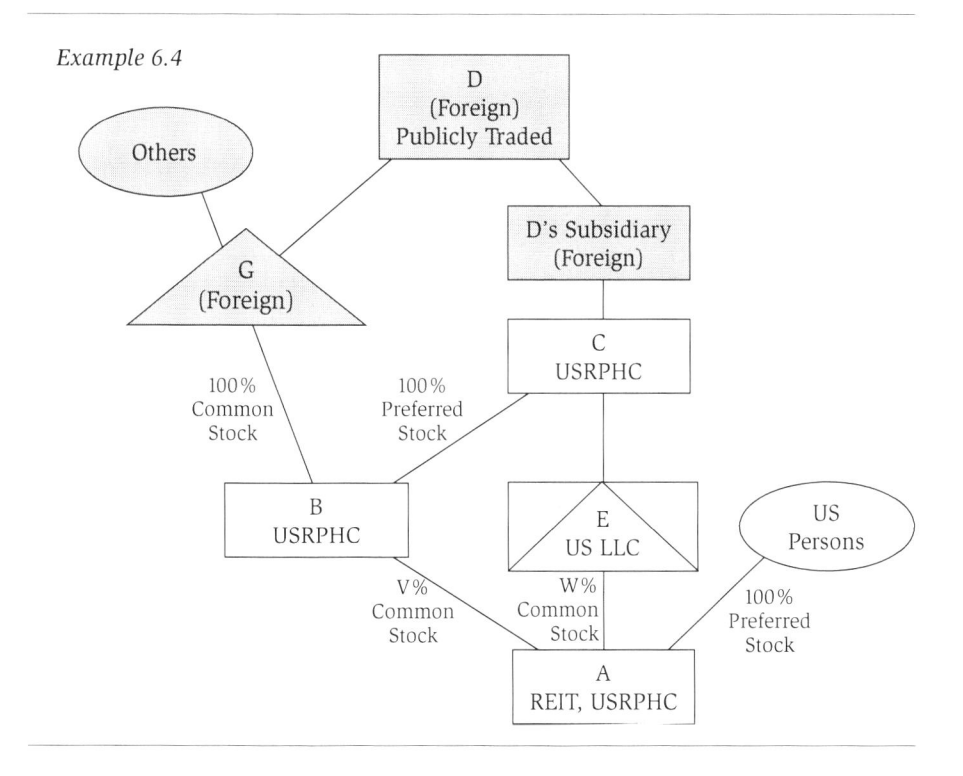

Example 6.4

```
                         D
                      (Foreign)
                   Publicly Traded
   Others

         G
      (Foreign)           D's Subsidiary
                            (Foreign)

                                C
    100%         100%         USRPHC
   Common      Preferred
    Stock        Stock

       B                                      US
     USRPHC              E                  Persons
                       US LLC
         V%         W%              100%
       Common     Common           Preferred
        Stock      Stock             Stock
                    A
                REIT, USRPHC
```

---

49. The Supreme Court has held that, if a statute is ambiguous, an agency's interpretation will be respected if it is a reasonable interpretation of the statute. *See Mayo Found. For Med. Educ. & Research v. United States*, 562 U.S. 44, 52-54 (2011) (deference to Treasury regulations was appropriate because Congress did not define the term 'student' in I.R.C. §3121(b)(10)). This analysis applies uniformly to regulations promulgated under both the specific and general rulemaking authority delegated by Congress.
50. June 5, 2009.

Entity E in **Example 6.4** is a disregarded entity of C which is a Subchapter C corporation. Under US tax principles, all of E's assets are treated as assets of C. As a result, C and B are treated as directly owning all of the common stock of A (i.e., the REIT).[51] In reaching its conclusion, the IRS cited the fact that both B and C were fully taxable US corporations, and were not REITs, RICs, hybrid entities, conduits, disregarded entities, or other flow-through or look-through entities. Accordingly, the ruling states that it is not necessary to look through B and C to determine whether the REIT (i.e., A) is domestically controlled. This ruling generated a lot of interest because B and C are both ultimately owned by foreign persons.

2.   *2015 PATH Act Changes*

The 2015 PATH Act, *inter alia*, made certain amendments to the Domestically Controlled REIT Exception. As a result of these amendments, it is now much easier for publicly traded parent REITs and their lower-tier REITs to qualify as Domestically Controlled REITs. In addition, the amendments apply a look-through rule to determine the ownership of REITs owned by private parent REITs. However, the 2015 PATH Act did not apply a similar look-through rule to determine the ownership of REITs held by Subchapter C corporations.

Interestingly, the Joint Committee Report to the 2015 PATH Act refers to PLR 200923001 as the existing rule in applying the Domestically Controlled REIT Exception with respect to a Subchapter C corporation's ownership of REITs.[52] This reference, together with the fact that the new law applies a look-through rule *only* to determine the ownership of REITs held by a parent REIT that is not publicly traded, has led some to infer that Congress agrees with the position in PLR 200923001. In other words, it may not be necessary to look through the ownership of a Subchapter C corporation to determine whether a foreign person is treated as an indirect owner of a REIT for purposes of the Domestically Controlled REIT Exception. It would be helpful if the Treasury Department and the IRS provide further public guidance to confirm this position to eliminate any lingering uncertainty.

The new rules enacted by the 2015 PATH Act are effective with respect to each testing period ending on or after December 18, 2015.[53] The new rules are summarized below and illustrated in the diagrams that follow. Under the new provisions:

- A publicly traded REIT would be permitted to presume, absent actual knowledge to the contrary, that a person that holds less than 5% of a class

---

51. The common stock of a privately owned REIT typically represents the vast majority, e.g., over 99%, of its value.
52. Joint Committee on Taxation, *Technical Explanation of the Revenue Provisions of the Protecting Americans from Tax Hikes Act of 2015, House Amendment #2 to the Senate Amendment to H.R. 2029 (Rules Committee Print 114-40)*, (JCX-144-15), at 186-187, December 17, 2015.
53. As amended by the 2016 TCA. Prior to the 2016 TCA amendment, the PATH Act merely stated that the new rules would 'take effect' on the enactment date without further specificity.

6. Exceptions to FIRPTA

of its stock regularly traded on an established securities market during the requisite testing period[54] is a US person;[55]
- REIT stock held by a publicly traded REIT is generally treated as owned by foreign persons unless the parent REIT itself is domestically controlled;[56] and
- REIT stock held by a *non-publicly traded parent REIT* is generally treated as owned by US persons to the extent the stock of the parent REIT is owned by US persons (i.e., applying a look-through approach).[57]

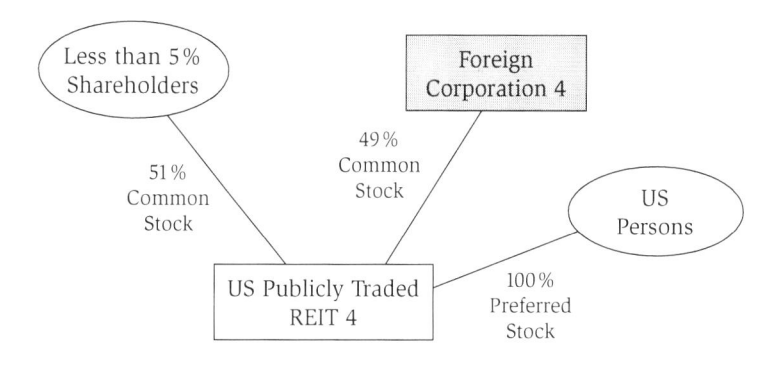

Example 6.5: Presumption of US Ownership for Publicly Traded REITs

```
    Less than 5%                          Foreign
    Shareholders                        Corporation 4

                       49%
         51%          Common
        Common         Stock                  US
         Stock                              Persons

                  US Publicly Traded    100%
                       REIT 4          Preferred
                                         Stock
```

Absent actual knowledge to the contrary, US publicly traded REIT 4 in **Example 6.5** may presume that all of the persons holding less than 5% of its publicly traded class of stock during the testing period are US person.[58] Hence, a REIT that does not have knowledge of any 5%-or-greater shareholder, e.g., from its SEC filings,[59] during the testing period may presume that it is a Domestically Controlled REIT.[60] This new rule also makes it easier for a publicly traded REIT to demonstrate whether it satisfies the domestic ownership *at all times* during the testing period.[61]

---

54. The testing period is the shorter of the five-year period ending on the date of the disposition or the period during which the REIT was in existence. I.R.C. §897(h)(4)(D).
55. I.R.C. §897(h)(4)(E)(i).
56. I.R.C. §897(h)(4)(E)(ii).
57. I.R.C. §897(h)(4)(E)(iii).
58. I.R.C. §897(h)(4)(E)(i).
59. *See* Section 13(g) of the Securities Exchange Act of 1934. Although the standards for determining the ownership percentage for purposes of the SEC disclosure are different from the standards used to determine tax ownership, it seems reasonable for taxpayers to rely on the SEC disclosure for purposes of satisfying the presumption.
60. This new rule is very sensible. Substantial administrative and compliance difficulties that would entail if a REIT were required to look through a publicly traded Subchapter C corporation when determining its own domestic ownership.
61. *See* I.R.C. §897(h)(4)(B).

The US Foreign Investment in Real Property Tax Act: A Practical Guide

Example 6.6: No *Ownership Look-Through for Publicly Traded REITs*

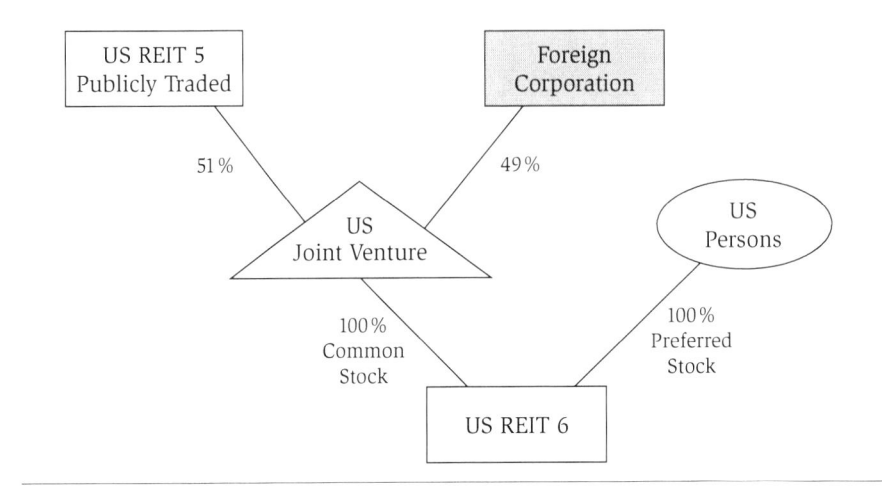

```
   US REIT 5              Foreign
 Publicly Traded         Corporation
        \                    /
      51%                  49%
          \              /
           US                          US
       Joint Venture              Persons
              \                     /
           100%                  100%
          Common               Preferred
           Stock                 Stock
                \              /
                  US REIT 6
```

Example 6.7: Look-Through *Rule for Non-Publicly Traded REITs*

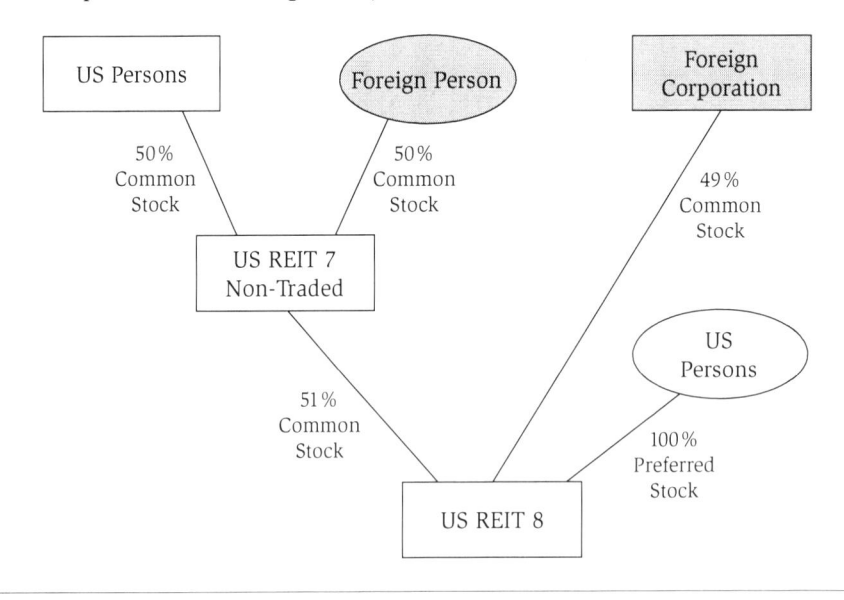

```
  US Persons        Foreign Person       Foreign
                                        Corporation
       \                  |                 |
      50%               50%               49%
    Common            Common            Common
     Stock             Stock             Stock
         \              |
          US REIT 7
          Non-Traded
              \                         US
               \                      Persons
               51%                       |
             Common                   100%
              Stock                 Preferred
                 \                    Stock
                  \                  /
                     US REIT 8
```

In **Example 6.6,** if US REIT 5 has only one class of publicly traded stock outstanding and no one person owns 5% or more of that class of stock, then US REIT 5 may

6. Exceptions to FIRPTA

presume that all its shareholders are US persons.[62] As a result, US REIT 5 should be a Domestically Controlled REIT. In turn, US REIT 6 also should be a Domestically Controlled REIT because more than 50% of its stock is considered owned by a US person.[63] This new rule makes it more attractive for foreign investors to form joint venture partnerships with publicly traded REITs.

US REIT 8 in **Example 6.7** needs to look through the ownership of US REIT 7, a non-publicly traded REIT, to determine its own US ownership.[64] Applying the look-through rule, only 25.5% (i.e., 50% of US REIT 7's US ownership multiplied by 51% of US REIT 8's stock owned by US REIT 7) of US REIT 8's stock is considered owned by US persons for this purpose. As a result, US REIT 8 is not a Domestically Controlled REIT. A foreign investor that wishes to co-invest in a lower-tier REIT with a private REIT needs to diligence the ownership of the private REIT in order to determine whether the lower-tier REIT may qualify as a Domestically Controlled REIT.

§6.03 NEW EXCEPTIONS UNDER THE 2015 PATH ACT

The 2015 PATH Act enacted two new exceptions to FIRPTA. These constitute significant amendments to the FIRPTA regime enacted over 35 years ago. Some of the new rules contain very convoluted definitions giving the impression that Congress intended to provide relief to targeted groups of taxpayers. Congress introduced the 2016 TCA within one year after the passage of the 2015 PATH Act to clarify certain aspects of these new rules.[65] Notwithstanding the clarifications, additional guidance is still necessary to understand how these exceptions apply.

A. QFPF Exemption

1. *General Rule*

The first new exception provides broad exemption of FIRPTA tax to certain foreign pension funds. Under this exception, a QFPF, or any entity wholly owned by a QFPF,[66] is exempt from FIRPTA tax on:

- disposition gains from all USRPIs;[67]
- REIT distributions that are attributable to gain from a disposition of USRPI;[68] and
- any FIRPTA withholding tax.[69]

---

62. I.R.C. §897(h)(4)(E)(i).
63. This discussion assumes that all the other requirements of I.R.C. §897(h)(4) are satisfied.
64. I.R.C. §897(h)(4)(E)(iii).
65. *See* footnote 3, *supra*.
66. This chapter uses the term QFPF to include an entity wholly owned by a QFPF for ease of discussion.
67. Such gain is otherwise taxable under I.R.C. §897(a).
68. Such amount is otherwise taxable under I.R.C. §897(h)(1).
69. *See* I.R.C. §1445(f)(3)(B).

Foreign pension funds, as an investor class, have a significant amount of capital which they deploy in global investments.[70] These pension funds may be owned by foreign governments or private enterprises. In a speech in March 2013, President Obama unveiled the proposal to attract additional investments from foreign pension funds in US infrastructure assets.[71] A related statement released by the White House indicated that the reasoning for the proposal included the following:

> Infrastructure assets can be attractive investments for long-term investors such as pension funds that value the long-term, predictable, and stable nature of the cash flows associated with infrastructure. Under current law, gains of foreign investors from the disposition of U.S. real property interests are generally subject to U.S. tax under FIRPTA, and foreign investors including large foreign pension funds regularly cite FIRPTA as an impediment to their investment in U.S. infrastructure and real estate assets. With U.S. pension funds generally exempt from U.S. tax upon the disposition of U.S. real property investments, the Administration proposes to put foreign pension funds on an approximately equal footing: exempting their gains from the dispositions of U.S. real property interests, including infrastructure and real estate assets, from U.S. tax under FIRPTA.[72]

Notwithstanding the fact that the White House announcements, on more than one occasion, mentioned attracting foreign pensions' investments in US *infrastructure* assets, the drafters of the 2015 PATH Act opted to exempt QFPFs from FIRPTA tax on gain from a disposition of *all* USRPIs. An abridged definition of a QFPF is given in box **Definition 6.1**.

Definition 6.1: QFPF

A QFPF is any trust, corporation, organization or arrangement that satisfies *all* of the following conditions:[73]

(1) which is created or organized under the law of a country other than the US;[74]

(2) which is established either:

    a. by such country to provide retirement or pension benefits to participants or beneficiaries that are current or former employees (including self-employed individuals) or persons designated by such employees, or

---

70. *See* Willis Towers Watson, Global Pension Assets Study 2016 (February, 2016), global pension fund investors have $13.6 trillion in assets under management in 18 foreign countries. https://www.willistowerswatson.com/en/insights/2016/02/global-pensions-asset-study-2016.
71. This is not the first time that the Obama Administration commented on this issue. President Obama announced a 'comprehensive infrastructure plan to expand and renew our nation's roads, railways and runways.' See Press Release, White House, *President Obama to Announce Plan to Renew and Expand America's Roads, Railways and Runways,* (9/7/10).
72. *See* the White House Office of the Press Secretary, *The 'Rebuild America Partnership': The President's Plan to Encourage Private Investment in America's Infrastructure* (March 29, 2013).
73. I.R.C. §897(l)(2).
74. I.R.C. §897(l)(2)(A).

6. Exceptions to FIRPTA

    b. by one or more employers to provide retirement or pension benefits to participants or beneficiaries that are current or former employees (including self-employed individuals) or persons designated by such employees;[75]

(3) which does not have a single participant or beneficiary with a right to more than 5% of its assets or income;[76]

(4) which is subject to government regulation and with respect to which annual information about its beneficiaries is provided, or is otherwise available, to the relevant tax authorities in the country in which it is established or operates;[77] and

(5) under the laws of the country in which the QFPF is established or operates either:

    a. contributions to such trust, corporation, organization, or arrangement which would otherwise be subject to tax under such laws are deductible or excluded from the gross income of such entity or arrangement or taxed at a reduced rate; or

    b. taxation of any investment income of such trust, corporation, organization or arrangement is deferred or such income is excluded from the gross income of such entity or arrangement or is taxed at a reduced rate.[78]

An aspect that is sometimes overlooked is worth mentioning here. A QFPF that is exempt from FIRPTA tax still may be subject to US net-basis tax if it directly owns an investment that in fact generates ECI (i.e., not just income that is deemed to be ECI under FIRPTA).[79] For example, a QFPF that owns an interest in a partnership that generates active rental income would be subject to US tax on its allocable portion of the rental

---

75. I.R.C. §897(l)(2)(B) as amended by the 2016 TCA. Prior to the 2016 TCA amendment, a QFPF did not include a retirement or pension plan established by the foreign country. According to the General Explanation of Tax Legislation Enacted in 2015, Prepared by the Staff of the Joint Committee on Taxation, March 2016, JCS-1-16 (the '2015 Blue Book'), '[M]ulti-employer and government-sponsored public pension funds that provide pension and pension-related benefits may satisfy this prong of the definition. For example, such pension funds may be established for one or more companies or professions of for the general working public of a foreign country.' See the 2015 Blue Book, page 283, footnote 968.
76. I.R.C. §897(l)(2)(C).
77. I.R.C. §897(l)(2)(D) as amended by the 2016 TCA. Prior to the 2016 TCA amendment, I.R.C. §897(l)(2)(D) required that the information on the QFPF's beneficiaries actually be provided to the relevant tax authorities as opposed to being available for review.
78. I.R.C. §897(l)(2)(E) as amended by the 2016 TCA. The 2016 TCA added that a foreign pension fund whose investment income is excluded from gross income may qualify as a QFPF.
79. Such an investment also may be subject to the additional 30% branch profits tax imposed by I.R.C. §884 unless a statutory or treaty exception applies. See discussion in Ch. 9, *infra*, for possible treaty reduction of the branch profits tax.

income and capital gain (from the sale of the partnership interest or the underlying asset). In essence, the QFPF would be deemed to be engaged in a US trade or business itself,[80] and would have US tax reporting obligations with respect to such investment. Therefore, a QFPF should hold any investment that generates ECI through one or more US Blocker Corporations.[81] Whenever possible, consideration should be given to using a REIT as the US Blocker which may give rise to a more efficient structure.[82]

Some QFPFs also may be eligible for reduced US withholding tax on passive income from the investment. For example, a QFPF that is a foreign government pension trust[83] may be exempt from US tax otherwise imposed on interest and dividends earned under the foreign sovereign exemption.[84] Non-government owned pension funds may be eligible for reduced US withholding tax under an applicable income tax treaty.[85]

2. Unanswered Questions

The multi-prong definition of a QFPF raises numerous questions.[86] A threshold issue is the legal form of a QFPF. The statutory definition of a QFPF includes an 'organization or an arrangement' but there is no definitive guidance of what constitutes an arrangement for this purpose. The 2015 Blue Book states that:

> [F]oreign pension funds may be structured in a variety of ways, and may comprise one or more separate entities. The word 'arrangement' encompasses such alternative structures.[87]

The above statement suggests that an 'arrangement' may be made up of separate entities. However, it does not indicate whether other structures, such as a separate division within a legal entity, may be considered an 'arrangement' for this purpose. In some foreign countries, a single legal entity may have multiple divisions to engage in different functions. For instance, one of these divisions may provide pension benefits while another offers non-pension investment or insurance products. A division that provides pension benefits is typically required by the local governing body to keep separate books and records and is subject to special regulatory supervision. There does not appear to be any policy reason to deny QFPF status to a division that offers pension benefits if all the other requirements of QFPF are met.

---

80. *See* I.R.C. §§864(c)(2), 875(1) and 882 and discussion in §2.03.A., *supra*.
81. Using a US Blocker also would avoid the application of branch profits tax on the ECI. See discussion in §2.04.C., *supra*.
82. *See* Example 5.1, *supra*. In addition, gain from the sale of REIT shares also is exempt from branch profits tax. *See* I.R.C. §884(d)(2)(C).
83. As defined in Temp. Treas. Reg. §1.892-2T(c).
84. *See* I.R.C. §892 discussed in §6.04.A., *infra*.
85. *See* discussion in Ch. 9, *infra*, on applications of special treaty benefits for certain foreign pension fund entities. For example, a number of US tax treaties eliminate the US withholding tax on REIT dividends paid to foreign pension funds.
86. *See* NYSBA, *Report on the changes to FIRPTA under Protecting Americans from Tax Hikes Act of 2015*, no. 1354, dated October 3, 2016. The 2016 TCA, introduced after the issuance of the report, has addressed some of the issues.
87. *See* 2015 Blue Book, page 283, footnote 967.

The requirement that the organization or arrangement is established to provide retirement or pension benefits to current or former *employees* does not appear to extend the QFPF status to a governmental organization that provides certain social benefits, e.g., old-age or medical benefits, to anyone within the general population who may never have been employed.

B. Qualified Shareholder Exemption

1. *General Rule*

The meaning of a Qualified Shareholder is incredibly complex and contains definitions within a definition. The benefit afforded to this category of investors, like the exemption for QFPFs, can be generous. In general, a Qualified Shareholder is completely exempt from FIRPTA tax on gain from a sale of any REIT shares, public or private, regardless of the percentage of its ownership in the REIT. The REIT shares may be owned directly by the Qualified Shareholder or indirectly through one or more partnerships.[88] Additionally, any REIT distribution to a Qualified Shareholder is also exempt from FIRPTA tax;[89] however, such distribution is taxed as an ordinary dividend of a REIT.[90] See an abridged definition of a Qualified Shareholder in **Definition 6.2**.

Definition 6.2: Qualified Shareholder

A Qualified Shareholder is a foreign person that satisfies conditions (1), (2) *and* (3) below.

(1) a. is eligible for benefits of a comprehensive US income tax treaty which includes an exchange of information program, and whose principal class of interest is listed and regularly traded on one or more recognized stock exchanges; or

   b. is foreign limited partnership created or organized under the laws of foreign jurisdiction that has an agreement for exchange of information with the US, which has a class of limited partnership units representing greater than 50% of the value of all the partnership units that is regularly traded on the New York Stock Exchange or Nasdaq Stock Market;

(2) qualifies as a qualified collective investment vehicle (QCIV); and

(3) maintains records on the identity of each person who, at any time during the entity's taxable year, holds directly 5% or more of the class of interests or units in the entity.

---

88. I.R.C. §897(k)(2)(A)(i).
89. I.R.C. §897(k)(2)(A)(ii).
90. *See* I.R.C. §§897(k)(2)(C) and 857(b)(3)(F). However, any distributions attributable to a 10%-or-greater owner of the stock in a REIT through its ownership in the Qualified Shareholder (i.e., an Applicable Investor) are not eligible for the FIRPTA exception for qualified investors and, hence, are subject to FIRPTA tax. See I.R.C. §897(k)(2)(C)(i) and (B).

An abridged definition of a QCIV is stated in **Definition 6.3**.

Definition 6.3: QCIV

A QCIV is a foreign person that is so designated by the IRS[91] or satisfies condition (1) *or* (2) below.

(1) eligible for a reduced US treaty withholding tax rate with respect to ordinary dividends paid by a REIT even if such person holds more than 10% of the stock of the REIT (but only if the dividends article of such treaty imposes conditions on the benefits allowable in the case of dividends paid by a REIT);[92] or

(2) a publicly traded partnership[93] which:

   a. is a withholding partnership for purposes of Chapters 3, 4, and 6 of the Internal Revenue Code;[94] and

   b. would be a USRPHC[95] at any time during the five-year period ending on the date of disposition of, or distribution with respect to, the partnership's interests in a REIT if the foreign partnership were a US corporation.[96]

These rules are very densely worded. The NYSBA PATH Act Report[97] contains a concise summary of the Qualified Shareholder exemption as follows:[98]

- Under the Treaty Rule (i.e., category (1) of QCIV in **Definition 6.3**), a publicly traded foreign property trust[99] that is eligible for reduced US withholding tax under an income tax treaty on ordinary REIT dividends, even if it owns more than 10% of the REIT stock, may be a Qualified Shareholder. Only the equivalent of a widely held public REIT in a foreign treaty country may be entitled to the benefits of this new exception. Potential beneficiaries

---

91. The IRS appears to have broad authority to designate an entity which is either fiscally transparent, or required to include dividends in its gross income, but entitled to a deduction for distributions to persons holding interests (other than interests solely as a creditor) in it as a QCIV. See I.R.C. §897(k)(3)(B).
92. I.R.C. §897(k)(3)(B)(i) as amended by the 2016 TCA, which added the parenthetical language.
93. As defined in I.R.C. §7704(b) and to which I.R.C. §7704(a) does not apply.
94. I.R.C. §897(k)(3)(B)(ii)(ll).
95. Determined without regard to I.R.C. §897(k)(1).
96. I.R.C. §897(k)(3)(B)(ii)(lll).
97. *See* footnote 86, *supra*.
98. The NYSBA PATH Act Report actually describes three different ways for the new Qualified Shareholder exception to apply if one takes into account the special designation by the IRS. As the IRS has not yet exercised its authority to designate any such entity, and it is not clear if the IRS will ever exercise such authority, the discussion herein only focuses on the two ways currently provided by the statute without regard to the designation.
99. *See* 2015 Blue Book page 283, footnote 966.

of this exception include Australian listed property trusts[100] and Dutch *beleggingsinstelling*.[101]
– Under the Publicly Traded Partnership Rule (i.e., category (2) of QCIV in **Definition 6.3**), a foreign partnership that, among other things, is publicly traded on one of the US stock exchanges, and that owns more than 50% of its relevant assets in USRPIs, also may be a Qualified Shareholder.[102]

2. Who Will Benefit?

The Qualified Shareholder exemption is interesting. Like the QFPF rules, a Qualified Shareholder may be completely exempt from FIRPTA tax on the gain from a disposition of REIT shares. The benefit for a Qualified Shareholder is reduced if it has one or more Applicable Investors.[103] An Applicable Investor generally is a person who holds an interest in the Qualified Shareholder and holds more than 10% of the stock of such REIT (whether or not by reason of the person's ownership interest in the Qualified Shareholder).[104] The reduction in benefits is determined by a formula which equals the portion of REIT stock multiplied by a fraction. The numerator of the fraction is the value of the Applicable Investor's non-creditor interests in the Qualified Shareholder and the denominator is the total value of such interests.[105]

In a way, the Qualified Shareholder exemption can be viewed as more generous than the Domestically Controlled REIT Exception. As discussed earlier, the definition of a Domestically Controlled REIT requires US persons to own more than 50% in the value of the shares of the REIT. Accordingly, up to almost half of the gain on the sale of the shares of a Domestically Controlled REIT may be exempt from US tax. However, the other half of the gain is subject to tax in the hands of the US owners.[106] Under

---

100. *See* Art. 6 of the Convention Between the United States of America and the Government of Australia for the Avoidance of Double Taxation and the Prevention of Fiscal Evasion with Respect to Taxes on Income, August 6, 1982, Art. 10(4)(d), as amended by Protocol, September 27, 2001. The Convention is referred to as the US-Australia Treaty.
101. *See* Art. 3 of the Convention Between the United States of America and the Kingdom of the Netherlands for the Avoidance of Double Taxation and the Prevention of Fiscal Evasion with Respect to Taxes on Income, December 18, 1992, Art. 10(4)(c)(iv), as amended by Protocol, March 8, 2004. The Convention is referred to as the US-Netherlands Treaty.
102. See I.R.C. §897(k)(3)(B)(ii) as amended by the 2016 TCA. The amendments made by the 2016 TCA clarified that the requirements of I.R.C. §897(k)(3)(B)(ii)(I), (II) and (III), which are outlined in paragraph (2) of the QCIV definition in Definition 6.3, must all be satisfied.
103. *See* I.R.C. §897(k)(2)(B).
104. I.R.C. §897(k)(2)(D). Regulations have yet to be issued that explain how to apply the language in the parenthetical clause.
105. I.R.C. §897(k)(2)(B)(i). The same haircut applies to (1) the amount realized by the Qualified Shareholder with respect to a disposition of REIT stock, or (2) a distribution from a REIT attributable to gain from sales or exchanges of USRPIs that is treated as amounts realized from a disposition of a USRPI. I.R.C. §897(k)(2)(B)(ii) and (C).
106. *See* discussion in §6.02.C., *supra*.

the Qualified Shareholder exemption, 100% of the gain on the sale of the shares of a REIT maybe exempt from US tax.[107]

At the moment, it is likely that only a handful of structures may qualify for the REIT Treaty Rule and the Publicly Traded Partnership Exception. It will be interesting to see whether fund sponsors will create new structures that are widely held to qualify under this new exception. Obviously, it is expensive to establish and maintain a US publicly traded partnership platform and, hence, such a structure may be suitable only for investments that are sizable. A structure created to take advantage of this exemption may incorporate the following elements:

- a fund sponsor establishes a limited partnership under the laws of Barbados;
- the partnership has a class of general partnership units and a class of limited partnership outstanding;
- the sponsor owns all the general partnership units which equals 9% of the total value of the partnership;
- the limited partnership units, which equals 91% of the value, are regularly traded on the Nasdaq stock market;
- no one person owns more than 10% of the value of the limited partnership interest;
- the partnership owns 100% of the common stock in two private REITs (i.e., REIT A and REIT B); and
- REIT A and REIT B each owns a portfolio of class an office buildings (one portfolio consists of buildings located in New York and the other consists of buildings located in California).

The limited partnership is formed with the intention of satisfying the requirements of a Qualified Shareholder. If the partnership indeed satisfies such requirements when it disposes of the shares of REIT A, then *all* the gain from the sale may be exempt from FIRPTA tax. A foreign investor that sells the limited partnership interest may be exempt from FIRPTA tax under the Publicly Traded Exception discussed above if the interest in the limited partnership satisfies all the requirements of that exception.[108]

§6.04   OTHER SPECIAL RULES

Two situations are often viewed as equivalent FIRPTA exemptions although they are not *per se* exceptions under the FIRPTA regime. The discussion below provides a brief summary of the issues relating to these structures.

The definition of a USRPI is limited to the shares of a US corporation that is a USRPHC. Therefore, a foreign investor may sell the shares of a *foreign* corporation that owns a USRPI without triggering FIRPTA tax.[109] The buyer would inherit the

---

107. For example, all USD 100 of the appreciation of REIT 2 stock (in Example 6.2) would be exempt from US tax under the Qualified Shareholder exemption as compared to an exemption of USD 49 under the Domestically Controlled REIT exemption.
108. The limited partnership interest should be treated as traded on domestic securities markets. See Temp. Treas. Reg. §1.897-9T(d)(2) and discussion in §6.02.B.3., *supra*.
109. Such gain is generally treated as foreign source income that is not subject to tax as ECI. *See* I.R.C. §§864 and 865(a). However, see discussion in §6.04.B.2., *infra*, regarding a

historical tax basis of the USRPI held by the foreign corporation. A liquidation of the foreign corporation that steps up the tax basis of the USRPI to its fair market value generally would be subject to US tax.[110] Therefore, this type of arrangement is suitable in cases where a buyer is willing not to step up the US tax basis of the underlying USRPI.

A special rule exempts certain passive income, including capital gains, from the sale of US stock investments realized by foreign sovereign investors (referred to as the 892 Exemption).[111] The 892 Exemption pre-dates the QFPF exemption but there are some connections between these two sets of rules. The discussion below expands on the implication of this exemption to FIRPTA tax.

A. Foreign Sovereign Exemption

The 892 Exemption excludes the gain from a sale or disposition of the stock of non-controlled USRPHCs (including REITs) by foreign sovereign[112] investors from US tax. This exemption operates similarly to the Domestically Controlled REIT Exception because both apply to gains from sale of less-than-50% owned shares of REITs. However, the 892 Exemption is broader, i.e., more taxpayer favorable, because there is no holding period requirement for the stock sold, no requirement for any domestic ownership, and the exemption also applies to USRPHCs that are not REITs. Fund sponsors sometimes use a parallel REIT for all the foreign sovereign investors who are eligible for the 892 Exemption to reduce the percentage of foreign ownership in a REIT that may qualify for the Domestic Controlled REIT Exception.[113]

A foreign sovereign investor's gain from the disposition of the stock of a less-than-50% owned REIT is not subject to US income tax under the 892 Exemption.[114] However, if a REIT disposes of its USRPI and distributes the proceeds to a foreign sovereign investor, the portion of the proceeds that is attributable to the gain is treated as gain from a sale of the underlying USRPI and subject to FIRPTA tax.[115] A foreign government is generally treated as a corporate resident of its own country;[116] hence,

---

special rule regarding the treatment of certain foreign corporations owned by a foreign sovereign investor. *See* Temp. Treas. Reg. §1.892-5T(b)(1).

110. *See* I.R.C. §§897(d)(1) and 336 which require the corporation to recognize as gain the difference between the fair market value and the adjusted basis for all appreciated assets distributed in liquidation. *See* Ch. 7, *infra*, for a discussion of the FIRPTA nonrecognition provisions.

111. The 892 Exemption also applies to a foreign sovereign's US source dividends or interest from less-than-50% controlled non-commercial entities. *See* I.R.C. §892(a)(1)(A)(i).

112. The temporary regulations use the term 'foreign sovereign' to refer to the universe of foreign governmental investors. *See* Temp. Treas. Reg. §1.892-2T(a)(1).

113. In general, as long as none of the foreign sovereign investors control the REIT, each of the foreign sovereign investors may claim the 892 Exemption.

114. *See* I.R.C. §892(a)(2)(A)(iii). The 892 Exemption does not apply to gains from the disposition of any other USRPIs including gain from the sale of interests in trusts or partnerships.

115. *See* discussion in §5.04.B., *supra*, for a discussion of the tax imposed by I.R.C. §897(h)(1) and the 2007 Notice.

116. I.R.C. §892(a)(3).

the gain is subject to 35% FIRPTA tax and potentially a 30% branch profits tax unless an exception applies.[117] To avoid that onerous result, foreign sovereign investors that own an interest in a REIT through an investment fund may require the fund manager to dispose only of REIT shares and not the underlying assets of the REITs.

The 892 Exemption does not apply to: (1) income derived by an Integral Part (defined below) of the foreign sovereign from the conduct of any commercial activity;[118] (2) income received *by* a Controlled Commercial Entity or received (directly or indirectly) *from* a Controlled Commercial Entity;[119] and (3) income derived from the disposition of any interest in a Controlled Commercial Entity.[120]

The Treasury Department and the IRS promulgated temporary regulations in 1988 to implement the 892 Exemption.[121] They received numerous comments on the current regulations and, in response, issued the 2011 Proposed Regulations[122] to address some of these issues. Although the 2011 Proposed Regulations technically become effective as of the date of their publication as final regulations in the Federal Register, the preamble to the regulations notes that taxpayers may rely on them currently. This is a welcome relief as the proposed regulations provide a number of clarifications that are taxpayer favorable.

1. Definition of Foreign Government

A foreign sovereign investor first must satisfy a status requirement to qualify for the 892 Exemption. The regulations define an eligible foreign government as an Integral Part of or a Controlled Entity of a foreign sovereign.[123] The distinction between the two is important because an Integral Part of a foreign sovereign may be eligible for the 892 Exemption on FIRPTA gains even if it is considered engaged in other commercial activities.[124] However, a Controlled Entity that receives any amount of income from commercial activities, conducted *anywhere in the world*, is not eligible to claim the 892 Exemption.[125]

An Integral Part of a foreign sovereign is defined as 'any person, body of persons, organization, agency, bureau, fund, instrumentality or other body, however designated, that constitutes a governing authority'. In addition, the net earnings of

---

117. Example 5.4., *supra*, illustrates the US federal income tax consequences with respect to such a distribution.
118. I.R.C. §892(a)(2)(A)(i).
119. I.R.C. §892(a)(2)(A)(ii).
120. I.R.C. §892(a)(2)(A)(iii).
121. *See* T.D. 8211, 1988-2 C.B. 214.
122. Notice of Proposed Rulemaking, REG-146537-06 (Nov. 3, 2011).
123. Temp. Treas. Reg. §1.892-2T(a) and Temp. Treas. Reg. §1.892-6T. The 892 Exemption also extends to international organizations and transnational entities. A 'transnational entity' is defined as 'an organization created by more than one foreign sovereign that has broad powers over external and domestic affairs of all participating foreign countries stretching beyond economic subjects to those concerning legal relations and transcending state or political boundaries,' e.g., European Union. Temp. Treas. Reg. §1.892–2T(d).
124. Temp. Treas. Reg. §1.892-5T(d)(4) Example (1)(a).
125. See discussion in §6.04.A.4., *infra*, for a brief discussion of the rules regarding commercial activities.

the governing authority must be credited to its own account or to other accounts of the foreign sovereign, with no portion insuring to the benefit of any private person.[126] Although the 892 Exemption applies more favorably to an Integral Part of a foreign sovereign investor, in the event the US investment generates ECI the foreign sovereign itself, classified as a foreign corporation for US tax purposes, would have US tax reporting obligations.[127]

A Controlled Entity that performs certain non-profit functions may be eligible to claim the 892 Exemption if the non-profit functions constitute 'governmental functions' determined under US standards. In general, activities performed for the general public with respect to the common welfare or which relate to the administration of some phase of government will be considered governmental functions. Examples of such activities include the operation of libraries, toll bridges, or local transportation services and activities substantially equivalent to the Federal Aviation Authority, Interstate Commerce Commission, or United States Postal Service.[128]

Under a special rule, a pension trust established exclusively for employees or former employees of a foreign sovereign constitutes a Controlled Entity if the funds are managed by employees or appointees of the foreign government, the trust provides for retirement, disability, or death benefits in consideration for prior services rendered, and the income of the trust satisfies the foreign government's obligations to participants rather than inuring to the benefit of a private person.[129] The definition of a pension trust under the section 892 regulations is somewhat similar to the definition of a QFPF under new Code section 897(l)(2). However, a pension trust that is a Controlled Entity does not necessarily qualify as a QFPF.

A Controlled Entity does not include a partnership or other entity owned and controlled by more than one foreign sovereign, e.g., a foreign financial organization organized and controlled by several foreign governments.[130]

2. *Controlled Entities v. Controlled Commercial Entities*

Although the labels are similar, there is a world of difference between a Controlled Entity and a Controlled Commercial Entity. A Controlled Entity that does not have any commercial income is, in essence, an extension of a foreign sovereign.[131] Such an entity may claim 892 Exemption on FIRPTA gain from a disposition of *non-controlled*

---

126. Temp. Treas. Reg. §1.892-2T(a)(2).
127. *See* I.R.C. §892(a)(3) and discussion in §6.04.A.4., *infra*.
128. *See* Temp. Treas. Reg. §1.892-4T(c)(4). This rule can be tricky as different countries perform different governmental functions for the benefit of their respective citizens. A specific program or function that is provided by a foreign country but not provided in the US may not qualify as a governmental function.
129. Temp. Treas. Reg. §1.892-2T(c).
130. Temp. Treas. Reg. §1.892-2T(a)(3).
131. A Controlled Entity must be wholly owned by the foreign sovereign and organized under the laws of the same country. Therefore, a wholly owned entity formed under the laws of a country other than the laws of the foreign sovereign's resident country is not eligible for 892 Exemption. Such a wholly owned subsidiary may be eligible for reduced US withholding tax under an applicable income tax treaty if it satisfies all the requirements thereunder. *See* discussion in Ch. 9, *infra*.

USRPHC shares and other qualifying income.[132] In practice, this comes up when a separate juridical entity, i.e., not a division, of a foreign sovereign invests in the US directly.

A Controlled Entity is an entity (such as a corporation) that is separate in form from a foreign sovereign or otherwise constitutes a separate juridical entity that meets all of the following requirements:

- it is *wholly* owned and controlled, directly or indirectly through one or more Controlled Entities, by a single foreign sovereign;
- it is organized under the laws of the foreign sovereign by which it is owned;[133]
- its net earnings do not inure to the benefit of any individual in his personal capacity; and
- its assets would vest in the foreign sovereign on dissolution.[134]

A foreign sovereign investor may not claim any 892 Exemption on passive income, e.g., interest and dividends, paid by a Controlled Commercial Entity. A foreign sovereign investor is considered to control an entity if it holds, directly or indirectly, a 50% or greater interest (by value or vote) in the entity or otherwise has 'effective control' of it.[135] There is no bright-line test for determining the existence of an 'effective control.'[136] A more-than-50% owned entity (foreign or US) is a Controlled Commercial Entity either because it engages in commercial activities or owns a substantial amount of USRPI under the special *per se* rule (discussed in the next section).

The determination of whether an item of passive income, e.g., interest or dividend, from a US payor to a Controlled Entity requires an analysis of the status of both the payor and the recipient. This is because the 892 Exemption does not apply to income received by or from a Controlled Commercial Entity.[137] Therefore, if either party is a Controlled Commercial Entity, then the income does not qualify for 892 Exemption.[138]

---

132. Dividends or interest received by a foreign government from a controlled US corporation should be subject to US withholding tax at a 30% or lower treaty rate, if applicable. I.R.C. §881. Also *see* Ch. 9 for a discussion of selected treaty provisions. The 892 Exemption does not apply to other types of FDAP income.
133. The rule requires the entity to be organized in the same country as the foreign government; therefore, an unincorporated entity that is considered a *per se* corporation owned by a foreign government, as provided by Treas. Reg. §301.7701-2(b)(6), does not appear to satisfy this requirement. Temp. Treas. Reg. §1.892-2T(a)(3)(ii).
134. Temp. Treas. Reg. §1.892-2T(a)(3)(iv).
135. I.R.C. §892(a)(2)(B). *See also* Rev. Rul. 87-6, 1987-1 C.B. 179.
136. Temp. Treas. Reg. §1.892-5T(c)(2) provides that if a foreign government, in addition to holding a small minority interest, is also a substantial creditor of the entity or controls a strategic natural resource which such entity uses in the conduct of its trade or business, then the foreign government may be viewed as having effective practical control over the entity.
137. I.R.C. §892(a)(2)(A)(ii).
138. *See* CCA 200243003 (October 25, 2002).

3. The Per Se Rule for Controlled Commercial Entities

Under a special *per se* rule, a USRPHC[139] or a foreign corporation that would be a USRPHC if it was a US corporation, is deemed to be treated as engaged in commercial activities. Foreign sovereign investors that make multiple investments in the US often establish special purpose vehicles to own the investments. For example, a foreign sovereign may use a special purpose Controlled Entity to own all of its investments that do not generate income from commercial activities. Such an entity may own a mix of foreign and US based investments and be eligible to claim 892 Exemption.

If the entity owns any USRPIs, it must be careful to avoid the special *per se* rule which treats a foreign corporation that *would be* a USRPHC if it were a US corporation as a Controlled Commercial Entity.[140] This rule is not intuitive and has been branded as a trap for the unwary.[141]

The same rules used to determine the USRPHC status of a US corporation apply to determine whether the foreign corporation would be a USRPHC.[142] Under the general rule, a corporation is considered a USRPHC if the value of its USRPIs equals or exceeds the sum of the value of all of its real properties and its trade or business assets.

$$\frac{\text{Fair Market Value of USRPIs}}{\text{Fair Market Value of USRPIs + FRPIs + Trade or Business Assets}} \geq 50.0\%$$

As the USRPHC fraction above shows, passive investment assets are generally not taken into account in determining the USRPHC status of a corporation. As a result, a foreign corporation that owns any amount of USRPI, e.g., shares of REIT stock, together with only other passive investments would be treated as a USRPHC under the general rule. A special investment company rule is intended to alleviate this situation. Under this special rule, if a company's principal business is trading or investing for its own account, then the company may treat certain investment assets,[143] other than USRPIs, as trade or business assets; the company may include the value of such investment assets in the denominator of the USRPHC fraction.[144] The result would be to decrease the ratio of USRPI owned which, in turn, reduces the chances that the company would qualify as a USRPHC.

A company is *presumed* to be trading or investing in the investment assets for its own account if the fair market value of such assets held by the entity equals or exceeds 90% of the sum of all of the entity's assets.[145] Although this special rule is

---

139. As defined in I.R.C. §897(c)(2).
140. Temp. Treas. Reg. §1.892-5T(b)(1).
141. Kimberly S. Blanchard, *Section 892 Controlled Commercial Entities: The USRPHC Trap*, 38 Tax Management Int'l J. 451.
142. *See* §4.03., *supra*, for a discussion of these rules.
143. The assets include cash, securities, receivables, options or contracts to acquire any of the foregoing, and options or contracts to acquire commodities. *See* Treas. Reg. §1.897-1(f)(1)(iii).
144. Treas. Reg. §1.897-1(f)(3)(ii).
145. *Id.*

intended to be helpful, it is often difficult to satisfy the 90% safe harbor[146] unless the value of an entity's non-USRPI investment assets equals or exceeds nine times the value of its USRPIs. To avoid the *per se* rule, a foreign sovereign investor may contribute FRPIs to a foreign subsidiary to balance the mix of the entity's assets so that the value of the entity's USRPIs falls below 50% under the USRHPC fraction.

4. *Commercial Activities*

Commercial activities, for this purpose, is defined very broadly to include any activities that are 'ordinarily conducted by the taxpayer or by other persons with a view towards the current or future production of income or gain.'[147] The threshold for such activities is lower than that required to have a US trade or business.[148] The temporary regulations provide a number of exceptions to the definition of commercial activities. One of the exceptions is the 'holding of net leases on real property or land which is not producing income (other than on its sale or from an investment in net leases on real property)'.[149] Effecting transactions in stocks, securities, or commodities for a foreign government's own account generally does not constitute a commercial activity.[150] Governmental functions also do not constitute commercial activities.[151]

Special rules apply to attribute the commercial activities of certain related parties to one another. Under these rules:

(1) commercial activities of a subsidiary are not attributable to its parent;[152]
(2) commercial activities of a controlled entity are not attributed to such entities' brother/sister related entities;[153]
(3) commercial activities of a parent entity *are* attributed to its subsidiary;[154] and
(4) commercial activities of partnerships are generally attributable to its partners, except for partners of publicly traded partnerships.[155]

---

146. Note, however, that the 90% safe harbor is only a presumption.
147. Temp. Treas. Reg. §1.892-4T(b).
148. As defined under I.R.C. §864(b) and the regulations thereunder. *See* Temp. Treas. Reg. §1.892-4T(b).
149. Temp. Treas. Reg. §1.892-4T(c)(1)(i).
150. This is true regardless of whether such activities constitute a trade or business for purposes of I.R.C. §162 or a US trade or business for purposes of I.R.C. §864. Temp. Treas. Reg. §1.892-4T(c)(1)(ii).
151. Temp. Treas. Reg. §1.892-4T(c)(4).
152. Temp. Treas. Reg. §1.892-5T(d)(2)(i). However, dividends paid by the parent are not eligible for 892 Exemption to the extent the amount is attributable to dividends received by the parent from the subsidiary.
153. Temp. Treas. Reg. §1.892-5T(d)(1).
154. Temp. Treas. Reg. §1.892-5T(d)(2)(ii). This rule is intended to prevent a commercial arm of a foreign government from transferring its investment assets to a subsidiary that does not engage in any commercial activities for the latter to enjoy the 892 Exemption.
155. Temp. Treas. Reg. §1.892-5T(d)(3). In other words, the regulations apply an 'aggregate' theory of the partnership principles to determine whether a foreign governmental entity is considered to be engaged in commercial activities. However, the regulations apply an 'entity' theory and treat gain recognized on the disposition of a partnership interest as the sale of an entity instead of the sale of the underlying assets. As a result, gain from

The 2011 Proposed Regulations, *inter alia*, include a safe harbor rule for certain 'inadvertent' and *de minimis* commercial activities. In general, a commercial activity is treated as inadvertent if the entity's failure to avoid such an activity was, based on all facts and circumstances, reasonable, such failure was timely cured, and adequate records are retained.[156] For this purpose, a failure to avoid the activity is deemed reasonable if the assets used in the entity's total commercial activity do not exceed 5% of its total assets, and the income from commercial activity does not exceed 5% of the total gross income.[157] This safe harbor provides practical relief to taxpayers.

The 2011 Proposed Regulations provide that the commercial activity determination is made annually. As a result, the commercial activity taint has an impact on the entity's status for the entire taxable year but does not carry over to future taxable years.[158] The proposed regulations also include a 'limited partner' exception to the attribution rules from partnerships.[159] Under this exception, commercial activities of a limited partnership are not attributed to its limited partners. However, this exception applies only to partners who do not have rights to participate in the management and conduct of the partnership's business.[160] The proposed regulations make it clear that consent rights in case of certain extraordinary events, however, do not rise to participation in management and conduct of the partnership business.[161]

5. Treatment of a Sovereign as a Foreign Corporation

A foreign government is generally treated as a corporate resident of its own country for US tax and treaty purposes if the government in question grants equivalent treaty treatment to the US government.[162]

A foreign government that has ECI may deduct interest expenses allocable to the income to determine its US net taxable income. The rules applicable to determine a foreign corporation's interest deduction are complex. The regulations generally require a foreign corporation to allocate its total worldwide interest expense between the foreign corporation's US and foreign assets to determine the portion of its interest expense that may be deducted against its US source income.[163] In order to comply with this regulation, a foreign government would have to disclose in its US tax return, *inter alia*, all of its worldwide assets and interest expenses that the foreign government

---

　　the sale of a partnership interest is not eligible for the 892 Exemption. *See* Temp. Reg. §1.892-3T(a)(2).
156. Prop. Treas. Reg. §1.892-5(a)(2).
157. Prop. Treas. Reg. §1.892-5(a)(2).
158. Prop. Treas. Reg. §1.892-5.
159. Prop. Treas. Reg. §1.892-5(d)(5)(iii)(A).
160. Prop. Treas. Reg. §1.892-5(d)(5)(iii)(B).
161. Prop. Treas. Reg. §1.892-5(d)(5)(iii)(B) ('Rights to participate in the management and conduct of a partnership's business do not include consent rights in the case of extraordinary events such as admission or expulsion of a general or limited partner, amendment of the partnership agreement, dissolution of the partnership, disposition of all or substantially all of the partnership's property outside of the ordinary course of the partnership's activities, merger, or conversion.')
162. I.R.C. §892(a)(3).
163. *See* Treas. Reg. §1.882-5.

pays on its outstanding sovereign debt. It is unlikely that a foreign government would comply with this type of requirement. On the other hand, this may be avoided if the foreign government uses a Blocker Corporation to own the USRPI that potentially gives rise to any ECI and, hence, not have to deal with these filing requirements.

§6.05 SUMMARY

Different FIRPTA exceptions apply to different categories of foreign investors. The Cleansing Exception is intended to apply one level of tax to the gain on USRPIs if all the requirements are met. Taxpayers need to be cognizant of the different requirements to satisfy the Publicly Traded Exception. Taxpayers may form joint ventures that satisfy the ownership of the Domestic Controlled REIT Exception and enjoy a FIRPTA exemption on the REIT shares owned by foreign investors.

Foreign pension funds should assess their eligibility for the QFPF exemption. Questions relating to qualification for the exemption should be posed to the Treasury Department and IRS and, hopefully, will be addressed in any upcoming guidance. Fund sponsors may consider whether any of their investment platforms can be structured to qualify for the Qualified Shareholder exemption. Foreign sovereign investors need to plan their USRPI investments carefully in order to qualify for the 892 Exemption.

Chapter 7
FIRPTA Nonrecognition Rules

§7.01	Overview	140
§7.02	General Code Nonrecognition Provisions	141
	A. Contributions to Corporations	141
	B. Corporate Reorganizations	142
	C. Corporate Liquidations	144
§7.03	The FIRPTA Nonrecognition Rules	145
	A. Exchanges of USRPIs in Code Section 351 Transfers and Acquisitive Reorganizations	147
	1. Transfers of USRPIs to a US Corporation in a Code Section 351 Exchange or B Reorganization	147
	2. Foreign-to-Foreign Nonrecognition Exchanges	148
	a. Transfer of USRPHC Stock in a Code Section 351 Exchange or B Reorganization	148
	b. Acquisitive Asset Reorganizations	149
	3. D and F Reorganizations	150
	4. A and C Reorganizations	152
	B. Foreign-to-Foreign Liquidations	153
	C. Inbound Liquidations and Reorganizations	154
	1. The General Rules	154
	2. The Way Forward?	156
	D. Code Section 355 Distributions	157
	E. Other Transfers to and from US Corporations	159
	1. E and F Reorganizations of USRPHCs	159
	2. Outbound Liquidations of US Corporations	160
§7.04	Other Special Rules	160
	A. The Filing Requirement	160
	B. The Section 897(i) Election	162
§7.05	Summary	163
Appendices		165

§7.01 OVERVIEW

US tax principles generally treat a sale, exchange, or other transfer[1] of property as a taxable disposition and, thus, the transferor generally recognizes gain or loss with respect to the transfer.[2] The Code's 'nonrecognition'[3] provisions are exceptions to this general rule. These provisions defer a transferor's recognition of gain or loss on the transfer of property if certain conditions are met.

Subchapter C of the Code governs the US tax consequences of certain corporate transactions (e.g., property distributions and contributions, liquidations, and tax-free reorganizations) and includes many of the nonrecognition provisions relevant to the transfer of property to and by corporations. As a condition for nonrecognition, these provisions generally preserve the transferred property's built-in gain or loss for recognition when the transferee subsequently disposes of the property in a transaction to which a nonrecognition provision does not apply. For example, a corporation generally takes a transferred tax basis in property received in a tax-free reorganization or contribution.[4]

FIRPTA turns off the application of the Code's nonrecognition provisions, including those in Subchapter C, when a foreign person transfers a USRPI, unless additional requirements (referred to as the FIRPTA Nonrecognition Rules) are satisfied.[5] If the transfer of a USRPI does not satisfy the FIRPTA Nonrecognition Rules, gain realized

---

1. The US applies a substance over form approach with respect to the application of tax principles. *See*, e.g., *Commissioner v. Court Holding Company*, 324 U.S. 331 (1945). Therefore, it is necessary to analyze the substance of a transaction to determine whether a taxpayer is treated as selling or transferring a USRPI for tax purposes. For instance, a taxpayer who purchased an option to acquire stock at 30% of the fair market value of the stock is treated as having bought the stock. *See* Rev. Rul. 82-150, 1982-2 CB 110. Separately, US tax rules sometimes create fictional transfers of properties between parties. For example, under the Check-the-Box rules, if an eligible entity that is treated as a disregarded entity from its owner elects to be classified as a corporation for US tax purposes, then the owner of the disregarded entity is *deemed* to have contributed all of the assets and liabilities of the entity to a newly formed corporation under I.R.C. §351. *See* Treas. Reg. §301.7701-3(g)(1)(iv). In the event the owner is a foreign corporation and the disregarded entity owns a USRPI, the election would result in a deemed transfer of the USRPI to a new corporation; such a transfer may trigger FIRPTA tax unless an exception applies.
2. I.R.C. §1001(c).
3. The terms 'tax deferred', 'tax free' and 'nonrecognition' are synonymous in this context. Similarly, the terms 'transferee', 'distributee' and 'acquiror' are synonymous in this context and refer to the party that receives the transferred asset. The term used depends on the specific provision that governs the transfer.
4. *See*, e.g., I.R.C. §362(a) and (b).
5. Nonrecognition provision is broadly defined, for this purpose, as any US tax provision that forestalls the recognition of gain or loss if the requirements of that provision are satisfied. Temp. Treas. Reg. §1.897-6T(a)(2). The Treasury Department Regulations note that nonrecognition provisions include, but are not limited to, I.R.C. §§332, 351, 354, 355, 361, 721, 731, 1031, 1033, and 1036. Thus, the FIRPTA Nonrecognition Rules also apply to nonrecognition transactions that are not in Subchapter C (*e.g.*, when a partnership with foreign partners disposes of a USRPI pursuant to a nonrecognition provision of the Code). The discussion in this chapter is limited to the application of the FIRPTA Nonrecognition Rules to Subchapter C nonrecognition transactions.

7. FIRPTA Nonrecognition Rules

on the transfer is subject to FIRPTA tax notwithstanding that the transfer otherwise qualifies for tax-free treatment under a nonrecognition provision.

The FIRPTA Nonrecognition Rules are extremely complicated and onerous.[6] This chapter highlights some of the most common corporate transactions that are affected by these rules. In particular, this chapter summarizes the application of the Subchapter C nonrecognition provisions and FIRPTA Nonrecognition Rules to certain corporate restructuring transactions.[7]

§7.02 GENERAL CODE NONRECOGNITION PROVISIONS

Common Subchapter C nonrecognition provisions affecting the transfer of property involving corporations include:

- a shareholder's transfer of property to a controlled corporation in exchange for stock of the corporation;[8]
- a transfer of property pursuant to a corporate reorganization;[9] and
- a subsidiary corporation's liquidating distribution of property to its parent corporation.[10]

A. Contributions to Corporations

A person that transfers property to a corporation generally does not recognize any gain or loss realized on the property transferred if three conditions are satisfied. First, the person (or group of persons, referred to as Transferors) transfers 'property' to a corporation (Transferee). Second, the transfer is solely in exchange for stock of the Transferee. Third, the Transferor controls[11] the Transferee corporation immediately after the transfer.[12] **Example 7.1** is a simplified illustration of a transaction in which a shareholder transfers property to a wholly owned corporation that qualifies for

---

6. One commentator has questioned whether the complexities within these rules are still warranted today, especially after the repeal of the *General Utilities* doctrine. *See* Blanchard, Ch. 1 footnote 39, *supra*.
7. *See* Levy, *Planning for Nonrecognition Transactions Involving U.S. Real Property Holding Corporations: Opportunities, Pitfalls, and Unexpected Results*, 2008 TNT 107-32 (June 3, 2008), for a more in-depth break down and technical discussion of the FIRPTA nonrecognition requirements. Mr. Levy's article is regarded as a seminal work in the area.
8. *See* I.R.C. §351.
9. *See* generally I.R.C. §368. There are seven types of reorganization transactions described in I.R.C. §368(a)(1) (and a few more described in other parts of the same Code section). Each type of reorganization contains its own unique requirements a discussion of which is beyond the scope of this book. *See*, e.g., Ginsberg, Levin, and Rocap, *Mergers, Acquisitions, and Buyouts,* (Wolters Kluwer 2017) for an in-depth discussion of the reorganization provisions.
10. *See* I.R.C. §332.
11. Control, for this purpose, means the ownership of 80% of all voting stock and 80% of each class of non-voting stock. *See* I.R.C. §368(c); Rev. Rul. 59-259, 1959-2 C.B. 115.
12. I.R.C. §351(a).

nonrecognition treatment under Code section 351.[13] Shareholder's tax basis in the stock of USCo received is the same as the basis of the Assets transferred.[14] USCo's tax basis in Assets is the same as Shareholder's basis immediately prior to the transfer.[15]

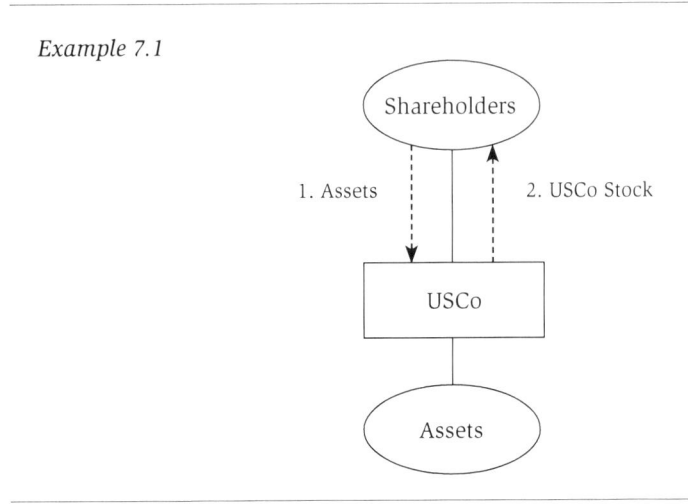

Example 7.1

```
              ┌─────────────┐
              │ Shareholders │
              └─────────────┘
                    ▲
   1. Assets        │        2. USCo Stock
                    │
                    ▼
              ┌─────────┐
              │  USCo   │
              └─────────┘
                    │
                    ▼
              ┌─────────┐
              │ Assets  │
              └─────────┘
```

B.   Corporate Reorganizations

The term 'reorganization' for tax purposes is a defined term that captures a special set of transactions.[16] The parties in the transactions treated as reorganizations would have recognized gain or loss but for the nonrecognition provisions that apply to such reorganizations.[17] The legislative history of the earliest incarnations of the nonrecognition provisions for 'reorganizations' provided that:

> Congress has heretofore adopted the policy of exempting from tax the gain from exchanges made in connection with a reorganization in order that ordinary business transactions will not be prevented on account of the provisions of the tax law ... These provisions are based upon the theory that the types of exchanges specified ... are *merely changes in form and not in substance*, and consequently should not be considered as affecting a realization of income at the time of the exchange. In other words, *these provisions result not in an exemption from tax but in a postponement of tax* until the gain is realized by a pure sale or by such an exchange as amounts to a pure sale. It follows, therefore, that in the case

---

13. I.R.C. §721 provides a comparable rule for a partner's transfer of property to a partnership in exchange for an interest in the partnership. See, e.g., PLR 200851023 (December 19, 2008).
14. I.R.C. §358(a)(1).
15. I.R.C. §362(a).
16. See Bittker & Eustice, *Federal Income Taxation of Corporations & Shareholders*, section 12.01[2] (RIA 2017).
17. See I.R.C. §1001.

of such an exchange the property received should be considered as taking the place of the property exchanged.[18]

If a transaction qualifies as a tax-free reorganization,[19] each 'party to the reorganization'[20] generally does not recognize gain or loss on the transfer of property, including corporate stock and securities, pursuant to the reorganization.[21] These transactions can generally be categorized as the acquisition of stock or assets of one corporation by another corporation or a change in the capital structure or legal identity of a single corporation.[22] Asset reorganizations include A, C and D reorganizations,[23] stock reorganizations include B reorganizations,[24] and single corporation reorganizations such as E and F reorganizations.[25]

A reorganization in which one corporation (sometimes referred to as the Acquiring Corporation) takes over the ownership of the stock or assets of another corporation (referred to as the Target Corporation) is referred to as an 'acquisitive' reorganization. On the other hand, a reorganization that involves a division, e.g., a spin-off, of one corporate entity into multiple entities is referred to as a 'divisive' reorganization.[26]

Example 7.2 is a simplified illustration of the transfers involved in a typical tax-free acquisitive asset reorganization. In the example, Target, a US corporation, transfers all of its assets to Acquiring, another US corporation, in exchange for the latter's common stock.[27] Target then distributes the stock of Acquiring to its shareholders in exchange for its own stock and thereafter ceases to exist.[28] Since the transaction qualifies as a tax-free reorganization: (i) Target does not recognize gain or loss on the transfer of its Assets to Acquiring in exchange for Acquiring Stock or its

---

18. H.R. Rep. No. 179, 68th Cong., 1st Sess. (1924), 1939-1 (Part 2) C.B. 241. (Emphasis added.)
19. To qualify as a reorganization, a transaction must meet all the statutory and judicial requirements including certain anti-abuse doctrines. The judicial requirements reflect a line of court decisions which generally hold that the reorganization provisions are not applicable to transactions that meet the statutory requirements in form only. Some of the judicial requirements have been incorporated into the regulations as continuity of interest, continuity of business enterprise and the business purpose tests. *See*, e.g., Treas. Reg. §1.368-1(b), (d) and (e).
20. I.R.C. §368(b) defines the term to include both corporations involved in the reorganization that results in the acquisition by one corporation of the stock or property of another corporation.
21. The exchange must be made pursuant to a plan of reorganization. *See* I.R.C. §361(a).
22. *See* I.R.C. §368(a)(1).
23. *See* I.R.C. §368(a)(1)(A),(C) and (D).
24. *See* I.R.C. §368(a)(1)(B).
25. *See* I.R.C. §368(a)(1)(E) and (F).
26. A divisive reorganization is typically governed by the rules of I.R.C. §§368(a)(1)(D) and 355.
27. In some cases, a certain amount of other property, referred to as 'boot', also may be transferred in connection with the transfer. A transferor is typically taxable on the gain to the extent of the fair market of the boot received in a transaction that otherwise qualifies for nonrecognition treatment. I.R.C. §356.
28. In some cases, the issuance, distribution and exchange of the stock of the transferee does not actually occur but is deemed to occur.

distribution of the Acquiring Stock to its shareholders, and (ii) Target Shareholders do not recognize gain or loss on their transfer of Target Stock in exchange for Acquiring Stock. Acquiring's tax basis in Target's Assets is the same as the tax basis of Assets in Target's hands.[29] Shareholders' tax basis in the stock of Acquiring is the same as their basis in the stock of Target.[30]

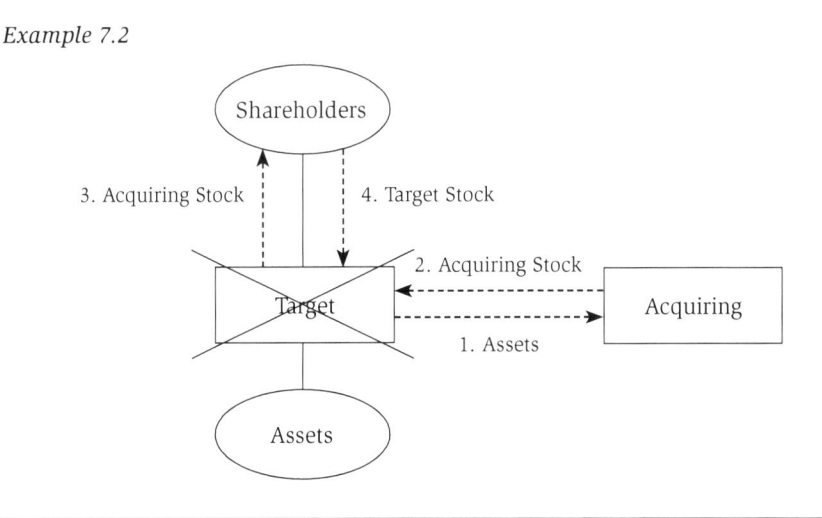

Example 7.2

[Diagram: Shareholders at top connected to Target (crossed out) via "3. Acquiring Stock" and "4. Target Stock"; Acquiring box on right connected to Target via "2. Acquiring Stock" and "1. Assets"; Assets oval at bottom connected to Target.]

C. Corporate Liquidations

As discussed earlier in this book, a corporation that distributes appreciated property to its shareholders generally is subject to tax on the property's built-in gain as a result of the repeal of the *General Utilities* doctrine.[31] An exception to this gain recognition rule applies to certain corporate liquidations.[32] In particular, if a subsidiary corporation completely liquidates into its *parent corporation*, neither the subsidiary nor the parent recognizes gain or loss on the liquidation if the requisite conditions are satisfied.[33] These conditions include the following:

---

29. I.R.C. §362(b).
30. I.R.C. §358(a)(1).
31. See discussion in §1.04.A., *supra*. After the repeal of the *General Utilities* doctrine, I.R.C. §§311(b) and 336(b) generally require a distributing corporation to recognize the gain inherent in any distributed property, in a non-liquidating and a liquidating distribution, respectively, as if the property had been sold to the shareholder.
32. Another exception to *General Utilities* repeal is a transaction that qualifies for I.R.C. §355 distribution. See §7.03.D, *infra*, regarding a discussion on special rules applicable to certain spin-off transactions involving the stock of a USRPHC.
33. I.R.C. §337(a) generally provides for tax-free treatment to the liquidating corporation and I.R.C. §332 generally provides for tax-free treatment to an 80%-or-greater corporate shareholder of the liquidating corporate subsidiary.

7. FIRPTA Nonrecognition Rules

- the parent corporation owns at least 80% of the vote and value of all of the liquidating subsidiary's stock;[34] and
- the liquidating subsidiary distributes all of its property in complete cancellation or redemption in accordance with a plan of liquidation.[35] The distribution either occurs within the tax year in which the plan is adopted, or is one of a series of distributions completed within three years from the close of the tax year during which the first of the series of distribution under the plan is made.[36]

Example 7.3 is a simplified illustration of a complete liquidation of a wholly owned subsidiary into its parent corporation under Code section 332. Subsidiary distributes its appreciated Assets to Parent in the year that it adopts a plan of liquidation in complete cancellation of its stock. Both Parent and Subsidiary do not recognize gain or loss upon the transfer of Assets in exchange for Subsidiary stock. Parent's tax basis in the Assets received in the liquidation would be the same as the basis in the hands of Subsidiary.[37]

Example 7.3

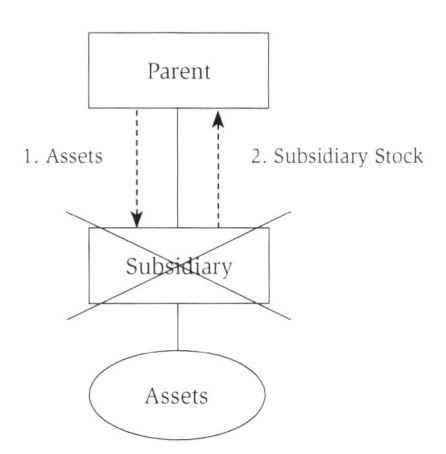

§7.03   THE FIRPTA NONRECOGNITION RULES

As noted above, FIRPTA overrides the Subchapter C nonrecognition provisions with respect to a foreign person's transfer of a USRPI, unless the transaction satisfies the

---

34. I.R.C. §332(b)(1). The parent corporation is required to satisfy the ownership requirement on the date of the adoption of the plan of liquidation and at all times until all the liquidating payments have been distributed by the subsidiary corporation.
35. I.R.C. §332(b)(2). Treas. Reg. §1.332-2(b) requires the shareholder to receive partial payment for its stock in the liquidating corporation; hence, the liquidating corporation must be solvent (i.e., the value of its asset must exceed the liabilities) at the time of its liquidation in order to satisfy this requirement.
36. I.R.C. §332(b)(3).
37. I.R.C. §334(b)(1).

FIRPTA Nonrecognition Rules. Thus, a foreign person's disposition of a USRPI in a corporate restructuring transaction will qualify for nonrecognition treatment only if the transaction satisfies one of the Subchapter C nonrecognition provisions *and* the applicable FIRPTA Nonrecognition Rules.

There are two sets of FIRPTA Nonrecognition rules: (i) Code section 897(d), which applies to a distribution of a USRPI, and (ii) Code section 897(e), which applies to an exchange of a USRPI. The FIRPTA Nonrecognition Rules are contained in temporary regulations that were issued in 1988 and a series of IRS notices that modify the temporary regulations.[38] Therefore, the application of FIRPTA Nonrecognition Rules requires reading the temporary regulations in conjunction with the notices.[39] The fact that the FIRPTA Nonrecognition Rules have not been incorporated into a single regulatory package makes the application of these already complicated rules even more challenging.[40]

The FIRPTA Nonrecognition Rules have two requirements that apply to all distributions and exchanges of USRPIs.[41] First, any gain from the subsequent disposition of the interest distributed or received by the transferor in the exchange would be included in the gross income of the distributee or transferor and be subject to US taxation (referred to as the Subject-to-Tax Requirement).[42] Gain is considered subject to US taxation for these purposes if it is included on a US income tax return, even if there is no actual US tax liability, e.g., the gain is offset with a net operating loss.[43] Secondly, certain procedural requirements are satisfied (referred to as the Filing Requirement).[44]

As discussed below, the FIRPTA Nonrecognition Rules include other requirements that apply in addition to the Subject-to-Tax Requirement and the Filing Requirement. The application of these additional requirements depends on the type

---

38. Notice 2006-46, 2006-1 C.B. 1044, Appendix 7-A; Notice 99-43, 1999-2 C.B. 344, Appendix 7-B; Notice 89-85, 1989-2 C.B. 403, Appendix 7-C; Notice 89-64, 1989-1 C.B. 270, Appendix 7-D; Notice 89-57, 1989-1 C.B. 698, Appendix 7-E; Notice 88-72, 1988-2 C.B. 383, Appendix 7-F; Notice 88-50, 1988-1 C.B. 535, Appendix 7-G.
39. Notice 2006-46 contains the most recent amendments to the FIRPTA Nonrecognition Rules. The modifications in the notice are supposed to be included in the final regulations which have not yet been issued, but taxpayers may choose to apply the exceptions, as well as other changes in the notice, to all dispositions, transfers, or exchanges occurring on or after May 23, 2006.
40. To quote Mr. Levy, 'In the end, significant portions of the original regulatory language are no longer applicable, and many of the other rules set forth in the regulations come with exceptions and with exceptions to exceptions that appear only in the notices or notices that modify other notices.' Levy, footnote 7, *supra*.
41. Temp. Treas. Reg. §§1.897-5T(d) and -6T(a)(1).
42. *Id.*
43. *Id.* On the other hand, the gain is not considered subject to US taxation if the gain is derived by a tax-exempt entity. Under a special transition rule, a USRPI is not considered subject to US taxation for these purposes if, at the time the USRPI is distributed or exchanged, a US income tax treaty entitles the recipient to an exemption from US taxation with respect to a subsequent disposition of the USRPI. Temp. Treas. Reg. §1.897-5T(d)(1)(ii)(A). *See*, e.g., Art. 13(9) of the US-Canada Treaty for an example of such a rule.
44. *See* §7.04.A, *infra*, for a discussion of the Filing Requirement.

7. FIRPTA Nonrecognition Rules

of corporate restructuring transaction at issue. The following discussion summarizes the situations in which these additional requirements apply.

A. Exchanges of USRPIs in Code Section 351 Transfers and Acquisitive Reorganizations

The FIRPTA Nonrecognition Rules have an additional requirement that applies to exchanges of USPRIs. Specifically, a transferor recognizes gain on the exchange of a USRPI unless the property received by the transferor in the exchange is itself a USRPI (referred to as the Hot-for-Hot Requirement) and the Subject-to-Tax Requirement and the Filing Requirement are satisfied.[45] The FIRPTA Nonrecognition Rules provide several exceptions to the Hot-for-Hot Requirement in connection with a foreign person's transfer of a USRPI to a foreign corporation, i.e., a foreign-to-foreign transfer. The application of these exceptions depends on the type of foreign-to-foreign transfer at issue.

1. Transfers of USRPIs to a US Corporation in a Code Section 351 Exchange or B Reorganization

No exceptions to the Hot-for-Hot Requirement apply to a foreign person's transfer of a USRPI to a US corporation in a Code section 351 exchange or a B reorganization. Thus, the foreign person recognizes gain on the transfer unless the transferee US corporation is a USRPHC *immediately after* the exchange.[46]

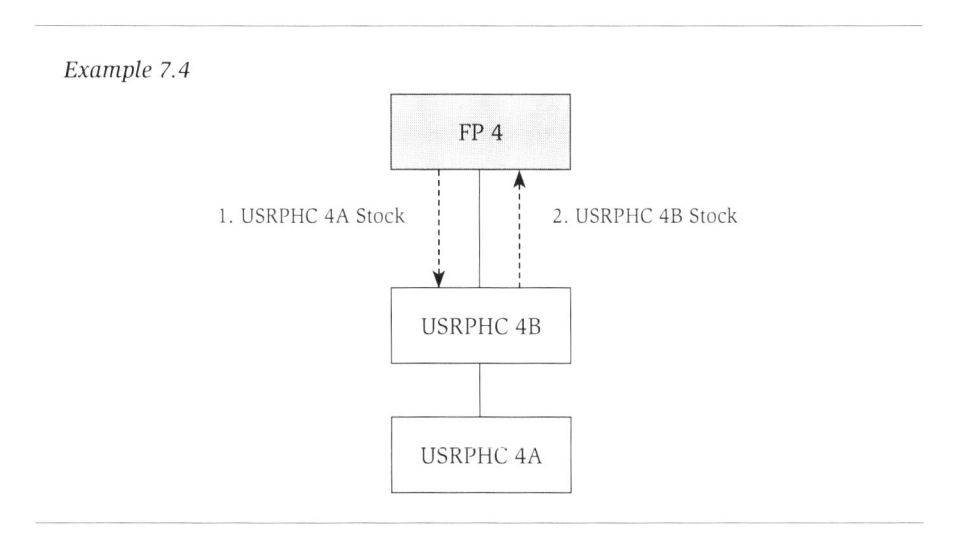

Example 7.4

```
                          ┌─────────┐
                          │  FP 4   │
                          └─────────┘
         1. USRPHC 4A Stock ↓   ↑ 2. USRPHC 4B Stock
                          ┌─────────┐
                          │USRPHC 4B│
                          └─────────┘
                               │
                          ┌─────────┐
                          │USRPHC 4A│
                          └─────────┘
```

---

45. Temp. Treas. Reg. §1.897-6T(a)(1).
46. *Id.* In other words, the receipt of shares of a former USRPHC, whose stock is a USRPI because of the Five-Year Look-Back Period of I.R.C. §897(c)(1)(A), does not satisfy the Hot-for-Hot Requirement.

In **Example 7.4**, a foreign corporate shareholder, FP 4, transfers the stock of USRPHC 4A to USRPHC 4B, a wholly owned US corporation that is a USRPHC, solely in exchange for USRPHC 4B common stock in a transaction that otherwise qualifies for tax-free treatment under Code section 351.[47] Assuming the Filing Requirements are satisfied, the exchange satisfies the FIRPTA Nonrecognition Rules because: (i) FP 4's USRPHC 4B stock would be subject to US taxation upon a subsequent disposition, and (ii) USRPHC 4B is a USRPHC immediately after the exchange.[48]

2. Foreign-to-Foreign Nonrecognition Exchanges

The FIRPTA Nonrecognition Rules provide a number of exceptions to the application of the Hot-for-Hot Requirement to foreign-to-foreign exchanges of: (i) USRPHC stock in a Code section 351 exchange or B reorganization, and (ii) USRPIs in acquisitive asset reorganizations.[49]

a. Transfer of USRPHC Stock in a Code Section 351 Exchange or B Reorganization

The FIRPTA Nonrecognition Rules provide that the Hot-for-Hot Requirement is satisfied with respect to a foreign person's transfer of USRPHC stock in a Code section 351 exchange or B reorganization, including a triangular B reorganization, if:

- the foreign transferee corporation's subsequent disposition of the USRPI would be subject to US taxation (determined under the above discussed principles);
- immediately after the transfer *substantially all* the outstanding stock of the foreign transferee corporation (or the parent corporation in the case of a triangular B reorganization) is owned by the same persons that, immediately before the transfer, owned the stock of the USRPHC; and
- the foreign transferor does not dispose of the foreign transferee corporation stock received in the exchange within *one year* from the date of the exchange.[50]

In **Example 7.5**, FP 5 transfers the stock of USRPHC 5 to a wholly owned foreign corporation, FP 5 Sub. After the transfer, FP 5 owns all the stock of FP 5 Sub, which owns all the stock of USRPHC 5. To satisfy the FIRPTA Nonrecognition Rules applicable to foreign-to-foreign exchanges, FP 5 must *not* dispose of any of the FP 5 Sub stock that it receives in the exchange within the one-year period following the transfer. FP 5 would violate this requirement if it transfers the FP 5 Sub stock in a transaction that constitutes a disposition for any purposes of the Code.[51] Hence, even an internal transfer of the FP 5 Sub stock by FP 5 within the one-year period would violate this requirement and cause the original contribution to be subject to FIRPTA.

---

47. I.R.C. §351.
48. *See* I.R.C. §897(e) and Temp. Treas. Reg. §1.897-6T(a)(1).
49. Temp. Treas. Reg. §1.897-6T(b)(1), as modified by Notice 2006-46, 2006-1 C.B. 1044.
50. Temp. Treas. Reg. §1.897-6T(b)(1)(iii), as modified by Notice 2006-46, Sec. 3(c), footnote 38, *supra*. (Emphasis added.)
51. *See* Treas. Reg. §1.897-1(g).

7. FIRPTA Nonrecognition Rules

Example 7.5

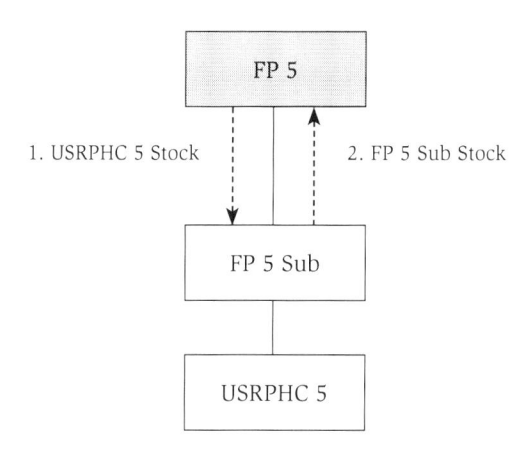

```
            ┌────────┐
            │  FP 5  │
            └────────┘
              ↑    │
1. USRPHC 5 Stock  │  2. FP 5 Sub Stock
              │    ↓
            ┌────────┐
            │ FP 5 Sub│
            └────────┘
                │
            ┌────────┐
            │USRPHC 5│
            └────────┘
```

In summary, this exception to the Hot-for-Hot Requirement has two potential traps for the unwary. First, the exception only applies to the transfer of *USRPHC stock*. The transfer of another type of USRPI, e.g., a building, is taxable unless another provision of the Nonrecognition Rules is satisfied. Secondly, the one-year holding period is absolute. If FP 5 Sub in **Example 7.5** transfers the USRPHC 5 stock to another foreign corporation, FP 5 Sub, will have to comply with the one-year holding period requirement with respect to the stock of the transferee corporation. However, this subsequent transfer does not affect the application of the one-year holding period requirement to FP 5 with respect to the FP 5 Sub stock.

Subsequent to the original enactment of FIRPTA, a concern arose that a foreign person could avoid FIRPTA by contributing for no consideration a USRPI to a foreign corporation in which the person was already a shareholder. This concern led to the codification of Code section 897(j), which treats the transfer of a USRPI to a foreign corporation as paid in surplus or as a contribution to capital as an exchange of the USRPI for stock of the foreign corporation.[52] As a result, a contribution of a USRPI to a foreign corporation generally is taxable unless it satisfies the FIRPTA Nonrecognition Rules. This is another potential trap for the unwary. If the parties to a contribution are not aware that the contribution is treated as *a transfer of the USRPI* for US tax purposes, they could inadvertently fail to satisfy the Filing Requirement, and the contribution could be subject to FIRPTA notwithstanding that the contribution otherwise satisfied the Subject-to-Tax Requirement and the Hot-for-Hot Requirement.

b. *Acquisitive Asset Reorganizations*

A foreign corporation that owns a USRPI may be subject to FIRPTA if it transfers, or is deemed to transfer, the USRPI to another foreign corporation as part of an

---

52. The transferee foreign corporation may or may not issue any stock in return for the contribution received. *See* I.R.C. §897(j) and Temp. Treas. Reg. §1.897-6T(b)(5).

acquisitive asset reorganization. This comes up frequently when USRPHC stock is transferred in an internal restructuring transaction. The application of the Hot-for-Hot Requirement to these transfers is subject to a number of exceptions, depending on the type of acquisitive asset reorganization in question. The following discussion summarizes the application of the Hot-for-Hot Requirement to the various types of acquisitive asset reorganizations. The examples in the discussion assume that the transfer otherwise qualifies as a tax-free reorganization under Subchapter C.

3. D and F Reorganizations

The Hot-for-Hot Requirement does not apply to a foreign Target Corporation's transfer of a USRPI to a foreign Acquiring Corporation in a Code section 361(a) exchange that is part of an acquisitive D reorganization[53] or an F reorganization if two requirements are satisfied. First, the foreign Acquiring Corporation's subsequent disposition of the USRPI must be subject to US taxation (determined under the above discussed principles). Secondly, the foreign Target Corporation must distribute the stock of the foreign Acquiring corporation in a transaction that qualifies *only* under Code section 354 (referred to as the Distribution Requirement).[54]

The application of the FIRPTA Nonrecognition Rules to acquisitive D reorganizations and F reorganizations raises a few issues that are worth further consideration. In the case of acquisitive D reorganization, the Distribution Requirement requires that no property other than foreign Acquiring Corporation stock or securities (i.e., boot) is transferred in exchange for any of the foreign Target Corporation's assets.[55] Accordingly, taxpayers should carefully consider the US tax characterization of the consideration received in a foreign-to-foreign acquisitive D reorganization that includes the transfer of a USRPI to the Acquiring Corporation. For example, taxpayers need to ensure that the foreign Acquiring Corporation stock received in the reorganization is qualifying consideration under US tax principles. In this regard, 'nonqualified preferred stock,'[56] a type of preferred stock for corporate law purposes, is treated as boot for US tax purposes.

---

53. When a series of integrated steps result in a corporation acquiring substantially all of a transferor corporation's assets followed by a liquidation of the transferor, and the transferor's shareholders control the acquiring corporation, the steps typically constitute a type D reorganization. Many internal corporate restructuring transactions occur in a manner that may fall within the description of a D reorganization. For instance, the steps of the transaction in Example 7.2 (assuming the Shareholders control Target and Acquiring) resemble those involved in a D reorganization.
54. Temp. Treas. Reg. §1.897-6T(b)(1)(i).
55. In a non-FIRPTA context, Target Corporation shareholders in a D reorganization can receive boot in exchange for their Target Corporation stock. In that case, the target shareholders are required to recognize the gain in their target corporation stock to the extent of the boot; this gain may be recharacterized as a dividend in certain circumstances. *See* I.R.C. §356(a)(1) and (2).
56. Nonqualified preferred stock is defined as: (1) stock that is limited and preferred as to dividends and does not participate in corporate growth to any significant extent, and (2) within the twenty-year period beginning on the issue date of the stock: (a) the holder has the right to require the issuer, or a related person, to redeem the stock; (b) the issuer, or

7. FIRPTA Nonrecognition Rules

In **Example 7.6** Target ForCo transfers an appreciated USRPI, i.e., the stock of USRPHC 6, to Acquiring ForCo in a transaction that satisfies the Subchapter C requirements for an acquisitive D reorganization. To make sure that Target ForCo does not trigger any gain under the FIRPTA Nonrecognition Rules, it must not receive any consideration other than the common stock of Acquiring ForCo. If Target ForCo *receives USD 1 of boot* (e.g., if it receives any Acquiring Corporation nonqualified preferred stock), then Target ForCo would not satisfy the Distribution Requirement and *all its inherent gain in USRPHC 6 would be subject to US tax under FIRPTA.* Finally, Target ForCo also must comply with the Filing Requirement with respect to the transfer of the stock of USRPHC 6.[57]

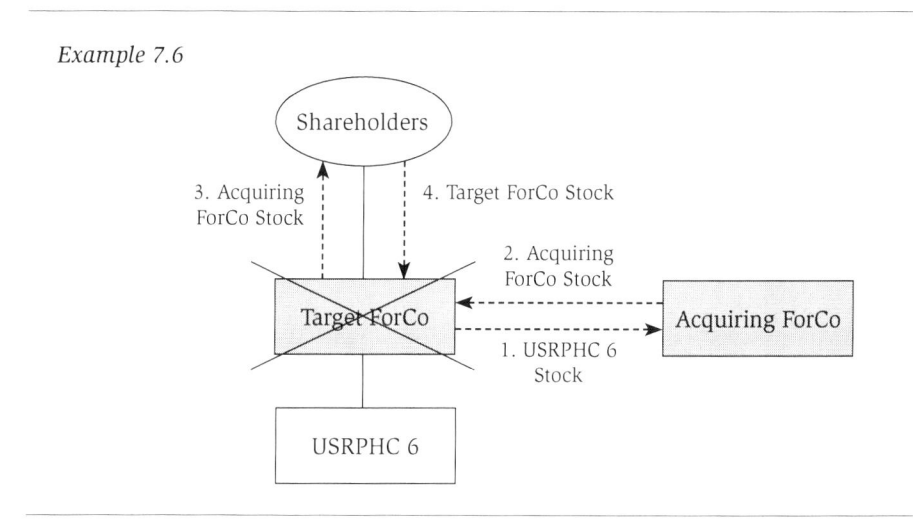

Example 7.6

Because an F reorganization is a mere change in identify, form, or place of organization of one corporation, e.g., the continuance of a Canadian corporation formed under the Companies Act of one province to one formed under the Canada Business Corporations Act,[58] an F reorganization does not involve boot. Thus, a foreign-to-foreign F reorganization of a foreign corporation that owns a USRPI should satisfy the Distribution Requirement. This result notwithstanding, if an F reorganization involves the transfer, or deemed transfer, of a USRPI, the reorganization must satisfy the other requirements of the FIRPTA Nonrecognition Rules, *including the Filing Requirement*, to avoid triggering FIRPTA tax. Because an F reorganization may occur within a larger transaction that affects more than a mere change of ownership,[59] a foreign

---

related person, is required to redeem the stock; (c) the issuer, or a related person, has the right to redeem such stock and it is more likely than not that such right will be exercised; or (d) the dividend rate on such stock varies with reference to interest rates, commodity prices, or other similar indices. *See* I.R.C. §351(g)(2).

57. See discussion in §7.04.A., *infra.*
58. *See* PLR 7752074 (September 30, 1977).
59. Treas. Reg. §1.368-2(m)(3)(ii).

corporation that owns a USRPI and engages in an internal restructuring transaction would be well advised to identify any potential deemed transfers of USRPIs that may be subject to FIRPTA and ensure that the parties satisfy the Filing Requirement.

4. A and C Reorganizations

There are three exceptions to the Hot-for-Hot Requirement with respect to a foreign Target Corporation's transfer of a USRPI to a foreign Acquiring Corporation in an exchange that is part of an A reorganization (i.e., a merger) or C reorganization, including a triangular A or C reorganization. The exceptions apply to different ownership structures of the foreign Target Corporations. Each of these exceptions has three requirements that must be satisfied, two of which are common to each of the exceptions and the last of which is unique to each exception.

The requirements common to each of the exceptions are as follows: (i) the foreign Acquiring Corporation's subsequent disposition of the USRPI would be subject to US taxation (determined under the above discussed principles), and (ii) the foreign Target Corporation shareholders exchange their foreign Target Corporation stock for foreign Acquiring Corporation stock (or stock of its parent corporation in a triangular reorganization) in a transaction that qualifies *only* under Code section 354(a) (i.e., the same Distribution Requirement that applies to foreign-to-foreign D and F reorganizations).

The first exception's unique requirement is that the foreign Target Corporation shareholders own *more than 50%* of the voting stock of the foreign Acquiring Corporation (or its parent corporation in a triangular reorganization) immediately after the reorganization.[60] The 50% requirement restricts the application of this exception to internal A and C reorganizations.

The second exception's unique requirement is that the stock of the foreign Target Corporation, including a Code section 381(a) predecessor, would not have been a USRPI at any time during the five-year period ending on the date of the reorganization if it were a US corporation (referred to as the Non-USRPHC Exception).[61] A commentator observed that this exception may be an acknowledgement by the Treasury Department and the IRS that the US taxing authority is preserved 'in any nonrecognition transaction in which the transferee corporation takes a carryover basis

---

60. Temp. Treas. Reg. §1.897-6T(b)(1)(ii) as modified by Notice 2006-46, Sec. 3(b). The intent of the 50% limitation is to restrict the application to the exception internal restructurings where the transferor corporation shareholders control the transferee corporation after the transaction. *See* Notice 2006-46, Sec. 3(a). The notice also provides that in determining whether the 50% limitation is met where the foreign Acquiring Corporation owns more than 50% of the foreign Target Corporation before the merger or C reorganization (i.e., an upstream transaction), the foreign Acquiring Corporation's shareholders before the reorganization that continue to be foreign Acquiring Corporation shareholders after the reorganization will be treated as foreign Target Corporation shareholders to the extent of their pre-reorganization indirect ownership in the foreign Target Corporation owned through the foreign Acquiring Corporation. *Id.*
61. Notice 2006-46, Sec. 3(b), first bullet, footnote 38, *supra*.

7. FIRPTA Nonrecognition Rules

in a transferred USRPI and would be subject to US tax on a subsequent disposition of that USRPI.'[62]

The third exception's unique requirement is: (i) prior to the exchange, the stock of the foreign Target Corporation and foreign Acquiring Corporation[63] and, after the exchange, the stock of the foreign Acquiring Corporation are regularly traded[64] on an Established Securities Market,[65] and (ii) if the foreign Target Corporation would have been a USRPHC at any time during the previous five years if it were a US corporation, no foreign Target Corporation shareholder owned greater than 5% interest of the foreign Target Corporation at such time (referred to as the Foreign Publicly Traded Nonrecognition Exception).[66]

Foreign corporations that engage in merger transactions often design the transaction to qualify for tax-free treatment under local country law. Because the corporate and tax laws of different countries vary and often are different from the US rules that govern tax-free mergers,[67] it is important to first make sure that the steps designed to satisfy the local country nonrecognition rules also satisfy Subchapter C nonrecognition provisions. A transaction that fails to satisfy the applicable Subchapter C nonrecognition rules will be taxable for US tax purposes notwithstanding the application of the FIRPTA Nonrecognition Rules. Once it is clear that a foreign merger qualifies for nonrecognition treatment under general US tax principles, then it is necessary to make sure that the transaction also satisfies the FIRPTA Nonrecognition Rules.

B. Foreign-to-Foreign Liquidations

A foreign subsidiary corporation's distribution of a USRPI to its 80% or greater foreign parent corporation in a complete liquidation[68] is not subject to FIRPTA tax if the foreign parent corporation satisfied the Subject-to-Tax and Filing Requirements and the foreign parent corporation's tax basis in the USRPI is not greater than the

---

62. See Levy, footnote 7, *supra*, at 9.
63. In the context of a forward triangular merger and triangular C reorganization, this requirement is determined by reference to the stock of the foreign Target Corporation and the corporation in control of the foreign Acquiring Corporation. Notice 2006-46, Sec. 3(c). In the context of a reverse triangular merger, this requirement is determined by reference to the stock of the corporation in control of the foreign Target Corporation and the foreign Acquiring Corporation. *Id.*
64. As defined in Treas. Reg. §1.897-1(n) and Temp. Reg. §1.897-9T.
65. See Notice 2006-46, Sec. 3(c), footnote 38, *supra*.
66. The ownership is determined under the rules of Treas. Reg. §1.897-1(c)(2)(iii) and Temp. Reg. §1.897-9T. *See* Notice 2006-46, Sec. 3(b), second bullet, footnote 38, *supra*.
67. For example, it is possible to defer Canadian income tax in an amalgamation transaction that combines the legal existence of two or more corporate entities into a single entity. If one of the amalgamating Canadian entities owns a USRPI, then it is necessary to make sure that the legal steps of the amalgamation also would qualify the transaction as a tax-deferred reorganization for US tax purposes. *See* Chong, *Surviving North or the Border: Structuring a Statutory Merger in Canada to Qualify s A U.S. Tax-Free Reorganization*, 41 Tax Mgm't Int'l J. 611.
68. *See* I.R.C. §332 and general description under §7.02.C., *supra*.

tax basis of the USRPI in the hands of the foreign subsidiary corporation before the distribution, increased by the amount of gain (if any) recognized by the foreign subsidiary corporation for US federal income tax purposes (referred to as the Basis Requirement).[69] **Example 7.7** illustrates a liquidating distribution by a foreign corporation of USRPI (i.e., a USRPHC) to its 100% foreign parent.

Example 7.7

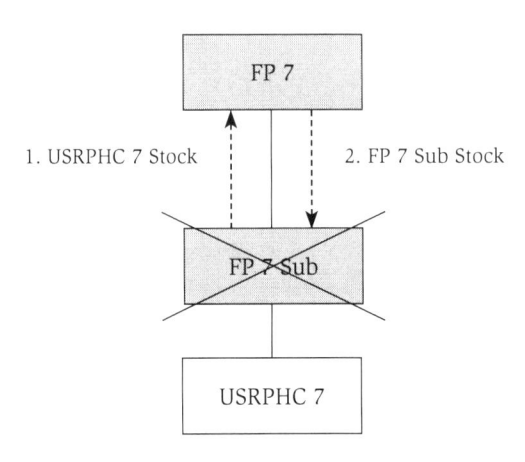

```
        ┌──────────┐
        │   FP 7   │
        └──────────┘
         ▲        │
1. USRPHC 7 Stock │ 2. FP 7 Sub Stock
         │        ▼
        ┌──────────┐
        │ ╲FP 7 Sub╱│
        │  ╲    ╱  │
        │   ╲  ╱   │
        │    ╳     │
        │   ╱  ╲   │
        │  ╱    ╲  │
        └──────────┘
             │
        ┌──────────┐
        │ USRPHC 7 │
        └──────────┘
```

FP Sub 7 in **Example 7.7** will not be required to recognize gain on the distribution of the USRPHC 7 stock to its Parent, FP 7, in connection with its liquidation if: (i) FP 7 would be subject to US tax on a subsequent disposition of the USRPHC 7 stock (i.e., the Subject-to-Tax Requirement is satisfied), (ii) FP 7's basis in the USRPHC 7 stock is not greater than the FP 7 Sub's US tax basis of the same stock at the time of the distribution (the Basis Requirement is satisfied), and (iii) FP 7 satisfies the Filing Requirement.[70]

C. Inbound Liquidations and Reorganizations

1. *The General Rules*

The FIRPTA Nonrecognition Rules include specific provisions regarding a foreign corporation's transfer of a USRPI in connection with an 'inbound' liquidation or acquisitive asset reorganization. The requirements of these provisions differ depending on the whether the inbound transaction is a complete liquidation[71] or tax-free

---

69. I.R.C. §897(d)(2).
70. *See* I.R.C. §897(d)(2) and Temp. Treas. Reg. §1.897-5T(c)(2).
71. As described in I.R.C. §332.

7. FIRPTA Nonrecognition Rules

reorganization and, in the case of a reorganization, whether the USRPI is transferred in an exchange[72] or if the stock of a USRPHC is distributed.[73]

A foreign subsidiary corporation does not recognize gain on the distribution of a USRPI to its US parent corporation in an inbound Code section 332 liquidation if the Subject-to-Tax, Basis, and Filing Requirements are satisfied, *and* the foreign subsidiary corporation pays a special tax (referred to as the Toll Charge, which is discussed below). An inbound asset reorganization involves a two-step analysis. An inbound asset reorganization is treated as if: (1) the foreign Target Corporation transfers its assets (including USRPIs) to the domestic Acquiring Corporation in exchange for domestic Acquiring Corporation stock, and (2) the foreign Target Corporation thereafter distributes the domestic Acquiring Corporation stock to its shareholders in exchange for the shareholders' Target Corporation stock in complete liquidation. The foreign Target Corporation must recognize gain on the inbound transfer of any USRPI in step 1 unless the Hot-for-Hot Requirement, the Subject-to-Tax Requirement, and the Filing Requirement are satisfied.[74] To qualify for nonrecognition treatment, the domestic Acquiring Corporation must be a USRPHC immediately after the exchange. The foreign Target Corporation generally must recognize gain on distribution of the USRPHC stock in step 2 unless:

- the Subject-to-Tax Requirement is satisfied with respect to the foreign Target Corporation shareholder's subsequent disposition of the USRPHC stock;
- the Basis Requirement is satisfied with respect to the foreign Target Corporation shareholder's basis in the stock of the foreign Target Corporation;
- the Filing Requirement is satisfied; and
- the foreign Target Corporation pays the Toll Charge.[75]

The Toll Charge is an amount equal to the tax and interest that would have been imposed upon all persons that disposed of the foreign corporation's stock[76] during a look-back period (referred to as the Toll Charge Look-Back Period),[77] if the foreign subsidiary corporation had been a domestic corporation.[78] The Toll Charge Look-Back Period for an inbound Code section 332 liquidation is different than the Toll Charge Look-Back Period for an inbound asset reorganization.

The Toll Charge Look Back-Period for an inbound Code section 332 liquidation is the period beginning on the date that is ten years before the date on which the US parent corporation or a related person[79] is in control[80] of the foreign liquidating

---

72. As described in I.R.C. §361(a).
73. Pursuant to I.R.C. §361(c).
74. I.R.C. §897(e) and Temp. Treas. Reg. §1.897-6T(a)(1).
75. Notice 89-85 as modified by Notice 2006-46, Sec. 2, footnote 38, *supra*.
76. This also includes the stock of a corporation from which the foreign subsidiary corporation acquired the distributed assets in a transaction that is described in I.R.C. §381 transaction (i.e., a I.R.C. §332 liquidation or acquisitive asset reorganization).
77. Prior to the amendment by Notice 2006-46, the look-back period for the Toll Charge went all the way to the June 18, 1980, the enactment date of FIRPTA. *See* Notice 89-85, footnote 38, *supra*.
78. Notice 2006-46, footnote 38, *supra*.
79. Within the meaning of I.R.C. §267(b).
80. Within the meaning of I.R.C. §304(c).

corporation and ending on the date of the liquidation.[81] The Toll Charge Look Back-Period for an inbound asset reorganization is the earliest of the period: (i) beginning on the date that is ten years before the date on which the domestic Acquiring Corporation or a related person[82] is in control[83] of the foreign Target Corporation and ending on the date of the reorganization; or (ii) beginning on the date that is ten years before the date of the reorganization and ending on the date of the reorganization.[84]

The Toll Charge associated with inbound transactions is a retroactive FIRPTA tax imposed on the gain from a disposition of the stock of a fictional USRPHC (i.e., the rules treat the foreign Target Corporation as if it were a US corporation). The Toll Charge has been the subject of extensive controversy from the time it was first introduced.[85] When FIRPTA was enacted in 1980, a US purchaser could purchase from a foreign seller the stock of a foreign corporation that owned a USRPI and then liquidate the foreign corporation tax-free. As a result of these transactions, the US purchaser obtained a stepped up tax basis in the USRPI and the foreign seller avoided FIRPTA. This result is no longer possible after the repeal of the *General Utilities* doctrine. Despite the repeal of the *General Utilities* doctrine in 1986, the Toll Charge, which was introduced to prevent the abuse available prior to the repeal, is still effective.

The practical application of the Toll Charge in situations involving widely held corporations raises significant issues. For example, it is not possible for a publicly traded corporation to gather the information to determine the amount of the gain that *all of its shareholders* realized from the prior sale of their shares. Furthermore, the Toll Charge applies even though the distributee of the USRPI takes a carryover basis in the USRPI and, thus, would be subject to US tax on the USRPI's built-in gain upon a subsequent disposition of the USPRI.

2. The Way Forward?

A 2013 private letter ruling provides an interesting twist in the application of the FIRPTA Nonrecognition Rules to an inbound F reorganization.[86] The taxpayer in the ruling was a foreign corporation with stock listed on both foreign and US stock exchanges. The taxpayer's sole asset was the stock of a USRPHC. The taxpayer wanted to reincorporate as a US corporation and delist its shares from the foreign

---

81. Notice 2006-46, footnote 38, *supra*.
82. Within the meaning of I.R.C. §267(b).
83. Within the meaning of I.R.C. §304(c).
84. Notice 2006-46, Sec. 2, footnote 38, *supra*.
85. *See*, e.g., the New York State Bar Association Tax Section's comprehensive report on the temporary regulations, *Report on the Temporary and Proposed Regulations under §§897(d) and (e) and Certain Related Provisions,* dated January 16, 1989, no. 600 (hereinafter referred to as the NYSBA FIRPTA Nonrecognition Report), Klein, *FIRPTA and Code Nonrecognition Provisions,* TPI Briefing (1983); Klein, *Beware of Inbound Reorganization Involving Real Estate,* TMIJ, 16 Tax Mgm't Int'l J. 376 (1987); Blanchard, Ch. 1 footnote 39, *supra*.
86. PLR 201321007 (May 24, 2013). *See* Blanchard, *FIRPTA in the 21st Century – Installment Seven: A Valentine to Domestication,'* 42 Tax Mgm't Int'l J. 556 (2013), and Friedline and McKniff, *IRS Rules Favorably on an Inbound Reorganization Involving U.S. Real Estate,* 41 Real Estate Tax'n 52 (2014).

stock exchange.[87] In accordance with the existing authorities, the IRS held that the FIRPTA Nonrecognition Rules applied to the taxpayer's transfer of the USRPHC stock as part of the F reorganization if the taxpayer paid the Toll Charge.

Then things got interesting. The IRS ruled that the taxpayer could exclude the gain realized by less-than-5% foreign shareholders during the Toll Charge Look-Back Period in determining the amount of its Toll Charge. In effect, the ruling treated these foreign shareholders as if they were shareholders of a publicly traded US corporation, and permitted such shareholders to avail themselves of the Publicly Traded Exception.[88] This ruling addresses, to a large extent, the key criticism with respect to the Toll Charge: it is difficult for a foreign corporation to determine the amount of gain realized by *all its shareholders* during the Toll Charge Look-Back Period.

The US Securities Exchange Commission requires publicly traded corporations to report the changes in the ownership structure when a shareholder's ownership exceeds or drops below 5%. Regulators in other countries may have similar requirements. Thus, a publicly traded foreign corporation may be able to track the dates (and the corresponding stock prices) of when its 5%-or-greater shareholders acquired and disposed of their stock and reasonably estimate the gain realized by these shareholders during the Toll Charge Look-Back Period – a practical approach to determining the Toll Charge. It would be interesting to see if, going forward, the Treasury Department and the IRS will be willing to apply this method to all situations that involve a Toll Charge.

D. Code Section 355 Distributions

Under Code section 355, a corporation (referred to as Distributing) can distribute the stock of a controlled subsidiary (referred to as Controlled) to its shareholders (referred to as Distributees) without Distributing or the Distributees recognizing gain or loss.[89] This divisive distribution of Controlled stock can be a standalone distribution or part of a D reorganization (e.g., Distributing transfers part of its assets to Controlled prior to the distribution) and can be structured in a number of ways, including a pro-rata distribution to the Distributees of Controlled stock with respect to Distributing's stock (referred to as a spin-off). If a Distributee receives Controlled stock in a Code section 355 distribution, the Distributee determines its basis in the Controlled stock under Code section 358. For example, in a spin-off, the Distributee generally is required to allocate the pre-distribution basis of its Distributing stock between its Distributing and Controlled stock after the distribution.[90]

If Distributing is a foreign corporation and Controlled is a USRPHC, Distributing recognizes gain on its distribution of Controlled to the extent that the Distributees'

---

87. In other words, the taxpayer becomes a US corporation whose stock is listed only on a US stock exchange after the reorganization.
88. *See* I.R.C. §897(c)(3) and discussion in §6.02.B., *supra*. This favorable treatment is conditioned on the fact that the shares of the newly domesticated corporation will qualify for the Publicly Traded Exception after the reorganization.
89. I.R.C. §355 only applies if certain requirements are satisfied. I.R.C. §355 and the regulations thereunder are very complex and beyond the scope of this discussion.
90. I.R.C. §358 and Treas. Reg. §1.358-2.

The US Foreign Investment in Real Property Tax Act: A Practical Guide

aggregate post-distribution Controlled stock basis, determined under Code section 358, exceeds Distributing's pre-distribution Controlled stock basis. Thus, Distributing recognizes gain to the extent that its pre-distribution Controlled stock gain is not preserved in the hands of the Distributees after the distribution, and the Subject-to-Tax Requirement and the Filing Requirement are satisfied. In other words, the Code section 355 distribution must satisfy the Basis Requirement.[91]

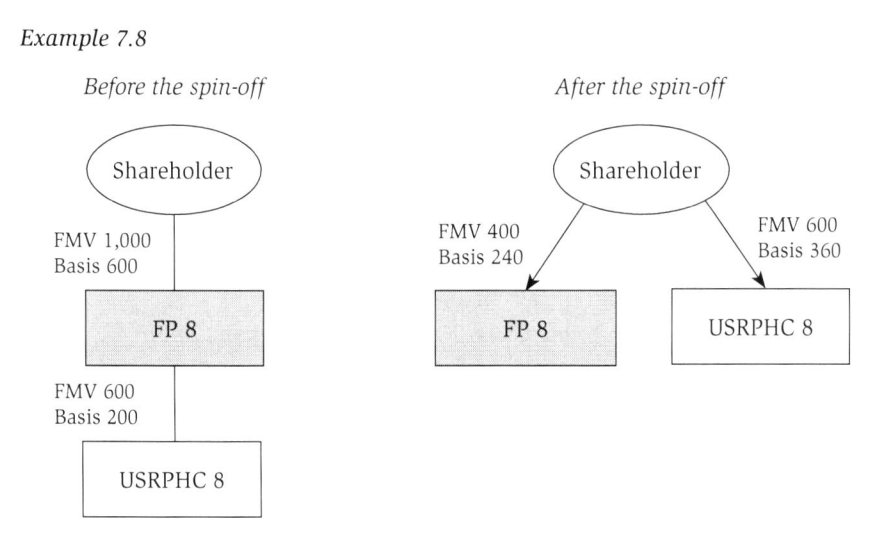

Example 7.8

Before the spin-off   *After the spin-off*

Shareholder   Shareholder

FMV 1,000   FMV 400   FMV 600
Basis 600   Basis 240   Basis 360

FP 8   FP 8   USRPHC 8

FMV 600
Basis 200

USRPHC 8

FP8 recognizes 160 of FIRPTA gain, calculated as follows:

$$
\begin{array}{rl}
360^* & \text{– shareholders' new basis in USRPHC 8} \\
-200 & \text{– FP 8's old basis in USRPHC 8} \\
\hline
160 &
\end{array}
$$

$$* \; 360 = 600 \times \frac{600}{1000} \quad \begin{array}{l} \text{– FMV of USRPHC 8} \\ \text{– Combined FMV} \end{array}$$

Example 7.8 illustrates the application of the FIRPTA Nonrecognition Rules to a spin-off.[92] Shareholder in the example owns all the stock of FP 8, a foreign corporation, which owns all the stock of USRPHC 8, a US corporation. The fair market value of the FP 8 stock is USD 1,000 (including the value of USRPHC 8) and Shareholder has a USD 600 basis in the stock. USRPHC 8 stock has a fair market value of USD 600 and FP 8 has a USD 200 basis in the stock. FP 8 distributes all the USRPHC 8 stock

---

91. See §7.03.B., *supra*, for a brief discussion of the Basis Requirement.
92. This is adopted from the Example in Temp. Treas. Reg. §1.897-5T(c)(3)(ii).

7. FIRPTA Nonrecognition Rules

to Shareholder in a spin-off transaction.[93] Under Code section 358, Shareholder takes a USD 360 basis in the USRPHC 8 stock as shown in the diagram.

In **Example 7.8**, FP 8's gain is limited to USD 160, which is the amount by which Shareholder's tax basis in the USRPHC 8 stock (after the spin-off) exceeds FP 8's basis in the USRPHC 8 stock (before the spin-off). This approach offers reprieve from full gain recognition[94] and is suitable for a situation where Distributing is closely held.[95] The approach, however, is not workable in a situation where Distributing is publicly traded for reasons that are similar to those affecting the Toll Charge.[96] That is, Distributing may not be able to ascertain the Distributee's aggregate post-distribution Controlled stock basis. With this said, the rule may be workable with respect to a widely held Distributing's distribution of Controlled if the Treasury Department and the IRS are willing to exclude the gains from the less-than-5% shareholders for purposes of determining the pre- and post-distribution basis disparity with respect to Controlled.

If Distributing is a USRPHC and Controlled is a foreign corporation or a domestic corporation that is not a USRPHC, then a foreign Distributee is treated as having exchanged a proportionate part of its Distributing stock for a non-USRPI.[97] Because the distribution is treated as an exchange of a USRPI (Distributing stock) for a non-USRPI (Controlled stock), the distribution cannot satisfy the Hot-for-Hot Requirement. As a result, the distribution of Controlled to the foreign Distributee is subject to FIRPTA.

E. Other Transfers to and from US Corporations

1. E and F Reorganizations of USRPHCs

The application of the Hot-for-Hot Requirement poses an issue when the stock of a former USRPHC,[98] whose stock is a USRPI because of the Five-Year Look-Back Period, is exchanged, or deemed exchanged, by a foreign person in a single-entity reorganization (i.e., an E or F reorganization) of the former USRPHC. As part of these reorganizations, a foreign shareholder of the former USRPHC transfers stock of the former USRPHC for stock of a new US corporation that is not a USRPHC immediately after the transfer in a Code section 354 exchange.[99] Thus, the Hot-for-Hot Requirement cannot be satisfied.

---

93. It is assumed that the transaction satisfies all the requirements of I.R.C. §355(a).
94. Without this special limitation, FP 8 would have to recognize USD 400 of gain upon the distribution of the USRPHC8 stock (USD 600 of fair market value less USD 200 tax basis).
95. Note that the Example in Temp. Treas. Reg. §1.897-5T(c)(3)(ii), the facts of which are reproduced in Example 7.8, only has one shareholder involved in the transaction.
96. See, e.g., the NYSBA Report on FIRPTA Nonrecognition Rules, footnote 85, supra, which observed that many of the temporary regulations appear to have been 'devised with a mind almost exclusively to closely held entities.'
97. Temp. Treas. Reg. §1.897-6T(a)(4).
98. A former USPRHC is US corporation the fair market value of whose USRPI is below the 50% threshold required by I.R.C. §897(c)(1)(A)(ii), but it is still considered a USRPHC due to the Five-Year Look Back Period of I.R.C. §897(c)(1)(A). See discussion in §4.04., supra.
99. This is because the percentage of USRPI that the new corporation owns during the one-day testing period is less than the 50% threshold required by I.R.C. §897(c)(1)(A)(ii).

Recognizing this issue, the Treasury Department and the IRS issued a notice that provides that when the new stock interests received by foreign shareholders in an E or F reorganization are substantially identical to the shares exchanged, then the determination of whether the interest received back in such exchange is a USRPI will include the period prior to exchange.[100] As a result, foreign shareholders that receive stock in a single-entity reorganization of a former USRPHC that is not a USRPHC immediately after the transfer can satisfy the Hot-for-Hot Requirement and, hence, will satisfy the FIRPTA Nonrecognition Rules if the Subject-to-Tax Requirement and Filing Requirement are also satisfied. This is an example that the requirements of the FIRPTA Nonrecognition Rules sometimes have unforeseen consequences.

2. *Outbound Liquidations of US Corporations*

A domestic corporation's Code section 332 liquidation into its foreign parent corporation can include two transfers of a USRPI. First, if the liquidating domestic corporation's stock is a USRPI with respect to the foreign parent corporation, the foreign parent corporation is deemed to exchange a USRPI for the liquidating domestic corporation's assets. Secondly, if the liquidating domestic corporation owns USRPIs, it is deemed to distribute the USRPIs to its foreign parent corporation in connection with its liquidation. With regard to the first transfer, the foreign parent corporation is not subject to FIRPTA on its disposition of the liquidating domestic corporation's stock.[101] With regard to the second transfer, the liquidating domestic corporation is not subject to FIRPTA on its liquidating distribution of USRPIs, but does recognize gain under Code section 367(e)(2) on the distribution of the stock of a former USRPHC.[102]

§7.04 OTHER SPECIAL RULES

A. The Filing Requirement

As discussed above, the FIRPTA Nonrecognition Rules require that the parties to the transaction satisfy the Filing Requirement. The Filing Requirement set forth in the temporary regulations has been modified by a subsequent IRS notice. The temporary regulations provide that if a USRPI is distributed or exchanged, the foreign distributing corporation or foreign transferor, as applicable, must file a US federal income tax return for the taxable year of the distribution or exchange.[103] This return must include a statement with the following information:

- a statement that the distribution or transfer is one to which Code section 897 applies;
- a description of the USRPI distributed or transferred, including its location, its adjusted basis in the hands of the distributor or transferor immediately before the distribution or transfer, and the date of the distribution or transfer;

---

100. *See* IRS Notice 99-43, footnote 38, *supra*.
101. Temp. Reg. §1.897-5T(b)(3)(iv)(A).
102. Treas. Reg. §1.367(e)-2(b)(2)(ii).
103. Temp. Reg. §1.897-5T(d)(1)(iii).

7. FIRPTA Nonrecognition Rules

- a description of the USRPI received in an exchange;
- a declaration signed by an officer of the corporation that the distributing foreign corporation has substantiated the adjusted basis of the shareholder in its stock if the distributing corporation has nonrecognition or recognition limitation under Temporary Regulation section 1.897-5T(c)(3) or (4);
- the amount of any gain recognized and tax withheld by any person with respect to the distribution or transfer;
- the treaty and article (if any) under which the distributee or transferor would be exempt from US taxation on a sale of the distributed USRPI or the USRPI received in the transfer; and
- a declaration, signed by the distributee or transferor or its authorized legal representative, that the distributee or transferor shall treat any subsequent sale, exchange, or other disposition of the USRPI as a disposition that is subject to US taxation, notwithstanding the provisions of any US income tax treaty or intervening change in circumstances.[104]

An IRS notice has suspended the tax return filing requirement in the temporary regulations for the disposition of a USRPI in a nonrecognition transaction other than those described in Code section 1445(e) if the following conditions are satisfied:[105]

- the transfer or distribution otherwise qualifies in its *entirety* for nonrecognition treatment under the FIRPTA Nonrecognition Rules;
- the transferor or distributor does not have any other ECI[106] during the taxable year that includes the transfer or distribution; and
- the relevant party either obtains a Withholding Certificate from the IRS under the rules of Treasury Regulation section 1.1445-3(a)[107] or submits a 'notice of nonrecognition' under the rules of Treasury Regulation section 1.1445-2(d)(2)[108] to the IRS.[109]

A taxpayer that wants to rely on the notice's waiver of the tax return filing requirement must satisfy *all* of the above requirements. For example, a foreign transferor that has ECI would not satisfy the second of the above requirements. As a result, the foreign transferor would be required to report the transfer of a USRPI on its US federal

---

104. *Id.*
105. *See* Notice 89-57, 1989-1 C.B. 698 , footnote 38, *supra*. The notice on its face does not cover Code section 1445(e) withholding. Thus, it appears that the tax return filing requirement continues to apply to dispositions of USRPIs described in Code section 1445(e).
106. *See* discussion in Chs. 1 and 2, *supra,* regarding the general US tax issues regarding ECI.
107. A Withholding Certificate issued under Treas. Reg. §1.1445-3(a) may reduce or eliminate the FIRPTA withholding tax imposed by I.R.C. §1445(a). *See* Ch. 8, *infra*, for a discussion of the FIRPTA Withholding Certificate.
108. A taxpayer that satisfies the Treas. Reg. §1.1445-2(d)(2) notification requirements may avoid the application of FIRPTA withholding tax imposed by I.R.C. §1445(a).
109. As discussed in §8.04.C., *infra*, a notice of nonrecognition must be filed within *twenty days* of the transaction in question. A taxpayer that did not submit a notice of nonrecognition to the IRS on a timely basis may request relief for late filing if the failure is due to reasonable cause. *See* Rev. Proc. 2008-27, 2008-1 C.B. 1014.

income tax return. The foreign transferor's failure to do so would violate the Filing Requirement, and its transfer of a USRPI would be subject to FIRPTA.

B. The Section 897(i) Election

Despite the intent to level the playing field regarding the taxation of foreign and US investors in real estate, certain FIRPTA provisions treat foreign corporations differently from domestic corporations. For example, if a foreign transferor sells a USRPI, the transferee is required to withhold tax under the FIRPTA withholding rules, but no withholding is required if the seller is a domestic corporation.[110] Another key difference is that US corporations, but not foreign corporations, may qualify for certain nonrecognition treatment under the FIRPTA Nonrecognition Rules.[111]

Code section 897(i) allows a foreign corporation to elect to be treated as a domestic corporation *solely* for purposes of Code sections 897, 1445 and 6039C if certain requirements are met (referred to as the Section 897(i) Election). First, the foreign corporation must own a USRPI at the time the election is made.[112] Secondly, the foreign corporation must be entitled to nondiscriminatory treatment with respect to its USRPI under a US income tax treaty.[113] Thirdly, the foreign corporation must qualify as a USRPHC if it were a US corporation.[114] Fourthly, the foreign corporation must pay a Toll Charge applicable to inbound acquisitive asset reorganizations.[115] A foreign corporation that wants to make this election must provide the following information to the IRS:[116]

- a general statement indicating the election under Code section 897(i) is being made;[117]
- a binding waiver of the benefits of any US treaty regarding gain or loss from the disposition of USRPIs while the election is in effect;[118]
- a binding agreement to pay income tax as a domestic corporation on gain of a USRPI while the election is in effect;[119]
- a signed consent to the making of the election and a waiver of US treaty benefits with respect to disposition of the interest in the corporation by each interest holder;[120] and

---

110. *See* I.R.C. §1445(a) and (b)(2).
111. *See* Rev. Rul. 87-66, 1987-2 C.B. 168.
112. Treas. Reg. §1.897-3(b)(1).
113. *See* Treas. Reg. §1.897-3(b)(2). The legislative history of I.R.C. §897(i) provides that a foreign corporation also may make the election under the non-discrimination clause of a 'friendship, commerce and navigation' treaty. *See* Conf. Rep. 97-176, reprinted in 1981-2 C.B. 481 (as H. Conf. Rep. 97-215).
114. Temp. Treas. Reg. §1.897-8T(b). This condition is more restrictive than the requirement stated in the statute which merely mandates that the foreign corporation owns a USRPI.
115. Notice 2006-46, Sec. 2, *see* footnote 38, *infra*.
116. *See* Treas. Reg. §1.897-3(c).
117. *See* Treas. Reg. §1.897-3(c)(1).
118. *See* Treas. Reg. §1.897-3(c)(2).
119. *See* Treas. Reg. §1.897-3(c)(3).
120. *See* Treas. Reg. §1.897-3(c)(4)(i). An exception applies to shareholders owning 5% or less of the stock of a publicly traded corporation.

7. FIRPTA Nonrecognition Rules

– a statement that no interest in the corporation was disposed of during the five years (or, if shorter, the period between the corporation's first acquisition of a USRPI and the date of the election).[121]

A foreign corporation can make the Section 897(i) Election any time before the first disposition of an interest in the corporation that would be subject to FIRPTA if the election were in effect at that time.[122] Unless revoked, the election applies during the remainder of the corporation's existence, and the election can be revoked only with IRS consent.[123] The regulations also provide conditions under which the election may be made after the disposition of an interest in the corporation that would have been subject to FIRPTA tax if the election had been in effect.[124]

A foreign corporation that has made a Section 897(i) Election is eligible for certain FIRPTA Nonrecognition Rules that are available to US corporations only. In addition, a foreign shareholder that receives the stock of a foreign corporation that has made a Section 897(i) Election is treated as if it received stock of a USRPHC for purposes of the Hot-for-Hot Requirement. Such a shareholder is not subject to FIRPTA withholding tax imposed on dispositions by a foreign seller of USRPI.[125]

The benefits of making the Section 897(i) Election, however, should be evaluated against any potential costs associated with the election. For example, a foreign corporation that makes the Section 897(i) Election is treated as a domestic corporation for all purposes of Code section 897; hence, its stock will be a USRPI. Any sale of the foreign corporation's stock, therefore, would be subject to FIRPTA tax unless the Cleansing Exception[126] applies. In addition, the gain from the sale of the stock would be treated as US source income.[127] If the foreign seller of the stock is also subject to its resident country tax on the gain, then the seller could be subject to double taxation unless its resident country permits the use of the US tax as a credit against such tax. Furthermore, the FIRPTA rules impose US tax on gain on the sale of the stock which may include non-USRPI assets.

§7.05 SUMMARY

If an asset transferred or deemed transferred in an otherwise nontaxable transaction is a USRPI, the FIRPTA rules could be triggered and the transaction may be taxable unless the FIRPTA Nonrecognition Rules apply. The FIRPTA Nonrecognition Rules, with all kinds of special rules and exceptions and exceptions to exceptions resemble a Rubik's cube. Nonetheless, it is possible to mitigate adverse US tax consequences through careful planning. This is an exercise that requires the taxpayer to be vigilant of any potential transfers that may involve USRPIs. A step-by-step program may look something like this:

---

121. *See* Treas. Reg. §1.897-3(c)(5).
122. Treas. Reg. §1.897-3(d).
123. Treas. Reg. §1.897-3(f) and -3(d)(1).
124. *See* Treas. Reg. §1.897-3(d)(2).
125. *See* discussion in Ch. 8, *infra,* regarding FIRPTA withholding tax.
126. See discussion in §6.02.A., *supra,* regarding the Cleansing Exception.
127. *See* I.R.C. §861(a)(5).

(1) be aware of any foreign transaction that may be viewed, under US tax principles, as a transfer or deemed transfer of assets;
(2) determine if any of the assets transferred or deemed transferred is a USRPI;
(3) determine if there is any inherit gain in the USRPI transferred;
(4) determine if the transaction in question would qualify for tax-free treatment under general US tax principles; and
(5) ensure that the transaction in question also satisfies the FIRPTA Nonrecognition Rules.

In the event a transaction does not qualify for tax-free treatment under both the general US Subchapter C tax principles and the FIRPTA Nonrecognition Rules, the taxpayer may consider applying for a private letter ruling with the IRS. Depending on the specific circumstances involved, the IRS may decide to provide relief to the taxpayer.

APPENDIX 7-A

Notice 2006-46

Notice 2006-46; 2006-1 C.B. 1044; 2006 IRB LEXIS 224; 2006-24 I.R.B. 1044

June 12, 2006

[*1]

SUBJECT MATTER: Announcement of rules to be included in final regulations under sections 897 (d) and (e) of the Code

TEXT:

PURPOSE

This notice announces that the Internal Revenue Service (IRS) and the Treasury Department (Treasury) will issue final regulations under *sections 897 (d)* and *(e)* of the Internal Revenue Code (Code) that set forth and, to the extent described in this notice, revise, the current rules under sections 1.897-5T and 1.897-6T of the temporary income tax regulations and *Notice 89-85, 1989-2 C.B. 403*, regarding certain transactions involving the transfer of U.S. real property interests (USRPIs), as defined in *section 897 (c) (1) of the Code*. When issued, the regulations will revise the rules of *Notice 89-85* and Temp. Treas. Reg. § 1.897-5T (c) (4) relating to inbound asset reorganizations described in *section 368 (a) (1) (C), (D)*, or *(F)* to take into account statutory mergers and consolidations described in *section 368 (a) (1) (A)*. The final regulations will also revise the rules of Temp. Treas. Reg. § 1.897-6T (b) (1) to take into account foreign-to-foreign statutory mergers and consolidations described in *section 368 (a) (1) (A)* and to create two additional exceptions that provide a foreign [*2] corporation with nonrecognition treatment on its transfer of a USRPI in certain foreign-to-foreign asset reorganizations. Moreover, the final regulations will incorporate a revised version of Temp. Treas. Reg. § 1.897-6T (b) (1) (iii). The final regulations will eliminate all the conditions required for nonrecognition treatment in Temp. Treas. Reg. § 1.897-6T (b) (2). Finally, the final regulations will modify the period that must be considered for imposing taxes and accrued interest on prior dispositions of the stock of foreign corporations under Temp. Treas. Reg. § 1.897-5T (c) (2), (4), and *Treas. Reg. §1.897-3 (c) (5)*, (d).

The portion of the final regulations that will address distributions, transfers, or exchanges occurring in the context of a statutory merger or consolidation described in *section 368 (a) (1) (A)* will generally apply to distributions, transfers, or exchanges occurring on or after January 23, 2006. Final regulations regarding the revisions to Temp. Treas. Reg. §1.897-5T (c) (2), (4), *Treas. Reg. §1.897-3 (c) (5), (d)*, and Temp. Treas. Reg. § 1.897-6T (b), except as such regulations are applicable to exchanges in *section 368 (a) (1) (A)* reorganizations, will apply [*3] to distributions, transfers, or exchanges occurring on or after May 23, 2006. However, taxpayers may choose to apply these regulatory changes to all dispositions, transfers, or exchanges occurring before May 23, 2006 during any taxable year that is not closed by the period of limitations, provided they do so consistently with respect to all such dispositions, transfers, and exchanges.

BACKGROUND

Under *section 897 (a)*, the disposition of a USRPI by a nonresident alien individual or a foreign corporation is taxable as effectively connected income under *section 871 (b) (1)* or *section 882 (a) (1)*, respectively, as if the taxpayer were engaged in a trade or business within the United States during the taxable year and the gain or loss were effectively connected with the trade or business.

Section 897 (c) (1) generally defines a USRPI to include any interest (other than an interest solely as a creditor) in any domestic corporation, unless the taxpayer establishes that such corporation was not a U.S. real property holding corporation (USRPHC) at any time during the shorter of the period the taxpayer held such interest or the 5-year period ending on the date of the disposition of such interest. [*4] Under *section 897 (c) (2)*, a USRPHC is defined as any corporation if the fair market value of its USRPIs equals or exceeds 50-percent of the sum of the fair market value of (i) its USRPIs, (ii) its real property interests located outside of the United States, and (iii) any of its other assets used or held for use in a trade or business.

Under *section 897 (d) (1)*, except to the extent provided in regulations, gain is recognized by a foreign corporation on the distribution (including a distribution in liquidation or redemption) of a USRPI in a transaction that otherwise qualifies for nonrecognition under the Code. *Section 897 (d) (2)* provides that gain is not recognized under *section 897 (d) (1)* if either: (i) at the time of the receipt of the distributed property, the distributee would be subject to taxation on a subsequent disposition of the distributed property, and the basis of the distributed property in the hands of the distributee is not greater than the adjusted basis of such property before the distribution, increased by the amount of gain (if any) recognized by the distributing corporation; or (ii) nonrecognition treatment is provided for in regulations prescribed by the Secretary [*5] under *section 897 (e) (2)*. Temp. Treas. Reg. § 1.897-5T provides rules, exceptions, and limitations regarding *section 897 (d)* distributions in the context of *sections 332, 355*, and *361*. See Temp. Treas. Reg. § 1.897-5T (c) (2), (3), and (4). *Notice 89-85* announced rules that would revise the application of certain of the exceptions set forth in the temporary regulations. As relevant to the changes announced in this notice, the provisions of those regulations and *Notice 89-85* are discussed below.

Subject to the rules of *section 897 (d)* and any regulations issued under *section 897 (e) (2)*, *section 897 (e) (1)* provides that any nonrecognition provision will apply only in the case of an exchange of a USRPI for an interest the sale of which would be taxable under Chapter 1 of the Code. Under *section 897 (e) (2)*, Treasury has authority to prescribe regulations providing the extent to which nonrecognition provisions shall apply to transfers of USRPIs.

Pursuant to *section 897 (e) (2)*, Temp. Treas. Reg. § 1.897-6T (a) (1) states the general rule of *section 897 (e)* and imposes certain requirements for nonrecognition. Among other things, that regulation provides that except as otherwise provided [*6] in Temp. Treas. Reg. §§ 1.897-5T and -6T, any nonrecognition provision applies to a transfer by a foreign person of a USRPI on which gain is realized only to the

7. FIRPTA Nonrecognition Rules

extent that the transferred USRPI is exchanged for a USRPI which, immediately following the exchange, would be subject to U.S. taxation upon its disposition, and the transferor complies with the filing requirements of Temp. Treas. Reg. § 1.897-5T (d) (1) (iii). Temp. Treas. Reg. § 1.897-6T (b) provides exceptions to this rule for certain exchanges in foreign-to-foreign nonrecognition transactions. The exceptions described in Temp. Treas. Reg. § 1.897-6T (b) are discussed below in the context of the changes announced by this notice to such provisions.

The IRS and Treasury issued final regulations on January 23, 2006, concerning statutory mergers and consolidations described in *section 368 (a) (1) (A)*. See *T.D. 9242, 2006-7 I.R.B. 422 (February 13, 2006). Treasury Decision 9242* provides a revised definition of the term "statutory merger or consolidation" that permits transactions effected pursuant to the statutes of a foreign jurisdiction or of a United States possession to qualify as a statutory merger or consolidation. Further, [*7] that regulation generally applies to transactions occurring on or after January 23, 2006. Prior to the issuance of *T.D. 9242*, temporary regulations defined a statutory merger or consolidation as including only transactions effected pursuant to the laws of the United States or a State or the District of Columbia.

DISCUSSION

The IRS and Treasury have determined that the rules of *Notice 89-85* and Temp. Treas. Reg. §§ 1.897-5T (c) and 1.897-6T (b) should be revised to reflect the recently issued regulations under *section 368 (a) (1) (A)*. This action is necessary because *Notice 89-85* and the temporary regulations did not contemplate statutory mergers or consolidations under foreign or possessions law as qualifying under *section 368 (a) (1) (A)*. In addition, the IRS and Treasury believe that certain other changes to the scope of the rules under *Treas. Reg. § 1.897-3* and Temp. Treas. Reg. §§ 1.897-5T and -6T are appropriate. Accordingly, this notice announces that the IRS and Treasury will issue final regulations under *sections 897 (d), (e)*, and *(i)* that generally incorporate the rules of *Treas. Reg. § 1.897-3* and Temp. Treas. Reg. §§ 1.897-5T and -6T, and *Notice 89-85*, except as described [*8] below.

1. Revision to the rules of Temp. Treas. Reg. § 1.897-5T (c) (4) relating to inbound asset reorganizations

Temp. Treas. Reg. § 1.897-5T (c) (4) applies the rules of *section 897 (d)* to certain distributions of stock of a USRPHC by a foreign corporation under *section 361 (c)*. Under the temporary regulations, a foreign corporation that transfers property to a domestic corporation (that is a USRPHC immediately after the transfer) in an exchange under *section 361 (a) or (b)* pursuant to a reorganization under *section 368 (a) (1) (C), (D),* or *(F)* must recognize gain under *section 897 (d) (1)* and Temp. Treas. Reg. § 1.897-5T (c) (4) (i) when it distributes the stock of the USRPHC to its shareholders under *section 361 (c)*. Temp. Treas. Reg. § 1.897-5T (c) (4) (ii) and (iii) provide an exception and a limitation to this gain recognition.

In *Notice 89-85*, the IRS and Treasury announced that the exception and the limitation set forth in Temp. Treas. Reg. § 1.897-5T (c) (4) (ii) and (iii) would be replaced by a new exception. The new exception announced in *Notice 89-85* provides that recognition of gain will not be required on the distribution under *section 361 (c)*

(1) of the stock of the USRPHC [*9] under Temp. Treas. Reg. § 1.897-5T (c) (4) (i) if the foreign corporation pays an amount equal to any taxes that *section 897* would have imposed upon all persons who had disposed of interests in the transferor foreign corporation (or a corporation from which such assets were acquired in a transaction described in *section 381*) after June 18, 1980, as if it were a domestic corporation on the date of each such disposition, and if the conditions of Temp. Treas. Reg. § 1.897-5T (c) (4) (ii) (A) and (C) (relating to the distributee being subject to tax on a subsequent disposition and certain filing requirements) are met. Other requirements relating to the time and manner of payment of tax and interest are also set forth in the notice. The revisions announced in *Notice 89-85* generally apply to all distributions of stock under Temp. Treas. Reg. § 1.897-5T (c) (4) occurring after July 31, 1989.

The IRS and Treasury have determined that when final regulations are issued, inbound statutory mergers and consolidations described in *section 368 (a) (1) (A)* (including such reorganizations by reason of *368 (a) (2) (D)* or *(E)*) will be subject to the same rules set forth in Temp. Treas. Reg. § 1.897-5T (c) (4) [*10] and *Notice 89-85* that apply to other inbound asset reorganizations. Further, as described in part 2, below, the period that a foreign corporation must consider with respect to prior stock dispositions under Temp. Treas. Reg. § 1.897-5T (c) (4) will be revised.

2. Revisions to the Notice 89-95 stock disposition look-back period applicable to Temp. Treas. Reg. § 1.897-5T (c) (2) (ii) liquidations, Temp. Treas. Reg. § 1.897-5T (c) (4) inbound asset reorganizations, and section 897 (i) elections.

Section 1.897-5T (c) (2) of the temporary regulations applies the rules of *section 897 (d)* to liquidating distributions of USRPIs by a foreign corporation to a domestic corporation pursuant to *section 332 (a)*. Under Temp. Treas. Reg. § 1.897-5T (c) (1), a foreign corporation that makes a liquidating distribution of a USRPI to a foreign or domestic shareholder must recognize gain on the distribution under *section 897 (d)*, unless the distribution comes within an exception described in Temp. Treas. Reg. § 1.897-5T (c) (2), (3), or (4). Temp. Treas. Reg. § 1.897-5T (c) (2) (i) and (ii) provide exceptions to this recognition rule that are applicable to liquidating distributions under *section 332 (a)*.

In [*11] *Notice 89-85*, the IRS and Treasury announced that the exceptions set forth in Temp. Treas. Reg. § 1.897-5T (c) (2) (i) and (ii) would be replaced by a new exception. The new exception announced in *Notice 89-85* provides that recognition of gain shall not be required on the liquidating distribution of a USRPI by a foreign corporation to a domestic corporation meeting the stock ownership requirements of *section 332 (b)* in a *section 332 (a)* liquidation if the distributing foreign corporation pays the tax and interest on any prior disposition of its stock (or stock of a corporation from which such assets were acquired in a transaction described in *section 381*) after June 18, 1980, as if it were a domestic corporation on the date of such dispositions, and if the conditions of Temp. Treas. Reg. § 1.897-5T (c) (2) (i) are met (relating to the distributee being subject to tax on a subsequent disposition and certain basis carryover and filing requirements). The revisions announced in *Notice 89-85* generally apply to all distributions of stock under Temp. Treas. Reg. § 1.897-5T (c) (2) occurring after July 31, 1989. Similarly, as described in part 1 of this notice, above, *Notice 89-85* revised [*12] the look-back period applicable to inbound reorganizations under Temp. Treas. Reg. § 1.897-5T (c) (4) to encompass certain dispositions of the stock of the foreign corporation that occur after June 18, 1980. The rules of *Notice 89-85*

7. FIRPTA Nonrecognition Rules

also require the payment of interest, as determined under *section 6621*, that would have accrued had tax actually been due with respect to the prior stock dispositions.

Further, *section 897 (i)*, which permits a foreign corporation to elect to be treated as a domestic corporation for purposes of *section 897*, requires as a condition to making the election that the electing foreign corporation verify that no interest in the corporation was disposed of during the shorter of: (1) the period from June 19,1980 through the date of the election, (2) the period from the date on which the corporation first holds a USPRI through the date of the election, or (3) the five year period ending on the date of the election. See *Treas. Reg. § 1.897-3 (c) (5)*. If the foreign corporation cannot make such verification, then it must comply with the conditions of *Treas. Reg. § 1.897-3 (d)* which, among other things, requires the payment of an amount equal to any taxes that *section 897* [*13] would have imposed on all persons who had disposed of interests in the corporation during such period. The payment must also include any interest, as determined under *section 6621*, that would have accrued had the tax actually been due with respect to the dispositions. These rules were modified by *Notice 89-85* to require the reporting and payment of tax and accrued interest on all dispositions of stock occurring after June 18, 1980 that would have been subject to taxation under *section 897 (a)*.

The IRS and Treasury have determined that when final regulations are issued, the look-back, tax, and interest payment periods applicable under *Notice 89-85* to Temp. Treas. Reg. § 1.897-5T (c) (2) liquidating distributions, Temp. Treas. Reg. § 1.897-5T (c) (4) inbound asset reorganizations, and *section 897 (i)* elections will be modified as described below.

Regarding distributions of USRPIs by a foreign corporation to a domestic corporation in a *section 332* liquidation, the final regulations will amend the rules of Temp. Treas. Reg. § 1.897-5T (c) (2) (ii) and *Notice 89-85* to provide that recognition of gain will not be required on the distribution of any USRPI by the distributing foreign corporation [*14] to the domestic corporation if the distributing foreign corporation pays an amount equal to the tax and interest that would have been imposed upon all persons who disposed of an interest in the foreign corporation (or a corporation from which such assets were acquired in a transaction described in *section 381*) during the period beginning on the date that is 10 years prior to the date on which the domestic corporation or any related person (within the meaning of *section 267 (b)*) is in control (as determined under *section 304 (c)*) of the liquidating foreign corporation, and ending on the date of the liquidation, as if the foreign corporation were a domestic corporation on the date of each such disposition and if the conditions of Temp. Treas. Reg. § 1.897-5T (c) (2) (i) are met.

Regarding inbound asset acquisitions described in Temp. Treas. Reg. § 1.897-5T (c) (4) as modified by this notice, the final regulations will amend the rules of Temp. Treas. Reg. § 1.897-5T (c) (4) (ii) and *Notice 89-85* to provide that recognition of gain will not be required on the distribution of stock of a USRPHC if the foreign corporation pays an amount equal to any taxes and interest that would have been [*15] imposed upon all persons who disposed of an interest in the foreign corporation (or a corporation from which the assets were acquired in a transaction described in *section 381*) during the applicable period as if the foreign corporation were a domestic corporation on the date of each such disposition, and the conditions of Temp. Treas. § 1.897-5T (c) (4) (ii) (A) and (C) are met. The applicable period means the earliest of either:

- The period beginning on the date that is 10 years prior to the date on which the acquiring domestic corporation or a related person (within the meaning of *section 267 (b)*) is in control (as determined under *section 304 (c)*) of the foreign corporation and ending on the date of the reorganization. For purposes of the preceding sentence, the acquiring domestic corporation means the domestic corporation that is the transferee in the 361 (a) exchange; or
- The period beginning on the date that is 10 years prior to the date of the reorganization and ending on the date of the reorganization.

Regarding the revisions to *Treas. Reg. §1.897-3 (c) (5)*, and *(d)* pertaining to a foreign corporation's election under *section 897 (i)*, the final regulations will provide that the [*16] applicable period will be the earliest of either:

The period beginning on the date that is 10 years prior to the date on which one or more domestic shareholders or related persons (within the meaning of *section 267 (b)*) are in control (as determined under *section 304 (c)*) of the foreign corporation and ending on the date of the election; or

The period beginning on the date that is 10 years prior to the date of the *section 897 (i)* election and ending on the date of the election.

3. Revisions to the rules of Temp. Treas. Reg. § 1.897-6T

(a) Revision to the rules of Temp. Treas. Reg. § 1.897 6T (b) (1) (ii) to take into account statutory mergers and consolidations described in section 368 (a) (1) (A)

As noted above, Temp. Treas. Reg. § 1.897-6T (a) (1) generally provides that any nonrecognition provision shall apply to a transfer by a foreign person of a USRPI only to the extent that the foreign person receives a USRPI in such exchange. Pursuant to the regulatory authority under *section 897 (e) (2) of the Code*, Temp. Treas. Reg. § 1.897-6T (b) (1) and (2) provide exceptions to the rule of Temp. Treas. Reg. § 1.897-6T (a) (1) for certain foreign-to-foreign reorganizations and certain exchanges [*17] under *section 351* where a foreign person transfers a USRPI for stock in a foreign corporation. These exceptions require that (1) the transferee's subsequent disposition of the transferred USRPI be subject to U.S. income taxation in accordance with Temp. Treas. Reg. § 1.897-5T (d) (1); (2) the filing requirements of Temp. Treas. Reg. § 1.897-5T (d) (1) (iii) be satisfied; (3) one of the five conditions set forth in paragraph (b) (2) exists; and (4) the exchange takes one of the three forms of exchange described in paragraph (b) (1).

Temp. Treas. Reg. § 1.897-6T (b) (1) (ii) describes one of the three permissible forms of exchange referenced above. That paragraph describes an exchange by a foreign corporation pursuant to *section 361 (a)* or *(b)* in a reorganization described in *section 368 (a) (1) (C)*, where there is an exchange of the transferor corporation stock for the transferee corporation stock (or stock of the transferee corporation's parent in the case of a parenthetical C reorganization) under *section 354 (a)*, and the transferor corporation's shareholders own more than fifty percent of the voting stock of the transferee corporation (or stock of the transferee corporation's parent [*18] in the case of a parenthetical C reorganization) immediately after the reorganization. The fifty percent limitation restricts this exception to reorganizations described in *section*

368 (a) (1) (C) that are restructurings where the transferor corporation shareholders control the transferee corporation after the transaction (e.g., internal restructurings).

The IRS and Treasury have determined that when final regulations are issued, foreign-to-foreign statutory mergers and consolidations described in *section 368 (a) (1) (A)* (including such reorganizations by reason of *section 368 (a) (2) (D) or (E)*) will be subject to the same rules set forth in Temp. Treas. Reg. § 1.897-6T (b) (1) (ii) that apply to foreign-to-foreign reorganizations described in *section 368 (a) (1) (C)* (including parenthetical C reorganizations). The exception for statutory mergers and consolidations described in *section 368 (a) (1) (A)* will be limited to restructurings where the 50 percent control requirement is satisfied after the transaction. Further, the final regulations will provide that in determining whether the fifty percent requirement set forth in Temp. Treas. Reg. § 1.897-6T (b) (1) (ii) is met where the [*19] transferee corporation owns more than fifty percent of the transferor corporation before a reorganization under *section 368 (a) (1) (A) or 368 (a) (1) (C)* (i.e., an upstream reorganization), the shareholders of thetransferee corporation before the reorganization (that continue to be shareholders of the transferee corporation after the reorganization) will be treated as shareholders of the transferor corporation before the reorganization to the extent of their indirect interest in the stock of the transferor corporation (owned by the transferee corporation) before the reorganization.

Accordingly, when issued, the final regulations will provide that gain shall not be recognized where an exchange is made by a foreign corporation pursuant to *section 361 (a) or (b)* in a reorganization described in *section 368 (a) (1) (A)* (including such reorganization by reason of *section 368 (a) (2) (D) or (E)*); there is an exchange of the transferor corporation stock for the transferee corporation stock (or the stock of the transferee corporation's parent in the case of a reorganization by reason of *section 368 (a) (2) (D)*) under *section 354 (a)*; immediately after the reorganization, the transferor corporation's [*20] shareholders own more than fifty percent of the voting stock of the transferee corporation (or the transferee corporation's parent in a reorganization by reason of *section 368 (a) (2) (D)*), or in the case of a reorganization by reason of *section 368 (a) (2) (E)*, the shareholders of the corporation that controls the transferor corporation before the reorganization own more than fifty percent of the voting stock of that controlling corporation after the reorganization; and the other requirements of Temp. Treas. Reg. § 1.897-6T (b) (1) are satisfied.

(b) Additional exceptions to be added to the rules of Temp. Treas. Reg. § 1.897-6T (b) (1)

The IRS and Treasury have determined that when final regulations are issued, the rules of Temp. Treas. Reg. § 1.897-6T (b) (1) will be expanded to include two additional exceptions. Those exceptions will apply only in certain foreign-to-foreign statutory mergers and consolidations described in *section 368 (a) (1) (A)* (including such reorganizations by reason of *section 368 (a) (2) (D) or (E)*) and foreign-to-foreign reorganizations described in *section 368 (a) (1) (C)* (including parenthetical C reorganizations). Accordingly, the new exceptions to be incorporated [*21] in the final regulations will revise the rules of Temp. Treas. Reg. § 1.897-6T (b) (1) to provide that such foreign-to-foreign reorganizations will be excepted from the general gain recognition rule of Temp. Treas. Reg. § 1.897-6T (a) (1) provided that the other requirements set forth in Temp. Treas. Reg. § 1.897-6T (b) (1) are met. The two additional exceptions apply where an exchange is made by a foreign corporation pursuant to *section 361 (a)* or *(b)* in a reorganization described in *section 368 (a) (1) (A)* (including a reorganization by reason of *section 368 (a) (2) (D)* or *(E)*) or *section 368 (a) (1) (C)* (including parenthetical C reorganizations); there is an exchange of the transferor corporation stock for the transferee corporation stock (or the transferee corporation's parent in the case of a reorganization by reason of *section 368 (a) (2) (D)* or a parenthetical C reorganization) under *section 354 (a)*; and either:

- Stock in the transferor corporation (including a predecessor corporation in a transaction described in *section 381 (a)*) would not be a USRPI at any time within the five year period ending on the date of the reorganization if the transferor corporation were a domestic [*22] corporation; or
- Regarding reorganizations under *section 368 (a) (1) (A)* (other than by reason of *section 368 (a) (2) (D)* or *(E)*) or *section 368 (a) (1) (C)* (other than parenthetical reorganizations described in that section): prior to the exchange the stock of the transferor corporation and the stock of the transferee corporation, and after the exchange the stock of the transferee corporation are regularly traded under *Treas. Reg.* § *1.897-1 (n)* and Temp. Treas. Reg. § 1.897-9T (d) (1) and (2) on an established securities market under § *1.897-1 (m)*, and in the case where the transferor corporation would have been a USRPHC at any time within the five year period ending on the date of the reorganization if the transferor corporation had been a domestic corporation, no foreign shareholder of the transferor corporation owned a more than five percent interest in the transferor corporation at such time under the rules of *Treas. Reg.* § *1.897-1 (c) (2) (iii)* and Temp. Treas. Reg. § 1.897-9T.Regarding parenthetical C reorganizations and reorganizations under *section 368 (a) (1) (A)* by reason of *section 368 (a) (2) (D)*: prior to the exchange the stock of the transferor corporation and the stock [*23] of the corporation in control of the transferee corporation, and after the exchange the stock of the corporation in control of the transferee corporation are regularly traded under *Treas. Reg.* § *1.897-1 (n)* and Temp. Treas. Reg. § 1.897-9T (d) (1) and (2) on an established securities market under § *1.897-1 (m)*, and in the case where the transferor corporation would have been a USRPHC at any time within the five year period ending on the date of the reorganization if the transferor corporation had been a domestic corporation, no foreign shareholder of the transferor corporation owned a more than five percent interest in the transferor corporation at such time under the rules of *Treas. Reg.* § *1.897-1 (c) (2) (iii)* and Temp. Treas. Reg. § 1.897-9T.Regarding reorganizations under *section 368 (a) (1) (A)* by reason of *section 368 (a) (2) (E)*: prior to the exchange the stock of the transferee corporation and the stock of the corporation in control of the transferor corporation, and after the exchange the stock of the corporation that controls the transferee corporation are regularly traded under *Treas. Reg.* § *1.897-1 (n)* and Temp. Treas. Reg. § 1.897-9T (d) (1) and (2) on an established securities [*24] market under § *1.897-1 (m)*, and in the case where the transferor corporation or the corporation in control of the transferor corporation would have been a USRPHC at any time within the five year period ending on the date of the reorganization if either corporation had been a domestic corporation, no foreign shareholder of the corporation

7. FIRPTA Nonrecognition Rules

in control of transferor corporation owned a more than five percent interest in the transferor corporation at such time under the rules of *Treas. Reg. § 1.897-1 (c) (2) (iii)* and Temp. Treas. Reg. § 1.897-9T.

(c) Revision to the rules of Temp. Treas. Reg. § 1.897-6T (b) (1) (iii) relating to foreign-to-foreign section 351 transactions and section 368 (a) (1) (B) reorganizations

As discussed above, Temp. Treas. Reg. § 1.897-6T (b) (1) contains exceptions to the general rule provided in Temp. Treas. Reg. § 1.897-6T (a) (1) if one of three forms of exchange occurs and certain other requirements are met. Specifically, Temp. Treas. Reg. § 1.897-6T (b) (1) (iii) provides a foreign person with nonrecognition treatment if the foreign person exchanges stock in a USRPHC under section 351 (a) or section 354 (a) in a reorganization described in section 368 (a) (1) (B), [*25] and, immediately after the exchange, all of the outstanding stock of the transferee corporation (or the stock of the transferee corporation's parent in the case of a parenthetical B reorganization) is owned in the same proportions by the same nonresident alien individuals and foreign corporations that immediately before the exchange owned the stock of the USRPHC. However, if any of the stock in the foreign corporation received by the individual or corporate transferor in the exchange is disposed of within three years from the date of its receipt, then the transferor must recognize that portion of the realized gain with respect to the stock of the USPRHC for which the foreign stock disposed of was received.

The IRS and Treasury have determined that the final regulations will revise Temp. Treas. Reg. § 1.897-6T (b) (1) (iii) in two respects. First, the exception will be revised so that "all of the stock of the transferee corporation" is removed and replaced with "substantially all of the outstanding stock of the transferee corporation" and the words "in the same proportions" will be removed. Second, the three year period will be revised to one year.

(d) Removal of the conditions set forth in Temp. Treas. Reg. § 1.897-6T (b) (2)

As [*26] discussed above, to come within an exception to Temp. Treas. Reg. § 1.897-6T (a) (1), not only must an exchange be described in Temp. Treas. Reg. § 1.897-6T (b) (1), but it must also satisfy one of the five conditions set forth in Temp. Treas. Reg. § 1.897-6T (b) (2). The IRS and Treasury have determined that the conditions of Temp. Treas. Reg. § 1.897-6T (b) (2) are no longer necessary. Accordingly, the final regulations will eliminate the conditions of Temp. Treas. Reg. § 1.897-6T (b) (2).

COMMENTS

Written comments on issues addressed in this notice may be submitted to the Office of Associate Chief Counsel International, Attention: Margaret Hogan (Notice 2006-46), room 4567, CC:INTL:B04, Internal Revenue Service, 1111 Constitution Avenue, NW, Washington, DC 20224. Alternatively, taxpayers may submit comments electronically to Notice.Comments@m1.irscounsel.treas.gov Comments will be available for public inspection and copying.

EFFECTIVE DATE

Final regulations to be issued incorporating the guidance set forth in this notice regarding exchanges occurring in the context of a statutory merger or consolidation described in *section 368 (a) (1) (A)* will generally apply to distributions, transfers, [*27] or exchanges occurring on or after January 23, 2006. Final regulations regarding the revisions to Temp. Treas. Reg. §§ 1.897-5T (c) (2), (4), *Treas. Reg.* §*1.897-3 (c) (5), (d)*, and Temp. Treas. Reg. § 1.897-6T (b), except as applicable to *section 368 (a) (1) (A)* transactions, will apply to distributions, transfers, or exchanges occurring on or after May 23, 2006. However, taxpayers may choose to apply these regulatory changes to all dispositions, transfers, or exchanges occurring before May 23, 2006 during any taxable year that is not closed by the period of limitations, provided they do so consistently with respect to all dispositions, transfers, and exchanges.

Prior to the issuance of the final regulations, taxpayers may rely on the guidance contained in this notice. Taxpayers applying this notice, however, must do so consistently with respect to all transactions within its scope.

PAPERWORK REDUCTION ACT

The collections of information contained in this notice have been reviewed and approved by the Office of Management and Budget in accordance with the Paperwork Reduction Act (*44 U.S.C. § 3507*) under control number 1545-2017. An agency may not conduct or sponsor, and a person is not [*28] required to respond to, a collection of information unless the collection of information displays a valid OMB control number.

The rules of this notice will apply to a foreign corporation distributing stock of a USRPHC to its shareholders pursuant to an inbound asset reorganization or a foreign corporation transferring a USRPI to another foreign corporation pursuant to an asset reorganization and will require such foreign corporations to satisfy the filing requirements of Temp. Treas. Reg. § 1.897-5T (d) (1) (iii), as modified by *Notice 89-57, 1989-1 C.B. 698*. The specific collections of information are contained in Temp. Treas. Reg. §§ 1.897-5T (c) (4) (ii) (C) and 1.897-6T (b) (1). These filing requirements notify the IRS of the transfer and enable it to verify that the transferor qualifies for nonrecognition and the transferee will be subject to U.S. tax on a subsequent disposition of the USRPI. Generally, they may be satisfied by: (1) filing the information statement required by Temp. Treas. Reg. § 1.897-5T (d) (1) (iii); (2) filing a notice of nonrecognition to the IRS in accordance with the provisions of *Treas. Reg. § 1.1445-2 (d) (2)*; or (3) filing a withholding certificate in [*29] accordance with the requirements of *Treas. Reg. § 1.1445-3*. The collections of information are required in order to obtain the benefit of the nonrecognition provisions. The likely respondents are businesses.

The estimated total annual reporting and/or recordkeeping burden is 500hours. The estimated annual burden hour per respondent and/or recordkeeper is 1 hour. The estimated number of respondents and/or recordkeepers is 500. The estimated frequency of response is occasional.

Books or records relating to a collection of information must be retained as long as their statements may become material in the administration of any internal revenue law. Generally, tax returns and tax information are confidential, as required by *26 U.S.C. § 6103.*

EFFECT ON OTHER DOCUMENTS

Notice 89-85, 1989-2 C.B. 403 is amplified.

DRAFTING INFORMATION

The principal author of this notice is Margaret A. Hogan of the Office of Associate Chief Counsel (International). For further information regarding this notice contact Ms. Hogan at (202) 622-3860 (not a toll-free call).

APPENDIX 7-B

Notice 99-43

Notice 99-43; 1999-2 C.B. 344; 1999 IRB LEXIS 303; 1999-36 I.R.B. 344

September 7, 1999

[*1]

SUBJECT MATTER: Rule to be Included in Final Regulations Under Section 897 (e) of the Code

TEXT:

This notice announces a modification of the current rules under Temp. Reg. §1.897-6T (a) (1) regarding transfers, exchanges, and other dispositions of U.S. real property interests in nonrecognition transactions occurring after June 18, 1980. The new rule will be included in regulations finalizing the temporary regulations.

SECTION I. BACKGROUND

Section 897 (a) of the Code provides generally that the disposition of a U.S. real property interest by a nonresident alien individual or a foreign corporation is taxable as effectively connected income under *section 871 (b) (1)* or *section 882 (a) (1)*, respectively, as if the taxpayer was engaged in a trade or business within the United States and the gain or loss was effectively connected with the trade or business.

Section 897 (c) (1) of the Code defines a U.S. real property interest as including an interest (other than an interest solely as a creditor) in any domestic corporation, unless the taxpayer establishes that such corporation was at no time a U.S. real property holding corporation during the shorter of the period the taxpayer held such interest or the 5-year period [*2] ending on the date of the disposition of such interest. Under *section 897 (c) (2)*, a U.S. real property holding corporation is defined as any corporation if the fair market value of its U.S. real property interests equals or exceeds 50-percent of the sum of (i) its U.S. real property interests, (ii) its real property interests located outside the United States, and (iii) any of its other assets used or held for use in a trade or business.

Section 897 (e) (1) of the Code provides generally that a nonrecognition provision applies only in the case of an exchange of a U.S. real property interest for an interest the sale of which would be taxable under Chapter 1 of the Code. Under *section 897 (e) (2)*, the Secretary may prescribe regulations providing the extent to which nonrecognition provisions apply to transfers of U.S. real property interests.

Pursuant to the regulatory authority under *section 897 (e) (2)*, Temp. Reg. §1.897-6T (a) (1) provides that, subject to certain exceptions, any nonrecognition provision shall apply to a transfer by a foreign person of a U.S. real property interest on which gain is realized only to the extent that the transferred U.S. real property interest is exchanged [*3] for a U.S. real property interest which, immediately following the exchange, would be subject to U.S. taxation upon its disposition (and the transferor complies with the filing requirement of *Temp. Reg. §1.897-5*). In the case of an exchange of a U.S. real property interest for stock in a domestic corporation (that is otherwise treated as a U.S. real property interest), such stock shall not be considered a U.S. real property interest unless the domestic corporation is a U.S. real property holding corporation immediately after the exchange. Thus, if an interest in a U.S. real property holding corporation is exchanged in a nonrecognition transaction for stock of a domestic corporation, that is not a U.S. real property holding corporation immediately after the exchange, the exchange would be taxable under *section 897*.

Under Temp. Reg. §1.897-6T (a) (2), a nonrecognition provision for purposes of *section 897 (e)* is any provision of the Code which provides that gain or loss is not recognized if the requirements of that provision are met. Thus, *section 897 (e)* applies only to an exchange that receives nonrecognition treatment pursuant to another provision of the Code and does not create (or [*4] expand) a nonrecognition provision.

SECTION II. FINALIZATION OF TEMP. REG. §1.897-6T (a) (1)

It is recognized that the requirement in Temp. Reg. §1.897-6T (a) (1), providing that the corporation whose stock is received in a nonrecognition exchange must be a U.S. real property holding corporation immediately after the exchange, may not be appropriate for stock exchanges under *section 354 (a)* in certain reorganizations described in *sections 368 (a) (1) (E) and (F) of the Code*. This may be illustrated by two examples. In both examples, the corporation, the stock of which was received in the exchange, is not a U.S. real property holding corporation immediately after the exchange, but was a U.S. real property holding corporation within the period provided in *section 897 (c) (1) (A) (ii)* (the shorter of five years or the taxpayer's holding period prior to the exchange).

In example one, a domestic corporation engages in a recapitalization, whereby one share of common stock is issued in exchange for two outstanding shares of the existing common stock (in what is commonly referred to as a "reverse stock split"), pursuant to a *section 354 (a)* exchange in a *section 368 (a) (1) (E)* reorganization. [*5] The shares received in the exchange are substantially identical to the shares exchanged therefor, possessing (in the aggregate and with respect to any other outstanding stock of the corporation) the same dividend rights, voting power, liquidation preference (if any), convertibility and other legal and economic entitlements as the shares exchanged, and do not contain any additional rights or obligations.

In example two, a domestic corporation changes its state of incorporation from State A to State B, pursuant to a state law merger of the corporation into a corporation newly incorporated in State B solely to facilitate the transaction, and which is the survivor in the merger. In the merger, stock of the merged corporation is exchanged for stock in the surviving corporation, possessing (in the aggregate and with respect to any other outstanding stock of the corporation) substantially identical dividend rights, voting power, liquidation preference (if any), convertibility and other legal and economic entitlements as the shares exchanged, and does not contain any additional rights or obligations. The reincorporation qualifies as a reorganization under *section 368 (a) (1) (F)*.

Under Temp. Reg. §1.897-6T (a) (1), [*6] the exchange of stock in both examples would be taxable to foreign shareholders because, with respect to the interests exchanged, the domestic corporation whose stock is received is not a U.S. real property holding corporation immediately after the exchange. Accordingly, when the final regulations under *section 897 (e)* are issued, the regulations will include an exception that will provide that a foreign taxpayer will not recognize gain under section 1.897-6T (a) (1) (as finalized) for a stock exchange under *section 354 (a)* in certain reorganizations described in *section 368 (a) (1) (E) or (F)*. The exception will apply where the taxpayer receives stock in the corporation that is substantially identical to the shares exchanged, possessing (in the aggregate and with respect to any other outstanding stock of the corporation) the same dividend rights, voting power, liquidation preferences (if any), and convertibility as the shares exchanged without any additional rights or obligations.

The final regulations will provide, for purposes of *section 897 (a) and (e)*, that stock received in a *section 368 (a) (1) (E) or (F)* reorganization qualifying for nonrecognition pursuant to *section 354 (a)* [*7] under the examples described above, constitutes the same interest in the corporation whose stock was exchanged for purposes of determining whether the interest received is a U.S. real property interest under *section 897 (c) (1) (A) (ii)*. Thus, the determination of whether the interest received in such an exchange is a U.S. real property interest under *section 897 (c) (1) (A) (ii)* will include the period prior to the exchange.

For example, if a foreign person receives substantially identical stock in a *section 354 (a)* exchange pursuant to the recapitalization of a domestic corporation that qualifies as a reorganization within the meaning of *section 368 (a) (1) (E)*, and the corporation ceased to be a U.S. real property holding corporation two years prior to the exchange, the sale of the stock by the foreign person two years after the exchange will constitute the disposition of a U.S. real property interest that is subject to tax under *section 897 (a)*. If the same interest were to be sold by the foreign person four years after the exchange, the sale would not be subject to tax under *section 897 (a)*, because the interest would not have been a U.S. real property interest. In such case, the [*8] interest would not have been an interest in a domestic corporation that was a U.S. real property holding corporation during the period specified in *section 897 (c) (1) (A) (ii)*.

The rule described in this notice is effective for transfers occurring on or after September 6, 1999 (the date of publication of this notice), although a taxpayer may elect to apply the rule of this notice to transfers occurring after June 18, 1980.

SECTION III. PAPERWORK REDUCTION ACT

The collections of information required by this notice have been reviewed and approved by the Office of Management and Budget in accordance with the Paperwork Reduction Act (*44 U.S.C. 3507*) under control number 1545-1660.

An agency may not conduct or sponsor, and a person is not required to respond to, a collection of information unless the collection of information displays a valid OMB control number.

The collections of information required by this notice are in Temp. Reg. §1.897-6T (a) (1) and 1.897-5T (d) (1) (iii), *Treas. Reg. §1.1445-2 (d) (2) (i) (A)* and Temp. Reg. §1.1445-9T. This information will be used to obtain exemptions from tax under certain nonrecognition transactions and to satisfy reporting requirements regarding these [*9] nonrecognition transactions. This information will be used by the Internal Revenue Service to verify whether a taxpayer is entitled to exemption from tax under a nonrecognition transaction. The likely respondents are individuals, corporations, and business or other for-profit institutions.

The estimated total annual reporting burden is 200 hours. The estimated annual burden per respondent is 2 hours. The estimated number of respondents is 100. The estimated frequency of responses is on occasion.

Books or records relating to a collection of information must be retained as long as their contents may become material in the administration of any internal revenue law. Generally, tax returns and tax return information are confidential, as required by *26 U.S.C. 6103*.

SECTION IV. DRAFTING INFORMATION

The principal author of this notice is Robert Lorence of the Office of Associate Chief Counsel (International). For further information regarding this notice, contact Mr. Lorence at (202) 622-3860 (not a toll-free call). Comments are requested regarding this Notice, including the application of the exception to be provided for in the final regulations as described herein to other nonrecognition transactions.

APPENDIX 7-C

Notice 89-85

Notice 89-85; 1989-2 C.B. 403; 1989 IRB LEXIS 319; 1989-31 I.R.B. 9

July 1989

[*1]

SUBJECT MATTER: Revision of Temporary Regulations Pending Issuance of Final Regulations under Section 897 of the Internal Revenue Code of 1986 and Final Regulations Concerning Elections under Section 897 (i) of the Code

TEXT:

The purpose of this notice is to announce certain rules that will be incorporated in the Temporary Income Tax Regulations issued under *section 897 (d)* and *(e)* of the Internal Revenue Code of 1986 and in the Income Tax Regulations issued under *section 897 (i) of the Code*. The temporary regulations under *section 897 (d)* and *(e)* were published in the Federal Register for Thursday, May 5, 1988 (*53 FR 16233*).

Distribution of U.S. real property interests in general

Section 897 (d) (1) of the Code and section 1.897-5T (c) (1) of the temporary regulations generally require that, if a foreign corporation makes a distribution (including a distribution in liquidation or redemption) of a United States real property interest (USRPI) to a shareholder, then the foreign corporation must recognize any gain (but not loss) on the distribution. The gain recognized is the excess of the fair market value of the USRPI at the time of the distribution over its adjusted basis. *Section 897 (d) (2)* and certain sections [*2] of the temporary regulations provide exceptions to the recognition rule of section 1.897-5T (c) (1) under certain conditions.

Further, *section 897 (e) (1) of the Code*, in general, provides that any nonrecognition provision of the Code shall apply to a transaction only in the case of an exchange of a USRPI for an interest the sale of which would be subject to United States taxation. The temporary regulations provide the extent to which transfers of property in reorganizations shall be treated as sales of property at fair market value.

Distributions of the stock of a U.S. real property holding corporation by a foreign corporation in a reorganization under section 1.897-5T (c) (4)

Section 1.897-5T (c) (4) of the temporary regulations applies the rules of *section 897 (d) of the Code* to the distribution of stock of a U.S. real property holding corporation (USRPHC) by a foreign corporation in an inbound reorganization under *section 368 (a) (1) (C), (D)* or *(F)*. A foreign corporation that transfers property to another corporation in an exchange under *section 361 (a)* or *(b)* for stock of a domestic corporation that is a USRPHC immediately after the transfer in such reorganization must recognize [*3] gain under *section 897 (d) (1)* and section 1.897-5T (c) (4) (i) when it distributes the stock of the domestic corporation received to its shareholders. Section 1.897-5T (c) (4) (ii) and (iii) provide an exception and a limitation to this recognition rule.

Paragraph (c) (4) (ii) and (iii) of section 1.897-5T of the temporary regulations will be replaced by a new exception to the recognition rule of section 1.897-5T (c) (4) (i). The exception will provide that recognition of gain will not be required on the distribution of the stock of the USRPHC under section 1.897-5T (c) (4) (i) if the foreign corporation pays an amount equal to any taxes that *section 897 of the Code* would have imposed upon all persons who had disposed of interests in the foreign corporation (or a corporation from which such assets were acquired in a transaction described in *section 381*) after June 18, 1980, as if it were a domestic corporation on the date of each of such dispositions, and if the conditions of current section 1.897-5T (c) (4) (ii) (A) and (C) are met. The payment must include any interest, as determined under *section 6621*, that would have accrued had tax actually been due with respect to the disposition. [*4] The time and manner of payment of any tax and interest determined to be due shall be made in accordance with the rules for the payment of tax and interest under section 1.897-3 (d) (2) of the regulations.

This revision of section 1.897-5T (c) (4) of the temporary regulations shall apply to all distributions of stock under section 1.897-5T (c) (4) occurring after July 31, 1989. The distributing foreign corporation may choose to apply this revision to distributions of stock under section 1.897-5T (c) (4) occurring before that date.

Distributions of U.S. real property interests by a foreign corporation to a domestic corporation in a liquidation under section 1.897-5T (c) (2)

The rules of *section 897 (d) of the Code* are applied to the distribution by a foreign corporation of a USRPI to a domestic corporation in a liquidation under *section 332 (a)* by section 1.897-5T (c) (1) of the temporary regulations. Section 1.897-5T (c) (2) (i) contains an exception to the general gain recognition rule of section 1.897-5T (c) (1) that is applicable to liquidation distributions under *section 332 (a)* to a domestic or foreign corporation if certain conditions are met. However, where there have been certain [*5] dispositions of the stock of the distributing foreign corporation within five years of a liquidating distribution to a domestic corporation, section 1.897-5T (c) (2) (ii) (B) requires gain to be recognized on the distribution of the USRPI even if the requirements of section 1.897-5T (c) (2) (i) are met.

Section 1.897-5T (c) (2) (i) and (ii) of the temporary regulations will be revised to provide that gain shall be recognized under section 1.897-5T (c) (1) upon the distribution of a USRPI by a foreign corporation to a domestic corporation meeting the stock ownership requirements of *section 332 (b) of the Code* in a liquidation under *section 332 (a)*. Thus, gain will be recognized by the foreign corporation even if the requirements of current section 1.897-5T (c) (2) (i) are met. There will be one exception to this gain recognition rule.

The exception will apply to the distribution of any USRPI by the distributing foreign corporation to the domestic-corporation if the distributing foreign corporation pays the tax and interest on any prior disposition of its stock (or stock of a corporation from which such assets were acquired in a transaction described in *section 381*) that would be required [*6] under the new exception to section 1.897-5T (c) (4) (i) of the temporary regulations that is described above and if the conditions of current section 1.897-5T (c) (2) (i) are met. Thus, if the appropriate tax and interest are paid and the conditions of section 1.897-5T (c) (2) (i) are met, then gain is not recognized on the distribution of any USRPIs by the foreign corporation to the domestic corporation.

7. FIRPTA Nonrecognition Rules

The revisions of section 1.897-5T (c) (2) of the temporary regulations shall apply to all distributions of USRPIs by foreign corporations in liquidations under *section 332 (a) of the Code* occurring after July 31, 1989. However, the distributing foreign corporation may choose instead to apply the rules of the current temporary regulations, including sections 1.897-5T (b) (3) (v) and (c) (2) (ii) (B), to its distribution of a USRPI to a domestic corporation in a liquidation under *section 332 (a)* where the corporation meeting the ownership requirements of *section 332 (b)* had such ownership in the distributing foreign corporation on July 31, 1989.

Certain requirements for elections under section 897 (i)

A foreign corporation may elect under *section 897 (i) of the Code* to be treated as a [*7] domestic corporation for purposes of *section 897*. Section 1.897-3 of the regulations specifies rules and procedures that foreign corporations are required to follow in making elections under *section 897 (i)*.

Section 1.897-3 (c) (5) of the regulations will be revised to require that a foreign corporation making the election under *section 897 (i) of the Code* must state that no interest in the corporation was disposed of during the shorter of (1) the period from June 19, 1980, through the date of election, or (2) the period from the date on which the corporation first holds a USRPI through the date of the election. There will no longer be a provision allowing for the use of the five-year period ending on the date of the election as the shortest period for the required statement concerning a disposition of an interest in the foreign corporation. Thus, where an election under *section 897 (i)* applies, all dispositions of stock after June 18, 1980, that would have been subject to taxation under *section 897 (a)*, will now be taxed.

This revision of section 1.897-3 (c) (5) of the regulations shall be effective for elections under *section 897 (i)* occurring after July 31, 1989.

Elections under section 897 (i) of the Code and the United States-Canada Income Tax Convention

Section 1.897-3 (d) (2) of the regulations, [*8] in general, provides that a corporation may make an election under *section 897 (i) of the Code* after a disposition of an interest in the corporation which would have been subject to taxation under *section 897 (a)* if the election had been made before that disposition but only if the requirements of either subdivision (i) or (ii) of that paragraph are met. Section 1.897-3 (d) (2) (i) provides that a payment must be made of an amount equal to any taxes which would have been imposed by reason of the application of *section 897* upon all persons who had disposed of interests in the foreign corporation during the period described in section 1.897-3 (c) (5) had the foreign corporation made the election prior to such dispositions.

The United States-Canada Income Tax Convention, 1986-2 C.B. 258, and the predecessor convention, *1943 C.B. 526*, provide in certain instances for a reduction in the amount of gain subject to United States taxation when a resident of Canada alienates certain USRFIs. Section 1.897-3 (d) (2) (i) of the regulations will be revised to provide that under that subdivision no payment of tax is required in the case of (1) a disposition before January 1, 1985, of an interest in [*9] a foreign corporation that would be exempt from taxation under *section 897 (a)* under Article VII of the former United States-Canada Income Tax Convention, if the foreign corporation had made an election under *section 897 (i) of the Code* prior to the date of the disposition; (2) a disposition after December 31, 1984, of an interest in a foreign corporation that would be exempt from taxation under *section 897 (a)* under Article VII of the former convention by virtue of Article XXX (5) of that Convention if the foreign corporation had made an election under *section 897 (i)* prior to the date of the disposition; or (3) a disposition after December 31, 1984, of an interest in a foreign corporation to the extent that it is not subject to taxation under *section 897 (a)* pursuant to Article XIII (9) of the current United States-Canada Income Tax Convention, with respect to gain attributable to appreciation of the stock of the foreign corporation occurring before January 1, 1985, if the foreign corporation had made an election under *section 897 (i)* prior to the date of the disposition.

This revision of section 1.897-3 (d) (2) (i) of the regulations shall be effective for elections under *section 897 (i) of the Code* [*10] occurring after July 31, 1989.

ADMINISTRATIVE PRONOUNCEMENT

This document serves as an "administrative pronouncement" as that term is described in section 1.6661-3 (b) (2) of the regulations and may be relied upon to the same extent as a revenue ruling or revenue procedure.

APPENDIX 7-D

Notice 89-64

Notice 89-64; 1989-1 C.B. 720; 1989 IRB LEXIS 241; 1989-22 I.R.B. 33

January 1989

[*1]

SUBJECT MATTER: Nonrecognition Exchange of U.S. Real Property Interests and Article XIII (9) of the United States-Canada Income Tax Convention

TEXT:

This notice provides guidance relating to nonrecognition distributions and exchanges by Canadian residents of U.S. real property interests (USRPIs) that qualify for reduced taxation under Article XIII (9) of the United States-Canada Income Tax Convention (the Treaty), 1986-2 C.B. 258, 264. The rules contained in this notice will be incorporated in final regulations to be issued under *section 897 (d)* and *(e)* of the Internal Revenue Code, and will be effective for any period in which a USRPI may be disposed of with reduced taxation under Article XIII (9) of the Treaty.

A foreign person that disposes of a USRPI is generally subject to U.S. income taxation under *section 897 (a) of the Code*. *Article XIII* (9) of the Treaty provides for a reduction in the amount of gain subject to U.S. taxation when a resident of Canada alienates certain USRPIs, to the extent the gain is attributable to the period before January 1, 1985. In order to qualify for the reduced U.S. income taxation under the Treaty, the Canadian resident had to own the USRPI on September 26, 1980, and be [*2] a resident of Canada on that date, or the USRPI had to be acquired by the

Canadian resident in an alienation of property that qualified as a nonrecognition transaction for purposes of taxation in the United States.

Section 337 of the Code generally provides for nonrecognition treatment on the distribution of property in a distribution pursuant to *section 332*. The non-recognition treatment provided under *section 337* may be overridden by *section 897 (d) (1)*, which specifies that a foreign corporation shall recognize gain on the distribution of a USRPI except to the extent provided in regulations or in *section 897 (d) (2)*. Under the regulations implementing *section 897 (d)*, a Canadian corporation that distributes a USRPI, the gain inherent in which would qualify for reduced taxation under the Treaty, must recognize gain on the distribution unless the following requirements of section 1.897-5T (c) (2) (i) of the Temporary Income Tax Regulations are met: (1) the distributee must be subject to U.S. income taxation on a subsequent disposition of the USRPI; (2) the distributee's basis in the USRPI must be no greater than the Canadian corporation's basis in the USRPI before the distribution, [*3] increased by the amount of gain (if any) recognized by the Canadian corporation on the distribution and added to the adjusted basis under the otherwise applicable provision, and (3) the Canadian corporation must comply with the filing requirements of paragraph (d) (1) (iii) of section 1.897-5T.

The Code also provides for nonrecognition treatment on the exchange of property in certain instances, including an exchange pursuant to *section 351 (a) of the Code*. The nonrecognition treatment provided in those instances may be overridden by *section 897 (e)*. If a Canadian resident transfers a USRPI, the gain inherent in which would qualify for reduced taxation under the Treaty, and such transfer would, but for *section 897 (e)*, qualify for nonrecognition under the Code, the transferee must recognize gain realized on the transfer unless the transfer complies with the following requirements of *section 897 (e) (1) of the Code* and section 1.897-6T (a) (1) of the temporary regulations: (1) the Canadian resident must receive a USRPI in the exchange that, immediately following the exchange, would be subject to U.S. taxation upon its disposition; and (2) the Canadian resident must comply with the filing [*4] requirements of paragraph (d) (1)-(iii) of section 1.897-5T.

Section 1.897-5T (d) (1) (ii) (B) of the temporary regulations provides that, if a distributee of a USRPI in a distribution or a transferor in an exchange who receives a USRPI would be entitled to reduced U.S. taxation under a treaty upon the disposition of the USRPI, then only a portion of the USRPI received is treated as subject to U.S. taxation upon its disposition, and only that portion is entitled to nonrecognition treatment on the original distribution or transfer. The temporary regulation states that this provision is applicable to certain transfers of USRPIs qualifying for reduced taxation under Article XIII (9) of the Treaty. Thus, if a Canadian corporation distributes to a Canadian distributee a USRPI, the gain inherent in which would qualify for reduced taxation under Article XIII (9), and such distribution would otherwise qualify for nonrecognition under section 1.897-5T (c) (2) (i), the Canadian corporation is required to recognize gain on the distribution if the Canadian distributee would be entitled to reduced U.S. taxation under the Treaty on the subsequent disposition of the USRPI. Similarly, if a Canadian [*5] person transfers a USRPI, the gain inherent in which would qualify for reduced taxation under Article XIII (9), in an exchange that otherwise qualifies for nonrecognition under section 1.897-6T (a) (1), the transferor is required to recognize gain if it is a Canadian individual or corporation that would be entitled to reduced U.S. taxation under the Treaty on a subsequent disposition of the USRPI received in the exchange.

The final regulations under *section 897 (d)* and *(e) of the Code* will be revised to provide generally that if a Canadian corporation distributes a USRPI, the gain inherent in which would qualify for reduced taxation under Article XIII (9) of the Treaty, in a liquidation under *section 332 (a)*, the Canadian corporation will not recognize gain solely because the distributee is a Canadian resident corporation qualifying for reduced taxation under Article XIII (9) in regard to the USRPI distributed. Thus, the distributee Canadian corporation will not be required to waive its U.S. treaty benefits under Article XIII (9) pursuant to section 1.897-5T (d) (1) (ii) (C) of the temporary regulations and any such waiver if filed shall be disregarded. All of the other provisions and [*6] requirements of the regulations under *section 897* will apply to the liquidation under *section 332 (a)*.

The final regulations under *section 897 (d)* and *(e) of the Code* will also be revised to provide generally that if a Canadian person transfers a USRPI, the gain inherent in which would qualify for reduced taxation under Article XIII (9) of the Treaty, to a U.S. corporation (or to a corporation that has made an election under *section 897 (i)*) in exchange under *section 351 (a)* for stock in such corporation that is a USRPI and also qualifies for reduced taxation under Article XIII (9), the transferor will not recognize gain on such exchange solely because the later transfer of the USRPI received in the exchange will qualify for reduced taxation under Article XIII (9). This exception will apply only where the Canadian person transfers solely USRPIs, the gain inherent in which would qualify in whole or in part for reduced taxation under Article XIII (9) of the Treaty (and such cash as is reasonably appropriate working capital), in actual (and not deemed) exchange for stock in such corporation that is equivalent in value to the USRPIs and the cash (if any) transferred. Thus, the Canadian [*7] transferor will not be required, in such case, to waive its U.S. treaty benefits under Article XIII (9) pursuant to section 1.897-5T (d) (1) (ii) (C) of the temporary regulations, and any such waiver if filed shall be disregarded.

These provisions of the final regulations under *section 897 (d)* and *(e) of the Code* will apply to transfers, exchanges, distributions, and other dispositions occurring after June 18, 1980. Except as otherwise provided, all of the other provisions and requirements of the regulations under *section 897* will apply to the transfer.

The final regulations to be issued under *section 897 (d)* and *(e) of the Code* may provide other exceptions to section 1.897-5T (d) (1) (ii) (B) of the temporary regulations for gains from transfers of USRPIs which qualify for reduced taxation under the Treaty. Additionally, exceptions may also be provided for transfers or distributions that do not consist solely of USRPIs (and reasonable working capital) which qualify for reduced taxation under the Treaty.

Section 1.897-3 (c) (4) (i) of the regulations provides that a foreign corporation must submit both a signed consent to the making of an election under *section 897 (i) of the Code* and [*8] a waiver of U.S. treaty benefits with respect to any gain or loss from the disposition of an interest in the corporation from each person who holds an interest in the corporation on the date the election is made. *Section 1.897-3 (c) (4) (i)* will be revised to provide that an interest-holder will not be required to waive benefits under Article XIII (9) upon the making of an election under *section*

897 (i) by a Canadian corporation. This provision will apply to all elections under *section 897 (i)* by Canadian corporations occurring after June 18, 1980.

ADMINISTRATIVE PRONOUNCEMENT

This document serves as an "administrative pronouncement" as that term is described in section 1.6661-3 (b) (2) of the Income Tax Regulations and may be relied on to the same extent as a revenue ruling or revenue procedure.

APPENDIX 7-E

Notice 89-57

Notice 89-57; 1989-1 C.B. 698; 1989 IRB LEXIS 227; 1989-21 I.R.B. 23

January 1989

[*1]

SUBJECT MATTER: Revision of Temporary Regulations Pending Issuance of Final Regulations under Section 897 of the Internal Revenue Code of 1986

TEXT:

The purpose of this notice is to announce the temporary suspension of a requirement contained in the Temporary Income Tax Regulations issued under *section 897 (d)* and *(e)* of the Internal Revenue Code. The temporary regulations under *section 897 (d)* and *(e)* were published in the Federal Register for Thursday, May 5, 1988 (*53 FR 16233*).

Background

The temporary regulations under *section 897 (d)* and *(e) of the Code* concern the transfer or distribution of U.S. real property interests by nonresident alien individuals or foreign corporations in dispositions that otherwise qualify for nonrecognition under the Code. Under the temporary regulations a condition of nonrecognition is that the filing requirements of paragraph (d) (1) (iii) of section 1.897-5T must be satisfied.

Section 1.897-5T (d) (1) (iii) of the temporary regulations provides that if a U.S. real property interest is distributed or transferred after December 31, 1987, the foreign transferor or distributor shall file an income tax return for the taxable year of the distribution or transfer in order to receive [*2] the nonrecognition treatment. It also provides that if a U.S. real property interest is distributed or transferred in a transaction before January 1, 1988, with respect to which nonrecognition treatment would not have been available under the express provisions of *section 897 (d)* or *(e) of the Code* but is available under the provisions of section 1.897-5T or section 1.897-6T, then the person that would otherwise be subject to tax by reason of the operation of *section 897* must file an income tax return or an amended return for the taxable year of the distribution or transfer by May 5, 1989, or by the date that the filing of the return is otherwise required. A statement providing certain information is required to be attached to the return.

Suspension of return filing requirement

The return filing requirement of section 1.897-5T (d) (1) (iii) of the temporary regulations is temporarily suspended for nonrecognition transfers and distributions by foreign transferors or distributors where (1) the transfer or distribution otherwise qualifies in its entirety for non-recognition under the temporary regulations under *section 897 (d) and (e) of the Code*; (2) the transferor or distributor does [*3] not have any other income that is effectively connected with a U.S. trade or business during the taxable year that includes the transfer or distribution subject to the temporary regulations under *section 897 (d) and (e)*; and (3) one of the following conditions is satisfied: (A) a withholding certificate is obtained pursuant to *section 1.1445-3 (a) of the regulations*, (B) a notice of nonrecognition is submitted to the Service pursuant to the provisions of *section 1.1445-2 (d) (2)* (or section 1.1445-2T (d) (2) of former temporary regulations), or (C) the transfer or distribution occurred before January 1, 1985. Additional guidance concerning the return filing requirement will be provided in the future.

ADMINISTRATIVE PRONOUNCEMENT

This document serves as an "administrative pronouncement" as that term is described in section 1.6661-3 (b) (2) of the regulations and may be relied upon to the same extent as a revenue ruling or revenue procedure.

APPENDIX 7-F

Notice 88-72

Notice 88-72; 1988-2 C.B. 383; 1988 IRB LEXIS 3659; 1988-27 I.R.B. 26

July 1988

[*1]

SUBJECT MATTER: Application of FIRPTA to Dispositions of Interests in Partnerships, Trusts, and Estates

TEXT:

This notice alerts foreign persons who are partners, trust beneficiaries, or estate beneficiaries that they are subject to the Foreign Investment in Real Property Tax Act of 1980 (FIRPTA), 1980-2 C.B. 524. United States income tax is therefore imposed when they dispose of an interest in the partnership, trust, or estate, on gain that is attributable to a United States real property interest (USRPI).

Section 897 (a) of the Internal Revenue Code of 1986 imposes tax generally on the disposition of a USRPI by a foreign person, and *section 897 (g)* extends this treatment to dispositions of an interest in a partnership, trust, or estate to the extent attributable to a USRPI held by the entity. Although *section 897 (g)* specifically authorizes the Service to issue implementing regulations, the section is not contingent on regulations. It therefore applies to dispositions after June 18, 1980, pursuant to section 1125 of FIRPTA. Thus, when a foreign person receives cash or property in exchange for all or part of an interest in a partnership, trust, or estate, gain or loss will be recognized to the extent attributable [*2] to a USRPI.

APPENDIX 7-F

Notice 88-72

Notice 88-72; 1988-2 C.B. 383; 1988 IRB LEXIS 3659; 1988-27 I.R.B. 26

July 1988

[*1]

SUBJECT MATTER: Application of FIRPTA to Dispositions of Interests in Partnerships, Trusts, and Estates

TEXT:

This notice alerts foreign persons who are partners, trust beneficiaries, or estate beneficiaries that they are subject to the Foreign Investment in Real Property Tax Act of 1980 (FIRPTA), 1980-2 C.B. 524. United States income tax is therefore imposed when they dispose of an interest in the partnership, trust, or estate, on gain that is attributable to a United States real property interest (USRPI).

Section 897 (a) of the Internal Revenue Code of 1986 imposes tax generally on the disposition of a USRPI by a foreign person, and *section 897 (g)* extends this treatment to dispositions of an interest in a partnership, trust, or estate to the extent attributable to a USRPI held by the entity. Although *section 897 (g)* specifically authorizes the Service to issue implementing regulations, the section is not contingent on regulations. It therefore applies to dispositions after June 18, 1980, pursuant to section 1125 of FIRPTA. Thus, when a foreign person receives cash or property in exchange for all or part of an interest in a partnership, trust, or estate, gain or loss will be recognized to the extent attributable [*2] to a USRPI.

APPENDIX 7-G

Notice 88-50

Notice 88-50; 1988-1 C.B. 535; 1988 IRB LEXIS 170; 1988-16 I.R.B. 32

January 1988

[*1]

SUBJECT MATTER: Guidance Concerning Reorganization Transactions Effected Through Use of State Domestication Statutes

TEXT:

This notice announces that, through publication of *Rev. Rul. 88-25*, page 8, this Bulletin, the Internal Revenue Service will provide guidance concerning the application of *section 368 (a) (1) (F) of the Internal Revenue Code* to the "domestication" of a foreign corporation pursuant to a state domestication statute. State domestication statutes (which are also known as corporate migration or corporate continuance statutes) allow an entity to transfer its place of incorporation without requiring the incorporation of a new legal entity. The Revenue Ruling concludes that there is a transfer of assets and liabilities from the foreign corporation to the domesticated U.S. corporation and a distribution by the foreign corporation to its shareholders of the stock in the domesticated corporation.

In addition, the ruling holds that a domestication constitutes a reorganization under *section 368 (a) (1) (F) of the Code*. Generally, applicable reorganization provisions of the Code will provide nonrecognition treatment to the foreign corporation and its shareholders. In certain circumstances, however, [*2] nonrecognition treatment will be contingent upon compliance with *section 367 (b)*, which generally govern international reorganizations, or *section 897 (d)* or *(e)*, which affect international reorganizations involving U.S. real property interests.

The regulations under *section 367 of the Code* will be revised to require the closing of the taxable year in all reorganizations of a foreign corporation into a domestic corporation (or vice versa) and to clarify that there is an actual or constructive transfer of assets and exchange of stock in all inbound, outbound and foreign to foreign reorganizations. See *Notice 87-29, 1987-1 C.B. 474*. The closing of the taxable year requirement will not generally apply to reorganizations under *section 368 (a) (1) (F)* within the same Country.

This document serves as an "administrative pronouncement" as that term is described in section 1.6661-3 (b) (2) of the Income Tax Regulations and may be relied upon to the same extent as a revenue ruling or revenue procedure. See *Rev. Rul. 87-138, 1987-2 C.B. 287*.

Finally, the Service is willing to provide further guidance on additional issues raised by the domestication of a foreign corporation. Written questions and [*3] comments should be addressed to: Associate Chief Council (International and Technical)

Attn: CC:C:3:Br.13 Rm. 5135

1111 Constitution Avenue, N.W.

Washington, DC 20224

Chapter 8
FIRPTA Withholding

§8.01	Overview	190
§8.02	Purchaser's Responsibility to Withhold	192
	A. Dispositions of Interests in USRPIs	192
	B. Dispositions of Interests in Partnerships	193
§8.03	Special Rules Relating to Certain Dispositions and Distributions	194
	A. Dispositions by Partnerships	194
	B. Dispositions by Trusts	195
	C. Distributions of USRPIs by Foreign Corporations	196
	D. Distributions by USRPHCs	197
§8.04	Exemptions from FIRPTA Withholding	198
	A. Sale of USRPIs	199
	1. Certification of Non-Foreign Status	199
	2. Certification of Non-USRPHC Interests	201
	B. Distributions with respect to USRPIs	202
	1. Certification of Non-Foreign Status	202
	2. Certification of Non-USRPHC Status	202
	C. Notice of Nonrecognition Transfer	203
	D. Foreclosures	205
	E. Government Transferors	207
§8.05	The Withholding Certificate	207
	A. Request Submitted Prior to the Transfer	209
	B. Request Submitted After the Transfer	209
§8.06	Coordination with FATCA	210
	A. FIRPTA Generally Overrides FATCA	210
	B. Certain Real Estate Related Payments Are Subject to FATCA	212
§8.07	Summary	213
Appendices		214

§8.01 OVERVIEW

'Withholding' is a term which typically describes a mechanism employed by tax authorities for the collection of tax imposed by law on the recipient of a payment. The collection responsibilities generally lie with the payor or distributor of the taxable amounts. Upon collection, or withholding, the payor or distributor would generally be required to remit such amounts to the tax authority.[1] In some instances, the tax withheld may be the final tax obligation of the income recipient, for example, non-US persons may be subject to withholding tax on FDAP income but the non-US person usually does not have any further US tax obligations. In other instances, the tax withheld may not be the final tax liability of the income recipient and the income recipient may be required to file a US tax return and pay additional taxes if the initial withholding was insufficient, or obtain a refund if taxes were over withheld.

There is a general misconception that FIRPTA itself is only a withholding regime. However, FIRPTA is a tax on net gain from the disposition of an asset, so it is a substantive tax.[2] The FIRPTA rules apply a withholding mechanism to collect part of the tax due when a USRPI is sold or when certain distributions are made to foreign interest holders. The foreign taxpayer that incurs the FIRPTA substantive tax then credits the amount withheld against the actual liability reported on its US federal income tax return.[3] FIRPTA withholding tax can be imposed in one of two ways:

– A purchaser that acquires USRPI from a foreign person is required to withhold *15% of the gross amount realized* from the disposition.[4]
– A corporation, partnership, trust and estate that distributes USRPI to a foreign person is generally required to withhold *35% of the gain realized from the transaction* that is distributed or allocated to the foreign recipient.[5]

The FIRPTA withholding rules mirror the FIRPTA substantive rules to a degree but contain their own definitions and detailed procedures. The FIRPTA withholding rules also are drafted very broadly. For example, all transactions involving a sale of the stock of *any* US corporation are subject to FIRPTA withholding unless an exemption applies. There are also exceptions to the exemptions, so anyone relying on an exemption should make sure the exceptions do not apply.

A withholding agent[6] that fails to withhold and pay over the required amount will be jointly and severally liable for the FIRPTA tax owed.[7] In the case of a transfer

---

1. Tello, Bloomberg BNA Tax Management Portfolio 915-3rd T.M., *Payments Directed Outside the United States — Withholding and Reporting Provisions Under Chapters 3 and 4*.
2. *See* I.R.C. §897 and the regulations thereunder. The FIRPTA withholding tax provisions can be found in I.R.C. §1445 and the regulations thereunder.
3. Treas. Reg. §1.1445-1(f).
4. *See* I.R.C. §1445(a).
5. *See* I.R.C. §1445(e).
6. The term withholding agent generally refers to a person with a FIRPTA withholding obligation under I.R.C. §1445. In the context of transactions covered by I.R.C. §1445(a) the withholding agent is the transferee; in the context of transactions covered by I.R.C. §1445(e) the withholding agent is the entity or fiduciary whose disposition of property triggers a withholding obligation under I.R.C. §1445(e).
7. I.R.C. §1461 and Treas. Reg. §1.1445-1(e).

of USRPI by a group of transferors, some domestic and some foreign, the amount subject to withholding is determined by allocating the amount realized based on the capital contribution of each transferor with respect to the property.[8] The phrase *caveat emptor,* or let the buyer beware, best describes this situation. Penalties and late payment interest also may apply.[9] A withholding agent also may be subject to various civil and criminal penalties.[10] For example, the corporate officers or other responsible persons may be subject to a civil penalty equal to 100% of the amount of tax required to be withheld.[11] Any such civil penalty imposed would be in addition to, and not in lieu of, any other penalty that could be imposed on the agent for the entity's failure to withhold.[12]

The transferee[13] of a USRPI is required to report the amount of tax withheld on Forms 8288 and 8288-A[14] and pay the amount over to the IRS by the twentieth day after the date of the transfer.[15] The IRS will then stamp a copy of the Form 8288-A to indicate receipt of the withheld tax and return the stamped copy to the foreign transferor.[16] The transferor[17] is required to attach the stamped copy of Form 8288-A to its income tax return reflecting the disposition of the USRPI to receive credit for the tax withheld.[18] It is advisable for a foreign seller to contractually obligate the transferee to properly execute the Forms 8288 and 8288-A and pay over the withheld

---

8. Treas. Reg. §1.1445-1(b)(3). There is a special rule for joint transferors that are husband and wife: the capital contributions will be aggregated and each transferor will be deemed to have contributed 50% of the aggregated amount.
9. For example, the liability may be satisfied by the transferor's filing of an income tax return and payment of any tax due with respect to the transfer. *See* Treas. Reg. §1.1445-1(e). Also see discussion in Ch. 11, *infra,* with respect to other civil and criminal penalties that may apply.
10. *See* Treas. Reg. §1.1445-1(e)(2).
11. I.R.C. §6672(a).
12. *Id.*
13. A transferee means any person, foreign or domestic, that acquires a USRPI by purchase, exchange, gift, or any other transfer. Treas. Reg. §1.1445-l(g)(4). This chapter uses the term purchaser if the context involves a purchase of USRPI; the term transferee is used in all other cases.
14. *See* Appendix 8-A to 8-C.
15. Treas. Reg. §1.1445-1(c)(1). The date of transfer of a USRPI generally is the first date on which consideration is paid or a liability is assumed by the transferee. However, the payment of consideration does not include the payment, prior to the passage of title of the USRPI, of earnest money, a good faith deposit or any similar sum that primarily is intended to bind the transferee or the transferor to the entering or performance of a contract, even if the earnest money, good faith deposit or similar sum ultimately is to be applied against the purchase price for the USRPI. A payment will be presumed to be earnest money, a good faith deposit or other similar sum if it is subject to forfeiture in the event of a failure to enter or breach of the contract with respect to which it is made. Treas. Reg. §1.1445-1(g)(8).
16. Treas. Reg. §1.1445-1(f)(2).
17. A transferor means any person, foreign or domestic, that disposes of a USRPI by sale, exchange, gift, or any other transfer. Treas. Reg. §1.1445-l(g)(3). This chapter uses the term seller if the context involves a sale of USRPI; the term transferor is used in all other cases.
18. Treas. Reg. §1.1445-1(f)(2).

tax to the IRS.[19] If a transferor does not receive a stamped copy of Form 8288-A, it may establish the amount of tax withheld by the purchaser by attaching to the return other substantial evidence (e.g., closing documents) of such amount.[20]

§8.02 PURCHASER'S RESPONSIBILITY TO WITHHOLD

A. Dispositions of Interests in USRPIs

A purchaser who acquires an interest in any USRPI, including the stock of a USRPHC, generally is required to withhold 15% of the amount realized[21] by the foreign seller[22] unless an exemption applies.[23] In some cases, a threshold issue is whether the interest being acquired constitutes an interest in a USRPI. As discussed earlier, the definition of a USRPI, particularly in the case of intangible assets, is not always clear cut.[24] Unless the parties agree that the subject being sold is not a USRPI, a purchaser is likely going to withhold the FIRPTA tax. The seller may avoid the withholding if it either certifies that the stock being sold is not a USRPHC,[25] or obtains a special certificate from the IRS to excuse the withholding (referred to as a Withholding Certificate).[26]

If *any* class of interest in an entity is regularly traded on an Established Securities Market,[27] a foreign seller of such interest is generally exempt from FIRPTA withholding tax.[28] This exemption applies to the disposition of a publicly traded interest in a domestic corporation, partnership or trust.[29] The exemption applies regardless of the percentage of the foreign person's ownership and even if the foreign seller is liable for the substantive FIRPTA tax with respect to such disposition. In other words, this

---

19. The taxes withheld should appear as an item in the closing statement prepared in connection with the transaction and should be transmitted to the IRS along with the completed and signed Forms 8288 and 8288-A at the time of closing.
20. Treas. Reg. §1.1445-1(f)(3)(i).
21. The amount realized by a foreign transferor is the sum of the cash and the fair market value of other property transferred or to be transferred to the foreign transferor, plus the outstanding amount of any liability assumed by the transferee or to which the USRPI is subject both before and after the transfer. Treas. Reg. §1.1445-l(g)(5).
22. The statute refers to dispositions by a foreign person. I.R.C. §1445(a). I.R.C. §1445(f)(3) defines foreign persons, for this purpose, to include foreign corporations, foreign partnerships and nonresident alien individuals. This book focuses on the US taxation of foreign corporate investors and, thus, this chapter only refers to tax rates applicable to corporate taxpayers and does not refer to tax rates applicable to investors who are nonresident aliens.
23. *See* Treas. Reg. §1.1445-2 and discussions in §8.04. and §8.05., *infra*.
24. *See*, e.g., discussion in §3.04., *supra*.
25. *See* discussion in §8.04.A.2., *infra*.
26. *See* discussion in §8.05, *infra*.
27. *See* Treas. Reg. §1.897-1(m) and Temp. Treas. Reg. §1.897-9T(d)(4). *See* discussion in §6.02.B., *supra*, for a discussion regarding the requirements for the Publicly Traded Exception to avoid FIRPTA substantive tax.
28. This exemption applies to FIRPTA withholding tax applicable under either I.R.C. §1445(a) or (e). *See* Treas. Reg. §1.1445-2(c)(2) and Treas. Reg. §1.1445-5(b)(4)(ii).
29. *Id*.

FIRPTA withholding exemption is more generous than the Publicly Traded Exception[30] from the FIRPTA substantive tax, which only applies to persons owning no more than 5% or 10%, respectively, of the class of stock of publicly traded Subchapter C corporations and REITs.

Furthermore, FIRPTA withholding tax also does not apply where a foreign person disposes of a non-publicly traded interest in an entity where the disposition is incident to an initial public offering of such interest pursuant to a registration statement filed with the Securities and Exchange Commission.[31]

B. Dispositions of Interests in Partnerships

A purchaser who acquires an interest in a partnership, domestic or foreign, generally is required to withhold 15% on the amount realized by the foreign seller if the partnership is a 50/90 Partnership.[32] A partnership is a 50/90 Partnership if 50% or more of the value of the gross assets of the partnership consists of USRPIs and 90% or more of the value of the gross assets consist of USRPIs plus any cash or cash equivalents.[33] Cash equivalents include any assets such as bank accounts, certificates of deposit, money market accounts, commercial paper, treasury bonds, corporate bonds, precious metals or commodities and publicly traded instruments.[34]

Proceeds from the sale of a non-50/90 Partnership interest are completely exempt from FIRPTA withholding tax. This distinction creates a cliff effect that is not in sync with the rules that determine the seller's FIRPTA substantive tax liability. Under the substantive FIRPTA rules, only the amount *attributable to* USRPI shall be considered received from the sale of USRPI in the case of the sale of a partnership interest.[35] A purchaser that receives a statement certifying that the partnership is not a 50/90 Partnership is not required to withhold any FIRPTA tax.[36] The regulations are silent on *when* to measure whether the partnership is a 50/90 Partnership. However, based on the guideline provided with respect to the certification by a US corporation (i.e., that it is not a USRPHC), it is reasonable to interpret that to mean that the percentages are applied to the assets of the partnership as of the date of the disposition of the partnership interest.[37]

---

30. I.R.C. §897(c)(3) and (k)(1)(A). *See* discussion in §6.02.B., *supra*.
31. *See* Treas. Reg. §1.1445-2(c)(2) and -5(b)(4)(ii).
32. *See* Treas. Reg. §1.1445-11T(d)(1). A partnership interest, unlike the interest in a corporation, is not itself a USRPI. FIRPTA applies an aggregate approach to investments through partnerships and taxes only gains attributable to a sale of USRPIs owned by the partnership. *See* I.R.C. §897(g).
33. Treas, Reg, §1.1445-11T(d)(1).
34. *Id.*
35. I.R.C. §897(g).
36. The statement must be issued by the partnership and signed by a general partner, under penalties of perjury, no earlier than thirty days before the transfer. *See* Treas. Reg. §1.1445-11T(d)(2)(i) and (ii). The purchaser may not rely on the statement if it either has actual knowledge that the statement is false or receives a notice that the statement is false.
37. Treas. Reg. §1.1445-5(b)(4)(iii) permits a transferee to rely on a statement, dated not more than thirty days of the date of the transfer, by a US corporation whose stock is being transferred providing that the corporation is not a USRPHC.

§8.03 SPECIAL RULES RELATING TO CERTAIN DISPOSITIONS AND DISTRIBUTIONS

FIRPTA applies to a disposition of a USRPI by a *foreign* person. Thus, dispositions of a USRPI by a US partnership, trust or estate generally do *not* result in any withholding obligation on the purchaser. In such a case, the seller (i.e., the US partnership, trust or estate), instead of the purchaser, has the responsibility to withhold the FIRPTA tax.[38]

The timing of the withholding depends on:

- whether the entity that sells the USRPI is a partnership or a trust;
- whether the partnership or trust has more than one hundred partners or beneficiaries; and
- whether the partnership or trust is publicly traded.

A. Dispositions by Partnerships

A partner's distributive share of certain partnership income retains the same character as determined in the hands of the partnership.[39] As a result, a foreign partner is liable for FIRPTA substantive tax on income allocable from a US partnership upon a disposition of USRPIs. Such distributive share of the gain must be determined under US partnership tax principles.[40] In general, a US partnership with one hundred or fewer partners, domestic and foreign, is required to withhold FIRPTA tax when it *disposes* of a USRPI.[41] The partnership is required to withhold 35% of the USRPI gain that is includible in the distributive share of any foreign partner.

A partnership with more than one hundred partners may elect to apply a simplified procedure, referred to as Large Entity Election, to collect the FIRPTA withholding tax.[42] An electing partnership is required to maintain a special account referred to as the Section 1445(e)(1) Transfers. The account equals the total amount of gain the partnership realizes on all USRPI dispositions net of the total amount of distributions made to domestic and foreign partners.[43] A distribution from the partnership is deemed to be first attributable to the Section 1445(e)(1) Transfers

---

38. I.R.C. §1445(e)(1).
39. *See* I.R.C. §702. Similar rules apply to beneficiaries of trusts and estates under I.R.C. §§652, 662, 671.
40. *See* I.R.C. §704.
41. Treas. Reg. §1.1445-5(c)(1)(ii).
42. *See* Treas. Reg. §1.1445-5(c)(3). The election, which is revocable only with the consent of the IRS, is made by filing a notice with the Internal Revenue Service Center, P.O. Box 409101, Ogden, UT 84409. The notice of the election must include the name, office address and taxpayer identification number of the electing partnership or trust and, in the case of a partnership, must also include the name, office address and taxpayer identification number of the general partner submitting the notice of election. A similar election is available to a partnership that makes recurring sales of unsevered growing crops and timber. Treas. Reg. §1.1445-5(c)(3)(iv). If the election is made, the partnership or trust may withhold from each distribution to a foreign partner or beneficiary an amount equal to 15% of such partner's proportionate share of the current balance another special account referred to as the Gross Section 1445(e)(1) Account.
43. Treas. Reg. §1.1445-5(c)(3)(iii)(A) and (B).

account.[44] The partnership collects the 35% withholding tax, imposed on each partner's proportionate share of the account, when it makes *distributions* to its foreign partners.[45] A publicly traded partnership is automatically required to establish a Section 1445(e)(1) Transfers account regardless of whether it elects to apply the Large Entity Election procedure.[46]

As discussed earlier, a partnership that engages in a US trade or business is required to withhold quarterly tax payments (currently at 35% for corporate partners) on ECI allocable to foreign partners (referred to as ECI Withholding Tax)[47] as the income is *earned*.[48] If the interest in a partnership is publicly traded, then the ECI Withholding Tax applies when the partnership *distributes* the income to its foreign partners.[49] To avoid duplicate withholding, the regulations provide that the ECI Withholding Tax trumps the FIRPTA withholding tax.[50] Thus, a partnership that complies with the ECI Withholding Tax is considered to have satisfied the FIRPTA withholding tax with respect to the disposition of a USRPI.[51] A foreign partnership that is subject to the 15% FIRPTA withholding from its sale of a USRPI[52] may credit the amount withheld against its ECI Withholding Tax liability.[53]

B. Dispositions by Trusts

The trustee, fiduciary,[54] executor or equivalent fiduciary (collectively referred to as the fiduciary) of a trust or estate is required to withhold 35% of the gain from a sale of a USRPI that is includible in the distributive share of any foreign beneficiary.[55]

The fiduciary of a non-grantor trust is required to establish a special account (referred to as the USRPI Account) and enter the gains and losses realized from the dispositions of USRPIs during the taxable year in such an account. The fiduciary is required to withhold 35% on any *distribution* to a foreign beneficiary attributable to the balance in the USRPI Account at the time of the distribution.[56] Distributions by

---

44. *Id.*
45. Treas. Reg. §1.1445-5(c)(3)(ii).
46. Treas. Reg. §1.1445-8(c)(1).
47. *See* I.R.C. §1446 and discussion in §2.03.A., *supra*.
48. Treas. Reg. §1.1446-3(b)(1). The withholding applies regardless of whether the income is distributed to the partners.
49. Treas. Reg. §1.1446-4(a).
50. Treas. Reg. §1.1446-3(c)(2)(i).
51. *Id.*
52. That is, a foreign partnership that is subject to FIRPTA withholding tax imposed by I.R.C. §1445(a) as discussed in §8.02.A., *supra*.
53. Treas. Reg. §1.1446-3(c)(2)(ii).
54. The withholding obligation applies to the fiduciary of a trust even if the grantor of the trust or another person is treated as the owner of the trust for US tax purposes. Thus, the withholding obligation applies to the trustee of a land trust or similar arrangement, even if such a trustee is not ordinarily treated under the applicable provisions of local law as a true fiduciary. Treas. Reg. §1.1445-5(c)(1)(i).
55. I.R.C. §1445(e)(1) and Treas. Reg. §1.1445-5(c)(1)(i).
56. Treas. Reg. §1.1445-5(c)(1)(iii). The fiduciary is required to pay the amount withheld over to the IRS by the twentieth day after the date of disposition. Treas. Reg. §1.1445-5(b)(5)(i).

a trust or estate are deemed to be attributable first to the balance of the account.[57] Any balance remaining in the account at the end of the year is *cancelled,*[58] and is not subject to withholding, although it may be subject to US income tax in the hands of the trust or estate under general trust taxation provisions.

A trust with more than one hundred beneficiaries may elect to use the simplified Large Entity Election procedure applicable to partnerships described above. A publicly traded trust is automatically required to establish a Section 1445(e)(1) Transfers account even if it does not elect to apply the Large Entity Election procedure.[59] In certain instances, a publicly traded trust may transfer the withholding obligation to another person if the person:

 - is a nominee;[60]
 - receives a distribution attributable to a disposition of a USRPI by the entity;
 - receives the distribution for payment to any foreign person; and
 - receives a qualified notice of the obligation to withhold.[61]

If all the above conditions are satisfied, then the sole obligation to withhold the FIRPTA tax is imposed on the nominee to the extent of the amount specified in the qualified notice.[62]

C. Distributions of USRPIs by Foreign Corporations

As stated earlier, a foreign corporation that distributes a USRPI to its shareholders generally is required to recognize gain on the distribution unless an exception applies.[63] The foreign corporation is required to deduct and withhold from the amount distributed a tax equal to 35% of the gain that it recognized on the distribution.[64] This is the only instance in which the FIRPTA withholding obligation is placed on the *same person* having the substantive FIRPTA tax liability. A foreign corporation that distributes a USRPI may avoid the FIRPTA tax (both substantive and withholding) if the transaction qualifies for an exception under the FIRPTA Nonrecognition Rules.[65]

---

57. The balance in the account is reduced by the total amount distributed to all beneficiaries (domestic and foreign) during the taxable year which is attributable to the account. Treas. Reg. §1.1445-5(c)(1)(iii).
58. *Id.*
59. Treas. Reg. §1.1445-8(c)(1).
60. Treas. Reg. §1.1445-8(d) defines the term nominee, for this purpose, as a domestic person that holds an interest in the relevant publicly traded trust.
61. Treas. Reg. §1.1445-8(b)(3). *See* also Treas. Reg. §1.1445-8(f), which describes what satisfies as a qualified notice for this purpose. A withholding agent, in such a situation, may rely on a Certification of Non-Foreign Status to avoid withholding or on a Form W-8 or Form W-9 to determine whether an interest holder in the entity is a foreign person. *See* Treas. Reg. §1.1445-8(e) and discussion in §8.04.B.1., *infra.*
62. *Id.*
63. I.R.C. §897(d). *See* discussion in §7.03, *supra,* on FIRPTA Nonrecognition Rules which operate as exceptions to gain recognitions.
64. I.R.C. §1445(e)(2); Treas. Reg. §1.1445-5(d).
65. *See* discussion in §7.03, *supra.*

8. FIRPTA Withholding

The statute also imposes FIRPTA withholding on a domestic or foreign partnership, trust or estate that distributes a USRPI to a foreign partner or beneficiary. The rule requires the distributing entity to withhold 15% of the fair market value of the USRPI distributed to a foreign partner or beneficiary.[66] However, the regulations delay such withholding until further guidance is issued.[67] No such guidance has been published to date and, hence, these distributions are *not* currently subject to FIRPTA withholding tax.

D.   Distributions by USRPHCs

A USRPHC is, by definition, a Subchapter C corporation and the general ordering rule on shareholder distributions under the Subchapter C rules apply to distributions by a USRPHC:[68]

(1) first out of the USRPHC's earnings and profits[69] which are treated as taxable dividends to the shareholders;
(2) any distribution in excess of earnings and profits are treated as non-taxable return of capital up to each shareholder's adjusted basis is the stock; and
(3) any remaining amount is treated as capital gain to the shareholders.[70]

The amount of a USRPHC's dividend paid to a foreign investor is treated as FDAP income which generally is subject to a 30% US statutory withholding tax.[71] A special rule applies to coordinate the FIRPTA withholding tax[72] with the FDAP income withholding tax rules.[73] Under the special rule, a USRPHC that makes a distribution to a foreign shareholder that is at least partially out of its earnings and profits generally may withhold either:

– 30% (or a lower treaty rate if applicable)[74] on the *entire* amount of the distribution, i.e., regardless of whether any portion of the distribution represents a return of basis or a capital gain;[75] or

---

66. I.R.C. §1445(e)(4).
67. *See* Treas. Reg. §1.1445-11T(c).
68. A foreign corporation that has made the Section 897(i) Election to be treated as a US corporation for FIRPTA substantive and withholding tax purposes is also subject to the withholding rules described in this section. Treas. Reg. §1.1445-7(c).
69. Determined in accordance with the rules of I.R.C. §312.
70. *See* I.R.C. §301(c)(1), (2) and (3).
71. *See* I.R.C. §§871 or 881 and discussion in §2.02.A., *supra*. A number of existing US tax treaties reduce the dividend withholding rate to 15%, 10%, 5%, or 0% if certain conditions are satisfied. For further discussion, *see* Ch. 9, *infra*.
72. Imposed by I.R.C. §1445(e).
73. Imposed by I.R.C. §§1441 and 1442.
74. *See* Ch. 9, *infra*, for a discussion on coordination with income tax treaty provisions. However, the amount of reduced treaty withholding rate under this rule may not be less than 10% (15% for distributions after February 16, 2016).
75. *See* Treas. Reg. §1.1441-3(c)(4)(i)(A).

- 30% (or a lower treaty rate if applicable) on the dividend portion of the distribution, and 35% on the remainder of the distribution (or on a smaller portion based on a withholding certificate).[76]

When a USRPHC distributes property to a foreign shareholder in redemption of the shareholder's stock or in liquidation of the USRPHC, the foreign shareholder is treated as exchanging USRPHC stock for the property distributed.[77] As such, the USRPHC generally must deduct and withhold from the distribution a tax equal to 15% of the fair market value of the property being distributed.[78] This is the case even if the distribution constitutes a partial return of capital with respect to the stock[79] and is not treated as gain on a disposition of the USRPHC stock by the foreign shareholder.[80]

As discussed earlier, a former USRPHC that has disposed of all of its USRPIs in one or more taxable transactions, including a taxable liquidation, may cleanse its USRPI taint immediately.[81] The former USRPHC is deemed to have sold all of its assets at their fair market value at the time of the liquidation and would be subject to corporate-level tax on the gain. As a result, FIRPTA withholding tax is not applicable to the liquidating distributions of such a former USRPHC.

As discussed in Chapter 5, the FIRPTA withholding rules require a REIT to withhold the largest amount of its distributions that may be designated as a Capital Gain Dividend under Code section 857(b)(3)(C).[82] By requiring a REIT to withhold on capital gain distributions, a foreign investor may be subject to overwithholding. The FIRPTA substantive tax on such distributions is imposed on distributions *attributable to* gain from a sale of USRPI by a REIT. This is another place where the FIRPTA withholding rules are not in sync with the FIRPTA substantive tax rules.[83]

§8.04   EXEMPTIONS FROM FIRPTA WITHHOLDING

A number of exemptions apply to the FIRPTA withholding tax regime.[84] The rules are written in a very pedantic manner but there is a common thread among them. Generally speaking, no FIRPTA withholding applies if the transferor (e.g., the seller)

---

76. See Treas. Reg. §1.1441-3(c)(4)(i)(B)(1) and (2).
77. See I.R.C. §302 with respect to redemptions and I.R.C. §331 with respect to liquidations.
78. I.R.C. §1445(e)(3); Treas. Reg. §1.1445-5(e)(1). The fair market value of property is the price at which the property would change hands between an unrelated willing buyer and a willing seller, neither being under any compulsion to buy or sell and both having reasonable knowledge of all relevant facts. Reg. §1.1445-1(g)(7).
79. See I.R.C. §301(c)(2).
80. There should be no substantive FIRPTA tax liability if the distribution is not treated as a deemed sale of the stock of the USRPHC. This is another situation where the taxpayer should obtain a Withholding Certificate to reduce any excess withholding.
81. See I.R.C. §897(c)(1)(B) and discussion in §6.02.A., *supra*, regarding the Cleansing Exception.
82. Treas. Reg. §1.1445-8(c)(2)(i) and (ii). See discussion in §5.04.B.2., *supra*, regarding the taxation of REIT capital gain distributions.
83. Some commentators have questioned the status of this regulation. See, e.g., Blanchard, Ch. 1 footnote 59, *supra*.
84. I.R.C. §1445(b).

8. FIRPTA Withholding

can demonstrate that it does not owe any FIRPTA substantive tax. It is up to the transferee (e.g., the purchaser) to make sure that it obtains the proper documentation (e.g., in the form of a certification)[85] from the transferor that the exemption applies. The transferor's or transferee's agent must notify the transferee (i.e., the buyer) if they know the certifications are false.[86]

These exemptions do not cover all the situations where withholding exceeds substantive tax liability. A seller/transferor may obtain a Withholding Certificate from the IRS in those other situations to minimize the amount of cash outlay.

A. Sale of USRPIs

A purchaser that acquires a USRPI from a foreign seller may avoid the 15% FIRPTA withholding obligation if it receives either a statement from the seller certifying that either the seller is not a foreign person[87] or the interest acquired is not a USRPHC.[88]

1. Certification of Non-Foreign Status

The Certification of Non-Foreign Status, signed by the seller under penalties of perjury, may be provided to the purchaser or the purchaser's qualified substitute.[89] The certification must state that the seller is not a foreign person, set forth the seller's address and taxpayer identification number.[90] A purchaser that either has actual knowledge that the Certification of Non-Foreign Status is false, or receives notice to that effect prior to the transfer of the USRPI, may not rely on the certification.[91] Under either of these circumstances, the purchaser is fully liable for any failure to withhold.[92] A seller or purchaser's agent involved in the transaction has a duty to notify the recipient that the certification is false if either:

---

85. Treas. Reg. §1.1445-2(c)(3). The regulations substitute the term 'certification' for the statutory term 'affidavit' to clarify that the document does not need to be sworn to before a notary.
86. Treas. Reg. §1.1445-4(a).
87. I.R.C. §1445(b)(2). A purchaser also may rely on other means, e.g., actual knowledge, to ascertain the non-foreign status of the transferor without actually receiving a certification. However, in the event the transferor turns out to be a foreign person, only a transferee obtaining a valid Certification of Non-Foreign Status may avoid liabilities for failure to withhold. Treas. Reg. §1.1445-1(e).
88. I.R.C. §1445(b)(3). The principle is the same as the certification that a partnership is not a 50/90 Partnership as discussed in §8.02.B., *supra*.
89. A qualified substitute generally means the party (including any attorney or title company) that is responsible for the closing, other than the transferor's agent. The term also include the transferee's agent. I.R.C. §1445(f)(6). If the certificate is provided to the qualified substitute, then the latter is required to furnish a statement to the purchaser that it has received such an affidavit. I.R.C. §1445(b)(9).
90. I.R.C. §1445(b)(2); Treas. Reg. §1.1445-2(b)(2). The transferee must retain the Certification of Non-Foreign Status in its records for five taxable years after the taxable year in which the transfer takes place. Treas. Reg. §1.1445-2(b)(3).
91. I.R.C. §1445(b)(7)(A); Treas. Reg. §1.1445-2(b)(4).
92. *See* Treas. Reg. §1.1445-1(e).

- the agent actually knows that the certification is false; or
- the agent represents a foreign corporation that has given a Certification of Non-Foreign Status.[93]

Any agent who is required to give notice as stated above but who fails to do so also may be liable for the withholding tax. However, the agent's actual liability for the tax that should have been withheld is limited to the amount of any compensation that the agent derived from the underlying transaction.[94]

A QFPF,[95] or an entity all of the interests of which are held by a QFPF, is not treated as a foreign person for this purpose.[96] Hence, a QFPF may provide a Certification of Non-Foreign Status under this rule.[97] A foreign corporation that has made a Section 897(i) Election to be treated as a US corporation for FIRPTA purposes[98] may provide a valid Certification of Non-Foreign Status provided that the electing corporation attaches to the certification a copy of the IRS's acknowledgement of the Section 897(i) Election.[99] The owner of certain disregarded entities is treated as

---

93. Treas. Reg. §1.1445-4(a) and (b). A transferor's or transferee's agent that is required to give notice that a Certification of Non-Foreign or Non-USRPI status is false must do so in writing as soon as possible after learning that a false certification has been given, but not later than the date of the implementation of the transaction with respect to which the certification was given. If the agent learns only after the closing of the transaction that a false Certification of Non-Foreign Status was given, the agent must give the notice within three days after learning of that fact. The notice given by a transferor's or transferee's agent must be in writing, must state that the certification in question is false and may not be relied upon and must explain the possible consequences to the recipient of a failure to withhold under I.R.C. §1445 in reliance upon the false certification. A copy of the notice must also be filed at the same time with the Internal Revenue Service Center, P.O. Box 409101, Ogden, UT 84409, and be accompanied by a cover letter stating that the copy is being filed pursuant to Treas. Reg. §1.1445-4(c)(2).
94. Treas. Reg. §1.1445-4(e). A transferee who properly relies on a Certification of Non-Foreign Status and does not withhold tax at the time of the disposition of the USRPI, nevertheless may be faced with a renewed FIRPTA withholding obligation subsequent to the disposition if: (1) the transferee acquires actual knowledge or is given notice that the certification of non-foreign status was false; and (2) the transferee still has control over any consideration remaining to be paid for the USRPI. In that case, the transferee must withhold the full 15% of the total amount realized by the transferor for the USRPI from the consideration remaining to be paid, if there is sufficient unpaid consideration to do so. Treas. Reg. §1.1445-2(b)(4)(iv).
95. See I.R.C. §897(l) and discussion in §6.03.A., supra, regarding the definition of QFPF.
96. Treas. Reg. §1.1445-2(b)(2)(i).
97. The 2015 PATH Act enacted two new exceptions to the FIRPTA substantive tax. See discussion in §6.03, supra. The FIRPTA withholding tax, however, only treats one of the new investor groups, QFPFs, as non-foreign person for purposes of I.R.C. §1445. It is not clear what the policy reason is for not granting the same treatment to Qualified Shareholders, the other category of investors that may qualify for exception under I.R.C. §897(k)(2).
98. See discussion in §7.04.B., supra, regarding the mechanisms and benefits of the Section 897(i) Election.
99. Treas. Reg. §1.1445-2(b)(2)(ii). Also see Treas. Reg. §1.897-3(d)(4). If the IRS acknowledgement of the foreign corporation's Section 897(i) Election is not attached to the

8. FIRPTA Withholding

the transferor and must be the party that provides the Certification of Non-Foreign Status.[100]

2. *Certification of Non-USRPHC Interests*

This exemption only applies to the stock of US corporations and not any other USRPIs. The FIRPTA withholding regime presumes that *all* US corporations are USRHPCs.[101] To rebut the presumption, the purchaser of a private US corporation[102] may obtain a Certification of Non-USRPI Status, signed under penalties of perjury, no more than thirty days prior to the date of the disposition.[103]

The certification must state that the corporation is not a USRPHC,[104] and was not a USRPHC at any time during the shorter of the period during which the transferor held the interest in the corporation or the five-year period ending on the date of the disposition. The determination may take into account the application of the Cleansing Exception.[105] A corporation may *not* certify that an interest in the corporation is not a USRPI based on the corporation's determination that the interest in question is an interest in the corporation *solely as a creditor*.[106]

A purchaser that has actual knowledge that the certification is false or receives notice to that effect prior to the purchase, may not rely on the certification.[107] If, after the date of transfer, a purchaser receives notice that a Certification of Non-USRPI Status is false, the purchaser is required to withhold a full 15% of the amount realized by the seller from the consideration that remains to be paid to the transferor.[108]

---

corporation's Certification of Non-Foreign Status, the transferee may not rely on it. Treas. Reg. §1.1445-2(b)(4)(ii).
100. Treas. Reg. §1.1445-2(b)(2)(iii). For this purpose, a disregarded entity means an entity that is disregarded from its owner under Treas. Reg. §301.7701-3, a qualified REIT subsidiary as defined in I.R.C. §856(i) or a qualified Subchapter S subsidiary under I.R.C. §1361(b)(3)(B).
101. This includes a foreign corporation that has made a Section 897(i) Election to be treated as a US corporation for FIRPTA purposes.
102. FIRPTA withholding tax does not apply to the acquisition of an interest in a US corporation if any class of the corporation's stock is regularly traded on an established securities market. Treas. Reg. §1.1445-2(c)(2).
103. Treas. Reg. §1.1445-2(c)(3)(i).
104. The statement is issued pursuant to the provisions of Treas. Reg. §1.897-2(h).
105. I.R.C. §1445(b)(3). If the seller so requests, the corporation may provide the certification directly to the purchaser. The corporation may also voluntarily provide such a certification to the purchaser. Treas. Reg. §1.l445-2(c)(3)(i).
106. Treas. Reg. §1.1445-2(c)(3)(i).
107. I.R.C. §1445(b)(7)(A); Treas. Reg. §1.1445-2(c)(3)(ii).
108. Treas. Reg. §1.1445-2(c)(3)(iii). Amounts so withheld must be reported and paid over to the IRS by the twentieth day following the date on which each payment to the transferor is made.

B. Distributions with respect to USRPIs

Exemptions also apply to FIRPTA withholding imposed on certain distributions by corporations, partnerships, trusts or estates.

1. Certification of Non-Foreign Status

An entity or a fiduciary may treat an interest holder as a US person if that interest holder furnishes to the entity or fiduciary a Certification of Non-Foreign Status. The certificate, signed under penalties of perjury, must set forth that the interest holder is not a foreign person, the interest holder's address and taxpayer identification number.[109] If the entity or fiduciary either has actual knowledge that the Certification of Non-Foreign Status is false, or receives notice to that effect prior to the transfer of the USRPI, the entity or fiduciary may not rely on the certification to establish its exemption from the FIRPTA withholding obligation.[110]

Special rules apply to certain belated notice of false certification. If, after the date of a distribution, a US corporation learns that an interest-holder's Certification of Non-Foreign Status is false, then the corporation may rely on the certificate only if the person providing the false certification holds (or held) less than 10% of the outstanding stock of the corporation.[111] On the other hand, a US corporation that learns that the certificate it received from a 10%-or-greater shareholder is false has the same 15% FIRPTA withholding obligation as if a certificate had never been given.[112]

A partnership that belatedly learns that a Certification of Non-Foreign Status on which it relied was false must withhold from the partner who gave the false certification only the lesser of: (1) the amount of tax it would have been required to withhold had that partner or beneficiary not given a Certification of Non-Foreign Status in the first place; and (2) the amount equal to that partner's remaining interest in the income or assets of the partnership.[113] Thus, the withholding obligation exists only if the particular partner who gave the false Certification of Non-Foreign Status continues thereafter to hold an interest in the partnership.

2. Certification of Non-USRPHC Status

No withholding is required if an entity (i.e., a corporation or a partnership) or fiduciary receives a statement that the stock being distributed is not a USRPI (i.e., a Certification

---

109. The transferee must retain the Certification of Non-Foreign Status in his records for three calendar years following the close of the last calendar year that the entity relied upon the certification. Treas. Reg. §1.1445-5(b)(3)(ii)(B).
110. Treas. Reg. §1.1445-5(b)(3)(iii). Reliance on the certification is also not permitted if the US corporation has received the certification from a corporation that does not attach to it a copy of the IRS acknowledgement of the corporation's Section 897(i) Election.
111. Treas. Reg. §1.1445-5(e)(3)(iii)(B).
112. Id.
113. The partnership must pay over the withheld tax to the IRS within sixty days after it learns the certification was false. The same rules apply to beneficiaries of a trust or estate. Treas. Reg. §1.1445-5(c)(2)(iii)(B).

of Non-USRPHC Status).[114] If an entity has disposed of an equity interest in a US corporation and only learns after the disposition that a Certification of Non-USRPHC Status upon which it relied was false, different consequences may ensue.

A foreign corporation that has distributed an equity interest in a US corporation to its shareholders remains fully liable for the tax that should have been withheld and must pay it over to the IRS within sixty days after the date on which it learns that the Certification of Non-USRPHC Status was false.[115] No penalties and interest would be assessed for failures to withhold prior to that date.[116]

A partnership that receives belated notice that a Certification of Non-USRPHC Status upon which it relied was false is only required to withhold with respect to each foreign partner tax equal to the lesser of: (1) the amount it would have been required to withhold had it not received the Certification of Non-USRPHC Status; and (2) the amount equal to the remaining interest (if any) in the income or assets of the partnership that continues to be held by the foreign partner who previously received the distribution of the USRPHC interest free of withholding.[117]

A transferor's or transferee's agent involved in a transaction in which a Certification of Non-USRPHC Status is given has a duty to notify the person receiving the certification that the certification is false if the agent actually knows that the Certification of Non-USRPHC Status is false.[118]

C. Notice of Nonrecognition Transfer

A transferee of a USRPI is not required to collect the otherwise applicable FIRPTA withholding tax if: (1) the transferor has provided the transferee with a notice stating that the transferor is not required to recognize gain or loss on the transfer because of the operation of a FIRPTA Nonrecognition Rules,[119] and (2) the transferee provides a copy of the transferor's statement to the IRS within twenty days after the date of the transfer.[120] The transferor's statement must contain the following specific items of information with respect to the transfer:

- a statement that the document constitutes a notice of nonrecognition transfer pursuant to the requirements of Treasury Regulation section 1.1445-2(d)(2);
- the name, taxpayer identification number, and address (the home address in the case of an individual) of the transferor;
- a statement that the transferor is not required to recognize any gain or loss on the transfer;

---

114. Treas. Reg. §1.1445-5(b)(4)(iii).
115. Treas. Reg. §1.1445-5(d)(2)(i)(B).
116. Id.
117. The tax withheld must be paid over to the IRS within sixty days after the date the partnership learns that the Certification of Non-USRPHC Status was false. Treas. Reg. §1.1445-5(c)(2)(iii)(B).
118. I.R.C. §1445(d)(1) and Treas. Reg. §1.1445-4(a) and (b).
119. See I.R.C. §897(d) and (e) related discussion in Ch. 7, *supra*.
120. Treas. Reg. §1.1445-2(d)(2)(i). The IRS procedures concerning the contents and handling of notices of nonrecognition transfer may be found in paragraph 21.8.5 of the Internal Revenue Manual (revised September 2015).

- a brief description of the transfer; and
- a brief summary of the law and facts supporting the claim of nonrecognition treatment.[121]

A transferee of a USRPI may not rely on such a notice: (1) if the transferor qualifies for nonrecognition treatment only with respect to *part of the gain* realized by the transferor on the transfer, or (2) if the transferee knows or has reason to know that the transferor is not entitled to the nonrecognition treatment claimed.[122]

A similar statement may also be used to relieve an entity or fiduciary of the FIRPTA withholding obligation imposed by Code section 1445(e).[123] However, due to the different nature of the transactions covered, the applicable procedures are different from those used in transfers of USRPIs governed by the withholding rule of Code section 1445(a). In particular, the withholding agent itself (e.g., the entity or fiduciary) subject to the special rules of Code section 1445(e) makes the determination and submits the required statement directly to the IRS.[124] The relevant statement must be submitted to the IRS within twenty days after the date of the underlying transfer and must also contain the name, address and taxpayer identification number of the entity or fiduciary submitting the notice and the name, address (the home address in the case of an individual) and taxpayer identification number of each foreign person with respect to which withholding would otherwise be required.[125]

Rev. Proc. 2008-27, in part, provides taxpayers with a simplified method to request relief for a late filing of this statement and is in lieu of the letter ruling procedure that otherwise would be required to obtain relief under Treasury Regulation section 301.9100-3.[126] In general, to be eligible for relief under Rev. Proc. 2008-27, the taxpayer must file the completed notice with the IRS upon becoming aware of its failure to file, and must attach an explanation describing why the taxpayer's failure to timely file the notice was due to reasonable cause. The IRS generally has 120 days upon receipt of the completed application to respond.

A purchaser is exempt from FIRPTA withholding obligation where the USRPI is acquired for use as a residence and the purchase price is not greater than USD 300,000.[127] Purchasers who use the property as a residence may be entitled to a reduced withholding rate of 10% if the amount realized for such property does not

---

121. Treas. Reg. §1.1445-2(d)(2)(iii).
122. Treas. Reg. §1.1445-2(d)(2)(ii). The Treasury Regulations do not specify when a transferee will be considered to have reason to know that a transferor is not entitled to the nonrecognition treatment claimed in a notice of nonrecognition transfer.
123. Treas. Reg. §1.1445-5(b)(2).
124. Treas. Reg. §1.1445-5(b)(2). This is different from the case of transfers covered by I.R.C. §1445(a) where the foreign person against which withholding would otherwise be required must make the determination of his entitlement to nonrecognition treatment and submit a notice of nonrecognition transfer to the withholding agent (the transferee).
125. Reg. §1.1445-5(b)(2)(ii).
126. 2008-1 C.B. 1014. In particular, the revenue procedure provides taxpayer relief for late filings under Treas. Reg. §§1.897-2(g)(1)(ii)(A), 1.897-2(h), 1.445-2(c)(3)(i), 1.1445-2(d)(2), 1.1445-5(b)(2), and 1.1445-5(b)(4). No user fees apply to submissions and taxpayers preserve their right to request relief under Treas. Reg. §301.9100-3 should the IRS deny the taxpayer relief pursuant to the revenue procedure.
127. I.R.C. §1445(b)(5); Treas. Reg. §1.1445-2(d)(1).

exceed USD 1,000,000.[128] A USRPI is considered to be acquired for use as a residence if on the date of the transfer the transferee has definite plans to reside at the property for at least 50% of the number of days that the property is actually in use during each of the two twelve-month periods following the date of the transfer.[129] A purchaser is considered to reside at the property on any day on which the purchaser or a member of his/her family resides at the property.[130]

A purchaser does not have to take any action to establish that he has definite plans to meet the residence requirements and thus is entitled to take advantage of this exemption. However, a transferee who, in reliance on this exemption, does not withhold tax and who later fails to reside at the property for the required minimum number of days will be liable for the tax that should have been withheld, unless either: (1) the foreign person transferor paid the full US tax due on the gain recognized on the transfer; or (2) the transferee establishes that his failure to reside at the property for the required minimum number of days was due to a change of circumstances that could not reasonably have been anticipated at the time of the transfer.[131]

D. Foreclosures

The regulations provide a special procedure applicable to sales of USRPIs conducted pursuant to foreclosure proceedings. A lender that acquires a USRPI from a foreign borrower in a foreclosure sale is a purchaser/transferee of the USRPI and, thus, is required to withhold FIRPTA tax. However, the regulations provide that if the transferee complies with certain notice requirements, it is only required to withhold tax imposed on the *lesser* of the amount realized by the foreign borrower on the transfer and an Alternative Amount.[132] This effectively operates as an exemption from withholding.

The Alternative Amount, for this purpose, is any amount that a court or trustee determines that accrues to the foreign borrower/transferor out of the amount realized from the foreclosure sale.[133] The amount of any mortgage, lien or other security interest that is terminated is excluded.[134] A property typically is sold in foreclosure proceedings for an amount that equals the outstanding debt secured by the property. Therefore, a borrower usually does *not* realize any amount in excess of the debt. The lender/transferee must report and pay over to the IRS the amount, if any, withheld on the twentieth day following the final determination by a court or trustee with jurisdiction over the foreclosure action.

---

128. *See* I.R.C. §1445(c)(4) enacted by the 2015 PATH Act.
129. Treas. Reg. §1.1445-2(d)(1).
130. Members of the transferee's family for this purpose include only the transferee's brothers and sisters, spouse, ancestors and lineal descendants. Treas. Reg. §1.1445-2(d)(1). See I.R.C. §267(c)(4). Aunts, uncles and cousins do not qualify as family members for this purpose.
131. Treas. Reg. §1.1445-2(d)(1).
132. Treas. Reg. §1.1445-2(d)(3)(i).
133. *Id.*
134. Any amount of the loan assumed by (or taken subject to by) another person is also excluded. *Id.*

A lender/transferee acquiring a USRPI in such a foreclosure sale must notify the court or the trustee on the day the property is transferred.[135] Furthermore, a lender/transferee must notify the IRS within twenty days after the final determination by a court or trustee with jurisdiction over the foreclosure action regarding the distribution of the amount realized from the foreclosure that the lender/transferee is relying on the special procedure to eliminate or reduce its withholding obligation.[136] The notice submitted to the IRS must contain the following information with respect to the foreclosure:

- a statement that the document is a notice of foreclosure pursuant to Treasury Regulation section 1.1445-2(d)(3);
- the name, address[137] and taxpayer identification number of the person who acquired the USRPI from the foreign person debtor;
- the name, address[138] and taxpayer identification number of the foreign person debtor from which the USRPI was acquired;
- the date of the final determination regarding the distribution of the amount realized from the foreclosure sale;
- a brief description of the property;
- the amount realized from the foreclosure sale; and
- the Alternative Amount.[139]

The special foreclosure procedure is not available if a USRPI is transferred pursuant to foreclosure proceedings for a principal purpose of avoiding the FIRPTA withholding obligation. It is presumed that there is a principal purpose of avoiding the FIRPTA withholding obligation if: (1) the lender's security interest in the USRPI did not arise in connection with the foreign debtor's acquisition, improvement or maintenance of the USRPI; and (2) the total amount of all debts secured by the USRPI exceeds 90% of the fair market value of the USRPI. This presumption may be rebutted by evidence.[140]

Instead of a foreclosure sale, the foreign borrower may transfer the title of the property to satisfy the debt (i.e., deed in lieu of foreclosure). The lender/transferee in such a transfer is required to withhold FIRPTA tax at 15% based on the amount realized by the debtor/transferor.[141] However, no withholding is required if: (1) the

---

135. No particular form is necessary but the notice must set forth the transferee's name, home address for an individual (office address for an entity), a brief description of the property, the date of the transfer, the amount realized on the sale and the amount withheld. Treas. Reg. §1.1445-2(d)(3)(ii)(A). In addition the creditor/transferee must provide notice to the court or trustee regarding the amount that is reported and paid over to the IRS. Treas. Reg. §1.1445-2(d)(3)(ii)(B).
136. Treas. Reg. §1.1445-2(d)(3)(ii).
137. An individual must provide his/her home address.
138. An individual must provide his/her home address.
139. Treas. Reg. §1.1445-2(d)(3)(iii). There is a special rule for lending institutions to ameliorate the reporting requirements. A person required under I.R.C. §6050J to file Form 1099-A does not have to comply with the notice requirements of Reg. §1.1445-2(d)(3)(iii) if the Alternative Amount is zero. However, the reporting rules of Treas. Reg. §1.1445-2(d)(3)(ii) must be complied with. Treas. Reg. §1.1445-2(d)(3)(iii)(B).
140. Treas. Reg. §1.1445-2(d)(3)(v).
141. Treas. Reg. §1.1445-2(d)(3)(i)(B).

transferee is the only person with a security interest in the property; (2) no cash or other property (other than incidental fees) is paid, directly or indirectly, to any person; and (3) certain notice requirements are met.[142] If cash or other property is paid to any person, or a person other than the creditor/transferee has a security interest, a certificate of reduced withholding may be requested.

E. Government Transferors

A foreign sovereign investor is subject to US tax only with respect to income arising from commercial activities or deemed commercial activities within the United States.[143] If a foreign sovereign investor is eligible to claim the 892 Exemption, any gain from a disposition of a USRPI will not be subject to the FIRPTA substantive tax or FIRPTA withholding tax.[144] To avoid FIRPTA withholding by the transferee, the foreign sovereign investor needs to provide the transferee with a Notice of Nonrecognition Transfer claiming nonrecognition treatment on the transfer and giving a brief summary of the law and facts supporting the claim.[145]

A foreign sovereign investor that acquires a USRPI from a foreign person is fully subject to the FIRPTA withholding tax obligation.[146] On the other hand, no FIRPTA withholding tax is required with respect to any acquisition of property (whether a USRPI or not) by the United States, a state or possession of the United States (or a political subdivision thereof) or the District of Columbia.[147]

§8.05 THE WITHHOLDING CERTIFICATE

A foreign transferor whose substantive FIRPTA tax liability[148] is less than the amount of the FIRPTA withholding tax[149] has the option to obtain a Withholding Certificate to avoid any excess withholding.[150] The IRS generally has ninety days after the receipt

---

142. The notice requirements are essentially those specified in Treas. Reg. §1.1445-2(d)(3)(iii), discussed above in connection with foreclosure sales. To satisfy the fourth requirement, the creditor/transferee must provide the date the property is transferred.
143. *See* discussion in Ch.5, *supra*.
144. Treas. Reg. §1.1445-10T(b)(1). *See* I.R.C. §892(a)(2) and discussion in §6.04.A., *supra*.
145. Treas. Reg. §1.1445-10T(b)(1). A proper notice of nonrecognition transfer would need to: (1) establish that the entity claiming nonrecognition treatment is a foreign government or international organization, (2) cite to I.R.C. §892 and the Treasury Regulations thereunder as providing for nonrecognition of income arising from non-commercial activities of foreign governments and international organizations and (3) summarize the facts supporting the claim that the USRPI in question is not being held by the foreign government or international organization for use in a commercial activity. The notice of nonrecognition transfer should otherwise conform with the requirements of Treas. Reg. §1.1445-2(d)(2).
146. Treas. Reg. §1.1445-10T(b)(2).
147. Treas. Reg. §1.1445-2(d)(5).
148. Determined under I.R.C. §§897 and 882.
149. Imposed by I.R.C. §1445.
150. *See* also Rev. Proc. 2000-35, 2000-2 C.B. 211. *See* Appendix 8-D for a copy of Form 8288-B which is used to apply for a FIRPTA Withholding Certificate.

The US Foreign Investment in Real Property Tax Act: A Practical Guide

of an application to act upon it.[151] In complicated or unusual cases, the IRS will notify the applicant no later than forty-five days after receiving the application that it needs more time. The IRS's notice also will provide a final date for its action.[152]

It is generally preferable to apply for a reduced amount of withholding ahead of time than to seek a refund of the amount of taxes withheld after the end of the tax year. The application for the Withholding Certificate, made on Form 8288-B, is sent to a special unit of the IRS[153] that handles these applications. The unit has been known, based on anecdotal evidence, to respond within the ninety-day window. On the other hand, a refund claim filed after the end of the year, done on the taxpayer's US tax return, e.g., Form 1120F, is filed with the IRS district center which handles a broad spectrum of tax matters. In addition, refund claims over a certain amount may require different layers of review within the IRS which may slow things down even further.

An applicant[154] must submit a statement of law and facts to support the request for a Withholding Certificate.[155] An applicant is required to include a calculation of its maximum FIRPTA tax liability[156] and any potential FIRPTA withholding tax that it still may owe.[157] A Withholding Certificate only has the effect of adjusting the FIRPTA withholding obligation and does not reduce the substantive FIRPTA tax liability.

Some taxpayers have raised concerns that applying for a Withholding Certificate may lead to an IRS examination of its tax returns. There is no evidence that the IRS FIRPTA Unit actually contacts the IRS district where the taxpayer files its tax returns to raise any issues, FIRPTA or otherwise, prior to issuing the Withholding Certificate.

---

151. The ninety-day period will not begin until an application for a Withholding Certificate is substantially complete. Treas. Reg. §1.1445-3(a).
152. Id.
153. The Withholding Certificate must be sent to the Internal Revenue Service Center, P.O. Box 409101, Ogden UT 84409. This unit, which handles varies administrative matters involving FIRPTA, is informally referred to as the FIRPTA Unit. The actual size and the operations of the unit are not publicized.
154. An application for a Withholding Certificate may be filed either by the foreign person who would be subject to tax with respect to the underlying transaction or by the person who would have the tax withholding obligation on the transaction. Rev. Proc. 2000-35, §4.01.
155. An applicant that seeks a Withholding Certificate on the basis of an agreement to pay the tax with the IRS must attach a copy of the security instrument, if any. See Treas. Reg. §1.1445-3(b)(4)(iii).
156. The maximum FIRPTA tax liability generally is the amount of gain multiplied by the highest applicable tax rate with certain adjustments. The adjustments include any losses previously recognized on dispositions of USRPIs by the taxpayer during the same tax year, the effect of any nonrecognition provisions applicable to the transaction and any other factor that may affect the tax liability with respect to the disposition. See Treas. Reg. §1.1445-3(c)(2) and Rev. Proc. 2000-35, §3.06.
157. This is generally the amount of any FIRPTA withholding tax that the transferor was required to, but did not, withhold and pay over to the IRS at the time the transferor (when it was in the position of transferee) acquired the USRPI (or a predecessor interest). See Treas. Reg. §1.1445-3(b)(4)(i). A predecessor interest is an interest that was exchanged for the USRPI in question in a transaction in which the transferor was not required to recognize the full amount of the gain or loss realized upon the transfer. Treas. Reg. §1.1445-3(c)(3).

8. FIRPTA Withholding

As a practical matter, ninety days do not provide a sufficient time frame for the IRS to conduct a meaningful examination of any technical issues.

A. Request Submitted Prior to the Transfer

Ideally, a transferor should obtain a Withholding Certificate *prior* to the sale or transfer of the USRPI (i.e., the application should be submitted with sufficient time for the IRS to respond within the ninety-day window). If an application for a Withholding Certificate is still pending on the date that the USRPI is transferred, the transferor may notify the transferee about the status.[158] The transferee must still withhold the full amount of tax required, but may delay paying the withheld tax until the IRS makes a final determination on the application. Once the IRS does make a final determination on the application, the withholding agent then has twenty days to pay over the amount of tax due as determined.[159]

Under a special procedure, a transferor who anticipates making multiple dispositions of USRPIs during a single period of up to twelve months may apply to the IRS for a so-called Blanket Withholding Certificate. Such a certificate provides advance authorization for reduced withholding with respect to each such disposition made during that period.[160] A Blanket Withholding Certificate issued to a transferor will provide that no withholding is required with respect to any disposition of a USRPI by the transferor if certain specified notice conditions are satisfied.

B. Request Submitted After the Transfer

A transferor who has been subjected to excess FIRPTA withholding tax may obtain an early refund.[161] The actual amount of tax that was withheld will be reflected on the stamped Form 8288-A which must be attached to the refund application.[162]

To obtain a refund, the transferor must apply for a Withholding Certificate from the IRS setting out the transferor's FIRPTA tax liability with respect to the transaction to demonstrate the amount of tax that should have been withheld. In a case where the transferor has already applied for a Withholding Certificate, the foreign person must wait until the Withholding Certificate is issued and then apply for the refund.[163]

---

158. Treas. Reg. §1.1445-1(c)(2)(i).
159. *Id.*
160. Rev. Proc. 2000-35, §9. Unlike an application for a Withholding Certificate in other circumstances which can be submitted either by a foreign person who would be subject to withholding with respect to a disposition of a USRPI or by the person who would have the tax withholding obligation on the disposition, only a transferor of a USRPI may apply for a Blanket Withholding Certificate. This makes sense because the Blanket Withholding Certificate, by definition, covers multiple dispositions of USRPIs, and the transferor generally will be the only person with a connection to all of the dispositions.
161. Treas. Reg. §1.1445-3(a). The IRS will not process an application for an early refund if the stamped Form 8288-A is not attached to the application. Treas. Reg. §§1.1445-3(g) and 1.1445-6(g).
162. Treas. Reg. §§1.1445-3(g) and 1.1445-6(g).
163. This should be equal to the maximum tax liability reflected in the Withholding Certificate.

A transferor also may combine its application for a Withholding Certificate with the refund application.[164] No particular form is required for the application. Most of the information required should have been included in the Withholding Certificate which must be included for the application. Taxpayers typically include a cover letter attaching the Withholding Certificate along with the stamped copy of Form 8288-A stating the intent to apply for the refund and the amount of refund claimed. The IRS generally will act within a ninety-day period for such a refund claim.[165]

§8.06 COORDINATION WITH FATCA

A. FIRPTA Generally Overrides FATCA

Enacted in 2010,[166] Chapter 4 of the Code (Code sections 1471 through 1474) also referred to as the Foreign Account Tax Compliance Act (FATCA) requires US withholding agents to withhold 30% tax on Withholdable Payments to: (1) non-US financial institutions that do not report to the IRS their US accounts, and (2) certain nonfinancial foreign entities that do not report their substantial United States owners.[167]

Withholdable Payments generally include (1) US-source FDAP income; and (2) gross proceeds from the sale or disposition of property that can give rise to US source dividends or interest.[168] However, income treated as ECI, including gains from the disposition of USRPI, is explicitly exempted from FATCA withholding,[169] and thus, income that is subject to FIRPTA escapes FATCA.

At its core, FATCA is a US information reporting regime, which is enforced by an imposition of a 30% withholding tax for non-compliance. The FATCA framework classifies all foreign entities[170] (other than those that are specifically exempted)[171] into two main categories: Foreign Financial Institutions (FFIs) and all other entities, referred to as Nonfinancial Foreign Entities (NFFEs). Very generally,[172] FFIs include entities that:

– accept deposits in the ordinary course of a banking or similar business;

---

164. Treas. Reg. §1.1445-3(g).
165. Treas. Reg. §1.1445-6(g).
166. The IRS has revised the timeline for implementation of FATCA requirements several times, but the final FATCA regulations are currently in effect. See T.D. 9657.
167. See I.R.C. §§1471 and 1472.
168. Treas. Reg. §1.1473-1(a).
169. Treas. Reg. §1.1473-1(a)(4)(ii).
170. FATCA generally does not apply to income realized directly by individuals, but may be implicated where, for example, such income is generated by assets held by foreign entities as nominees. See Bissell, *When FATCA Meets FIRPTA: Some Preliminary Comments*, 43 Tax Mgmt. Intl. J. 621 (2014).
171. Entities exempt from FATCA withholding include, for example, foreign governments and their political subdivisions, international organizations and their wholly owned agencies or instrumentalities, foreign central banks, certain publicly traded corporations, and certain foreign retirement funds. I.R.C. §§1471(f) and 1472(c).
172. As discussed below, the definitions of the FFI in the regulations and IGAs differ, raising multiple interpretive issues.

- hold, as a substantial portion of their business, financial assets for the benefit of one or more other persons; or
- are engaged primarily in the business of investing, reinvesting, or trading in securities, partnership interests, commodities, or any interest therein.[173]

An entity that does not fall under the definition of an FFI, is treated as an NFFE and then has to be further classified as an active NFFE or a passive NFFE. Generally, FFIs and passive NFFEs are subject to FATCA withholding. An FFI and a passive NFFE may take certain steps to avoid FATCA withholding.[174] Specifically, an FFI may register with the IRS and obtain a Global Intermediary Identification Number and either enter into an agreement with the IRS to provide information regarding its US owners, or, if it is located in a jurisdiction with an Intergovernmental Agreement or IGA, comply with the due diligence and reporting requirements in the applicable IGA. An NFFE should not be subject to FATCA withholding if it provides information regarding its direct and indirect US owners or that it is otherwise exempt from FATCA withholding.

Prior to receiving a Withholdable Payment, a foreign entity must determine whether it is an FFI, NFFE, or Exempt Beneficial Owner. It must then certify its FATCA status with the withholding agent by providing the withholding agent a Form W-8BEN-E.[175] Generally, in order to be compliant with FATCA and avoid the 30% FATCA withholding, FFIs must adopt due diligence, validation and monitoring procedures for tax documentation, and may need to report certain information to the IRS with respect to US account holders/owners. Moreover, an FFI may be required to withhold on payments to FFIs that are not compliant with the FATCA reporting requirements. NFFEs may need to disclose their 'substantial US owners' (US persons owning > 10%), which they can do on the Form W-8BEN-E.

The IRS has issued several notices and promulgated regulations interpreting FATCA.[176] The United States also entered into IGAs with several countries, which generally rely on one of the IRS models (specifically, Model 1, which has version 1A and 1B, and Model 2).[177] Under the Regulations, the definition of FFI includes any entity treated as an FFI under the applicable IGA.[178] The counter-parties to the IGAs have also issued their guidance on the interpretation of the respective IGAs (referred to as guidance notes),[179] which provide persuasive authority interpreting the

---

173. I.R.C. §1471(d)(5).
174. *See* I.R.C. §§1471 and 1474.
175. The Form W-8BEN-E is 8 pages long and provides 25 different classifications. As such, an entity's FATCA classification requires a detailed analysis of the facts and circumstances of the entity's operations. See Appendix 8-E and 8-F for a copy of Form W-8BEN-E.
176. *See* e.g., T.D. 9657, T.D. 9610.
177. Model 1A provides for reciprocal exchange of information between the United States and the IGA partner, while Model 1B envisions that the IGA partner's FFIs will provide information to the United States.
178. Treas. Reg. §1.1471-5(d) which provides that 'With respect to any entity that is resident in a country that has in effect a Model 1 IGA or Model 2 IGA, an FFI is any entity that is treated as a Financial Institution pursuant to such Model 1 IGA or Model 2 IGA.'
179. *See*, e.g., HM Revenue & Customs, *The Implementation of the International Tax Compliance (United States of America) Regulations 2014 Guidance Notes,* (28 August 2014), available at https://www.gov.uk/government/uploads/system/uploads/attachment_data/file/357542/uk-us-fatca-guidance-notes.pdf (last visited August 31, 2015).

IGA and are authoritative in the issuing country, but formally do not bind the IRS or US courts. As a result, the interpretation of the FATCA status of such companies as, for example, treasury centers, holding companies, and pension funds, raise various technical interpretive and practical issues that extend beyond the present discussion.[180]

Putting the complexity of the FATCA compliance aside, it is clear that following the enactment of FATCA, foreign investors in US real estate have to take into consideration the interplay between the FIRPTA and FATCA rules. For example, prior to enactment of FATCA, a foreign investor that did not file US tax returns and preferred not to be subject to US income tax payment or filing obligations, could structure its investment in US real estate via a leveraged US corporation, and thus, not trigger direct US tax payment and filing exposure upon an exit via the disposition of the investment and liquidation of the corporation.[181] Following the enactment of FATCA, the foreign investor may be required to register its FATCA status with the IRS and otherwise comply with the FATCA due diligence and reporting requirements.[182] In this sense, FATCA is similar to other US reporting requirements, such as the US information reporting, in that it becomes one of the considerations in investing in US real estate.

If a withholding agent determines that a particular payment is subject to both FATCA withholding and withholding under Code sections 1441, 1442, and 1443 (referred to as the Chapter 3 Withholding), such agent may credit the amount withheld pursuant to FATCA against the Chapter 3 liability.[183] However, the definition of a Withholdable Payment for FATCA purposes is more expansive than the definition of FDAP income subject to withholding under Chapter 3; e.g., FATCA also applies to proceeds from dispositions of property that may give rise to FDAP income.[184] As such, a FATCA charge may apply even if Chapter 3 Withholding is not triggered.

B.   Certain Real Estate Related Payments Are Subject to FATCA

FATCA is implicated in a range of investment structures for an inbound investment in US real estate. Foreign investors should be prepared to navigate the FATCA rules to the extent they derive income from an investment in US real property that is not treated as ECI under FIRPTA rules. Examples of these include distributions from corporations or REITs, and gains on the disposition of Domestically Controlled REITs.[185] While FIRPTA and FATCA rules do not overlap due to an explicit statutory exemption under the FATCA rules, the broad reach of the FATCA rules requires that both regimes should be taken into account in structuring an investment in US real estate. Specifically, in order to not fall subject to the 30% FATCA withholding, it is

---

180. *See* e.g., Tanenbaum, *FATCA 'Versus' IGAs*, 44 Tax Mgmt. Intl. J. 503 (2015), Acharya, *Reporting Obligations Imposed by FACA on Foreign Retirement Plans and U.S. Participants of Such Plans,* 43 Tax Mgmt. Intl. J. 540 (2014).
181. Lipton & Mcdonald, *Foreign Investment in U.S. Real Estate: The FATCA/FIRPTA Dichotomy,* 120 J. Tax 248, 262 (2014).
182. *Id.*
183. Treas. Reg. §1.1474-6(b)(1).
184. *See* Treas. Reg. §1.1441-2(a) and Treas. Reg. §1.1473-1(a).
185. *Id.* Generally, the beneficial owner of a Withholdable Payment may not be entitled to a credit or refund of the tax withheld under FATCA if it is not in compliance with the FATCA reporting requirements. *See* Treas. Reg. §1.1474-5(a).

imperative that foreign entities determine their FATCA classification, determine what procedures and reporting are required under FATCA based on that classification, and provide the withholding agent with a Form W-8 certifying the entity's FATCA status and compliance with the FATCA reporting rules.

§8.07 SUMMARY

The FIRPTA withholding rules generally require a purchaser or other transferee of a USRPI or any related distribution to withhold either 15% of the gross consideration or 35% of the net gain involving a sale, transfer or related distribution with respect to the USRPI. A purchaser or transferee that fails to properly withhold and remit the FIRPTA withholding tax to the IRS can be held liable for the amount of tax due plus interest and penalties. A number of exemptions apply to the withholding requirements. The withholding agents are responsible to keep the necessary records to demonstrate the applicability of any exemption. A seller or transferor also may obtain a Withholding Certificate to reduce the amount of excess FIRPTA tax withheld. The Withholding Certificate is a useful procedure that often results in tax and cash savings to a foreign investor that disposes of a USRPI.

APPENDIX 8-A

Instructions for Form 8288
(Rev. February 2017)

Department of the Treasury
Internal Revenue Service

U.S. Withholding Tax Return for Dispositions by Foreign Persons of U.S. Real Property Interests

Section references are to the Internal Revenue Code unless otherwise noted.

Future Developments

For the latest information about developments related to Form 8288 and its instructions, such as legislation enacted after they were published, go to www.irs.gov/form8288.

What's New

We made the following changes to the prior version of Form 8288.
- Added a line at the top of the form to indicate the Form 8288 filed is an amended return.
- Deleted old line 5, Part I, as the amount realized will be reported on new line 5a, and/or 5b.
- On line 5, Part II, we rearranged the withholding rates to better reflect the types of transactions reported on Form 8288.
- The blank line to the right of line 5d, Part II, has been replaced with a check box, by which the filer will indicate that the withholding is at a reduced rate. The amount of such withholding is included in the total on line 6, Part II.

General Instructions

Purpose of Form

A withholding obligation under section 1445 is generally imposed on the buyer or other transferee (withholding agent) when a U.S. real property interest is acquired from a foreign person. The withholding obligation also applies to foreign and domestic corporations, qualified investment entities, and the fiduciary of certain trusts and estates. This withholding serves to collect U.S. tax that may be owed by the foreign person. Use Form 8288 to report and transmit the amount withheld.

TIP *If an exception applies, you may be required to withhold at a reduced rate, or you may not be required to withhold. See Exceptions, later.*

Who Must File

A buyer or other transferee of a U.S. real property interest, and a corporation, qualified investment entity, or fiduciary that is required to withhold tax, must file Form 8288 to report and transmit the amount withheld. If two or more persons are joint transferees, each is obligated to withhold. However, the obligation of each will be met if one of the joint transferees withholds and transmits the required amount to the IRS.

Do not use Forms 8288 and 8288-A for the following distributions.

1. A distribution of effectively connected income by a publicly traded partnership is subject to the withholding requirements of section 1446.

2. A distribution with respect to gains from the disposition of a U.S. real property interest from a trust that is regularly traded on an established securities market is subject to section 1445, but is not reported on Forms 8288 and 8288-A.

3. A dividend distribution by a qualified investment entity to a nonresident alien or a foreign corporation that is attributable to gains from sales or exchanges by the qualified investment entity of U.S. real property interests is not subject to withholding under section 1445 as a gain from the sale or exchange of a U.S. real property interest if:

   a. The distribution is on stock regularly traded on a securities market in the United States, and

   b. The alien or corporation did not own more than 10% (for dispositions and distributions before December 17, 2015, did not own more than 5% of such stock in case of a real restate investment trust (REIT)) of that stock at any time during the 1-year period ending on the date of the distribution.

Use Form 1042, and Form 1042-S, to report and pay over the withheld amounts.

Amount To Withhold

Generally, you must withhold 15% of the amount realized on the disposition by the transferor (see *Definitions*, later).

Note. Prior to February 17, 2016, the transferor was generally required to withhold 10% of the amount realized on the disposition.

For information about:

- Withholding at 35%, see *Entities Subject to Section 1445(e)*, later.
- Withholding at a reduced amount, see *Purchase of residence for $1,000,000 or less*.

For information about applying for reduction or elimination of withholding see *Withholding certificate issued by the IRS*, later.

Joint transferors. If one or more foreign persons and one or more U.S. persons jointly transfer a U.S. real property interest, you must determine the amount subject to withholding in the following manner.

1. Allocate the amount realized from the transfer among the transferors based on their capital contribution to the property. For this purpose, a husband and wife are treated as having contributed 50% each.

2. Withhold on the total amount allocated to foreign transferors.

3. Credit the amount withheld among the foreign transferors as they mutually agree. The transferors must request that the withholding be credited as agreed upon by the 10th day after the date of transfer. If no agreement is reached, credit the withholding by evenly dividing it among the foreign transferors.

When To File

A transferee must file Form 8288 and transmit the tax withheld to the IRS by the 20th day after the date of transfer.

You must withhold even if an application for a withholding certificate is or has been submitted to the IRS on the date of transfer. However, you do not have to file Form 8288 and transmit the withholding until the 20th day after the day the IRS mails you a copy of the withholding certificate or notice of denial. But, if the principal purpose for filing the application for a withholding certificate was to delay paying the IRS the amount withheld, interest and penalties will apply to the period beginning on the 21st day after the date of transfer and ending on the day full payment is made.

Installment payments. You must withhold the full amount at the time of the first installment payment. If you

Jan 13, 2017   Cat. No. 57528F

8. FIRPTA Withholding

cannot because the payment does not involve sufficient cash or other liquid assets, you may obtain a withholding certificate from the IRS. See the instructions for Form 8288-B for more information.

Where To File

Send Form 8288 with the amount withheld, and copies A and B of Form(s) 8288-A to:

Ogden Service Center
P.O. Box 409101
Ogden, UT 84409.

Forms 8288-A Must Be Attached

Anyone who completes Form 8288 must also complete a Form 8288-A for each person subject to withholding. Copies A and B of Form 8288-A must be attached to Form 8288. Copy C is for your records. Multiple Forms 8288-A related to a transaction can be filed with one Form 8288. You are not required to furnish a copy of Form 8288 or 8288-A directly to the transferor.

The IRS will stamp Copy B of each Form 8288-A and will forward the stamped copy to the foreign person subject to withholding at the address shown on Form 8288-A. To receive credit for the withheld amount, the transferor generally must attach the stamped Copy B of Form 8288-A to a U.S. income tax return (for example, Form 1040NR or 1120-F) or application for early refund filed with the IRS.

Transferor's TIN missing. If you do not have the transferor's taxpayer identification number (TIN), you still must file Forms 8288 and 8288-A. A stamped copy of Form 8288-A will not be provided to the transferor if the transferor's TIN is not included on that form. The IRS will send a letter to the transferor requesting the TIN and providing instructions for how to get a TIN. When the transferor provides the IRS with a TIN, the IRS will provide the transferor with a stamped Copy B of Form 8288-A.

Penalties

Under section 6651, penalties apply for failure to file Form 8288 when due and for failure to pay the withholding when due. In addition, if you are required to but do not withhold tax under section 1445, the tax, including interest, may be collected from you. Under section 7202, you may be subject to a penalty of up to $10,000 for willful failure to collect and pay over the tax. Corporate officers or other responsible persons may be subject to a penalty under section 6672 equal to the amount that should have been withheld and paid over to the IRS.

Definitions

Transferee. Any person, foreign or domestic, that acquires a U.S. real property interest by purchase, exchange, gift, or any other transfer.

Transferor. For purposes of this withholding, this means any foreign person that disposes of a U.S. real property interest by sale, exchange, gift, or any other disposition. A disregarded entity cannot be the transferor for purposes of section 1445. Instead, the person considered as owning the assets of the disregarded entity for federal tax purposes is regarded as the transferor. A **disregarded entity** for these purposes means an entity that is disregarded as an entity separate from its owner under Regulations section 301.7701-3, a qualified real estate investment trust subsidiary as defined in section 856(i), or a qualified subchapter S subsidiary under section 1361(b)(3)(B).

Qualified substitute. For this purpose, a qualified substitute is (a) the person (including any attorney or title company) responsible for closing the transaction, other than the transferor's agent, and (b) the transferee's agent.

Withholding agent. For purposes of this return, this means the buyer or other transferee who acquires a U.S. real property interest from a foreign person.

Foreign person. A nonresident alien individual, a foreign corporation that does not have a valid election under section 897(i) to be treated as a domestic corporation, a foreign partnership, a foreign trust, or a foreign estate. A resident alien individual is not a foreign person.

A qualified foreign pension fund or any entity wholly owned by such fund that disposes U.S. real property interest or receives a distribution from a REIT is not a foreign person. See sections 897(l) and 1445(f)(3) for more information.

U.S. real property interest. Any interest, other than an interest solely as a creditor, in:

1. Real property located in the United States or the U.S. Virgin Islands.

2. Certain personal property associated with the use of real property.

3. A domestic corporation, unless it is shown that the corporation was not a U.S. real property holding corporation during the previous 5 years (or during the period in which the transferor held the interest, if shorter).

A U.S. real property interest does not include:

1. An interest in a domestically controlled qualified investment entity.

2. An interest in a REIT that is held by a qualified shareholder. For the definition of a qualified shareholder see section 897(k)(3). But see section 897(k)(2)(B) for the cut-back rule if the qualified shareholder has one or more applicable investors.

3. An interest in a corporation that:
• Did not hold any U.S. real property interest as of the date the interest in such corporation is disposed,
• Has disposed of all its U.S. real property interests in transactions in which the full amount of any gain was recognized as provided in section 897(c)(1)(B), and
• Neither such corporation nor any predecessor of such corporation was a REIT or a RIC at any time during the shorter of the previous 5 years or the period in which the transferor held the interest.

4. An interest in certain publicly traded corporations, partnerships, and trusts.

See Regulations sections 1.897-1 and 1.897-2 for more information. Also see _Transferred property that is not a U.S. real property interest_, later.

Qualified investment entity (QIE). A QIE is:
• Any REIT, and
• Any RIC which is a United States real property holding corporation or which would be a United States real property holding corporation.

In determining if a RIC is a U.S. real property holding corporation, the RIC is required to include as U.S. real property interests its holdings of stock in a RIC or REIT that is a U.S. real property holding company, even if such stock is regularly traded and the RIC did not own more than 10% of such stock in the case of a REIT (5% for dispositions before December 17, 2015) or 5% of such stock in case of a RIC, and even if such stock is domestically controlled.

For more information, see Pub. 515.

Domestically controlled qualified investment entity. A QIE is domestically controlled if at all times during the testing period less than 50% in value of its stock was held, directly or indirectly,

The US Foreign Investment in Real Property Tax Act: A Practical Guide

by foreign persons. The testing period is the shorter of:
- The 5-year period ending on the date of the disposition (or distribution), or
- The period during which the entity was in existence.

For purpose of determining whether a QIE is domestically controlled, the following rules apply.

1. A person holding less than 5% of any class of stock of a QIE which is regularly traded on an established securities market in the United States at all times during the testing period will be treated as a U.S. person unless the QIE has actual knowledge that such person is not a U.S. person.

2. Any stock in a QIE that is held by another QIE will be treated as held by a foreign person if:
- Any class of stock of such other QIE is regularly traded on an established securities market, or
- Such other QIE is a RIC that issues certain redeemable securities.

Notwithstanding the above, the stock of the QIE will be treated as held by a U.S. person if such other QIE is domestically controlled.

3. Stock in a QIE that is held by any other QIE not described above will be treated as held by a U.S. person in proportion to the stock ownership of such other QIE which is (or is treated as) held by a U.S. person.

Amount realized. The sum of the cash paid or to be paid (not including interest or original issue discount), the fair market value of other property transferred or to be transferred, and the amount of any liability assumed by the transferee or to which the U.S. real property interest is subject immediately before and after the transfer. Generally, the amount realized for purposes of this withholding is the sales or contract price.

Date of transfer. The first date on which consideration is paid or a liability is assumed by the transferee. However, for purposes of sections 1445(e)(2), (3), and (4), and Regulations sections 1.1445-5(c)(1)(iii) and 1.1445-5(c)(3), the date of transfer is the date of distribution that creates the obligation to withhold. Payment of consideration does not include the payment before passage of legal or equitable title of earnest money (other than pursuant to an initial purchase contract), a good-faith deposit, or any similar amount primarily intended to bind the parties to the contract and subject to forfeiture. A payment that is not forfeitable may also be considered earnest money, a good-faith deposit, or a similar sum.

Exceptions
Withholding At a Reduced Rate

Purchase of residence for $1,000,000 or less. Withholding is required at a reduced rate of 10% in the case of a disposition of:
- A property which is acquired by the transferee for use by the transferee as a residence, and
- The amount realized for the property is $1,000,000 or less. However, see *Purchase of residence for $300,000 or less* next.

Withholding Not Required

Purchase of residence for $300,000 or less. If one or more individuals acquire U.S. real property for use as a residence and the amount realized (in most cases the sales price) is $300,000 or less, no withholding is required.

A U.S. real property interest is acquired for use as a residence if you or a member of your family has definite plans to reside in the property for at least 50% of the number of days the property is used by any person during each of the first two 12-month periods following the date of transfer. Do not take into account the number of days the property will be vacant in making this determination. No form or other document is required to be filed with the IRS for this exception; however, if you do not in fact use the property as a residence, the withholding tax may be collected from you.

This exception applies whether or not the transferor (seller) is an individual, partnership, trust, corporation, or other transferor. However, this exception does not apply if the actual transferee (buyer) is not an individual, even if the property is acquired for an individual.

Transferor not a foreign person. Generally, no withholding is required if you receive a certification of nonforeign status from the transferor, signed under penalties of perjury, stating that the transferor is not a foreign person and containing the transferor's name, address, and identification number (social security number (SSN) or employer identification number (EIN)). The transferor can give the certification to a qualified substitute (defined on this page). The qualified substitute gives you a statement, under penalties of perjury, that the certification is in the qualified substitute's possession.

If you receive a certification (or statement), the withholding tax cannot be collected from you unless you knew that the certification (or statement) was false or you received a notice from your agent, the transferor's agent, or the qualified substitute that it was false. The certification must be signed by the individual, a responsible officer of a corporation, a general partner of a partnership, or the trustee, executor, or fiduciary of a trust or estate.

A disregarded entity may not certify that it is the transferor for U.S. tax purposes. Rather, the owner of the disregarded entity is treated as the transferor of the property and must provide the certificate of nonforeign status to avoid withholding under section 1445.

A foreign corporation electing to be treated as a domestic corporation under section 897(i) must attach to the certification a copy of the acknowledgment of the election received from the IRS. The acknowledgment must state that the information required by Regulations section 1.897-3 has been determined to be complete. If the acknowledgment is not attached, you may not rely on the certification. Keep any certification of nonforeign status you receive in your records for 5 years after the year of transfer.

You may also use other means to determine that the transferor is not a foreign person. But if you do, and it is later determined that the transferor is a foreign person, the withholding tax may be collected from you.

Late notice of false certification. If, after the date of transfer, you receive a notice from your agent, the transferor's agent, or the qualified substitute that the certification of nonforeign status is false, you do not have to withhold on consideration paid before you received the notice. However, you must withhold the full 15% of the amount realized from any consideration that remains to be paid, if possible. You must do this by withholding and paying over the entire amount of each successive payment of consideration until the full 15% has been withheld and paid to the IRS. These amounts must be reported and transmitted to the IRS by the 20th day following the date of each payment.

Transferred property that is not a U.S. real property interest. If you acquire an interest in property that is not a U.S. real property interest (defined

Instructions for Form 8288 (Rev. 2-2017)   -3-

216

8. FIRPTA Withholding

under *U.S. real property interest*, earlier), withholding generally is not required. A U.S. real property interest includes certain interests in U.S. corporations, as well as direct interests in real property and certain associated personal property.

No withholding is required on the acquisition of an interest in a domestic corporation if (a) any class of stock of the corporation is regularly traded on an established securities market, or (b) the transferee receives a statement issued by the corporation that the interest is not a U.S. real property interest, unless you know the statement is false or you receive a notice from your agent or the transferor's agent that the statement is false. A corporation's statement may be relied on only if it is dated not more than 30 days before the date of transfer.

Late notice of false statement. If, after the date of transfer, you receive a notice that the statement is false, see *Late notice of false statement*, earlier.

Generally, no withholding is required on the acquisition of an interest in a foreign corporation. However, withholding may be required if the foreign corporation has made the election under section 897(i) to be treated as a domestic corporation.

Transferor's nonrecognition of gain or loss. You may receive a notice from the transferor signed under penalties of perjury stating that the transferor is not required to recognize gain or loss on the transfer because of a nonrecognition provision of the Internal Revenue Code (see Temporary Regulations section 1.897-6T(a)(2)) or a provision in a U.S. tax treaty. You may rely on the transferor's notice, and not withhold, unless (a) only part of the gain qualifies for nonrecognition or (b) you know or have reason to know that the transferor is not entitled to the claimed nonrecognition treatment.

No particular form is required for this notice. By the 20th day after the date of transfer, you must send a copy of the notice of nonrecognition (with a cover letter giving your name, address, and identification number) to:

Ogden Service Center
P.O. Box 409101
Ogden, UT 84409

See Regulations section 1.1445-2(d)(2) for more information on the transferor's notice of nonrecognition.

Note. A notice of nonrecognition cannot be used for the exclusion from income under section 121, like-kind exchanges that do not qualify for nonrecognition treatment in their entirety, and deferred like-kind exchanges that have not been completed when it is time to file Form 8288. In these cases, a withholding certificate issued by the IRS, as described next, must be obtained.

Withholding certificate issued by the IRS. A withholding certificate may be issued by the IRS to reduce or eliminate withholding on dispositions of U.S. real property interests by foreign persons. Either a transferee or transferor may apply for the certificate. The certificate may be issued if:

• Reduced withholding is appropriate because the 10%, 15%, or 35% amount exceeds the transferor's maximum tax liability,
• The transferor is exempt from U.S. tax or nonrecognition provisions apply, or
• The transferee or transferor enters into an agreement with the IRS for the payment of the tax.

An application for a withholding certificate must comply with the provisions of Regulations sections 1.1445-3 and 1.1445-6, and Rev. Proc. 2000-35, 2000-35 I.R.B. 211. You can find Rev. Proc. 2000-35 at *www.irs.gov/pub/irs-irbs/irb00-35.pdf*. In certain cases, you may use Form 8288-B to apply for a withholding certificate. The IRS will normally act on an application by the 90th day after a complete application is received.

If you receive a withholding certificate from the IRS that excuses withholding, you are not required to file Form 8288. However, if you receive a withholding certificate that reduces (rather than eliminates) withholding, there is no exception to withholding, and you are required to file Form 8288. Attach a copy of the withholding certificate to Form 8288. See *When To File*, earlier, for more information.

No consideration paid. Withholding is not required if the amount realized by the transferor is zero (for example, the property is transferred as a gift and the recipient does not assume any liabilities or furnish any other consideration to the transferor).

Options to acquire U.S. real property interests. No withholding is required with respect to any amount realized by the grantor on the grant or lapse of an option to acquire a U.S. real property interest. However, withholding is required on the sale, exchange, or exercise of an option.

Property acquired by a governmental unit. If the property is acquired by the United States, a U.S. state or possession or political subdivision, or the District of Columbia, withholding is generally not required.

For rules that apply to foreclosures, see Regulations section 1.1445-2(d)(3).

Applicable wash sale transaction. If a distribution from a domestically controlled qualified investment entity is treated as a distribution of a U.S. real property interest only because an interest in the entity was disposed of in an applicable wash sale transaction, withholding generally is not required. See section 897(h)(5).

Late Filing of Certification or Notices

You may be eligible for relief for a late filing if a statement or notice was not provided to the relevant person or the IRS by the specified deadline and if you have reasonable cause for the failure to make a timely filing. Once you become aware that you have failed to timely file certain certificates or notices, you must file the required certification or notice with the appropriate person or the IRS. Also include the following.

• A statement at the top of the document(s) that it is "FILED PURSUANT TO REV. PROC. 2008-27."
• An explanation describing why the failure was due to reasonable cause. Within the explanation, provide that you filed with, or obtained from, an appropriate person the required certification or notice.

The completed certification or notice attached to the explanation must be sent to:

Ogden Service Center
P.O. Box 409101
Ogden, UT 84409.

For more information, see Rev. Proc. 2008-27, 2008-21 I.R.B. 1014, available at *www.irs.gov/irb/2008-21_IRB/ar14.html*.

Liability of Agents

If you (or the qualified substitute) received: (a) a transferor's certification of nonforeign status or (b) a corporation's statement that an interest is not a U.S. real property interest, and the transferee's or transferor's agent, or the substitute, knows the document is false, the agent (or substitute) must

The US Foreign Investment in Real Property Tax Act: A Practical Guide

notify you. If notification is not provided, the agent (or substitute) will be liable for the tax that should have been withheld, but only to the extent of the agent's (or substitute's) compensation from the transaction.

If you (or the substitute) receive a notice of false certification or statement from your agent, the transferor's agent, or qualified substitute, you must withhold tax as if you had not received a certification or statement. See *Late notice of false certification*, earlier.

An "agent" is any person who represents the transferor or transferee in any negotiation with another person (or another person's agent) relating to the transaction or in settling the transaction. For purposes of section 1445(e), a transferor's or transferee's agent is any person who represents or advises an entity, a holder of an interest in an entity, or a fiduciary with respect to the planning, arrangement, or completion of a transaction described in sections 1445(e)(1) through (4).

A person is not treated as an agent if the person only performs one or more of the following acts in connection with the transaction:

1. Receiving and disbursing any part of the consideration.

2. Recording any document.

3. Typing, copying, and other clerical tasks.

4. Obtaining title insurance reports and reports concerning the condition of the property.

5. Transmitting documents between the parties.

6. Functioning exclusively in his or her capacity as a representative of a condominium association or cooperative housing corporation. This exemption includes the board of directors, the committee, or other governing body.

Entities Subject to Section 1445(e)

Withholding is required on certain distributions and other transactions by domestic or foreign corporations, qualified investment entities, trusts, and estates. A domestic trust or estate must withhold 35% of the amount distributed to a foreign beneficiary from a "U.S. real property interest account" that it is required to establish under Regulations section 1.1445-5(c)(1)(iii). A foreign corporation that has not made the election under section 897(i) must withhold 35% of the gain it recognizes on the distribution of a U.S. real property interest to its shareholders. Certain domestic corporations are required to withhold tax on distributions to foreign shareholders.

No withholding is required on the transfer of an interest in a domestic corporation if any class of stock of the corporation is regularly traded on an established securities market. Also, no withholding is required on the transfer of an interest in a publicly traded partnership or trust.

No withholding will be required with respect to an interest holder if the entity or fiduciary receives a certification of nonforeign status from the interest holder. An entity or fiduciary may also use other means to determine that an interest holder is not a foreign person, but if it does so and it is later determined that the interest holder is a foreign person, the withholding may be collected from the entity or fiduciary.

Section 1445(e)(1) Transactions

Partnerships. A domestic partnership that is not publicly traded must withhold tax under section 1446 on effectively connected income allocated to its foreign partners and must file Form 8804, and Form 8805. A publicly traded partnership or nominee generally must withhold tax under section 1446 on distributions to its foreign partners and must file Forms 1042 and 1042-S. Because a domestic partnership that disposes of a U.S. real property interest is required to withhold under section 1446, it is not required to withhold under section 1445(e)(1).

Trusts and estates. If a domestic trust or estate disposes of a U.S. real property interest, the amount of gain realized must be paid into a separate "U.S. real property interest account." For these purposes, a domestic trust is one that does not make the "large trust election" (explained below), is not a qualified investment entity, and is not publicly traded. The fiduciary must withhold 35% of the amount distributed to a foreign person from the account during the tax year of the trust or estate in which the disposition occurred. The withholding must be paid over to the IRS within 20 days of the date of distribution. Special rules apply to grantor trusts. See Regulations section 1.1445-5 for more information and how to compute the amount subject to withholding.

Large trust election. Trusts with more than 100 beneficiaries may make an election to withhold upon distribution rather than at the time of transfer. The amount to be withheld from each distribution is 35% of the amount attributable to the foreign beneficiary's proportionate share of the current balance of the trust's section 1445(e)(1) account. This election does not apply to any qualified investment entity or to any publicly traded trust. Special rules apply to large trusts that make recurring sales of growing crops and timber.

A trust's section 1445(e)(1) account is the total net gain realized by the trust on all section 1445(e)(1) transactions after the date of the election, minus the total of all distributions made by the trust after the date of the election from such total net gain. See Regulations section 1.1445-5(c)(3) for more information.

Section 1445(e)(2) Transactions

A foreign corporation that distributes a U.S. real property interest must generally withhold 35% of the gain recognized by the corporation. No withholding or reduced withholding is required if the corporation receives a withholding certificate from the IRS.

Section 1445(e)(3) Transactions

Generally, a domestic corporation that distributes any property to a foreign person that holds an interest in the corporation must withhold 15% (10% for distributions before February 17, 2016) of the fair market value of the property distributed if:

• The foreign person's interest in the corporation is a U.S. real property interest under section 897, and

• The property is distributed in redemption of stock under section 302, in liquidation of the corporation under sections 331 through 341, or with respect to stock under section 301 that is not made out of the earnings and profits of the corporation.

No withholding or reduced withholding is required if the corporation receives a withholding certificate from the IRS.

Section 1445(e)(4) Transactions

No withholding is required under section 1445(e)(4), relating to certain taxable distributions by domestic or foreign partnerships, trusts, and estates, until the effective date of a Treasury Decision under section 897(e)(2)(B)(ii) and (g).

Instructions for Form 8288 (Rev. 2-2017)

8. FIRPTA Withholding

Section 1445(e)(5) Transactions

The transferee of a partnership interest must withhold 15% (10% for dispositions before February 17, 2016) of the amount realized on the disposition by a foreign partner of an interest in a domestic or foreign partnership in which at least 50% of the value of the gross assets consists of U.S. real property interests and at least 90% of the value of the gross assets consists of U.S. real property interests plus any cash or cash equivalents. However, no withholding is required under section 1445(e)(5) for dispositions of interests in other partnerships, trusts, or estates until the effective date of a Treasury Decision under section 897(g). No withholding is required if, no earlier than 30 days before the transfer, the transferee receives a statement signed by a general partner under penalties of perjury that at least 50% of the value of the gross assets of the partnership does not consist of U.S. real property interests or that at least 90% of the value of the gross assets does not consist of U.S. real property interests plus cash or cash equivalents. The transferee may rely on the statement unless the transferee knows it is false or the transferee receives a false statement notice pursuant to Regulations section 1.1445-4.

Section 1445(e)(6) Transactions

A qualified investment entity must withhold 35% of a distribution to a nonresident alien or a foreign corporation that is treated as gain realized from the sale or exchange of a U.S. real property interest. No withholding under section 1445 is required on a distribution to a nonresident alien or foreign corporation if the distribution is on stock regularly traded on a securities market in the United States and the alien or corporation did not own more than 10% (for distributions before December 17, 2015, did not own more than 5% of such stock in case of a REIT) of that stock at any time during the 1-year period ending on the date of distribution.

A distribution made after December 17, 2015, by a REIT generally is not treated as gain from the sale or exchange of a U.S. real property interest if the shareholder is a qualified shareholder (as described in section 897(k)(3)).

Specific Instructions

Amended return. Check the box at the top of the page to indicate the Form 8288 you are filing is an amended return.

Complete Part I or Part II, but not both. Also, you must complete and attach Copies A and B of Form(s) 8288-A. Attach additional sheets if you need more space.

Part I, To Be Completed By The Buyer or Other Transferee Required to Withhold Under Section 1445(a)

Line 1. In Part I, enter the name, address, and identifying number of the buyer or other transferee responsible for withholding under section 1445(a). Do not enter the name, address, and identifying number of a title company, mortgage company, etc. unless it happens to be the actual buyer or transferee.

In Part II, enter the name, address, and identifying number of the entity or fiduciary responsible for withholding under section 1445(e). Do not enter the name, address, and identifying number of a title company, mortgage company, etc. unless it happens to be the actual entity responsible for withholding under section 1445(e).

The IRS will contact the person or entity listed on line 1 to resolve any problems that may arise concerning underwithholding and/or penalties.

Name and address. If you are a fiduciary, list your name and the name of the trust or estate. Enter the home address of an individual or the office address of an entity.

Identifying number. For a U.S. individual, the identifying number is a social security number (SSN). For any entity other than an individual (for example, corporation, qualified investment entity, estate, or trust), the identifying number is an employer identification number (EIN). If you do not have an EIN, you can apply for one online at *www.irs.gov/businesses/small-businesses-self-employed/apply-for-an-employer-identification-number-ein-online* or by telephone at 1-800-829-4933. Also, you can file Form SS-4 by fax or mail.

For a nonresident alien individual who is not eligible for an SSN, the identifying number is an IRS individual taxpayer identification number (ITIN). If the individual does not already have an ITIN, he or she should complete Forms 8288 and 8288-A and mail the forms along with any payment to the address shown under *Where To File,* earlier. In a separate package mail a completed Form W-7 with supporting documentation and a copy of Forms 8288 and 8288-A to the IRS at the address given in the Form W-7 instructions.

Line 2. Enter the location and a description of the property, including any substantial improvements (for example, "12-unit apartment building"). In the case of interests in a corporation that constitute a U.S. real property interest, enter the class or type and amount of the interest (for example, "10,000 shares Class A Preferred Stock XYZ Corporation").

Line 4. Enter the number of Forms 8288-A attached to Form 8288. Copies A and B of each Form 8288-A should be counted as one form.

Line 5a. Enter amounts subject to withholding at 15%. Generally, this is the rate of withholding for transactions required to be reported under section 1445(a) in Part I.

Include withholding for the purchase of a residence with an amount realized of more than $1,000,000.

Line 5b. Enter amounts subject to withholding at 10%. Amounts entered on line 5b, include the following.

• Withholding for the purchase of a residence with an amount realized of more than $300,000, but less than or equal to $1,000,000. Generally, no withholding is required for the purchase of a residence if the amount realized is $300,000 or less. For more information, see *Exceptions,* earlier.

• Any dispositions of property prior to February 17, 2016, subject to a 10% rate of withholding under section 1445(a).

Line 5c. If withholding is at a reduced rate check the box. See *Exceptions,* earlier. Include the amount withheld in the total reported on line 6, Part I.

Example 1. B, a corporation, purchases a U.S. real property interest from F, a foreign person. On settlement day, the settlement agent pays off existing loans, withholds 15% of the amount realized on the sale, and disburses the remaining amount to F. B, not the agent, must complete Part I of Form 8288 and Form 8288-A.

The US Foreign Investment in Real Property Tax Act: A Practical Guide

Part II, To Be Completed By an Entity Subject to The Provisions of Section 1445(e)

Line 3. If you are a qualified investment entity, domestic trust or estate, or you make the large trust election, enter the date of distribution for the date of transfer.

Line 5a. Enter amounts subject to withholding at 15%. Generally, this is the rate of withholding for transactions required to be reported under section 1445(e) in Part II. However, see the discussion of various section 1445(e) transactions under *Entities Subject to Section 1445(e)*, earlier.

Line 5b. Enter amounts subject to withholding at 10%. Report on line 5b withholding for any dispositions of property prior to February 17, 2016, subject to a 10% rate of withholding under section 1445(e).

Line 5c. Enter amounts subject to withholding at 35%. See the discussion of various section 1445(e) transactions under *Entities Subject to Section 1445(e)*, earlier.

Line 5d. If withholding is at a reduced rate check the box. Include the amount withheld in the total reported on line 6, Part II. See the discussion of various section 1445(e) transactions under *Entities Subject to Section 1445(e)*, earlier.

Line 5e. If withholding is from a large trust election to withhold upon distribution, check the box, and include the amount withheld in the total reported on line 6, Part II. See *Large trust election*, under *Section 1445(e)(1) Transactions*, earlier.

Example 2. C, a domestic corporation, distributes property to F, a foreign shareholder whose interest in C is a U.S. real property interest. The distribution is in redemption of C's stock (section 1445(e)(3) transaction). C must withhold 15% of the fair market value of the property distributed to F. C must complete Part II of Form 8288, and Form 8288-A.

Paid Preparer

Generally, anyone you pay to prepare Form 8288 must sign it and include their Preparer Tax Identification Number (PTIN) in the space provided.

Privacy Act and Paperwork Reduction Act Notice. We ask for the information on this form to carry out the Internal Revenue laws of the United States. Section 1445 generally imposes a withholding obligation on the buyer or other transferee (withholding agent) when a U.S. real property interest is acquired from a foreign person. Section 1445 also imposes a withholding obligation on certain foreign and domestic corporations, qualified investment entities, and the fiduciary of certain trusts and estates. This form is used to report and transmit the amount withheld.

You are required to provide this information. Section 6109 requires you to provide your identification number. We need this information to ensure that you are complying with the Internal Revenue laws and to allow us to figure and collect the right amount of tax. Failure to provide this information in a timely manner, or providing false information, may subject you to penalties. Routine uses of this information include giving it to the Department of Justice for civil and criminal litigation, and to cities, states, the District of Columbia, and U.S. commonwealths and possessions for administration of their tax laws. We may also disclose this information to other countries under a tax treaty, to federal and state agencies to enforce federal nontax criminal laws, or to federal law enforcement and intelligence agencies to combat terrorism.

You are not required to provide the information requested on a form that is subject to the Paperwork Reduction Act unless the form displays a valid OMB control number. Books or records relating to a form or its instructions must be retained as long as their contents may become material in the administration of any Internal Revenue law. Generally, tax returns and return information are confidential, as required by section 6103.

The time needed to complete and file these forms will vary depending on individual circumstances. The estimated burden for business taxpayers filing this form is approved under OMB control number 1545-0123. The estimated burden for all other taxpayers who file these forms is shown below.

	Form 8288	Form 8288-A
Recordkeeping	6 hr., 13 min.	2 hr., 52 min.
Learning about the law or the form	5 hr., 13 min.	30 min.
Preparing and sending the form to the IRS	6 hr., 46 min.	34 min.

If you have comments concerning the accuracy of these time estimates or suggestions for making these forms simpler, we would be happy to hear from you. You can send us comments from *www.irs.gov/formspubs/*. Click on "More information," and then on "Give us feedback." Or, you can write to the Internal Revenue Service, Tax Forms and Publications, 1111 Constitution Ave. NW, IR-6526, Washington, DC 20224. Do not send the form to this address. Instead, see *Where To File*, earlier.

8. FIRPTA Withholding

APPENDIX 8-B

Form 8288 (Rev. February 2017)
Department of the Treasury
Internal Revenue Service

U.S. Withholding Tax Return for Dispositions by Foreign Persons of U.S. Real Property Interests

► Information about Form 8288 and its separate instructions is at www.irs.gov/form8288.

OMB No. 1545-0902

If this is an amended return, check here . . . . ► ☐

Complete Part I **or** Part II. Also complete and attach Copies A and B of Form(s) 8288-A. Attach additional sheets if you need more space.

Part I — To Be Completed by the Buyer or Other Transferee Required To Withhold Under Section 1445(a)

1 Name of buyer or other transferee responsible for withholding. See instructions.

Identifying number

Street address, apt. or suite no., or rural route. Do not use a P.O. box.

City or town, province or state, country, and ZIP or foreign postal code

Phone number (optional)

2 Description and location of property acquired

3 Date of transfer

4 Number of Forms 8288-A attached

5 Complete all items that apply. Enter dollar amounts on applicable lines.

6 Total amount withheld

a Amount subject to withholding at 15% . . . . . . ►
b Amount subject to withholding at 10% . . . . . . ►
c Withholding is at a reduced rate. See instructions . . . . ► ☐

Part II — To Be Completed by an Entity Subject to the Provisions of Section 1445(e)

1 Name of entity or fiduciary responsible for withholding. See instructions.

Identifying number

Street address, apt. or suite no., or rural route. Do not use a P.O. box.

City or town, province or state, country, and ZIP or foreign postal code

Phone number (optional)

2 Description of U.S. real property interest transferred or distributed

3 Date of transfer

4 Number of Forms 8288-A attached

5 Complete all items that apply. Enter dollar amounts on applicable lines.

6 Total amount withheld

a Amount subject to withholding at 15% . . . . . . ►
b Amount subject to withholding at 10% . . . . . . ►
c Amount subject to withholding at 35% . . . . . . ►
d Withholding is at a reduced rate. See instructions . . . . ► ☐
e Large trust election to withhold at distribution . . . . ► ☐

Sign Here

Under penalties of perjury, I declare that I have examined this return, including accompanying schedules and statements, and to the best of my knowledge and belief, it is true, correct, and complete. Declaration of preparer (other than taxpayer) is based on all information of which preparer has any knowledge.

► Signature of withholding agent, partner, fiduciary, or corporate officer | Title (if applicable) | Date

Paid Preparer Use Only

Print/Type preparer's name	Preparer's signature	Date	Check ☐ if self-employed	PTIN
Firm's name ►		Firm's EIN ►		
Firm's address ►		Phone no.		

For Privacy Act and Paperwork Reduction Act Notice, see separate instructions. Cat. No. 62260A Form **8288** (Rev. 2-2017)

APPENDIX 8-C

Withholding agent's name, street address, city, state, and ZIP code		1 Date of transfer		**Statement of Withholding on Dispositions by Foreign Persons of U.S. Real Property Interests**
		2 Federal income tax withheld		OMB No. 1545-0902
Withholding agent's Federal identification number	Identification number of foreign person subject to withholding (see instructions)	3 Amount realized	4 Gain recognized by foreign corporation	**Copy A** **For Internal Revenue Service Center**
Name of person subject to withholding		5 Description of property transferred		
Foreign address (number, street, and apt. or suite no.)		6 Person subject to withholding is: An individual ☐ A corporation ☐ Other (specify) ▶		For Privacy Act and Paperwork Reduction Act Notice, see the Instructions for Form 8288.
City, province or state, postal code, and country (not U.S.)		7 Country code	Mailing address of person subject to withholding (if different)	

Form **8288-A** (Rev. 2-2016) Cat. No. 62261L **Attach Copies A and B to Form 8288** Department of the Treasury - Internal Revenue Service

Withholding agent's name, street address, city, state, and ZIP code		1 Date of transfer		**Statement of Withholding on Dispositions by Foreign Persons of U.S. Real Property Interests**
		2 Federal income tax withheld		OMB No. 1545-0902
Withholding agent's Federal identification number	Identification number of foreign person subject to withholding (see instructions)	3 Amount realized	4 Gain recognized by foreign corporation	**Copy B** Send to Internal Revenue Service Center (For Use by Person Subject to Withholding)
Name of person subject to withholding		5 Description of property transferred		
Foreign address (number, street, and apt. or suite no.)		6 Person subject to withholding is: An individual ☐ A corporation ☐ Other (specify) ▶		This information is being furnished to the Internal Revenue Service.
City, province or state, postal code, and country (not U.S.)		7 Country code	Mailing address of person subject to withholding (if different)	

Form **8288-A** (Rev. 2-2016) Department of the Treasury - Internal Revenue Service

Instructions for the Person Subject to Withholding

Generally, if you are a foreign person that disposes of real property located in the United States as seller or transferor, the buyer or other transferee must withhold 15% of the amount realized. Certain foreign interest holders that are beneficiaries or shareholders are subject to federal income tax withholding at a rate of 35%.

You must file a U.S. tax return (Form 1040NR, 1041, 1065, 1065-B, or 1120-F) to report the sale or other disposition as effectively connected with the conduct of a trade or business in the United States. To receive credit for any federal income tax withheld shown in box 2, attach Form 8288-A to your tax return, unless you make a request for early refund. Foreign partnerships, other than publicly traded partnerships, should report the withholding on Form 8804, Annual Return for Partnership Withholding Tax (Section 1446), and attach Form 8288-A. Publicly traded partnerships, and nominees of such partnerships, should use Forms 1042 and 1042-S to report the withholding. See Pub. 515, Withholding of Tax on Nonresident Aliens and Foreign Entities, and Pub. 519, U.S. Tax Guide for Aliens, for more information.

If the amount shown in box 2 is greater than your maximum tax liability, you may apply for an early refund. However, you must still file your tax return when due. To apply for an early refund, you must first get a withholding certificate. No particular form is required for an application for early refund, but it must include the following information in separate paragraphs numbered as shown below:

1. Your name, address, and U.S. taxpayer identification number;
2. The amount required to be withheld as stated in the withholding certificate issued by the IRS;
3. The amount withheld shown in box 2 (attach a copy of this Form 8288-A); and
4. The amount to be refunded.

Send your application for a withholding certificate and/or application for early refund to Ogden Service Center, P.O. Box 409101, Ogden, UT 84409.

See Pub. 515 and Form 8288-B, Application for Withholding Certificate for Dispositions by Foreign Persons of U.S. Real Property Interests, for information about withholding certificates.

8. FIRPTA Withholding

Withholding agent's name, street address, city, state, and ZIP code		1 Date of transfer		**Statement of Withholding on Dispositions by Foreign Persons of U.S. Real Property Interests**
		2 Federal income tax withheld		OMB No. 1545-0902
Withholding agent's Federal identification number	Identification number of foreign person subject to withholding (see instructions)	3 Amount realized	4 Gain recognized by foreign corporation	Copy C For Withholding Agent
Name of person subject to withholding		5 Description of property transferred		
Foreign address (number, street, and apt. or suite no.)		6 Person subject to withholding is: An individual ☐ A corporation ☐ Other (specify) ▶		For Privacy Act and Paperwork Reduction Act Notice, see the Instructions for Form 8288.
City, province or state, postal code, and country (not U.S.)	7 Country code	Mailing address of person subject to withholding (if different)		

Form **8288-A** (Rev. 2-2016)   **Keep for your records**   Department of the Treasury - Internal Revenue Service

Instructions for the Withholding Agent

Prepare Form 8288-A for each foreign person subject to withholding. Attach Copies A and B to Form 8288, U.S. Withholding Tax Return for Dispositions by Foreign Persons of U.S. Real Property Interests. Copy B will be stamped by the IRS and sent to the person subject to withholding if the form is complete, including the transferor's identification number. Retain Copy C for your records. You do not have to give a copy of this form to the person subject to withholding.

Identification number. A U.S. taxpayer identification number (TIN) is a social security number (SSN), employer identification number (EIN), or IRS individual taxpayer identification number (ITIN). For more information, see *Forms 8288-A Must Be Attached* and *Identifying number* in the Instructions for Form 8288.

Address. You must enter the foreign home address (for an individual) or the foreign office address (for other than an individual) of the person subject to withholding. You may enter a separate mailing address in the space provided. If provided, the IRS will use the separate mailing address to forward Copy B to the person subject to withholding.

Note: The home or office address of the person subject to withholding must be an address outside the United States. If the person does not have an address outside the United States, enter the country of residence of the foreign person in this section and provide a complete mailing address.

Box 1. Enter the date of transfer. However, enter the date of distribution if you withheld under section 1445(e)(2), (e)(3), or (e)(6) or if you made the large trust election to withhold at the date of distribution.

Box 2. Enter the federal income tax you withheld for the foreign person whose name appears on this form.

Box 3. Enter the amount realized by the foreign person whose name appears on this form.

Box 4. Complete only if you are a foreign corporation required to withhold under section 1445(e)(2).

Box 6. Check the applicable box to indicate whether the foreign person subject to withholding is an individual or a corporation. If "other," specify whether the person is a partnership, trust, or estate.

Box 7. Enter the applicable two-letter code from the list at *www.irs.gov/countrycodes* for the foreign home address or foreign office address of the person subject to withholding.

See the Instructions for Form 8288 for more information.

APPENDIX 8-D

Form 8288-B (Rev. February 2016)
Department of the Treasury
Internal Revenue Service

Application for Withholding Certificate for Dispositions by Foreign Persons of U.S. Real Property Interests

▶ Please type or print.

OMB No. 1545-1060

1 Name of transferor (attach additional sheets if more than one transferor) | Identification number

Street address, apt. or suite no., or rural route. Do not use a P.O. box.

City, state or province, and country (if not U.S.). Include ZIP code or postal code where appropriate.

2 Name of transferee (attach additional sheets if more than one transferee) | Identification number

Street address, apt. or suite no., or rural route. Do not use a P.O. box.

City, state or province, and country (if not U.S.). Include ZIP code or postal code where appropriate.

3 Applicant is: ☐ Transferor ☐ Transferee

4a Name of withholding agent (see instructions) | **b** Identification number

c Name of estate, trust, or entity (if applicable) | **d** Identification number

5 Address where you want withholding certificate sent (street address, apt. or suite no., P.O. box, or rural route number) | Phone number (optional)

City, state or province, and country (if not U.S.). Include ZIP code or postal code where appropriate.

6 Description of U.S. real property transaction:
  a Date of transfer (month, day, year) (see inst.) _____ **b** Contract price $ _____
  c Type of interest transferred: ☐ Real property ☐ Associated personal property
                                     ☐ Domestic U.S. real property holding corporation
  d Use of property at time of sale: ☐ Rental or commercial ☐ Personal ☐ Other (attach explanation)
  e Adjusted basis $ _____
  f Location and general description of property (for a real property interest), description (for associated personal property), or the class or type and amount of the interest (for an interest in a U.S. real property holding corporation). See instructions.

  g For the 3 preceding tax years:
   (1) Were U.S. income tax returns filed relating to the U.S. real property interest? . . . . ☐ Yes ☐ No
   If "Yes," when and where were those returns filed? ▶
   (2) Were U.S. income taxes paid relating to the U.S. real property interest? . . . . ☐ Yes ☐ No
   If "Yes," enter the amount of tax paid for each year ▶

7 Check the box to indicate the reason a withholding certificate should be issued. See the instructions for information that must be attached to Form 8288-B.
  a ☐ The transferor is exempt from U.S. tax or nonrecognition treatment applies.
  b ☐ The transferor's maximum tax liability is less than the tax required to be withheld.
  c ☐ The special installment sales rules described in section 7 of Rev. Proc. 2000-35 allow reduced withholding.
8 Does the transferor have any unsatisfied withholding liability under section 1445? . . . . ☐ Yes ☐ No
  See the instructions for information required to be attached.
9 Is this application for a withholding certificate made under section 1445(e)? . . . . ☐ Yes ☐ No
  If "Yes," check the applicable box in **a** and the applicable box in **b** below.
  a Type of transaction: ☐ 1445(e)(1) ☐ 1445(e)(2) ☐ 1445(e)(3) ☐ 1445(e)(5) ☐ 1445(e)(6)
  b Applicant is: ☐ Taxpayer ☐ Other person required to withhold. Specify your title (e.g., trustee) ▶

Under penalties of perjury, I declare that I have examined this application and accompanying attachments, and, to the best of my knowledge and belief, they are true, correct, and complete.

Signature | Title (if applicable) | Date

For Privacy Act and Paperwork Reduction Act Notice, see the instructions. | Cat. No. 101287 | Form **8288-B** (Rev. 2-2016)

# 8. FIRPTA Withholding

Form 8288-B (Rev. 2-2016) Page **2**

Section references are to the Internal Revenue Code unless otherwise noted.

Future Developments

For the latest information about developments related to Form 8288 and its instructions, such as legislation enacted after they were published, go to *www.irs.gov/form8288*.

General Instructions

Purpose of form. Use Form 8288-B to apply for a withholding certificate to reduce or eliminate withholding on dispositions of U.S. real property interests by foreign persons, but **only** if the application is based on:

1. A claim that the transferor is entitled to nonrecognition treatment or is exempt from tax,

2. A claim solely on a calculation that shows the transferor's maximum tax liability is less than the tax otherwise required to be withheld, or

3. A claim that the special installment sales rules described in section 7 of Rev. Proc. 2000-35 allowed reduced withholding.

Do not use this form for applications:

• Based on an agreement for the payment of tax with conforming security,

• For blanket withholding certificates under Rev. Proc. 2000-35, or

• Other than the three types described above.

See Regulations sections 1.1445-3 and 1.1445-6 and Rev. Proc. 2000-35 for information and procedures for applying for a withholding certificate.

Who can apply for a withholding certificate. Either the transferee or the transferor (or other authorized person) can file this application.

Withholding certificate. The IRS can issue a withholding certificate to reduce or eliminate withholding under section 1445. A certificate issued before the transfer notifies the transferee that reduced withholding or no withholding is required. A certificate issued after the transfer may authorize an early or a normal refund. If, on the date of transfer, an application for a withholding certificate is or has been submitted to the IRS, the applicable withholding is not required to be paid over to the IRS until the 20th day after the day that the IRS mails the withholding certificate or notice of denial. A transferor that applies for a withholding certificate must notify the transferee in writing that the certificate has been applied for on the day of or prior to the transfer.

The IRS will normally act on an application within 90 days of receipt of all information necessary to make a proper determination. The IRS will determine whether withholding should be reduced or eliminated or whether a withholding certificate should not be issued.

Identification number. The U.S. taxpayer identification number (TIN) of all parties to the transaction must be on the application for a withholding certificate. For U.S. individuals, the TIN is a social security number (SSN). For all other entities, it is an employer identification number (EIN). If you do not have an EIN, you can apply for one online at *www.irs.gov/smallbiz* or by telephone at 1-800-829-4933. Also, you can file Form SS-4, Application for Employer Identification Number, by fax or mail.

If you are a nonresident alien individual who is required to have a TIN, but is not eligible to obtain an SSN, you must apply for an IRS individual taxpayer identification number (ITIN). If you do not have a TIN and are eligible for an ITIN, you can apply for an ITIN by attaching the completed Form 8288-B to a completed Form W-7 and forwarding the package to the IRS at the address given in the Form W-7 instructions. Get Form W-7, Application for IRS Individual Taxpayer Identification Number, for more information.

Any withholding certificate issued by the IRS applies only for the limited purpose of determining the withholding obligation under section 1445 and does not apply to any substantive issue that may arise in connection with the transfer. The acceptance by the IRS of any evidence submitted in connection with this application is not binding on the IRS for any purpose other than issuing the withholding certificate. The information submitted in support of the application may be subject to verification by the IRS prior to issuance of a withholding certificate.

If you receive a withholding certificate from the IRS and withholding is still required, a copy of the withholding certificate must be attached to Form 8288, U.S. Withholding Tax Return for Dispositions by Foreign Persons of U.S. Real Property Interests.

Installment sales. A transferee is required to withhold on the full sales price regardless of the amount of the payment. However, if the transferor is not a dealer and will report gain using the installment method under section 453, a withholding certificate allowing reduced withholding may be obtained. Any withholding certificate based on the installment sale method will provide for payment of interest on the deferred tax liability under section 453A(c) when applicable.

For installment sales subject to withholding under section 1445(a) or (e), the IRS will consider applications for a withholding certificate based on the transferee's (or entity's or fiduciary's) agreement to all of the following:

1. Withhold and pay over 15% or lower amount determined by the IRS (or the amount the IRS determines to be appropriate under section 1445(e)) of the down payment. The amount of the down payment includes any liabilities of the transferor (entity in the case of section 1445(e)) assumed by the transferee, or liabilities to which the U.S. real property interest was subject immediately before and after the transfer.

2. Withhold 15% or lower amount determined by the IRS (or the amount the IRS determines to be appropriate under section 1445(e)) of each subsequent payment and the interest on the deferred tax liability.

3. Use Forms 8288 and 8288-A (relating to withholding on dispositions by foreign persons of U.S. real property interests) to pay over all amounts withheld. The identification number of the transferor (or interest holder subject to withholding under section 1445(e)) must be included on Forms 8288 and 8288-A.

4. Notify the IRS before the disposition or encumbrance of the U.S. real property interest (of the installment obligation under section 1445(e)), and when it occurs, pay over the remaining amount to be withheld.

5. Continue to withhold under a reduced withholding certificate until an amended certificate is issued, even if the transferor pledges the installment obligation in exchange for all or part of the proceeds due on the obligation and includes in gross income under section 453A(d) the net proceeds of the secured indebtedness.

Where to send applications for a withholding certificate. Form 8288-B and other applications for a withholding certificate must be sent to Internal Revenue Service, P.O. Box 409101, Ogden, UT 84409.

Specific Instructions

Complete all information for each line. An application that is not substantially complete when submitted will be rejected. For example, an application without a specific or estimated date of transfer will not be considered to be substantially complete.

Line 1. Enter the name, street address, and identification number of the transferor. If there are multiple transferors, attach additional sheets giving the required information about each one. For a transaction under section 1445(e), enter the required information for each foreign person for whom you are requesting reduced withholding.

Line 2. Enter the name, street address, and identification number of the transferee. If there are multiple transferees, attach additional sheets giving the required information about each one.

Line 4a. The withholding agent will normally be the buyer or other transferee as described in section 1445(d)(4). For distributions under section 1445(e), the withholding agent also includes a trustee, executor, or other authorized person.

Line 4b. If you are not applying for this withholding certificate in your personal capacity, enter your SSN or ITIN (see *Identification number* on this page for more information).

Form 8288-B (Rev. 2-2016)

Line 4c. If you are acting on behalf of an estate or trust, or are signing as an authorized person for an entity other than an individual (for example, a corporation, qualified investment entity, or partnership), enter the name of the estate, trust, or entity.

Line 4d. Enter the EIN of the estate, trust, or entity.

Line 5. Enter the address you want the IRS to use for purposes of returning the withholding certificate.

Line 6a. Enter the year as a four-digit number (for example, "2013").

Line 6c. "Associated personal property" means property (for example, furniture) sold with a building. See Regulations section 1.897-1.

Line 6d. Check "Other" if the property was used for both personal and rental use and attach an explanation.

Line 6f. Enter the address and description of the property (for example, "10-story, 100-unit luxury apartment building"). For a real estate holding corporation interest transferred, enter the class or type and amount of the interest (for example, "10,000 shares Class A Preferred Stock XYZ Corporation"). You may attach additional sheets. Be sure to include your name and TIN on each sheet you attach.

Line 6g. A U.S. income tax return includes Forms 1040NR, and 1120-F.

Line 7a. If you checked 7a, attach:

1. A brief description of the transfer,
2. A summary of the law,
3. Facts supporting the claim of exemption or nonrecognition,
4. Evidence that the transferor has no unsatisfied withholding liability, and
5. The most recent assessed value for state or local property tax purposes of the interest to be transferred, or other estimate of its fair market value. You need not submit supporting evidence of the value of the property.

A nonresident alien or foreign corporation must also attach a statement of the adjusted basis of the property immediately before the distribution or transfer.

Line 7b. If you checked 7b, attach a calculation of the maximum tax that can be imposed on the disposition. You must include a statement signed by the transferor under penalties of perjury that the calculation and all supporting evidence is true and correct to the best knowledge of the transferor.

The calculation of the maximum tax that can be imposed must include:

1. Evidence of the amount to be realized by the transferor, such as a copy of the signed contract of transfer;

2. Evidence of the adjusted basis of the property, such as closing statements, invoices for improvements, and depreciation schedules, or if no depreciation schedules are submitted, a statement of the nature of the use of the property and why depreciation was not allowed;

3. Amounts to be recaptured for depreciation, investment credit, or other items subject to recapture;

4. The maximum capital gain and/or ordinary income tax rates applicable to the transfer;

5. The tentative tax owed; and

6. Evidence showing the amount of any increase or reduction of tax to which the transferor is subject, including any reduction to which the transferor is entitled under a U.S. income tax treaty.

If you have a net operating loss, see Rev. Proc. 2000-35, section 4.06, for special rules about the maximum tax calculation.

If the purchase price includes personal property not subject to tax under section 897, for the calculation of maximum tax, the transferor must also include a statement listing each such item of personal property transferred and the fair market value attributable to each item. The fair market value claimed should be supported by an independent appraisal or other similar documentation.

Line 7c. If you checked 7c, see *Installment sales*, earlier.

Line 8. You must provide a calculation of the transferor's unsatisfied withholding liability or evidence that it does not exist. This liability is the amount of any tax the transferor was required to, but did not, withhold and pay over under section 1445 when the U.S. real property interest now being transferred was acquired, or upon a prior acquisition. The transferor's unsatisfied withholding liability is included in the calculation of maximum tax liability so that it can be satisfied by the withholding on the current transfer.

Evidence that there is no unsatisfied withholding liability includes any of the following:

1. Evidence that the transferor acquired the subject or prior real property interest before 1985;

2. A copy of Form 8288 filed and proof of payment;

3. A copy of a withholding certificate issued by the IRS plus a copy of Form 8288 and proof of payment of any amount required by that certificate;

4. A copy of the nonforeign certificate furnished by the person from whom the U.S. real property interest was acquired (the certificate must be executed at the time of acquisition);

5. Evidence that the transferor purchased the subject or prior real property interest for $300,000 or less and a statement, signed by the transferor under penalties of perjury, that the transferor purchased the property for use as a residence within the meaning of Regulations section 1.1445-2(d)(1);

6. Evidence that the person from whom the transferor acquired the subject or prior U.S. real property interest fully paid any tax imposed on that transaction under section 897;

7. A copy of a notice of nonrecognition treatment provided to the transferor under Regulations section 1.1445-2(d)(2) by the person from whom the transferor acquired the subject or prior U.S. real property interest; or

8. A statement, signed by the transferor under penalties of perjury, explaining why the transferor was not required to withhold under section 1445(a) with regard to the transferor's acquisition of the subject or prior real property interest.

Line 9a. If the transaction is subject to withholding under section 1445(e), check the box to indicate which provision of section 1445(e) applies.

Line 9b. Indicate whether the applicant is the taxpayer or the person required to withhold, and in what capacity that person is required to withhold.

Signature. The application must be signed by an individual, a responsible corporate officer, a general partner of a partnership, or a trustee, executor, or other fiduciary of a trust or estate. The application may also be signed by an authorized agent with a power of attorney. Form 2848, Power of Attorney and Declaration of Representative, can be used for this purpose.

Privacy Act and Paperwork Reduction Act Notice. We ask for the information on this form to carry out the Internal Revenue laws of the United States. Section 1445 generally imposes a withholding obligation on the buyer or other transferee (withholding agent) when a U.S. real property interest is acquired from a foreign person. Section 1445 also imposes a withholding obligation on certain foreign and domestic corporations, qualified investment entities, and the fiduciary of certain trusts and estates. This form is used to apply for a withholding certificate to reduce or eliminate withholding on dispositions of U.S. real property interests by foreign persons if certain conditions apply.

You are required to provide this information. Section 6109 requires you to provide your identification number. We need this information to ensure that you are complying with the Internal Revenue laws and to allow us to figure and collect the right amount of tax. Failure to provide this information in a timely manner, or providing false information, may subject you to penalties. Routine uses of this information include giving it to the Department of Justice for civil and criminal litigation, and to cities, states, the District of Columbia, and to U.S. commonwealths and possessions for use in the administration of their tax laws. We may also disclose this information to other countries under a tax treaty, to federal and state agencies to enforce federal nontax criminal laws, or to federal law enforcement and intelligence agencies to combat terrorism.

8. FIRPTA Withholding

Form 8288-B (Rev. 2-2016)

You are not required to provide the information requested on a form that is subject to the Paperwork Reduction Act unless the form displays a valid OMB control number. Books or records relating to a form or its instructions must be retained as long as their contents may become material in the administration of any Internal Revenue law. Generally, tax returns and return information are confidential, as required by section 6103.

The time needed to complete and file this form will vary depending on individual circumstances. The estimated average time is:

Recordkeeping . . . . . 2 hr., 4 min.
Learning about the law or the form . . . . . 2 hr., 7 min.
Preparing the form . . . 1 hr., 7 min.
Copying, assembling, and sending the form to the IRS . . . . 20 min.

If you have comments concerning the accuracy of these time estimates or suggestions for making this form simpler, we would be happy to hear from you. You can send your comments to the Internal Revenue Service, Tax Forms and Publications, SE:W:CAR:MP:TFP, 1111 Constitution Ave. NW, IR-6526, Washington, DC 20224. Do not send this form to this office. Instead, see *Where to send applications for a withholding certificate*, earlier.

The US Foreign Investment in Real Property Tax Act: A Practical Guide

APPENDIX 8-E

Instructions for Form W-8BEN-E
(Rev. July 2017)

Certificate of Status of Beneficial Owner for United States Tax Withholding and Reporting (Entities)

Department of the Treasury
Internal Revenue Service

Section references are to the Internal Revenue Code unless otherwise noted.

Future Developments

For the latest information about developments related to Form W-8BEN-E and its instructions, such as legislation enacted after they were published, go to *IRS.gov/FormW8BENE*.

What's New

Limited FFIs and limited branches. Limited FFI and limited branch statuses expired on December 31, 2016, and have been removed from this form and the instructions.

Sponsored FFIs and sponsored direct reporting NFFEs. As of January 1, 2017, sponsored FFIs that are registered deemed-compliant FFIs and sponsored direct reporting NFFEs are required to obtain their own GIINs to be provided on this form and can no longer provide the sponsoring entity's GIIN. This form has been updated to reflect this requirement.

Nonreporting IGA FFIs. This form and these instructions have been updated to reflect the requirements for withholding agents to document nonreporting IGA FFIs in the Treasury regulations. These instructions also clarify that nonreporting IGA FFIs that are sponsored entities should provide their own GIIN (if required) and should not provide the GIIN of the sponsoring entity. See the instructions to Part XII. In addition, these instructions provide that a trustee of a trustee-documented trust that is a foreign person should provide the GIIN it received when it registered as a participating FFI (including a reporting Model 2 FFI) or reporting Model 1 FFI.

Foreign taxpayer identification numbers (TINs). These instructions have been updated to require a foreign TIN (except in certain cases) to be provided on this form for certain foreign account holders of a financial account maintained at a U.S. office or branch of a financial institution. See the instructions to line 9b for exceptions to this requirement.

Reminder

Note. If you are a resident in a FATCA partner jurisdiction (that is, a Model 1 IGA jurisdiction with reciprocity), certain tax account information may be provided to your jurisdiction of residence.

General Instructions

For definitions of terms used throughout these instructions, see *Definitions*, later.

Purpose of Form

This form is used by foreign entities to document their statuses for purposes of chapter 3 and chapter 4, as well as for certain other Code provisions as described later in these instructions.

Foreign persons are subject to U.S. tax at a 30% rate on income they receive from U.S. sources that consists of:
- Interest (including certain original issue discount (OID));
- Dividends;
- Rents;
- Royalties;
- Premiums;
- Annuities;
- Compensation for, or in expectation of, services performed;
- Substitute payments in a securities lending transaction; or
- Other fixed or determinable annual or periodical gains, profits, or income.

This tax is imposed on the gross amount paid and is generally collected by withholding under section 1441 or 1442 on that amount. A payment is considered to have been made whether it is made directly to the beneficial owner or to another person, such as an intermediary, agent, or partnership, for the benefit of the beneficial owner.

In addition, section 1446 requires a partnership conducting a trade or business in the United States to withhold tax on a foreign partner's distributive share of the partnership's effectively connected taxable income. Generally, a foreign person that is a partner in a partnership that submits a Form W-8 for purposes of section 1441 or 1442 will satisfy the documentation requirements under section 1446 as well. However, in some cases the documentation requirements of sections 1441 and 1442 do not match the documentation requirements of section 1446. See Regulations sections 1.1446-1 through 1.1446-6.

A withholding agent or payer of the income may rely on a properly completed Form W-8BEN-E to treat a payment associated with the Form W-8BEN-E as a payment to a foreign person who beneficially owns the amounts paid. If applicable, the withholding agent may rely on the Form W-8BEN-E to apply a reduced rate of, or exemption from, withholding. If you receive certain types of income, you must provide Form W-8BEN-E to:

Jul 19, 2017

Cat. No. 59691Z

8. FIRPTA Withholding

- Claim that you are the beneficial owner of the income for which Form W-8BEN-E is being provided or a partner in a partnership subject to section 1446; and
- If applicable, claim a reduced rate of, or exemption from, withholding as a resident of a foreign country with which the United States has an income tax treaty.

You may also use Form W-8BEN-E to identify income from a notional principal contract that is not effectively connected with the conduct of a trade or business in the United States to establish the exception to reporting such income on Form 1042-S. See Regulations section 1.1461-1(c)(2)(ii)(F).

Form W-8BEN-E may also be used to claim exemption from withholding for portfolio interest pursuant to section 881(c). The portfolio interest exemption does not apply to payments of interest for which the recipient is a 10 percent shareholder of the payer or to payments of interest received by a controlled foreign corporation from a related person. See sections 881(c)(3) and 881(c)(5). A future version of this form may require that persons receiving interest payments to which this form relates identify any obligation with respect to which they have one of these prohibited relationships.

You may also be required to submit Form W-8BEN-E to claim an exception from domestic information reporting on Form 1099 and backup withholding (at the backup withholding rate under section 3406) for certain types of income. Such income includes:
- Broker proceeds.
- Short-term (183 days or less) original issue discount (short-term OID).
- Bank deposit interest.
- Foreign source interest, dividends, rents, or royalties.

Provide Form W-8BEN-E to the withholding agent or payer before income is paid or credited to you. Failure to provide a Form W-8BEN-E when requested may lead to withholding at a 30% rate or the backup withholding rate in certain cases when you receive a payment to which backup withholding applies.

In addition to the requirements of chapter 3, chapter 4 requires withholding agents to identify the chapter 4 status of entities that are payees receiving withholdable payments. A withholding agent may request this Form W-8BEN-E to establish your chapter 4 status and avoid withholding at a 30% rate on such payments.

Chapter 4 also requires participating FFIs and certain registered deemed-compliant FFIs to document their entity account holders in order to determine their chapter 4 statuses regardless of whether withholding applies to any payments made to the entities. If you are an entity maintaining an account with an FFI, the FFI may request that you provide this Form W-8BEN-E in order to document your chapter 4 status.

Additional information. For additional information and instructions for the withholding agent, see the Instructions for the Requester of Forms W-8BEN, W-8BEN-E, W-8ECI, W-8EXP, and W-8IMY.

Who Must Provide Form W-8BEN-E

You must give Form W-8BEN-E to the withholding agent or payer if you are a foreign entity receiving a withholdable payment from a withholding agent, receiving a payment subject to chapter 3 withholding, or if you are an entity maintaining an account with an FFI requesting this form.

Do not use Form W-8BEN-E if:
- You are a U.S. person (including U.S. citizens, resident aliens, and entities treated as U.S. persons, such as a corporation organized under the law of a state). Instead, use Form W-9, Request for Taxpayer Identification Number and Certification.
- You are a foreign insurance company that has made an election under section 953(d) to be treated as a U.S. person. Instead, provide a withholding agent with Form W-9 to certify to your U.S. status even if you are considered an FFI for purposes of chapter 4.
- You are a nonresident alien individual. Instead, use Form W-8BEN, Certificate of Foreign Status of Beneficial Owner for United States Tax Withholding and Reporting (Individuals), or Form 8233, Exemption From Withholding on Compensation for Independent (and Certain Dependent) Personal Services of a Nonresident Alien Individual, as applicable.
- You are a disregarded entity, branch, or flow-through entity for U.S. tax purposes. However, you may use this form if you are a disregarded entity or flow-through entity using this form either solely to document your chapter 4 status (because you hold an account with an FFI) or, if you are a disregarded entity or a partnership, to claim treaty benefits because you are a hybrid entity liable to tax as a resident for treaty purposes. See *Special Instructions for Hybrid Entities*, later. A flow-through entity may also use this form for purposes of documenting itself as a participating payee for purposes of section 6050W. If you are a disregarded entity with a single owner or branch of an FFI, the single owner, if such owner is a foreign person, should provide Form W-8BEN or Form W-8BEN-E (as appropriate). If the single owner is a U.S. person, a Form W-9 should be provided. If you are a partnership, you should provide a Form W-8IMY, Certificate of Foreign Intermediary, Foreign Flow-Through Entity, or Certain U.S. Branches for United States Tax Withholding and Reporting.
- You are acting as an intermediary (that is, acting not for your own account, but for the account of others as an agent, nominee, or custodian), a qualified intermediary (including a qualified intermediary acting as a qualified derivatives dealer), or a qualified securities lender (QSL). Instead, provide Form W-8IMY.
- You are receiving income that is effectively connected with the conduct of a trade or business in the United States, unless it is allocable to you through a partnership. Instead, provide Form W-8ECI, Certificate of Foreign Person's Claim That Income Is Effectively Connected With the Conduct of a Trade or Business in the United States. If any of the income for which you have provided a Form W-8BEN-E becomes effectively connected, this is a change in circumstances and the Form W-8BEN-E is no longer valid.
- You are filing for a foreign government, international organization, foreign central bank of issue, foreign tax-exempt organization, foreign private foundation, or government of a U.S. possession claiming the applicability of section 115(2), 501(c), 892, 895, or 1443(b). Instead, provide Form W-8EXP, Certificate of

The US Foreign Investment in Real Property Tax Act: A Practical Guide

Foreign Government or Other Foreign Organization for United States Tax Withholding and Reporting, to certify to your exemption and identify your chapter 4 status. However, you should provide Form W-8BEN-E if you are claiming treaty benefits, and you may provide this form if you are only claiming you are a foreign person exempt from backup withholding or documenting your chapter 4 status. For example, a foreign tax-exempt organization under section 501(c) receiving royalty income that is not exempt because it is taxable as unrelated business income but that is eligible for a reduced rate of withholding under a royalty article of a tax treaty should provide Form W-8BEN-E. You should use Form W-8ECI if you are receiving effectively connected income (for example, income from commercial activities that is not exempt under an applicable section of the Code).

- You are a foreign reverse hybrid entity transmitting documentation provided by your interest holders to claim treaty benefits on their behalf. Instead, provide Form W-8IMY. A foreign reverse hybrid entity also may not use this form to attempt to claim treaty benefits on its own behalf. See *Foreign Reverse Hybrid Entities*, later.
- You are a withholding foreign partnership or a withholding foreign trust within the meaning of sections 1441 and 1442 and the accompanying regulations. Instead, provide Form W-8IMY.
- You are a foreign partnership or foreign grantor trust providing documentation for purposes of section 1446. Instead, provide Form W-8IMY and accompanying documentation.
- You are a foreign branch of a U.S. financial institution that is an FFI (other than a qualified intermediary branch) under an applicable Model 1 IGA. For purposes of identifying yourself to withholding agents, you may submit Form W-9 to certify to your U.S. status.

Giving Form W-8BEN-E to the withholding agent. Do not send Form W-8BEN-E to the IRS. Instead, give it to the person who is requesting it from you. Generally, this will be the person from whom you receive the payment, who credits your account, or a partnership that allocates income to you. An FFI may also request this form from you to document the status of your account.

When to provide Form W-8BEN-E to the withholding agent. Give Form W-8BEN-E to the person requesting it before the payment is made to you, credited to your account, or allocated. If you do not provide this form, the withholding agent may have to withhold at the 30% rate (as applicable under chapters 3 or 4), backup withholding rate, or the rate applicable under section 1446. If you receive more than one type of income from a single withholding agent for which you claim different benefits, the withholding agent may, at its option, require you to submit a Form W-8BEN-E for each type of income. Generally, a separate Form W-8BEN-E must be given to each withholding agent.

Note. If you own the income with one or more other persons, the income will be treated by the withholding agent as owned by a foreign person that is a beneficial owner of a payment only if Form W-8BEN or W-8BEN-E (or other applicable document) is provided by each of the owners. An account will be treated as a U.S. account for chapter 4 purposes by an FFI requesting this form if any of the account holders is a specified U.S. person or a U.S.-owned foreign entity (unless the account is otherwise excepted from U.S. account status for chapter 4 purposes).

Change in circumstances. If a change in circumstances makes any information on the Form W-8BEN-E you have submitted incorrect for purposes of either chapter 3 or chapter 4, you must notify the withholding agent or financial institution maintaining your account within 30 days of the change in circumstances by providing the documentation required in Regulations section 1.1471-3(c)(6)(ii)(E)(2). See Regulations sections 1.1441-1(e)(4)(ii)(D) for the definition of change in circumstances for purposes of chapter 3, and 1.1471-3(c)(6)(ii)(E) for purposes of chapter 4.

⚠ *With respect to an FFI claiming a chapter 4 status under an applicable IGA, a change in circumstances includes when the jurisdiction where the FFI is organized or resident (or the jurisdiction identified in Part II of the form) was included on the list of jurisdictions treated as having an intergovernmental agreement in effect and is removed from that list or when the FATCA status of the jurisdiction changes (for example, from Model 2 to Model 1). The list of agreements is maintained at www.treasury.gov/resource-center/tax-policy/treaties/Pages/FATCA-Archive.aspx.*

Expiration of Form W-8BEN-E. Generally, a Form W-8BEN-E will remain valid for purposes of both chapters 3 and 4 for a period starting on the date the form is signed and ending on the last day of the third succeeding calendar year, unless a change in circumstances makes any information on the form incorrect. For example, a Form W-8BEN signed on September 30, 2014, remains valid through December 31, 2017.

However, under certain conditions a Form W-8BEN-E will remain in effect indefinitely absent a change of circumstances. See Regulations sections 1.1441-1(e)(4)(ii) and 1.1471-3(c)(6)(ii) for the period of validity for chapters 3 and 4 purposes, respectively.

Definitions

Account holder. An account holder is generally the person listed or identified as the holder or owner of a financial account. For example, if a partnership is listed as the holder or owner of a financial account, then the partnership is the account holder, rather than the partners of the partnership. However, an account that is held by a disregarded entity (other than a disregarded entity treated as an FFI for chapter 4 purposes) is treated as held by the entity's single owner.

Amounts subject to chapter 3 withholding. Generally, an amount subject to chapter 3 withholding is an amount from sources within the United States that is fixed or determinable annual or periodical (FDAP) income. FDAP income is all income included in gross income, including interest (as well as OID), dividends, rents, royalties, and compensation. Amounts subject to chapter 3 withholding do not include amounts that are not FDAP, such as most gains from the sale of property (including market discount and option premiums), as well as other specific items of

Instructions for Form W-8BEN-E (Rev. 7-2017) -3-

8. FIRPTA Withholding

income described in Regulations section 1.1441-2 (such as interest on bank deposits and short-term OID).

For purposes of section 1446, the amount subject to withholding is the foreign partner's share of the partnership's effectively connected taxable income.

Beneficial owner. For payments other than those for which a reduced rate of, or exemption from, withholding is claimed under an income tax treaty, the beneficial owner of income is generally the person who is required under U.S. tax principles to include the payment in gross income on a tax return. A person is not a beneficial owner of income, however, to the extent that person is receiving the income as a nominee, agent, or custodian, or to the extent the person is a conduit whose participation in a transaction is disregarded. In the case of amounts paid that do not constitute income, beneficial ownership is determined as if the payment were income.

Foreign partnerships, foreign simple trusts, and foreign grantor trusts are not the beneficial owners of income paid to the partnership or trust. The beneficial owners of income paid to a foreign partnership are generally the partners in the partnership, provided that the partner is not itself a partnership, foreign simple or grantor trust, nominee or other agent. The beneficial owners of income paid to a foreign simple trust (that is, a foreign trust that is described in section 651(a)) are generally the beneficiaries of the trust, if the beneficiary is not a foreign partnership, foreign simple or grantor trust, nominee, or other agent. The beneficial owners of income paid to a foreign grantor trust (that is, a foreign trust to the extent that all or a portion of the income of the trust is treated as owned by the grantor or another person under sections 671 through 679) are the persons treated as the owners of the trust. The beneficial owners of income paid to a foreign complex trust (that is, a foreign trust that is not a foreign simple trust or foreign grantor trust) is the trust itself.

For purposes of section 1446, the same beneficial owner rules apply, except that under section 1446 a foreign simple trust rather than the beneficiary provides the form to the partnership.

The beneficial owner of income paid to a foreign estate is the estate itself.

Note. A payment to a U.S. partnership, U.S. trust, or U.S. estate is treated as a payment to a U.S. payee that is not subject to 30% withholding for purposes of chapters 3 and 4. A U.S. partnership, trust, or estate should provide the withholding agent with a Form W-9. For purposes of section 1446, a U.S. grantor trust or disregarded entity shall not provide the withholding agent a Form W-9 in its own right. Rather, the grantor or other owner shall provide the withholding agent the appropriate form.

Chapter 3. Chapter 3 means chapter 3 of the Internal Revenue Code (Withholding of Tax on Nonresident Aliens and Foreign Corporations). Chapter 3 contains sections 1441 through 1464.

Chapter 4. Chapter 4 means chapter 4 of the Internal Revenue Code (Taxes to Enforce Reporting on Certain Foreign Accounts). Chapter 4 contains sections 1471 through 1474.

Chapter 4 status. The term chapter 4 status means a person's status as a U.S. person, specified U.S. person, foreign individual, participating FFI, deemed-compliant FFI, restricted distributor, exempt beneficial owner, nonparticipating FFI, territory financial institution, excepted NFFE, or passive NFFE.

Deemed-compliant FFI. Under section 1471(b)(2), certain FFIs are deemed to comply with the regulations under chapter 4 without the need to enter into an FFI agreement with the IRS. However, certain deemed-compliant FFIs are required to register with the IRS and obtain a GIIN. These FFIs are referred to as *registered deemed-compliant FFIs*. See Regulations section 1.1471-5(f)(1).

Disregarded entity. A business entity that has a single owner and is not a corporation under Regulations section 301.7701-2(b) is disregarded as an entity separate from its owner. Generally, a disregarded entity does not submit this Form W-8BEN-E to a withholding agent. Instead, the owner of such entity provides the appropriate documentation (for example, a Form W-8BEN-E if the owner is a foreign entity). However, if a disregarded entity receiving a withholdable payment is an FFI outside the single owner's country of organization or has its own GIIN, its foreign owner will be required to complete Part II of Form W-8BEN-E to document the chapter 4 status of the disregarded entity receiving the payment.

Certain entities that are disregarded for U.S. tax purposes may be treated as treaty residents for purposes of claiming treaty benefits under an applicable tax treaty or may be recognized as FFIs under an applicable IGA. A hybrid entity claiming treaty benefits on its own behalf is required to complete Form W-8BEN-E. See *Hybrid Entities* under *Special Instructions*, later.

A disregarded entity with a U.S. owner or a disregarded entity with a foreign owner that is not otherwise able to fill out Part II (that is, because it is in the same country as its single owner and does not have a GIIN) may provide this form to an FFI solely for purposes of documenting itself for chapter 4 purposes. In such a case, the disregarded entity should complete Part I as if it were a beneficial owner and should not complete line 3.

Financial account. A financial account includes:
- A depository account maintained by an FFI;
- A custodial account maintained by an FFI;
- Equity or debt interests (other than interests regularly traded on an established securities market) in investment entities and certain holding companies, treasury centers, or financial institutions as defined in Regulations section 1.1471-5(e);
- Certain cash value insurance contracts; and
- Annuity contracts.

For purposes of chapter 4, exceptions are provided for accounts such as certain tax-favored savings accounts, term life insurance contracts, accounts held by estates, escrow accounts, and certain annuity contracts. These exceptions are subject to certain conditions. See Regulations section 1.1471-5(b)(2). Accounts may also be excluded from the definition of financial account under an applicable IGA.

Financial institution. A financial institution generally means an entity that is a depository institution, custodial institution, investment entity, or an insurance company (or holding company of an insurance company) that issues cash value insurance or annuity contracts. See Regulations section 1.1471-5(e).

An investment entity organized in a territory that is not also a depository institution, custodial institution, or specified insurance company is not treated as a financial institution. Instead, it is a territory NFFE. If such an entity cannot qualify as an excepted NFFE as described in Regulations section 1.1472-1(c)(1) (including an excepted territory NFFE), it must disclose its substantial U.S. owners using this definition (applying the 10 percent threshold) under Regulations section 1.1473-1(b)(1).

Foreign financial institution (FFI). A foreign financial institution (FFI) means a foreign entity that is a financial institution.

Fiscally transparent entity. An entity is treated as fiscally transparent with respect to an item of income for which treaty benefits are claimed to the extent that the interest holders in the entity must, on a current basis, take into account separately their shares of an item of income paid to the entity, whether or not distributed, and must determine the character of the items of income as if they were realized directly from the sources from which realized by the entity. For example, partnerships, common trust funds, and simple trusts or grantor trusts are generally considered to be fiscally transparent with respect to items of income received by them.

Flow-through entity. A flow-through entity is a foreign partnership (other than a withholding foreign partnership), a foreign simple or foreign grantor trust (other than a withholding foreign trust), or, for payments for which a reduced rate of, or exemption from, withholding is claimed under an income tax treaty, any entity to the extent the entity is considered to be fiscally transparent with respect to the payment by an interest holder's jurisdiction.

Foreign person. A foreign person includes a foreign corporation, a foreign partnership, a foreign trust, a foreign estate, and any other person that is not a U.S. person. It also includes a foreign branch or office of a U.S. financial institution or U.S. clearing organization if the foreign branch is a qualified intermediary. Generally, a payment to a U.S. branch of a foreign person is a payment to a foreign person.

GIIN. The term GIIN means a global intermediary identification number. A GIIN is the identification number assigned to an entity that has registered with the IRS for chapter 4 purposes.

Hybrid entity. A hybrid entity is any person (other than an individual) that is treated as fiscally transparent for purposes of its status under the Code but is not treated as fiscally transparent by a country with which the United States has an income tax treaty. Hybrid entity status is relevant for claiming treaty benefits. A hybrid entity is required to provide its chapter 4 status if it is receiving a withholdable payment.

Intergovernmental agreement (IGA). An intergovernmental agreement (IGA) means a Model 1 IGA or a Model 2 IGA. For a list of jurisdictions treated as having in effect a Model 1 or Model 2 IGA, see www.treasury.gov/resource-center/tax-policy/treaties/Pages/FATCA-Archive.aspx.

A **Model 1 IGA** means an agreement between the United States or the Treasury Department and a foreign government or one or more agencies to implement FATCA through reporting by FFIs to such foreign government or agency, followed by automatic exchange of the reported information with the IRS. An FFI in a Model 1 IGA jurisdiction that performs account reporting to the jurisdiction's government is referred to as a *reporting Model 1 FFI*.

A **Model 2 IGA** means an agreement or arrangement between the United States or the Treasury Department and a foreign government or one or more agencies to implement FATCA through reporting by FFIs directly to the IRS in accordance with the requirements of an FFI agreement, supplemented by the exchange of information between such foreign government or agency and the IRS. An FFI in a Model 2 IGA jurisdiction that has entered into an FFI agreement with respect to a branch is a participating FFI but may be referred to as a *reporting Model 2 FFI*.

The term **reporting IGA FFI** refers to both reporting Model 1 FFIs and reporting Model 2 FFIs.

Nonparticipating FFI. A nonparticipating FFI means an FFI that is not a participating FFI, deemed-compliant FFI, or exempt beneficial owner.

Nonreporting IGA FFI. A nonreporting IGA FFI is an FFI that is a resident of, or located or established in, a Model 1 or Model 2 IGA jurisdiction that meets the requirements of:
- A nonreporting financial institution described in a specific category in Annex II of the Model 1 or Model 2 IGA;
- A registered deemed-compliant FFI described in Regulations section 1.1471-5(f)(1)(i)(A) through (F);
- A certified deemed-compliant FFI described in Regulations section 1.1471-5(f)(2)(i) through (v); or
- An exempt beneficial owner described in Regulations section 1.1471-6.

Participating FFI. A participating FFI is an FFI that has agreed to comply with the terms of an FFI agreement with respect to all branches of the FFI, other than a branch that is a reporting Model 1 FFI or a U.S. branch. The term participating FFI also includes a reporting Model 2 FFI and a QI branch of a U.S. financial institution unless such branch is a reporting Model 1 FFI.

Participating payee. A participating payee means any person that accepts a payment card as payment or accepts payment from a third party settlement organization in settlement of a third party network transaction for purposes of section 6050W.

Payee. A payee is generally a person to whom a payment is made regardless of whether such person is the beneficial owner. For a payment made to a financial account, the payee is generally the holder of the financial account. See Regulations sections 1.1441-1(b)(2) and 1.1471-3(a)(3).

8. FIRPTA Withholding

Payment settlement entity (PSE). A payment settlement entity is a merchant acquiring entity or third party settlement organization. Under section 6050W, a PSE is generally required to report payments made in settlement of payment card transactions or third party network transactions. However, a PSE is not required to report payments made to a beneficial owner that is documented as foreign with an applicable Form W-8.

Qualified intermediary (QI). A qualified intermediary (QI) is a person that is a party to an agreement with the IRS that is described in Regulations section 1.1441-1(e)(5)(iii). A *qualified derivatives dealer (QDD)* is a QI that has agreed to certain reporting and withholding requirements pursuant to Regulations section 1.1441-1(e)(6).

Recalcitrant account holder. A recalcitrant account holder includes an entity (other than an entity required to be treated as a nonparticipating FFI) that fails to comply with a request by an FFI maintaining the account for documentation and information for determining whether the account is a U.S. account. See Regulations section 1.1471-5(g).

Reverse hybrid entity. A reverse hybrid entity is any person (other than an individual) that is not fiscally transparent under U.S. tax law principles but that is fiscally transparent under the laws of a jurisdiction with which the United States has an income tax treaty. See Form W-8IMY and the accompanying instructions for information on a reverse hybrid entity making a claim of treaty benefits on behalf of its owners.

Specified U.S. person. A specified U.S. person is any U.S. person other than a person identified in Regulations section 1.1473-1(c).

Substantial U.S. owner. A substantial U.S. owner (as defined in Regulations section 1.1473-1(b)) means any specified U.S. person that:
• Owns, directly or indirectly, more than 10 percent (by vote or value) of the stock of any foreign corporation;
• Owns, directly or indirectly, more than 10 percent of the profits or capital interests in a foreign partnership;
• Is treated as an owner of any portion of a foreign trust under sections 671 through 679; or
• Holds, directly or indirectly, more than a 10 percent beneficial interest in a trust.

U.S. person. A U.S. person is defined in section 7701(a)(30) and includes domestic partnerships, corporations, and trusts.

> **CAUTION.** Certain foreign insurance companies issuing annuities or cash value insurance contracts that elect to be treated as a U.S. person for federal tax purposes but are not licensed to do business in the United States are treated as FFIs for purposes of chapter 4. For purposes of providing a withholding agent with documentation for both chapter 3 and chapter 4 purposes, however, such an insurance company is permitted to use Form W-9 to certify its status as a U.S. person. Likewise, a foreign branch of a U.S. financial institution (other than a branch that operates as a qualified intermediary) that is treated as an FFI under an applicable IGA is permitted to use Form W-9 to certify its status as a U.S. person for chapter 3 and chapter 4 purposes.

Withholdable payment. A withholdable payment is defined in Regulations section 1.1473-1(a). For exceptions applicable to the definition of a withholdable payment, see Regulations section 1.1473-1(a)(4) (for example, certain nonfinancial payments).

Withholding agent. Any person, U.S. or foreign, that has control, receipt, custody, disposal, or payment of U.S. source FDAP income subject to chapter 3 or 4 withholding is a withholding agent. The withholding agent may be an individual, corporation, partnership, trust, association, or any other entity, including (but not limited to) any foreign intermediary, foreign partnership, and U.S. branches of certain foreign banks and insurance companies.

For purposes of section 1446, the withholding agent is the partnership conducting the trade or business in the United States. For a publicly traded partnership, the withholding agent may be the partnership, a nominee holding an interest on behalf of a foreign person, or both. See Regulations sections 1.1446-1 through 1.1446-6.

Specific Instructions

Part I – Identification of Beneficial Owner

Line 1. Enter your name. If you are a disregarded entity or branch, do not enter your business name. Instead, enter the legal name of your owner (or, if you are a branch, the entity that you form a part of) (looking through multiple disregarded entities if applicable). If you are a disregarded entity that is a hybrid entity filing a treaty claim, however, see *Hybrid entities* under *Special Instructions*, later.

> **TIP.** If you are an account holder providing this form to an FFI solely for purposes of documenting yourself as an account holder and you are not receiving a withholdable payment or reportable amount (as defined in Regulations section 1.1441-1(e)(3)(vi)), you should complete Part I by substituting the references to "beneficial owner" with "account holder."

> **CAUTION.** The named holder on the account is not necessarily the account holder for purposes of chapter 4. See *Definitions*, earlier, or, for an account maintained by an FFI covered by a Model 1 or Model 2 IGA with respect to the account, the definition of account holder in an applicable IGA to determine if you are the account holder. If you hold an account with an FFI and are unsure whether the definition of "account holder" under an IGA is applicable to your account, consult with the FFI requesting this form.

Line 2. If you are a corporation, enter your country of incorporation. If you are another type of entity, enter the country under whose laws you are created, organized, or governed.

Line 3. If you are a disregarded entity receiving a withholdable payment, enter your name on line 3 if you: 1)

-6- Instructions for Form W-8BEN-E (Rev. 7-2017)

The US Foreign Investment in Real Property Tax Act: A Practical Guide

have registered with the IRS and been assigned a GIIN associated with the legal name of the disregarded entity; 2) are a reporting Model 1 FFI or reporting Model 2 FFI; and 3) are not a hybrid entity using this form to claim treaty benefits.

> ⚠ **CAUTION** *If you are not required to provide the legal name of the disregarded entity, you may want to notify the withholding agent that you are a disregarded entity receiving a payment or maintaining an account by indicating the name of the disregarded entity on line 10. If you wish to report the name of a disregarded entity holding an account with the withholding agent requesting this form for only information purposes (that is, the disregarded entity is not reported on line 1 or in Part II of this form), you may enter the disregarded entity's name on line 3.*

Line 4. Check the one box that applies. By checking a box, you are representing that you qualify for the classification indicated. You must check the box that represents your classification (for example, corporation, partnership, trust, estate, etc.) under U.S. tax principles (not under the law of a treaty country). If you are providing Form W-8BEN-E to an FFI solely for purposes of documenting yourself for chapter 4 purposes as an account holder of an account maintained by an FFI, you do not need to complete line 4.

If you are a partnership, disregarded entity, simple trust, or grantor trust receiving a payment for which treaty benefits are being claimed by such entity, you must check the "Partnership," "Disregarded entity," "Simple trust," or "Grantor trust" box. For such a case, you must also check the "yes" box to indicate that you are a hybrid entity making a treaty claim. You may only check the "no" box if (1) you are a disregarded entity, partnership, simple trust, or grantor trust and are using the form solely for purposes of documenting yourself as an account holder of an FFI and the form is not associated with a withholdable payment or a reportable amount or (2) you are using this form solely for purposes of documenting your status as a participating payee for purposes of section 6050W. In such cases, you are not required to complete line 4, but you may check the "no" box if you choose to complete line 4. You may also use Form W-8IMY to document yourself as an account holder of an FFI.

> ⚠ **CAUTION** *Only entities that are tax-exempt under section 501(c) should check the "Tax-exempt organization" box for purposes of line 4. Such organizations should use Form W-8BEN-E only if they are claiming a reduced rate of withholding under an income tax treaty or a Code exception other than section 501(c) or if they are using this form solely for purposes of documenting themselves as an account holder with an FFI. However, if you are a private foundation you should check "Private Foundation" instead of "Tax-exempt organization."*

Line 5. Check the one box that applies to your chapter 4 status. You are only required to provide a chapter 4 status on this form if you are the payee of a withholdable payment or are documenting the status of a financial account you hold with an FFI requesting this form. By checking a box on this line, you are representing that you qualify for this classification in your country of residence.

> 💡 **TIP** *For most of the chapter 4 statuses, you are required to complete an additional part of this form certifying that you meet the conditions of the status indicated on line 5. Complete the required portion of this form before signing and providing it to the withholding agent. See* Entities Providing Certifications Under an Applicable IGA *under* Special Instructions, *later.*

FFIs Covered by an IGA and Related Entities

A reporting IGA FFI resident in, or established under the laws of, a jurisdiction covered by a Model 1 IGA should check "Reporting Model 1 FFI." A reporting FFI resident in, or established under the laws of, a jurisdiction covered by a Model 2 IGA should check "Reporting Model 2 FFI." If you are treated as a registered deemed-compliant FFI under an applicable IGA, you should check "Nonreporting IGA FFI" rather than "registered deemed-compliant FFI" and provide your GIIN.

In general, if you are treated as a nonreporting IGA FFI under an applicable IGA, you should check "Nonreporting IGA FFI" even if you meet the qualifications for deemed-compliant status or are an exempt beneficial owner under the chapter 4 regulations. In such a case, you should not also check your applicable status under the regulations but should provide your GIIN on line 9, if applicable. If you are an owner-documented FFI that is treated as a nonreporting IGA FFI under an applicable IGA you must check "Owner-documented FFI" and complete Part X.

An FFI that is related to a reporting IGA FFI and that is treated as a nonparticipating FFI in its country of residence should check "Nonparticipating FFI" in line 5.

If you are an FFI in a jurisdiction treated as having an IGA in effect, you should not check "Participating FFI" but rather should check "Reporting Model 1 FFI" or "Reporting Model 2 FFI" as applicable. See *www.treasury.gov/resource-center/tax-policy/treaties/Pages/FATCA-Archive.aspx* for a list of jurisdictions treated as having an IGA in effect.

Non-Profit Organizations Covered by an IGA

If you are a non-profit entity that is established and maintained in a jurisdiction treated as having an IGA in effect and you meet the definition of "active NFFE" under Annex I of the applicable IGA, you should not check a box on line 5 if you are providing this form to an FFI for purposes of documenting yourself as an account holder. Instead, you should provide a certification of your status under the IGA. See *Entities Providing Certifications Under an Applicable IGA* under *Special Instructions*, later.

Account That Is Not a Financial Account

If you are providing this form to document an account you hold with a foreign financial institution that is not a financial account under Regulations section 1.1471-5(b)(2), check the "Account that is not a financial account" box on line 5.

Line 6. Enter the permanent residence address of the entity identified in line 1. Your permanent residence

8. FIRPTA Withholding

address is the address in the country where you claim to be a resident for purposes of that country's income tax. If you are giving Form W-8BEN-E to claim a reduced rate of, or exemption from, withholding under an income tax treaty, you must determine residency in the manner required by the treaty. Do not show the address of a financial institution (unless you are a financial institution providing your own address), a post office box, or an address used solely for mailing purposes unless it is the only address you use and it appears in your organizational documents (that is, your registered address). If you do not have a tax residence in any country, the permanent residence address is where you maintain your principal office.

Line 7. Enter your mailing address only if it is different from the address on line 6.

Line 8. Enter your U.S. employer identification number (EIN). An EIN is a U.S. taxpayer identification number (TIN) for entities. If you do not have a U.S. EIN, apply for one on Form SS-4, Application for Employer Identification Number, if you are required to obtain a U.S. TIN.

A partner in a partnership conducting a trade or business in the United States will likely be allocated effectively connected taxable income. The partner is required to file a U.S. federal income tax return and must have a TIN.

You must provide a U.S. TIN if you are:
- Claiming an exemption from withholding under section 871(f) for certain annuities received under qualified plans, or
- Claiming benefits under an income tax treaty and have not provided a foreign TIN on line 9b.

However, a TIN is not required to be shown in order to claim treaty benefits on the following items of income:
- Dividends and interest from stocks and debt obligations that are actively traded;
- Dividends from any redeemable security issued by an investment company registered under the Investment Company Act of 1940 (mutual fund);
- Dividends, interest, or royalties from units of beneficial interest in a unit investment trust that are (or were upon issuance) publicly offered and are registered with the SEC under the Securities Act of 1933; and
- Income related to loans of any of the above securities.

See Regulations section 1.1441-1(e)(4)(vii) for other circumstances when you are required to provide a U.S. TIN.

TIP *If you need an EIN, you are encouraged to apply for one online instead of submitting a paper Form SS-4. For more information, visit IRS.gov/EIN.*

Line 9a. If you are a participating FFI, registered deemed-compliant FFI (including a sponsored FFI described in the Treasury regulations), reporting Model 1 FFI, reporting Model 2 FFI, direct reporting NFFE, trustee of a trustee-documented trust that is a foreign person providing this form for the trust, or sponsored direct reporting NFFE, you are required to enter your GIIN (with regard to your country of residence) on line 9a. If you are a trustee of a trustee-documented trust and you are a foreign person, you should provide the GIIN that you received when you registered as a participating FFI or reporting Model 1 FFI. If your branch is receiving the payment and is required to be identified in Part II, you are not required to provide a GIIN on line 9a. Instead, provide the GIIN of your branch (if applicable) on line 13.

You must provide your GIIN on line 9 if you are a nonreporting IGA FFI that is (1) treated as registered deemed-compliant under Annex II to an applicable Model 2 IGA or (2) a registered deemed-compliant FFI under Regulations section 1.1471-5(f)(1).

TIP *If you are in the process of registering with the IRS as a participating FFI, registered deemed-compliant FFI (including a sponsored FFI), reporting Model 1 FFI, reporting Model 2 FFI, direct reporting NFFE, sponsored direct reporting NFFE, or nonreporting IGA FFI but have not received a GIIN, you may complete this line by writing "applied for." However, the person requesting this form from you must receive and verify your GIIN within 90 days.*

Line 9b. If you are providing this Form W-8BEN-E to document yourself as an account holder with respect to a financial account (as defined in Regulations section 1.1471-5(b)) that you hold at a U.S. office of a financial institution (including a U.S. branch of an FFI) and you receive U.S. source income reportable on Form 1042-S associated with this form, you **must** provide the TIN issued to you by the jurisdiction in which you are a tax resident identified on line 6 unless:
- You have not been issued a TIN (including if the jurisdiction does not issue TINs), or
- You properly identified yourself as a government, central bank of issue, or international organization on line 4, or you are a resident of a U.S. possession.

If you are providing this form to document a financial account described above but you do not enter a TIN on line 9b, and you are not a government, central bank of issue, international organization, or resident of a U.S. possession, you must provide the withholding agent with an explanation of why you have not been issued a TIN. For this purpose, an explanation is a statement that you are not legally required to obtain a TIN in your jurisdiction of tax residence. The explanation may be written on line 9b, in the margins of the form, or on a separate attached statement associated with the form. If you are writing the explanation on line 9b, you may shorten it to "not legally required." Do not write "not applicable."

In addition, if you are not using this form to document a financial account described above, you may provide the TIN issued to you by your jurisdiction of tax residence on line 9b for purposes of claiming treaty benefits (rather than providing a U.S. TIN on line 6b, if required).

TIP *Lines 9a and 9b should accommodate the GIIN or foreign TIN, as appropriate. You may need to use a smaller font when completing the form. If the GIIN or foreign TIN does not fit in the space provided, you may provide a GIIN or foreign TIN that is indicated and clearly identified somewhere else on the form, or on a separate attached sheet, as long as the GIIN or foreign TIN is clearly identified as being furnished with respect to line 9a or 9b, respectively. For example, a handwritten GIIN located just outside of line 9a with a corresponding* arrow pointing to line 9a is a properly provided GIIN for this purpose.

Line 10. This line may be used by you or by the withholding agent or FFI to include any referencing information that is useful to the withholding agent to document the beneficial owner. For example, withholding agents who are required to associate the Form W-8BEN-E with a particular Form W-8IMY may want to use line 10 for a referencing number or code that will make the association clear. You may also want to use line 10 to include the number of the account for which you are providing the form. If you are a single owner of a disregarded entity you may use line 10 to inform the withholding agent that the account to which a payment is made or credited is held in the name of the disregarded entity (unless the name of the disregarded entity is required to be provided on line 3).

You may also use line 10 to identify income from a notional principal contract that is not effectively connected with the conduct of a trade or business in the United States.

Part II – Disregarded Entity or Branch Receiving Payment

Complete Part II for a disregarded entity that has its own GIIN and is receiving a withholdable payment, or for a branch (including a branch that is a disregarded entity that does not have a GIIN) operating in a jurisdiction other than the country of residence identified in line 2. For example, assume ABC Co., which is a participating FFI resident in Country A, operates through a branch in Country B (which is a Model 1 IGA jurisdiction) and the branch is treated as a reporting Model 1 FFI under the terms of the Country B Model 1 IGA. ABC Co. should not enter its GIIN on line 9, and the Country B branch should complete this Part II by identifying itself as a reporting Model 1 IGA FFI and providing its GIIN on line 13. If the Country B branch receiving the payment is a disregarded entity you may be required to provide its legal name on line 3.

TIP *If the disregarded entity receiving a withholdable payment has its own GIIN, Part II should be completed regardless of whether it is in the same country as the single owner identified in Part I.*

If you have multiple branches/disregarded entities receiving payments from the same withholding agent and the information in Part I is the same for each branch/disregarded entity that will receive payments, a withholding agent may accept a single Form W-8BEN-E from you with a schedule attached that includes all of the Part II information for each branch/disregarded entity rather than separate Forms W-8BEN-E to identify each branch/disregarded entity receiving payments associated with the form and an allocation of the payment to each branch/disregarded entity.

Line 11. Check the one box that applies. If no box applies to the disregarded entity, you do not need to complete this part. If you check reporting Model 1 FFI, reporting Model 2 FFI, or participating FFI, you must complete line 13 (see below). If your branch is a branch of a reporting IGA FFI that cannot comply with the requirements of an applicable IGA or the regulations under chapter 4 (a related entity), you must check "Branch treated as nonparticipating FFI."

Line 12. Enter the address of the branch or disregarded entity.

Line 13. If you are a reporting Model 1 FFI, reporting Model 2 FFI, or participating FFI, you must enter the GIIN on line 13 of your branch that receives the payment. If you are a disregarded entity that completed Part I, line 3 of this form and are receiving payments associated with this form, enter your GIIN. Do not enter your GIIN on line 9. If you are a U.S. branch, enter a GIIN applicable to any other branch of the FFI (including in its residence country).

TIP *If you are in the process of registering your branch with the IRS but have not received a GIIN, you may complete this line by writing "applied for." However, the person requesting this form from you must receive and verify your GIIN within 90 days.*

Part III – Claim of Tax Treaty Benefits

Line 14a. If you are claiming a reduced rate of, or exemption from, withholding under an income tax treaty you must enter the country where you are a resident for income tax treaty purposes and check the box to certify that you are a resident of that country.

Line 14b. If you are claiming a reduced rate of, or exemption from, withholding under an income tax treaty you must check the box to certify that you:
- Derive the item of income for which the treaty benefit is claimed, and
- Meet the limitation on benefits provision contained in the treaty, if any.

An item of income may be derived by either the entity receiving the item of income or by the interest holders in the entity or, in certain circumstances, both. An item of income paid to an entity is considered to be derived by the entity only if the entity is not fiscally transparent under the laws of the entity's jurisdiction with respect to the item of income. An item of income paid to an entity shall be considered to be derived by the interest holder in the entity only if:
- The interest holder is not fiscally transparent in its jurisdiction with respect to the item of income, and
- The entity is considered to be fiscally transparent under the laws of the interest holder's jurisdiction with respect to the item of income. An item of income paid directly to a type of entity specifically identified in a treaty as a resident of a treaty jurisdiction is treated as derived by a resident of that treaty jurisdiction.

Limitation on benefits treaty provisions. If you are a resident of a foreign country that has entered into an income tax treaty with the United States that contains a limitation on benefits (LOB) article, you must complete one of the checkboxes in line 14b. You may only check a box if the limitation on benefits article in that treaty includes a provision that corresponds to the checkbox on which you are relying to claim treaty benefits. A particular treaty might not include every type of test for which a checkbox is provided. For example, "Company that meets the derivative benefits test" is generally not available to a

8. FIRPTA Withholding

company resident in a treaty country that is not a member of the EU, EEA, or NAFTA. In addition, each treaty LOB article that contains a specific test listed below may have particular requirements that must be met that differ from the requirements in another treaty with regard to the same test. Accordingly, you must check the relevant treaty LOB article for the particular requirements associated with each test. In general, only one LOB checkbox is required to claim a treaty exemption even if more than one checkbox would suffice to claim the benefits of the treaty for that item of income.

Each of the tests is summarized below for your general convenience but may not be relied upon for making a final determination that you meet an LOB test. Rather you must check the text of the LOB article itself to determine which tests are available under that treaty and the particular requirements of those tests. See Table 4, Limitation on Benefits, at *IRS.gov/Individuals/International-Taxpayers/ Tax-Treaty-Tables*, for a summary of the major tests within the Limitation on Benefits article that are relevant for documenting any entity's claim for treaty benefits.

- Government—this test is met if the entity is the Contracting State, political subdivision, or local authority.
- Tax-exempt pension trust or pension fund—this test generally requires that more than half the beneficiaries or participants in the trust or fund be residents of the country of residence of the trust or fund itself.
- Other tax-exempt organization—this test generally requires that more than half the beneficiaries, members, or participants of religious, charitable, scientific, artistic, cultural, or educational organizations be residents of the country of residence of the organization.
- Publicly-traded corporation—this test generally requires the corporation's principal class of shares to be primarily and regularly traded on a recognized stock exchange in its country of residence, while other treaties may permit trading in either the United States or the treaty country, or in certain third countries if the primary place of management is the country of residence.
- Subsidiary of publicly-traded corporation—this test generally requires that more than 50% of the vote and value of the company's shares be owned, directly or indirectly, by five or fewer companies that are publicly-traded corporations and that themselves meet the publicly-traded corporation test, as long as all companies in the chain of ownership are resident in either the United States or the same country of residence as the subsidiary.
- Company that meets the ownership and base erosion test—this test generally requires that more than 50% of the vote and value of the company's shares be owned, directly or indirectly, by individuals, governments, tax-exempt entities, and publicly-traded corporations resident in the same country as the company, as long as all companies in the chain of ownership are resident in the same country of residence, and less than 50% of the company's gross income is accrued or paid, directly or indirectly, to persons who would not be good shareholders for purposes of the ownership test.
- Company that meets the derivative benefits test—this test is generally limited to NAFTA, EU, and EEA country treaties, and may apply to all benefits or only to certain items of income (interest, dividends, and royalties). It generally requires that more than 95% of the aggregate vote and value of the company's shares be owned, directly or indirectly, by seven or fewer equivalent beneficiaries (ultimate owners who are resident in an EU, EEA, or NAFTA country and are entitled to identical benefits under their own treaty with the United States under one of the ownership tests included within the LOB article (other than the stock ownership and base erosion test)). In addition, this test requires that less than 50% of the company's gross income be paid or accrued, directly or indirectly, to persons who would not be equivalent beneficiaries.
- Company with an item of income that meets the active trade or business test—this test generally requires that the company be engaged in an active trade or business in its country of residence, that its activities in that country be substantial in relation to its U.S. activities, if the payer is a related party, and the income be derived in connection to or incidental to that trade or business.
- Favorable discretionary determination received—this test requires that the company obtain a favorable determination granting benefits from the U.S. competent authority that, despite the company's failure to meet a specific objective LOB test in the applicable treaty, it may nonetheless claim the requested benefits. Unless a treaty or technical explanation specifically provides otherwise, you may not claim discretionary benefits while your claim for discretionary benefits is pending.
- Other—for other LOB tests that are not listed above (for example, a headquarters test). Identify the other test relied upon, or enter N/A if the treaty has no LOB article. For example, if you meet the headquarters test under the United States-Netherlands income tax treaty, you should write "Headquarters test, Article 26(5)" in the space provided.

If an entity is claiming treaty benefits on its own behalf, it should complete Form W-8BEN-E. If an interest holder in an entity that is considered fiscally transparent in the interest holder's jurisdiction is claiming a treaty benefit, the interest holder should complete Form W-8BEN (if an individual) or Form W-8BEN-E (if an entity) on its own behalf as the appropriate treaty resident, and the fiscally transparent entity should associate the interest holder's Form W-8BEN or Form W-8BEN-E with a Form W-8IMY completed by the fiscally transparent entity (see *Hybrid entities* under *Special Instructions*, later).

CAUTION: *An income tax treaty may not apply to reduce the amount of any tax on an item of income received by an entity that is treated as a domestic corporation for U.S. tax purposes. Therefore, neither the domestic corporation nor its shareholders are entitled to the benefits of a reduction of U.S. income tax on an item of income received from U.S. sources by the corporation.*

TIP: *If you are an entity that derives the income as a resident of a treaty country, you may check this box if the applicable income tax treaty does not contain a "limitation on benefits" provision.*

Line 14c. If you are a foreign corporation claiming treaty benefits under an income tax treaty that entered into force before January 1, 1987 (and has not been renegotiated) on (1) U.S. source dividends paid to you by another foreign corporation or (2) U.S. source interest paid to you

The US Foreign Investment in Real Property Tax Act: A Practical Guide

by a U.S. trade or business of another foreign corporation, you must generally be a "qualified resident" of a treaty country. See section 884 for the definition of interest paid by a U.S. trade or business of a foreign corporation ("branch interest") and other applicable rules.

In general, a foreign corporation is a qualified resident of a country if any of the following apply:
- It meets a 50% ownership and base erosion test.
- It is primarily and regularly traded on an established securities market in its country of residence or the United States.
- It carries on an active trade or business in its country of residence.
- It gets a ruling from the IRS that it is a qualified resident.

See Regulations section 1.884-5 for the requirements that must be met to satisfy each of these tests.

⚠ **CAUTION** *If you are claiming treaty benefits under an income tax treaty entered into force after December 31, 1986, do not check box 14c. Instead, check box 14b.*

Line 15. Line 15 must be used only if you are claiming treaty benefits that require that you meet conditions not covered by the representations you make in line 14 (or other certifications on the form). This line is generally not applicable to claiming treaty benefits under an interest or dividends (other than dividends subject to a preferential rate based on ownership) article of a treaty or other income article, unless such article requires additional representations. For example, certain treaties allow for a zero rate on dividends for certain qualified residents provided that additional requirements are met, such as ownership percentage, ownership period, and that the resident meet a combination of tests under an applicable LOB article. You should indicate the specific treaty article and paragraph or subparagraph, as applicable. You should also use this space to set out the requirements you meet under the identified treaty article.

The following are examples of persons who should complete this line:
- Exempt organizations claiming treaty benefits under the exempt organization articles of the treaties with Canada, Mexico, Germany, and the Netherlands.
- Foreign corporations that are claiming a preferential rate applicable to dividends based on ownership of a specific percentage of stock in the entity paying the dividend and owning the stock for a specified period of time. Such persons should provide the percentage of ownership and the period of time they owned the stock. For example, under the United States-Italy treaty, to claim the 5% dividend rate, the Italian corporation must own 25% of the voting stock for a 12-month period.

In addition, for example, if you qualify for and are claiming a zero rate on dividend payments under Article 10(3) of the United States-Germany income tax treaty, you should fill out line 15 with "Article 10(3)," "0," and "dividends" in the spaces provided. In the space provided for an explanation, you may write that you are the beneficial owner of the dividends, you are a resident of Germany, you have directly owned shares representing 80% or more of the voting power of the company paying the dividends for the 12-month period ending on the date

the entitlement to the dividend is determined, and that you satisfy the conditions of Article 28(2)(f)(aa) and (bb) and Article 28(4) of the treaty with respect to the dividends.
- Persons claiming treaty benefits on royalties if the treaty contains different withholding rates for different types of royalties.
- Persons claiming treaty benefits on interest other than the generally applicable rate. For example, under the United States-Australia treaty, the generally applicable interest rate is 10% under Article 11(2). However, interest may be exempt from withholding if the specific conditions under Article 11(3) are met.

Parts IV Through XXVIII – Certification of Chapter 4 Status

You should complete only one part of Parts IV through XXVIII certifying to your chapter 4 status (if required). You are not required to complete a chapter 4 status certification if you are not the payee of withholdable payment or you do not hold an account with an FFI requesting this form. Identify which part (if any) you should complete by reference to the box you checked on line 5. An entity that selects nonparticipating FFI, participating FFI, registered deemed-compliant FFI (other than a sponsored FFI), reporting Model 1 FFI, reporting Model 2 FFI, or direct reporting NFFE (other than a sponsored direct reporting NFFE) on line 5 is not required to complete any of the certifications in Parts IV through XXVIII.

IGA. In lieu of the certifications contained in Parts IV through XXVIII of Form W-8BEN-E, in certain cases you may provide an alternate certification to a withholding agent. See *Entities Providing Certifications Under an Applicable IGA* under *Special Instructions*, later.

Part IV – Sponsored FFI

Line 16. If you are a sponsored FFI described in Regulations section 1.1471-5(f)(1)(i)(F), enter the name of the sponsoring entity that has agreed to fulfill the due diligence, reporting, and withholding obligations (as applicable) on behalf of the sponsored FFI identified in line 1. You must provide your GIIN on line 9.

Line 17. You must check the applicable box to certify that you are either a sponsored investment entity or sponsored controlled foreign corporation (within the meaning of section 957(a)) and that you satisfy the other relevant requirements for this status.

Part V – Certified Deemed-Compliant Nonregistering Local Bank

Line 18. If you are a certified deemed-compliant nonregistering local bank, you must check the box to certify that you meet all of the requirements for this certified deemed-compliant status.

Part VI – Certified Deemed-Compliant FFI With Only Low-Value Accounts

Line 19. If you are a certified deemed-compliant FFI with only low-value accounts, you must check the box to certify

Instructions for Form W-8BEN-E (Rev. 7-2017) -11-

8. FIRPTA Withholding

that you meet all of the requirements for this certified deemed-compliant classification.

Part VII – Certified Deemed-Compliant Sponsored, Closely Held Investment Vehicle

Line 20. Enter the name of your sponsoring entity that has agreed to fulfill the due diligence, reporting, and withholding obligations of the entity identified in line 1 as if the entity in line 1 were a participating FFI. You must also enter the GIIN of your sponsoring entity on line 9a.

Line 21. If you are a sponsored, closely held investment vehicle, you must check the box to certify that you meet all of the requirements for this certified deemed-compliant status.

Part VIII – Certified Deemed-Compliant Limited Life Debt Investment Company

Line 22. If you are a limited life debt investment entity, you must check the box to certify that you meet all of the requirements for this certified deemed-compliant status.

Part IX – Certain Investment Entities That Do Not Maintain Financial Accounts

Line 23. If you are an FFI that is a financial institution solely because you are described in Regulations section 1.1471-5(e)(4)(i)(A) and you do not maintain financial accounts, you must check the box to certify that you meet all of the requirements for this certified deemed-compliant status.

Part X – Owner-Documented FFI

Line 24a. If you are an owner-documented FFI, you must check the box to certify that you meet all of the requirements for this status and are providing this form to a U.S. financial institution, participating FFI, reporting Model 1 FFI, or reporting Model 2 FFI that agrees to act as a designated withholding agent with respect to you. See Regulations section 1.1471-5(f)(3) for more information about an owner-documented FFI, including with respect to a designated withholding agent.

Line 24b. Check the box to certify that you have provided or will provide the documentation set forth in the certifications, including the FFI owner reporting statement and the valid documentation for each person identified on the FFI owner reporting statement described on line 24b.

Line 24c. Check the box to certify that you have provided or will provide the auditor's letter (in lieu of the information required by line 24b) that satisfies the requirements reflected on this line.

TIP *Check either line 24b or line 24c. Do not check both boxes.*

Line 24d. Check the box if you do not have any contingent beneficiaries or designated classes with unidentified beneficiaries. While this certification is not required, an owner reporting statement provided by an owner-documented FFI will remain valid indefinitely for chapter 4 purposes absent a change in circumstances with respect to offshore obligations (as defined in Regulations section 1.6049-5(c)(1)) only if this certification is provided and the account balance of all accounts held by the owner-documented FFI with the withholding agent does not exceed $1,000,000 on the later of June 30, 2014, or the last day of the calendar year in which the account was opened, and the last day of each subsequent calendar year preceding the payment, applying the account aggregation rules of Regulations section 1.1471-5(b)(4)(iii).

Part XI – Restricted Distributor

Line 25a. If you are a restricted distributor you must check the box to certify that you meet all of the requirements for this status.

Lines 25b and 25c. Check the appropriate box to certify your status. Do not check both boxes.

CAUTION *A restricted distributor may certify only with respect to an account it maintains in connection with a distribution agreement with a restricted fund. A restricted distributor that, in connection with such a distribution agreement, receives a payment subject to chapter 3 withholding or a withholdable payment should complete Form W-8IMY and not this form except to the extent it holds interests in connection with such an agreement as a beneficial owner.*

Part XII – Nonreporting IGA FFI

Line 26. Check the box to indicate that you are treated as a nonreporting IGA FFI. You must identify the IGA by entering the name of the jurisdiction that has the IGA treated as in effect with the United States, and indicate whether it is a Model 1 or Model 2 IGA. You must also provide the withholding agent with the specific category of FFI described in Annex II of the IGA. In providing the specific category of FFI described in Annex II, you should use the language from Annex II that best and most specifically describes your status. For example, indicate "investment entity wholly owned by exempt beneficial owners" rather than "exempt beneficial owner." If you are a nonreporting IGA FFI claiming a deemed-compliant status under the regulations, you must instead indicate on this line which section of the regulations you qualify under.

If you are a nonreporting financial institution under an applicable IGA because you qualify as an owner-documented FFI under the regulations, do not check "Nonreporting IGA FFI." Instead, you must check "Owner-documented FFI" and complete Part X rather than this Part XII.

See instructions for line 9a for when a GIIN is required for a nonreporting IGA FFI (including a trustee of a trustee-documented trust that is a foreign person).

Instructions for Form W-8BEN-E (Rev. 7-2017)

Part XIII – Foreign Government, Government of a U.S. Possession, or Foreign Central Bank of Issue

Line 27. If you are a foreign government or political subdivision of a foreign government (including wholly owned agencies and instrumentalities thereof), government of a U.S. possession, or foreign central bank of issue (each as defined in Regulations section 1.1471-6) you must check the box and certify that you meet all of the requirements for this status (including that you do not engage in the type of commercial financial activities described on this line except to the extent permitted under Regulations section 1.1471-6(h)(2)).

TIP *If you are a foreign government or political subdivision of a foreign government (including wholly owned agencies and instrumentalities thereof), government of a U.S. possession, or foreign central bank of issue, you should only complete Form W-8BEN-E for payments for which you are not claiming the applicability of section(s) 115(2), 892, or 895; otherwise you should use Form W-8EXP.*

Part XIV – International Organization

Line 28a. Check this box to certify that you are an international organization described in section 7701(a)(18).

TIP *If you are an entity that has been designated as an international organization by executive order (pursuant to 22 U.S.C. 288 through 288f), check box 28a. If you are claiming an exemption from withholding for purposes of chapter 3, however, use Form W-8EXP.*

Line 28b. If you are an international organization other than an international organization described in line 28a, you must check the box to certify that you satisfy all of the requirements for this status.

Part XV – Exempt Retirement Plans

Lines 29a, b, c, d, e, and f. If you are an exempt retirement plan you must check the appropriate box to certify that you meet all of the requirements for this status.

Part XVI – Entity Wholly Owned by Exempt Beneficial Owners

Line 30. If you are an entity wholly owned by exempt beneficial owners you must check the box to certify that you meet all of the requirements for this status. You must also provide the owner documentation described in this line establishing that each of your direct owners or debt holders is an exempt beneficial owner described in Regulations section 1.1471-6(b).

Part XVII – Territory Financial Institution

Line 31. If you are a territory financial institution you must check the box to certify that you meet all of the requirements for this status.

Part XVIII – Excepted Nonfinancial Group Entity

Line 32. If you are an excepted nonfinancial group entity you must check the box to certify that you meet all of the requirements for this status.

Part XIX – Excepted Nonfinancial Start-Up Company

Line 33. If you are an excepted nonfinancial start-up company you must check the box to certify that you meet all of the requirements for this status. You must also provide the date you were formed or your board passed a resolution (or equivalent measure) approving a new line of business (which cannot be that of a financial institution or passive NFFE).

Part XX – Excepted Nonfinancial Entity in Liquidation or Bankruptcy

Line 34. If you are an excepted nonfinancial group entity in liquidation or bankruptcy you must check the box to certify that you meet all of the requirements for this status. You must also provide the date that you filed a plan of liquidation, plan of reorganization, or bankruptcy petition.

Part XXI – 501(c) Organization

Line 35. If you are an entity claiming chapter 4 status as a section 501(c) organization pursuant to Regulations section 1.1471-5(e)(5)(v) you must check the box and provide the date that the IRS issued you a determination letter or provide a copy of an opinion from U.S. counsel certifying that you qualify as a section 501(c) organization (without regard to whether you are a foreign private foundation).

TIP *If you are a section 501(c) organization claiming an exemption from withholding for purposes of chapter 3, however, use Form W-8EXP.*

Part XXII – Nonprofit Organization

Line 36. If you are a nonprofit organization (other than an entity claiming chapter 4 status as a section 501(c) organization pursuant to Regulations section 1.1471-5(e)(5)(v)) you must check the box to certify that you meet all of the requirements for this status.

Nonprofit organization under an IGA. If you are an entity that is established and maintained in a jurisdiction that is treated as having in effect an IGA and you are described in Annex I as a nonprofit organization that is an Active NFFE, see *Entities Providing Certifications Under an Applicable IGA* under *Special Instructions*, later.

Part XXIII – Publicly-Traded NFFE or NFFE Affiliate of a Publicly-Traded Corporation

Line 37a. If you are a publicly-traded NFFE you must check the box to certify that you are not a financial institution and provide the name of a securities exchange on which your stock is publicly traded.

Instructions for Form W-8BEN-E (Rev. 7-2017)

8. FIRPTA Withholding

Line 37b. If you are an NFFE that is a member of the same expanded affiliated group as a publicly-traded U.S. or foreign entity you must check this box, provide the name of the publicly-traded entity, and identify the securities market on which the stock of the publicly-traded entity is traded. See Regulations section 1.1472-1(c)(1)(i) to determine if the stock of an entity is regularly traded on an established securities market (substituting the term "U.S. entity" for "NFFE," as appropriate, for purposes of testing whether an entity is publicly traded).

Part XXIV – Excepted Territory NFFE

Line 38. If you are an excepted territory NFFE you must check the box to certify that you meet all of the requirements for this classification. See Regulations section 1.1472-1(c)(1)(iii) for the definition of an excepted territory NFFE.

Part XXV – Active NFFE

Line 39. If you are an active NFFE you must check the box to certify that you meet all of the requirements for this status, including the assets and passive income test described in the certification for this part. For purposes of applying this test, passive income includes dividends, interest, rents, royalties, annuities, and certain other forms of passive income. See Regulations section 1.1472-1(c)(1)(iv)(A) for additional detail for the definition of passive income. Also see Regulations section 1.1472-1(c)(1)(iv)(B) for exceptions from the definition of passive income for certain types of income.

Part XXVI – Passive NFFE

Line 40a. If you are a passive NFFE you must check the box to certify that you are not a financial institution and are not certifying your status as a publicly-traded NFFE, NFFE affiliate of a publicly-traded company, excepted territory NFFE, active NFFE, direct reporting NFFE, or sponsored direct reporting NFFE.

Note. If you would be a passive NFFE but for the fact that you are managed by certain types of FFIs (see Regulations section 1.1471-5(e)(4)(i)(B)), you should not complete line 40a as you would be considered a financial institution and not a passive NFFE.

TIP *If you are an NFFE that may qualify as an active NFFE (or other NFFE described in another part of this form), you may still check line 40a and disclose your substantial U.S. owners or certify that you have no substantial U.S. owners.*

Line 40b. Check this box to certify that you have no substantial U.S. owners.

Line 40c. If you do not check the box and make the certification on line 40b, you must check this box 40c and complete Part XXIX to identify and provide the name, address, and TIN of each of your substantial U.S. owners.

Note. If you are an NFFE that is providing Form W-8BEN-E to an FFI treated as a reporting Model 1 FFI or reporting Model 2 FFI, you may also use Part XXIX to report controlling U.S. persons (as defined in an applicable IGA). The references to "controlling U.S. persons" in this part and Part XXIX apply only if the form is being provided to an FFI treated as a reporting Model 1 FFI or reporting Model 2 FFI.

Part XXVII – Excepted Inter-Affiliate FFI

Line 41. If you are an excepted inter-affiliate FFI you must check the box to certify that you meet all of the requirements for this classification. This classification will only apply for an excepted inter-affiliate FFI that holds deposit accounts described in the certification for this part and that is documenting itself to the financial institution that maintains the deposit account. You are not eligible for this classification if you receive or make withholdable payments to or from any person other than a member of your expanded affiliated group, other than the depository institution described in the previous sentence. See Regulations section 1.1471-5(e)(5)(iv) for all the requirements of this status.

Part XXVIII – Sponsored Direct Reporting NFFEs

Lines 42 and 43. If you are a sponsored direct reporting NFFE you must enter the name of the sponsoring entity on line 42 and check the box to certify that you meet all of the requirements for this classification. You must also provide your GIIN in line 9a.

Part XXIX – Substantial U.S. Owners of Passive NFFE

If you identified yourself as a passive NFFE (including an investment entity that is a territory NFFE but is not an excepted territory NFFE under Regulations section 1.1472-1(c)) with one or more substantial U.S. owners in Part XXVI, you must identify each substantial U.S. owner. Provide the name, address, and TIN of each substantial U.S. owner in the relevant column. You may attach this information on a separate statement, which remains subject to the same perjury statement and other certifications made in Part XXX. If you are reporting controlling U.S. persons (as defined in an applicable IGA) to a Model 1 FFI or reporting Model 2 FFI with which you maintain an account that requests such ownership information with this form, you may use this space or attach a separate statement to report such persons.

Part XXX – Certification

Form W-8BEN-E must be signed and dated by an authorized representative or officer of the beneficial owner, participating payee (for purposes of section 6050W), or account holder of an FFI requesting this form. You must check the box to certify that you have the legal capacity to sign for the entity identified on line 1 that is the beneficial owner of the income. If Form W-8BEN-E is completed by an agent acting under a duly authorized power of attorney, the form must be accompanied by the power of attorney in proper form or a copy thereof specifically authorizing the agent to represent the principal in making, executing, and presenting the form. Form 2848, Power of Attorney and Declaration of

Representative, may be used for this purpose. The agent, as well as the beneficial owner, payee, or account holder (as applicable), may incur liability for the penalties provided for an erroneous, false, or fraudulent form. By signing Form W-8BEN-E, the authorized representative, officer, or agent of the entity also agrees to provide a new form within 30 days following a change in circumstances affecting the correctness of the form.

A withholding agent may allow you to provide this form with an electronic signature. The electronic signature must indicate that the form was electronically signed by a person authorized to do so (for example, with a time and date stamp and statement that the form has been electronically signed). Simply typing your name into the signature line is not an electronic signature.

Broker transactions or barter exchanges. Income from transactions with a broker or a barter exchange is subject to reporting rules and backup withholding unless Form W-8BEN-E or a substitute form is filed to notify the broker or barter exchange that you are an exempt foreign person.

You are an exempt foreign person for a calendar year in which:

- You are a foreign corporation, partnership, estate, or trust; and
- You are neither engaged, nor plan to be engaged during the year, in a U.S. trade or business that has effectively connected gains from transactions with a broker or barter exchange.

Special Instructions

Hybrid Entity Making a Claim of Treaty Benefits

If you are a hybrid entity making a claim for treaty benefits as a resident on your own behalf, you may do so as permitted under an applicable tax treaty. You should complete this Form W-8BEN-E to claim treaty benefits in the manner described in the instructions for Part III and complete Part I to the extent indicated below. Note that you should not complete line 5 indicating your chapter 4 status unless you are a disregarded entity that is treated as the payee for chapter 4 purposes.

If you are a flow-through entity claiming treaty benefits on a payment that is a withholdable payment, you should also provide Form W-8IMY along with a withholding statement (if required) establishing the chapter 4 status of each of your partners or owners. Allocation information is not required on this withholding statement unless one or more partners or owners are subject to chapter 4 withholding (such as a nonparticipating FFI). If you are a disregarded entity claiming treaty benefits on a payment that is a withholdable payment, unless you are treated as the payee for chapter 4 purposes and have your own GIIN, your single owner should provide Form W-8BEN-E or Form W-8BEN (as applicable) to the withholding agent along with this form. You or the withholding agent may use line 10 to inform the withholding agent to associate the two forms.

Line 1. Enter your legal name (determined by reference to your legal identity in your country of incorporation or organization).

Line 2. Enter the country under whose laws you are created, organized, or governed.

Line 3. Leave this line blank. For purposes of completing this form as a hybrid entity making a treaty claim (including a disregarded entity), you are treated as the beneficial owner and should be identified in line 1.

Line 4. Check the box that applies among disregarded entity, partnership, grantor trust, or simple trust. You must also check the box indicating that you are a hybrid making a treaty claim and complete Part III.

Line 5. Leave this line blank, except in the circumstances described above.

Lines 6, 7, and 8. Complete lines 6, 7, and 8 as provided in the specific instructions, earlier.

Line 9b. If your country of residence for tax purposes has issued you a tax identifying number, enter it here. Do not enter the tax identifying number of your owner(s).

Line 10. This reference line is used to associate this Form W-8BEN-E with another applicable withholding certificate or other documentation provided for purposes of chapter 4. For example, if you are a partnership making a treaty claim, you may want to provide information for the withholding agent to associate this Form W-8BEN-E with the Form W-8IMY and owner documentation you provide for purposes of establishing the chapter 4 status of your owner(s).

You must complete Parts III and XXX in accordance with the specific instructions above. Complete Part II if applicable.

Foreign Reverse Hybrid Entities

A foreign reverse hybrid entity should only file a Form W-8BEN-E for payments for which it is not claiming treaty benefits on behalf of its owners and must provide a chapter 4 status when it is receiving a withholdable payment. A foreign reverse hybrid entity claiming treaty benefits on behalf of its owners should provide the withholding agent with Form W-8IMY (including its chapter 4 status when receiving a withholdable payment) along with a withholding statement and Forms W-8BEN or W-8BEN-E (or documentary evidence to the extent permitted) on behalf of each of its owners claiming treaty benefits. See Form W-8IMY and accompanying instructions for more information.

Entities Providing Certifications Under an Applicable IGA

An FFI in an IGA jurisdiction with which you have an account may provide you with a chapter 4 status certification other than as shown in Parts IV through XXVIII in order to satisfy its due diligence requirements under the applicable IGA. In such a case, you may attach the alternative certification to this Form W-8BEN-E in lieu of completing a certification otherwise required in Parts IV through XXVIII provided that you: (1) determine that the certification accurately reflects your status for chapter 4 purposes or under an applicable IGA; and (2) the withholding agent provides a written statement to you that it has provided the certification to meet its due diligence requirements as a participating FFI or registered

Instructions for Form W-8BEN-E (Rev. 7-2017)   -15-

8. FIRPTA Withholding

deemed-compliant FFI under an applicable IGA. For example, Entity A organized in Country A holds an account with an FFI in Country B. Country B has a Model 1 IGA in effect. The FFI in Country B may ask Entity A to provide a chapter 4 status certification based on the terms of the Country B IGA in order to fulfil its due diligence and documentation requirements under the Country B IGA.

You may also provide with this form an applicable IGA certification if you are determining your chapter 4 status under the definitions provided in an applicable IGA and your certification identifies the jurisdiction that is treated as having an IGA in effect and describes your status as an NFFE or FFI in accordance with the applicable IGA. However, if you determine your status under an applicable IGA as an NFFE, you must still determine if you are an excepted NFFE under the Regulations in order to complete this form unless you are provided an alternative certification by an FFI described in the preceding paragraph that covers your certification as an NFFE (such as "active NFFE") as defined in an applicable IGA. Additionally, you are required to comply with the conditions of your status under the law of the IGA jurisdiction to which you are subject if you are determining your status under that IGA. If you cannot provide the certifications in Parts IV through XXVIII, or if you are a nonprofit entity that meets the definition of "active NFFE" under the applicable IGA, do not check a box in line 5. However, if you determine your status under the definitions of the IGA and can certify to a chapter 4 status included on this form, you do not need to provide the certifications described in this paragraph unless required by the FFI to whom you are providing this form.

Any certifications provided under an applicable IGA remain subject to the penalty of perjury statement and other certifications made in Part XXX.

Entities Providing Alternate or Additional Certifications Under Regulations

If you qualify for a status that is not shown on this form, you may attach applicable certifications for such status from any other Form W-8 on which the relevant certifications appear. If the applicable certifications do not appear on any Form W-8 (if, for example, new regulations provide for an additional status and this form has not been updated to incorporate the status) then you may provide an attachment certifying that you qualify for the applicable status described in a particular Regulations section. Include a citation to the applicable provision in the Regulations. Any such attached certification becomes an integral part of this Form W-8BEN-E and is subject to the penalty of perjury statement and other certifications made in Part XXX.

Paperwork Reduction Act Notice. We ask for the information on this form to carry out the Internal Revenue laws of the United States. You are required to provide the information. We need it to ensure that you are complying with these laws and to allow us to figure and collect the right amount of tax.

You are not required to provide the information requested on a form that is subject to the Paperwork Reduction Act unless the form displays a valid OMB control number. Books or records relating to a form or its instructions must be retained as long as their contents may become material in the administration of any Internal Revenue law. Generally, tax returns and return information are confidential, as required by section 6103.

The time needed to complete and file this form will vary depending on individual circumstances. The estimated average time is:**Recordkeeping**, 12 hr., 40 min.; **Learning about the law or the form**, 4 hr., 17 min.; **Preparing and sending the form**, 8 hr., 16 min.

If you have comments concerning the accuracy of these time estimates or suggestions for making this form simpler, we would be happy to hear from you. You can send us comments from *IRS.gov/FormComments*. You can write to the Internal Revenue Service, Tax Forms and Publications, 1111 Constitution Ave. NW, IR-6526, Washington, DC 20224. Do not send Form W-8IMY to this office. Instead, give it to your withholding agent.

APPENDIX 8-F

Form W-8BEN-E
(Rev. July 2017)
Department of the Treasury
Internal Revenue Service

Certificate of Status of Beneficial Owner for United States Tax Withholding and Reporting (Entities)

▶ For use by entities. Individuals must use Form W-8BEN. ▶ Section references are to the Internal Revenue Code.
▶ Go to *www.irs.gov/FormW8BENE* for instructions and the latest information.
▶ Give this form to the withholding agent or payer. Do not send to the IRS.

OMB No. 1545-1621

Do NOT use this form for: | **Instead use Form:**
- U.S. entity or U.S. citizen or resident W-9
- A foreign individual . . . . W-8BEN (Individual) or Form 8233
- A foreign individual or entity claiming that income is effectively connected with the conduct of trade or business within the U.S.
(unless claiming treaty benefits) W-8ECI
- A foreign partnership, a foreign simple trust, or a foreign grantor trust (unless claiming treaty benefits) (see instructions for exceptions) . . W-8IMY
- A foreign government, international organization, foreign central bank of issue, foreign tax-exempt organization, foreign private foundation, or government of a U.S. possession claiming that income is effectively connected U.S. income or that is claiming the applicability of section(s) 115(2), 501(c), 892, 895, or 1443(b) (unless claiming treaty benefits) (see instructions for other exceptions) . . . . W-8ECI or W-8EXP
- Any person acting as an intermediary (including a qualified intermediary acting as a qualified derivatives dealer) W-8IMY

Part I Identification of Beneficial Owner

1 Name of organization that is the beneficial owner | **2** Country of incorporation or organization

3 Name of disregarded entity receiving the payment (if applicable, see instructions)

4 Chapter 3 Status (entity type) (Must check one box only):
☐ Corporation ☐ Disregarded entity ☐ Partnership
☐ Simple trust ☐ Grantor trust ☐ Complex trust ☐ Estate ☐ Government
☐ Central Bank of Issue ☐ Tax-exempt organization ☐ Private foundation ☐ International organization

If you entered disregarded entity, partnership, simple trust, or grantor trust above, is the entity a hybrid making a treaty claim? If "Yes" complete Part III. ☐ Yes ☐ No

5 Chapter 4 Status (FATCA status) (See instructions for details and complete the certification below for the entity's applicable status.)
☐ Nonparticipating FFI (including an FFI related to a Reporting IGA FFI other than a deemed-compliant FFI, participating FFI, or exempt beneficial owner).
☐ Participating FFI.
☐ Reporting Model 1 FFI.
☐ Reporting Model 2 FFI.
☐ Registered deemed-compliant FFI (other than a reporting Model 1 FFI, sponsored FFI, or nonreporting IGA FFI covered in Part XII). See instructions.
☐ Sponsored FFI. Complete Part IV.
☐ Certified deemed-compliant nonregistering local bank. Complete Part V.
☐ Certified deemed-compliant FFI with only low-value accounts. Complete Part VI.
☐ Certified deemed-compliant sponsored, closely held investment vehicle. Complete Part VII.
☐ Certified deemed-compliant limited life debt investment entity. Complete Part VIII.
☐ Certain investment entities that do not maintain financial accounts. Complete Part IX.
☐ Owner-documented FFI. Complete Part X.
☐ Restricted distributor. Complete Part XI.

☐ Nonreporting IGA FFI. Complete Part XII.
☐ Foreign government, government of a U.S. possession, or foreign central bank of issue. Complete Part XIII.
☐ International organization. Complete Part XIV.
☐ Exempt retirement plans. Complete Part XV.
☐ Entity wholly owned by exempt beneficial owners. Complete Part XVI.
☐ Territory financial institution. Complete Part XVII.
☐ Excepted nonfinancial group entity. Complete Part XVIII.
☐ Excepted nonfinancial start-up company. Complete Part XIX.
☐ Excepted nonfinancial entity in liquidation or bankruptcy. Complete Part XX.
☐ 501(c) organization. Complete Part XXI.
☐ Nonprofit organization. Complete Part XXII.
☐ Publicly traded NFFE or NFFE affiliate of a publicly traded corporation. Complete Part XXIII.
☐ Excepted territory NFFE. Complete Part XXIV.
☐ Active NFFE. Complete Part XXV.
☐ Passive NFFE. Complete Part XXVI.
☐ Excepted inter-affiliate FFI. Complete Part XXVII.
☐ Direct reporting NFFE.
☐ Sponsored direct reporting NFFE. Complete Part XXVIII.
☐ Account that is not a financial account.

6 Permanent residence address (street, apt. or suite no., or rural route). **Do not use a P.O. box or in-care-of address** (other than a registered address).

City or town, state or province. Include postal code where appropriate. | Country

7 Mailing address (if different from above)

City or town, state or province. Include postal code where appropriate. | Country

8 U.S. taxpayer identification number (TIN), if required | **9a** GIIN | **b** Foreign TIN

10 Reference number(s) (see instructions)

Note: Please complete remainder of the form including signing the form in Part XXX.

For Paperwork Reduction Act Notice, see separate instructions. Cat. No. 59689N Form **W-8BEN-E** (Rev. 7-2017)

# 8. FIRPTA Withholding

Form W-8BEN-E (Rev. 7-2017) Page **2**

| **Part II** | **Disregarded Entity or Branch Receiving Payment.** (Complete only if a disregarded entity with a GIIN or a branch of an FFI in a country other than the FFI's country of residence. See instructions.) |

11 Chapter 4 Status (FATCA status) of disregarded entity or branch receiving payment
    ☐ Branch treated as nonparticipating FFI.   ☐ Reporting Model 1 FFI.   ☐ U.S. Branch.
    ☐ Participating FFI.   ☐ Reporting Model 2 FFI.

12 Address of disregarded entity or branch (street, apt. or suite no., or rural route). **Do not use a P.O. box or in-care-of address** (other than a registered address).

_____
City or town, state or province. Include postal code where appropriate.

_____
Country

13 GIIN (if any) _____

| **Part III** | **Claim of Tax Treaty Benefits** (if applicable). (For chapter 3 purposes only.) |

14 I certify that (check all that apply):
 a   ☐ The beneficial owner is a resident of _____ within the meaning of the income tax treaty between the United States and that country.
 b   ☐ The beneficial owner derives the item (or items) of income for which the treaty benefits are claimed, and, if applicable, meets the requirements of the treaty provision dealing with limitation on benefits. The following are types of limitation on benefits provisions that may be included in an applicable tax treaty (check only one; see instructions):
     ☐ Government   ☐ Company that meets the ownership and base erosion test
     ☐ Tax exempt pension trust or pension fund   ☐ Company that meets the derivative benefits test
     ☐ Other tax exempt organization   ☐ Company with an item of income that meets active trade or business test
     ☐ Publicly traded corporation   ☐ Favorable discretionary determination by the U.S. competent authority received
     ☐ Subsidiary of a publicly traded corporation   ☐ Other (specify Article and paragraph): _____
 c   ☐ The beneficial owner is claiming treaty benefits for U.S. source dividends received from a foreign corporation or interest from a U.S. trade or business of a foreign corporation and meets qualified resident status (see instructions).

15 **Special rates and conditions** (if applicable—see instructions):
    The beneficial owner is claiming the provisions of Article and paragraph _____ of the treaty identified on line 14a above to claim a _____ % rate of withholding on (specify type of income): _____.
    Explain the additional conditions in the Article the beneficial owner meets to be eligible for the rate of withholding: _____
    _____
    _____

| **Part IV** | **Sponsored FFI** |

16 Name of sponsoring entity: _____
17 **Check whichever box applies.**
    ☐ I certify that the entity identified in Part I:
    • Is an investment entity;
    • Is not a QI, WP (except to the extent permitted in the withholding foreign partnership agreement), or WT; **and**
    • Has agreed with the entity identified above (that is not a nonparticipating FFI) to act as the sponsoring entity for this entity.
    ☐ I certify that the entity identified in Part I:
    • Is a controlled foreign corporation as defined in section 957(a);
    • Is not a QI, WP, or WT;
    • Is wholly owned, directly or indirectly, by the U.S. financial institution identified above that agrees to act as the sponsoring entity for this entity; **and**
    • Shares a common electronic account system with the sponsoring entity (identified above) that enables the sponsoring entity to identify all account holders and payees of the entity and to access all account and customer information maintained by the entity including, but not limited to, customer identification information, customer documentation, account balance, and all payments made to account holders or payees.

Form **W-8BEN-E** (Rev. 7-2017)

Form W-8BEN-E (Rev. 7-2017) Page **3**

Part V — Certified Deemed-Compliant Nonregistering Local Bank

18 ☐ I certify that the FFI identified in Part I:

- Operates and is licensed solely as a bank or credit union (or similar cooperative credit organization operated without profit) in its country of incorporation or organization;
- Engages primarily in the business of receiving deposits from and making loans to, with respect to a bank, retail customers unrelated to such bank and, with respect to a credit union or similar cooperative credit organization, members, provided that no member has a greater than 5% interest in such credit union or cooperative credit organization;
- Does not solicit account holders outside its country of organization;
- Has no fixed place of business outside such country (for this purpose, a fixed place of business does not include a location that is not advertised to the public and from which the FFI performs solely administrative support functions);
- Has no more than $175 million in assets on its balance sheet and, if it is a member of an expanded affiliated group, the group has no more than $500 million in total assets on its consolidated or combined balance sheets; **and**
- Does not have any member of its expanded affiliated group that is a foreign financial institution, other than a foreign financial institution that is incorporated or organized in the same country as the FFI identified in Part I and that meets the requirements set forth in this part.

Part VI — Certified Deemed-Compliant FFI with Only Low-Value Accounts

19 ☐ I certify that the FFI identified in Part I:

- Is not engaged primarily in the business of investing, reinvesting, or trading in securities, partnership interests, commodities, notional principal contracts, insurance or annuity contracts, or any interest (including a futures or forward contract or option) in such security, partnership interest, commodity, notional principal contract, insurance contract or annuity contract;
- No financial account maintained by the FFI or any member of its expanded affiliated group, if any, has a balance or value in excess of $50,000 (as determined after applying applicable account aggregation rules); **and**
- Neither the FFI nor the entire expanded affiliated group, if any, of the FFI, have more than $50 million in assets on its consolidated or combined balance sheet as of the end of its most recent accounting year.

Part VII — Certified Deemed-Compliant Sponsored, Closely Held Investment Vehicle

20 Name of sponsoring entity: _____

21 ☐ I certify that the entity identified in Part I:

- Is an FFI solely because it is an investment entity described in Regulations section 1.1471-5(e)(4);
- Is not a QI, WP, or WT;
- Will have all of its due diligence, withholding, and reporting responsibilities (determined as if the FFI were a participating FFI) fulfilled by the sponsoring entity identified on line 20; **and**
- 20 or fewer individuals own all of the debt and equity interests in the entity (disregarding debt interests owned by U.S. financial institutions, participating FFIs, registered deemed-compliant FFIs, and certified deemed-compliant FFIs and equity interests owned by an entity if that entity owns 100% of the equity interests in the FFI and is itself a sponsored FFI).

Part VIII — Certified Deemed-Compliant Limited Life Debt Investment Entity

22 ☐ I certify that the entity identified in Part I:

- Was in existence as of January 17, 2013;
- Issued all classes of its debt or equity interests to investors on or before January 17, 2013, pursuant to a trust indenture or similar agreement; **and**
- Is certified deemed-compliant because it satisfies the requirements to be treated as a limited life debt investment entity (such as the restrictions with respect to its assets and other requirements under Regulations section 1.1471-5(f)(2)(iv)).

Part IX — Certain Investment Entities that Do Not Maintain Financial Accounts

23 ☐ I certify that the entity identified in Part I:

- Is a financial institution solely because it is an investment entity described in Regulations section 1.1471-5(e)(4)(i)(A), **and**
- Does not maintain financial accounts.

Part X — Owner-Documented FFI

Note: This status only applies if the U.S. financial institution, participating FFI, or reporting Model 1 FFI to which this form is given has agreed that it will treat the FFI as an owner-documented FFI (see instructions for eligibility requirements). In addition, the FFI must make the certifications below.

24a ☐ (All owner-documented FFIs check here) I certify that the FFI identified in Part I:

- Does not act as an intermediary;
- Does not accept deposits in the ordinary course of a banking or similar business;
- Does not hold, as a substantial portion of its business, financial assets for the account of others;
- Is not an insurance company (or the holding company of an insurance company) that issues or is obligated to make payments with respect to a financial account;
- Is not owned by or in an expanded affiliated group with an entity that accepts deposits in the ordinary course of a banking or similar business, holds, as a substantial portion of its business, financial assets for the account of others, or is an insurance company (or the holding company of an insurance company) that issues or is obligated to make payments with respect to a financial account;
- Does not maintain a financial account for any nonparticipating FFI; **and**
- Does not have any specified U.S. persons that own an equity interest or debt interest (other than a debt interest that is not a financial account or that has a balance or value not exceeding $50,000) in the FFI other than those identified on the FFI owner reporting statement.

Form **W-8BEN-E** (Rev. 7-2017)

8. FIRPTA Withholding

Form W-8BEN-E (Rev. 7-2017) Page **4**

Part X Owner-Documented FFI *(continued)*

Check box 24b or 24c, whichever applies.

- **b** ☐ I certify that the FFI identified in Part I:
  - Has provided, or will provide, an FFI owner reporting statement that contains:
    - (i) The name, address, TIN (if any), chapter 4 status, and type of documentation provided (if required) of every individual and specified U.S. person that owns a direct or indirect equity interest in the owner-documented FFI (looking through all entities other than specified U.S. persons);
    - (ii) The name, address, TIN (if any), and chapter 4 status of every individual and specified U.S. person that owns a debt interest in the owner-documented FFI (including any indirect debt interest, which includes debt interests in any entity that directly or indirectly owns the payee or any direct or indirect equity interest in a debt holder of the payee) that constitutes a financial account in excess of $50,000 (disregarding all such debt interests owned by participating FFIs, registered deemed-compliant FFIs, certified deemed-compliant FFIs, excepted NFFEs, exempt beneficial owners, or U.S. persons other than specified U.S. persons); **and**
    - (iii) Any additional information the withholding agent requests in order to fulfill its obligations with respect to the entity.
  - Has provided, or will provide, valid documentation meeting the requirements of Regulations section 1.1471-3(d)(6)(iii) for each person identified in the FFI owner reporting statement.

- **c** ☐ I certify that the FFI identified in Part I has provided, or will provide, an auditor's letter, signed within 4 years of the date of payment, from an independent accounting firm or legal representative with a location in the United States stating that the firm or representative has reviewed the FFI's documentation with respect to all of its owners and debt holders identified in Regulations section 1.1471-3(d)(6)(iv)(A)(2), and that the FFI meets all the requirements to be an owner-documented FFI. The FFI identified in Part I has also provided, or will provide, an FFI owner reporting statement of its owners that are specified U.S. persons and Form(s) W-9, with applicable waivers.

Check box 24d if applicable (optional, see instructions).

- **d** ☐ I certify that the entity identified on line 1 is a trust that does not have any contingent beneficiaries or designated classes with unidentified beneficiaries.

Part XI Restricted Distributor

- **25a** ☐ (All restricted distributors check here) I certify that the entity identified in Part I:
  - Operates as a distributor with respect to debt or equity interests of the restricted fund with respect to which this form is furnished;
  - Provides investment services to at least 30 customers unrelated to each other and less than half of its customers are related to each other;
  - Is required to perform AML due diligence procedures under the anti-money laundering laws of its country of organization (which is an FATF-compliant jurisdiction);
  - Operates solely in its country of incorporation or organization, has no fixed place of business outside of that country, and has the same country of incorporation or organization as all members of its affiliated group, if any;
  - Does not solicit customers outside its country of incorporation or organization;
  - Has no more than $175 million in total assets under management and no more than $7 million in gross revenue on its income statement for the most recent accounting year;
  - Is not a member of an expanded affiliated group that has more than $500 million in total assets under management or more than $20 million in gross revenue for its most recent accounting year on a combined or consolidated income statement; **and**
  - Does not distribute any debt or securities of the restricted fund to specified U.S. persons, passive NFFEs with one or more substantial U.S. owners, or nonparticipating FFIs.

Check box 25b or 25c, whichever applies.

I further certify that with respect to all sales of debt or equity interests in the restricted fund with respect to which this form is furnished that are made after December 31, 2011, the entity identified in Part I:

- **b** ☐ Has been bound by a distribution agreement that contained a general prohibition on the sale of debt or securities to U.S. entities and U.S. resident individuals and is currently bound by a distribution agreement that contains a prohibition of the sale of debt or securities to any specified U.S. person, passive NFFE with one or more substantial U.S. owners, or nonparticipating FFI.

- **c** ☐ Is currently bound by a distribution agreement that contains a prohibition on the sale of debt or securities to any specified U.S. person, passive NFFE with one or more substantial U.S. owners, or nonparticipating FFI and, for all sales made prior to the time that such a restriction was included in its distribution agreement, has reviewed all accounts related to such sales in accordance with the procedures identified in Regulations section 1.1471-4(c) applicable to preexisting accounts and has redeemed or retired any, or caused the restricted fund to transfer the securities to a distributor that is a participating FFI or reporting Model 1 FFI securities which were sold to specified U.S. persons, passive NFFEs with one or more substantial U.S. owners, or nonparticipating FFIs.

Form **W-8BEN-E** (Rev. 7-2017)

Form W-8BEN-E (Rev. 7-2017) Page **5**

Part XII Nonreporting IGA FFI

26 ☐ I certify that the entity identified in Part I:
- Meets the requirements to be considered a nonreporting financial institution pursuant to an applicable IGA between the United States and _____. The applicable IGA is a ☐ Model 1 IGA or a ☐ Model 2 IGA; and is treated as a _____ under the provisions of the applicable IGA or Treasury regulations (if applicable, see instructions);
- If you are a trustee documented trust or a sponsored entity, provide the name of the trustee or sponsor _____.
The trustee is: ☐ U.S. ☐ Foreign

Part XIII Foreign Government, Government of a U.S. Possession, or Foreign Central Bank of Issue

27 ☐ I certify that the entity identified in Part I is the beneficial owner of the payment, and is not engaged in commercial financial activities of a type engaged in by an insurance company, custodial institution, or depository institution with respect to the payments, accounts, or obligations for which this form is submitted (except as permitted in Regulations section 1.1471-6(h)(2)).

Part XIV International Organization

Check box 28a or 28b, whichever applies.

28a ☐ I certify that the entity identified in Part I is an international organization described in section 7701(a)(18).

b ☐ I certify that the entity identified in Part I:
- Is comprised primarily of foreign governments;
- Is recognized as an intergovernmental or supranational organization under a foreign law similar to the International Organizations Immunities Act or that has in effect a headquarters agreement with a foreign government;
- The benefit of the entity's income does not inure to any private person; **and**
- Is the beneficial owner of the payment and is not engaged in commercial financial activities of a type engaged in by an insurance company, custodial institution, or depository institution with respect to the payments, accounts, or obligations for which this form is submitted (except as permitted in Regulations section 1.1471-6(h)(2)).

Part XV Exempt Retirement Plans

Check box 29a, b, c, d, e, or f, whichever applies.

29a ☐ I certify that the entity identified in Part I:
- Is established in a country with which the United States has an income tax treaty in force (see Part III if claiming treaty benefits);
- Is operated principally to administer or provide pension or retirement benefits; **and**
- Is entitled to treaty benefits on income that the fund derives from U.S. sources (or would be entitled to benefits if it derived any such income) as a resident of the other country which satisfies any applicable limitation on benefits requirement.

b ☐ I certify that the entity identified in Part I:
- Is organized for the provision of retirement, disability, or death benefits (or any combination thereof) to beneficiaries that are former employees of one or more employers in consideration for services rendered;
- No single beneficiary has a right to more than 5% of the FFI's assets;
- Is subject to government regulation and provides annual information reporting about its beneficiaries to the relevant tax authorities in the country in which the fund is established or operated; **and**
  (i) Is generally exempt from tax on investment income under the laws of the country in which it is established or operates due to its status as a retirement or pension plan;
  (ii) Receives at least 50% of its total contributions from sponsoring employers (disregarding transfers of assets from other plans described in this part, retirement and pension accounts described in an applicable Model 1 or Model 2 IGA, other retirement funds described in an applicable Model 1 or Model 2 IGA, or accounts described in Regulations section 1.1471-5(b)(2)(i)(A));
  (iii) Either does not permit or penalizes distributions or withdrawals made before the occurrence of specified events related to retirement, disability, or death (except rollover distributions to accounts described in Regulations section 1.1471-5(b)(2)(i)(A) (referring to retirement and pension accounts), to retirement and pension accounts described in an applicable Model 1 or Model 2 IGA, or to other retirement funds described in this part or in an applicable Model 1 or Model 2 IGA); **or**
  (iv) Limits contributions by employees to the fund by reference to earned income of the employee or may not exceed $50,000 annually.

c ☐ I certify that the entity identified in Part I:
- Is organized for the provision of retirement, disability, or death benefits (or any combination thereof) to beneficiaries that are former employees of one or more employers in consideration for services rendered;
- Has fewer than 50 participants;
- Is sponsored by one or more employers each of which is not an investment entity or passive NFFE;
- Employee and employer contributions to the fund (disregarding transfers of assets from other plans described in this part, retirement and pension accounts described in an applicable Model 1 or Model 2 IGA, or accounts described in Regulations section 1.1471-5(b)(2)(i)(A)) are limited by reference to earned income and compensation of the employee, respectively;
- Participants that are not residents of the country in which the fund is established or operated are not entitled to more than 20% of the fund's assets; **and**
- Is subject to government regulation and provides annual information reporting about its beneficiaries to the relevant tax authorities in the country in which the fund is established or operates.

Form **W-8BEN-E** (Rev. 7-2017)

8. FIRPTA Withholding

Form W-8BEN-E (Rev. 7-2017) Page **6**

Part XV Exempt Retirement Plans *(continued)*

d ☐ I certify that the entity identified in Part I is formed pursuant to a pension plan that would meet the requirements of section 401(a), other than the requirement that the plan be funded by a trust created or organized in the United States.

e ☐ I certify that the entity identified in Part I is established exclusively to earn income for the benefit of one or more retirement funds described in this part or in an applicable Model 1 or Model 2 IGA, or accounts described in Regulations section 1.1471-5(b)(2)(i)(A) (referring to retirement and pension accounts), or retirement and pension accounts described in an applicable Model 1 or Model 2 IGA.

f ☐ I certify that the entity identified in Part I:

• Is established and sponsored by a foreign government, international organization, central bank of issue, or government of a U.S. possession (each as defined in Regulations section 1.1471-6) or an exempt beneficial owner described in an applicable Model 1 or Model 2 IGA to provide retirement, disability, or death benefits to beneficiaries or participants that are current or former employees of the sponsor (or persons designated by such employees); **or**

• Is established and sponsored by a foreign government, international organization, central bank of issue, or government of a U.S. possession (each as defined in Regulations section 1.1471-6) or an exempt beneficial owner described in an applicable Model 1 or Model 2 IGA to provide retirement, disability, or death benefits to beneficiaries or participants that are not current or former employees of such sponsor, but are in consideration of personal services performed for the sponsor.

Part XVI Entity Wholly Owned by Exempt Beneficial Owners

30 ☐ I certify that the entity identified in Part I:

• Is an FFI solely because it is an investment entity;

• Each direct holder of an equity interest in the investment entity is an exempt beneficial owner described in Regulations section 1.1471-6 or in an applicable Model 1 or Model 2 IGA;

• Each direct holder of a debt interest in the investment entity is either a depository institution (with respect to a loan made to such entity) or an exempt beneficial owner described in Regulations section 1.1471-6 or an applicable Model 1 or Model 2 IGA.

• Has provided an owner reporting statement that contains the name, address, TIN (if any), chapter 4 status, and a description of the type of documentation provided to the withholding agent for every person that owns a debt interest constituting a financial account or direct equity interest in the entity; **and**

• Has provided documentation establishing that every owner of the entity is an entity described in Regulations section 1.1471-6(b), (c), (d), (e), (f) and/or (g) without regard to whether such owners are beneficial owners.

Part XVII Territory Financial Institution

31 ☐ I certify that the entity identified in Part I is a financial institution (other than an investment entity) that is incorporated or organized under the laws of a possession of the United States.

Part XVIII Excepted Nonfinancial Group Entity

32 ☐ I certify that the entity identified in Part I:

• Is a holding company, treasury center, or captive finance company and substantially all of the entity's activities are functions described in Regulations section 1.1471-5(e)(5)(i)(C) through (E);

• Is a member of a nonfinancial group described in Regulations section 1.1471-5(e)(5)(i)(B);

• Is not a depository or custodial institution (other than for members of the entity's expanded affiliated group); **and**

• Does not function (or hold itself out) as an investment fund, such as a private equity fund, venture capital fund, leveraged buyout fund, or any investment vehicle with an investment strategy to acquire or fund companies and then hold interests in those companies as capital assets for investment purposes.

Part XIX Excepted Nonfinancial Start-Up Company

33 ☐ I certify that the entity identified in Part I:

• Was formed on (or, in the case of a new line of business, the date of board resolution approving the new line of business) _____

(date must be less than 24 months prior to date of payment);

• Is not yet operating a business and has no prior operating history or is investing capital in assets with the intent to operate a new line of business other than that of a financial institution or passive NFFE;

• Is investing capital into assets with the intent to operate a business other than that of a financial institution; **and**

• Does not function (or hold itself out) as an investment fund, such as a private equity fund, venture capital fund, leveraged buyout fund, or any investment vehicle whose purpose is to acquire or fund companies and then hold interests in those companies as capital assets for investment purposes.

Part XX Excepted Nonfinancial Entity in Liquidation or Bankruptcy

34 ☐ I certify that the entity identified in Part I:

• Filed a plan of liquidation, filed a plan of reorganization, or filed for bankruptcy on _____ ;

• During the past 5 years has not been engaged in business as a financial institution or acted as a passive NFFE;

• Is either liquidating or emerging from a reorganization or bankruptcy with the intent to continue or recommence operations as a nonfinancial entity; **and**

• Has, or will provide, documentary evidence such as a bankruptcy filing or other public documentation that supports its claim if it remains in bankruptcy or liquidation for more than 3 years.

Form **W-8BEN-E** (Rev. 7-2017)

Form W-8BEN-E (Rev. 7-2017) Page **7**

Part XXI   **501(c) Organization**

35   ☐ I certify that the entity identified in Part I is a 501(c) organization that:

- Has been issued a determination letter from the IRS that is currently in effect concluding that the payee is a section 501(c) organization that is dated _____ ; **or**
- Has provided a copy of an opinion from U.S. counsel certifying that the payee is a section 501(c) organization (without regard to whether the payee is a foreign private foundation).

Part XXII   **Nonprofit Organization**

36   ☐ I certify that the entity identified in Part I is a nonprofit organization that meets the following requirements.

- The entity is established and maintained in its country of residence exclusively for religious, charitable, scientific, artistic, cultural or educational purposes;
- The entity is exempt from income tax in its country of residence;
- The entity has no shareholders or members who have a proprietary or beneficial interest in its income or assets;

- Neither the applicable laws of the entity's country of residence nor the entity's formation documents permit any income or assets of the entity to be distributed to, or applied for the benefit of, a private person or noncharitable entity other than pursuant to the conduct of the entity's charitable activities or as payment of reasonable compensation for services rendered or payment representing the fair market value of property which the entity has purchased; **and**

- The applicable laws of the entity's country of residence or the entity's formation documents require that, upon the entity's liquidation or dissolution, all of its assets be distributed to an entity that is a foreign government, an integral part of a foreign government, a controlled entity of a foreign government, or another organization that is described in this part or escheats to the government of the entity's country of residence or any political subdivision thereof.

Part XXIII   **Publicly Traded NFFE or NFFE Affiliate of a Publicly Traded Corporation**

Check box 37a or 37b, whichever applies.

37a   ☐ I certify that:

- The entity identified in Part I is a foreign corporation that is not a financial institution; **and**
- The stock of such corporation is regularly traded on one or more established securities markets, including _____ (name one securities exchange upon which the stock is regularly traded).

b   ☐ I certify that:

- The entity identified in Part I is a foreign corporation that is not a financial institution;
- The entity identified in Part I is a member of the same expanded affiliated group as an entity the stock of which is regularly traded on an established securities market;
- The name of the entity, the stock of which is regularly traded on an established securities market, is _____ ; **and**
- The name of the securities market on which the stock is regularly traded is _____ .

Part XXIV   **Excepted Territory NFFE**

38   ☐ I certify that:

- The entity identified in Part I is an entity that is organized in a possession of the United States;
- The entity identified in Part I:
  - (i) Does not accept deposits in the ordinary course of a banking or similar business;
  - (ii) Does not hold, as a substantial portion of its business, financial assets for the account of others; **or**
  - (iii) Is not an insurance company (or the holding company of an insurance company) that issues or is obligated to make payments with respect to a financial account; **and**
- All of the owners of the entity identified in Part I are bona fide residents of the possession in which the NFFE is organized or incorporated.

Part XXV   **Active NFFE**

39   ☐ I certify that:

- The entity identified in Part I is a foreign entity that is not a financial institution;
- Less than 50% of such entity's gross income for the preceding calendar year is passive income; **and**
- Less than 50% of the assets held by such entity are assets that produce or are held for the production of passive income (calculated as a weighted average of the percentage of passive assets measured quarterly) (see instructions for the definition of passive income).

Part XXVI   **Passive NFFE**

40a   ☐ I certify that the entity identified in Part I is a foreign entity that is not a financial institution (other than an investment entity organized in a possession of the United States) and is not certifying its status as a publicly traded NFFE (or affiliate), excepted territory NFFE, active NFFE, direct reporting NFFE, or sponsored direct reporting NFFE.

Check box 40b or 40c, whichever applies.

b   ☐ I further certify that the entity identified in Part I has no substantial U.S. owners (or, if applicable, no controlling U.S. persons); **or**

c   ☐ I further certify that the entity identified in Part I has provided the name, address, and TIN of each substantial U.S. owner (or, if applicable, controlling U.S. person) of the NFFE in Part XXIX.

Form **W-8BEN-E** (Rev. 7-2017)

8. FIRPTA Withholding

Form W-8BEN-E (Rev. 7-2017)   Page **8**

Part XXVII   Excepted Inter-Affiliate FFI

41   ☐ I certify that the entity identified in Part I:
- Is a member of an expanded affiliated group;
- Does not maintain financial accounts (other than accounts maintained for members of its expanded affiliated group);
- Does not make withholdable payments to any person other than to members of its expanded affiliated group;
- Does not hold an account (other than depository accounts in the country in which the entity is operating to pay for expenses) with or receive payments from any withholding agent other than a member of its expanded affiliated group; **and**
- Has not agreed to report under Regulations section 1.1471-4(d)(2)(ii)(C) or otherwise act as an agent for chapter 4 purposes on behalf of any financial institution, including a member of its expanded affiliated group.

Part XXVIII   Sponsored Direct Reporting NFFE (see instructions for when this is permitted)

42   Name of sponsoring entity: _____

43   ☐ I certify that the entity identified in Part I is a direct reporting NFFE that is sponsored by the entity identified on line 42.

Part XXIX   Substantial U.S. Owners of Passive NFFE

As required by Part XXVI, provide the name, address, and TIN of each substantial U.S. owner of the NFFE. Please see the instructions for a definition of substantial U.S. owner. If providing the form to an FFI treated as a reporting Model 1 FFI or reporting Model 2 FFI, an NFFE may also use this part for reporting its controlling U.S. persons under an applicable IGA.

Name	Address	TIN

Part XXX   Certification

Under penalties of perjury, I declare that I have examined the information on this form and to the best of my knowledge and belief it is true, correct, and complete. I further certify under penalties of perjury that:

- The entity identified on line 1 of this form is the beneficial owner of all the income to which this form relates, is using this form to certify its status for chapter 4 purposes, or is a merchant submitting this form for purposes of section 6050W;
- The entity identified on line 1 of this form is not a U.S. person;
- The income to which this form relates is: (a) not effectively connected with the conduct of a trade or business in the United States, (b) effectively connected but is not subject to tax under an income tax treaty, or (c) the partner's share of a partnership's effectively connected income; **and**
- For broker transactions or barter exchanges, the beneficial owner is an exempt foreign person as defined in the instructions.

Furthermore, I authorize this form to be provided to any withholding agent that has control, receipt, or custody of the income of which the entity on line 1 is the beneficial owner or any withholding agent that can disburse or make payments of the income of which the entity on line 1 is the beneficial owner.

I agree that I will submit a new form within 30 days if any certification on this form becomes incorrect.

Sign Here ▶ _____   _____   _____
               Signature of individual authorized to sign for beneficial owner   Print Name   Date (MM-DD-YYYY)

☐ I certify that I have the capacity to sign for the entity identified on line 1 of this form.

Form **W-8BEN-E** (Rev. 7-2017)

Chapter 9
Impact of US Income Tax Treaties

§9.01	Overview	254
§9.02	US Treaty Interpretation	255
§9.03	Limitation on Benefits	256
	A. Qualified Persons	256
	B. Limited Benefits for Non-Qualified Persons	258
	1. Active Trade or Business Test	259
	2. Derivative Benefits Provision	263
	3. Competent Authority Relief	264
§9.04	Provisions that Affect Real Estate Gains	264
	A. Relief for Capital Gains	264
	B. Non-Discrimination Provisions	266
	C. Branch Profits Tax	266
	D. Business Profits and Permanent Establishment	268
§9.05	Treaty Benefits for FDAP Income	269
	A. Real Estate Rental Income	269
	B. Interest Income	270
	1. Amounts Paid by US Corporations	271
	2. Amounts Paid by Foreign Corporations	272
	C. Dividend Income	273
	D. Special Rules for Tax-Exempt Organizations and Pensions	274
§9.06	2016 US Model	275
	A. Special Tax Regimes	275
	B. Revisions to LOB Provisions	276
	1. New Derivative Benefits Test	276
	2. New Headquarters Company Test	277
	3. Active Trade or Business and Publicly Traded Company Subsidiary Tests	278
	C. Triangular Permanent Establishments	278
	D. Denial of Treaty Benefits Following Law Change	279
	E. Dividend Article	279
§9.07	Summary	280
Appendix 9-A		281

§9.01 OVERVIEW

FIRPTA overrides US treaty obligations and imposes US graduated income tax on a foreign investor's gain from a sale or other disposition of a USRPI. US tax treaties negotiated post-FIRPTA include provisions intended to ensure that gain from a sale or disposition of a USRPI will be subject to tax under US domestic law. Therefore, income tax treaties generally cannot reduce the FIRPTA tax liability of a foreign investor *per se*. However, an income tax treaty may significantly impact the overall US tax burden imposed on a foreign investor either on the exit gain (through a reduction or even elimination of the 30% US branch profits tax) or other income generated during the holding period of the USRPI.[1]

US treaties generally require foreign residents of a treaty country to satisfy *both* the limitation on benefits, or LOB, provisions in the treaty *and* any requirements of the relevant article to claim treaty benefits.[2] These treaty provisions require information and data that a foreign investor may not otherwise maintain. A taxpayer that fails to produce the necessary documentation to support its tax position may lose the treaty benefit it is otherwise entitled to claim. In addition, taxpayers may be required to disclose their treaty-based positions on their US tax returns. A failure to report the position, even if the position is correct, may result in monetary penalties.

Unless otherwise indicated, the discussion in this chapter is based on the language of the 2006 US Model Income Tax Treaty[3] which is the latest comprehensive model used as the baseline for most of the recent US negotiations.[4] The Technical Explanation, or TE, to the 2006 US Model also reflects the Treasury Department's latest views on various provisions.[5] Key changes introduced by the new 2016 US Model are discussed at the end of this chapter.[6] The discussion in this chapter is intended to be general in nature and is *not intended* to provide an in-depth analysis of any particular treaty provisions.

---

1. *See* discussion in §2.02., *supra*.
2. The United States has entered into bilateral income tax treaties with over sixty countries. See Appendix 9-A for a list of US income tax treaties currently in force as of July, 2017. The stated goals of these treaties are the avoidance of double taxation of treaty residents and evasion of tax by taxpayers involved in cross-border transactions.
3. United States Model Income Tax Convention of November 15, 2006.
4. Previous US model treaties were issued in 1981 and 1996 also can be instructive in evaluating contemporaneous bilateral treaties. The language from a given edition of the US model language is typical of many US treaties of comparable vintage. References also will be made to the US Model Technical Explanation Accompanying the Income Tax Convention of November 15, 2006 (TE to 2006 US Model).
5. In practice, when a specific treaty includes language that is similar to the language of the 2006 US Model, taxpayers often refer to the TE of the 2006 US Model for guidance.
6. Future editions of this book may integrate the provisions of the 2016 US Model into the discussions.

§9.02 US TREATY INTERPRETATION

US treaty provisions, together with US treaty interpretation principles, make the task of applying the provisions anything but straightforward. Oftentimes, the TE to a particular treaty[7] is the only place where taxpayers can find any guidance relating to a technical issue with respect to the treaty. It is not clear whether taxpayers may rely on the TE on a particular treaty the same way that they may rely on other public guidance such as revenue rulings, notices and regulations issued by the Treasury Department and the IRS.[8] General US tax principles applicable to treaty interpretations include:

- US treaties are *ambulatory*, meaning that any term not defined in the treaty is generally interpreted under the internal law in effect at the time the taxpayer seeks to rely on the treaty, rather than the date when the treaty was signed.[9] As a result, the treaties reflect the developments of US internal tax law in effect when the treaty is being applied.
- Under the *consistency* principle, a taxpayer generally may not choose among the provisions of the Code and a treaty in an inconsistent manner in order to minimize its US tax liabilities.[10]
- The *later-in-time* rule provides that where there is a conflict between a Code provision and a treaty provision, the provision enacted later normally prevails.[11]
- A taxpayer that takes the position that a US treaty overrules or otherwise modifies a Code provision is required to disclose the treaty-based position on its timely filed tax return.[12] Penalties may be imposed for each failure to comply with this disclosure requirement.[13]

In the context of ongoing international dialogue about the approach to treaty anti-abuse rules,[14] the Treasury Department introduced a new draft model treaty on May 20, 2015 (referred to as the 2015 Draft Model). The 2015 Draft Model proposed

---

7. The TE is submitted to the Senate Foreign Relations Committee of the US Congress as part of the ratification process. The TE also reflect the US Treasury Department's official interpretation of the provisions of a particular income tax treaty.
8. *See* NYSBA, *Report on Guidance under U.S. Income Tax Treaties*, dated May 28, 2010, no. 1214.
9. *See* 2006 US Model, Art. 3(2); TE to 2006 US Model, Art. 3.
10. *See* 2006 US Model, Art. 1(2) and the associated TE to that provision. *See* Revenue Ruling 84-17, 1984-1, C.B. 308; *see* also NYSBA, *Report on the Tax Treaty Consistency Principle*, dated July 14, 2015 (no. 1325). The report provides recommendations regarding the scope of the application of the consistency principle.
11. *Reid v. Covert*, 354 U.S. 1, 17-18 (1957).
12. I.R.C. §6114. If no return is required the IRS is authorized to prescribe a method for reporting the taxpayer's position.
13. The penalty for each failure (i.e., there can be multiple failures in a tax year) is USD 10,000 for a corporate taxpayer. The penalty may be imposed even if the taxpayer's position is correct. *See* I.R.C. §6712. The IRS may waive a penalty if the taxpayer can show that there was a reasonable cause for the failure and that the taxpayer acted in good faith.
14. For more background *see* Finet, *ABA Meeting: U.S. Model Tax Treaty Proposals Were Meant To Influence OECD*. 2015 TNT 183-7 (2015).

changes to the existing 2006 US Model. Following a comment period, the US Treasury released a revised US Model Income Tax Convention on February 17, 2016 (referred to as the 2016 US Model). The 2016 US Model retained many of the proposed changes introduced in the 2015 Draft Model. The Treasury had indicated that it intended to release the TE to the 2016 US Model in the spring of 2016; however, the TE to the 2016 US Model has not yet been issued as of July 2017.

The discussion below first describes the key requirements of the LOB provisions. Then the discussion focuses on other provisions that may impact a foreign investor's US tax liability with respect to its exit gain and certain passive income generated during the holding period of the USRPI. The chapter ends with a brief discussion on certain changes proposed by the 2016 US Model.

§9.03 LIMITATION ON BENEFITS

Satisfying the LOB provisions is a threshold requirement for a foreign person to claim treaty benefits.[15] In general, a foreign person is eligible to claim *all* the benefits under a US income tax treaty if it is a Qualified Person under that treaty. A foreign person that is not a Qualified Person still may claim benefits with respect to specific items of income under a particular treaty. A foreign taxpayer must satisfy the LOB provisions *each year* that it intends to claim treaty benefits. The rules are complex with various definitions, requirements, sub-requirements and exceptions. Some of the provisions contain bright-line tests (such as the Ownership and Base-Erosion test) while some other provisions apply based on the facts and circumstances of the particular case.

A. Qualified Persons

While the specific provisions of LOB articles differ between treaties, the definition of a Qualified Person typically includes:

- individual residents and governments of the treaty country;
- entities that satisfy both prongs of an Ownership and Base-Erosion test;
- companies whose Principal Class of Shares and any Disproportionate Class of Shares are Regularly and Primarily Traded on one or more Recognized Stock Exchanges (referred to as the Publicly Traded Company test); and
- certain subsidiaries of companies that satisfy the Publicly Traded Company test (Publicly Traded Company Subsidiary test).

---

15. As a pre-requisite, the foreign person must be a tax resident of its resident country. A corporation generally qualifies as resident of a country if it is liable to tax by reason of its domicile, residence, place of management, place of incorporation, or other criteria of a similar nature. The term also includes the government of the country and any political subdivision or local authority thereof, a pension fund established in that country and certain religious, charitable or similar organizations. The term does not include any person who is liable to tax in that country only of income from sources in that country or of profits attributable to a permanent establishment in that country. *See* 2006 US Model, Art. 1(1) and Art. 4.

9. Impact of US Income Tax Treaties

Most relevant for the purposes of this discussion are the Ownership and Base-Erosion test and the Publicly Traded Company test. **Definition 9.1** contains the definitions relevant for the Ownership and Base-Erosion test. A foreign taxpayer relying on this test must demonstrate that it satisfies both prongs of the test. The facts and circumstances of a particular taxpayer will influence the amount and type of documentation for this purpose.

Definition 9.1

Ownership and Base-Erosion test

- A company satisfies the Ownership prong if at least 50% of the aggregate voting power and value of its shares (and at least 50% of any Disproportionate Class of Shares) or other beneficial interest is owned, directly or indirectly, by one or more Qualified Persons of that same country on at least half of the days of the taxable year.[16]

- A company satisfies the Base-Erosion prong if less than 50% of its gross income for the taxable year is paid or accrued, as deductible payments, directly or indirectly to third-country residents who are not Qualified Persons of either its resident country or the US. Arm's-length payments in the ordinary course of business for services or tangible property are excluded from the definition of deductible expenses for this purpose.[17]

Definition 9.2 contains the definitions applicable to the Publicly Traded Company test.[18] The requirements are specific and nuanced. A company whose stock is publicly traded should *not assume* that it satisfies the requirements of this test without carefully analyzing each requirement. The same set of definitions apply to a foreign taxpayer that intends to qualify for treaty benefits under the Publicly Traded Company Subsidiary test. A company satisfies the Publicly Traded Company Subsidiary test if at least 50% of the aggregate vote and value of the shares (and at least 50% of any Disproportionate Class of Shares) is owned, directly or indirectly, by five or fewer companies that satisfy the Publicly Traded Company test. In the case of indirect ownership, each intermediate owner must also be a resident of the US or the treaty partner.

Definition 9.2

Publicly Traded Company Test

The Publicly Traded Company test contains numerous definitions and requirements. A publicly traded company that intends to claim treaty benefits under

---

16. 2006 US Model, Art. 22(2)(e)(i).
17. 2006 US Model, Art. 22(2)(e)(ii).
18. *See* I.R.C. §897(c)(3) and §6.02. B., *supra,* for a discussion of the Publicly Traded Exception to the FIRPTA substantive tax.

this provision should maintain on a contemporary basis all records necessary to demonstrate that it meets all the requirements of this provision.

- The term Principal Class of Shares means the ordinary or common shares that represent the majority of the voting power and value of the company.[19] If no single class of ordinary or common shares represent the majority of the aggregate voting power and value of the company, the principal class of shares are those classes that represent a majority of the aggregate voting power and value of the company.[20]
- The term Disproportionate Class of Shares means any shares of the company that entitles the shareholder to disproportionately higher participation, through dividends, redemption repayments or others, in the earnings generated by particular assets or activities of the company (e.g., tracking stock).[21]
- A Recognized Stock Exchange means the NASDAQ System owned by the National Association of Securities Dealers, Inc., a stock exchange registered with the US Securities and Exchange Commission as a national securities exchange under the US Securities Exchange Act of 1934 and any other stock exchange specified in the particular treaty.[22]
- A class of shares is Regularly Traded if (1) trades in the class are made in more than *de minimis* quantities on at least 60 days during the taxable year, and (2) the aggregate number of shares traded during the year is at least 10% of the average number of shares outstanding.[23]
- A class of shares is Primarily Traded if the number of shares in such class that are traded during the taxable year on all recognized stock exchanges in the company's resident country exceeds the number of shares in such class traded on any other established securities market.[24]

B. Limited Benefits for Non-Qualified Persons

A foreign corporation that cannot meet the definition of a Qualified Resident, e.g., a corporation that is privately owned by third-country residents, may still be eligible

---

19. 2006 US Model, Art. 22(5)(b).
20. 2006 US Model, Art. 22(5)(b). *See* Yu and Loh, *Ambiguity in the U.S.-Canada Treaty's Public-Traded Test Should Be Resolved In Favor of Canadian Dual-Class Public Companies*, 40 Tax Mgmt. Intl. J. 589 (October 14, 2011) for a discussion of some issues that arise under this test for public companies with dual-class stock ownership structures.
21. 2006 US Model, Art. 22(5)(c).
22. 2006 US Model, Art. 22(5)(a).
23. The 2006 US Model does not define the terms Primarily Traded and Regularly Traded. Under the ambulatory principle of treaty interpretation, the source country's (i.e., US) definition applies unless the context requires otherwise or the competent authorities have agreed to a different interpretation. As a result, the definitions above incorporate the meaning of those terms from the US branch profits tax regulations. *See* 2006 US Model, Art. 3(2) and Treas. Reg. §1.884-5(d)(3).
24. *Id.*

for limited treaty benefits if it satisfies one of three special provisions. The Active Trade or Business test contains a number of prescriptive rules. A taxpayer that intends to rely on this test needs to delve into various aspects of its ownership and operations to determine whether it qualifies for treaty benefits. A corporation that is owned by residents of another treaty country may satisfy the Derivative Benefits test. A foreign taxpayer that cannot satisfy either of these tests may apply to the US competent authority for discretionary relief.

1.   Active Trade or Business Test

The Active Trade or Business test grants treaty benefits on an *item-by-item* basis. A foreign corporation that is considered to engage in an active trade or business in its resident country may claim treaty benefits on *an item* of US source income that it derives *in connection with,* or that is *incidental to,* such active trade or business. In the case of a payment that is either received from a related US payor or derived from a US trade or business carried on by the foreign company, the business activities in the foreign person's resident country also must be *substantial* in relation to the US business activities of the payee (referred to as the Substantiality test).[25] An active trade or business excludes the business of making or managing investments for the person's own account, unless these activities are banking, insurance or securities activities carried on by a bank, insurance company or registered securities dealer.

The first step in the analysis is to establish that the party claiming treaty benefits in engaged in an *active trade or business.* Under US internal law, the term 'trade or business' generally refers to a specific unified group of activities that constitutes or could constitute an independent economic enterprise carried on for profit.[26] In order for a business to be considered *active,* the officers and employees of the corporation must conduct *substantial managerial and operational activities* for the business to qualify.[27] There is no clear guidance on what constitutes *substantial management and operational activities* for this purpose and a determination must be made on a case-by-case basis.

Special rules attribute the activities conducted by certain *connected* entities to determine whether the recipient satisfies the active trade or business test.[28] Under this provision, activities conducted by persons *connected to* a person are deemed to be conducted by the second person. A person is *connected to* another if one possesses at least 50% of the beneficial interest (or vote and value) in the other, if another person possesses at least 50% of the beneficial interest (or vote and value) in both

---

25. 2006 US Model, Art. 22(3)(b).
26. Treas. Reg. §1.367(a)-2T(b)(2).
27. TE to 2006 US Model, Art. 22, also refer to Art. 3(2) and I.R.C. §367(a). Treas. Reg. §1.367(a)-2T(b)(3) provides that a corporation may be engaged in the active conduct of a trade or business even though incidental activities of the trade or business are carried out on behalf of the corporation by independent contractors, though such activities are disregarded in determining whether the officers and employees of the corporation carry out substantial managerial and operational activities.
28. 2006 US Model, Art. 22(3)(c).

persons, or if, based on all relevant facts and circumstances, one person has control of the other person or both persons are under common control.

In the second step, a foreign corporation must establish that the item of US source income for which treaty benefit is claimed is derived *in connection with* or *incidental to* that business.[29] An item of income is derived in connection with a trade or business if the income producing activity in the US is a line of business that either:

- *forms a part of* the business conducted in the resident country. This generally means that the two activities involve the design, manufacture, or sale of the same products or type of product, or the provision of similar services;
- the businesses may be upstream, downstream, or parallel in relation to one another; or
- is *complementary to* the other business. This generally means that the businesses must be a part of the same overall industry and be related in the sense that the success or failure of one businesses will tend to result in the success or failure of the other.[30]

Whether a foreign person's business is considered *substantial* in relation to the related payor's US business is based on the facts and circumstances of the particular situation.[31] The TE provides that the analysis takes into account the comparative sizes of the businesses and also the economies of the United States and its treaty partner. This requires subjective judgment and it is no explicit guideline on the standards the US tax authorities currently apply for purposes of this determination. A previous US model treaty, the 1996 US Model Income Tax Treaty, as well as several US treaties in force, provide a safe harbor for the *Substantiality* test comparing the assets, gross income, and payroll expense of the two businesses.[32]

The example below, from PLR 200525002,[33] illustrates certain aspects of the Active Trade or Business test. Parent Co, a corporation resident in Country B, and its

---

29. An item of income is considered *incidental to* the trade of business carried on by the foreign person if the item facilitates the conduct of the trade or business in its resident country. An example of such income is the income derived when a foreign person temporarily invests its working capital in the US. In practice, it is more common to test whether an item of income is considered *in connection with* the taxpayer's business conducted in the resident country.
30. TE to 2006 US Model, Art. 22.
31. 2006 US Model, Art. 22(3)(b).
32. The United States Model Income Tax Convention, Sept. 20, 1996, Art. 22(3)(c). The safe harbor compares the assets, gross income, and payroll of the businesses to those carried on in the other country. Each of the three amounts from the foreign business is divided by those of the business, each ratio must exceed 7.5%, and the average of the three ratios must exceed 10%. This determination is made by using values from the taxable year preceding the year of receiving US source payment. If any individual ratio does not exceed 7.5%, the average for the three preceding taxable years may be used instead; see *e.g.*, Convention Between the Government of the United States of America and the Government of Ireland for the Avoidance of Double Taxation and the Prevention of Fiscal Evasion with Respect to Taxes on Income and on Capital Gains, July 28, 1997, US-Ireland, as amended by Protocol, Art. 23(3)(b)(ii).The Convention is referred to as the US-Ireland Treaty.
33. June 24, 2005.

9. Impact of US Income Tax Treaties

global subsidiaries[34] engage in a number of principal lines of business. The key issue in the ruling is whether the taxpayer may claim benefits under the Active Trade or Business test of the US-Country A income tax treaty. The terms of the Active Trade or Business test of the US-Country A income tax treaty are very similar to the terms of the same test in the 2006 US Model. Here are the simplified facts in the ruling:

- Country A Operating Affiliates and US Operating Affiliates are directly engaged in a number of the group's principal lines of business in their respective countries.
- Country A Operating Affiliates and US Operating Affiliates engage in parallel activities in their respective countries.[35] There are significant business relationships between Country A Operating Affiliates and US Operating Affiliates that are engaged in the same businesses.
- Taxpayer and US Finance Co are indirect subsidiaries of Parent Co and are resident in Country A and the US, respectively. Taxpayer and US Finance Co are themselves not directly engaged in any of the group's principal lines of business.
- Taxpayer and US Finance Co act as the finance companies for the Parent Co group companies. Taxpayer and US Finance Co issue debt obligations in their respective public markets. They on-lend the funds from the external debt issuances to borrowers that are members of the Parent Co's group.

Example 9.1 below is a simplified illustration of the cash flow between the entities. Of issue here is the interest that US Finance Co pays to Taxpayer. The IRS concludes that Taxpayer, a Country A resident that does not engage in an active trade or business itself, satisfies the Active Trade or Business test due to the activities of the Country A Operating Affiliates.[36]

---

34. The ruling does not specify the ownership percentages of the different entities.
35. The fact that the Country A Operating Affiliates and the US Operating Affiliates engage in parallel activities supports the position that interest income paid by the US Operating Affiliates to Taxpayer is derived in connection the active trade or business conducted by Taxpayer.
36. The IRS also provides that no opinion is expressed on a number of factual issues. The list, which does not contain any surprises, describes certain factual information that a taxpayer needs to gather and the associated analysis necessary to support the position that it is eligible to claim benefits under the Active Trade or Business test. Specially, the IRS states that no opinion is expressed as to (1) whether Taxpayer is connected to any of its Country A Operating Affiliate within the meaning of the treaty; (2) whether the Country A Operating Affiliates are engaged in the active conduct of Country A trade or business; (3) whether a particular item of US source interest income received by Taxpayer is attributable to income producing activities of a US Operating Affiliate whose line of business forms part of or is complementary to a trade or business conducted in the US; and (4) whether the trades or businesses of the Country A Operating Affiliates that are treated as conducted by Taxpayer satisfy the Substantiality test.

Example 9.1

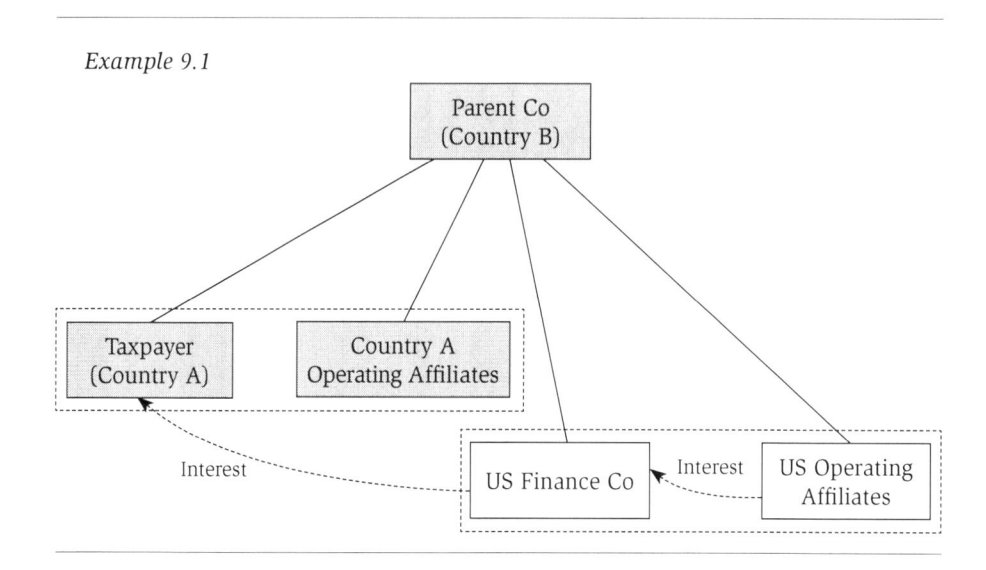

```
                    ┌─────────────┐
                    │  Parent Co  │
                    │ (Country B) │
                    └─────────────┘
                   /      |      \
                  /       |       \
┌──────────────┐  ┌──────────────────┐        \
│   Taxpayer   │  │    Country A     │         \
│  (Country A) │  │Operating Affiliates│        \
└──────────────┘  └──────────────────┘          \
       ▲                    ┌─────────────┐  Interest  ┌─────────────┐
       │       Interest     │US Finance Co│◄----------│US Operating │
       └────────────────────│             │           │  Affiliates │
                            └─────────────┘           └─────────────┘
```

The rulings are summarized below.

- Provided that Taxpayer is *connected to* the Country A Operating Affiliates,[37] Taxpayer would be considered to conduct the activities of the Country A Operating Affiliates for purposes of: (1) determining if it is engaged in the *active trade or business* in Country A, and (2) determining the line of business *in connection with* which the item of US source income must be derived to entitle Taxpayer to treaty benefits.
- Whether interest that Taxpayer receives from US Finance Co is derived *in connection with* the Taxpayer's trade or business will depend on whether the interest is attributable to income producing activities of a US Operating Affiliate whose line of business *forms part of* or *is complementary to* a trade or business treated as conducted by Taxpayer through the activities of the Country A Operating Affiliates.
- Taxpayer would determine whether its Country A trade or business is *substantial* in relation to the US trade or business that gives rise to the interest income by comparing the size and nature of the trade or business conducted by the Country A Operating Affiliates in Country A with that trade or business conducted in the US by the US Operating Affiliates that give rise to the item of income (e.g., relative asset values, income, and payroll expenses of the Country A Operating Affiliates and the US Operating Affiliates, and the relative contributions made to that trade or business in Country A and the US).[38]

---

37. The definition of the term *connected to* under the treaty between US and Country A is very similar to the definition in the 2006 US Model. *See* footnote 30, *supra*.
38. According to the ruling, the assets, income and payroll of US Finance Co and Taxpayer are not taken into account in making this comparison because these finance companies' own activities do not constitute the active conduct of a trade or business.

2. Derivative Benefits Provision

US treaties with North American countries and a number of European countries contain a Derivative Benefits provision.[39] This type of provision permits an eligible foreign company that may not be a Qualified Person to claim treaty benefits depending on whether it meets a modified version of the Ownership and Base Erosion test that focuses on whether the foreign company is owned by Equivalent Beneficiaries that may be residents of specified third countries that also have tax treaties with the United States. In the case of certain specific items of income (generally interest, dividends, and royalties), the test also incorporates a rate comparison to ensure that benefits are available only where the company would not be entitled to a lower tax rate under the treaty than the one the company's owners otherwise would enjoy if they had received the income directly.

Generally speaking, a company that is a resident in the treaty country may claim treaty benefits under this type of provision if it satisfies the following three requirements:

- under the Ownership Requirement, seven or fewer persons, that are Equivalent Beneficiaries[40] must own shares representing at least 95% of the aggregate voting power and value of the company and at least 50% of any Disproportionate Class of Shares.[41] The ownership percentage may be measured directly or indirectly (e.g., looking through intermediary entities).[42]
- the Base-Erosion Requirement for the Derivative Benefit provision is essentially the same as the Base-Erosion prong under the Qualified Person test discussed earlier, except that the company may pay up to 50% of its deductible payments to Equivalent Beneficiaries.
- to claim benefits under the Derivative Benefit provision with respect to dividends, interest, or royalties, under the Rate Requirement, the 95% owners must be entitled under their country's tax treaty with the United States to a rate of tax that is less than or equal to the rate applicable with respect to the income for which benefits are being claimed under the treaty in question. This requirement creates a cliff effect because a company that fails to satisfy this rate test with respect to an item of income is not entitled to any treaty benefits with respect to that item of income.

---

39. This provision is not included in the 2006 US Model but has been added to the 2016 US Model. See discussion in §9.06.B.1., *infra*.
40. Most commonly, residents of member countries of the European Union (EU) or of parties to the North America Free Trade Agreement (NAFTA) that qualify for benefits under a specific subset of tests under the LOB provision of the applicable tax treaty with the US.
41. *See, e.g.*, Convention Between the Government of the United Kingdom of Great Britain and Northern Ireland and the Government of the United States of America for the Avoidance of Double Taxation and the Prevention of Fiscal Evasion with Respect to Taxes on Income and on Capital Gains, July 24, 2001, U.S.-U.K., as amended by Protocol, Art. 23(3). The Convention is referred to as the US-UK Treaty.
42. *Id.* Note that unlike the Ownership-Base Erosion test and the Publicly Traded Company test, the Derivative Benefits provision typically does not contain restrictions on who can be an intermediate owner in cases where Equivalent Beneficiaries own the company indirectly.

3. *Competent Authority Relief*

The US competent authority may, using its own discretion, grant treaty relief to a foreign person that does not otherwise qualify for treaty benefits.[43] In making the determination, the competent authority will take into account whether the establishment, acquisition or maintenance of the foreign person seeking treaty benefits, or the conduct of such person's operations, has or had the obtaining of treaty benefits as one of its principal purposes. The competent authority's discretion under this provision is quite broad; for example, it may grant relief with respect to one or more items of income and the relief may be retroactive to the effective date of the treaty provision.[44]

The US competent authority has indicated that for it to grant benefits under this type of provision, a taxpayer must demonstrate that it does not qualify for the requested benefits under the relevant LOB provisions of the applicable US tax treaty, that the taxpayer has a substantial nontax nexus to the treaty country, and that, if benefits are granted, neither the taxpayer nor its direct or indirect owners will use the treaty inconsistently with its purposes.[45]

§9.04 PROVISIONS THAT AFFECT REAL ESTATE GAINS

A. Relief for Capital Gains

A little known provision, included in the capital gains article of just a handful of US tax treaties, can alleviate a foreign investor's FIRPTA tax burden in limited situations.[46] Although this provision is not widely known and, for that matter, probably seldom used, the fact that it exists at all is intriguing, and hence, worthy of discussion.

Article XIII(8) of the US-Canada Treaty[47] provides relief for a Canadian resident that disposes of property in the course of a reorganization, amalgamation, division or similar transaction where the profit, gain or income with respect to such transaction is not taxable under Canadian rules. Under this provision, the US competent authority, in its *sole* discretion, may agree to defer the recognition of the profit, gain or income with respect to such a transaction for US tax purposes until such time and manner as stipulated in the agreement with the taxpayer.

The US-Netherlands Treaty[48] contains a similar provision. The Memorandum of Understanding (MOU) to the US-Netherlands Treaty goes even further and provides a closing agreement mechanism that allows taxpayers to defer the recognition of gain in certain situations. The TE to the Netherlands Treaty explains that the provision is intended to coordinate the rules of both countries where one country taxes the gain from the transaction, but the other country defers the taxation.[49] In such a case, the shareholders of a foreign corporation may agree to reduce the tax basis of certain

---

43. 2006 US Model, Art. 22(4).
44. TE to 2006 US Model, Art. 22(4).
45. Rev. Proc. 2015-40, 2015-35 I.R.B. 236.
46. This provision is not found in the 2006 US Model.
47. *See* Art. XIII(8) of the US-Canada Treaty.
48. *See* Art. 14(8) of the US-Netherlands Treaty.
49. TE to the US-Netherlands Treaty, Art. 14.

properties by a closing agreement to defer tax in the country that otherwise would tax the gain immediately.[50]

Under the provision, e.g., a Canadian corporation that engages in a type of corporate division transaction that qualifies for Canadian tax-free treatment may petition the US competent authority to defer the US tax on the transaction if it involves a disposition of a USRPI. Such a provision can be helpful in a situation where the taxpayer, for whatever reason, cannot satisfy the FIRPTA Nonrecognition Rules.[51] Without the relief, the taxpayer would incur US tax in the year the transaction occurs while the resident country tax is deferred. The mismatch in the timing of the taxation could result in double taxation of the same gain.[52]

Where a treaty does not contain a specific competent authority relief provision in the capital gains article, one should query whether an eligible taxpayer may seek similar relief under the general competent authority provision, referred to as the Mutual Agreement Procedure,[53] under the treaty between the US and its resident country. The Mutual Agreement Procedure grants the competent authorities a mechanism to alleviate instances of double taxation. The language of the 2006 US Model version of that procedure states that:

> [T]he competent authorities of the Contracting States shall endeavor to resolve by mutual agreement ...They also may consult together for the elimination of double taxation in cases not provided for in the Convention. In particular the competent authorities of the Contracting States may agree...[54]

In accordance with this provision, a foreign investor may seek competent authority relief in cases of double taxation with respect to an item of income. FIRPTA overrides treaties to allow US taxation of a foreign investor's gain from a disposition of USRPI. There is no policy reason to preclude a taxpayer from seeking relief with respect to double taxation that arises due to FIRPTA. Furthermore, US internal law generally treats a foreign taxpayer's capital gain from the disposition of non-USRPIs as foreign source income exempt from US tax. Therefore, the ability to alleviate double taxation of gain from a disposition of USRPIs appears to be the primary purpose, from a US tax perspective, of a special competent authority provision in the capital gains articles.

---

50. The TE to the US-Netherlands Treaty provides that 'Furthermore, paragraph VIII of the Memorandum of Understanding provides that the relief provided under paragraph 8 of Article 14 shall not be available if the tax that otherwise would be imposed cannot be reasonably imposed or collected in the future. In order to ensure that any deferred United States tax may be collected in the future, the United States Competent Authority may require the alienator or shareholders of a corporation that is a party to the transaction to reduce the basis of any stock received pursuant to the reorganization by closing agreement in order to ensure that the tax that otherwise would have been imposed may be collected at a later time. If such adjustments cannot be made, then the relief described in paragraph 8 will not be available.'
51. As discussed in Ch. 7, *supra*, the FIRPTA Nonrecognition Rules can be difficult to satisfy.
52. The foreign tax credit mechanism in many countries may allow a taxpayer to use the US tax to reduce or offset its resident country tax on the same gain if the amount is taxed by both countries in the same tax year.
53. 2006 US Model, Art. 25.
54. 2006 US Model, Art. 25(3).

The US Foreign Investment in Real Property Tax Act: A Practical Guide

Nonetheless, there is no publicly available information about competent authority requests and related decisions. Therefore, it cannot be determined how often taxpayers use these special provisions and the circumstances under which the competent authority is willing to grant relief either under a specific provision under the capital gains article or under the Mutual Agreement Procedure.

B. Non-Discrimination Provisions

Most US income tax treaties contain a non-discrimination provision.[55] The intent of the provision is to provide that persons that are comparably situated should be taxed similarly. FIRPTA contains a number of provisions that treat foreign corporations differently from the US tax treatment accorded to domestic corporations. For example, US corporations, but not foreign corporations, may qualify for certain nonrecognition treatment under the FIRPTA Nonrecognition Rules.[56]

As discussed in Chapter 7, a foreign corporation that satisfies certain conditions, including qualifying for non-discrimination provision in a treaty, may make the Section 897(i) Election to be treated as a domestic corporation solely for purposes of FIRPTA.[57] According to the FIRPTA statute, the Section 897(i) Election is the *exclusive* remedy for any foreign taxpayer claiming *discriminatory* treatment with respect to the FIRPTA provisions.[58] Legal and tax requirements of other countries differ from US requirements. A foreign taxpayer that engages in a restructuring transaction generally chooses a form that satisfies the requirements of its resident country. The transaction may not qualify for tax-free treatment under the FIRPTA Nonrecognition Rules even if the foreign corporation makes a Section 897(i) Election to be treated as a US corporation. In these instances, it would make sense that the foreign taxpayer may apply for relief if the FIRPTA rules would give rise to double taxation of the same income.

C. Branch Profits Tax

A foreign corporation is generally subject to 35% net basis federal income tax on its FIRPTA gain. The gain also may be subject to a 30% branch profits tax[59] in the hands of a foreign corporation unless the foreign corporation satisfies the Branch Termination Exception.[60] On the other hand, if the Branch Termination Exception does not apply, then the only way to reduce a foreign corporation's branch profits tax liability is if it is eligible to claim benefits available under the income tax treaty between its resident country and the US.[61]

---

55. *See* 2006 US Model, Art. 24.
56. *See* Rev. Rul. 87-66, 1987-2 C.B. 168. *See* Ch. 7, *supra,* for a discussion on I.R.C. §897(d) and (e).
57. *See* §7.05.B., *supra.*
58. I.R.C §897(i)(4).
59. *See* §2.02.B.1., *supra.*
60. *See* Treas. Reg. §1.884-2T. Also *see* §2.02.B.2., *supra.*
61. Note that branch profits tax does not apply to the disposition of the stock in a USRPHC. I.R.C. §884(d)(1)(C).

9. Impact of US Income Tax Treaties

The 2006 US Model permits the US to impose a branch profits tax on the dividend equivalent amount of the profits generated by a foreign company, but limits the rate to 5%.[62]

Example 9.1 illustrates the US federal income tax consequences with respect to the amount taxable from a foreign corporation's sale of a USRPI.

Example 9.1

	(in USD 000s)		
	A. FIRPTA Tax	B. FIRPTA Tax + 5% Branch Profits Tax	C. FIRPTA Tax + 30% Branch Profits Tax
Gain	100	100	100
Taxable Income	100	100	100
35% FIRPTA Tax	(35)	(35)	(35)
Branch Profits Tax	n/a	(3.25)	(19.5)
Net cash received	65	61.75	45.5
Effective tax rate	35%	38.25%	54.5%

A. The foreign corporation is subject to FIRPTA tax but eligible for the Branch Termination Exception.

B. The foreign corporation is not eligible for the Branch Termination Exception; however, it is eligible for treaty reduction of the branch profits tax rate to 5%.

C. The foreign corporation is not eligible for the Branch Termination Exception; it is also not eligible for treaty reduction of the branch profits tax rate.

There is another potential treaty benefit regarding the branch profits tax. US internal law generally imposes the branch profits tax on a foreign *corporation* that has ECI.[63] The 2006 US Model narrows this application and generally permits the imposition of the branch profits tax on a *company* that has ECI.[64] The 2006 US Model defines the term *company*, for this purpose, as:

> [A]ny body corporate or any entity that is treated as a body corporate for tax purposes according to *the laws of the state in which it was organized*.[65]

Under the above treaty definition, a foreign entity is a *company*, only if it is taxed as a corporation under the laws of its resident country. Under US tax principles, a foreign partnership may elect to be treated as a corporation *solely* for US tax purposes

---

62. Art. 10(8) of the 2006 US Model.
63. *Id.*
64. Art. 10(8)(a) of the 2006 US Model.
65. Art. 3(1)(b) of the 2006 US Model. (Emphasis added.)

under the Check-the-Box rules (such an entity is referred to as a Reverse Hybrid).[66] A Reverse Hybrid may be subject to the 30% branch profits tax under US internal law because it is treated as a foreign *corporation* for US tax purposes.[67] However, a Reverse Hybrid is not a *company* under the above treaty definition. The question that follows is whether a Reverse Hybrid that is eligible for treaty benefits may avoid the branch profits tax as a result of the treaty definition of a company. In a case where the owners/partners of the Reverse Hybrid are individuals (presumably residents of the same country as the Reverse Hybrid), it appears that the individuals also should be exempt from branch profits tax as well.

A handful of treaties provide a special allowance regarding the branch profits tax. As an example, the US-Canada treaty exempts the first USD 500,000 of a foreign corporation's earnings from the branch profits tax.[68] Certain older treaties preclude the application of the branch profits tax.[69]

D.   Business Profits and Permanent Establishment

The 2006 US Model, like most US tax treaties, provides that the US may tax business profits derived by a foreign treaty resident only if that resident carries on business through a permanent establishment, or PE, situated in the US, and only to the extent those profits are attributable to that PE.[70] Consequently, the PE concept establishes the threshold for, and the extent of, source country taxation of business profits under US tax treaties. The 2006 US Model defines the term PE in general terms as a 'fixed place of business through which the business of an enterprise is wholly or partly carried on.'[71] It then provides a number of examples,[72] limitations,[73] and exceptions.[74] These take the form of assets, activities and relationships deemed to be either included in or excluded from the scope of the concept.

A special rule under the PE article provides that certain construction sites or installment projects that last for twelve months or less do not constitute a PE, regardless of whether they are conducted through a fixed place of business.[75] The twelve-month period applies to each site or project. A series of contracts or projects by a contractor that are interdependent both commercially and geographically may be

---

66. *See* Ch. 10, *infra*, for a further discussion on the US entity classification rules.
67. Temp. Treas. Reg. sec. §301.7701-2T(a)(2) generally provides that the Check-the-Box rules apply to taxes imposed under subtitle A, all income taxes, including I.R.C. §884(a).
68. US-Canada Treaty, Art. X(6)(d).
69. *See*, e.g., the Agreement Between The Government of The United States of America And The Government of The People's Republic of China For The Avoidance of Double Taxation And The Prevention of Tax Evasion with respect to Taxes on Income, Together With a Supplementary Protocol And Exchange of Notes, Signed at Beijing on April 30, 1984, as amended by the Second Protocol Signed at Beijing on May 10, 1986. Referred to as the US-China Treaty.
70. 2006 US Model, Art. 7(1).
71. 2006 US Model, Art. 5(1).
72. 2006 US Model, Art. 5(2).
73. 2006 US Model, Art. 5(3).
74. 2006 US Model, Art. 5(4).
75. 2006 US Model, Art. 5(3).

treated as a single project for purposes of this twelve month rule.[76] A foreign investor relying on this rule should monitor the timing of the project carefully.

Even in the absence of a fixed place of business, a foreign enterprise can be deemed to have a PE if a person acts in the United States on behalf of that enterprise and habitually exercises authority to conclude contracts that are binding on that enterprise. An enterprise is not deemed to have a PE in the US, however, merely because it carries on business there through an independent agent acting in the ordinary course of its business.[77] In general, an agent is considered independent if it is both legally and economically independent of the foreign principal, and the agent is acting in its ordinary course of business in carrying out activities on behalf of its principal.[78]

Under US internal law, on the other hand, the threshold for the taxation of business income of non-resident aliens or foreign enterprises is based on whether the non-resident alien or foreign enterprise is engaged in a 'trade or business within the United States' (US trade or business).[79] This standard is similar to, but different from, the PE standard. In the absence of a treaty, hence, a foreign enterprise that does not maintain a PE may nevertheless be considered engaged in a US trade or business, and therefore taxable on its business profits under US internal law.[80] Where a tax treaty applies, however, a foreign taxpayer who is eligible to claim treaty benefits under the PE and business profits articles may be considered to engage in a US trade or business and still be exempt from US tax if it either does not have a PE in the US or does not have any business profits attributable to the PE.

§9.05 TREATY BENEFITS FOR FDAP INCOME

As discussed in Chapter 2, a foreign person is generally subject to a 30% gross-basis tax on US source FDAP (i.e., passive) income.[81] An applicable treaty provision may reduce or even eliminate the statutory tax if all the specific conditions of the provisions are satisfied.

A. Real Estate Rental Income

The 2006 US Model, like most treaties, applies the situs principle and grants primary taxing jurisdiction to the country where the real property is located. In other words,

---

76. TE to 2006 US Model, Art. 5(3).
77. 2006 US Model, Art. 7(6).
78. TE to 2006 US Model, Art. 7(6).
79. *See*, e.g., I.R.C. §§871(b), 882 and 864(b).
80. *See*, e.g., Rev. Rul. 55-617, 1955-2 CB 774 (Belgian enterprise with no PE in the United States exempt from United States taxation even though engaged in a trade or business). See also *de Amodio v. Commissioner*, 34 T.C. 894 (1960), aff'd, 299 F.2d 623 (3d Cir. 1962), the facts of which involved a non-resident alien residing in Switzerland purchased income-producing real property in the US and managed it through independent real estate agents. The court held that the taxpayer was engaged in a trade or business in the US but did not have a PE within the meaning of the US-Switzerland treaty.
81. *See* I.R.C. §§1441 and 1442.

there is *no reduction* in the 30% gross-basis tax if a foreign person receives rental income from real estate located in the US. Income derived from real property includes income from the direct use or rental of the property.[82] Real estate rental income can be either FDAP or business income depending the specific facts and circumstances of the situation.

In general, income from a net lease where the lessee pays all the expenses with respect to the property such as real estate taxes, operating expenses, ground rent, repairs, and insurance, in addition to a monthly rental to the lessor is treated as FDAP income for US tax purposes. The IRS has also held that an investor who leases real property in the United States will not be considered to be engaged in a trade or business if his management activity is minimal.[83] A foreign taxpayer, instead of being subject to tax at 30% rate, could elect to be taxed on the rental income on a net basis.[84]

A foreign taxpayer has the choice of making a net-basis election with respect to rental income under either US internal law[85] or an applicable treaty.[86] The language of the treaty net-basis election provides that the investor's US real estate income will be taxed on a net basis, whereas the language of the Code election treats income subject to the election as ECI. A foreign corporation that is, or is deemed to be, engaged in a US trade or business may be subject to the 30% branch profits tax.[87]

B.   Interest Income

US tax policy applies the substance over form principle and may recast an instrument that is drafted as a debt as equity for federal income tax purposes. Hence, the reduced withholding tax on interest only applies to amounts that constitute interest with respect to an instrument that is respected as a debt obligation for federal income

---

82. 2006 US Model, Art. 6(3).
83. *See*, e.g., Rev. Rul. 73-522, 1973-2 C.B. 226 in which the IRS concluded that a foreign investor was not engaged in a trade or business where his tenant conducted substantially all of the management and maintenance activities with respect to the underlying property.
84. *See* 2006 US Model, Art. 6(5) and discussion in Ch. 2, *supra*, with respect to a similar election under I.R.C. §§871(d) and 882(d). A taxpayer that makes the net-basis election generally should be entitled to certain deductions such as interest expense, depreciation and routine maintenance expenses. In such case, the net profits from the activity will be treated as business profits taxed at 35% and no portion of such income will be treated as FDAP income. *See* Example 2.1, *supra*.
85. *See* I.R.C. §§871(d) and 882(d).
86. *See* 2006 US Model, Art. 6(5).
87. I.R.C. §884(d)(1) defines 'effectively connected earnings and profits' as 'income which is effectively connected (or treated as effectively connected) with the conduct of a trade or business in the United States'. There is no requirement that the electing investor actually be engaged in a US trade or business. Typically, a treaty provision may provide that a foreign investor may elect to have income taxed 'on a net basis as if such income were attributable to a permanent establishment ...'. *See*, e.g., 2006 US Model, Art. 6(5). The US tax law equivalent of 'attributable to a permanent establishment' is 'effectively connected with the conduct of a trade or business'. Accordingly, the IRS may view the treaty election the same as the Code election and apply the branch profits tax to a foreign corporation that has made a treaty election.

tax purposes.[88] In addition, the IRS may disregard, for US withholding purposes, the participation of one or more intermediate entities in a financing arrangement if it determines that such entities are acting as conduit entities.[89] Foreign investors should consider the application of the conduit financing regulations when structuring loans to a US borrow to avoid any potential disallowance of treaty benefits on the interest payments under the rules.[90]

1. Amounts Paid by US Corporations

The 2006 US Model generally exempts interest income from source country tax, and allows the resident country of the foreign taxpayer the exclusive right to tax interest income.[91] Guarantee fees paid with respect to loan obligations are sourced in the same way as interest.[92] Under a special rule, any 'contingent interest' may be subject to a 15% withholding tax.[93] Hence, a foreign person that is eligible to claim treaty benefits may be exempt from US tax on regular interest and subject to 15% US withholding tax on certain contingent interest paid by a US subsidiary or a REIT.[94]

As discussed earlier, the definition of an interest in a USRPI excludes an interest solely as a creditor with respect to real properties and other entities.[95] Under this definition, a mortgage loan that entitles the lender to any appreciation with respect to the underlying USRPI constitutes an interest other than a creditor, and any *gain* from a disposition of the mortgage is subject to FIRPTA tax.[96] However, a payments on the loan that are respected as interest, including any contingent interest, are *not subject* to FIRPTA tax.[97] Thus, a foreign investor that makes a mortgage loan to a US borrower with a contingent interest element (e.g., an equity kicker) may structure the investment so that it is subject to 15% US withholding tax[98] instead of being subject to the 35% FIRPTA tax.[99] This may be an attractive alternative for certain foreign investors.

---

88. *See* discussion in Ch. 10, *infra*, regarding US debt versus equity considerations and various limitations on the deductibility of interest payments.
89. Treas. Reg. §1.881-3(a)(1).
90. *See* I.R.C. §7701(l) and Treas. Reg. §1.881-3. *See* §10.06.B., *infra*, for a further discussion on this issue.
91. *See* Art. 11 of the 2006 US Model.
92. *See* I.R.C. §861(c)(9) and US-Canada Treaty, Art. XI.
93. The TE to the 2006 US Model provides that contingent interest is defined by reference to I.R.C. §871(h)(4) including the exceptions thereunder. *See* Yu and Kerzner, *Protocol to U.S.-Canada Treaty Introduces New 15 Percent Withholding Tax Rate for Contingent Interest*, Journal of Financial Products, Vol. 7, Issue 4, 2009, for a further discussion of this topic.
94. *See* discussion in §10.06.A., *infra*, for a discussion of the definition of contingent interest.
95. Treas. Reg. §1.897-1(d)(1). *See* Ch. 3, *supra*, for a further discussion about this issue.
96. Treas. Reg. §1.897-1(d)(2).
97. Treas. Reg. §1.897-1(h).
98. This assumes that the foreign investor is eligible to claim benefits under an income tax treaty that adopts the interest provisions as provided by the 2006 US Model.
99. If the contingent interest is determined solely upon the gain or appreciation from the underlying property.

Article 11, as a more specific provision on interest, generally takes precedence over Article 7 on business profits.[100] Accordingly, the taxation of interest received by a foreign person in the course of its business is generally governed by Article 11 with one exception – Article 11(3) provides that if a recipient of interest operates a business through PE in the source country, and the interest is *attributable to* the PE then taxation of the amount is determined under Article 7.[101]

2. *Amounts Paid by Foreign Corporations*

A foreign corporation that has, or is deemed to have, ECI in a tax year generally is subject to US federal income tax on a net basis at graduated rates applicable to US corporations.[102] The foreign corporation may deduct expenses allocable to its ECI in determining its US taxable income.[103] For example, a foreign corporation may allocate a portion of its worldwide interest expense to reduce the amount of its net income under Treasury Regulation section 1.882-5.

A special rule treats deductible interest payments of a foreign corporation as US source FDAP interest subject to the 30% gross-basis tax.[104] There are two components of this interest expense. The first is the actual interest payment that the US branch made to a lender; the second is the excess of the amount of interest allocated under Treasury Regulation section 1.882-5 over the amount that is actually paid by the US branch (referred to as Excess Interest). Such Excess Interest is deemed to be paid from the branch to the home office of the foreign corporation.[105] Different income tax treaties apply to reduce the US tax imposed on each component:

- The income tax treaty between the US and the residence country of the *foreign lender* applies to reduce or eliminate the US withholding tax otherwise imposed on the amount of interest actually paid by the US branch of a foreign corporation.[106]
- The income tax treaty between the US and the resident country of the *foreign corporation* that has the US branch applies to reduce or eliminate the withholding tax otherwise imposed on the Excess Interest.[107]

The rules that coordinate a foreign corporation's interest deduction under Treasury Regulation section 1.882-5 and the branch-level interest rules of Code section 884 are complex. For example, if a foreign corporation owns a 10% or more interest[108] in the capital, profits, or losses of a partnership, the foreign corporation is treated as

---

100. 2006 US Model, Art. 7(7).
101. 2006 US Model, Art. 11(3).
102. I.R.C. §882(a)(1).
103. I.R.C. §882(c)(1).
104. I.R.C. §884(f)(1).
105. I.R.C. §884(f)(1)(A).
106. I.R.C. §884(e)(3)(B) and 884(f)(3)(B).
107. I.R.C. §884(f)(1)(B). If the foreign corporation is a Qualified Person of a treaty country and the treaty follows the US Model, there will be no US taxation under Art. 11(1) on the deemed interest payment from the US branch to the foreign corporation.
108. I.R.C. §318 attribution rules are taken into account in determining the foreign corporate partner's ownership in the partnership for this purpose. Treas. Reg. §1.884-4(b)(8)(v).

if it paid *directly* its distributive share of partnership interest expense to any foreign persons, and the foreign corporate partner needs to determine whether the recipient is eligible for treaty benefits for such interest.[109] A foreign person that invests in a USRPI directly or through a partnership should take these rules into account if it intends to use debt financing in such an investment structure.

C.   Dividend Income

US corporate Blockers that are Subchapter C corporations may distribute their after-tax earnings and profits to their foreign owners as dividends.[110] US source dividends are subject to the 30% gross-basis tax.[111] Dividends paid to a corporate shareholder that owns 10% or more of the voting stock of the payor corporation are eligible for 5% withholding tax on direct investment dividends.[112] While dividends from portfolio investments (i.e., if the recipient is an individual or a corporation that owns less than 10% of the voting stock of the payor corporation) are subject to a 15% withholding tax.[113] Some newer US treaties provide for a 0% withholding on dividends if certain additional conditions are met, although the 2006 US Model does not contain such a provision.[114]

The 2006 US Model imposes additional restrictions on dividends paid by a REIT.[115] Although REITs are treated as corporations for US purposes, a REIT generally may avoid paying corporate-level tax in a year that it distributes 100% of its earnings and profits to its shareholders.[116] A policy reason behind the imposition of the full 30% US gross-basis tax on REIT dividends paid to a foreign person may be to ensure the imposition of at least one full level of tax on REIT earnings. According to the TE to the 2006 US Model, these rules are intended to prevent the use of a REIT to inappropriately convert an amount that is otherwise subject to FIRPTA tax into ordinary REIT dividends eligible for a lower withholding tax rate.[117] Under the 2006 US Model, a reduced 15% withholding rate on REIT ordinary dividends are available to three categories of shareholders:

---

109. *See* also Treas. Reg. §1.884-4(b)(8)(vi), Example (2).
110. Distributions from a US corporation is considered to first come out of the earnings and profits of the distributing corporation, followed by a return of the stock's corporation and then any excess is considered capital gain. I.R.C. §301(c).
111. I.R.C. §§871(a)(1) and 881(a)(1).
112. This relief does not apply to dividends paid to a shareholder who is an individual or partnership made up of individuals, even if such shareholder owns a substantial interest in the payer corporation's shares.
113. 2006 US Model, Art. 10(3).
114. *See*, e.g., US-UK Treaty, Art. 10(3).
115. 2006 US Model, Art. 10(4); *see* I.R.C. §856. Similar provisions also apply to Regulated Investment Companies (RICs or mutual funds). The discussion in this chapter only focus on REITs and does not cover the rules applicable to RICs.
116. *See* §5.03.D., *supra,* for a discussion on REIT distributions.
117. This statement reflects the policy behind I.R.C. §897(h), which imposes a FIRPTA tax on a REIT's distribution that is attributable to gain from the sale of a USRPI.

- the beneficial owner of the dividend holds an interest of not more than 10% in the REIT and is either a pension fund or an individual;[118]
- the dividends are paid with respect to a class of stock that is publicly traded and the beneficial owner of the dividend does not own more than 5% of any class of the REIT's stock; and[119]
- the beneficial owner of the dividend holds an interest of not more than 10% in the REIT and the REIT's interest in a single property does not exceed 10% of its interests in real property.[120]

US withholding tax applies to both actual and constructive dividends paid or deemed paid to a foreign person.[121] A situation where a constructive dividend arises may be due to an IRS audit adjustment for certain payments made by a US person to a related party. In that situation, only a foreign owner of the dividend that qualifies for treaty benefits may claim benefit for a reduced rate of US withholding. Similar to the provision for interest payments, the dividend article, as a more specific provision, generally takes precedence over the business profits article.[122]

D. Special Rules for Tax-Exempt Organizations and Pensions

Some US treaties, such as the US-Canada Treaty, also provide exemptions for special types of non-profit entities. Under such a provision, income derived by a Canadian tax-exempt organization formed for religious, scientific, literary, educational or charitable purposes is exempt from US tax if such income is also exempt from Canadian income tax.[123] In addition, US source interest and dividends derived by a Canadian resident trust, company, organization or other arrangement that operates exclusively to administer or provide pension, retirement or employee benefits is also exempt from US tax.[124]

If an entity that qualifies for this exemption is also a QFPF,[125] then it may be possible to structure the investment to avoid US tax on both the operating income and gain from a disposition of USRPI. An example is the investment in the stock

---

118. *See* 2006 US Model, Art. 10(4)(a)(i).
119. *See* 2006 US Model, Art. 10(4)(a)(ii).
120. The REIT is considered 'diversified'. *See* 2006 US Model, Art. 10(4)(a)(iii) and (4)(b).
121. *See*, e.g., *Central De Gas De Chihuahua, S.A.*, 102 TC 515.
122. 2006 US Model, Art. 7(7). On the other hand, Article 7 will override Article 10 if the recipient of the dividends has a PE in US and if the dividends are attributable to the PE. 2006 US Model, Art. 10(6). This situation rarely happens because it is difficult to attribute the dividends to a PE under US internal tax principles. *See*, e.g., Treas. Reg. §1.864-4(c). However, if dividend is attributable to a foreign taxpayer's PE, then the US would tax such income in the hands of the foreign taxpayer in the same manner as a domestic enterprise. 2006 US Model, Art. 24(4).
123. *See* US-Canada Treaty Art. XXI(1).
124. *See* US-Canada Treaty Art. XX1(2). The exemption also applies to US withholding tax on REIT dividends otherwise imposed by Art. X of the US-Canada Treaty.
125. *See* Ch. 6, *infra,* for the definition of a QFPF and the FIRPTA exception available to such an entity.

9. Impact of US Income Tax Treaties

of a REIT. Other treaties that include a similar provision include the US-Germany Treaty[126] and the US-Netherlands Treaty.[127]

§9.06 2016 US MODEL

The terms of the 2016 US Model deviate substantially from the 2006 US Model and current treaties in force by adopting many of the proposals for the 2015 Draft Model. These changes stem from the Treasury Department's desire to further prevent the use of US treaties to achieve double non-taxation or reduced taxation through tax evasion or avoidance.[128] It is difficult to predict how US treaty partners will react to these modified standards in future negotiations. If adopted, these new standards will lead to additional analysis and record keeping by foreign taxpayers that intend to claim US treaty benefits. Some of the more significant changes are described below.

A.   Special Tax Regimes

The 2016 US Model modifies Articles 11 (Interest), 12 (Royalties), and 21 (Other Income) to deny treaty benefits for such income arising in one contracting state and paid to a 'connected person' resident in the other contracting state if the recipient is subject to a Special Tax Regime, or STR, with respect to that category of income in its country of residence at any time during the tax period in which the item of income is paid.[129]

2016 US Model defines a STR as any statute, regulation or administrative practice in a contracting state that either provides preferential tax treatment for interest, royalties, or guarantee fees, or provides preferential tax treatment for companies that are not engaged in an active trade or business in that state.[130] An STR does not include preferential tax treatment for royalties that is conditioned on the extent of research and development activities that take place in the resident country.[131] Furthermore, an STR does not include a regime that applies primarily to pension funds or charitable organizations, or to the foreign equivalents of RICs and REITs.[132] Finally, a regime will not constitute an STR unless the resulting rate of taxation with respect to an item

---

126. Art. 10(3)(b) of the Convention between the United States of America and the Federal Republic of Germany for the Avoidance of Double Taxation and the Prevention of Fiscal Evasion with respect to Taxes on Income, August 29, 1989, as amended by Protocol exempts a pension fund from source-country tax on dividends. The Convention is referred to as the US-Germany Treaty.
127. Art. 35(1) of the US-Netherlands Treaty exempts a pension trust or similar organization from source-country tax on interest and dividends.
128. *See* the preamble to the 2016 US Model.
129. Two persons are 'connected', for this purpose, if one owns 50% or more of the beneficial interest in the other, or the same person owns 50% or more of the beneficial interest in both. Additionally, two persons will be treated as connected if both are under common control, regardless of the ownership percentage. 2016 US Model, Art. 3(m).
130. 2016 US Model, Art. 3(1)(l)(i). This definition is narrower than the definition provided in the May 2015 draft.
131. 2016 US Model, Art. 3(1)(l)(ii).
132. 2016 US Model, Art. 3(1)(l)(iv).

of income is lower than the lesser of: (1) 15%, or (2) 60% of the general statutory rate of company tax applicable in the resident country.[133]

B. Revisions to LOB Provisions

The 2016 US Model adds a Derivative Benefits provision and a new Headquarters Company test to the LOB article. The 2016 US Model also modifies the Active Trade or Business test and the Publicly Traded Company Subsidiary test of the 2006 US Model. Each of these is described below.

1. New Derivative Benefits Test

The 2016 US Model incorporates the Derivative Benefits provision, already included in various US treaties with European and North American countries, in the LOB. The changes in the new model include the following:

- Under the Ownership Requirement, seven or fewer persons that are Equivalent Beneficiaries must own shares representing at least 95% of the aggregate voting power and value of the company (and at least 50% of any Disproportionate Class of Shares) of the company claiming treaty benefits.[134] In the case of indirect ownership, each intermediate owner must be a Qualifying Intermediate Owner. The definition of Equivalent Beneficiary is substantially more complicated than in existing US tax treaties, but in broad terms includes a resident of a country that has a comprehensive tax treaty with the US under which the resident would be treated as a qualifying person under certain specific clauses of the LOB, and would be entitled to the benefits at least as favorable as the benefits being claimed. It also generally includes residents of the same country as the entity seeking benefits,[135] and residents of the source country.[136] A Qualifying Intermediate Owner means a company resident in the same country as the taxpayer seeking benefits or a company resident in a country that has a comprehensive tax treaty in force with the US that contains certain anti-abuse provisions analogous to ones included in the 2016 US Model.[137]

---

133. 2016 US Model, Art. 3(1)(l)(iii).
134. 2016 US Model, Art. 22(4)(a). The requirements of the Derivative Benefits provision must be satisfied at the time when the benefit would be accorded, and on at least half of the days of a twelve-month period commencing or ending on the date when the benefit otherwise would be accorded. Previous versions of the Derivative Benefits test did not specify the time at which the test must be satisfied.
135. Provided that those residents qualify for benefits under certain specific clauses of the LOB.
136. Provided those residents qualify for benefits under specific clauses of the LOB and do not own more than 25% of the company in the aggregate. 2016 US Model, Art. 22(7)(e).
137. 2016 US Model, Art. 22(7)(f). The Derivative Benefits test in the 2016 US Model also provides that where the taxpayer seeking benefits earns income through an entity treated as fiscally transparent in the taxpayer's jurisdiction, an owner will not qualify as an Equivalent Beneficiary with respect to that income if that owner would not be treated as deriving that income (under a provision analogous to Art. 1(6) of the US Model) if the owner had directly owned the entity through which the income was derived.

- Under the Base-Erosion Requirement, in general, a company's deductible payments (excluding arm's-length payments in the ordinary course of business for tangible property or services) to persons that are not Equivalent Beneficiaries (or to Equivalent Beneficiaries that are connected persons benefiting from an STR or notional deduction in their resident country) must be less than 50% of the company's gross income and less than 50% of the Tested Group's gross income.[138] The Tested Group means the resident of the contracting country that is claiming treaty benefits and any company that is a member of a tax consolidation regime or similar group regime that allows group members to aggregate profits or losses.[139]
- The Rate Requirement in the Derivative Benefits provisions in existing treaties has been modified significantly. Some of these changes include addressing the cliff effect that applies under previous Derivative Benefits provisions. For example, the articles on interest,[140] dividends,[141] and royalties[142] of the 2016 US Model now provide that where an owner of the taxpayer seeking benefits meets all of the requirements of the Derivative Benefits provision other than the Rate Requirement, the taxpayer will get the worst of the benefits to which its owners would have been entitled, rather than losing benefits entirely. In some cases, the modifications go beyond merely removing the cliff effect. For example, the Rate Requirement has been modified to make the 5% rate on direct dividends available to certain companies engaged in an active trade or business, even where the owner is an individual who would not have been entitled to the 5% rate directly.[143]

2. New Headquarters Company Test

Under the new Headquarters Company test, a company resident in a contracting state and acting as a headquarters company for a multinational corporate group is entitled to treaty benefits with respect to interest[144] and dividends paid by members of the multinational corporate group if certain conditions are satisfied.

To qualify for benefits as a headquarters company, the company's multinational corporate group must consist of companies resident in, and engaged in the active conduct of a trade or business in at least four countries, and the trades or businesses carried on in each of the four countries (or four groupings of countries) must generate at least 10% of the gross income of the group. In addition, the trades or businesses of the multinational corporate group that are carried on in any one state other than

---

138. 2016 US Model, Art. 22(4)(b). The term 'gross income' does not include the portion of any dividends effectively exempt from tax in the person's resident country. 2016 US Model, Art. 22(7)(h).
139. 2016 US Model, Art. 22(7)(g).
140. 2016 US Model, Art. 11(3).
141. 2016 US Model, Art. 10(6).
142. 2016 US Model, Art. 12(3).
143. 2016 US Model, Art. 22(7)(e)(i)(B)(1).
144. Under this test, the lowest withholding rate on interest paid to the headquarters company is 10%. 2016 US Model, Art. 11(2)(f).

the company's state of residence must generate less than 50% of the gross income of the group, and the company must derive 25% or less of its gross income from the other contracting state. These numerical tests will be treated as satisfied if they are either satisfied in the relevant taxable year or by averaging the preceding four taxable years. The 2016 US Model requires a headquarters company to exercise primary management and control functions in its residence country with respect to itself and its subsidiaries. A taxpayer that wishes to claim benefits under this test also must satisfy a Base-Erosion test.[145]

3. Active Trade or Business and Publicly Traded Company Subsidiary Tests

The 2016 US Model retains the basic framework of the Active Trade or Business test in the 2006 US Model, which generally allowed a resident of one country engaged in the active conduct of a trade or business in its resident country to receive treaty benefits with respect to an item of income derived from the other contracting country *in connection with,* or *incidental to,* that trade or business.[146] The 2016 US Model, however, narrows the scope of income that can qualify for benefits by requiring that the income 'emanates from, or is incidental to' the active trade or business in the residence country. The preamble to the 2016 US Model states that under this revised test, the mere fact that two companies are in similar lines of business would not be sufficient to establish that dividends or interest paid between them are related to the active conduct of a trade or business. The preamble further states that the upcoming TE to the 2016 US Model will provide guidance regarding when an item of income, in particular intra-group dividend or interest payments, is considered to qualify for benefits under this test.

The 2016 US Model also adds a new Base-Erosion test to the Publicly Traded Company Subsidiary test, which applies to corporations claiming treaty benefits for income other than dividends.[147] The Base-Erosion test is substantially similar to the Base-Erosion test found in the new Derivative Benefits provision discussed above.

C. Triangular Permanent Establishments

The 2016 US Model adds a new Triangular PE provision. This new provision would deny treaty benefits for US source income if the taxpayer's residence country treats the income as attributable to a PE situated outside that country, and either:

- the profits of the PE are subject to a combined aggregate effective tax rate in the residence state and the state in which the PE is situated that is less than the lesser of (1) 15% or (2) 60% of the general company tax rate applicable in the residence state; or

---

145. 2016 US Model, Art. 22(5).
146. 2016 US Model, Art. 22(3)(a).
147. 2016 US Model, Art. 22(2)(d).

- the PE is situated in a third country that does not have a comprehensive income tax treaty with the US and the taxpayer's resident country does not include the income attributable to the PE in its tax base.[148]

Nonetheless, the US competent authority may grant treaty benefits with respect to a specific item of income if such grant of benefits is justified (e.g., because the low effective tax rate is due to incurring losses).[149]

D. Denial of Treaty Benefits Following Law Change

The 2016 US Model adds Article 28, which generally triggers a consultation between the two treaty countries to determine whether to amend the treaty when:

- the general statutory rate of company tax of a treaty partner falls below the lesser of either a 15% rate or 60% of the general statutory rate of company tax applicable in the other treaty partner; or
- a treaty partner provides an exemption from taxation to resident companies for substantially all foreign source income (including interest and royalties).

If the consultation does not progress, the US has the right to cease to apply the provisions of Articles 10 (Dividends), 11 (Interest), 12 (Royalties) and 21 (Other Income) by notifying the treaty partner through diplomatic channels; the cessation takes effect six months after diplomatic notice. The application of Article 28 would affect only the aforementioned articles; it would not terminate the treaty or affect any other provisions of the treaty (e.g., the PE and business profits articles would continue to apply as intended).

E. Dividend Article

The 2016 US Model maintains two levels of withholding tax rates for dividends – 5% and 15% – and adopts the requirements from the OECD BEPS initiative that impose additional ownership and residency requirements in order to obtain the 5% rate. The beneficial owner claiming the 5% rate must for a twelve-month period ending on the date on which it is entitled to the dividends: (1) be resident in the other contracting country or a qualifying third country; and (2) own at least 10% of the vote and value of the shares of the payor or a Qualifying Predecessor Owner. For the purposes of this requirement, the qualifying third country must be a country with a comprehensive income tax treaty with the US that provides for a preferential 5% rate with similar terms.

A Qualifying Predecessor Owner is any connected person from whom the beneficial owner of the dividends acquired the shares and such connected person was a connected person at the time of acquisition. For purposes of this test, a resident of a contracting country is considered to directly own shares held by a fiscally transparent entity that is not a resident of the other contracting country in proportion to the company's ownership interest in that entity. In addition, the term dividends

---

148. 2016 US Model, Art. 1(8).
149. *Id.*

now explicitly excludes distributions that are treated as gains under the law of the contracting country where the company is making the distribution.

§9.07 SUMMARY

In general, treaties can significantly reduce a foreign taxpayer's overall US tax burden. In the case of a foreign corporate investor in USRPIs, an important benefit is to reduce the 30% branch profits tax rate that is otherwise applicable. To qualify for treaty benefits, a taxpayer must conduct an annual, and in some cases, an item-by-item analysis to determine whether it is eligible to claim benefits with respect to a particular item of income or a specific provision. The LOB rules in US treaties are complex and may require a taxpayer to provide information that is not otherwise maintained. It is advisable for affected taxpayers to perform the proper analysis and to maintain the required information to satisfy all the treaty requirements they are claiming on a contemporaneous basis.

APPENDIX 9-A

UNITED STATES INCOME TAX TREATIES IN FORCE AS OF MARCH 31, 2017.
The entry into force date is provided in parentheses.

Armenia (January 29, 1976)
Australia (October 31, 1983)
Austria (February 1, 1998)
Azerbaijan (January 29, 1976)
Bangladesh (August 7, 2006)
Barbados (February 28, 1986)
Belarus (January 29, 1976)
Belgium (December 28, 2007)
Bulgaria (December 15, 2008)
Bermuda (January 1, 1986)
Canada (August 16, 1984)
People's Republic of China (November 21, 1986)
Cyprus (December 31, 1985)
Czech Republic (December 23, 1993)
Denmark (March 31, 2000)
Egypt (December 31, 1981)
Estonia (December 30, 1999)
Finland (December 30. 1990)
France (December 30, 1995)
Georgia (January 29, 1976)
Germany (August 21, 1991)
Greece (December 30, 1953)
Hungary (September 12, 1979)
Iceland (December 15, 2008)
India (December 18, 1990)
Indonesia (December 30, 1990)
Ireland (December 17, 1997)
Israel (December 30, 1994)
Italy (December 16, 2009)
Jamaica (December 29, 1981)
Japan (March 30, 2004)
Kazakhstan (December 30, 1996)
Korea, Rep. (October 20, 1979)
Kyrgyzstan (January 1, 1976)

Latvia (December 30, 1999)
Lithuania (December 30, 1999)
Luxembourg (December 20, 2000)
Malta (November 23, 2010)
Mexico (December 28, 1993)
Moldova (January 29, 1976)
Morocco (December 30, 1981)
Netherlands (December 31, 1993)
New Zealand (November 2, 1983)
Norway (November 29, 1972)
Pakistan (May 21, 1959)
Philippines (October 16, 1982)
Poland (July 22, 1976)
Portugal (December 18, 1995)
Romania (January 26, 1976)
Russia (December 16, 1993)
Slovak Republic (December 29, 1993)
Slovenia (June 22, 2001)
South Africa (December 28, 1997)
Spain (November 21, 1990)
Sri Lanka (July 12, 2004)
Sweden (October 26, 1995)
Switzerland (December 19, 1997)
Tajikistan (January 29, 1976)
Thailand (December 15, 1997)
Trinidad & Tobago (December 30, 1970)
Tunisia (December 26, 1990)
Turkey (December 19, 1997)
Turkmenistan (January 29, 1976)
Ukraine (June 5, 2000)
United Kingdom (March 31, 2003)
Uzbekistan (January 29, 1976)
Venezuela (December 30, 1999)

Chapter 10
Entity Classifications and Interest Deductions

§10.01	Overview	283
§10.02	Entity Classification Rules	284
§10.03	Debt Equity Considerations	286
	A. Common Law and the Codification of Section 385	287
	B. The 385 Regulations	288
	1. Documentation Requirements	289
	2. Recast Rules	290
§10.04	Other Applicable Doctrines	292
	A. Transfer Pricing – Section 482	293
	B. Acquisitions Made to Evade or Avoid Tax – Section 269	294
	C. Economic Substance Doctrine – Section 7701(o)	295
§10.05	Limitations on Interest Deductions	295
	A. Interest Owed to Related Person	296
	B. Earnings Stripping Limitation	297
§10.06	Withholding Tax on Interest	299
	A. Portfolio Interest Exemption	299
	B. Anti-Conduit Financing Rules	301
§10.06	Summary	303
Appendix 10-A		305

§10.01 OVERVIEW

When a foreign person invests in one or more USRPIs through a US corporation, commonly referred to as a Blocker Corporation, the income from the underlying investment is subject to US entity-level tax.[1] The US entity classification rules generally allow a taxpayer to elect the US tax characterization of an entity regardless of the

---

1. After initial brackets, the current top marginal federal income tax rate for corporations is 35%. I.R.C. §11. As discussed in §2.04.C., *supra,* there are a number of benefits for using a Blocker. As the US tax reporting vehicle, the Blocker prevents attribution of the trade or business of any underlying flow-through entity. *Cf.* I.R.C. §875. In addition, an

legal form of the entity. Therefore, investors may use limited liability companies or limited partnerships as their Blockers provided that they make the proper entity classification elections.

Blockers typically are funded with a combination of equity (common and/or preferred) as well as debt (internal and external). Indebtedness is typically evidenced by a loan document which provides for a fixed schedule of principal and interest payments over a defined time period. In the event of bankruptcy, debt holders typically have a priority to the proceeds of the entity. Equity investments, on the other hand, may not provide for regular payments, and typically only entitle the equity holder to income when the entity is profitable (e.g., in the form of dividends). Equity holders also have a lower priority than debt holders in the event the entity files for bankruptcy. The tax laws of most other countries follow the legal form of a transaction. Thus, intercompany loans generally are respected as debt for local country tax purposes. Some countries apply thin capital rules to determine whether all or a portion of the amount of related party interest is deductible.

The US tax rules on interest deductibility are uniquely complicated. At its core, the US applies a substance over form principle in administering its tax law. Therefore, an instrument that is legally structured as an intercompany loan may *not* be respected as debt unless the substance of the transaction supports such a characterization. Once a loan is respected as debt for US tax purposes, a variety of provisions apply to potentially limit the amount of the interest deduction allowed. Hence, a Blocker needs to navigate the different provisions developed under case law, the statute and the regulations in order to sustain its US interest deduction incurred on intercompany debt. This chapter discusses the highlights of some of these provisions and their application to a Blocker.[2]

§10.02 ENTITY CLASSIFICATION RULES

Treasury regulations govern the US tax characterization of legal entities.[3] A business entity[4] that is not a *per se* corporation[5] is an eligible entity which may elect its classification for US tax purposes under the so-called Check-the-Box rules.[6] For example, a US limited partnership and a limited liability company are eligible entities that may

---

uncontrolled Blocker protects a foreign sovereign investor that is available for the 892 Exemption from being connected to a commercial activity. See discussion in §6.04, *supra*.

2. The objective of this chapter is to raise awareness of the most common issues that arise in situations involving straightforward debt funding of a US Blocker by a foreign corporate shareholder. This chapter does not cover issues that may arise in situations where taxpayers enter into a transaction that may enable them to deduct the same interest expense in the US and abroad, i.e., a double-dip transactions, or to create an interest deduction in the US without an associated income inclusion in another country.
3. *See*, generally, Treas. Reg. §301.7701-2 and -3.
4. Treas. Reg. §301.7701-2(a). Generally, a business entity is an entity other than a trust. *See* Treas. Reg. §301.7701-4 for the trust classification rules.
5. *See, generally*, Treas. Reg. §301.7701-2(b). For example, US business entities that are treated as *per se* entities include an entity organized under a statute that refers to the entity as incorporated or as a corporation or body corporate.
6. Treas. Reg. §301.7701-3(a).

10. Entity Classifications and Interest Deductions

elect to be taxed as either a corporation or a pass-through entity for US tax purposes. In the absence of an election, an eligible US entity will default to be *a partnership* if it has two or more members and as a disregarded entity if it has just one member.[7] To make a Check-the-Box election, the eligible entity must file Form 8832 with the IRS. The effective date of the election cannot be more than seventy-five days prior to the date on which the election is filed and cannot be more than twelve months after the date on which the election is filed.[8]

An entity that did not file the initial Form 8832 by the due date may seek late-filing relief.[9] To be eligible for an expedited process for such relief, the entity must either have not filed a federal tax or information return for the first year the election was intended because the due date has not passed for that year's return, or the entity (or each affected person if the entity is not required to file a US return) must have timely filed all required federal tax and information returns consistent with its requested classification for all the years the entity intended the election to be effective and no inconsistent tax or information returns have been filed during such period.[10] The entity must have reasonable cause for its failure to file a timely election and must request relief within three years and seventy-five days of the election's desired effective date. If these requirements cannot be met, the entity alternatively may request relief by applying for a private letter ruling.[11] There is also a USD 10,000 fee for applying for a letter ruling.[12]

An entity generally cannot change its tax classification again during the sixty months following the effective date of its Check-the-Box election with two exceptions.[13] The sixty-month limitation does not apply in the case of an initial classification election, i.e., an election made effective on the entity's formation date.[14] In addition, the IRS may waive the sixty-month restriction if there has been a substantial ownership change, i.e., more than 50%, since the effective date of change in classification.[15]

---

7. Treas. Reg. §301.7701-3(b)(1). An entity that elects REIT status is generally not required to file Form 8832. *See* Treas. Reg. §301.7701-3(c)(v)(B).
8. If no such date is specified on the election form, the election will be effective on the date filed.
9. Rev. Proc. 2009-41, 2009-2 C.B. 439. Late election relief is available when an otherwise valid Form 8832 was filed based on the reasonable assumption that the entity had either a single owner (if disregarded status was elected) or two or more owners (if partnership status was elected) and that assumption was incorrect. *See* Rev. Proc. 2010-32, 2010-2 C.B. 320.
10. For purposes of this requirement, a return will be considered timely if filed within six months of its due date (excluding extensions).
11. Such an entity is required to include a representation that their tax and information returns have been timely and consistently filed under the desired classification, or an explanation for the reason for not so filed.
12. *See* Rev. Proc. 2017-1, Appendix A, 2017-1 I.R.B. 1.
13. Treas. Reg. §301.7701-3(c)(1)(iv).
14. *Id.* For this reason, it may be beneficial to make a Check-the-Box election effective *as of* the formation date, if practicable, in order to provide more flexibility for subsequent elections, if needed.
15. *Id.*

As mentioned earlier, a Blocker is typically funded with a combination of debt and equity. 'Leveraging' a Blocker – meaning to capitalize the Blocker entity with debt in additional to equity – is a common tax planning strategy which has the dual benefit of reducing the borrower's US taxable income and increasing the amount of tax-free cash that may be repatriated to the foreign investor. The different US tax consequences on the payments with respect to an instrument that is characterized as debt versus equity are summarized below.

§10.03 DEBT EQUITY CONSIDERATIONS

US tax principles generally view a loan as a legal liability for a specific amount.[16] Interest on the loan is defined as 'compensation for the use or forbearance of money.'[17] Case law has disallowed interest deductions where the facts suggested that the underlying debt instrument was more appropriately treated as equity.[18] Recently issued regulations under Code section 385, referred to as the 385 Regulations, grant the IRS authority to recast intercompany debt as equity if certain conditions are met.[19]

If an instrument is respected as debt, then periodic interest payments on the instrument generally should be *deductible* by the Blocker in determining its US taxable income.[20] The interest payments may be *exempt* from US tax under a treaty or the statutory Portfolio Interest Exemption.[21] Repayment of the principal of the debt is *tax-free* to the lender. On the other hand, if an instrument is treated, or recast, as equity investment in the Blocker, then the Blocker may not deduct the periodic payments. Such payments are characterized, in the hands of the shareholder, as:

(1) *taxable* dividends to the extent of its earnings and profits.[22] Dividends are usually subject to *higher* treaty withholding rates than interest and are exempt only in a narrow set of cases;[23]

(2) distributions in excess of earnings and profits are *tax-free* returns of capital[24] that reduce the shareholder's stock basis;[25] and

---

16. Black's Law Dictionary (10th ed. 2014), DEBT.
17. *See Deputy v. du Pont*, 308 U.S. 488 (1940).
18. *See, e.g., Plantation Patterns Inc. v. Comm'r*, 462 F.2d 712 (5th Cir. 1972) (Court attributed a debt obligation of a corporate borrower to its shareholder because the corporate borrower was unlikely to be able to repay the debt and it was unlikely the lender would have lent the money absent the shareholder's guarantee); *Laidlaw Transportation, Inc. v. Comm'r*, T.C. Memo 1998-232, (Tax Ct. 1998) (cash advances from Dutch subsidiary to Taxpayer were not treated as debt because, in part, interest payments were made to the Canadian parent).
19. This is the first set of permanent Treasury guidance issued since the codification of I.R.C. §385 almost five decades ago.
20. I.R.C. §163(a) (but see the later discussion on various limitations on the interest deduction).
21. *See* discussion in §10.06.A., *infra*, regarding the requirements to qualify for this exemption.
22. I.R.C. §316.
23. *See* discussion in §9.05.C., *supra*.
24. I.R.C. §301(c)(2).
25. *Id.*

(3) distributions in excess of basis are capital gains, and *taxable* to a foreign shareholder, if the corporation is a USRPHC.[26] Repayment/redemption of stock can give rise to *taxable* dividends or capital gain as stated above.[27]

A. Common Law and the Codification of Section 385

Prior to 1969, the guidance on what constitutes debt and equity in various fact patterns was primarily developed in the courts. It was established, early on in the process, that no single criteria was dispositive in determining whether a corporate interest is debt or equity for tax purposes.[28] Furthermore, there is no uniform system for courts to weigh the importance of particular factors when performing a debt-equity analysis.[29] As a result, the legal analysis for determining whether a corporate interest constitutes debt or equity varies across the different courts in the US, and the outcome of such analyses depends on the specific facts and circumstances of each case.

In *Fin Hay Realty Co. v. U.S.*,[30] the Third Circuit referenced sixteen factors commonly cited in previous case law.[31] Other courts have developed similar lists of factors in varying quantities.[32] Shortly thereafter, the Tax Reform Act of 1969[33] enacted Code section 385 to provide guidance on the characterization of debt versus equity. Rather than prescribing a finite set of rules defining what constitutes debt versus equity, the statute authorizes the Treasury Department to promulgate regulations in order to address the different scenarios in which a debt-equity analysis may arise.[34] The regulations are required to set forth factors to be considered when determining whether a debtor-creditor or corporation-shareholder relationship exists.[35]

---

26. I.R.C. §301(c)(3).
27. *See* I.R.C. §302.
28. *See John Kelley Co. v. Comm'r*, 326 US 521, 530 (1946).
29. *See Tyler v. Tomlinson*, 414 F2d 844, 848 (5th Cir. 1969).
30. 398 F.2d 694 (3rd Cir. 1968).
31. The factors are: (i) the intent of the parties, (ii) the identity between creditors and shareholders, (iii) the extent of participation in management by the holder of the instrument, (iv) the ability of the corporation to obtain funds from outside sources, (v) the thinness of the capital structure in relation to debt, (vi) the risk involved, (vii) the formal indicia of the arrangement, (viii) the relative position of the borrowers as to other creditors regarding the payment of interest and principal, (ix) the voting power of the holder of the instrument, (x) the provision of a fixed rate of interest, (xi) a contingency on the obligation to repay, (xii) the source of the interest payments, (xiii) the presence or absence of a fixed maturity date, (xiv) a provision for redemption by the corporation, (xv) a provision for redemption at the option of the holder, and (xvi) the timing of the advance with reference to the organization of the corporation.
32. *See, e.g., Estate of Mixon*, 464 F.2d 394 (5th Cir. 1972) (13 factors); *Hardman v. U.S.*, 827 F.2d 1409 (9th Cir. 1987) (11 factors).
33. P.L. 91-172, 83 Stat. 487 (Dec. 30, 1969).
34. *Id.*
35. I.R.C. §385(b). Such factors may include whether there is a written unconditional promise to pay on demand or on a specified date a sum certain in money in return for an adequate consideration in money or money's worth, and to pay a fixed rate of interest, whether there is subordination to or preference over any indebtedness of the corporation, the ratio of debt to equity of the corporation, whether there is convertibility into the stock of

The IRS later issued its own set of factors for instruments designed to be treated as debt for tax purposes but as equity for regulatory purposes stating that no particular factor is conclusive. The factors are whether:

- there is an unconditional promise on the part of the issuer to pay a sum certain on demand or at a fixed maturity date that is in the reasonably foreseeable future;
- holders of the instruments possess the right to enforce the payment of principal and interest;
- the rights of the holders of the instruments are subordinate to the rights of general creditors;
- the instruments give the holders the right to participate in the management of the issuer;
- the issuer is thinly capitalized;
- there is identity between the holders of the instruments and stockholders of the issuer;
- the name of the instrument; and
- the instruments are intended to be treated as debt or equity for non-tax purposes.[36]

No one factor is determinative. The weight given to a particular factor varies from case to case. Whether an instrument should be treated as debt or equity depends on the totality of the underlying facts and circumstances. The recently promulgated regulations, discussed below, perpetuate the common law, factor-based analysis:

> Except as otherwise provided ... whether an interest in a corporation is treated for purposes of the Internal Revenue Code as stock or indebtedness (or as part stock and in part indebtedness) is determined based on common law, including the factors prescribed under such common law.[37]

B. The 385 Regulations

The Treasury Department and the IRS issued the first set of debt-equity regulations in 1980, but subsequently withdrew them after several years' worth of unsuccessful attempts to develop a workable regime.[38] More than three decades later, they issued proposed regulations in April, 2016, and promulgated the final and temporary regulations in October, 2016 (such final and temporary regulations being the 385 Regulations).[39] These regulations, substantially pared down from the April 2016 proposed version, still represent a very significant change from prior law. The 385 Regulations now primarily target cross-border debt owed by a US borrower to its foreign related

---

the corporation, and the relationship between holdings of stock in the corporation and holdings of the interest in question.
36. Notice 94-47, 1994-1 CB 357.
37. Treas. Reg. §1.385-1(b). *See* William T. Plumb Jr., *The Federal Income Tax Significance of Corporate Debt: A Critical Analysis and a Proposal,* 26 Tax L. Rev. 369 (1971), for an in-depth analysis of debt versus equity characterization.
38. T.D. 7920, 1983-2 C.B. 69 (November 3, 1983).
39. T.D. 9790, 81 Fed. Reg. 72,858 (October 21, 2016).

parties (i.e., these regulations target US Blockers). There are two key components to the 385 Regulations: (i) the Documentation Requirements and (ii) the Recast Rules.

The substantive effect of a taxpayer failing to satisfy the Documentation Requirements or running afoul of the Recast Rules is the same: an instrument at issue, which would otherwise be treated as debt for US tax purposes, is instead treated as equity. The Documentation Requirements apply to debt issued on after January 1, 2019.[40] The Recast Rules apply to transactions occurring and debt issued after April 4, 2016.[41] The new rules generally do not apply to a related group that does not have any publicly traded members and a group the assets or revenue of which does not exceed a minimum threshold.[42] Certain key features of these new rules are discussed below.

1.   Documentation Requirements

In general, related parties must document their intention to create debt and their continuing behavior must demonstrate that intent. The new rules are applicable to debt issued by a Blocker to foreign affiliates and certain related US entities. A Blocker's failure to comply with these rules will automatically result in the related party debt being treated as equity for US tax purposes. Even if the Blocker meets the Documentation Requirements, the debt instrument must still be evaluated under the common law factors discussed above for determining debt treatment.

Generally, the Document Requirements apply to debt, referred to as an Expanded Group Interest (or EGI),[43] issued by a Blocker to a related party, referred to as member of an Expanded Group,[44] outside of the issuer's US consolidated group. The 385 Regulations require the Blocker to maintain information to establish that the EGI is debt for US tax purposes. Such documentation should include evidence of:

- an unconditional obligation to pay a sum certain;[45]
- minimum rights of the creditor (e.g., rights to trigger default) and obligations of the debtor (e.g., to pay interest and/or maintain financial ratios);[46]

---

40. Treas. Reg. §1.385-3(d)(2)(iii). The IRS delayed the application of the Documentation Requirements by one year from the original effective date of January 1, 2018. The documentation regulations will apply only to interests issued or deemed issued on or after January 1, 2019. See Notice 2017-36, 2017 I.R.B. 33.
41. However, pursuant to a ninety-day transition rule beginning after the October 21, 2016 final release, any debt that would run afoul of the Recast Rules from April 5, 2016 through January 19, 2017, was not recast into equity until January 20, 2017. Treas. Reg. §1.385-3(j)(2).
42. In general, the total assets or the total revenue of the related group must exceed USD 100 million or USD 50 million, respectively. See Treas. Reg. §1.385-2(a)(3)(ii).
43. Treas. Reg. §1.385-2(d)(3). EGIs include interests issued in the legal form of a debt instrument, and intercompany payables/receivables documented as debt in a ledger. Treas. Reg. §1.385-2(d)(2)(iii). EGIs exclude certain instruments such as intercompany obligations, payables deemed to arise due to transfer pricing adjustments, certain production payments and REMIC regular interests. See Treas. Reg. §1.385-2(d)(2)(iii).
44. Treas. Reg. §1.385-1(c)(4).
45. Treas. Reg. §1.385-2(c)(2)(i).
46. Treas. Reg. §1.385-2(c)(2)(ii).

- reasonable expectations of the borrower's ability to repay;[47] and
- timely payments of the required interest and principal amounts (or, in the event of default, evidence that the creditor is enforcing its rights).[48]

The required documentation must be in place by the time the Blocker files its US federal income tax return, including extensions, for the tax year that includes the Relevant Date.[49] The 385 Regulations provide limited exceptions to the Documentation Requirements. The most important exception is that if the Expanded Group of which a Blocker is highly compliant with the Documentation Requirements, then the Blocker may overcome the presumption that the EGI is stock if it clearly establishes that there are sufficient common law factors present to treat the EGI as indebtedness.[50]

2. Recast Rules

At a high level, there are two components to the Recast Rules. The general rule provides that any debt instrument, referred to as a Covered Debt Instrument (or CDI),[51] issued by a Covered Member in connection with one out of three categories of specified transactions would be automatically recharacterized as equity to the amount of the transactions. A Covered Member is a domestic corporation (including a Blocker) that is a member of an Expanded Group of entities connected by 80% vote or value, direct or indirect ownership.[52] The three categories of specified transactions are:

- distributions of a CDI to a shareholder of the Blocker (other than an exempt distribution);[53]
- issuance of a CDI to acquire stock in an Expanded Group member (other than in an exempt exchange);[54] or
- issuance of a CDI as 'boot'[55] in an inter-Expanded Group asset reorganization.[56]

---

47. Treas. Reg. §1.385-2(c)(2)(iii).
48. Treas. Reg. §1.385-2(c)(2)(iv).
49. Treas. Reg. §1.385-2(c)(4). In general, the Relevant Date is the date on which a covered member becomes the issuer of a new or existing EGI; the Relevant Date includes the date of a deemed exchange triggered by a significant modification under Treas. Reg. §1.1001-3 if the deemed exchange relates to a written modification of the EGI's terms; and if an applicable interest becomes an EGI after its issuance, the Relevant Date is the date it becomes an EGI.
50. Treas. Reg. §1.385-2(b)(2)(i). Other exceptions include a 'reasonable cause exception' and a 'ministerial or non-material error exception.' See Treas. Reg. §1.385-2(b)(2)(ii) and (iii).
51. A CDI is a debt instrument issued after April 4, 2016 by a Covered Member. See Treas. Reg. §1.385-3(g)(3)(i). CDIs exclude certain instruments such as qualified dealer debt instruments, production payments treated as a loan, regular interests in a REMIC, debt instruments deemed to arise due to transfer pricing adjustments, stripped bonds and coupons, leases treated as loans, and debt instruments issued by certain regulated financial or insurance companies. See Treas. Reg. §1.385-3(g)(3)(ii) and (iii).
52. Treas. Reg. §1.385-1(c)(2).
53. Treas. Reg. §1.385-3(b)(3)(i)(A).
54. Treas. Reg. §1.385-3(b)(3)(i)(B).
55. This is generally defined as money or other property within the meaning of I.R.C. §368.
56. Treas. Reg. §1.385-3(b)(3)(i)(C).

10. Entity Classifications and Interest Deductions

Example 10.1 illustrates the application of the general rule regarding a distribution of a CDI by US1, a Blocker, to its foreign parent company, FP. Unless an exemption applies, the USD 100 Note that US1 distributes to FP may be recast as stock for US tax purposes.

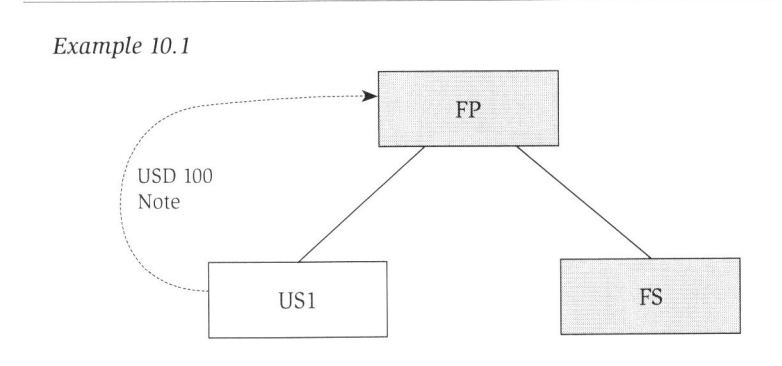

Example 10.1

[Diagram: FP at top, with US1 and FS below connected to FP. A dashed arrow labeled "USD 100 Note" goes from US1 to FP.]

The Funding Rule, the second part of the Recast Rule, treats as stock any debt instrument issued by a funded member in exchange for property that was treated as funding one of the three specified transactions described above. **Example 10.2** illustrates the application of the Funding Rule with respect to a loan by FS to US1 followed by US1's distribution of an equivalent amount of property to FP. The economic result of the transactions in **Example 10.2** is the same as that in **Example 10.1**. The loan from FS to US1 may be recast as stock under the Funding Rule.

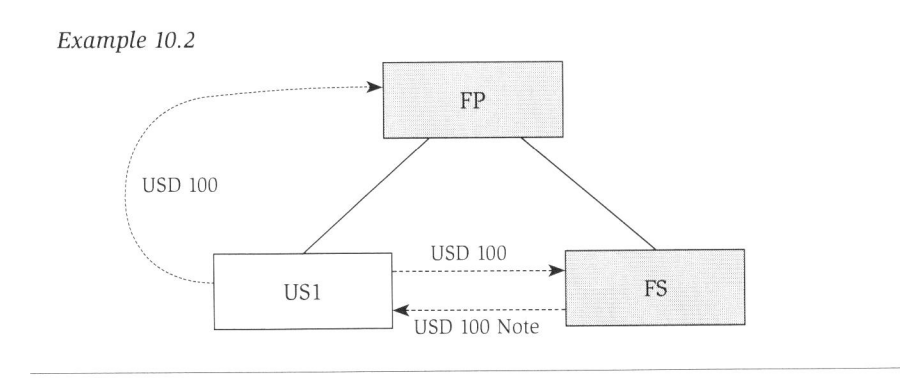

Example 10.2

[Diagram: FP at top, with US1 and FS below connected to FP. A dashed arrow labeled "USD 100" goes from US1 to FP. Between US1 and FS: "USD 100" arrow from US1 to FS, and "USD 100 Note" arrow from FS to US1.]

There is an objective prong and a subjective prong of the Funding Rule. Under the objective prong, a CDI is treated as funding an acquisition or distribution to the extent the issuer issues the CDI within the *per se* period that applies to the acquisition or distribution. The *per se* period covers the thirty-six months *before and* the thirty-six months *after* the date of the acquisition or distribution. There is no exception to this seventy-two-month *per se* period. Under the subjective prong, a CDI issued outside

291

of the *per se* period would be recast only if the Covered Member entered into a transaction with a principal purpose of avoiding the Recast Rule.[57]

There are a number of exclusions to the Recast Rules and various exceptions to the exclusions. The most significant exclusions include: (1) distribution of a Covered Member's earnings and profits accumulated in tax years ending after April 4, 2016;[58] (2) distributions of amounts of Qualified Contributions that were previously added to the Covered Member's capital;[59] and (3) a USD 50 million threshold exemption that must be exceeded before the 385 Regulations can apply at all.[60] Hence, a CDI, even if issued in connection with a specified transaction, is not recharacterized as stock to the extent of these exclusions apply.

Due to the broad reach of the Recast Rule, affected taxpayers should adopt (if they do not already have in place) robust processes and controls to enhance internal communications, e.g., between the treasury department and the tax department, to monitor distributions and any debt issuances by a Blocker to avoid any adverse US tax consequences.

§10.04 OTHER APPLICABLE DOCTRINES

In some cases, simply following the literal meaning of the law may not be enough to warrant a deduction if the taxpayer's actions are perceived to have a tax avoidance motive or are, in substance, different in a meaningful way from what the taxpayer has asserted them to be. Even without regard to intent, the IRS also may simply challenge a Blocker's interest deduction under common law doctrines, some of which have been codified in different statutory provisions. For example, the IRS may:

- apply the transfer pricing rules under Code section 482 to recharacterize a debt instrument as equity, or to partially disallow the interest expense on a loan, in order to properly reflect income between related parties; or
- apply one of the anti-abuse provisions, e.g., Code section 269 or 7701(o), to disregard or recast either an overall transaction or just disallow a Blocker's interest deduction.

Anti-abuse provisions are broadly drafted by design to give the IRS latitude to address situations that are not contemplated. Therefore, it is hard to foresee how the IRS may apply these authorities in a particular situation. Nonetheless, these provisions form a part of the IRS's arsenal of tools to potentially disallow interest deductions and, hence, are mentioned briefly here. These provisions may be applied in addition to, not in lieu of, the 385 Regulations.

---

57. Treas. Reg. §1.385-3(b)(4).
58. Treas. Reg. §1.385-3(c)(3)(i).
59. Treas. Reg. §1.385-3(c)(3)(ii). Generally, Qualified Contributions are property (but excluding stock and debt of affiliates) contributed to the US corporation Covered Member in exchange for stock. In particular, the initial capitalization of a Blocker with cash should be a Qualified Contribution if the Blocker is part of an Expanded Group with the contributing shareholder. In this case, the capital contribution can provide an additional buffer against the Recast Rules afterwards.
60. Treas. Reg. §1.385-3(c)(4).

A.   Transfer Pricing – Section 482

This provision in the Code grants the IRS significant authority to reallocate income or expense between controlled entities to clearly reflect their taxable income or to prevent the evasion of taxes.[61] The applicable definition of 'control' is very broad and includes persons owning more than 50% of the interest in a Blocker.[62] In the cross-border context, the Treasury Department and the IRS may invoke the transfer pricing rules for transactions between a foreign owner and a Blocker.

The regulations generally require that related parties price transactions using an arm's-length standard.[63] The regulations further set out methods for determining a range of arm's-length prices, and the US entity is required to choose the best method for determining this arm's-length range.[64] With respect to bona fide indebtedness between related entities, the IRS requires that the interest rate charged by the related lender reflect an arm's-length interest rate that would have been charged between two unrelated parties under similar circumstances.[65] If the related lender is not in the business of making loans to unrelated third parties, the regulations provide a safe harbor rate range between 100% and 130% of the applicable federal rate.[66] The safe harbor provision is only available for loans denominated in US dollars, which often presents foreign currency issues when such loans involve non-US affiliates.

Even when a taxpayer uses comparable commercial interest rates as a proxy for an arm's-length rate, or otherwise chooses a rate within the acceptable range of arm's-length results, the taxpayer nevertheless may be subject to an accuracy-related penalty if there is no documentation showing the taxpayer reasonably followed the requirements of the Transfer Pricing rules.[67] As a result, many taxpayers perform, internally or externally, a debt capacity analysis which may include:

- credit ratings of the debt issuer together with financial statements relied upon;
- cash flow projections over the life of the debt showing ability to service and repay the debt;
- key financial ratios (e.g., EBITDA leverage and interest coverage) and similar information for comparable uncontrolled companies – one could perform a benchmarking analysis or alternatively use industry averages as appropriate;
- size of debt market for uncontrolled issuances with similar credit ratings; and

---

61. See I.R.C. §482. The IRS has invoked I.R.C. §482 to reclassify intercompany advances as equity or debt depending on the facts and circumstances of the particular situation. See, e.g., PLR 8302015 (9/30/82); FSA 199921002 (5/28/99).
62. See also Forman Co., Inc. v. Comm'r, 453 F2d 1144 (2nd Cir. 1972) (two 50% shareholders acting in concert held to 'control' subsidiary).
63. Treas. Reg. §1.482-1(b)(1).
64. Treas. Reg. §1.482-1(c)(1).
65. Treas. Reg. §1.482-2(a)(2)(i).
66. Treas. Reg. §1.482-2(a)(2)(iii).
67. See Treas. Reg. §1.6662-6(d)(2)(iii). The contemporaneous documentation only protects a taxpayer from the imposition of the accuracy related penalty, and not from a potential reallocation of income or expense under I.R.C. §482. This is different from the Documentation Requirement of the 385 Regulations thereunder, discussed above, which must be satisfied in order for related party debt to be respected as debt.

- recent evidence of similarly large uncontrolled transactions for large intercompany debt issuances.

B. Acquisitions Made to Evade or Avoid Tax – Section 269

Another statutory anti-provision that should be considered when using a Blocker Corporation is Code section 269. This provision is applicable when any person or persons acquire, directly or indirectly, 'control' of a corporation and the principal purpose of the acquisition is the evasion or avoidance of federal income tax by securing the benefit of a deduction, credit or other allowance that such person would not otherwise enjoy. When this principal purpose test is met, the IRS may disallow such deduction, credit or other allowance. The principal purpose requirement is that the tax evasion or avoidance purpose must outrank, or exceed in importance, any other purpose.[68] 'Control', for this purpose, requires the ownership of stock possessing at least 50% of the total combined voting power of all classes of stock entitled to vote, or at least 50% of the total value of shares of all classes of stock of the corporation.[69]

Transactions that have been perceived as subject to the Code section 269 rules include: (1) a large, profitable corporation acquires control of a corporation with current, past, or prospective credits, deductions, net operating losses or other allowances and the acquisition is followed by transfers necessary to use these items to offset income of the acquiring corporation; and (2) a person or persons with income-generating assets transfer them to a newly organized controlled corporation while the transferors retain assets producing net operating losses which are utilized to secure refunds.[70] Thus, the two cases contemplate either combining income-producing with loss-producing assets to capture the benefit of the losses, or separating the income-producing assets from the loss-producing assets. While there are other provisions, such as Code section 382, that also restrict the ability to traffic in tax attributes such as net operating loss carryovers, Code section 269 is still in the statute and must still be considered when a corporate transaction falls within the scope of its application.

The provision requires a taxpayer to demonstrate that the avoidance of tax was not *the* principal purpose to overcome a disallowance by the IRS.[71] The purpose of an acquisition presents a question that takes into account all of the facts and circumstances of the transaction.[72] The inquiry is the intent or purpose of the acquiring person or corporation at the time of the acquisition.[73] Avoidance of US tax by acquiring control of a corporation may not be the principal purpose of a transaction if there are other significant business reasons for the acquisition of control of the corporation. Notwithstanding the presence of any business purpose

---

68. Treas. Reg. §1.269-3(a) (flush language).
69. I.R.C. §269(a).
70. Treas. Reg. §1.269-3(b).
71. *See Capri Inc. v. Comm'r*, 65 TC 162 (1975).
72. *See D'Arcy-MacManus & Masius, Inc. v. Comm'r*, 63 TC 440 (1975).
73. *See Southern Dredging Corp. v. Comm'r*, 54 TC 705 (1970).

factor, the principal purpose can still be tax avoidance if the value of the tax allowance greatly outweighs the value of the other asserted advantages.[74]

C. Economic Substance Doctrine – Section 7701(o)

The courts have developed several judicial doctrines to disallow tax benefits from tax-motivated transactions that otherwise satisfy the literal requirements of specific tax provisions. One of these is the Economic Substance Doctrine.[75] Because the courts did not apply the doctrine in a uniform manner, Congress codified the Economic Substance Doctrine for transactions entered into after March 30, 2010.[76] A transaction has economic substance if the taxpayer has, apart from federal income tax effects, both (1) an economic position changed by the transaction in a meaningful way; and (2) a substantial purpose for entering into the transaction. It is important to note that a 20% underpayment penalty applies to any tax benefits disallowed by reason of a transaction lacking economic substance.[77] In addition, a taxpayer may not assert a reasonable cause exception to avoid the penalty.[78]

§10.05   LIMITATIONS ON INTEREST DEDUCTIONS

Various limitations apply to determine the amount of interest expense that a Blocker may deduct with respect to related party debt in a particular year. These rules were added to the Internal Revenue Code at different times and for different policy reasons. Some of the definitions, e.g., whether certain parties are 'related' are similar in certain respects (e.g., the percentage owned) but different in other respects (e.g., the ownership may be measured by voting power or value or both for different provisions).[79] Further, different constructive ownership rules may apply to different rules causing additional confusion regarding the application of these rules.

---

74. *See Scroll, Inc. v. Comm'r*, 447 F.2d 612 (5th Cir. 1971).
75. *See* further discussion in Ch. 11, *infra*.
76. *See* I.R.C. §7701(o).
77. I.R.C. §6662(b)(6). In addition, the accuracy-related penalty is increased to 40% (from 20%) if an economic substance transaction is not adequately disclosed on the tax return. I.R.C. §6662(i).
78. See I.R.C. §§6664(d)(2) and 6676(c).
79. Note also that I.R.C. §6038A generally requires a Blocker that is at least 25% foreign owned to report transactions, including intercompany loans with 'related persons', on its US tax return. Although it is a reporting provision and does not limit the amount of interest deduction, a Blocker that fails to comply with this requirement may be subject to a USD 10,000 penalty for each failure. A related party for this purpose is defined to include a 25% shareholder of the reporting corporation, including a partnership (*e.g.*, a 'feeder fund' or other collective investment vehicle owning 25% or more of a Blocker Corporation). *See* I.R.C. §6038A(c)(2). Stated differently, the 25% shareholder test treats partnerships as 'entities' and not as 'aggregates' for this purpose.

A. Interest Owed to Related Person

Under US tax principles, domestic corporations generally are required to use the accrual (as opposed to the cash) method of accounting in computing their taxable income.[80] Interest expense ordinarily accrues and is deductible on a daily ratable basis by the debtor.[81] When the creditor is a related party, however, the debtor's interest expense deduction becomes contingent upon the timing of the lender's income inclusion – a so-called Matching Principle.

Under that principle, a Blocker may deduct accrued interest expense if the related lender[82] is accruing the interest income for US tax purposes even though the interest has not been paid. However, the same interest is not deductible if the related lender is a cash basis taxpayer. These related-party matching rules treat related foreign lenders as automatically on the cash method for US tax purposes, irrespective of their actual method of accounting. Consequently, where the related lender is a foreign person, a US Blocker may deduct interest expenses only when the amounts are paid.[83]

A US Blocker must analyze whether it is 'related' to the lender in order to determine whether the related party matching rules described above apply. There is a long, prescriptive list of ways individuals and entities are considered 'related' for purposes of these rules.[84] Some relevant relationship rules include:

- an individual and a corporation are related if more than 50% of the *value* of the outstanding stock is owned, directly or indirectly, by such individual;[85]
- a corporation and a partnership are related if the same persons own more than 50% of the *value* of the outstanding stock of the corporation, and more than 50% of the capital interest, or the profits interest, in the partnership;[86] and
- two corporations are related if they are part of a controlled group connected by more than 50% of *vote or value*.[87]

Moreover, when determining if a corporation is related to an individual or another entity, there are additional rules for determining the ownership of the stock of the corporation.[88] For example, if corporation A owns 80% of corporation B, and corporation B owns 80% of corporation C, corporation A will be deemed to own its proportionate share of the corporation C stock (i.e., 64%) for purposes of determining whether corporations A and C are 'related.'[89]

---

80. *See, e.g.,* I.R.C. §448.
81. *See* Treas. Reg. §1.446-2(b).
82. As defined in I.R.C. §267(a)(2).
83. I.R.C. §267(a)(3) and Treas. Reg. §1.267(a)-3(b). Note that an amount is treated as paid for purposes of this rule if the amount is considered paid for withholding tax purposes of I.R.C. §§1441 or 1442.
84. *See generally* I.R.C. §267(b).
85. *See* I.R.C. §267(b)(2).
86. *See* I.R.C. §267(b)(10).
87. See I.R.C. §267(b)(3), (f) and I.R.C. §1563(b).
88. *See generally* I.RC. §267(c).
89. *See* I.R.C. §267(c)(1).

10. Entity Classifications and Interest Deductions

B. Earnings Stripping Limitation

The US' version of 'thin cap' or Earnings Stripping rules, contained in Code section 163(j), limit deductions for interest paid to foreign related persons[90] that are not subject to US withholding tax under an income tax treaty.[91] If the Earnings Stripping limitations apply in a given taxable year, the US Blocker's Disqualified Interest may not be deducted to the extent of the corporation's Excess Interest Expense for the taxable year.[92] All Disallowed Interest deductions may be carried forward *indefinitely*, subject to future limitations.[93] The limitation may be expressed as a formula.[94]

Disallowed Interest = Disqualified Interest > 50% of Adusted Taxable Income

The definitions below apply for purposes of this determination.

- Disqualified Interest includes: (1) interest paid, directly or indirectly, to a related foreign person that is not subject to US federal income tax;[95] (2) interest paid to an unrelated US taxpayer where a related foreign person guarantees[96] the debt; or (3) interest paid, directly or indirectly, by a TRS to a REIT.[97]
- Excess Interest Expense is generally defined as the excess of (1) the corporation's Net Interest Expense, i.e., the amount by which the corporation's interest expense exceeds its interest income, over (2) the sum of 50% of the corporation's Adjusted Taxable Income plus any Excess Limitation carried forward.[98]

---

90. A related person, for this purpose, is defined as a person who, directly or indirectly, owns more than 50% of the value of the US Blocker's stock. I.R.C. §163(j)(4)(A). Interest paid or accrued to a partnership that would otherwise be considered a related person under this more-than-50% test will not be considered interest paid or accrued to a related person if persons not subject to tax hold less than 10% of the profits and capital interests in such partnership (except for interest allocable to a partner that is related to the US corporation paying the interest). I.R.C. §163(j)(4)(B).
91. Interest paid to a related party that is subject to a reduced rate of withholding is treated as partially not subject to US income tax to the extent of the rate reduction. I.R.C. §163(j)(5)(B). For example, if the US withholding tax on an interest payment is reduced from 30% to 15% under an income tax treaty, the earnings stripping rules would apply to one-half of the interest paid.
92. I.R.C. §163(j)(1)(A). The Earnings Stripping rules do not apply if the US Blocker's debt-to-equity ratio on the last day of its taxable year does not exceed 1.5 to 1. I.R.C. §163(j)(2)(A)(ii).
93. I.R.C. §163(j)(1)(B).
94. I.R.C. §163(j)(2)(A).
95. Interest paid to a pass-through entity, e.g., a partnership, is treated as being paid to the owners of such entity for purposes of determining whether the interest is Disqualified Interest. I.R.C. §163(j)(5)(A).
96. The term 'guarantee' is broadly defined to include, except as provided in regulations, any arrangement under which a person (directly or indirectly through an entity or otherwise) assures, on a conditional or unconditional basis, the payment of another person's obligation under any indebtedness. See I.R.C. §163(j)(6)(D)(iii).
97. I.R.C. §163(j)(3)(B).
98. I.R.C. §163(j)(5)(B).

- Adjusted Taxable Income generally equals a corporation's cash flow for the year before deducting interest expense.[99] If 50% of the Adjusted Taxable Income exceeds the Disqualified Interest paid during the taxable year, this is considered an Excess Limitation, and is an attribute that can be carried forward three years but cannot be carried back.[100]

Below is a simplified example illustrating the application of these rules:

Example 10.3

A, a domestic corporation, is a wholly owned subsidiary of F, a foreign corporation that is not subject to US tax on USD 60 of interest paid by A due to a tax treaty. A has the following relevant items of income and expense for 2016:

	USD
Adjusted Taxable Income (including the items below)	100
Interest Income	20
Interest Expense	90
Disqualified Interest Expense	60

- A's Excess Interest Expense for 2016 is USD 20, which is the difference between its Net Interest Expense (90 – 20 = 70) and 50% of its Adjusted Taxable Income (100 x 50% = 50).
- A's Disqualified Interest Expense (60) is greater than its Excess Interest Expense (20). Hence, 20 of A's Disqualified Interest Expense is disallowed a deduction for the 2016 tax year.
- A's 2016 Disallowed Interest of 20 is carried forward to A's succeeding taxable year.[101]

The statute treats members of an affiliated group as a single corporation for purposes of the Earnings Stripping rules.[102] An affiliated group is generally defined as a group of domestic corporations with a common domestic parent that owns 80% of the vote and value of such corporations.[103] The proposed regulations expanded this definition to domestic corporations indirectly owned by other domestic corporations.[104] For

---

99. I.R.C. §163(j)(6)(A).
100. I.R.C. §163(j)(2)(B)(ii). Permitting the carry forward of this positive attribute produces a similar result to allowing a three-year carry*back* of disqualified Excess Interest Expense arising in later years, without the need to file amended returns for the carryback refund claim.
101. *See* Prop. Treas. Reg. §1.163(j)-1(g), Example 1.
102. I.R.C. §163(j)(6)(C).
103. Prop. Treas. Reg. §1.163(j)-5(a)(2). If a corporation is treated as a member of more than one affiliated group, the principles of I.R.C. §1563(b)(4) and the regulations thereunder will determine the affiliated group of which such corporation will be treated as a member.
104. *See* Prop. Treas. Reg. §1.163(j)-5(a)(3)(i). The attribution rules of I.R.C. §318 apply for purposes of determining indirect stock ownership under this rule.

example, two wholly owned domestic subsidiaries of a foreign corporation are treated as indirectly owning 100% of each other's stock, and, therefore, are treated as members of an affiliated group for purposes of the Earnings Stripping rules.[105] This expansion can be difficult to apply in practice and can be a trap for the unwary.

A REIT may not be part of an affiliated group.[106] However, similar to domestic subsidiaries of a foreign corporation, the TRSs of a REIT may be treated as members of an affiliated group if the requisite ownership percentages are satisfied.

The Treasury Department and the IRS issued the proposed regulations to implement the Earnings Stripping rules on June 19, 1991.[107] These rules clarify certain aspects of the statute but also raise some new questions. These proposed regulations have not been on the list of the IRS priority project for years and may never be finalized. At this point, taxpayers have to come up with their own interpretations to apply the Earnings Stripping rules in some instances. Domestic corporations, including Blocker Corporations, that are subject to the Earnings Stripping rules during a taxable year are required to report their calculation on a special form.[108]

§10.06 WITHHOLDING TAX ON INTEREST

As discussed above, leveraging a Blocker may reduce the payor's US taxable income and, correspondingly, the effective US tax rate. When the lender is a foreign person, however, the interest income is subject to a 30% statutory withholding tax unless a treaty applies.[109] Even if a treaty is expected to reduce or eliminate US withholding tax on interest paid by a Blocker, it is still necessary to be make sure the transaction does not run afoul of the Anti-Conduit Financing rules. The Anti-Conduit Financing rules, if applicable, may result in the disallowance of treaty benefits to which the lender may otherwise be entitled.

In contrast to the multitude of provisions that limit a US corporation's interest deduction, foreign corporations may be exempt from withholding tax on interest under the Portfolio Interest Exemption. This lone statutory oasis in a desert of potential pitfalls is discussed immediately below.

A. Portfolio Interest Exemption

Payments of US source interest income to foreign corporations that are not effectively connected to a US trade or business are subject to a 30% withholding tax (i.e., as FDPA income), unless an exception applies.[110] An important exception to this general rule is the Portfolio Interest Exemption which exempts from withholding tax certain

---

105. *See* Prop. Treas. Reg. §1.163(j)-5(a)(3)(i).
106. *See* I.R.C. §1504(b).
107. 56 Federal Register 27907; 1991-2 C.B. 1040.
108. *See* Form 8926, Disqualified Corporate Interest Disallowed Under Section 163(j) and Related Information attached as Appendix 10-A. There is no specific monetary penalty provision for failure to file this form.
109. *See* discussion in Ch. 9, *supra*, regarding the availability of treaty benefits to a foreign person.
110. I.R.C. §881(a)(1).

types of US source interest payments received by an eligible foreign person.[111] The Portfolio Interest Exemption is a provision of US domestic tax law that may apply to all eligible foreign recipients of interest payments from US sources, in particular including residents of non-treaty countries.[112]

Portfolio interest is defined as any interest (including original issue discount) that would otherwise be subject to tax that meets certain requirements.[113] The debt on which the interest is payable must be a Registered Obligation and the US withholding agent must receive a Form W-8BEN or other statement showing that the beneficial owner of the debt is not a US person.[114] For this purpose, a debt constitutes a Registered Obligation if:

- the obligation is registered as to principal and interest with the issuer or its agent, and transfer of the obligation can be effected only by surrender of the old instrument and either the re-issuance of the old instrument or issuance of a new instrument to the holder;
- the right to the principal of, and stated interest on, the obligation may be transferred only through a book entry system maintained by the issuer (or its agent); or
- the obligation is registered as to principal and interest with the issuer or its agent and can be transferred through either surrender and issuance (or re-issuance) or a book entry system.[115]

There are several limitations on the application of the Portfolio Interest Exemption, two of which are most likely to limit a foreign corporation's ability to claim the

---

111. I.R.C. §881(c)(1).
112. *See* Ch. 9, *supra*, for a discussion of the general requirements a foreign corporation must satisfy in order to obtain treaty benefits.
113. Prior to March 19, 2012, the applicable requirements differed depending on whether the obligation was in registered form. If an obligation was not in registered form, the Portfolio Interest Exemption applied if there were arrangements designed to ensure that the obligation will be sold only to persons who are not US persons; the interest was payable only outside the US; and the face of the obligation contained a statement of limitation applicable to any US person who holds the obligation. I.R.C. §881(c)(2)(A), by cross reference to I.R.C. §163(f)(2)(B) (before amendments by P.L. 111-147, Hiring Incentives to Restore Employment Act). This rule only applies for obligations issued on or before March 18, 2012. The Portfolio Interest Exemption is no longer applicable to interest paid on unregistered obligations issued after March 18, 2012. *See* I.R.C. §163(f) by cross reference from I.R.C. §871(h)(2)(A).
114. I.R.C. §881(c)(2)(B). Notice 2012-20, 2012-1 C.B. 574 (March 7, 2012) (as amended by Notice 2013-43, 2013-2 C.B. 113, July 12, 2013), provides additional guidance regarding when obligations are issued in registered form, including discussion of the book-entry system rules and their application to certain obligations 'immobilized' in a clearing system. It also provides guidance with respect to the application of the portfolio interest exemption with respect to certain obligations in registered form issued after March 18, 2012 and before January 1, 2014. The IRS has yet to issue regulations implementing the guidance in this notice.
115. Treas. Reg. §1.871-14(c)(1)(i).

exemption.[116] First, interest received by a 10% shareholder of an entity is not eligible for the Portfolio Interest Exemption on interest received from that entity.[117] Modified attribution rules apply to determine whether the 10% ownership threshold is met.[118] The regulations apply the 10% limitation at the partner level with respect to interest received by a partnership.[119] This is a taxpayer-favorable rule and enhances the ability of a widely held investment fund, typically classified as a partnership for US tax purposes, to structure debt from its investors to a Blocker owned by the fund.

Secondly, any amount of Contingent Interest is not eligible for the Portfolio Interest Exemption.[120] Contingent Interest includes any interest determined in reference to:

- receipts, sales or other cash flow of the debtor or related person;
- income or profits of the debtor or related person;
- changes in value of any property of the debtor or related person; or
- dividend, partnerships distributions, or similar payments made by the debtor or a related person.[121]

Contingent interest does not include interest subject to a contingency with respect to the timing of the payments; and interest paid on non-recourse or limited recourse debt.[122]

B. Anti-Conduit Financing Rules

The US Anti-Conduit Financing rules allow the IRS to disregard intermediate entities in a Financing Arrangement where such entities are acting as Conduit Entities. The effect of this is the denial of treaty benefits for US source income paid to such Conduit Entities.

In summary, a Financing Arrangement means a series of Financing Transactions where a Financing Entity advances money or other property (or rights to use property) to a Financed Entity through one or more intermediaries.[123] A Financing Transaction includes debt and certain debt-like instruments.[124] A parent guarantee, however, is not a Financing Transaction.[125]

---

116. The other limitations include interest received by a bank on an extension of credit for a loan agreement entered into in the ordinary course of its business, I.R.C. §881(c)(3)(A) and interest paid to a controlled foreign corporation by a related person within the meaning of I.R.C. §864(d)(4), I.R.C. §881(c)(3)(C).
117. I.R.C. §881(c)(3)(B).
118. I.R.C. §318(a) attribution rules apply without the 50% limitation. See I.R.C. §871(h)(3)(C).
119. Treas. Reg. §1.871-14(g)(3)(i).
120. I.R.C. §881(c)(4).
121. I.R.C. §871(h)(4)(A).
122. I.R.C. §871(h)(4)(C).
123. Treas. Reg. §1.881-3(a)(2)(i).
124. Treas. Reg. §1.881-3(a)(2)(ii)(A).
125. See Treas. Reg. §1.881-3(e), Example (1).

A Financing Transaction does not include common stock with no redemption features.[126] This can sometimes create an 'equity blocker' that prevents linking together the transactions that might constitute a Financing Arrangement. If an equity investment is undertaken to avoid the status of an intermediate entity as a Conduit Entity, however, and involves an investment between related entities, then the two entities may be collapsed into a single intermediate entity for purposes of the Anti-Conduit Financing rules.[127]

A Conduit Entity is an intermediate entity (or entities) which is either related to the Financing Entity or Financed Entity, or would not have participated in the Financing Arrangement under substantially the same terms if the Financing Entity did not engage in the Financing Transaction with the intermediate entity, and whose participation in the Financing Arrangement: (1) reduces US tax imposed; and (2) is pursuant to a *tax avoidance plan*.[128] Four factors are taken into account to determine if there is a *tax avoidance* purpose:

- whether there is a significant reduction in tax;
- whether the intermediate entity had sufficient money itself to make the advance to the Financed Entity;
- the time period between Financing Transactions, where a short period of time indicates a *tax avoidance purpose*; and
- whether Financing Transactions are part of the ordinary course of business between related entities.[129]

Notwithstanding the presence of the above factors, an intermediate entity can create a rebuttable presumption that its participation in the Financing Arrangement was not pursuant to a *tax avoidance purpose* if:

- the intermediate entity performs Financing Transactions with respect to leases or licenses if the rents or royalties are earned in an active trade or business; or
- the intermediate entity's officers and employees actively conduct the day-to-day operations of the intermediate entity and actively manage material market risks of the intermediate entity's Financing Transactions within the country with respect to which the intermediate entity is claiming treaty benefits.[130]

The example below, adopted from FSA 200227006,[131] illustrates the application of the US Anti-Conduit Financing rules. Parent, a Country A corporation, wholly owns Taxpayer, a US holding company, and FC, a Country B corporation. The key issue in the FSA was whether a funding arrangement between Parent, FC, and Taxpayer ought to be recharacterized as a Financing Arrangement under the Anti-Conduit Financing rules. Parent formed FC, to which it contributed USD A to in exchange for ordinary shares of FC stock. The source of the funds from Parent is unknown. On

---

126. *See* Treas. Reg. §1.881-3(a)(2)(ii)(B).
127. Treas. Reg. §1.881-3(a)(4)(ii)(B).
128. Treas. Reg. §1.881-3(a)(4)(i).
129. Treas. Reg. §1.881-3(b)(2).
130. Treas. Reg. §1.881-3(b)(3).
131. 7/5/02.

the same day, FC lent USD A to Taxpayer in exchange for a note subordinate to all senior indebtedness of Parent. The note is not guaranteed by Parent. **Example 10.4** illustrates the relevant transactions.

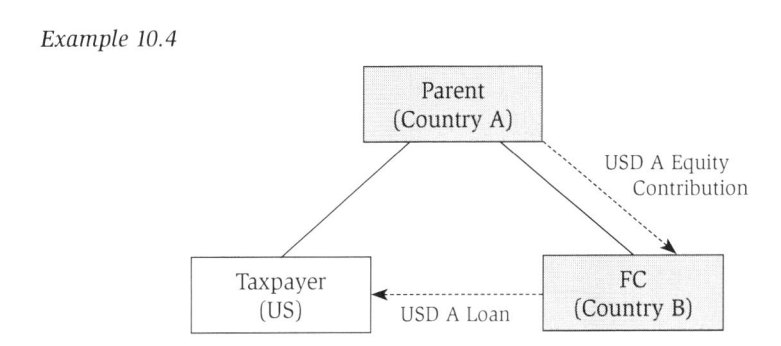

Example 10.4

```
                    Parent
                   (Country A)
                   /         \
                  /           \ USD A Equity
                 /             \ Contribution
                /               ↓
         Taxpayer  ←---------  FC
           (US)    USD A Loan  (Country B)
```

Certain conclusions in the ruling, summarized below, highlight the key aspects of the Anti-Conduit Financing rules.

- In order for there to be a Financing Arrangement, there needs to be at least two Financing Transactions connected through an intermediary corporation. Common stock with no redemption features is not a Financing Transaction. Based on the facts submitted, the IRS concluded that there was only one Financing Transaction, i.e., the loan from FC to Taxpayer. In effect, Parent's ownership of the FC ordinary shares created an 'equity blocker.' As a result, the multi-party funding arrangement between Parent, FC and Taxpayer did *not* constitute a Financing Arrangement.
- On the other hand, if the facts of the case were to show that Parent borrowed all or a part of the amount it contributed to FC from a foreign lender, and the purpose of the structure was to avoid characterization as a Financing Arrangement, then the Anti-Conduit Financing rules could apply to treat Parent and FC as a single intermediary entity. Under this characterization, Taxpayer would be treated as borrowing directly from the foreign lender because the participation of Parent and FC would be disregarded. As a result, Taxpayer would be liable for any withholding tax that might apply to interest payments that that it made to the foreign lender.

§10.06 SUMMARY

Foreign investors that use limited liability companies or limited partnerships as Blockers need to affirmatively elect corporate classification for the entity. It is generally preferable to make the election effective on the date of the entity's formation.

Although the composition of an entity's capital is more of a financing issue, the treatment of debt versus equity (and the corresponding interest payments and corporate distributions) results in very different US tax consequences. In general, interest payments on debts may be deductible but distributions on stock are not deductible. In addition, the repayment of the debt principal provides a pipeline to repatriate cash to the foreign shareholder without incurring any US tax.

The newly issued 385 Regulations generally require Blockers to satisfy certain Documentation Requirements with respect to intercompany debt or the instrument will be presumed to be equity for US tax purposes. Special Recast Rules also may apply to achieve the same result if certain conditions are met. A number of anti-abuse rules may apply, in addition to the Earnings Stripping rules, to reduce the US tax benefit of any interest payments made by a Blocker. It is important for foreign investors that use Blockers to proactively manage these issues in order to best achieve the anticipated tax outcome.

10. Entity Classifications and Interest Deductions

APPENDIX 10-A

Form 8926 (Rev. December 2011)
Department of the Treasury
Internal Revenue Service

Disqualified Corporate Interest Expense Disallowed Under Section 163(j) and Related Information

► Attach to the corporation's income tax return.
► See separate instructions.

OMB No. 1545-2127

Name of corporation (name of parent, if an affiliated group) | Employer identification number

Check here if the form is being filed on behalf of an affiliated group described in section 1504(a) . . . . ☐

- **1a** Enter the total amount of the corporation's money at the end of the tax year **1a**
- **b** Enter the adjusted basis of all the corporation's other assets at the end of the tax year **1b**
- **c** Add lines 1a and 1b **1c**
- **d** Enter the total amount of the corporation's indebtedness at the end of the tax year (see instructions) **1d**
- **e** Subtract line 1d from line 1c. If zero or less, enter $1 . . . . **1e**
- **f** **Debt to equity ratio.** Divide line 1d by line 1e (see instructions) **1f**
- **g** Is the corporation including as part of its assets on line 1b stock described in Regulations section 1.7874-1(d) that it holds in a corporation to whom it paid disqualified interest? . . . . ☐ Yes ☐ No
  If "Yes," enter the adjusted basis of that stock . . . . ► $_____
- **h** Is the corporation including as part of its assets on line 1b stock it holds in foreign subsidiaries? . . ☐ Yes ☐ No
  If "Yes," enter the adjusted basis of that stock . . . . ► $_____
- **i** Is the corporation including as part of its assets on line 1b tangible assets it directly holds that are located in a foreign country? (see instructions) . . . . ☐ Yes ☐ No
  If "Yes," enter the adjusted basis of those tangible assets . . . . ► $_____
- **j** Is the corporation including as part of its assets on line 1b any intangible assets? . . . . ☐ Yes ☐ No
  If "Yes," enter the adjusted basis of those intangible assets . . . ► $_____

- **2a** Enter the interest paid or accrued by the corporation for the tax year **2a**
- **b** Enter any interest includible in the gross income of the corporation for the tax year **2b**
- **c** **Net interest expense.** Subtract line 2b from line 2a. If zero or less, enter -0- **2c**

- **3a** Enter the corporation's taxable income (loss) before the application of section 163(j) **3a**
- **b** Enter the corporation's net interest expense from line 2c **3b**
- **c** Enter any net operating loss deduction taken by the corporation under section 172 . . . . **3c**
- **d** Enter any deduction taken under section 199 . . . . **3d**
- **e** Enter any deduction taken for depreciation, amortization, or depletion **3e**
- **f** Enter any additional adjustments the corporation has made to its taxable income (loss) (other than those listed on lines 3b through 3e above) in arriving at its adjusted taxable income (see instructions—attach schedule) **3f**
- **g** **Adjusted taxable income.** Combine lines 3a through 3f. If zero or less, enter -0- **3g**

For Paperwork Reduction Act Notice, see separate instructions. Cat. No. 37739W Form **8926** (Rev. 12-2011)

Form 8926 (Rev. 12-2011)   Page **2**

4a	Multiply line 3g by 50%	4a	
b	Enter any unused excess limitation carried forward to the current tax year from the prior 3 tax years (see instructions)	4b	
c	Add lines 4a and 4b	4c	
d	**Excess interest expense.** Subtract line 4c from line 2c. If zero or less, enter -0-	4d	
5a	Enter any disqualified interest paid or accrued by the corporation to a related person	5a	
b	Enter any disqualified interest paid or accrued by the corporation on indebtedness subject to a disqualified guarantee	5b	
c	Enter any interest paid or accrued by a taxable REIT subsidiary (as defined in section 856(l)) of a real estate investment trust to such trust	5c	
d	Add lines 5a, 5b, and 5c	5d	
e	Enter any disqualified interest disallowed under section 163(j) for prior tax years that is treated as paid or accrued in the current tax year	5e	
f	**Total disqualified interest for the tax year.** Add lines 5d and 5e	5f	

6   Information about related persons receiving disqualified interest:

	Name, Address, and ZIP code	Country of Incorporation or Organization
a		
b		
c		
d		
e		

7	**Amount of interest deduction disallowed under section 163(j) for the current tax year and carried forward to the next tax year.** If line 1f is 1.5 or less, enter the smaller of line 4d or line 5e. If line 1f is greater than 1.5, subtract the smaller of line 4d or line 5d from the interest the corporation would have otherwise deducted this tax year (see instructions)	7	
8a	Unused excess limitation carryforward from the prior 2 tax years	8a	
b	**Excess limitation for the current tax year.** Subtract line 2c from line 4a. If zero or less, enter -0-	8b	
c	**Excess limitation carryforward to the next tax year.** Add lines 8a and 8b (see instructions)	8c	

Form **8926** (Rev. 12-2011)

Chapter 11
Tax Administration, Penalties, and Interest

§11.01	Overview	307
§11.02	Types of Tax Authorities	308
	A. Legislative Authorities	309
	B. Administrative Authorities	309
	1. Regulations	310
	2. Generic Guidance	311
	3. Taxpayer Specific Guidance	312
	C. Judicial Authorities	313
§11.03	Common Types of Penalties	313
	A. Penalties Related to the Filing of Tax Returns	313
	1. Delinquency Penalties	314
	2. Reasonable Cause Exception	315
	B. Accuracy-Related Penalties	316
	1. Penalty for Negligence and Disregard of Tax Rules or Regulations	317
	2. Penalty for Substantial Understatement of Income Tax	319
	3. Penalty for Transactions Lacking Economic Substance	320
	4. Penalty for Undisclosed Foreign Financial Assets	321
	5. Special Rules for Tax Shelters	321
§11.04	Summary	322

§11.01 OVERVIEW

The IRS is a bureau of the US Department of Treasury and is organized to carry out the responsibilities of the Secretary of the Department of Treasury.[1] The Secretary has full authority to administer and enforce the internal revenue laws and has the power to create an agency to enforce these laws. The IRS was created based on this legislative grant and Code section 7803 provides for the appointment of a commissioner of Internal Revenue to administer and supervise the execution and application of the

---

1. I.R.C. §7801.

internal revenue laws, including the examination of returns, collection of tax and imposition of penalties and interest.

Under the US tax legislations, there are penalties for a variety of different incidences such as failure-to-file, failure-to-pay and underpayment of taxes. Despite a taxpayer's best efforts in conforming to the US tax legislations, due to the complexities of the tax administration and rules in the US, taxpayers may sometimes find themselves being subject to penalties and interest assessed by the IRS. For example, a foreign entity with a US trade or business may sometimes be caught unaware that it has a filing obligation in the US even if it does not have any US ECI.[2] Unlike some jurisdictions, the IRS is entitled to charge an interest amount equivalent to a percentage of underpaid taxes and the quantum of penalties, taxes and interest owed by a taxpayer to the IRS may unexpectedly snowball into an astronomical sum.

Notwithstanding the above, current legislation provided room for a taxpayer to mitigate the amount of penalties imposed by the IRS. For example, the penalty for negligence may be avoided if the position meets a 'reasonable basis' standard, but may not be avoided by adequate disclosure.[3] The reasonable basis standard is significantly higher than the not frivolous or patently improper standard under Code section 6694, but it is less stringent than both the 'more likely than not' standard (i.e., greater than a 50% likelihood of being upheld in litigation) and the substantial authority standard (i.e., an objective standard involving an analysis of the law and application of the law to relevant facts). This chapter seeks to provide an understanding of the various types of penalties and interest that may be imposed by the IRS as well as the mitigating factors that may be considered in such scenarios.

§11.02 TYPES OF TAX AUTHORITIES

Whether it is a taxpayer trying to determine an appropriate position for tax purposes or the IRS carrying out its responsibilities, it is important to determine whether a decision was based upon a primary or secondary tax authority. Although both sources may be referred to in arriving at a decision, a primary authority should undergird a decision as it is the main body of US federal income tax law.

Primary tax authorities consist of the Code as drafted by Congress, treaties,[4] regulations and other pronouncements of the Department of the Treasury, and judicial decisions devoted to tax issues. On the other hand, secondary tax authorities are typically publications which seek to interpret or explain the primary authorities and could include materials such as IRS publications, tax journals and newsletters. Although secondary tax authorities could shed light on a technical interpretation of a primary tax authority, they are not the equivalent of a primary tax authority and should not be solely relied on to arrive at a decision for US federal income tax purposes.

---

2. Treas. Reg. §1.6012-2(g)(1)(i).
3. Treas. Reg. §1.6662-3(b)(1) and §1.6662-7(b).
4. U.S. Constitution, Art. VI, CL2.

A. Legislative Authorities

The Code, which is Title 26 of the United States Code (USC), is the primary legislative authority for US federal income tax purposes. Other statutes such as the Bank Secrecy Act (Title 31 of the USC), which requires currency transaction reporting by financial institutions (FinCEN Form 104) and reporting of foreign financial accounts by US persons on FinCEN Form 114 (the FBAR), are also considered primary legislative authorities. In addition, the US income tax treaties are also considered a primary legislative authority as such treaties must be approved by the United States Senate.

An analysis of a US tax issue must always begin with the statutory text. It should be determined if the statutory language is clear and unambiguous on its face and if so, the plain and common meaning of the text as it is written by Congress should be applied. Certain publications, such as Congressional committee reports, the Blue Book,[5] and TEs to US income tax treaties[6] may be referred to for an understanding of the legislative history and intent of a particular statute.

Congressional committee reports are written when a statute is passed by Congress to indicate Congress' intent behind enacting the statute. The Blue Book is written by the staff of the Joint Committee on Taxation and provides a general explanation of a statute; though it is technically not legislative history, it is an authority for accuracy-related and preparer penalty purposes.[7] Last but not least, the TEs to US income tax treaties are issued by the Treasury as an official guide to a particular treaty. They reflect the policies behind the treaty's provisions as well as the mutual understanding reached by the two countries on the appropriate application and interpretation of the provisions.

B. Administrative Authorities

Taxpayers and others affected by the Code's legal requirements often find a need for guidance to navigate the Code's highly technical and complex provisions. Recognizing this need, Congress has required the Secretary of the Treasury to 'prescribe all needful rules and regulations for the enforcement' of the tax law.[8]

---

5. Generally, at the end of each Congress, the Joint Committee Staff, in consultation with the staffs of the House Committee on Ways and Means and the Senate Committee on Finance, prepare explanations of the enacted tax legislation and the document is commonly referred to as the 'Blue Book'. The explanation follows the chronological order of the tax legislation as signed into law. For each provision, the document includes a description of present law, explanation of the provision, and effective date. Present law describes the law in effect immediately prior to enactment. It does not reflect changes to the law made by the provision or subsequent to the enactment of the provision. For many provisions, the reasons for change are also included.
6. Technical Explanations are official guides, released by the US Treasury Department, to the Convention between the Government of the US and the Government of a foreign country for tax treaties. It reflects policies behind particular Convention provisions, as well as understandings reached with respect to the interpretation and application of the Convention.
7. I.R.C. §6662.
8. Saltzman & Book, *IRS Practice and Procedure (Thomson Reuters/Tax & Accounting*, Rev. 2nd ed. 2002 & Supp. 2016-3).

Administrative authorities comprise of a wide variety of materials, such as regulations, revenue rulings, and private letter rulings (PLRs) among others. However, equal authority is not accorded across the various types of administrative authorities and the highest degree of deference is accorded to the regulations. In *Mayo Foundation v. United States*, 131 S. Ct. 704 (2011), the US Supreme Court clarified the standard that courts are to apply in testing the validity of tax regulations; like regulations of other administrative agencies, tax regulations are to be accorded the highest degree of deference as prescribed in the 'two-part Chevron test' in *Chevron USA Inc. v. Natural Resource Deference Council, Inc.*[9]

The two-part Chevron test requires one to consider if Congress has directly addressed the precise question at issue and whether the tax regulation in question is a reasonable interpretation of the statue. As a first step, if a statute is unambiguous, its requirements prevail (i.e., the courts 'must give effect to the unambiguously expressed intent of Congress'). However, if the statute is ambiguous or silent, then one needs to determine if the agency's construction of the statute is 'permissible', and a court may strike down an agency's rule only if the rule is 'arbitrary and capricious in substance or manifestly contrary to the statute.'

1. Regulations

Under the supervision of the Treasury Department, the IRS issues Treasury regulations to provide guidance for Code provisions. Treasury regulations set forth the IRS's position on these provisions and guide taxpayers in their compliance with the Code. There are different levels of regulations (namely, the proposed, temporary and final regulations) and three types of regulations (namely, legislative, interpretive and procedural regulations).

Proposed regulations are generally not considered an authority unless no final or temporary regulations are available and the proposed regulations specifically allow taxpayers to rely on them.[10] The proposed regulations are published in the Federal Register via a Notice of Proposed Rulemaking. There is a public comment period (commonly between thirty to sixty days) and sometimes a public hearing, during which interested parties can review the proposed regulations and submit written comments. It can take a considerable amount of time (months or years) before a proposed regulation is adopted as a final regulation.

Temporary regulations provide guidance until final regulations are adopted and have the same authority as final regulations. Temporary regulations may sometimes be simultaneously issued with a proposed regulation containing identical wordings. In such a scenario, interested parties may still provide comments to the proposed regulations within the public comment period and the temporary regulations will be

---

9. 467 U.S. 837 (1984)
10. *See*, e.g., §10.05.B., *supra*, for a discussion of the Earnings Stripping rules in I.R.C. §163(j). The Treasury Department and the IRS issued the proposed regulations to implement the Earnings Stripping rules on June 19, 1991. These rules clarify certain aspects of the statute but also raise some new questions. These proposed regulations have not been on the list of the IRS priority project for years and may never be finalized.

11. Tax Administration, Penalties, and Interest

effective upon publication in the Federal Register and will be valid for three years[11] from its issuance.

Final regulations are the highest authority issued by the Treasury and must be approved by the Secretary of the Treasury. Final regulations interpret a corresponding Code section and provide guidance for tax compliance and planning purposes. Final regulations are typically valid for the period of the Code section that the regulation interprets, unless otherwise amended or repealed.

Legislative regulations are based upon a specific grant of authority by Congress and are entitled to greater deference by the courts since they normally have the force and effect of law.[12] Interpretive regulations, on the other hand, help to interpret a particular Code section and are issued under the general grant of authority found in Code section 7805(a), which empowers the Secretary of Treasury to adopt all 'needful rules and regulations' for enforcement of the internal revenue laws. Interpretive regulations are given less deference than legislative regulations by the courts. Lastly, procedural regulations address procedural matters, such as how to file returns, make elections, apply for refunds, etc. Generally, procedural regulations relating to particular Code sections are binding authority.

2. *Generic Guidance*

The IRS issues various forms of guidance, which may be applicable to a specific taxpayer or taxpayers generally. Publications that are issued for generic guidance include revenue rulings, revenue procedures, notices and announcements.

- A revenue ruling is an official interpretation by the IRS of the Code, related statutes, tax treaties and/or regulations. It is the conclusion of the IRS on how the law is applied to a specific set of facts and is published in the Internal Revenue Bulletin for the information of and guidance to taxpayers, IRS personnel and tax professionals. Revenue rulings must be followed by the IRS as they are the IRS's stated position and can be relied upon by a taxpayer with similar circumstances.
- A revenue procedure is an official statement of a procedure that affects the rights or duties of taxpayers or other members of the public under the Code, related statutes, tax treaties and/or regulations and that should be a matter of public knowledge. It is also published in the Internal Revenue Bulletin. While a revenue ruling generally states an IRS position, a revenue procedure can cover a broad spectrum of issues (e.g., procedures relating to methods of electronic filing) and provides return filing or other instructions concerning an IRS position.
- A notice is a public pronouncement that may contain guidance that involves substantive interpretations of the Code or other provisions of the law. For example, notices can be used to relate what regulations will say in situations where the regulations may not be published in the immediate future.

---

11. For temporary regulations issued on or after November 20, 1988.
12. *Rowan Cos. v U.S*, 452 U.S. 247, 253 (1981).

– An announcement is a public pronouncement that has only immediate or short-term value. For example, announcements can be used to summarize the law or regulations without making any substantive interpretation; to state what regulations will say when they are certain to be published in the immediate future; or to notify taxpayers of the existence of an approaching deadline.

In addition to the above, the IRS has also issued an Internal Revenue Manual, which is a compilation of procedures, policies, and guidelines governing the IRS. This document is not binding on the IRS, but usually followed by the IRS and can provide valuable insight to taxpayers.

3. *Taxpayer Specific Guidance*

Certain IRS written determinations, such as PLRs and technical advice memoranda (TAMs), are issued for a specific taxpayer's guidance. Such written determinations can only be relied upon by the specific taxpayer and although not controlling on other taxpayers, they may shed light on the IRS's position on certain tax matters.

A PLR is a written statement issued to a taxpayer that interprets and applies tax laws to the taxpayer's specific set of facts. A PLR is issued to establish with certainty the federal tax consequences of a particular transaction before the transaction is consummated or before the taxpayer's return is filed. A PLR is issued in response to a written request submitted by a taxpayer and is binding on the IRS if the taxpayer fully and accurately described the proposed transaction in the request and carries out the transaction as described. A PLR may not be relied on as precedent by other taxpayers or IRS personnel. PLRs are generally made public after all information that could identify the taxpayer to whom it was issued has been redacted.

A TAM is guidance furnished by the Office of Chief Counsel upon the request of an IRS Examination director or an IRS Appeals director, in response to technical or procedural questions that develop during a proceeding. A request for a TAM generally stems from an examination of a taxpayer's return, a consideration of a taxpayer's claim for a refund or credit, or any other matter involving a specific taxpayer under the jurisdiction of the territory manager or the area director, Appeals. TAMs are issued only on closed transactions and provide an interpretation of the proper application of tax laws, tax treaties, regulations, revenue rulings or other precedents. The advice rendered represents a final determination of the position of the IRS, but only with respect to the specific issue in the specific case in which the advice is issued. TAMs are generally made public after all information that could identify the taxpayer whose circumstances triggered a specific memorandum has been removed.

The IRS Office of Chief Counsel drafts numerous types of internal advice issued to attorneys and revenue agents within the IRS, such as Chief Counsel Advice and Field Service Advice Memoranda. These documents have no precedential value and cannot be relied on by taxpayers. Nonetheless, they may provide useful insight into a position the IRS might take on an undecided or novel issue for which no other agency guidance is available.

C. Judicial Authorities

When a statutory or administrative authority alone fails to resolve a tax issue, it may be necessary to consult judicial authority. As the meaning of statutory language is not always evident, judges have developed various interpretive tools in the form of canons of construction. The starting point in construing a statute is the language of the statute itself. If the language of the statute is plain and unambiguous, it must be applied according to its terms and, in general, a statute cannot go beyond its text. However, there may be instances where to effect the purpose of the statute, the statue may be implemented beyond its text.[13]

The exercise of the judicial power of the US often requires courts to construe statutes in their application to particular cases and controversies. Generally, the higher the court, the greater the weight of the precedent.[14] In the interest of achieving uniform application of the tax laws, the IRS is under no obligation to follow, on a nationwide basis, the decisions of any court other than the Supreme Court.

§11.03 COMMON TYPES OF PENALTIES

A. Penalties Related to the Filing of Tax Returns

The US has adopted a self-assessment system for federal income tax purposes. As such, the imposition of penalties may act as a deterrent to taxpayers' noncompliance. There are over *one hundred fifty* civil penalties in the Code ranging from the failure to timely file a tax return or pay a tax, to accuracy-related penalties, to penalties for omitting to file information returns, to special penalties covering the activities of tax return preparers, to penalties relating to tax shelter activities, etc.[15] Chapter 68 of the Code (sections 6651-6751) generally sets out the civil penalty provisions, and failures to file certain information returns with respect to cross-border transactions are found in Chapter 61 of the Code.[16] The discussion below aims to highlight some of the penalties that may commonly be faced by foreign investors.

---

13. Katharine Clark and Matthew Connolly, *A Guide to Reading, Interpreting and Applying Statutes*, April 2006; William N. Eskridge, Jr., Philip P. Frickey, & Elizabeth Garrett, *Cases and Materials on Legislation: Statutes and the Creation of Public Policy*, 3d.ed. 2001; Statutory Interpretation: General Principles and Recent Trends, December 19, 2011
14. There are three levels of federal courts that hear tax cases. At the bottom of the hierarchy, there are several trial courts, including the Tax Court, the U.S. Court of Federal Claims, District Courts and Bankruptcy Courts. Trial court cases are appealed to the U.S. Courts of Appeals. The highest court and final level of appeal is the Supreme Court of the United States.
15. Alan J. Tarr, J.D., LL.M. (Taxation) & Pamela Jensen Drucker, J.D., LL.M. (Taxation), *Civil Tax Penalties, US Income Portfolios*, Vol. 634 (2d ed. 2012), Bloomberg BNA.
16. For example, *see* §13.02.A., *infra*, for further information on some of the requirements.

1. Delinquency Penalties

The statute of limitations for the IRS to assess a deficiency is generally three years from the date the return was filed.[17] The statute of limitations to claim for refund by a taxpayer is generally three years after the date the return was actually filed or two years after the tax is paid, whichever is later.[18] If a return is never filed by a taxpayer, the IRS technically has an unlimited window period to assess additional taxes as the statute of limitations on assessment does not begin to run until the taxpayer files a return. Failure to file a return within eighteen months of the due date may also result in the disallowance of a taxpayer's ability to take any deductions on its operating expenses or net operating losses which may result in a higher tax liability of the taxpayer, on top of any related penalties and interest imposed.[19]

Failure to timely file a tax return results in a penalty computed as 5% of the net tax amount required to be shown on the tax return for each month (or fraction of a month) that the return is late, up to a maximum of 25% of such net tax amount,[20] unless such failure to file is due to reasonable cause and not willful neglect.[21] For any month in which the taxpayer has a failure-to-file penalty and a failure-to-pay penalty, the failure-to-pay penalty is reduced to 4.5%.[22] If the failure to file is fraudulent, the penalty is increased to 15% for each month (or part thereof), up to a maximum of 75%.[23] The burden of proof of the fraud element is on the IRS and must be carried by clear and convincing evidence.[24]

Any unpaid taxes are due by the last day the related return is due (without regard to extensions) even if the return is filed later on a valid extension. A taxpayer who fails to timely pay the amount shown as tax on a return is subject to penalty unless the failure is due to reasonable cause and not willful neglect.[25] The late payment penalty is generally 0.5% of the late payment for each month (or part of a month) that the payment is late, up to a maximum of 25%.[26] The failure-to-pay penalty is based on the lesser of the tax shown on the return as filed, or the amount of tax required to be shown on the return.[27] The penalty is based on the amount shown on the original return, less tax paid by beginning of month and it runs from the original due date of the return (filing extensions are ignored) until paid.[28]

A taxpayer who fails to pay a tax that is required to be (but was not) shown on a return within twenty-one days after the date of the IRS's notice and demand for that tax is subject to a penalty.[29] The penalty is imposed at the rate of 0.5% for

---

17. I.R.C. §6501.
18. I.R.C. §6511.
19. Treas. Reg. §1.882-4.
20. I.R.C. §6651(a)(1).
21. I.R.C. §6651(a)(1) and Treas. Reg. §301.6651-1(c)(1).
22. I.R.C. §6651(c).
23. I.R.C. §6651(f).
24. I.R.C. §7454(a).
25. I.R.C. §6651(a)(2).
26. Id.
27. I.R.C. §6651(c)(2).
28. I.R.C. §6151(a).
29. I.R.C. §6651(a)(3).

each month (or part thereof) that the assessment remains unpaid, up to a maximum of 25%.[30] The penalty runs from twenty one calendar days (ten business days if the amount shown on the notice and demand is USD 100,000 or more) after the date of the notice and demand. The penalty period ends when the IRS receives payment of the penalty.

2. *Reasonable Cause Exception*

A delay in filing a tax return or paying the tax shown on the return is due to reasonable cause if the taxpayer exercised ordinary business care and prudence but was, nevertheless, unable to file the return within the prescribed period.[31] To claim the reasonable cause exception, the taxpayer must file a written statement, signed under penalties of perjury that affirmatively shows facts sufficient to indicate the existence of a reasonable cause for failing to timely file the tax return.[32] In United States v. Boyle, the taxpayer had relied on his advisor to timely comply with his return filing obligation, but the advisor had failed to file the return in a timely manner. The Supreme Court then clarified that reliance on a qualified tax professional may be reasonable when an issue is technical or complex, but a taxpayer cannot delegate its filing obligation to a tax advisor.

The Internal Revenue Manual is another resource to understand what constitutes reasonable cause for purposes of the delinquency penalties.[33] For those penalties for which reasonable cause can be considered, any reason which establishes that the taxpayer exercised ordinary business care and prudence, but nevertheless was unable to comply with a prescribed duty within the prescribe time, will be considered. Ordinary business care and prudence means making provisions for business obligations to be met when reasonably foreseeable events occur and taking that degree of care that a reasonably prudent person would exercise. In determining this, the IRS may also take into account the taxpayer's compliance history, the length of time between the event cited as reason for non-compliance and subsequent compliance, and the circumstance that may have been beyond the taxpayer's control. Death, serious illness, fire, casualty and natural disaster may constitute reasonable cause.

A taxpayer may also qualify for the administrative relief from penalties for failing to timely file a tax return, pay on time, and/or to deposit taxes when due under the IRS's 'First Time Penalty Abatement' policy[34] if the following are true:

- the taxpayer did not previously have to file a return or had no penalties for the three tax years prior to the tax year in which it received a penalty;
- the taxpayer filed all currently required returns or filed an extension of time to file; and
- the taxpayer has paid, or arranged to pay, any tax due.

The first time penalty abatement may be requested in writing to the IRS.

---

30. I.R.C. §6651(a)(3).
31. Treas. Reg. §301.6651-1(c)(1) and *United States v. Boyle*, 469 US 241 (1985).
32. Treas. Reg. §301.6651-1(c)(1).
33. Internal Revenue Manual §20.1.1.3.2 (11-25-2011).
34. I.R.M. §20.1.1.3.6.1 (08-05-2014).

B. Accuracy-Related Penalties

Code section 6662 provides for accuracy-related penalties to address underpayments of tax and Code section 6662A provides similar penalties for understatements related to a reportable transaction. Generally, the accuracy-related penalty for underpayments is imposed at the rate of 20% on the portion of any underpayment of tax required to be shown on a return attributable to any of the following:[35]

- negligence;
- substantial understatement of tax;
- substantial valuation misstatement;
- substantial overstatement of pension liabilities;
- substantial estate or gift tax valuation understatement;
- transactions lacking economic substance;
- undisclosed foreign financial asset; or
- inconsistent estate basis.

In the case of a gross valuation misstatement and the inadequate disclosure of a transaction found to lack economic substance, the maximum rate of 40% is imposed on the tax underpaid.[36] Similarly, if any portion of an underpayment of tax is attributable to an undisclosed foreign financial asset, the penalty rate is increased to 40%.[37] For accuracy-related penalties, a 'no stacking' provision applies, which is illustrated as follows:[38]

- If a portion of the underpayment of tax required to be shown on a return is attributable to both negligence and a substantial understatement, the accuracy-related penalty would apply only once at the 20% rate to this portion of the underpayment. The examiner should assert the penalty that is most strongly supported by the facts and circumstances and write up the other as an alternative penalty position.
- The penalty is applied at the 40% rate on any portion of the underpayment attributable to a gross valuation misstatement. Any penalty at the 20% rate that could have applied to this portion is not asserted except as an alternative penalty position.
- A penalty is applied at the 75% rate on any portion of the underpayment attributable to civil fraud. Any penalty that could have applied to this portion at the 20% or 40% rate is not asserted except as an alternative penalty position.

No accuracy-related penalty under Code section 6662 is imposed if it is shown that the taxpayer had reasonable cause for the position taken and that the taxpayer acted in good faith.[39] The burden of proof lies with the taxpayer. A similar reasonable cause exception also applies to accuracy-related penalties on reportable transaction

---

35. I.R.C. §6662(b)(1)-(8).
36. I.R.C. §6662(h) and (i).
37. I.R.C. §6662(j)(3).
38. Treas. Reg. §1.6662-2(c).
39. I.R.C. §6664(c).

understatements.[40] The reasonable cause exception does not apply to understatements from transactions lacking economic substance or gross valuation misstatements with respect to charitable deduction property.[41] The determination of whether a taxpayer acted with reasonable cause and in good faith is made on a case-by-case basis, taking into account all pertinent facts and circumstances.[42] The most important factor is the extent of the taxpayer's efforts to assess his proper tax liability.[43]

1. Penalty for Negligence and Disregard of Tax Rules or Regulations

The accuracy-related penalties apply to any portion of an underpayment attributable to negligence or disregard of rules or regulations.[44] The term 'negligence' includes any failure to make a reasonable attempt to comply with the provisions of the Code.[45]

Under the regulations, negligence includes any failure to make a reasonable attempt to comply with the tax laws, exercise reasonable care in return preparation, keep proper books and records, or properly substantiate items. The regulations further provide that negligence is 'strongly indicated' when: (1) a taxpayer fails to report income shown on an information return, or fails to make a reasonable inquiry into the correctness of an item that seems 'too good to be true'; or (2) the returns of partners or S corporation shareholders and the applicable entity fail to satisfy the consistency requirements.[46]

Generally, the penalty for negligence may be avoided if the position meets a 'reasonable basis' standard and may not be avoided by adequate disclosure.[47] The reasonable basis standard is considered to be a relatively high standard of tax reporting (i.e., significantly higher than the not frivolous or patently improper standard under Code section 6694), but it is less stringent than both the 'more likely than not' standard (i.e., greater than a 50% likelihood of being upheld in litigation) and the substantial authority standard (i.e., an objective standard involving an analysis of the law and application of the law to relevant facts). The reasonable basis standard is not satisfied by a position that is merely arguable or merely a colorable claim.[48]

If a return position is reasonably based on one or more of the authorities set forth in Regulation section 1.6662-4(d)(3)(iii) (taking into account the relevance and persuasiveness of the authorities, and subsequent developments), it generally will satisfy the reasonable basis standard even though it may not satisfy the substantial authority standard (as defined under Regulation section 1.6662-4(d)(2)).[49] Also, the

---

40. I.R.C. §6664(d).
41. I.R.C. §6664(c)(2) and (3).
42. Treas. Reg. §1.6664-4(b)(1).
43. Treas. Reg. §1.6664-4(b)(1).
44. I.R.C. §6662(b)(1).
45. I.R.C. §6662(c).
46. Treas. Reg. §1.6662-3(b)(1).
47. Treas. Reg. §1.6662-3(b)(1) and §1.6662-7(b).
48. See Treas. Reg. §1.6662-3(b)(3); H.R. Conf. Rep. No. 213, 103d Cong., 1st Sess. 668–69 (1993).
49. See Treas. Reg. §1.6662-3(b)(3). In addition, the reasonable cause and good faith exception of Treas. Reg. §1.6664-4 may provide relief from the penalty, even if a return position does not satisfy the reasonable basis standard.

courts have held that a taxpayer can misinterpret an authority, reach the wrong conclusion, and still behave reasonably to avoid the Code section 6662(b)(1) negligence penalty. Moreover, reasonable minds can differ over tax reporting, even when the IRS disallows certain transactions, and when a legal issue is reasonably debatable, an underpayment generally will not be found negligent.[50]

Disregard is defined to include any careless, reckless, or intentional disregard.[51] It includes any careless, reckless, or intentional disregard of the Code, temporary or final regulations, revenue rulings or notices,[52] and in some cases, revenue procedures.[53] A 'careless' disregard exists when a taxpayer does not exercise reasonable diligence to determine the correctness of a return position that is contrary to the rule or regulation. A 'reckless' disregard exists when the taxpayer makes little or no effort to determine whether a rule or regulation exists, failing to satisfy the standard of conduct that a reasonable person would observe.

An 'intentional' disregard exists when a taxpayer knows of the rule or regulation that is disregarded. On the other hand, a taxpayer who takes a position contrary to a revenue ruling or notice has not disregarded the ruling or notice if the contrary position has a realistic possibility of being sustained on the merits.[54] Positions related to a reportable transaction are excluded from this 'realistic possibility of being sustained' exception.[55] The penalty for the disregard of rules and regulations is not imposed on any portion of an underpayment that is attributable to a position contrary to a rule or regulation if the relevant facts affecting the item's tax treatment are 'adequately disclosed', provided there is a reasonable basis for the taxpayer's position and the taxpayer maintains adequate books and records to substantiate the item.[56]

In the case of a position contrary to a regulation, the position must be disclosed and must represent a good faith challenge to the validity of the regulation.[57] The disclosure exception does not apply, however, where the disclosed position does not have a 'reasonable basis' or where the taxpayer fails to keep adequate books and records or to substantiate items properly.[58] Moreover, a taxpayer cannot rely on an opinion or advice that a regulation is invalid to establish that the taxpayer acted with reasonable cause and good faith unless the taxpayer adequately disclosed on his tax return the position that the regulation is invalid.[59] The minimum standard a

---

50. *See Mortensen v. Commissioner*, T.C. Memo 2004-279, aff'd, 440 F.3d 375 (6th Cir. 2006); *Bergersen v. Commissioner*, T.C. Memo 1995-424, aff'd, 109 F.3d 56 (1st Cir. 1997); *Everson v. United States*, 108 F.3d 234 (9th Cir. 1997). See also *TIFD III-E, Inc. v. United States*, 8 F. Supp. 3d 142 (D. Conn. 2014), rev'd, 604 Fed. Appx. 69 (2d Cir. 2015), cert. denied, 136 S. Ct. 796, 193 L. Ed. 2d 765 (2016) (taxpayer's position not considered reasonably based, which attributed to negligence penalty).
51. I.R.C. §6662(c).
52. Treas. Reg. §1.6662-3(b)(2).
53. Preamble to T.D. 8381, 56 Fed. Reg. 67492 (Dec. 31, 1991).
54. Treas. Reg. §1.6662-3(b)(2). *See also* Treas. Reg. §1.6694-2(b).
55. Treas. Reg. §1.6662-3(a) and (b)(2).
56. Treas. Reg. §1.6662-3(c) and-7(c).
57. Treas. Reg. §1.6662-3(c)(1).
58. *See* I.R.C. §6662(d)(2)(B); Treas. Reg. §1.6662-3(c)(1) – §1.6662-7(b).
59. Treas. Reg. §1.6664-4(c)(1)(iii).

disclosed return must satisfy to avoid the penalty for disregarding rules or regulations is the 'reasonable basis' standard.[60]

2.   *Penalty for Substantial Understatement of Income Tax*

The accuracy-related penalties also apply to substantial understatement of income tax.[61] For corporations, an understatement of income tax for a taxable year is 'substantial' if the understatement exceeds the greater of: (1) 10% of the tax required to be shown on the return for the taxable year (or USD 10,000, if greater); or (2) USD 10 million.[62] For all other taxpayers, an understatement of income tax is 'substantial' if it exceeds the greater of (1) 10% of the tax required to be shown on the return for the taxable year; or (2) USD 5,000.

Any understatement is reduced to the extent it is attributable to an item for which there is or was substantial authority for the taxpayer's treatment, or with respect to which the relevant facts affecting the item's tax treatment are adequately disclosed in the return or a statement attached to the return.[63] Special rules apply to items that are attributable to a tax shelter.[64]

The 'substantial authority' standard is an objective standard involving an analysis of the law and an application of the law to relevant facts of a particular situation. It is more stringent than the 'reasonable basis' standard but less stringent than the 'more likely than not' standard. In a 1999 Joint Committee on Taxation study evaluating the likelihood of the tax treatment of an item being upheld if challenged by the IRS in numerical probability, the Joint Committee on Taxation expressed reasonable basis as 20% and substantial authority as 40%. However, in the preamble to the 1998 Code section 6662 final treasury regulations, the IRS explained that the regulations excluded numerical qualification to avoid encouraging arbitrary and mechanical application of the standard. Moreover, the substantial authority regulations[65] specifically state that 'a taxpayer may have substantial authority for a position supported by no authorities except a well-reasoned construction of the applicable statutory provision.'

There is 'substantial authority' for the tax treatment of an item only if the weight of the authorities supporting the treatment is substantial in relation to the weight of authorities supporting contrary treatment. Examples of relevant authorities are statutes, treaties, regulations, revenue rulings, revenue procedures, cases, private letter rulings, and other IRS sources that have not been overruled. All authorities relevant to the tax treatment of an item, including the authorities contrary to the treatment, are taken into account in determining whether substantial authority exists. The weight accorded an authority depends on its relevance and persuasiveness, and the type of document providing the authority. For instance, as discussed earlier in

---

60. Treas. Reg. §1.6662-3(c)(1) – §1.6662-7(c).
61. I.R.C. §6662(b)(2), (d); Treas. Reg. §1.6662-4(a).
62. I.R.C. §6662(d)(1)(B).
63. I.R.C. §6662(d)(2)(B); Treas. Reg. §1.6662-4(a).
64. I.R.C. §6662(d)(2)(C)(i).
65. Treas. Reg. §1.6662-4(d)(3)(ii).

the chapter, a revenue ruling is accorded more weight than a private letter ruling addressing the same issue.

3. *Penalty for Transactions Lacking Economic Substance*

A strict liability penalty is imposed in an amount equal to 20% of the portion of an underpayment of tax that is attributable to the disallowance of claimed tax benefits by reason of a transaction lacking economic substance (within the meaning of Code section 7701(o)) or failing to meet the requirements of any similar rule of law.[66] The 20% penalty increases to 40% with respect to any portion of any underpayment attributable to a transaction that lacks economic substance and with respect to which the relevant facts affecting the tax treatment of the transaction are not adequately disclosed on the return or in a statement attached to the return.[67] Reasonable cause cannot be used to avoid the penalty with respect to an understatement attributable to a transaction lacking economic substance.[68]

The Economic Substance doctrine is a longstanding, judicially developed rule that may apply to deny the US federal income tax benefits of a transaction that does not have economic substance. The Economic Substance doctrine was recently codified in Code section 7701(o). [69] Code section 7701(o), which generally follows the judicially developed principles, provides that a transaction has economic substance if:

- the transaction changes in a meaningful way (apart from US federal income tax effects) the taxpayer's economic position; and
- the taxpayer has a substantial purpose (apart from US federal income tax effects) for entering into the transaction.[70]

Code section 7701(o) does not generally apply to transactions undertaken in the ordinary course of business. The Blue Book[71] released in conjunction with the enactment of Code section 7701(o) clarifies that Congress did not intend Code section 7701(o) to change the tax treatment of basic business transactions that are respected under longstanding judicial practice. These business transactions include the choice to utilize a related party entity in a transaction provided that the arm's length standard of Code section 482 and other applicable concepts are satisfied.

---

66. I.R.C. §6662(b)(6).
67. I.R.C. §6662(i)(1).
68. I.R.C. §6664(c)(2).
69. I.R.C. §7701(o)(1) and (5)(A). In addition, penalties apply to transactions that do not have economic substance under I.R.C. §7701(o).
70. A transaction may be treated as satisfying these criteria if the transaction has substantial after-tax profit potential. Specifically, a transaction is viewed as having economic substance if the present value of the reasonably expected pre-tax profit from the transaction is substantial in relation to the present value of the expected net tax benefit that would be allowed if the transaction were respected. *See* I.R.C. §7701(o)(2).
71. Joint Committee on Taxation Report on the Health Care and Education Reconciliation Act of 2010, P.L. 111-152 (March 30, 2010).

4. *Penalty for Undisclosed Foreign Financial Assets*

The accuracy-related 40% penalty applies to underpayments attributable to undisclosed foreign financial assets.[72] The term 'undisclosed foreign financial asset' means, with respect to any taxable year, any asset subject to information reporting requirements under Code sections 6038, 6038B, 6038D, 6046A and 6048 for such taxable year for which the required information was not provided by the taxpayer under those reporting provisions.[73] An understatement is attributable to an undisclosed foreign financial asset if it is attributable to any transaction involving such asset.[74] The reasonable cause exception can generally apply to any component of the accuracy-related penalty, except the penalty for transactions lacking economic substance.

5. *Special Rules for Tax Shelters*

Taxpayers should be mindful of the promotion of any tax shelter plans or arrangements to them as more severe penalties apply in the case of a tax shelter item.[75] A 'tax shelter' is any entity, plan, or arrangement with 'a significant purpose' of avoiding or evading income tax.[76] Taxpayers should take note of Circular No. 230, released by the Treasury Department, which provides the standards to which practitioners (such as certified public accountants, attorneys, enrolled agents, and enrolled actuaries) must adhere to when providing advice on a 'federal tax matter'.[77] When providing written advice, a practitioner must:

- base the written advice on reasonable factual and legal assumptions (including assumptions as to future events);
- reasonably consider all relevant facts and circumstances that the practitioner knows or reasonably should know;
- use reasonable efforts to identify and ascertain the facts relevant to written advice on each federal tax matter;
- not rely upon representations, statements, findings or agreements (including projections, financial forecasts, or appraisals) of the taxpayer or any other person if reliance on them would be unreasonable;
- relate applicable law and authorities to facts; and
- not, in evaluating a federal tax matter, take into account the possibility that a tax return will not be audited or that a matter will not be raised on audit.

If the practitioner knows or has reason to know an opinion will be used or referred to by a person other than the practitioner issuing the written advice in promoting,

---

72. I.R.C. §6662(b)(7).
73. I.R.C. §6662(j)(2).
74. I.R.C. §6662(j)(1).
75. Treas. Reg. §1.6664-4(f).
76. I.R.C. §6662(d).
77. Broadly defined to include the application or interpretation of a revenue provision within the Code (e.g., treaties, former and current provisions of the Code, regulations, revenue rulings, PLRs, etc.).

marketing, or recommending to one or more taxpayers, a partnership or other entity, an investment plan or arrangement a significant purpose of which is the avoidance or evasion of tax imposed under the Code, the practitioner may be at risk of not adhering to the requirements set out above. In addition, under Code section 6111, a person who is a material advisor with respect to a reportable transaction other than a transaction of interest must register the transaction by filing Form 8918 with the IRS, if the person provided aid, assistance, or advice with respect to the transaction after October 22, 2004. There are currently five categories of federal 'reportable transactions':

- listed (including substantially similar) transactions;
- confidential transactions;
- contractual protection transactions;
- large Code section 165 loss transactions; and
- transactions of interest (including substantially similar transactions).

§11.04 SUMMARY

The complexity of the US tax rules and regulations may be a trap for the unwary. Foreign investors who are not very familiar with such rules and regulations may face unexpected and unintended penalties. For example, certain foreign investors may receive reportable ECI on Schedule K-1s that reports each partner's share of income, losses, deductions and credits. Where such investors do not use a Blocker Corporation[78] to own the investment directly, the ultimate foreign investor (either a foreign corporation or a foreign national) who was later made aware of its US tax filing obligations on taxable ECI, is potentially subject to different sorts of penalties and interests and a disallowance of tax deduction on various losses and its expenses. To avoid such penalties, it is, therefore, important for foreign investors to seek professional US tax advice regarding the treatment of the investments, and have some understanding of the different US tax reporting standards, weight of the legal authorities, and penalty defenses which may be peculiar to the US tax regime.

---

78. *See* discussion in §2.04, *supra,* for a discussion of various investment vehicles typically used for owning one or more USRPIs.

Chapter 12
State and Local Tax Considerations

§12.01	Application of FIRPTA to State and Local Taxes, Generally	323
	A. Overview	323
	B. Effect of Tax Treaties on State and Local Taxation	324
§12.02	State and Local Tax Considerations on Sales of Real Property	324
§12.03	State and Local Withholding on Sales of Real Property	325
	A. California	325
	B. Delaware	327
	C. Hawaii	328
	D. New York State	330
§12.04	State and Local Transaction Taxes on Sales of Real Estate	331
	A. Direct Transfer of Realty	332
	B. Indirect Transfer of Realty	332
	C. Long-term Lease	332
	D. Exemptions	333
§12.05	Selected State-Specific Real Estate Transfer Tax Provisions	333
	A. California	333
	1. Los Angeles	334
	2. San Francisco	335
	B. New York	336

§12.01 APPLICATION OF FIRPTA TO STATE AND LOCAL TAXES, GENERALLY

A. Overview

FIRPTA does not apply to any taxes imposed at the state or local level. However, many states have enacted statutes similar to FIRPTA that apply to taxes imposed by the state and/or its localities. Unlike FIRPTA, the withholding requirements of these statutes may apply even when the seller is a US resident or domiciliary.

As is the usual case with state and local taxation, these requirements vary from state to state. Sometimes, the rules applicable to state taxes are different than those applicable to taxes imposed by localities in that same state. And the rules applicable to localities within a state may vary from locality to locality. As a result, buyers must always consider the rules applicable in the state and locality where the property they are purchasing is located.

B. Effect of Tax Treaties on State and Local Taxation

International tax treaties applicable to federal taxes do not apply to state and local taxes unless explicitly provided for in the treaty. The United States model tax treaty provides that 'The existing taxes to which this Convention shall apply are ... in the case of the United States: the Federal income taxes imposed by the Internal Revenue Code ... and the Federal excise taxes imposed with respect to private foundations.'[1] As a result, a foreign taxpayer may be subject to state and local income taxes even though it is protected from federal US income tax under the terms of a treaty. Similarly, federal tax treaties do not restrict a state or local government from imposing non-income taxes.

§12.02 STATE AND LOCAL TAX CONSIDERATIONS ON SALES OF REAL PROPERTY

A number of states require buyers or an intermediary to the sale of real estate to withhold a portion of the sales proceeds and remit those to the state as prepayment of income taxes relating to the seller's gain on the sale of the real estate. Unlike FIRPTA, which applies when a seller is not a US seller, the state withholding requirement may apply when the seller is not a resident of the state or is not otherwise conducting business in the state. Like FIRPTA, this includes foreign sellers but also includes US domestic sellers that are not resident or not otherwise located in the state.

Accordingly, transactions may be subject to state and/or local withholding even if they are not subject to FIRPTA withholding. And while states often provide exemptions from withholding, these exemptions frequently differ from the exceptions provided in FIRPTA. State statutes also may differ with respect to the base on which the tax is imposed, the party responsible for the tax, the process for reporting, and the timing for paying the tax. The first part of this chapter describes the states' FIRPTA-style withholding requirements.

It is important to note that state FIRPTA-style withholding is merely a prepayment of income taxes due from the seller. It is not an additional tax imposed on the transaction. However, some states and localities do impose an additional tax on the transfer of an interest in real property. Such a tax is similar to a sales tax and often must be paid before an instrument of transfer may be recorded. This chapter also describes the transfer taxes that may be imposed by a state or local government in addition to income taxes.

---

1. *See* 2006 US Model, Art. 2(3)(b).

§12.03 STATE AND LOCAL WITHHOLDING ON SALES OF REAL PROPERTY

The paragraphs below describe some of the state and local withholding rules applicable to sales of real estate in California, Delaware, Hawaii, and New York. These are not the only states that impose withholding requirements. Rather, the states below have FIRPTA-style taxes that are illustrative of the types of requirements that states impose on purchasers of real property.[2]

A. California

California law requires withholding when there is a transfer of title on California real property.[3] In general, the state requires withholding on any transaction where a party on a title to real property before the transaction is not on the title after the transaction is complete. For example, the buyer is responsible for withholding on gifts and exchanges, leasehold/options, short sales, and easements of real estate.[4]

Withholding on the sale of an ownership interest in California real property is generally required when the transfer meets the definition of Code section 897(c)(1)(A)(i). An ownership interest does not include an option to acquire real estate unless the option is exercised by the transferor and the real property is transferred.[5]

Unless an exemption applies, withholding requirements apply to most buyers, including individuals, corporations, partnerships, limited liability companies, estates, trusts, REITs, relocation companies, bankruptcy trusts and estates, and conservatorships.[6] However, withholding is not required if the seller is a tax exempt entity, insurance company, individual retirement account, qualified pension plan, or charitable remainder trust.[7]

Although the buyer is primarily responsible, in practice, the buyer usually delegates this responsibility to a real estate escrow person (REEP) who is an attorney, escrow company, or title company that is responsible for closing the real estate transaction, or any person who receives and disburses payment for the sale of real property.[8]

Real estate withholding is not required when the total sale price is USD 100,000 or less.[9] When multiple sellers are involved in the transaction, the withholding

---

2. Other states that require withholding on sales of real estate include Alabama (Ala. Code §40-18-86), Colorado (Colo. Rev. Stat. §39-22-604.5(1), Georgia (Ga. Code Ann. §48-7-128), Maine (Me. Rev. Stat. Ann. §5250-A), Maryland (Md. Code Ann. Tax-Gen. §10-912), Mississippi (Miss. Code Ann. §27-7-308); New Jersey (N.J. Rev. Stat. §54A:8-9); Oregon (Or. Rev. Stat. §314.258), Rhode Island (R.I. Gen. Laws §44-30-71.3), South Carolina (S.C. Code Ann. §12-8-580), Vermont (Vt. Stat. Ann. 32 §5847), West Virginia (W.Va. Code §11-21-71b).
3. Cal. Rev. & Tax. Cd. §18662.
4. California Franchise Tax Board, Real Estate Withholding Guidelines, FTB Publication 1016, Aug. 2016, https://www.ftb.ca.gov/forms/misc/1016.pdf, p. 2.
5. Cal. Code Regs. tit. 18, §18662-2(c).
6. Cal. Code Regs. tit. 18, §18662-3(c).
7. Cal. Code Regs. tit. 18, §18662-3(d)(2).
8. *See* Cal. Code Regs. tit. 18, §18662-3(c)(3).
9. Cal. Rev. & Tax. Cd. §18662(e)(A).

amount is determined by the total sales price and not by each seller's portion.[10] Furthermore, the sales of multiple parcels and/or family units, for example a duplex that is within the same escrow agreement, will constitute one transaction for purposes of determining the withholding requirements.[11] Withholding is required when the combined sales price of all parcels is over USD 100,000 even if the sales price of each separate parcel in the same escrow transaction is under USD 100,000.[12]

In lieu of withholding, the seller or transferor can certify that the transaction meets one or more exemptions, such as the property sold qualifies as the seller's principal residence or the seller has a loss on the property for California income tax purposes.[13] Withholding is not required if the seller is a corporation with a permanent place of business in California[14] or is qualified through the California Secretary of State[15] or is a California partnership or a partnership that is qualified to do business in California.[16] Withholding may not be required if the seller is a limited liability company that is taxed as a partnership as long as it is not a single member limited liability company that is disregarded for federal income tax purposes.[17]

Withholding is not required in certain foreclosure transactions, including a sale according to a power of sale under a mortgage or deed of trust, selling according to a decree of foreclosure, or acquiring a deed in lieu of foreclosure.[18] Real estate withholding is not required if the transferor is a bank acting as a trustee, but not as a trustee of a deed of trust.[19] Withholding is not required on transfers to a controlled corporation or partnership that qualify for nonrecognition treatment under Code section 351 or 721.[20]

A transaction may qualify for withholding if it qualifies for a simultaneous or deferred Like-Kind Exchange under Code section 1031.[21] However, if a taxpayer receives money or other property (in addition to property that is part of the Like-Kind Exchange) that exceeds USD 1,500 from the transaction, then withholding is required. Tax must be withheld only on the principal portion of an installment sale.[22]

Withholding may be calculated in two different ways. In general, tax is imposed at 3⅓% of the total sales price of the sale.[23] The sales price means the sum of the cash paid or to be paid, the fair market value of other property transferred, and the outstanding amount of any liability relating to the real property assumed by the transferee.[24]

---

10. FTB Publication 1016 (rev. 08-2016), p. 2.
11. Id.
12. Id.
13. Cal. Rev. & Tax. Cd. §18662(e)(3)(D)(i) and (iv).
14. Cal. Rev. & Tax. Cd. §18662(e)(3)(D)(v).
15. FTB Publication 1016, p. 4.
16. Id.
17. Id.
18. Cal. Rev. & Tax. Cd. §18662(e)(3)(C)(i).
19. Cal. Rev. & Tax. Cd. §18662(e)(3)(C)(ii).
20. Cal. Code Regs. tit. 18, §18662-3(d)(2)(D).
21. Cal. Rev. & Tax. Cd. §18662(e)(3)(D)(ii).
22. FTB Publication 1016, p. 4.
23. Cal. Rev. & Tax. Cd. §18662(e)(2)(A).
24. Cal. Rev. & Tax. Cd. §18662(e)(8).

12. State and Local Tax Considerations

The seller may elect to have the tax imposed on the net gain on the sale.[25] In that case, the rate varies depending on the classification of the seller. The table below lists the rates that must be applied to the gain on the sale when the seller so elects for escrow as of December 31, 2016.[26]

Individual	12.3%	Bank and financial corporation	10.84%
Non-California partnership	12.3%	S corporation	13.8%
Corporation	8.84%	Financial S corporation	15.8%

California law requires the REEP to provide buyers with specific written notification of their withholding requirements unless the buyer is an intermediary or accommodator in a deferred exchange. If no one is responsible for closing the transaction, the person who receives and disburses the funds for the property sold is required to notify the buyers. In the case of a deferred Like-Kind Exchange, a qualified intermediary may be responsible. The state may assess a penalty of USD 500 or 10% of the amount required to be withheld, whichever is greater, for failure to provide the required notice. In many situations, the REEP will assist the buyer to complete the withholding forms and remit the required amounts. Although the REEP may charge a fee, the statute provides that the fee may not exceed USD 45 for each seller. The fee is negotiable and may be paid by either the buyer or the seller.[27]

A buyer who fails to withhold or timely remit taxes withheld may be liable for the greater of the amount actually withheld or the amount of taxes due.[28]

If the seller seeks an exemption from withholding, the seller/transferor must complete and sign Form 593-C.[29] A seller must have a valid federal Taxpayer Identification Number (TIN) to qualify for a withholding exemption. A REEP is not required to verify the information provided by the seller on Form 593-C unless they have actual knowledge of the facts.[30] A REEP will be relieved of its withholding requirements if it relies in good faith on a completed and signed Form 593-C.[31] The form must be retained for five years following the closing date of the transaction.

B. Delaware

Rather than imposing a withholding requirement on the buyer, Delaware requires every nonresident individual, pass-through entity, and corporation that sells or exchanges Delaware real estate to file a Delaware Corporate Tentative Tax Return for the quarter in which the sale is settled and to pay tax on the estimated gain

---

25. Cal. Rev. & Tax. Cd. §18662(e)(2)(B).
26. https://www.ftb.ca.gov/individuals/wsc/California-Real-Estate.shtml
27. FTB Publication 1061, p. 10.
28. Cal. Rev. & Tax. Cd. §18662(d).
29. https://www.ftb.ca.gov/forms/2017/17_593c.pdf
30. Cal. Code Regs. tit. 18, §18662-3(f)(3).
31. Id.

recognized on the sale or exchange.[32] Such return and payment must be made before the deed is recorded.[33] If the recorder does not receive the estimated tax return and payment, the title may not be recorded.

A nonresident individual is an individual who is not a resident of Delaware for that individual's entire tax year.[34] Accordingly, an individual who sells a home and moves out of state during the year is considered a nonresident for the entire year and is required to file an estimated tax return and pay the tax.

A nonresident corporation means a corporation that is not organized under the laws of Delaware and is not qualified or registered with the Secretary of State to do business in Delaware.[35]

A nonresident pass-through entity means a pass-through entity having one or more owners who are either nonresident individuals or nonresident corporations.[36] The pass-through entity is required to file a Declaration of Estimated Income Tax or a Delaware Corporate Tentative Tax Return on behalf of its nonresident owners. The estimated payments are deemed to have been paid on behalf of the nonresident owner and credited against Delaware income tax of the owner.[37]

Because the payment requirement is imposed on the seller, the buyer is not liable for unpaid taxes. Similarly, the title insurance producer, title insurer, settlement agent, closing attorney, lending institution, real estate agent or broker are not liable for nonpayment.[38]

The Division of Revenue has issued Delaware Form 5403, which must be completed and presented to the recorder for all sales of real property regardless of whether the seller is a nonresident of Delaware. Although residents must complete the form, no estimated tax is due at the time the title is recorded. All nonresident sellers must pay tax at the rate of estimated tax due, 6.75%, regardless of whether the seller is an individual, corporation, or pass-through entity. Estimated tax may be paid based on the net gain realized by the seller or the net cash received, at the seller's option.[39]

C. Hawaii

Hawaii's withholding statute, commonly referred to as HARPTA (Hawaii Real Property Tax Act), is similar to FIRPTA.[40] The buyer or transferee is required to withhold 5% of the amount realized on the sale of property purchased from a nonresident of Hawaii.[41]

---

32. Del. Code Ann. §§1126(b) (individuals), 1606(b) (pass-through entities), and 1909(b)(1) (corporations).
33. Del. Code Ann. §§1126(c), 1606(c), and 1909(c).
34. Del. Code Ann. §1126(a)(2).
35. Del. Code Ann. §1909(a)(2).
36. Del. Code Ann. §1606(a)(2).
37. Del. Code Ann. §1606(d).
38. Del. Code Ann. §§1126(e), 1606(e), and 1909(e).
39. https://www.sussexcountyde.gov/sites/default/files/PDFs/5403.pdf
40. Ha. Rev. Stat. §235-68. See Hawaii Tax Information Release No. 2002-2 (Revised 1/2014), Hawaii Dep't of Taxation, Jan. 7, 2014.
41. Ha. Rev. Stat. §235-68(b) and (d)(1).

The residency status of a partnership or limited liability company, and not the status of its owners, determines whether the buyer must withhold. Withholding is not required for a partnership or limited liability company formed in Hawaii or registered to transact business in Hawaii.[42] In the case of joint sellers, withholding is required to the extent of the amount realized by nonresident persons. The amount realized may be allocated among the sellers based on the capital contributions made to purchase the property. If that amount is not known, the sellers will be deemed to realize the amounts equally. Prior to the transfer, the transferors should notify the buyer if different allocation amounts apply.[43]

No withholding is required if a transferor furnishes an affidavit stating that the transferor used the property as a principal residence for the year preceding the date of the transfer of the property and the amount realized does not exceed USD 300,000.[44] The department also is authorized to enter into written agreements with persons who engage in multiple real property transactions or with persons whom the withholding requirements are not practicable.[45] The department has issued Form N-289 to be used for this purpose.[46]

No withholding is required if the transferor provides an affidavit stating that the transferor is a resident of Hawaii[47] or is not required to recognize any gain or loss on the transfer by reason of provisions of the Code or any US tax treaty.[48] The transferor may apply for a withholding certificate to waive or reduce withholding by showing that the transferor will not realize any gain on the transfer or there will be insufficient proceeds to pay the withholding after payment of all costs, including selling expenses and the amount of any mortgage or lien secured by the property.[49] If the department is satisfied with the application, the department will issue a withholding certificate stating the amount to be withheld, if any.[50]

In the case of a purchase money mortgage, the buyer's withhold requirements depend on whether the seller reports the gain under the installment method. If the seller recognizes gain under the installment method, the buyer withholds the annual amount of tax from the first payment of each year. Withholding applies only to the principal portion of the payments, i.e., not the interest portion. The amount withheld must be paid to the department by the twentieth day after the first payment of the

---

42. Hawaii Tax Information Release No. 2002-2, §I(C).
43. Hawaii Tax Information Release No. 2002-2, §I(D).
44. Ha. Rev. Stat. §235-68(f).
45. Ha. Rev. Stat. §235-68(g).
46. See http://files.hawaii.gov/tax/forms/2013/n289.pdf.
47. Ha. Rev. Stat. §235-68(d)(1). The term 'resident' is defined in Ha. Rev. Stat. §235-1 and includes individuals domiciled or residing in the state.
48. Ha. Rev. Stat. §235-68(d)(2). Per Hawaii Tax Information Release No. 2002-2, §II(A), this includes nonrecognition under I.R.C. §§102 (gifts and inheritances), 332 (complete liquidations of subsidiaries), 337 (nonrecognition for property distributed to parent in complete liquidation of subsidiary), 351 (transfer to corporation controlled by transferor), 721 (nonrecognition of gain or loss on contribution), 1031 (exchange of property held for productive use or investment), and 1041 (transfers of property between spouses or incident to divorce).
49. Ha. Rev. Stat. §235-68(e)(2) and (3).
50. Ha. Rev. Stat. §235-68(e)(3).

year is made.[51] If the seller elects out of the installment method, the buyer must withhold on the entire amount realized and pay the amount to the department by the twentieth day after the date of the transfer.[52] If the buyer does not receive written notification from the seller that the seller will elect out of the installment method, the buyer may assume that the gain will be reported under the installment method and deduct withholding accordingly.[53]

But, Hawaii Tax Information Release 2002-2 distinguishes HARPTA from FIRPTA in a number of ways.

- HARPTA does not allow an adjustment of state income tax withholding based on FIRPTA's 'maximum tax liability,' which adjusts the FIRPTA withholding amount if the transferor's or seller's maximum tax liability is less than the tax required to be withheld.[54]
- HARPTA does not include the value of tangible personal property in the adjusted basis of property, but FIRPTA allows for 'associated personal property' to be included in the adjusted basis calculation.[55]
- Tax rate reductions authorized under a tax treaty are not recognized under HARPTA.[56]
- If a request for a waiver or reduction of withholding is pending, HARPTA requires tax be paid as otherwise required; FIRPTA does not require a payment until a determination is made by the IRS.[57]

If a buyer fails to report the withholding in a timely manner, the buyer may be subject to a penalty of 5% of the amount of tax per month, or any fraction of a month, not to exceed 25%, plus interest. An additional penalty is imposed if the buyer fails to pay the tax timely. This penalty may be doubled if the failure to file is due to fraud.[58] Criminal penalties also may apply if the failure is willful, an attempt to evade tax, or fraudulent.[59]

D.   New York State

Nonresident individuals, estates, and trusts are required to estimate the income tax liability on the gain from the sale of real property located in New York and on sales of stock in a cooperative housing corporation sold in connection with a leasehold in a property located in New York.[60] Real property that is used exclusively as a principal

---

51. Hawaii Tax Information Release No. 2002-2 (rev. 1/2014), §I(B)(1).
52. Hawaii Tax Information Release No. 2002-2 (rev. 1/2014), §I(B)(2).
53. Hawaii Tax Information Release No. 2002-2 (rev. 1/2014), §I(B).
54. Hawaii Tax Information Release No. 2002-2 (rev. 1/2014), §IV(C). *See also* I.R.S. Rev. Proc. 2000-35, §4.06.
55. *Id.*
56. *Id.*
57. *Id.*
58. Ha. Rev. Stat. §231-39.
59. Ha. Rev. Stat. §231-35 through 231-36.
60. N.Y. Tax Law §663(a) and TSB-M-03(2)R/TSB-M-03(4)I, August 1, 2003.

residence by the transferor under Code section 121 is exempt.[61] Certain foreclosure transactions also are exempt.[62]

The seller is required to complete NY Form IT-2663 and pay the full amount of estimated tax due (calculated at the highest applicable tax rate for the year[63]) at the time the deed is recorded.[64] If no tax is due, the seller must certify that estimated tax is not required either because the sale results in a loss or because the seller is not required to recognize gain under any provisions of the IRC except Code section 121.[65]

The certification received from the department must be presented at the time the deed is presented to be recorded.[66] In the alternative, the transferor can sign a certification on Form TP-584 that the provisions requiring estimated taxes do not apply.[67]

§12.04 STATE AND LOCAL TRANSACTION TAXES ON SALES OF REAL ESTATE

Some states and localities impose a real estate transfer tax (RETT) on the transfer of real estate within a jurisdiction. Additionally, some impose a transfer tax on a controlling interest in a legal entity holding such property. Unlike withholding for purposes of the seller's income tax, this is an additional tax imposed on the transfer. The tax is similar to a sales tax, and generally is based on the total consideration paid for the property. It may be due at the time of the transfer or when the deed or other documents relating to the transfer are filed with the county.

Generally, a transfer of real estate is reflected by a written document (e.g., deed) and the tax is implemented by the purchase of stamps from the state or locality that are affixed to the deed. Some jurisdictions refer to the RETT as a stamp tax. While the basic concept of RETT is a straightforward tax or fee assessed on the transfer of real property, complying with the different state and local rules and regulations can be quite complex.

According to the National Conference of State Legislatures,[68] thirty-seven states and the District of Columbia impose a RETT; numerous localities also impose some form of a RETT. These taxes, although similar in form and function, go by a variety of names, such as: Real Estate Conveyance Tax (Connecticut), Excise Tax on Documents (Florida); Documentary Stamp Tax (Nebraska), and Deed Recording Fee (South Carolina).[69] It should be noted that the name of the RETT may not be

---

61. N.Y. Tax Law §663(c)(1).
62. N.Y. Tax Law §663(c)(2) and (3).
63. N.Y. Tax Law §663(b).
64. TSB-M-03(2.1)R/TSB-M-03(4.1)I, Nov. 4, 2003.
65. See https://www.tax.ny.gov/pdf/current_forms/it/it2663_fill_in.pdf, Part 3.
66. N.Y. Tax Law §663(d) and TSB-M-03(2)R/TSB-M-03(4)I.
67. TSB-M-03(2)R/TSB-M-03(4)I.
68. The National Conference of State Legislatures, *Real Estate Transfer Taxes*, http://www.ncsl.org/research/fiscal-policy/real-estate-transfer-taxes.aspx (last accessed March 8, 2017). This site also includes a description of the tax imposed by each state and the tax rate and generally indicates whether local RETT may apply.
69. Conn. Gen. Stat. Title 12, Chapter 223; Fla. Stat. Title XIV, Chapter 201; Neb. Rev. Stat Chapter 76, Article 9; S.C. Code Ann. Title 12, Chapter 24.

consistent between a state and its locality, *e.g.,* New York State refers to a Real Estate Transfer Tax while New York City refers to a Real Property Transfer Tax.[70]

A.   Direct Transfer of Realty

Depending on the jurisdiction, the seller or purchaser may be responsible for paying the tax; in some jurisdictions the parties are jointly liable. Generally, the tax is based on the consideration paid for the real property, including in some cases the assumption of debt. However, a jurisdiction may require tax to be paid on the fair market value of the property, rather than consideration on transactions that involve minimal consideration or that are significantly below fair market value.

B.   Indirect Transfer of Realty

RETT may be imposed when there is an indirect transfer of realty, such as a change in a controlling ownership interest in an entity that owns real estate. Such a tax is commonly referred to as controlling interest transfer tax (CITT). Controlling interest is typically defined by a jurisdiction as an interest of more than 50% of the voting power, capital, and/or profits of the entity.[71] A jurisdiction may enact a CITT to prevent avoidance of tax by structuring a transaction as a sale of an entity rather than a direct sale of the real property.

C.   Long-term Lease

A transfer of a leasehold interest in real property also may be subject to a RETT. Like the CITT, a jurisdiction may assess RETT on leasehold interests to prevent tax avoidance by granting use of the property through a long-term lease instead of selling the property outright. The definition of 'long-term' varies significantly. For example, New Jersey imposes tax on a lease with a term of ninety-nine years or more; in New York, the term is roughly half of that, with tax imposed on a lease with a term that exceeds forty-nine years.[72] Virginia imposes tax to record any lease of real or personal property, regardless of the term.

---

70. N.Y. Tax Law §1400; New York City Admin. Code Title 11, Chapter 21.
71. *See, e.g.,* Conn. Gen. Stat. §12-638a (50% of total combined voting power of all classes of stock of a corporation or more than 50% of the capital, profits, or beneficial interest in a partnership, association, trust or other entity); D.C. Code Ann. §42-1101(11) (more than 50% of the total voting power or total fair market value of all classes of stock of a corporation or more than 50% of the capital or profits in a partnership, association, or other unincorporated entity, or more than 50% of the beneficial interests in a trust); 35 ILCS §200/31-5 (more than 50% of the fair market value of all ownership interests or beneficial interests in a real estate entity).
72. N.J. Rev. Stat. §46:15-5(a); 20 NYCRR 575.7(a)(1);

D. Exemptions

Jurisdictions provide a number of exemptions for certain conveyances of real property from the RETT. Common exemptions include like-kind exchanges, transfers to certain tax-exempt organizations, transfers from parent to subsidiary (or vice versa), mergers, consolidations, and transactions when there is no ultimate change in beneficial owner. Note that the exceptions offered by states vary.

§12.05 SELECTED STATE-SPECIFIC REAL ESTATE TRANSFER TAX PROVISIONS

The paragraphs below discuss provisions in selected states where the rules are unique or where foreign investors may be more likely to invest in real property.[73]

A. California

The state of California authorizes counties and cities to tax documents conveying an interest in real property.[74] Depending on the location of the property transferred, a document generally may be subject to both a city and a county tax. However, a credit may be allowed against tax imposed by a county for the amount of tax imposed by a city within that county.[75] The rate of the county tax is set by the state at 55 cents for each USD 500 or fractional part of consideration or the value of the property conveyed.[76] The city rate is one half of the county rate.[77]

Unlike other states, the statute allowing the county or city to tax does not require the document to be recorded in order for tax to be imposed. Also, the state statute

---

73. Other states that impose transfer and/or recordation taxes include Alabama (Al. Code §40-22-1), Arizona (Ariz. Rev. Stat. Ann. §11-1132), Arkansas (Ark. Code Ann. §26-60-106), Colorado (Colo. Rev. Stat. §39-13-102), Connecticut (Conn. Gen. Stat. §12-495), Delaware (Del. Code Ann. 30 §5402), District of Columbia (D.C. Code Ann. §§42-1103(c) and 47-903(c); Florida (Fla. Stat. §201.02), Georgia (Ga. Code Ann. §48-6-3), Hawaii (Haw. Rev. Stat. §247-1), Illinois (ILCS Chapter 35 §200/31-10), Iowa (Iowa Code §428A.1), Kansas (Kan. Stat. Ann. §79-3102, will phase out through 2018), Kentucky (Ky. Rev. Stat. Ann. §142.050), Maine (Me. Rev. Stat. Ann. 36 §4641-A), Maryland (Md. Code Ann. Tax-Prop. §12-102), Massachusetts (Mass. Gen. L. Chapter 64d §1), Michigan (Mich. Comp. Laws Ann. §207.502(2), Minnesota (Minn. Stat. §287.035), Nebraska Neb. Rev. Stat. §76-901), Nevada (Nev. Rev. Stat. §375.030), New Hampshire (N.H. Rev. stat. Ann. §78-B:1), New Jersey (N.J. Rev. Stat. §46:15-7), North Carolina (N.C. Gen. Stat. §105-228.30), Ohio (Ohio Re. Code Ann. §319.202), Oklahoma (Okla. Stat. 68 §1904), Pennsylvania (Pa. Stat. Ann. §8102-C), Rhode Island (R.I. Gen. Laws §45-25-1), South Carolina (S.C. Code Ann. §12-24-10), South Dakota (S.D. Codified Laws §43-4-21), Tennessee (Tenn. Code Ann. §67-4-409(a)), Vermont (Vt. Stat. Ann. §9602), Virginia (Va, Code Ann. §58.1-812), Washington (Wash. Rev. Code §82.45.060), West Virginia (W.Va. Code §11-22-2); Wisconsin (Wis. Stat. §77-22).
74. Cal. Rev. & Tax. Cd. §11911.
75. Cal. Rev. & Tax. Cd. §11911(c).
76. Cal. Rev. & Tax. Cd. §11911(a).
77. Cal. Rev. & Tax. Cd. §11911(b).

does not mandate who is responsible for paying the tax. Unless the county or city ordinance provides otherwise, this may be negotiable by the parties.

In general, the state statute provides exemptions for a number of different instruments or transactions, including

- an instrument to secure a debt;[78]
- a transfer pursuant to a plan of bankruptcy;[79]
- a transfer of an interest in a partnership, e.g., in a merger or division of the partnership, if the partnership is a continuing partnership within the meaning of Code section 708 and the continuing partnership continues to hold the property;[80]
- a transfer due to foreclosure;[81]
- a transfer between entities and/or their owners that merely changes the method of holding title without affecting proportional ownership of interests.[82]

The general state rates and rules may not apply in charter cities. Instead, voters in charter cities determine whether a tax is imposed and at what rate. According to the League of California Cities, there are over 120 chartered cities in the state.[83] The paragraphs below discuss the rules in the charter cities of Los Angeles and San Francisco.

The California statute does not impose a transfer tax on leases. A California court concluded that a lease of sufficient longevity that approximated a transfer in fee could warrant taxation under the documentary transfer tax. However, the court determined that a twenty year lease with an option to renew for ten years was not sufficiently long to constitute realty sold.[84]

1. *Los Angeles*

A transfer of realty located within the city limits of Los Angeles is subject to the Los Angeles County documentary transfer tax at the rate prescribed by the state plus City of Los Angeles real property transfer tax of USD 2.25 for each USD 500 of consideration.[85]

The exemptions in the Los Angeles county tax code are similar to the exemptions provided under the state statute. However, the county amends the exemption relating to Code section 708 to specifically provide that a termination of any partnership within

---

78. Cal. Rev. & Tax. Cd. §11921.
79. Cal. Rev. & Tax. Cd. §11922.
80. Cal. Rev. & Tax. Cd. §11925. Note that the exemption applies only when the partnership is considered to be a continuing partnership under IRC §708. Thus, by implication, a termination of the partnership under IRC §708 may trigger a tax liability.
81. Cal. Rev. & Tax. Cd. §11926.
82. Cal. Rev. & Tax. Cd. §11925(d).
83. A list of charter cities in California can be found at http://www.cacities.org/Resources-Documents/Resources-Section/Charter-Cities/Charter_Cities-List (last accessed March 8, 2017).
84. *See Thrifty Corp. v. County of Los Angeles*, 210 Cal. App. 3d 881 (Cal. Ct. App., 2nd Dist., 1989).
85. Los Angeles Municipal Code §21.9.2.

the meaning of Code section 708 is treated as though the partnership executed an instrument conveying, for fair market value, all realty held by the partnership at the time of the termination.[86]

Los Angeles County requires payment of tax on transfers of an interest in a legal entity when no document is recorded, but the transfer results in the transfer of a greater-than-50% interest in control of the legal entity.[87] Los Angeles County adopts this position based on a broad reading of the state law and county ordinance, both of which imposes tax on any instrument in which 'realty sold within the county shall be granted, assigned, transferred, or otherwise conveyed....'[88]

Nevertheless a California Court of Appeal has upheld the imposition of the tax on series of transfers of interests in a family trust, limited partnership, and limited liability company. The Court reviewed several cases addressing property taxes that concluded that 'realty sold' includes 'changes of ownership' such as were undertaken by the taxpayer.[89] Because this case addressed the state statute as well as the county ordinance, it potentially affects sales in counties other than Los Angeles County. At the time of writing, the case is on appeal to the state Supreme Court.

The provisions of the Los Angeles city municipal code are similar, and in many parts identical, to those in the county. In addition to the different rates of tax, the city provides an additional exemption for certain acquisition transactions with the city itself as well as an exemption for transactions required by the city.[90]

2. *San Francisco*

The laws relating to real estate transfer tax in San Francisco city and county are combined in a single statute, known as Real Property Transfer Tax Ordinance, which is Article 12-C of the City and County of San Francisco Business Tax Regulations Code. Tax is imposed at an incremental rate ranging from USD 2.50 for each USD 500 (or fractional part thereof) for consideration equal to or less than USD 250,000 up to USD 15 for each USD 500 (or fractional part thereof) for sales of USD 25 million or more.

San Francisco exempts the transactions that are exempt under the state law, and also provides additional exemptions. For example, San Francisco exempts up to one third of tax imposed on transfers of residential real property in which the transferor has installed an active solar panel system or made certain seismic or earthquake hazard mitigation improvements.[91]

In addition, the San Francisco ordinance specifically states that transfers of an ownership interest in a legal entity that owns real property is treated as a sale of

---

86. Los Angeles County Code of Ordinances §4.60.80(B).
87. See https://www.lavote.net/home/records/property-document-recording/documentary-transfer-taxes/corporate-documentary-transfer-tax.
88. Cal. Rev. & Tax. Cd. §11911(a) and Los Angeles County Code of Ordinances §4.60.20.
89. *926 North Ardmore Avenue, LLC v. County of Los Angeles*, No. B248536 (Cal Ct. App, 2nd Dist, 2014).
90. Los Angeles Municipal Code §§21.9.12 and 21.9.13.
91. San Francisco Business Tax Regulations §1105.

the underlying real property.[92] Further, San Francisco imposes tax on a transfer of a leasehold interest of 35 years or more. [93]

B. New York

New York imposes a realty transfer tax on the conveyance of real property or interest therein where the consideration is greater than USD 500 at the rate of USD 2 per USD 500 of consideration.[94] The liability generally is imposed on the seller, but if the grantor fails to pay or is exempt from tax, the tax is levied on the buyer.[95] The tax is imposed on conveyances of real property in fee, a leasehold interest, a beneficial interest, an encumbrance, development rights, air space and air rights, and any other interest with the right to use or occupy the property or the right to receive rents or other income from the property. It also includes an option or contract to purchase real property.[96] New York also imposes a transfer tax on the sale or transfer of a controlling interest in an entity having an interest in real property.[97]

An additional 1% tax is imposed on sales of residential real property when the total consideration is USD 1 million or more.[98] Unlike, the basic real estate transfer tax, the additional tax is imposed on the buyer. If the buyer is exempt, then the seller must pay the tax.[99]

The tax specifically does not apply to a number of types of transactions, including conveyances to secure a debt that effectuate a mere change in identity or form of ownership when there is no change of beneficial ownership, or made pursuant to bankruptcy.[100]

New York also imposes tax to record a mortgage, which actually consists of six separate taxes imposed on recording mortgages of real property located in the state.[101] The applicability and rate depends on the county and city where the real property is located. The basic tax is imposed at the rate of 50 cents per USD 100 secured by the mortgage plus an additional tax of 25 cents per USD 100 for counties outside the metropolitan commuter transportation district (MCTD) and 30 cents per USD 100 for counties within the MCTD.[102] A number of counties are authorized to impose an additional mortgage recording tax.[103]

The state authorizes a number of different counties and cities to adopt a real property transfer tax. [104] The rates for these taxes vary.

---

92. San Francisco Business Tax Regulations §1114.
93. San Francisco Business Tax Regulations §1108.3.
94. N.Y. Tax Law §1402. In the case of a real estate investment trust transfer, the tax rate is USD 1 for each USD 500 (or fraction thereof) of consideration.
95. N.Y. Tax Law §1404(a).
96. N.Y. Tax Law §1401(f).
97. N.Y. Tax Law §1401(e).
98. N.Y. Tax Law §1402-a(a).
99. N.Y. Tax Law §1402-a(b).
100. N.Y. Tax Law §1405-(b).
101. N.Y. Tax Law §253.
102. N.Y. Tax Law §253(1) and (2)(a).
103. N.Y. Tax Law §253-a through 253-x.
104. See, N.Y. Tax Law §1438-a through 1449-ppppp.

12. State and Local Tax Considerations

- New York City (NYC) imposes both a real property transfer tax and a mortgage recording tax.[105] In general, the real property transfer tax is imposed on a sale or transfer of more than USD 25,000.[106]
- The city provides specific rules for conveyances to corporations and partnerships. For example, a sale or transfer of at least 50% of the ownership in a corporation, partnership, trust, or other entity that owns or leases real property or a transfer of cooperative housing stock shares is subject to the transfer tax.[107]
- A transfer of realty to a corporation in exchange for shares of its capital stock is taxable. Likewise, a transfer of real property or an economic interest in real property pursuant to a complete or partial liquidation of a corporation, partnership, or other entity also is taxable.[108]
- However, a transfer to an existing corporation by a sole shareholder as a contribution to capital, where no additional shares of stock are issued, is deemed to be without consideration and not subject to tax unless the corporation was organized for the purpose of holding and/or operating the real estate.[109] Also, a transfer of real property in a statutory merger or consolidation to the new or continuing corporation is not subject to tax.[110] Similar rules apply for transfers involving partnerships.[111]
- The city provides several exemptions that are not applicable at the state level including sales to an exempt non-profit organization and a transaction or deed from an agent, dummy, straw man, or conduit to its principal.[112] Even though exempt, all real estate transfers must be reported on a real property transfer tax return within 30 days after the transfer.[113]
- New York City generally imposes a mortgage tax beginning at the rate of 50 cents for each USD 100 of debt.[114] Mortgages greater than USD 500,000 may be subject to tax at a higher rate.[115]

---

105. N.Y. City Admin. Code §§11-2102 and 11-2601; see also http://www1.nyc.gov/site/finance/taxes/property-real-property-transfer-tax-rptt.page.
106. N.Y. City Admin. Code §11-2102.
107. N.Y. City Admin. Code §11-2102(d).
108. RCNY23-03(g).
109. RCNY23-03(e)(1)(ii) and (iii).
110. RCNY23-03(e)(2).
111. RCNY23-03(e)(3) and (4).
112. NYC Admin. Code §11-2106.
113. *See* New York City Department of Finance web page at http://www1.nyc.gov/site/finance/taxes/property-real-property-transfer-tax-rptt.page (last accessed on March 20, 2017).
114. NYC Admin. Code §11-2601(a).
115. NYC Admin. Code §11-2601(b), (c), and (d).

Chapter 13
Income and Transfer Tax Issues Applicable to Foreign Individual Investors

§13.01	Overview	339
§13.02	Income Taxation	340
	A. Definition of a Resident Alien	341
§13.03	Estate and Gift Taxation	348
	A. Gift Tax	348
	1. Application to a US Citizen or Domiciliary	348
	2. Application to a Non-Domiciled Foreign Citizen	349
	B. Estate Tax	350
	1. Application to a US Citizen or Domiciliary	350
	2. Application to a Non-Domiciled Foreign Citizen	350
	C. Generation-Skipping Transfer Tax	351
§13.04	Estate and Gift Tax Treaties	352
§13.05	Summary	354

§13.01 OVERVIEW

This chapter describes certain key US income and estate tax consequences applicable to a foreign individual investor in USRPI, in part, through an example. Let's assume Helen, a Hungarian tax resident, is acquiring a five-star hotel located in Santa Barbara, California. The hotel is doing very well and generates taxable income each year. Helen expects to operate the hotel until 2025 at which point she hopes to sell it for a gain. As discussed earlier, the taxable income from the hotel is ECI,[1] and any gain from the subsequent sale of the hotel is *treated as* ECI subject to FIRPTA tax.[2] Helen should take into account the US income and estate tax consequences in determining how to structure the ownership of the hotel.

---

1. See discussion in §2.02.A, *supra*.
2. See discussion in §3.02, *supra*.

If Helen owns the hotel personally, the top US federal income tax rate for the annual ECI is 39.6%, and any capital gain upon the sale of the hotel is taxed at 20%. On the other hand, the top US federal income tax rate for a corporation is 35% for both operating income and the gain. Meanwhile, if Helen passes away while she owns the hotel, the value of the hotel may be subject to 40% US estate tax. On the other hand, if Helen owns the hotel through a foreign corporation, then no US estate tax would be applicable at all. Helen should model out the expected tax burden taking into account the projected cash flow and appreciation of the hotel, etc. for purposes of determining the appropriate ownership structure.

To the extent Helen owns the hotel personally, she cannot avoid being taxed in *the same manner* as a US resident on her ECI (and deemed ECI) generated by the hotel.[3] However, to the extent possible, Helen should avoid being actually classified (i.e., not just deemed) as a US tax resident inadvertently.[4] If Helen is classified as a US tax resident, she would be subject to US tax on her worldwide income.[5] In addition, foreign nationals owning US situs property, including a USRPI, may be subject to US estate tax.

§13.02 INCOME TAXATION

The United States taxes its citizens and residents on a worldwide basis and provides a credit for foreign taxes imposed on foreign source income.[6] US income tax rules applicable to individuals, like their counterpart on corporations, are dizzyingly complex. A 2016 Congressional document, in describing the current state of the US tax Code, states that:

> Even a concept as simple as 'married' takes 218 words and five paragraphs to define.[7]

The same document also recommends, *inter alia,* a permanent repeal of the parallel alternative minimum tax, or AMT, which currently requires millions of individuals to perform complex calculations to determine whether they are subject to the tax. This special tax was put in place more than three decades ago so that taxpayers at high income levels pay at least a minimum amount of tax. The AMT tax rates are lower than the regular income tax rate,[8] but fewer deductions are allowed when figuring the amount of income subject to AMT. The taxpayer is also allowed an exemption in computing his/her AMT liability. The exemption is intended to ensure

---

3. Recall that the intent for the enactment of FIRPTA is to establish the equity of tax treatment on sale of USRPIs between US and foreign investors. *See* discussion in §1.03, *supra*.
4. See discussion in §13.02.A., *infra*, regarding the US income tax definition of a resident.
5. A foreign national who is a nonresident is only subject to US tax on US source FDAP income and ECI. *See* I.R.C. §§871 and 881, respectively. In addition to the income taxation, a US resident is also subject to various information reporting requirements discussed in Example 13.3, *infra*.
6. *See*, e.g., I.R.C. §§901 and 904. The US foreign tax credit mechanism is complicated and does not always work to alleviate double taxation completely.
7. *See A Better Way – Our vision for a Confident America* (June 24, 2016) (published by the House of Representatives Republican Tax Reform Task Force) and I.R.C. §7703.
8. The current top AMT rate for individuals is 28%. I.R.C. §55(b).

A. Definition of a Resident Alien

The United States generally classifies a foreign national (i.e., an individual who is not a US citizen) as a resident alien[9] or a nonresident alien[10] for income tax purposes.[11] A foreign citizen is generally treated as a nonresident alien unless the person meets one of the two tests to be considered a resident alien: the lawful permanent resident test and the substantial presence test. These tests only apply to determine whether the person is a resident for federal *income* tax purposes and are not applicable for purposes of gift and estate tax or other legal purposes. It should be noted that states also apply their own residency tests.

An individual is considered to be a resident alien under the lawful permanent resident test if he/she is a green card holder.[12] This test is based on having the legal right to enter and remain permanently in the US, and applies regardless of whether the person is actually physically present in the United States. If someone has a green card, he/she is automatically considered to be a resident alien for US income tax purposes no matter where he/she actually lives, until the green card is either revoked or officially abandoned under US immigration law. On the other hand, the substantial presence test depends entirely on the number of days a person spends in the US, regardless of the immigration status or intent. Under the substantial presence test, an individual will be considered a resident alien if:

- he/she is present in the United States for at least thirty-one days during the current calendar year; and
- the sum of the number of the days he/she is present in the United States in the current year, plus one-third of the days he/she was present in the US in the immediately prior year, plus one-sixth of the days he/she was present in the US in the year before that, is at least 183 days.[13]

Now assume that Helen, after acquiring the Santa Barbara hotel, begins to make frequent long business trips to the United States in 2016, but maintains a home in Hungary where her family remains. Helen does not have a green card. Helen spent 150 days in the US in 2016, and she was present in the US for 90 days in 2014 and 60 days in 2015, respectively. Some of the time was spent looking for business opportunities in the US and the rest on vacation.

---

9. I.R.C. §7701(b)(1)(A).
10. I.R.C. §7701(b)(1)(B).
11. There are special rules for some employees of foreign governments and certain types of international organizations, for visiting students and teachers, as well as for residents of US possessions (i.e., Puerto Rico, Guam, American Samoa, the Northern Marianas Islands, and the US Virgin Islands).
12. *See* I.R.C. §7701(b)(1)(A)(i).
13. *See* I.R.C. §7701(b)(3)(A).

Example 13.1

Helen is considered to be a resident alien of the United States in 2016 because she was present in the US for at least 31 days in 2016, and her number of equivalent days in 2016 and the two preceding years was at least 183, calculated as follows:

Year	Actual Days	Equivalent Days
2016	150 x 1	150
2015	90 x ⅓	30
2014	60 x ⅙	10
Total	190	190

When doing this calculation, Helen must count a day if she is physically present in the United States at any time during that day – including days of arrival and departure. There are exceptions for people who are present in the US for less than twenty-four hours in transit between two other countries, and for residents of Canada and Mexico who commute daily to employment in the United States. Also, she does not have to count days that she is unable to leave the US due to a medical condition that arose while she was present in the United States.[14]

There are two key exceptions to the substantial presence test: the exempt individual exception and the closer connection exception.[15] The exempt individual exception applies to a foreign citizen or national who is temporarily present in the United States with one of the several types of specified status.[16] Any day that the person is an exempt individual is not counted as a day of presence when he/she is determining whether the substantial presence test applies.

- Teachers and trainees who hold a J or Q visa are considered exempt individuals in the current year, unless they have had exempt individual status as a teacher, trainee, or student for two years during the last six calendar years (under certain circumstances this can be extended to four of the past six years).
- Students who hold an F, J, M, or Q visa are considered exempt individuals in the current year, unless they have been present for more than five years as a student, teacher, or trainee. Exempt individual status can be extended beyond five years if the student can show that he/she has complied with the terms of her visa and does not intend to reside in the United States permanently.
- Foreign government-related individuals (including individuals who work for specified international organizations) remain nonresidents of the United States for as long as they are present with that status.
- Professional athletes are considered exempt individuals on any day of presence they are competing in a charitable sports event.

---

14. I.R.C. §7701(b)(3)(D).
15. I.R.C. §7701(b)(3)(B).
16. I.R.C. §7701(b)(5).

13. Income and Transfer Tax Issues Applicable to Foreign Individual Investors

The closer connection exception means that a person who meets the requirements of the substantial presence test still will not be considered a resident of the United States for federal income tax purposes if during the current year the person:

- is present in the US for less than 183 days;
- maintains a tax home in a foreign country; and
- has a closer connection to that same foreign country.

To establish that the person's tax home is in a foreign country, he/she generally must be able to demonstrate that his/her principal place of business and/or abode is in a foreign country. Whether a person has have a closer connection to a foreign country is determined by comparing his/her various connections to the United States with the connections to the foreign country. Both of these determinations (tax home and closer connection) depend on factual matters, and, therefore, are subject to a degree of uncertainty. An individual who has a valid green card, has a green card application pending, or has started the process of applying for a green card, may not rely on this test.

Under a special rule, residents of a country that has an income tax treaty with the US may be able to claim that they are not a US tax resident under the 'treaty tie-breaker provision' for all of part of a tax year. Green card holders living in another country technically may be able to claim a treaty tie-breaker position to override their US resident status. However, this decision should be considered carefully and discussed with a US immigration attorney, as claiming to be a nonresident alien under a treaty could affect the person's eligibility to maintain their green card status. Also, green card holders who claim that they are residents of another country under a treaty may be considered to have expatriated,[17] and may be subject to the special exit tax that applies to long-term permanent residents who give up their green card status. **Example 13.2** illustrates this rule.

Example 13.2

Sherry is a Swedish citizen and resident who vacationed in the United States for two weeks, February 1 to 14, 2016. On June 1, 2016 she returned to the United States to begin a three-year employment assignment. Sherry's US residency start date is February 1, her first day of presence in the US, yet she remained a resident of Sweden until May 31, where she continued to keep a home. Under the US-Sweden income tax treaty,[18] Sherry can 'break the tie' and claim June 1 as her US residency start date, since up to that point her permanent home was in Sweden.

---

17. *See* I.R.C. §877A which imposes a special exit tax on a US citizen or a green card holder who is a 'long-term resident' and who gives up their US citizenship or green card.
18. *See* Art. 4(2) of the Convention Between the Government of Sweden and the Government of the United States of America for the Avoidance of Double Taxation and the Prevention of Fiscal Evasion with Respect to Income (1994). The Convention is referred to as the US-Sweden Treaty.

A foreign national is likely to be a part-year resident in the first year he/she becomes a resident alien.[19] For example, if the substantial presence test applies to Helen in 2016, her US residency start date is generally the first day that she was physically present in the United States, although there is an exception which allows her to have been present in the US for a period of no more than ten days in total without triggering the start of her resident status.

The US anti-deferral tax rules apply to income of a US investor, including resident aliens, earned through a foreign corporation.[20] Once Helen becomes a resident alien, the anti-deferral rules potentially may apply and subject certain undistributed income of these foreign corporations to current US income tax. Hence, Helen also is required to file various information returns to disclose relationships and transactions with certain foreign entities.[21] Significant penalties can be imposed in some cases for failure to comply. Some of the required information returns are noted in **Example 13.3**.

Example 13.3

Sample List of Information Returns.

- FinCEN Form 114, Report of Foreign Bank and Financial Accounts. This form, commonly known as the FBAR, must be filed by US citizens and residents (including individuals who are US residents under the substantial presence test or lawful permanent residence test but who file as nonresidents for income tax purposes under a treaty tie-breaker provision) who have a financial interest in or signature authority over a foreign bank, securities, or other financial accounts, both business and personal, that exceeds USD 10,000 in aggregate value at any time during the calendar year. Form 114 must be filed electronically at http://bsaefiling.fincen.treas.gov/main.html. The report is due by April 15, and a six-month extension is allowed.

- Form 8938, Statement of Specified Foreign Financial Assets, must be filed by US citizens and residents, including dual-status taxpayers, whose foreign financial assets exceed in value certain thresholds that vary depending on marital status and whether the taxpayer lives in the United States or abroad. Foreign financial assets include (but are not limited to) bank accounts, investments, and pensions. This form is required in addition to the FBAR mentioned above.

- Form 5471, Information Return of US Persons with Respect to Certain Foreign Corporations[22] may have to be filed, in certain circumstances, by US resident aliens who own 10% or more of the stock of a foreign corporation or who acquire or dispose of stock in the corporation. For this purpose, an individual

---

19. I.R.C. §7701(b)(2).
20. *See* footnotes 22 and 23, *infra,* for a brief description of these rules.
21. *See,* e.g., I.R.C. §6038.
22. A foreign corporation is a CFC if US shareholders each owning at least 10% of the voting power own, in the aggregate, more than 50% of the voting power or value of the corporation's stock. *See* I.R.C. §957. Certain passive income of the CFC could be taxed to a US shareholder that owns, or is deemed to own, an interest in a CFC as the income is earned each year even though the amount has not yet been distributed. *See* I.R.C. §951.

13. Income and Transfer Tax Issues Applicable to Foreign Individual Investors

is considered to own the stock owned by certain related persons. Moreover, certain officers and directors of foreign corporations may have to file Form 5471. In certain cases, balance sheets of the foreign corporation and lists of transactions between the foreign company and the US resident alien may be required.

- Form 5713, International Boycott Report, must be filed by US citizens or residents who, directly or indirectly, have operations in certain countries that participate in an international boycott.
- Form 8621, Return by a Shareholder of a Passive Foreign Investment Company[23] or Qualified Electing Fund, must be filed by US residents who own, directly or indirectly, stock in a passive foreign investment company.

As a resident alien in 2016, Helen must first calculate her taxable income, which is gross income minus all allowable deductions and exemptions. The gross income of a resident alien includes income from all sources, wherever earned or paid throughout the world. In calculating her taxable income, Helen is allowed to claim certain personal expenses as deductions. In addition, Helen also is allowed a personal exemption of USD 4,050 (for both 2016 and 2017).[24] As mentioned earlier, Helen needs to use the tax rate schedules to determine her federal income tax liability for 2016. There are four tax rate schedules. Which one applies depends on Helen's filing status:

- married individuals (and certain surviving spouses) filing joint returns;
- heads of households;
- single individuals; and
- married individuals filing separate returns.

It is important to determine Helen's filing status because the tax rate schedules are different for each status. If Helen is married, she must use either 'married filing joint' or 'married filing separate' status. To file a joint return, Helen and her spouse must both be US citizens or resident aliens for the entire year. Otherwise, the person must use the 'married filing separate' status, which usually results in a higher tax burden. If Helen is unmarried and her home is the principal residence for a related dependent (e.g., a parent or a child), she may claim the 'head of household' status. A special exception allows Helen to claim the 'head of household' status if she is a married full-year US resident alien, and her spouse is a nonresident alien for at least part of the year.

---

23. A foreign corporation is a passive foreign investment company or PFIC if: (i) at least 75% of its gross income for the tax year is passive, or (ii) at least 50% of the assets held by it during the year produce passive income. *See* I.R.C. §1297. A US investor's share of certain distributions from a PFIC and gain from the sale of an interest in a PFIC could be subject to a substantial interest charge. *See* I.R.C. §1291. If a US investor makes a qualified electing fund or QEF election with respect to a PFIC, such US investor would be required to include in income annually its share of the PFIC's current income and gains, but would avoid the interest charge. *See* I.R.C. §1293.
24. Helen also may claim a personal exemption for her spouse and each dependent if certain conditions are met.

Tables **13.1** and **13.2** contain the different individual income tax schedules for the 2016 and 2017 tax years.

Table 13.1

2016 Tax Rates for Resident Aliens

A. Married Individual Filing Joint Returns and surviving spouses	
If taxable income is:	*The tax is:*
Not over $18,550	10% of the taxable income
Over $18,550 but not over $75,300	$1,855 plus 15% of excess over $18,550
Over $75,300 but not over $151,900	$10,367.50 plus 25% of the excess over $75,300
Over $151,900 but not over $231,450	$29,517.50 plus 28% of the excess over $151,900
Over $231,450 but not over $413,350	$51,791.50 plus 33% of the excess over $231,450
Over $413,350 but not over $466,950	$111,818.50 plus 35% of the excess over $413,350
Over $466,950	$130,578.50 plus 39.6% of the excess over $466,950
B. Heads of Households	
Not Over $13,250	10% of the taxable income
Over $13,250 but not over $50,400	$1,325 plus 15% of excess over $13,250
Over $50,400 but not over $130,150	$6,897.50 plus 25% of the excess over $50,400
Over $130,150 but not over $210,800	$26,835 plus 28% of the excess over $130,150
Over $210,800 but not over $413,350	$49,417 plus 33% of the excess over $210,800
Over $413,350 but not over $441,000	$116,258.50 plus 35% of the excess over $413,350
Over $441,000	$125,936 plus 39.6% of the excess over $441,000
C. Unmarried Individuals (other than Surviving Spouse and Head of Households)	
Not Over $9,275	10% of the taxable income
Over $9,275 but not over $37,650	$927.50 plus 15% of the excess over $9,275
Over $37,650 but not over $91,150	$5,183.75 plus 25% of the excess over $37,650
Over $91,150 but not over $190,150	$18,558.75 plus 28% of the excess over $91,150
Over $190,150 but not over $413,350	$46,278.75 plus 33% of the excess over $190,150
Over $413,350 but not over $415,050	$119,934.75 plus 35% of the excess over $413,350
Over $415,050	$120,529.75 plus 39.6% of the excess over $415,050
D. Married Individuals filing separate returns	
Not Over $9,275	10% of the taxable income
Over $9,275 but not over $37,650	$927.50 plus 15% of the excess over $9,275
Over $37,650 but not over $75,950	$5,183.75 plus 25% of the excess over $37,650
Over $75,950 but not over $115,725	$14,758.75 plus 28% of the excess over $75,950
Over $115,725 but not over $206,675	$25,895.75 plus 33% of the excess over $115,725
Over $206,675 but not over $233,475	$55,909.25 plus 35% of the excess over $206,675
Over $233,475	$65,289.25 plus 39.6% of the excess over $233,475

13. Income and Transfer Tax Issues Applicable to Foreign Individual Investors

Table 13.2

2017 Tax Rates for Residential Aliens

A. Married Individual Filing Joint Returns and surviving spouses	
If taxable income is:	The tax is:
Not Over $18,650	10% of the taxable income
Over $18,650 but not over $75,900	$1,865 plus 15% of excess over $18,650
Over $75,900 but not over $153,100	$10,452.50 plus 25% of the excess over $75,900
Over $153,100 but not over $233,350	$29,752.50 plus 28% of the excess over $153,100
Over $233,350 but not over $416,700	$52,222.50 plus 33% of the excess over $233,350
Over $416,700 but not over $470,700	$112,728 plus 35% of the excess over $416,700
Over $470,700	$131,628 plus 39.6% of the excess over $470,700
B. Heads of Households	
Not Over $13,350	10% of the taxable income
Over $13,350 but not over $50,800	$1,335 plus 15% of excess over $13,350
Over $50,800 but not over $131,200	$6,952.50 plus 25% of the excess over $50,800
Over $131,200 but not over $212,500	$27,052.50 plus 28% of the excess over $131,200
Over $212,500 but not over $416,700	$49,816.50 plus 33% of the excess over $212,500
Over $416,700 but not over $444,550	$117,202.50 plus 35% of the excess over $416,700
Over $444,550	$126,950 plus 39.6% of the excess over $444,550
C. Unmarried Individuals (other than Surviving Spouse and Head of Households)	
Not Over $9,325	10% of the taxable income
Over $9,325 but not over $37,950	$932.50 plus 15% of the excess over $9,325
Over $37,950 but not over $91,900	$5,226.25 plus 25% of the excess over $37,950
Over $91,900 but not over $191,650	$18,713.75 plus 28% of the excess over $91,900
Over $191,650 but not over $416,700	$46,643.75 plus 33% of the excess over $191,650
Over $416,700 but not over $418,400	$120,910.25 plus 35% of the excess over $416,700
Over $418,400	$121,505.25 plus 39.6% of the excess over $418,400
D. Married Individuals filing separate returns	
Not Over $9,325	10% of the taxable income
Over $9,325 but not over $37,950	$932.50 plus 15% of the excess over $9,325
Over $37,950 but not over $76,550	$5,226.25 plus 25% of the excess over $37,950
Over $76,550 but not over $116,675	$14,876.25 plus 28% of the excess over $76,550
Over $116,675 but not over $208,350	$26,111.25 plus 33% of the excess over $116,675
Over $208,350 but not over $235,350	$56,364 plus 35% of the excess over $208,350
Over $235,350	$65,814 plus 39.6% of the excess over $235,350

§13.03 ESTATE AND GIFT TAXATION

The United States applies a unified gift and estate tax system to *transfers* of property made by an individual during life and at death. This *transfer* tax regime is 'unified' in the sense that all transfers, during life or at death, are aggregated in determining the rate of tax applicable to a particular transfer, and also in the sense that the exclusion amount applies to an individual's cumulative lifetime and testamentary gratuitous transfers. In other words, to the extent the exclusion amount is not used during life, it may be applied to transfers at death.

One system of estate and gift taxation applies to US citizens and to foreign citizens *domiciled* in the United States. A separate system applies to foreign citizens who are not domiciled in the United States. An individual is considered domiciled in the United States if he or she actually resides there and has the intention to remain in the United States indefinitely.[25] This intention is determined based on a review of all the facts and circumstances (e.g., location of homes and assets, location of professional and social contacts, address on stationery, statements of intent, jurisdiction of driver's license and burial plot, etc.). Although the notion of domicile for transfer tax purposes is analogous to the notion of resident for income tax purpose, the two tests apply different standards. Therefore, a foreign individual domiciled in the United States for transfer tax purposes may be either a resident alien or a nonresident alien for US *income* tax purposes.[26]

A.   Gift Tax

1.   *Application to a US Citizen or Domiciliary*

A US citizen or domiciliary is allowed to give up to USD 14,000 per year (for 2016 and 2017) to each separate recipient free of any US gift tax (as long as the gift is of a present interest).[27] If the donor is married and the couple are both either US citizens or domiciled in the United States, then the couple may together give double those amounts to each separate recipient and make a gift-splitting election such that the gift is treated as being made one-half by the donor and one-half by the donor's spouse. This election is not available if either spouse is a nonresident alien at the time of the gift.[28]

A donor is allowed an unlimited deduction for outright gifts (and certain gifts in trust) to his/her spouse who is a US citizen. However, the amount of non-taxable gifts to a non-citizen spouse is limited to USD 148,000 and USD 149,000 in 2016 and 2017, respectively.[29] Any gifts in excess of these annual limits are subject to gift tax.

---

25. Treas. Reg. §20.0-1(b)(1).
26. As a practical matter, green card holders are probably considered to be domiciled in the United States; however, it is possible for other factors to be strong enough to overcome the possession of a green card.
27. I.R.C. §2503(b)(1). This amount is adjusted annually for inflation. I.R.C. §2503(b)(2). *See* Rev. Proc. 2016-55, 2014-45 I.R.B. 707, for gifts in 2017.
28. I.R.C. §2513(a)(1).
29. I.R.C. §2523(i)(2). This amount is adjusted annually for inflation. I.R.C. §2503(b)(2).

13. Income and Transfer Tax Issues Applicable to Foreign Individual Investors

The donor of a taxable gift is primarily liable for any gift tax due.[30] The donor is also responsible for filing a gift tax return.[31] The gift tax is cumulative; that is, the tax rate imposed on gifts for a particular year is determined by the total amount of taxable gifts that a donor has made over his entire lifetime. When a donor's cumulative taxable gifts exceed a lifetime maximum of USD 5,450,000 and USD 5,490,000 in 2016 and 2017, respectively, the excess is subject to gift tax at a maximum rate of 40%.[32] The gift tax due for a particular year is determined by:

- adding the amount of taxable gifts made in the year and the amount of taxable gifts made in previous years;
- computing a 'tentative tax' on this total; and
- subtracting from the first 'tentative tax' a second 'tentative tax' attributable solely to the earlier gifts.[33]

In addition to the gift tax annual exclusion, amounts that constitute qualified payments for tuition and medical care[34] and some transfers to which the marital deduction applies are excluded from gift tax.[35] Unless an extension of time is granted, the gift tax return must be filed by April 15 following the close of the calendar year.[36]

2. Application to a Non-Domiciled Foreign Citizen

Individuals who are not citizens of and are not domiciled in the United States (referred to as Non-Domiciled Foreign Citizens) are only subject to gift tax on real property and tangible personal property that is located within the United States.[37] Intangible property like stocks (whether issued by a domestic or foreign corporation) and bonds are generally not taxable when gifted by a Non-Domiciled Foreign Citizen.[38] A Non-Domiciled Foreign Citizen may transfer an unlimited amount of assets to his/her spouse who is a US citizen without incurring any gift tax. Non-taxable gifts of up to USD 14,000 per year (in both 2016 and 2017) are allowed to each separate recipient, and non-taxable gifts to a non-citizen spouse of up to USD 148,000 and USD 149,000 in 2016 and 2017, respectively, are allowed. All gifts in excess of these amounts are subject to gift tax at a maximum rate of 40%. The lifetime exclusion described above does not apply to Non-Domiciled Foreign Citizens.

---

30. I.R.C. §2502(c) and Treas. Reg. §25.2502-2.
31. I.R.C. §6019 and Treas. Reg. §25.6019-1.
32. I.R.C. §§2001(c) and 2502(a).
33. I.R.C. §2502(a).
34. I.R.C. §2503(e).
35. *See* I.R.C. §6019. *See also* Treas. Reg. §25.6019-1(a) and (f).
36. I.R.C. §6075(b) and Treas. Reg. §25.6075-1(a). The proper return to be filed is Form 709, *United States Gift (and Generation-Skipping Transfer) Tax Return*. Treas. Reg. §25.6019-1(a).
37. I.R.C. §§2501(a)(2) and 2511(a). Real property and tangible personal property are 'situated in the United States' for gift tax purposes only if such property is physically located within the United States. Treas. Reg. §25.2511-3(b)(1).
38. However, stock of a domestic corporation would be included in the gross estate of a Non-Domiciled Foreign Citizen for estate tax purposes.

B. Estate Tax

1. Application to a US Citizen or Domiciliary

The US imposes an estate tax on the value of an individual's estate upon his/her death. The taxable value of the estate is the value of the individual's property at the date of death, reduced by expenses and liabilities, certain transfers to the decedent's spouse, and certain bequests to charitable organizations. The portion of the taxable estate that exceeds the decedent's remaining exclusion amount (USD 5,450,000 or 5,490,000 for 2016 and 2017, respectively) is taxed at the maximum rate of 40%.

A deduction is permitted for the value of property bequeathed to a US citizen spouse (although there are certain limitations on the type of transfer that will qualify).[39] On the other hand, no deduction is allowed, for estate tax purposes, for property that is left to a spouse who is *not a US citizen* unless the property passes to a special trust that benefits the spouse, a Qualified Domestic Trust or QDOT.[40] A QDOT merely defers the estate tax liability until the surviving spouse dies or takes a distribution of corpus (other than on account of hardship).[41] A QDOT is required to have at least one US citizen or domestic corporation trustee who has the right to withhold the estate tax attributable to any distributions.[42]

2. Application to a Non-Domiciled Foreign Citizen

The gross estate of a Non-Domiciled Foreign Citizen includes all property in which the decedent had an interest at the time of his/her death, which is situated in the United States.[43] Property considered situated in the United States that is directly relevant for foreign investors includes US real estate[44] and shares of stock in a US corporation (i.e., not just the shares of a USRPHC), regardless of the actual location of the share certificates at the time of the decedent's death.[45]

Non-Domiciled Foreign Citizens, like US citizens or domiciled individuals, are treating as owning, for US estate tax purposes, property previously transferred, by trust or otherwise, where the decedent retained certain interests or control (e.g., a life estate, a right to revoke, a reversion) until their death (or relinquished such interests or control within three years of death).[46] Such previously transferred property will be includable in the US gross estate of a Non-Domiciled Foreign Citizen if the

---

39. I.R.C. §2056(a).
40. I.R.C. §2056(d)(2). *See* I.R.C. §2056A. Note that no provision is available to allow lifetime gifts to a non-US citizen spouse through a QDOT, such as the provision applicable in the case of the US estate tax.
41. I.R.C. §2056A(a)(1)(A) and (B).
42. I.R.C. §2056A(b)(1)(B), §2056A(b)(1)(A), and §2056A(b)(3).
43. I.R.C. §§2103, 2031 and 2033. *See* also I.R.C. §§2034-2044.
44. Treas. Reg. §20.2104-1(a)(1).
45. I.R.C. §2104(a).
46. *See* I.R.C. §§2035 through 2038.

underlying property had a US situs *either* at the time of the earlier transfer *or* at the time of the decedent's death.[47]

The value of a Non-Domiciled Foreign Citizen's taxable estate in excess of USD 60,000 is taxed at rates up to a maximum rate of 40%.[48] The United States has estate tax treaties with certain countries.[49] A Non-Domiciled Foreign Citizen domiciled in one of those countries may be excluded a greater amount of his/her estate from US estate tax.

Estates of Non-Domiciled Foreign Citizen are also entitled to the usual deductions for expenses, indebtedness, and losses, but may only claim the fraction of such deductions that the decedent's US estate constitutes of his/her worldwide estate.[50] Charitable bequests to US charities and governmental units are also deductible.[51] However, to claim these deductions the estate of a Non-Domiciled Foreign Citizen must disclose its worldwide property, not just the property situated in the US.[52] Under a special rule, estates of Non-Domiciled Foreign Citizens owning US real estate may reduce the value of the includable real property by the entire amount of any non-recourse mortgages.[53] The applicable estate tax due is determined by:

- adding two amounts, the amount of the taxable estate, and the amount of taxable gifts made after 1976;
- computing a tentative tax on this sum according to the estate tax rate schedule; and
- subtracting from this tentative tax a second 'tentative tax' computed by applying the estate tax rates to the amount of post-1976 taxable gifts alone.[54]

The estate of a Non-Domiciled Foreign Citizen is entitled to a credit of USD 13,000 – which equates to an exclusion of USD 60,000 – against the estate tax imposed on it.[55] This contrasts sharply with the much more generous credit/exclusion available against both gift and estate taxes in the case of US citizens and residents.[56]

C. Generation-Skipping Transfer Tax

The generation-skipping transfer tax (GSTT) is a transfer tax on the gratuitous transfer of property that skips a generation. The policy is to impose a substitute tax for the gift or estate tax that would have been imposed if no generation had been skipped. For example, if a grandparent makes a taxable gift to a grandchild, both gift tax and GSTT liability will arise, with the GSTT taking the place of the gift or

---

47. I.R.C. §2104(b).
48. I.R.C. §2001(c).
49. *See* discussion in §13.04, *infra*.
50. I.R.C. §§2106(a)(1), 2053 and 2054.
51. I.R.C. §2106(a)(2).
52. I.R.C. §2106(b) and Treas. Reg. §20.2106-1(b).
53. Treas. Reg. §20.2053-7.
54. I.R.C. §2101(b). These steps are very similar to the ones used to determine a donor's gift tax, discussed *infra*.
55. I.R.C. §2102(b).
56. *See* I.R.C. §§2010 and 2505.

estate tax that would have been incurred by the child if the property had been gifted from the grandparent to the parent and then from the parent to the grandchild in the traditional sequence of events.

The GSTT applies to gratuitous transfers made by a Non-Domiciled Foreign Citizen only to the extent such transfers are also subject to the estate or gift tax. For this purpose, exposure to estate or gift tax is determined at the time of the initial transfer (outright or into a trust). Thus, for example, if a Non-Domiciled Foreign Citizen creates a trust for the benefit of a child for life, remainder to grandchild, and transfers US situs real or tangible personal property to the trust such that the gift tax applies, the GSTT will also apply to that trust even if the trust reinvests in totally non-US situs property before any taxable transfer to the grandchild occurs.

There is an exemption of up to USD 5,000,000 (which amount is adjusted for inflation each year and is USD 5,490,000 in 2017) (the GST Exemption) for each person who makes generation-skipping transfers.[57] This exemption amount may be allocated by the transferor to lifetime generation-skipping transfers, or the exemption may be allocated to such transfers by his executor after the death of the transferor.[58] The Code imposes a hierarchy of deemed allocations of the GST Exemption if neither the transferor nor his executor makes the allocations.[59] Generally speaking, if a transfer in trust exceeds the amount of GST Exemption allocated to the transfer, a proportionate part of later transfers from the trust are subject to the GSTT. The proportion is the ratio of the amount of exemption allocated to the amount of the transfer in trust.[60]

The GSTT does not apply to certain inter vivos transfers that are exempt from gift tax pursuant to the annual gift tax exclusion (which is USD 14,000 – or USD 149,000 for gifts to non-US citizen spouses – in 2017) or the special exclusion for certain tuition or medical expense payments.[61] There is also an exemption for a transfer to a grandchild where the grandchild's parent who is a lineal descendant of the grantor is deceased.[62] The rate of tax on generation-skipping transfers is equal to the maximum estate tax rate of 40%.[63]

§13.04 ESTATE AND GIFT TAX TREATIES

The United States has estate tax treaties currently in force with a number of countries, but has treaties covering gift taxes (separately or included in an estate tax treaty) only with Australia, Austria, Denmark, France, Germany, Japan, and the United Kingdom. **Table 13.3** below contains a list of all US estate treaties and gift tax treaties in force as of July 31, 2016.

---

57. I.R.C. §2631.
58. I.R.C. §§2631 and 2632.
59. I.R.C. §2632.
60. *See* I.R.C. §§2641 and 2642. The actual mechanics of calculating the generation-skipping transfer tax are more complicated than this brief description might suggest.
61. I.R.C. §§2611(b) and 2642(c). Note that the GSTT annual exclusion does not apply in all cases where the gift tax annual exclusion applies; certain transfers in trust may meet the requirements for the gift tax exclusion but not the GSTT exclusion.
62. I.R.C. §2651(e).
63. I.R.C. §2641.

Table 13.3

US Treaties in Force as of July 31, 2017

	Estate Tax	Gift Tax
Australia	✓	✓
Austria	✓	✓
Canada	✓	–
Denmark	✓	✓
Finland	✓	–
France	✓	✓
Germany	✓	✓
Greece	✓	–
Ireland	✓	–
Italy	✓	–
Japan	✓	✓
Netherlands	✓	–
South Africa	✓	–
Switzerland	✓	–
United Kingdom	✓	✓

The types of questions and problems that estate and gift tax treaties generally address are the domicile of citizens at time of death, situs of property interests, creditability of taxes and avoidance of double taxation. The Treasury Department has developed a revised model estate and gift tax treaty as a starting point for negotiations with other nations.[64] To the extent any estate or gift tax treaties are in conflict with any estate or gift tax provisions of the Code or regulations, neither treaties nor statutes are entitled to preference simply by reason of there being a treaty or statute.[65] This reinstates the general rule that the last in time of a treaty or statute prevails in cases of unavoidable conflict between the two.[66]

---

64. Treasury Department's Model Estate and Gift Tax Convention of November 20, 1980, reproduced in 2014 U.S. Tax Treaties (CCH) P 214.
65. I.R.C. §7852(d).
66. See, e.g., *Whitley v. Robinson*, 124 U.S. 190, 194 (1988); *Rainey v. United States*, 232 U.S. 310, 316 (1914). *See generally* H. Rep. No. 100-795, 100th Cong., 2d. Sess. 300-09 (1988).

§13.05 SUMMARY

Non-Domiciled Foreign Citizens who are interested in acquiring one or more USRPIs should take the following into account in deciding the ownership structure of the investment:

- owning the investment directly may enable the investor to enjoy a 20% capital gain rate which is significantly lower than the corporate income tax rate of 35%[67] on any gain from the disposition of a USRPI;
- owning the investment through a foreign corporation[68] would generally avoid any exposure to US estate tax, while owning the same interest through a US corporation or directly may subject the fair market value of the USRPI to US estate tax; and
- transferring the USRPI or the entity that owns the USRPI during life or at death may have US gift, estate, and generation-skipping transfer tax consequences.

It is possible for an individual who has an investment in USRPI to inadvertently become a US resident alien for income tax purposes. This is a trap that may be avoided if the investor carefully monitors the days he/she spends in the US. Becoming a US resident alien unexpectedly could lead to myriad taxation and reporting issues that can be overwhelming.

---

67. State income taxes may boost the effective rate for a corporate structure up to 38% to 42%, whereas state income taxes in some cases do not apply to non-residents of those states.
68. A foreign corporation may be subject to the 30% branch profits tax on the gain from a disposition of the USRPI. However, the branch profits tax may be avoided through proper planning including a complete liquidation of the corporation in the year of the sale. *See* discussion in §2.02.B., *supra*.

Index

A

Acquiring Corporation, 143, 150–153, 155, 156, 294
Adjusted basis, 20, 37, 101, 160, 161, 166, 179, 183, 197, 226, 305, 330
Agents, 16, 53, 58, 60, 69, 94, 190, 191, 199, 200, 203, 204, 209, 210, 226, 228–231, 233–236, 238, 239, 241–244, 247, 249, 251, 269, 300, 312, 321, 328, 337
Alternative Investment Fund Managers Directive (AIMFD), 23n
Alternative minimum tax (AMT), 340, 341
American Bar Association (ABA), 104, 107
Anti-Conduit Financing Rule, 299, 301, 303
    conduit entities, 301, 302
        financing arrangement, 301–303
        financing entity, 301, 302
        financing transaction, 301–303
Applicable federal rates, 293
Attribution rules. *See* Code section 318

B

Blockers, 14, 15, 18, 24, 30–32, 34, 64, 126, 138, 273, 283, 284, 286, 289–297, 299, 301–304, 322
Boot, 150, 151, 290
Branch profits tax, 3, 4, 7–9, 13, 16, 17, 18, 22, 28–30, 32, 105–107, 132, 254, 266, 268, 270, 280. *See also* Code section 884
    dividend equivalent amount, 8, 19, 21, 28, 267
    effectively connected earnings and profits, 19–22
    excess interest, 272, 297, 298
    US assets, 20–22, 64, 90
    US liabilities, 20–22
    US net equity, 20–22
Branch Termination Exception, 22, 23, 28, 29, 31, 33, 105–107, 266, 267
    reinvestment rule, 22, 23
Burden of proof, 40, 314, 316

C

Capital Gain Dividend, 10, 101, 107, 198
Check-the-Box rules, 268, 284
    default rule, 285
    late-filing, 285
    per se corporation, 284
Circular No. 230, 321
Code section 318, 73, 114
Code section 482, 292, 320
Code section 884, 8, 272
Code section 897(h), 10, 11, 96, 102–105, 107, 112
Contingent Interest, 45, 271, 301
Commission Rule, 53
Consent dividends, 97, 101
Controlled Commercial Entity, 132–135
Controlled Entity, 88, 89, 132–136, 250
Controlled foreign corporation (CFC), 38, 229, 238, 245

D

Debt
    385 Regulations, 286, 288, 292, 304
    common law principle, 287, 288

covered debt instrument (CDI), 290, 292
documentation requirements, 289, 290, 304
expanded group interest (EGI), 289, 290
funding rule, 291
recast rules, 289, 290, 292, 304
Deemed Sale Election, 88
Dividend, 8, 10, 11, 15, 19, 21, 28, 30–35, 80–82, 85, 87, 89, 94, 95, 97, 99, 100, 107, 112, 118, 126–128, 134, 176, 177, 197, 198, 210, 214, 228–230, 235, 237, 238, 241, 245, 258, 263, 267, 273, 274, 277–280, 284, 286, 287, 301
Domestic corporation, 65, 66, 68, 71, 85, 112, 155, 159, 160, 162, 163, 166–170, 172, 175–177, 179–181, 188, 192, 214–218, 220, 226, 237, 266, 290, 296, 298, 299, 350
   dividend distribution, 31, 33, 104, 105, 214

E

Earnings and profits, 19–22, 44, 80–82, 85–87, 89, 96, 101–103, 106, 107, 197, 218, 273, 286, 292
Earnings Stripping rule
   adjusted taxable income, 297, 298, 305
   disallowed interest, 286, 297, 298
   disqualified interest expense, 298
   excess interest expense, 297, 298, 306
   excess limitation, 297, 298, 306
   net interest expense, 297, 298, 305
   proposed regulation, 288, 298, 299, 310
Economic Substance Doctrine, 295, 320
Effectively connected income (ECI), 5, 6, 14–19, 23–27, 29, 30, 34–42, 44, 65, 93, 125, 126, 133, 137, 138, 161, 166, 175, 195, 210, 212, 214, 218, 230, 251, 267, 270, 272, 308, 322, 339, 340
   Net-basis election, 17, 270
Entity classification rule. *See* Check-the-Box rules
Equivalent Beneficiaries, 237, 263, 276, 277

Established securities market, 11, 33, 47, 112, 113, 121, 153, 172, 192, 214, 216–218, 231, 238, 241, 250, 258
Estate tax
   non-domiciled Foreign Citizens, 349, 350, 351, 352, 354
   treaties, 351–353
European Union (EU), 237

F

Fair market value, 40, 41, 63, 64, 66, 68, 69, 71–73, 75, 86, 87, 89, 93, 95, 111, 131, 135, 158, 166, 175, 179, 197, 198, 206, 216, 218, 220, 226, 250, 326, 332, 335, 354
Five-Year Look-Back Period, 71, 111, 112, 114, 159
Fixed or determinable annual or periodic (FDAP) income, 67, 80, 269–270. *See* Gross-basis tax
   rental income, 67, 80, 269–270
Force of attraction principle, 5
Foreign Account Tax Compliance Act (FATCA), 210, 213, 228, 230, 232
Foreign corporation, 68, 10, 13, 16, 24, 26, 33, 35, 38, 54, 58, 74, 105, 110, 118, 130, 131, 133, 135, 137, 138, 147, 149, 151, 153, 159, 161, 163, 165, 175, 179–185, 188, 196, 197, 200, 203, 214, 215, 219, 226, 229, 231–233, 237, 238, 242, 250, 258, 260, 264, 266, 268, 270, 272, 298–300, 322, 340, 344, 345, 349, 354
Foreign government
   892 Exemption, 131–135, 138, 207
   foreign sovereign, 110, 126, 131, 138, 207
   governmental function, 133, 136
   integral part of, 132, 133
   special *per se* rule, 134, 135
Foreign Investment in Real Property Tax Act 1980 (FIRPTA)
   applicable investor, 129, 215
   cleansing exception, 104, 105, 110, 111, 138, 163, 201
   domestic controlled REIT exception, 131, 138
   publicly traded exception, 112, 116, 118, 130, 138, 157, 193

ownership requirements, 89, 90, 114, 116, 263, 276
regularly traded requirement, 33, 153
qualified foreign pension fund (QFPF), 11, 31, 33, 123, 124, 127, 131, 133, 138, 200, 274
qualified shareholder, 33, 127, 130, 138
qualified collective investment vehicle (QCIV), 127, 129
repeal of, 6, 7, 12, 156
Foreign real property interest (FRPI), 63, 64, 66–68, 71, 72, 116, 135, 136

G

Generally accepted accounting principles, 68
General Utilities Doctrine
repeal of, 7–8, 87, 144, 156
Generation-skipping transfer tax (GSTT), 351, 352, 354
Gift tax, 316, 348–349, 351–353
Grantor trust, 218, 230–232, 234, 242
Gross-basis tax, 15, 17, 19, 30, 269, 270, 272, 273

H

Headquarters Company test, 276–278
Hybrid entity. See Check-the-Box rules

I

Individual income tax rates, 346
Infrastructure, 44, 55, 57, 60, 61, 64, 93, 124
Interest income, 30, 93, 262, 270–273, 296–299
Interest deduction, 4, 17, 21, 22, 137, 272, 283, 306
Internal Revenue Manual (IRM), 312, 315
Internal Revenue Service (IRS)
IRS Appeals, 312
IRS Examination, 97, 208, 312
IRS Office of Chief Counsel, 312
Investment company rule, 135

J

Joint Committee on Taxation, 309, 319
Blue Book, 126, 309, 320

L

Like-Kind Exchange, 86, 106, 217, 326, 327, 333
Limitation on benefits (LOB) provision
Ownership and Base-Erosion Test, 256, 257
Publicly Traded Company Test
principal class of shares, 237, 256, 258
disproportionate class of shares, 256–258, 263, 276
recognized stock exchange, 256, 258
regularly traded, 258
primarily traded, 256, 258
Active Trade or Business Test
activities conducted by connected persons, 259
income derived in connection with or incidental to, 278
substantiality test, 259, 260
Derivative Benefits provision
ownership requirement, 89, 90, 114, 116, 263, 276
base-erosion requirement, 263, 277
Limited liability companies, 28, 284, 303, 325, 326, 329, 335
Limited partnerships, 23, 127, 130, 137, 284, 303, 335

M

Matching Principle, 296
Model treaties
OECD model, 42
US model, 256, 260
1977 Model, 46
1996 Model, 260
2006 Model, 254, 256, 261, 265, 267–269, 271, 273, 275, 276, 278
2015 Draft Model, 255, 256, 275
2016 Model, 254, 256, 275–280
Mutual Agreement Procedure, 265, 266

N

Net-basis election, 17, 270
Net-basis tax, 15, 19, 125
Net capital gains, 95, 101–104
Net operating loss, 96, 102, 146, 226, 294
Nonqualified preferred stock, 150, 151

Nonrecognition rules
  acquiring corporation, 143, 150–153, 155, 156
  basis requirement, 154, 155, 158
  Code section 332 liquidation, 155, 160
  Code section 351 exchange, 147–148
  Code section 355 distribution, 157–159
  controlled, 141, 157–159
  distributee, 157–159, 161
  distributing, 157, 158
  distribution requirement, 151
  filing requirement, 146–149, 151–155, 158, 160–162, 167, 168, 170, 174, 176, 183, 185, 186
  foreign-to-foreign exchange, 148–150
  Hot-for-Hot Requirement, 147–150, 152, 155, 159, 160, 163
  one-year holding period, 149
  subject-to-tax requirement, 146, 147, 149, 153–155, 158, 160
  toll charge, 155–157, 159, 162
North American Free Trade Agreement (NAFTA), 263n
New York State Bar Association (NYSBA), 56, 107, 128

O

Organization for Economic Cooperation and Development (OECD), 42, 279

P

Passive foreign investment company (PFIC), 345
Parties to a reorganization, 143
Partnership
  aggregate theory, 25, 47
  entity theory, 25
Penalties
  accuracy-related, 293, 313, 316–322
  failure to file, 18, 308, 314, 330
  failure to pay, 314
  negligence, 308, 317–319
  substantial understatement, 319–320
Permanent resident test, 341, 343
Portfolio Interest Exemption, 114, 286, 299–301

Q

Qualified Domestic Trust (QDOT), 350

Qualified investment entities (QIE), 116–123
Qualified Person, 256–258, 263
Qualified Shareholder, 33, 127–130, 138

R

Real estate investment fund, 23–27, 33
Real estate investment trust (REIT)
  annual distribution requirement, 95–97
  asset tests, 90–93
  beneficial owners, 89
  conversion transaction, 85, 88
  dividend paid deduction, 80, 96, 100, 101, 103
  Distribution Look-through Rule, 11
  (see also Code section 897(h))
  eligible independent contractor (EIK), 99–100
  excise tax, 97
  impermissible tenant services income (ITSI), 98
  income tests, 93–95
  independent contractor (IK), 95, 99–100
  opco-propco, 80, 89
  qualified healthcare facility, 94, 99
  qualified lodging facility, 94, 98–100
  qualified REIT subsidiary (QRS), 90
  quarterly asset tests, 90–93
  spin-offs, 80, 87–89
  sting tax, 85–87, 107
  taxable REIT subsidiary (TRS), 97
  tenant services, 98–99
  umbrella REIT (UPREIT), 85
Real estate transfer tax (RETT), 331–337
Reorganization
  A reorganization, 142, 143, 152–153, 155
  B reorganization, 143, 147–148, 173
  C Reorganization, 152–153, 170–172
  D Reorganization, 143, 150–152, 157
  E Reorganization, 143, 159–160, 176, 177
  F Reorganization, 143, 150–152, 156, 157, 159–160, 177
Reportable transaction, 316–318, 322
Resident alien, 26, 37, 38, 166, 173, 175, 185, 341–348, 354
Reverse hybrid entity, 230, 233, 242, 268

Index

S

Securities Exchange Commission, 157
Section 897(i) Election, 162–163, 200, 266
Special Tax Regime (STR), 275–277
State and local tax
    California, 325–327
        Los Angeles, 334–335
        San Francisco, 335–336
    Delaware, 327–328
    Hawaii, 328–330
    New York
        New York City, 330–331
Statute of limitation, 14, 314
Subchapter C, 140, 141, 145, 146, 151, 153, 164, 197
Subchapter C corporation, 80–82, 84, 85, 87, 88, 95, 96, 106, 112, 114, 116, 119, 120, 193, 197, 273
Subchapter S corporation, 86
Substance over form, 270, 284
Substantial presence test, 341–344
Supreme Court, 310, 313, 315, 335

T

Target Corporation, 143, 150, 152, 153, 155, 156
Tax avoidance, 292, 295, 302, 332
Tax avoidance purpose, 302
Tax shelter, 313, 319, 321–322
Tax return
    due dates, 18
    filing obligation, 34
    filing standards, 313–315
Tax treaty
    competent authority relief, 259, 264–266, 279
    non-discrimination provision, 266
    permanent establishment (PE), 268–269
    reduction of tax
        branch profits tax, 266–268
        FDAP income, 269–275
    saving clause, 276
    Technical Explanation (TE), 237, 254–256, 260, 264, 273, 278
Trade or Business Assets, 64, 66–72, 74, 75, 116, 135
Transfer pricing. *See* Code section 482

U

United States Real Property Holding Corporation (USRPHC)
    alternative book value test, 68, 69, 72
    asset test, 64–69
    cleansing exception (*see* Foreign Investment in Real Property Tax Act 1980 (FIRPTA))
    determination date, 68, 69, 71, 72
    fair market value test, 64, 66–69, 72, 158, 166
    former USRPHC, 59, 64, 65, 76, 110, 111, 159, 160, 198
    look-through rule, 73–76
    publicly traded exception (*see* Foreign Investment in Real Property Tax Act 1980 (FIRPTA))
US Real Property Interest (USRPI)
    commission rule, 53
    installment obligation, 52
    indirect right to share interest, 51–54, 57, 59, 60
    interest rate rule, 53–55
    interest in real property, 43, 45, 51–54, 56, 59, 83, 91, 92
    leasehold interest, 51, 55, 56, 59, 60, 111
    notional principal contract, 54, 55
US trade or business, 5, 6, 15, 16, 19–25, 44, 126, 136, 195, 259, 262, 269, 270, 299, 308
US-Australia Treaty, 129n
US-Canada Treaty, 268, 274
US-China Treaty, 268n
US-Germany Treaty, 275
US-Ireland Treaty, 260n
US-Netherlands Treaty, 264, 265
US-Sweden Treaty, 343n
US-Switzerland Treaty, 269n
US-UK Treaty, 263, 273n

W

Withholding
    agents' liability, 210, 213
    amount subject to FIRPTA withholding, 191
    Certification of Non-Foreign Status, 199–202

Certification of Non-USRPHC Status, 202–203
coordination with ECI Withholding Tax, 195
coordination with FATCA, 210–213
exemption, 198–207
FDAP income, 30, 35, 101, 112, 190, 197, 210, 212
foreclosure, 205–207
foreign government transferor, 207
notice of nonrecognition transfer, 203–205
penalties, 191, 199, 201, 202, 213
publicly traded interest, 192
refund, 208, 209
Withholding Certificate
blanket withholding certificate, 209
FIRPTA Unit, 208

FORMS

Form 1120, 30, 32
Form 1120F, 28–30, 32
Form 1120 REIT, 32
Form 5471, 344, 345
Form 5713, 345
Form 8621, 345
Form 8288, 221

Form 8288-A, 222
Form 8288-B, 224
Form 8832, 285
Form 8926, 299, 305, 306
Form 8938, 344
Form FinCEN Form 114 (FBAR), 309, 344
Form W-8BEN-E, 211, 228–251, 300

CASES

Bergersen v. Commissioner, 318
Boree v. Commissioner, 45
Capri Inc. v. Commissioner, 294
Casel v. Commissioner, 25, 39
Chevron USA Inc. v. Natural Resource Deference Council, Inc., 310
Commissioner v. Court Holding Company, 140
Cottle v. Commissioner, 95
D'Arcy-MacManus & Masius, Inc. v. Commissioner, 294
De Amodio v. Commissioner, 16, 269
Deputy v. du Pont, 286
Donroy, Ltd. v. United States, 25, 41
Estate of Mixon, 287
Everson v. United States, 318
Fin Hay Realty Co. v. U.S., 287
General Utilities & Operating Co. v. Helvering, 7
Grecian Magnesite Mining, Co. v. Commissioner, 26
Hardman v. U.S., 287
Herbert v. Commissioner, 16
Higgins v. Commissioner, 16
InverWorld, Inc. v. C.I.R., 16

John Kelley Co. v. Commissioner, 287
Laidlaw Transportation, Inc. v. Commissioner, 286
Lewenhaupt v. Commissioner, 16
Marineland of Pacific, Inc. v. Commissioner, 49
Mayo Found. For Med. Educ. & Research v. United States, 119, 310
Mortensen v. Commissioner, 318
Munford v. Commissioner, 48
Plantation Patterns Inc. v. Commissioner, 286
Pool v. Commissioner, 45
Rainey v. United States, 353
Rice v. Commissioner, 45
Scroll, Inc. v. Commissioner, 295
Southern Dredging Corp. v. Commissioner, 294
Swallows Holdings, Ltd. v. Commissioner, 18
Tyler v. Tomlinson, 287
Unger v. Commissioner, 25, 38, 41
United States v. Boyle, 315
Weirick v. Commissioner, 49
Whitley v. Robinson, 353

Index

IRS ANNOUNCEMENT, NOTICES, PRIVATE LETTER RULINGS, TECHNICAL ADVICE MEMORANDA, REVENUE RULINGS AND REVENUE PROCEDURES

Announcement 2008-115, 55–57, 64, 93
EMISC 2009-010, 16
Notice 88-19, 86
Notice 88-50, 146, 187
Notice 88-72, 47, 146, 186, 187
Notice 89-57, 146, 161, 174, 185
Notice 89-64, 146, 182
Notice 89-85, 146, 155, 165–169, 175, 179
Notice 99-43, 146, 160, 175
Notice 2006-46, 146, 148, 152, 153, 155, 156, 162, 165, 173
Notice 2007-55 (2007 Notice), 32, 104, 107
Notice 2013-43, 300
PLR 7752074, 151
PLR 8302015, 293
PLR 9534022, 90
PLR 9621032, 90
PLR 200507004, 89
PLR 200525002, 260
PLR 200534013, 102
PLR 200825034, 100
PLR 200851023, 142
PLR 200923001, 119, 120
PLR 201125013, 100
PLR 201147015 , 99
PLR 201202014, 86
PLR 201314002, 92
PLR 201321007, 156
PLR 201340004, 95
PLR 201346005, 95
PLR 201429017, 99
PLR 201503010, 84
PLR 201509019, 99
PLR 201609004, 95
TAM 9639010, 113
Rev. Rul. 55-617, 269
Rev. Rul. 59-259, 73, 141
Rev. Rul. 69-557, 49
Rev. Rul. 73-194, 99
Rev. Rul. 73-522, 15, 270
Rev. Rul. 75-136, 99
Rev. Rul. 79-183, 49
Rev. Rul. 81-78, 42
Rev. Rul. 82-150, 140
Rev. Rul. 85-60, 41
Rev. Rul. 85-93, 48
Rev. Rul. 87-6, 134
Rev. Rul. 87-66, 162, 266
Rev. Rul. 89-95, 168
Rev. Rul. 91-32, 25–26, 36
Rev. Proc. 2000-35, 207–209, 330
Rev. Proc. 2008-27, 161, 204
Rev. Proc. 2009-41, 285
Rev. Proc. 2010-32, 285
Rev. Proc. 2015-40, 264
Rev. Proc. 2016-55, 348
Rev. Proc. 2017-1, 285

LEGISLATIVE ACTS

US Securities Exchange Act of 1934, 258
Foreign Investor Tax Act of 1966 (FITA), 5
Tax Reform Act of 1969, 287
Foreign Investment in Real Property Tax Act of 1980 (FIRPTA), 2, 46, 186, 187
Economic Recovery Act of 1981, 6
Tax Reform Act of 1984, 6
Tax Reform Act of 1986 (TRA of 1986), 6, 8
American Jobs Creation Act of 2004 (2004 Jobs Act), 11, 103
Foreign Account Tax Compliance Act (FATCA), 210
Protecting Americans from Tax Hikes Act of 2015 (2015 PATH Act), 11, 88, 120, 126
The Tax Technical Corrections Act of 2016 (2016 TCA), 110